The Global History
of Portugal

From Prehistory to the Modern World

The Portuguese-Speaking World

ITS HISTORY, POLITICS AND CULTURE

The Series Editors
António Costa Pinto (University of Lisbon)
Onésimo T. Almeida (Brown University)
Miguel Bandeira Jerónimo (University of Coimbra)

This new series will publish high-quality scholarly books on the entire spectrum of the Portuguese-speaking world, with particular emphasis on the modern history, culture, and politics of Portugal, Brazil, and Africa. The series, which will be open to a variety of approaches, will offer fresh insights into a wide range of topics covering diverse historical and geographical contexts. Particular preferences will be given to books that reflect interdisciplinarity and innovative methodologies. The editors encourage the submission of proposals for single author as well as collective volumes.

Published

The Lusophone World: The Evolution of Portuguese National Narratives   Sarah Ashby

The Politics of Representation: Elections and Parliamentarism in Portugal and Spain, 1875–1926   Edited by Pedro Tavares de Almeida & Javier Moreno Luzón

Inequality in the Portuguese-Speaking World: Global and Historical Perspectives
Edited by Francisco Bethencourt

Marcello Caetano: A Biography (1906–1980)   Francisco Carlos Palomanes Martinho

From Lisbon to the World: Fernando Pessoa's Enduring Literary Presence
George Monteiro

The First Portuguese Republic: Between Liberalism and Democracy (1910–1926)
Miriam Pereira

The Locusts: British Critics of Portugal before the First World War   Gary Thorn

The Military and Political in Authoritarian Brazil: The Aliança Renovadora Nacional (ARENA), 1965–1979   Lucia Grinberg

The Portuguese at War: From the Nineteenth Century to the Present Day
Nuno Severiano Teixeira

Dictatorship and the Electoral Vote: Francoism and the Portuguese New State Regime in Comparative Perspective, 1945–1975   Carlos Domper Lasús

Literary Censorship in Francisco Franco's Spain and Getulio Vargas' Brazil, 1936–1945: Burning Books, Awarding Writers   Gabriela de Lima Grecco

On Guard Against the Red Menace: Anti-Communism in Brazil, 1917–1964
Rodrigo Patto Sá Motta

Frei Betto: The Political-Pastoral Work of a Dominican Friar in Brazil and Beyond
Américo Oscar Guichard Freire and Evanize Martins Sydow

The Eruption of Insular Identities: A Comparative Study of Azorean and Cape Verdean Prose   Brianna Medeiros

Fernando Pessoa: A Critical Introduction   Jerónimo Pizarro

Portuguese Orientalism: The Interplay of Power, Representation and Dialogue in the Nineteenth and Twentieth Centuries   Edited by Marta Pacheco Pinto and Catarina Apolinário de Almeida

Politics and Religion in the Portuguese Colonial Empire in Africa (1890–1930)
Hugo Gonçalves Dores

Rebuilding a Blue Nation: Maritime Policies of the Portuguese New State, 1933–1974
Álvaro Garrido

The Brazilian Revolution of 1930: The Legacy of Getúlio Vargas Revisited
Edited by Luciano Aronne De Abreu and Marco Aurélio Vannucchi

The Global History of Portugal: From Prehistory to the Modern World
Edited by Carlos Fiolhais, José Eduardo Franco and José Pedro Paiva

A full list of titles in the series, including those forthcoming, are presented on the Press website

The Global History of Portugal

From Prehistory to the Modern World

Edited by Carlos Fiolhais, José Eduardo Franco and José Pedro Paiva

sussex
ACADEMIC
PRESS
Brighton • Chicago • Toronto

2 4 6 8 10 9 7 5 3 1

First published in 2022 in Great Britain by
SUSSEX ACADEMIC PRESS
P.O. Box 139
Eastbourne BN24 9BP

Distributed in North America by
SUSSEX ACADEMIC PRESS
Independent Publishers Group
814 N. Franklin Street
Chicago, IL 60610

British Library Cataloguing in Publication Data
A CIP catalogue record for this book is available from the British Library.

Library of Congress Cataloging-in-Publication Data
To be applied for.

Hardcover ISBN 978-1-78976-103-0

Paperback ISBN 978-1-78976-104-7

Typeset and designed by Sussex Academic Press, Brighton & Eastbourne.
Printed by TJ Books Limited, Padstow, Cornwall.

Contents

Series Editors' Preface   xv

Acknowledgements   xvi

General Introduction   1
Carlos Fiolhais, José Eduardo Franco and José Pedro Paiva

Part I Prehistory and Protohistory
Introduction to Part I — From Modern Humans to the Advent   8
of Writing
João Luís Cardoso

240,000–10,000 BC — From Neanderthal Man to *Homo sapiens*   10
João Cascalheira and Nuno Bicho

5500–4500 BC — The Spread of Farming and Domestic Animals   14
António Faustino Carvalho

2700–1800 BC — The Bell Beaker Question: Origin and Diffusion during   17
the Third Millennium BC
João Luís Cardoso

2000–800 BC — Long-Distance Trading in the Bronze Age   20
Raquel Vilaça

Ninth to Fifth Centuries BC — The Phoenicians in Portugal   24
Ana Margarida Arruda

Part II Antiquity
Introduction to Part II — From the Roman Empire to Gothic Iberia   30
Carlos Fabião

218–19 BC — The Romans in the Iberian Peninsula: From Conquered Land   34
to Imperial Province
Carlos Fabião

155–139 BC — The Lusitanian Wars and the True Viriathus   37
Amílcar Guerra

Second Century BC to the Fourth Century AD — In the Marketplace   41
of the Roman Empire
Catarina Viegas

139 BC–14 AD — Aligning with the Empire: Language   44
Amílcar Guerra

First Century BC — Where Does the World End?   48
Amílcar Guerra

First Century BC — The Emergence of Cities   52
Catarina Viegas

80 BC — The Impact of the Roman Civil Wars   55
Carlos Fabião

16–15 BC — Founding of the Roman Province of Lusitania   59
Catarina Viegas

First Century BC to the Second Century AD — Environmental Threats   62
Catarina Viegas

17–23 — The Tides According to Strabo   65
Amílcar Guerra

First Century — Between Seas: A Historical and Geographical Constant   69
Carlos Fabião

Fourth Century — Administrative Reform of the Roman Empire   72
Pedro C. Carvalho

409–411 — Arrivals of the Barbarians   76
Pedro C. Carvalho

Second Half of the Sixth Century — A United Peninsula Under the Goths   80
Carlos Fabião

Part III The Middle Ages
Introduction to Part III — From the Advent of Islam to the Conquest   86
of Ceuta
Bernardo Vasconcelos e Sousa

711 — Confrontation and Interaction: Islam in the Iberian Peninsula   89
Hermenegildo Fernandes

Contents | ix

844 — What Remained from the Time of the Vikings? 92
Hélio Pires

882 — Evolution of the Handwritten Text 96
Maria José Azevedo Santos

1089 — From Romanesque to Gothic: Aesthetic Forms 99
José Custódio Vieira da Silva

1128 — Influences and External Relations in a County That Gave Birth 103
to a Kingdom
Luís Carlos Amaral

1128 — Fighting in the Name of Faith: Military Orders in Portugal 107
Luís Filipe Oliveira

1140 — Afonso Henriques, *Portugalensium Rex*, Son of Theresa of León 112
and Henry of Burgundy
António Resende de Oliveira and Bernardo Vasconcelos e Sousa

1146 — Marrying for Love of the Crown 116
Manuela Santos Silva

1147 — Lisbon: From Conquest to Head of the Realm 119
Amélia Aguiar Andrade and Maria João Branco

1153 — A Religion without Borders: Religious Orders 123
João Luís Inglês Fontes

1174 — The Language Spoken and Written by the Portuguese 126
António Manuel Ribeiro Rebelo

1196 — From Latin Literature to Portuguese Literature 130
António Resende de Oliveira

1231 — From Fernando Martins to Saint Anthony of Lisbon 133
and Padua: A Saint for All the World
Eleonora Lombardo and José Francisco Meirinhos

1276 — Pope John XXI, Portuguese Clergyman and Universal Pastor 137
Armando Norte

1290 — A University That Would Develop a World Profile 140
Saul António Gomes

1293 — The Merchants' Guild: The Ports, the King and Portuguese 144
Trade within European Networks
Amândio J. M. Barros

1297 — The Treaty of Alcañices and the Establishment of a Border with Neighbouring Threats 148
J. A. de Sottomayor-Pizarro

1348 — The Black Death: The Near "Global" Plague 151
Maria Helena da Cruz Coelho

1385 — Aljubarrota: An Ancestral Enemy, an Old Alliance and Reinforcement of the Country's Identity 155
João Gouveia Monteiro

1415 — New Horizons: The Conquest of Ceuta and the Sea 159
Luís Miguel Duarte

Part IV The Early Modern Period
Introduction to Part IV — Of Settlement and Slavery to Royal Exile 164
Cátia Antunes

1425 — Madeira: Settlement, Sugar and Enslaved Populations 167
Mariana P. Candido

1434 — Rounding Cape Bojador: New Horizons 171
Amélia Polónia

1468 — The Guinea Monopoly: Pluricontinental Economic Development 174
Susana Münch Miranda

1494 — The Treaty of Tordesillas: A New Vision of the Atlantic and Sharing of the Seas 178
†*Francisco Contente Domingues*

1496 — Expulsion of the Jews: The Diaspora of the Diasporas 181
José Alberto Rodrigues da Silva Tavim

1498–1500 — Calicut and Porto Seguro: The Birth of Pluricontinentalism 184
Edgar Cravo Bertrand Pereira

1502 — Asilah, Ceuta, Tangier and Ksar es-Seghir: The Global Phenomenon of the *Misericórdia* Brotherhoods 188
Isabel dos Guimarães Sá

1502 — The Cantino Planisphere: A Model of the World 191
Joaquim Alves Gaspar

1509 — Santarém Rice and the Globalization of Food Products 195
Isabel Drumond Braga

1514 — A Religion for the World: Royal Patronage and a Pluricontinental 198
Diocese
José Pedro Paiva

1517 — The Slave Revolt in São Tomé 202
Filipa Ribeiro da Silva

1519 — Ferdinand Magellan and the First Voyage Around the World 205
Rui Manuel Loureiro

1536 — The Inquisition Arrives in Portugal 209
Francisco Bethencourt

1540 — The Jesuits and the First Global Knowledge Database 212
José Eduardo Franco

1541 — Mazagan: An Architectural Revolution 216
Walter Rossa

1563 — *Colóquios dos Simples*, or the Globalization of the Printing Press 220
and Knowledge
Palmira Fontes da Costa

1572 — Camões: Arms, Letters and the Clash of Civilizations 223
Diogo Ramada Curto

1580 — Union of Crowns, Union of the World 226
Rafael Valladares

1582 — The Gregorian Calendar: Globalizing the Measurement of Time 230
Henrique Leitão and José Madruga Carvalho

1614 — The Scientific Revolution Reaches Asia 233
Carlos Fiolhais

1640–1648 — The Luso-Spanish Split and the Westphalia Treaties: 237
A Changed World Order?
Pedro Cardim

1645 — The Pernambucan Insurrection and the Rejection of Globalism 241
Bruno Miranda and Kleber Clementino

1680 — The Founding of Colonia de Sacramento 244
Tamar Herzog

1703 — The Methuen Treaty 248
Cátia Antunes and João Paulo Salvado

1717 — The Palace of Mafra, or a Global Vision of the Baroque   251
Luís de Moura Sobral

1727 — The Arrival of Freemasonry in Portugal   255
António Ventura

1732 — Preoccupations of the Overseas Council: Decline of the Portuguese   259
Diaspora in the World
Noelle Richardson

1755 — History and the Great Lisbon Earthquake   263
Mariana Françozo

1756 — The Demarcation of the Port Wine Region   267
Gaspar Martins Pereira

1759–1773 — The Suppression of the Society of Jesus   270
José Vicente Serrão

1807 — The Transfer of the Portuguese Royal Court to Brazil   274
Laura de Mello e Souza

Part V The Modern Period
Introduction to Part V — From the Independence of Brazil to   280
Portuguese Global Emigration
António Costa Pinto

1822 — Brazilian Independence: The Global and the Specific   282
Fernando Catroga

1823 — King Miguel and Miguelism   287
Maria Alexandre Lousada

1834 — The Institutionalization of Protestantism in Portugal   291
Timóteo Cavaco

1867 — Abolition of the Death Penalty   294
Rui de Figueiredo Marcos

1884 — Portugal at the Berlin Conference   299
Hugo Gonçalves Dores and Miguel Bandeira Jerónimo

1908 — The International Impact of the Regicide of Charles the First   302
Paulo Jorge Fernandes

1910 — The Republican Revolution   306
José Miguel Sardica

1911 — Resorts and Tourism: From Madeira to the Algarve   310
† *Alberto Vieira*

1914 — Amadeo, the Delaunays and Modernism   313
Joana Brites

1916 — Portugal and the Great War: Victory with a Taste of Defeat   317
Nuno Severiano Teixeira

1917 — Fatima, the Global Shrine   321
Marco Daniel Duarte

1933 — Salazarism and the Interwar Dictatorships   324
Rita Almeida de Carvalho

1934 — Cod: Global Connections within the National Myth   328
Álvaro Garrido

1940 — A Portuguese World on Display   332
Annarita Gori

1949 — Egas Moniz, a Nobel Prizewinner Who Founded a School   336
Carlos Fiolhais

1949 — Portugal and NATO: Rediscovering the Atlantic Option   340
Nuno Severiano Teixeira

1955 — Portugal in the "World Parliament"   343
Fernando Martins

1961 — Portugal as Pariah State During the Late Colonial Wars   346
Bruno Cardoso Reis

1966 — Eusébio, Lusotropicalism and the Globalization of Sports Idols   351
Nuno Domingos

1974 — The 25th of April: Transition to Democracy   355
Maria Inácia Rezola

1986 — Portugal's Membership to the European Economic Community   358
José Luís Cardoso

1988 — On the Internationalization of Portuguese Literature: Pessoa, Saramago and Lobo Antunes   362
Onésimo Teotónio Almeida

2011 — Portuguese Emigration: Global Interconnections 366
Rui Carita

The Editors, Scientific Coordinators and Contributors 371

Index 378

Series Editors' Preface

The field of global history is currently one of the most vibrant in the humanities. Despite the existence of acritical advocates and uninformed critics, the last decades have seen the publication of countless crucial works and many unpublished Ph.D. theses, which rigorously benefit from (albeit sometimes failing to test) the conceptual, methodological, and analytical possibilities offered by global history. However, side by side with other critical historiographical innovations (for example, transnational history), fruitfully dialoguing with them, global history is not a consensual domain. Multiple voices and arguments shape its perspectives, its proposals and indeed its future potential. The main scholarly aim of the field is the global contextualization of events and processes, to promote the ability to capture the interconnection and inter-dependence among actors, discourses, and practices across different geographies, linking the "local" with the "global". This dynamic can be achieved in diverse ways and the current volume leads the way scholastically.

An underlying theme throughout all the chapter contributions is that the global historical imagination must be expanded. The chapter contributions are exemplar in sponsoring and probing new ideas, hypotheses, and research methods. The potential embedded in better understanding global history is immense, and includes: acknowledging inclusive perspectives, from the "global north" to the "global south"; addressing issues of ethnocentric bias; recognizing the repercussions of nationalist hegemony; accepting how doctrines of exceptionality change over time; and developing an uncompromising new approach to "centre" and "periphery" analysis.

The original Portuguese publication of *The Global History of Portugal: From Prehistory to the Modern World* was met with much scholarly praise. Its publication in English marks a significant historiographical moment. Portuguese history has imperial and colonial dimensions, (geo)political crises, and social/cultural dynamics that make it an ideal platform for global history study. The result is a template for better understanding that historical legacy is global. The editors of this series, who also contribute to this volume, are delighted to include this important work in the series.

The Series Editors

António Costa Pinto
Onésimo Teotónio Almeida
Miguel Bandeira Jerónimo

Acknowledgements

At the end of a complex process of preparation, we would like to thank everyone who, from the first moment believed and supported this daring project that seeks to align Portugal with the new epistemology of international historiography.

Let us begin with heartfelt thanks to those colleagues who, unhesitatingly, accepted the challenge to constitute the academic advisory board overseeing this work: João Luís Cardoso for Pre- and Proto-history; Carlos Fabião for Classical Antiquity; Bernardo Vasconcelos e Sousa for the Middle Ages; Cátia Antunes for the Early Modern period; and António Costa Pinto for Modern Age. In close conjunction with the three of us, the Scientific Coordinators were responsible for selecting those events that served as springboards for the texts. Their expertise in undertaking a careful scientific review of the contributions was carried out with enthusiasm and dedication.

Our gratitude and acknowledgement also go to the ninety historians that authored the commissioned texts, accepting the daring proposal to rethink the subjects that they understood so well in keeping with the hermeneutic scope defined by the aims of this volume. It is thanks to them that readers can now for the first time perceive the history of Portugal through the prism of global history.

The proposal of this English version by Sussex Academic Press was enthusiastically stimulated by the series editors of *The Portuguese-Speaking World*, António Costa Pinto, Onésimo Almeida and Miguel Bandeira Jerónimo, and benefited from the very professional and generous help of the Editorial Director, Anthony Grahame. We are most grateful to all of you.

We are also indebted to the publisher of the Portuguese edition, *Temas & Debates / Círculo de Leitores*, and in particular its director, Guilhermina Gomes, for all the favours granted regarding the rights to publish the volume in languages other than Portuguese.

We also thank the secretaries of this project, coordinated by Cristiana Lucas Silva with the assistance of Paula Carreira and Milene Alves, who managed the correspondence and pre-editorial revision of the texts, and also Maria João Nobre, José Bernardino, Marta Marecos Duarte, Timóteo Cavaco and Carlos Serra for their help in text revisions and in index compilation. Without their work, this undertaking would have been impossible.

A special word of gratitude also to the three translators of the original Portuguese texts, Karen Bennett, Sheena Caldwell and Diana Silver, who did a brilliant job.

It is uncommon in Portugal for institutions to support projects of this kind. At a time when interest in historical culture is fading in societies, great praise is due to those who understand how a country's identity depends upon its memory and how historical knowledge is socially important, especially as regards knowledge of Portugal in the world. It is in this framework that we wish to pay sincere homage and express our unrestrained gratitude to the patrons that made this project possible: President of the Eugénio de Almeida Foundation; President of the Administration Board of the Montepio Mutualist Association; and President of the Administrative Council of the Navigator Company. A warm and sincere thanks to them. Without their clear-sightedness, and that of their collaborators, this *Global History of Portugal* would never have seen the light of day.

The Editors

CARLOS FIOLHAIS, JOSÉ EDUARDO FRANCO AND JOSÉ PEDRO PAIVA

General Introduction

The concept of globalization, a very recent term in our universal lexicon, has come to occupy a central place in the first decades of the twenty-first century. In fact, globalization – which is the intensification of a phenomenon that has been going on for centuries – has produced widespread perceptions and effects that have led to a reconsideration of identities (of individuals, countries, regions and even the whole planet, which is ultimately the common fatherland of humanity). We are now obliged to take account of the interconnectivity linking the numerous spaces around the globe that humans inhabit, as well as the consequent processes of uniformization and miscegenation, which accentuated in the nineteenth century, and, more obviously, in the twentieth.

The dizzyingly radical transformations brought about by this more recent globalization, provoked by, amongst other factors, digital communication technologies, have historical antecedents. These included the great sea voyages of the fifteenth and sixteenth centuries, protagonized by seafarers at the service of the Portuguese and Spanish Crowns. Sailing out into the unknown, and opening up new communication routes, (the Indian Ocean had been navigated since the early fifteenth century by many Arab vessels, and especially by the Chinese ships commanded by Zheng He at the beginning of the fifteenth century), Europeans broke through the frontiers of knowledge of the time. In the words of the sixteenth-century Portuguese mathematician Pedro Nunes, "they discovered new islands, new lands, new seas, new peoples, and what is more, new heavens and new stars". They ultimately opened up a whole new world, enabling humanity, for the first time in its history, to acquire an awareness of its own planetary dimension. From then on, at an ever-increasing pace, the world was unlocked – or, in the epigrammatic words of the seventeenth-century Portuguese Jesuit António Vieira, "the world was opened up to itself".

At the end of the nineteenth century, the inventions of first the electrical telegraph, then the wireless telegraph, enabled communications to be expanded around the world, a process that has accelerated to an astonishing pace since the end of the twentieth century with the information and telecommunications revolutions. At the same time, human travel has become progressively easier, both on land and sea, as well as (a novelty) by air. Today, the "global village" proclaimed by Canadian Marshall McLuhan back in the 1960s instigates cultural trends, behaviours and lifestyles as well as altering the classic paradigms of knowledge construction, while, in cyberspace, human communities across different continents have found a common forum that they can share.

Since the end of the twentieth century, the changes provoked by globalization have started to make themselves felt in the domain of historiography, transforming the analytical bias of the past. The village, the city, the region, the country, the continent – till recently viewed with the contingency imposed by mental and cultural barriers, as well as the tangible obstacles that enclosed them – have come to be understood as part of an interconnected dynamic to an unprecedented extent.

The appearance, in 2006, of the *Journal of Global History* (Cambridge University Press) was an important landmark in this regard, ushering in what later became known as the 'global turn' in historiography. This brought onto the historian's horizon new categories for understanding the world on a global scale, such as those of miscegenation, cultural conversion and connected history. Prior to this, the old school manuals, reflecting what was produced in the academies, had taught the history of a single country from an eminently national perspective, centred on the nation state, as Jeremy Adelman, professor at the University of Princeton, recalled in 2017 in a controversial text entitled "What is global history now?". The starting point was the configuration of rigid and apparently closed frontiers, which presupposed a certain cultural, mental, spiritual and symbolic territory, cantoned off within the land where one was born. Through this epistemological prism one studied first the history of one's own country, possibly acquiring some knowledge of others as seen through the window of one's native land. Each nation was the navel of the world, with everything else coming second or completely ignored, no more than a field upon which national vanity could be projected. Beyond the fatherland were a cluster of countries with which relations of cooperation, transaction, influence, dominion, conflict, separation, negation, or in some cases, acceptance, had been established. History was understood in a bipolar, dualist manner, separated into us and them. And others were often seen in a very black and white fashion, in terms of friends and foes. In more extreme cases, the national, or even local history, was conceived and taught as an almost autonomous reality with its own imaginary, quite separate from the history of the rest of the world, explained as if nothing else existed (or if it did exist, without this in any way determining our understanding of it). In Portuguese historiography, this pattern was broken in a determined manner by the distinguished historian Vitorino Magalhães Godinho, who set a new direction, particularly with his innovative concept of the historic-geographic complex. He understood how dense networks of relations were created, particularly from the fifteenth to sixteenth centuries, which transcended national (and European) borders, giving rise to what he had already classified in *Os Descobrimentos e a Economia Mundial* ("The Discoveries and World Economy", 1961), as a "market on a world scale".

Despite the critical debates that have emerged, of which the text by Jeremy Adelman is an example, as British historian Christopher Bayly recalled in 2004 in *The Birth of the Modern World 1780–1914* (a book that would transform historiographic paradigms), we all do global history, even if we don't always realize it. This new historiographic perspective on the time of globalization should not be confused with world history, which came earlier, nor with comparative history, from which it has borrowed some perspectives and methods. As defined by the German historian Sebastian Conrad in a book published in 2016 by Princeton University Press, with the clarity and simplicity only achievable by someone that has complete mastery of the subjects covered, global history is "a form of historical analysis in which phenomena, events, and processes are placed in global contexts". Global history is, therefore, very different from the sum of national histories.

To better understand the dynamics provoked by transnational interactions and interconnections, we need to remember that, in this domain, the historian's task does not consist, according to Conrad, of "writing a total history of the planet", exploring a particular (religious, cultural, political or other) movement. Instead, we should "bear in mind the global connections and structural conditions" to try to understand the long-term dynamics and the changes they undergo at pivotal moments which usually unfold after long maturation. In fact, as this historian recalls, global history "is not synonymous with 'macro-history'. [...] The most fascinating questions are often those that arise at the intersection between global processes and their local manifestations". It is in the interweaving of the global and the local that the most intriguing questions take root, making it necessary to discern global tendencies and local realizations, naturally very differentiated.

This perspective was emphasised by John-Paul Ghobrial, professor at the University of Oxford, in the introduction to a special issue of the prestigious journal *Past & Present* published at the end of 2019. In it, he argued that global history has not only resisted the criticism levelled at it from various sectors but has also animated historiographic debate. Offering an in-depth exploration of global history and its possible articulations with microhistory, the issue shows that only by using micro and macro visions simultaneously is it possible to analyse and understand the local impacts of universal phenomena and vice versa. Paraphrasing the American historian Tonio Andrade, in a 2010 article in the *Journal of World History* entitled "A Chinese farmer, two African boys and a warlord. Toward a global microhistory", we might say that it is useful to adopt perspectives from microhistory and biography to "populate our models, and theories with real people", in other words, to produce "global microhistory".

Doing global history, therefore, does not mean devaluing a solid knowledge of the local and factual, nor does it mean ceasing to recognize that it is at this scale and in this type of context, sometimes through the actions of individuals, that dynamics occur which often prove crucial for our understanding of change, rupture and continuities. Consequently, without a detailed and rigorous knowledge of events at local scale and recourse to documents kept in archives (which are themselves the result of historical constructions of local and national bias), it will never be possible to do good history, bringing global perspectives to the circulation and integration of ideas and processes germinated elsewhere or not. Thus, in this *Global History of Portugal*, we have invited specialists in particular places, facts and people to rethink their knowledge from an open perspective and recompose it in a way that is not closed in upon those same spaces, events and characters. In the light of these trends, we no longer consider countries, regions, cities and villages as closed spaces, confined within their own borders. Instead, they are viewed as territorial platforms to be observed throughout the long process of humanization, from the first human communities – who left behind indistinct and multiform traces which sophisticated archaeological methods have now started to reveal – to the new migratory waves, which (despite the atavistic responses they have generated, manifested above all by the building of walls) oblige the relativization of limits that previously separated humanity into national, regional, urban and even village communities.

Nations are young entities, defined and consolidated in the nineteenth century. But the territories circumscribed by them form the stage upon which different peoples, ethnic groups, clans, tribes, fiefdoms, kingdoms, empires, republics have acted, circulating and settling irrespective of current borders. Global history goes back thousands of years while the history of nations no more than a few centuries.

Despite having one of the oldest borders in Europe, the territory in which Portugal is currently inscribed was, like most others, crossed for thousands of years by the dynamic circulation of different peoples. In the prehistoric protoglobalization, as defined by French sociologist and historian Edgar Morin in his work *Penser Global* (2015), they circulated across continents in accordance with the rhythms of climatic cycles. The *locus* that is today called Portugal was a point of arrival and departure for various peoples, cultures, languages, ideas, fashions, behaviours, beliefs, institutions and products, which impressed upon it, and upon the places where they arrived, signs of multimodal miscegenation which gradually enriched the colours of the world, but also provoked disruptions and violence, and often war, suffering and resistance.

Thus, in recent decades, a penetrating reflection on global history has developed, obliging the rethinking of the past. This epistemological upheaval has led to the emergence of new global histories of various nations: in 2017, there appeared world histories of France and Italy, followed in 2018 by similar perspectives on the Netherlands and Spain. In America too, books have been published dealing with the global history of the United States.

This volume was naturally inspired by those that preceded it, especially by the pioneer French book edited by Patrick Boucheron, as regards both the perspective adopted and the very structure of the work. It contains 92 texts grouped into five chronological blocs: Prehistory and Protohistory (ed. João Luís Cardoso), Antiquity (ed. Carlos Fabião), The Middle Ages (ed. Bernardo Vasconcelos e Sousa), The Early Modern Period (ed. Cátia Antunes) and The Modern Period (ed. António Costa Pinto). The texts begin with an event, carefully chosen by the coordinators and section editors, which is interpreted in the light of the precepts described above. Each Part opens with a short introduction by the editor, explaining the logic and coherence of the chosen events and offering a reading of the whole based on the contributions supplied by the various texts.

Thus, this *Global History of Portugal*, through an exercise in analytic synthesis, offers a critical overview of the history which originated in Portuguese territory or passed through it, stimulating the process of encounter and dis-encounter in today's global world. This is Portugal in contact with (the) world(s), receiving and exerting influences that transcend physical and mental boundaries. This history is as decentred as possible from the national viewpoints through which we have been used to knowing our past, and gives special attention to the world that moulded Portugal and the Portuguese, and to the ways Portugal configured the world. It seeks to identify and understand the transversal dynamics of historic impact and the impulses these gave to the construction of the country and world. Each are today the result of multiple intersections. As these texts make clear, there was, until the fourteenth–fifteenth centuries, more reception of influxes than irradiation of innovation (though this territory at the extreme west of Europe had never been totally closed in upon itself). Then, between the mid-fifteenth and sixteenth centuries, this pattern altered, with the appearance, in what was by then the kingdom of Portugal, of numerous signs of innovation, triggering changes throughout the whole world. Later, however, this tendency subsided and it again became more about receiving than about creating or sowing innovation.

This publishing project has counted on the collaboration of almost ninety contributor authors based not only in Portugal but also in different countries around the globe. Portuguese and non-Portuguese, these are specialists in diverse subfields of history such as political history, institutional history, geographic history, cultural history, history of science, economic history, social history, history of art, religious history, amongst others. With them, the reader is invited to construct a non-parochial view of the history of Portugal in the belief that today we cannot understand the history of a place, even an old country, if we overlook the wider world with which that country has always interacted.

Portugal is the result of countless dialogue and clashes with other places. And there are traces of these mediations, spread around the world by the inhabitants of its space. It is this fascinating story that we tell here in order to better understand who we are and the world in which we live.

CARLOS FIOLHAIS
JOSÉ EDUARDO FRANCO
JOSÉ PEDRO PAIVA

PART I

Prehistory and Protohistory

Introduction to Part I

From Modern Humans to the Advent of Writing

Universidade Aberta

The essays which follow, covering the Prehistory and Protohistory of the territory which is nowadays Portugal, result from critical discussion of key themes associated with the two major periods prior to the introduction of writing (Prehistory) or contemporary with the first societies to adopt writing in the Western Peninsula (Protohistory).

The themes were chosen taking into consideration the main aspects which best reveal the role of the territory that would later become Portugal during this lengthy period of time, as an arena for interactions between different populations or even the setting for the diffusion of ideas and concepts. The information is based on material evidence gathered from archaeological excavations or, more recently, studies in molecular biology and genetics. The latter has provided a new and unexpected set of information that has proved invaluable to our understanding of the mobility of populations prior to the introduction of writing.

Five topics were selected, relating to decisive periods of social, economic and cultural change driven by the various communities existing at the time. They represent a series of events which, although part of a continuum intrinsic to the human occupation of the area nowadays known as Portugal, represent significant examples of social transformation, whilst not detracting from others such as the phenomenon of fortification during the Copper Age, closely related to the increasing social complexity that developed throughout the third millennium BC.

The role of geographical movements of past human groups to and from Portuguese territory, influenced in certain cases by major changes in climate occurring over time, is recognized as a common denominator.

Hence, 240,000–10,000 BC concerns interaction in the south-west of the Peninsula during the transition from the Middle to the Upper Palaeolithic between groups of anatomically modern humans and the last of the Neanderthals, leading to genetic crossbreeding, as suggested by the hybrid characteristics of the Lapedo child.

One key moment of change in the history of humanity involved the breakdown of the subsistence model based on hunter-gathering that had been present since its inception, followed by the adoption of an economy dominated by food production, which took place in Portuguese territory in approximately 5500 BC and still prevails today. This is the information conveyed by the presence of domestic species of cereals and animals originating from the Near East, accompanied by technological innovations such as pottery and polished stone artefacts, which is the subject of the second essay.

It discusses the practices which influenced the change, in the context of the actual dynamics established between populations in different phases of development.

In the period **2700–1800** BC occured the expansion of a characteristically European form of pottery in the third millennium bc, namely the Maritime Bell Beaker, whose name refers to the fact that it is shaped like an inverted bell and was distributed throughout Europe from centres located on the Atlantic coast. The oldest of these centres would have been situated in the Tagus estuary, expanding to the Breton coast, which in turn became established as a new distribution point for the Baltics and the interior of mainland Europe. Maritime Bell Beakers have been identified in locations extending as far as Eastern Europe and the Central Mediterranean, embodying the direct or indirect presence of populations that were undoubtedly genetically different yet collectively responsible for the European-wide diffusion of this type of vessel, organized by typologically distinct regional groups and resulting from locally instigated interaction processes that unfolded on an unprecedented scale.

Such wide-ranging interactions, covering the whole of Europe, did not fail to register in the archaeological records as an ongoing movement of people and, above all, objects, travelling more intensively in all directions throughout the Bronze Age, especially between **2000–800** BC. Based on archaeological evidence, it will be demonstrated that Portuguese territory was, at the time although only for a brief period, the hub of Atlantic-Mediterranean relations due to its geographical position and natural resources, embodying the variable geometry of core-periphery economic relations that had developed over time. The voyages to and from Portuguese territory undertaken at the time, essentially for trading purposes, together with the possible overland routes explained by the nature of certain hoards from Central Europe, facilitated the wide circulation of raw materials and manufactured products, both functional and religious. The presence of the latter reveals the creation of a mindset common to all who incorporated them into their cognitive universe, producing the first pan-European consciousness, shared by the elites at least, in the societies of the time.

The period between the **Ninth to the Fifth Centuries** BC is to some extent a corollary of the previous one, characterizes the relations established in certain points along the Portuguese coast from the end of the ninth century BC with the western Phoenicians, who regularly ventured out from Cádiz and Huelva across the ocean, following a pre-established programme, to found settlements in the Tagus and Mondego estuaries. They forged deep and lasting relationships with the local populations which soon resulted in the transfer of technology, including writing and ways of living (urbanism), as well as language itself and exogenous religious practices that were incorporated into everyday life, following on from practices already confirmed for the end of the Bronze Age.

According to the contributions provided it may therefore be concluded that interaction between populations – already existing and newly arrived, as well as those leaving for other destinations – was a constant feature in the history of humanity. For the first time, we believe, these texts offer a coherent, significant and organized vision of this reality with regard to the vast geographical space of Europe, in which the territory of Portugal has always been involved, in ways that extend beyond geographical determinants. The ongoing balance between the economic, social and cultural circumstances of the succession of populations that have lived there and the wider geographical conjunctures which have partly determined but also been repeatedly influenced by them, is the common denominator in these contributions.

This knowledge was only made possible through research and the materials gathered over the last twenty-five years, which comprise an extraordinary collection of new information clearly reflected in the essays which follow. The result, for the reader, is far more than the mere sum of its parts, offering an undogmatic, rigorous and up-to-date critical appreciation, but also one which, like all scientific knowledge, can always be surpassed, since it is constantly being enriched.

240,000–10,000 BC
From Neanderthal Man to *Homo sapiens*

Fossil remains of our ancestors have only been identified in three locations, namely Gruta Nova da Columbeira (Bombarral), the Figueira Brava Cave (Sesimbra) and the Oliveira Cave (Torres Novas), amounting to less than a dozen bones.

Approximately 800,000 years ago, in the prehistoric period known as the Lower Palaeolithic, a new hominid appeared on the face of the Earth: *Homo heidelbergensis*, or Heidelberg Man, identified in October 1907 following the discovery of the Mauer mandible, named after the place where it was found, close to Heidelberg (Germany). Between 300,000 to 40,000 years ago during the Middle Palaeolithic, this ancestor of ours, together with various subspecies scattered throughout Europe, would have given rise to *Homo sapiens*, as well as a diverse set of other humans possibly belonging to the same species. One such example was *Homo neanderthalensis*, or Neanderthal Man, named after the first fossils identified in the Neander Valley in Düsseldorf (Germany). Originating in Europe, he gradually spread throughout the entire continent before arriving in the Near East and Central Asia. It is also the case with the fossil known as Denisova Man, after the site of the same name, the Denisova Cave in Siberia (Russia). Recently identified by molecular biology studies, this species is likely to have been of Asian origin and had colonized the whole of Asia before reaching Eastern Europe, where it interbred with *Homo neanderthalensis* and *Homo sapiens*.

Approximately 150,000 years ago the latter, of African origin, would have been responsible for various migration waves from East Africa to the Arabian Peninsula, either crossing the Red Sea from the Horn of Africa or traveling overland through the area where the Suez Canal was constructed. However, human archaeogenetic studies appear to indicate that only one of these migrations, which took place between 70,000 and 60,000 years ago, would have been responsible for the present-day modern human population. Despite their differences, the presence of other fossil forms in Europe and Asia admit significant genetic exchanges between various contemporary human groups during the past 100,000 to 50,000 years. As a result, most of the current non-African human population, represented by *Homo sapiens*, has 1% to 6% Neanderthal DNA, while the human group from Asia and Oceania has up to 6% Denisovan DNA. In Portugal, information on the Neanderthals, in particular with regard to their origin, is still limited. Fossil remains of our ancestors have only been identified in three locations, namely Gruta Nova da Columbeira (Bombarral), the Figueira Brava Cave (Sesimbra) and the Oliveira Cave (Torres Novas), amounting to less than a dozen bones, including teeth and various phalanges. They all appear to date back to an already advanced phase in the Neanderthal occupation of Portugal and are probably between 80,000 and 40,000 years old. The only potential exceptions are two teeth found in the Aroeira Cave (Torres Novas) in 2001 and 2002 by Anthony Marks, which have a chronology of approximately 240,000 years. These fossil remains have not been definitively identified as Neanderthal although, given their age and cultural context, which is typical of the Middle Palaeolithic, they would be the oldest Neanderthal remains found in present-day Portuguese territory. This would appear to be confirmed by the presence of a skullcap in the same site dating from 400,000 years ago, stratigraphically older than the aforementioned teeth. Reported in 2018 by a team led by João Zilhão, it represents a phase in human evolution in the region that predates the Neanderthals.

The few archaeological contexts for the beginning of the Middle Palaeolithic in Portugal are poorly represented and dated, meaning that, apart from the above-mentioned Aroeira Cave and the recently excavated Cobrinhos site (Vila Velha de Ródão) which may be around 150,000 years old, there are still no known sites that can be confirmed as belonging to the time prior to the last interglacial period during Marine Isotope Stage 5 (a warm climate phase which occurred around 120,000 years ago). For this period, the significance of the Praia Rei Cortiço site located south of Foz do Arelho near Caldas da Rainha, where a Middle Palaeolithic archaeological horizon was found, should be noted. In addition to sites containing human remains dating from the end of the Middle Palaeolithic, there is also a group of sites confirmed as dating from 80,000 to 40,000 years ago, the most important of which are Foz do Enxarrique and Vilas Ruivas (Vila Velha de Ródão), Mira Nascente (Nazaré), the Caldeirão Cave (Tomar), Lapa do Picareiro (Fátima), Vale do Forno 8 (Alpiarça) and the Escoural Cave (near Évora). All of these sites, as well as others which have recently been located, such as the Companheira Cave (near Portimão), may be the object of archaeological work that will provide a more accurate chronological and cultural characterisation of the period and a better understanding of Neanderthal occupation in the area which is nowadays Portugal.

In this region, the stone knapping technology used to produce the most common Neanderthal tools during the Middle Palaeolithic appears to be characterized by two main phases. The first and earliest of these, possibly dating back more than 150,000 years, has been identified in the Aroeira Cave and in Milharós (Vale do Forno, Alpiarça) and is defined by the presence of so-called Micoquian bifaces (a name derived from the French site of La Micoque), small asymmetric bifaces, leaf-shaped implements, bifacial backed knives and bifacial scrapers, as well as a small amount of Levallois flaking (a technique which enabled the user to predefine the shape and size of the flakes that would be produced). The second or Mousterian phase (the name for a stone flaking industry derived from the French cave of Le Moustier), is characterized by the presence of flakes and projectile points produced from Levallois and discoidal cores. The retouched tools are mainly denticulates and notches, and rarely simple sidescrapers. Quartzite, quartz and flint, usually locally sourced, were used as raw materials.

The Neanderthals in Portuguese territory appear to have survived by hunting species which included deer, aurochs, horses and wild boars but rarely larger species, such as rhinoceros or elephant. Although there is little data, Neanderthals would also have consumed marine resources such as fish, shellfish, birds and aquatic mammals including seal and dolphin.

The point at which Neanderthal populations disappeared and were replaced by the new *Homo sapiens* population in the Iberian Peninsula has been one of the most frequently discussed topics in the past two decades. Various studies suggest the prolonged survival of the Neanderthals in the south of the Iberian Peninsula until at least 37,000 years ago. In this context, according to the Ebro Frontier Model, the south of the Iberian Peninsula was a Neanderthal refuge for several thousand years after the initial arrival of *Homo sapiens* north of the River Ebro, approximately 42,000 years ago at the beginning of the Upper Palaeolithic.

There is no consensus on the late presence of the Neanderthals in southern Iberia, primarily based on absolute dating obtained from sites which include the Oliveira and Foz do Enxarrique caves, both in Portugal, and Gorham's Cave in Gibraltar. According to Rachel E. Wood and other authors, the validity of the results obtained from some of the sites has been questioned on the basis of possible underestimations of the ages, associated with the problems of stratigraphic integrity, contamination with modern carbon, and poorly preserved collagen in the radiocarbon samples that were used. On the other hand, the Ebro Frontier Model proposes the relatively late emigration of groups of *Homo sapiens* bringing Aurignacian technology (an industry named after the French site of Aurignac) to the extreme west of the Iberian Peninsula, claiming the existence of Aurignacian occupations in the Portuguese sites of Gato Preto and Vale de Porcos (both in the Rio Maior district), and the Salemas, Pego do Diabo (Loures) and Escoural caves.

The flaking industries associated with these occupations are distinct from those found in the Neanderthal sites and are defined by the presence of the small retouched points known as Dufour bladelets, produced by working a carinated core using a system identical to the one identified in the Aurignacian III–IV, a phase of the Upper Palaeolithic in France. Only the Pego do Diabo site presents an absolute chronology obtained by using more modern dating methods, situating the first *Homo sapiens* occupations in the region approximately 34,500 years ago, as João Zilhão maintains. These results suggest the possible coexistence of *Homo neanderthalensis* and *Homo sapiens* in the west of the Peninsula, which would have allowed for genetic cross-breeding. The argument seems to be confirmed by the hybrid morphology of the skeleton of the Lapedo child (Lagar Velho, Leiria). However, the dating of approximately 29,000 years obtained from animal bones and charcoal remains associated with this burial (the only known example of its kind during the Upper Palaeolithic in Portugal) places it within the next cultural phase of the Upper Palaeolithic, the Gravettian (named after the French site of La Gravette).

A considerable number of sites, mainly located in Portuguese Estremadura (including Cabeço de Porto Marinho, Abrigo do Lagar Velho, the Caldeirão Cave and Lapa do Picareiro), the Algarve (Vale Boi) and the Côa Valley (including Olga Grande and Cardina I), reveal that the Gravettian would have begun around 34,000 years ago and lasted roughly until the beginning of the Last Glacial Maximum, approximately 26,000 years ago. The lithic industries associated with this period were defined by the extensive use of the abrupt retouch technique, also known as backed retouch, and the manufacture of projectile points known as La Gravette, Microgravette or double-backed bi-pointed points. In terms of subsistence, as in the previous phase, the total disappearance of large herbivores found in Middle Palaeolithic sites can be confirmed, together with the predominance of smaller herbivores such as deer, horse and aurochs, and even smaller species, including rabbit. In addition, there was an increasing and more varied use of marine resources, evident in the consumption of different types of shellfish and the use of molluscs as adornments.

The environmental changes that occurred over 26,000 years ago with the start of the Last Glacial Maximum, one of the coldest periods of all times, were accompanied by significant alterations to the technological and cultural structures of populations. This took place over two successive periods, namely the Upper Palaeolithic phases known as the Proto-Solutrean and Solutrean (named after the French site known as Le Solutré), lasting until approximately 20,000 years ago. In technological terms, the main changes involved mastery of flaked stone tools, with the appearance of new types of projectile points that were probably for use with a bow and arrow. They were larger than those from the previous phase and were produced during the Solutrean by using the invasive flat retouch, which gave the items a leaf-shaped, often bifacial, appearance. Important sites include the Caldeirão Cave, Casal do Cepo (Torres Novas), Lapa do Anecrial (Porto de Mós), Vale Comprido (Rio Maior), Vale Almoinha (Torres Vedras) and Vale Boi (Vila do Bispo). The first examples of portable art in Portuguese territory also date from this period, two of the most significant examples being the engraved schist plaquettes from the Caldeirão Cave and Vale Boi rockshelter, both featuring zoomorphic images.

The last phase of the Upper Palaeolithic, known as the Magdalenian, extended from approximately 20,000 to 10,000 years ago, ending with the new wave of climate and environmental changes that marked the beginning of the Holocene. Within Portuguese territory, although there are several dozen known sites that can be assigned to this chronology, only twelve have provided chronometric information, most of which is based on results from sites in Lapa do Picareiro and Cabeço de Porto Marinho (Rio Maior) and Lapa do Suão (Bombarral).

With regard to flaked stone tools, the disappearance of the leaf-shaped items characteristic of the previous phase can be observed, together with a general reduction in the size of tools and a return to the technological models of the Gravettian and the predominance of backed points. The subsistence patterns remained similar, but with an increase in the consumption of small species such as rabbit.

The human occupation of the Portuguese territory during the Upper Palaeolithic is comparable to findings elsewhere in Europe, particularly in the rest of the Iberian Peninsula. The most significant differences appear to have developed principally after the start of the Holocene, around 12,000 years ago, at a time which marked the beginning of a new phase in Prehistory with the development of the Epipalaeolithic and the Mesolithic, the final stage in the life of the hunter-gatherers in Portuguese territory.

João Cascalheira and Nuno Bicho
Interdisciplinary Centre for Archaeology and Evolution of Human Behaviour,
Faculty of Humanities and Social Sciences, University of Algarve

Bibliography
Print

BICHO, Nuno, HAWS, Jonathan, "The Magdalenian in central and southern Portugal: Human ecology at the end of the Pleistocene", *Quaternary International*, vols. 272–273, 2012, pp. 6–16.

PEREIRA, Telmo et al., "O Paleolítico Médio no território português", *Mainake*, no. 33, 2011, pp. 11–30.

WOOD, Rachel E. et al., "Radiocarbon dating casts doubt on the late chronology of the Middle to Upper Palaeolithic transition in Southern Iberia", *Proceedings of the National Academy of Sciences*, vol. 110, no. 8, 2013, pp. 2781–2786.

Digital

CASCALHEIRA, João, BICHO, Nuno, "On the chronological structure of the Solutrean in Southern Iberia", *PLoS One*, Sept. 2015: https://journals.plos.org/plosone/article?id=10.1371/journal.pone.0137308 (accessed 26 July 2019).

ZILHÃO, João et al., "Pego do Diabo (Loures, Portugal). Dating the emergence of anatomical modernity in Westernmost Eurasia", *PLoS One*, Jan. 2010: https://journals.plos.org/plosone/article?id=10.1371/journal.pone.0008880 (accessed 26 July 2019).

5500–4500 BC
The Spread of Farming and Domestic Animals

Although different socio-economic realities have been documented within the Portuguese Early Neolithic, it should be noted that domestic elements have been found in all regions from the beginning of this period, whose development over time would lead to irreversible changes on various different levels: ecological, subsistence, economic, demographic, social and ideological.

The dawn of the Neolithic established a structural division in human history between societies whose subsistence was based on hunter-gathering and those which practised some form of agriculture and/or animal husbandry. Essentially, it was a division between societies that made use of spontaneous food resources and those which produced their own food, with all the consequences this would imply for various aspects of their ways of life, from demography to ideology.

In the territory that would become Portugal, the first developments in this complex transition process took place roughly between 5500 and 4500 BC, a period of approximately one millennium, usually known as the Early Neolithic.

During this period, agriculture and herding already involved a wide range of animal and vegetable species which have since become basic elements of food production. Varieties of barley (*Hordeum sp.*), wheat (*Triticum sp.*) and various types of pulses, including pea (*Pisum sativum*), broad bean (*Vicia faba*) and lentil (*Lens culinaris*) have been recorded for the Early Neolithic. The range of domesticated animals included cattle (*Bos taurus*), goat (*Capra hircus*), sheep (*Ovis aries*) and pig (*Sus domesticus*), in addition to the dog (*Canis familiaris*), which had been domesticated in the previous epoch, although not to serve as a source of food.

One issue which is key to understanding the cultural processes behind the appearance of these domestic species stems from the fact that the agriotypes – that is, the ancestral wild forms – of some of these animals (goat and sheep) and plants (barley, wheat, pea, lentil) do not exist, and did not exist at the time, in Europe. Although at one point serious consideration was given to the possibility that some domestication processes may have, at least partly, occurred locally, nowadays various lines of research (zooarchaeological, palaeontological and genetic) have established that all domestic species in the Neolithic originated from the Near East, where the respective agriotypes existed at the time, and that their domestication first began approximately 10,000 years ago. They only expanded into Europe later, via the Aegean Sea and the Balkans. In fact, only crossbreeding between these first domestic animals and their wild European counterparts is conceivable and has actually been verified by palaeo-genetic studies. This would have been the case with the ox and the aurochs (*Bos primigenius*), which became extinct in Europe in the seventeenth century, and the pig and wild boar (*Sus scrofa*). The sheep, which appeared in large numbers during the Mediterranean Early Neolithic, had no wild ancestors here. It is derived from the Near East muflon (*Ovis orientalis*), whose habitat extended from Anatolia to the Iranian plateaux. Therefore, the cultural and historical processes that led to the introduction of these elements to Europe – and, more particularly, to the Iberian Peninsula – can only be established within this specific framework.

On the basis of this assumption, the interpretations constructed around this time of radical transformation (the "Neolithisation process") may be structured around three main perspectives, as presented by Joan Bernabeu:

- Migrationism: the emergence of the Neolithic is explained by migration processes or, in other words, movements of people or groups bringing all the innovations of the period with them – the so-called "Neolithic package". Interpretative models such as the "wave of advance" or "pioneer colonisation" form part of this concept. The former argues for continuous demographic growth from the moment agriculture was adopted in the Near East, leading to a steady rate of migratory episodes over short distances (the notion of "demic diffusion") which, in due time, resulted in the Neolithisation of the entire European continent. The second model supports the existence of rapid migration processes by sea covering larger geographical areas, by which small Neolithic groups were gradually established along the shores of the Mediterranean in territories on the fringes of the existing Mesolithic settlement centres;

- Indigenism: in contrast to the previous perspective, the claim that it was information and material items (from plants and animals to objects) rather than people that circulated, via networks of contacts. The so-called "availability model" applied by some authors to the example of Portugal should be emphasized. It envisages three consecutive stages in the relationship between Neolithic farmers and Mesolithic hunter-gatherers in "agricultural border zones", by which the Neolithisation of the latter took place through the economic and social interactions established between both. The three stages unfolded as follows, in accordance with the approximate given chronologies: (i) the availability phase (5500–5000 BC), in which hunter-gathering was still the main means of subsistence for the Mesolithics; (ii) the substitution phase (5000–4500 BC), corresponding to the effective expansion of production strategies; (iii) the consolidation phase (4500 BC onwards), in which agriculture finally constituted almost all subsistence strategies. Following this model, it was also proposed that these interaction processes could have resulted in the selection or filtering by Mesolithic societies – the "filter model" – of elements that made up the "Neolithic package", a process which would determine the adoption of only part of the technological and economic innovations, rather than all of them:

- Mixed perspectives: the claim that the two previous processes may have both played a role in the formation of the first agricultural societies to varying extents, according to the concrete situations under analysis. Therefore, the processes that took place in the Neolithic past may have differed according to region, depending on the respective ecological-geographical conditions and, above all, the historical trajectory and socio-economic conditions of the human communities involved in the process of Neolithisation.

The past twenty-five years of archaeological research into the Early Neolithic would appear to indicate that this last perspective is applicable to Portugal, as António Faustino Carvalho and João Luís Cardoso propose.

The arrival of exogenous populations in coastal areas, particularly in Estremadura, is one possibility. It was initially advanced by João Zilhão on the basis of strictly archaeological data, but has received further support from ongoing genetic research into the osteological remains of these populations. In other words, the triggering factor for Neolithisation would have been a concrete migration process which took place in the middle of the sixth millennium BC. The phase which immediately followed, involving the expansion of the agropastoral economy into adjacent territories inland, would have developed according to the specific features of each area.

Indeed, the coastline and limestone massifs of Estremadura do not appear to have been regularly exploited by the last hunter-gatherers of the Tagus valley. Moreover, the "Neolithic package" emerged there in its entirety from the start of the Early Neolithic. Although economic specialisation can be observed (for example, a greater tendency towards herding in mountain areas), the region presents what seems to be a fully established production economy from the beginning, which at times was even sedentary (for example, in the fertile terrains of Lower Estremadura) and for which there was no previous cultural tradition. In the Alentejo and Algarve a mosaic of hunter-gatherer and agropastoral components emerges, each with very varying degrees of importance, evident in the example of shell middens (accumulated remains of shells and other vestiges of human occupation) along the shoreline and various small temporary camps scattered throughout the region, while there are few known permanent settlements. Within this broader context, some Mesolithic cultural features appear to have survived, in particular those associated with technology. North of the Mondego, where the orographic and bioclimatic conditions are markedly different from the typically Mediterranean conditions in the southern half of the country and there were fewer Mesolithic settlements, the Neolithic would have arrived later (in the final centuries of the sixth millennium BC) and appears to have developed in a more diffuse and general way within the landscape, based on a strategy of residential mobility, regardless of the specific environmental context.

Although different socio-economic realities have been documented within the Portuguese Early Neolithic, it should be noted that domestic elements have been found in all regions from the beginning of this period, whose development over time would lead to irreversible changes on various different levels: ecological, due to the clearing of forests to create pastureland and agricultural fields (possibly using the "slash and burn" method); subsistence, with the use of animal "secondary products" (milk, wool, traction power, etc.); economic, with the storage of agricultural surpluses; demographic, with the population growth resulting from the agropastoral economy and the rise of "village life"; social, with rising inequalities between individuals and particular groups; and ideological, with the arrival of new "world views".

Perhaps the most striking changes are the biological adaptations that developed in these societies from whom we are descended, namely tolerance to gluten, ethanol and lactose, resulting in the culturally imposed adoption of the consumption of cereals, alcohol, milk and its derivatives.

António Faustino Carvalho
University of Algarve

Bibliography

BERNABEU, Joan, "Sobre el origen y difusión del Neolítico en la Península Ibérica, ca. 5600–5000 cal BC", *Promontoria*, no. 5, 2007, pp. 125–162.

CARDOSO, João Luís, *Pré-História de Portugal*, Lisbon, Universidade Aberta, 2007.

CARVALHO, António Faustino, "A emergência do Neolítico no actual território português: Pressupostos teóricos, modelos interpretativos e a evidência empírica", *O Arqueólogo Português*, series IV, no. 21, 2003, pp. 65–150.

ZILHÃO, João, "The spread of agro-pastoral economies across Mediterranean Europe: A view from the Far West", *Journal of Mediterranean Archaeology*, no. 6, fasc. 1, 1993, pp. 5–63.

2700–1800 BC

The Bell Beaker Question: Origin and Diffusion during the Third Millennium BC

The weak genetic influence of the Central European regions on Beaker populations within Portuguese territory means that the latter, whether due to their remote geographical location or, above all, their earlier chronology, did not receive any input from this diffusion, thus affirming that they are the direct descendants of their Neolithic ancestors.

Bell Beaker production, which took place between approximately 2700 and 1800 BC in the territory which is nowadays Portugal, is particularly well-known for its ceramics, whose most characteristic shape gave rise to the name for this set of products, which also includes ornaments, clothing and copper weapons. The most distinctive form of these vessels is the so-called Maritime or Standard Beaker, shaped like an inverted bell and decorated with stippled horizontal bands, filled in with alternating oblique lines. The term "Maritime" derives from the fact that its European-wide diffusion probably occurred by sea, via coastal voyages.

The important 1977 study by Richard J. Harrison, a professor at Bristol University, had been unable to take fully into account the Dutch model which defined research into the origins and diffusion of Bell Beaker production within Europe during the 1980s and 1990s. According to this model, Maritime beakers would have evolved out of Dutch Corded Ware, namely vessels decorated by pressing lengths of cord horizontally into the fresh clay, a perspective later rejected by Laure Salanova. In fact, the radiocarbon dates meanwhile obtained showed that the corded bell beakers in Holland were, in general, more modern than the oldest Iberian Maritime beakers. The earlier dating for the latter was recently confirmed, reinforcing the classic theory which had been put forward via different channels since the beginning of the twentieth century. In 1913, Hubert Schmidt first drew attention to the importance of the Iberian Peninsula with regard to the origins of Bell Beaker vessels, soon followed by Pedro Bosch Gimpera, who hypothesized that they had spread throughout Europe from Iberia. This inspired Alberto del Castillo Yurrita in his renowned overview *La Cultura del Vaso Campaniforme (Su Origen y Extensión en Europa)* (1928). Many years later, the author affirmed that bell beakers had always spread by sea routes – via the Atlantic and the Mediterranean – and that this was due to the copper industry. Moreover, he anticipated the importance of future excavation work in settlements in the Tagus estuary region in terms of resolving the question of the origin and chronology of the Bell Beaker culture.

This theory was gradually refined, in particular by Edward Sangmeister's "reflux" theory described in his study *Exposé sur la Civilisation du Vase Campaniforme. Les Civilisations Atlantiques du Néolithique à l'Âge du Fer* (1963), which was, to some extent, corroborated by Richard J. Harrison's dual model presented in *The Bell Beaker Cultures of Spain and Portugal* (1977). The model, which recognized two different origins, one in the Iberian Peninsula and the other in Central Europe, was recently supported by the DNA results for European Bell Beaker populations.

Returning to the classic theory, Laure Salanova argued that the origin of the Maritime Beaker was the Tagus estuary, as this was the European region in which the greatest concentration of this type of product can be found, given that this vessel corresponds to the only pure form of Bell Beaker production which she defines as the standard style. In this context, the significance of the radiocarbon dating becomes evident, indicating its true age in the said region, particularly in the case of the prehistoric settlement in Leceia (Oeiras), since it establishes the emergence of the Bell Beaker culture in the Tagus estuary region at approximately 2750 BC, a time in which Maritime Beakers already coexisted with regional Bell Beaker production and an earlier tradition of ceramic production.

DNA analyses on a European scale of the skeletal remains of Bell Beaker populations from the Tagus estuary region have confirmed that they are directly descended from their local ancestors. Therefore, this region is indirectly confirmed as the origin of the Maritime Beaker, from whence it expanded along the Atlantic coast, where Brittany was a key reception centre, until the amounts become insignificant in more eastern regions such as the Rhine Valley and the Netherlands.

The specific incidence of Maritime vessels in the Tagus estuary region cannot be separated from the wealth and use of fertile soils in this region, which resulted in very productive agriculture that generated surpluses requiring transregional circuits for trading. Hence, the agricultural importance of the region, as verified in other areas in Europe, would explain the abundance of examples of bell beakers in the estuary, in far greater amounts than in regions where there was copper, thus challenging the traditional Bell Beaker-copper industry pairing. This conclusion is confirmed in Portugal by analyses undertaken in the copper regions of the Upper and Lower Alentejo, where the Bell Beaker presence is limited, and it is even more marked in the Algarve, where it is only residual, despite the wealth of copper found there.

Moreover, in the Tagus estuary zone the hypothesis that Bell Beaker products correspond to prestige goods is not acceptable. In fact, they sometimes comprise all the decorative pottery found both in open Bell Beaker settlements (Freiria, in Cascais) and simple farm units (Leião, in Oeiras; Monte do Castelo, in Oeiras) where the possibility of a social hierarchy cannot be admitted. Within Bell Beaker ceramic production, the exceptions are the Maritime beakers, whose social value or functions, for authors such as Laure Salanova, "extend far beyond simple everyday use". In fact, the existence of two operational chains leading to different Bell Beaker products – the Maritime Beakers and the cruder vessels with technically and thematically different decorations – indicates the presence of different craftsmen. How can their coexistence be explained? What are the reasons for this? Since 2014 both questions have been fully explained by the author of this text. Firstly, the results of the radiocarbon analyses show the coexistence, since the second half of the third millennium BC, of Maritime Beakers and cruder recipients, usually large storage vessels and highly decorated broad flat slips known as Palmela bowls. On the basis of the survey carried out at the time, it was concluded that Maritime Beakers were concentrated in fortified settlements, whereas the cruder products are associated with open settlements or simple small farm units such as the ones mentioned above. Thus, bearing in mind that the differentiated distribution of Bell Beaker products has no chronological significance, since the datings have proved the coexistence of fortified settlements, open settlements and small farm units throughout the second half of the third millennium BC, it may be concluded that the Bell Beaker elites, who were based in fortified settlements, were responsible for managing the territories and used the more sophisticated (Maritime) products in their daily life as markers of their social status, whereas agriculture and livestock production, made viable by the good soils in the region adjacent to the Tagus estuary, were reserved for the socially less important communities, distributed in countless small farm units and settlements scattered around the hillsides. With regard to the absolute chronology provided by radiocarbon dating, the oldest chronologies in the Peninsula and even in the south-west of France may date back to around 2800 BC, although there is still some uncertainty with regard to this, in contrast to the chronology obtained for one of the huts in the settlement in Leceia (Oeiras), indicating that the Bell Beaker culture was already fully established in the Tagus estuary region by around 2750/2700 BC. The chronologies for the Ciempozuelos Bell Beaker culture, a Bell Beaker group characteristic of the Iberian Meseta, are more recent, and are reliable from 2600/2500 BC. This is therefore consistent with the influences observed by Edward Sangmeister associated with a second Bell Beaker period which originated in Central Europe. The Central European influences were recently confirmed by DNA results for approximately 280 individuals, covering the whole of Europe. With regard to the five individuals from Portuguese territory who were analysed, three of whom came from the Verdelha dos Ruivos cave in Vila Franca de Xira in the Tagus estuary, dating from between 2700 and 2300 BC, and the remaining two from the Galeria da Cisterna in Torres Novas (2500–2200 BC), the complete absence of any genetic contribution from Central European populations can be verified. However, the Central European contribution can be identified in certain populations within Spanish territory, some corresponding to the Iberian Meseta. This reality can therefore be related to Edward Sangmeister's hypothesis, placing these populations within an already advanced period of Bell Beaker culture.

Hence, cross-referencing genetic data with the absolute chronology obtained from the samples that were analysed has proved that the Bell Beaker influences from Central Europe were only felt from 2500 BC onwards, with the rapid and widespread penetration of individuals from the east into the west, particularly in England. The weak genetic influence of the Central European regions on populations within Portuguese territory means that the latter, whether due to their remote geographical location or, above all, their earlier chronology, did not receive any important input from this diffusion, thus affirming that they are the direct descendants of their Neolithic ancestors. This conclusion, together with their earlier chronology, constitutes an additional argument to support the origin of the Maritime beaker in the Tagus estuary and its subsequent diffusion by sea at a time which predates the major movement of populations from Central Europe recently revealed by genetics.

João Luís Cardoso
Universidade Aberta

Bibliography

CARDOSO, João Luís, "Absolute chronology of the beaker phenomenon north of the Tagus estuary: demographic and social implications", *Trabajos de Prehistoria*, vol. 71, no. 1, 2014, pp. 56–75.

CASTILLO YURRITA, Alberto del, *La Cultura del Vaso Campaniforme (Su Origen y Extensión en Europa)*, Barcelona, Universidad de Barcelona, 1928.

HARRISON, Richard J., *The Bell Beaker Cultures of Spain and Portugal*, Cambridge (Massachusetts), Peabody Museum/Harvard University, 1977.

OLALDE, Iñigo et al., "The beaker phenomenon and the genomic transformation of Northwest Europe", *Nature*, February 2018.

SANGMEISTER, Edward, "Exposé sur la civilisation du vase bell beaker. Les civilisations atlantiques du Néolithique à l'Âge du Fer", in *Actes du Premier Colloque Atlantique (Brest, 1961)*, Rennes, Laboratoire d'Anthropologie Préhistorique de la Faculté des Sciences de Rennes, 1963, pp. 25–56.

2000–800 BC
Long-Distance Trading in the Bronze Age

As today, Europe was defined by numerous cultural, economic and social asymmetries, partly dictated by differential access to the key resources that constituted one of the bases of power, namely metals, raw and processed (gold, copper, tin, lead, bronze), which, metaphorically speaking, "make the world go round".

By land and sea, following clearly defined yet multidirectional, intercrossing routes or more sporadic, diffuse and labyrinthine paths, distinct networks of interaction were established between the territory that is nowadays Portugal, and Atlantic and Mediterranean Europe during the course of the second millennium BC – the Bronze Age. Equally varying in rhythm, scale and nature, these connections first showed greater affinities with Atlantic Europe (the British Isles, France), clearly illustrated by the example of the "solar discs" found in Cabeceiras de Basto (Braga). These were never abandoned and were even extended, densifying from the third quarter of the millennium onwards to peak at the start of the next millennium. They are best represented by metals, namely bronze and gold, amortized in tombs and above all in deposits, leading some researchers to refer to the apparently unified Atlantic entity which they had created.

Signs of an Eastern Mediterranean presence in the Iberian Peninsula are less evident over time. After some earlier indications, including ivory from the Asian elephant, they become more visible from the fourteenth century BC onwards in other types of evidence such as Mycenaean pottery or the carnelian pendants produced in Egypt. The bronze knife found in the Belmeque hypogeum (Serpa), also considered to have Mycenaean origins, remains the exception. The question of whether these traces were the result of regular, direct contact with mainland Greece or sporadic, indirect voyages to Sardinia (Italy) is still being discussed.

From around 1100 BC onwards, links with the Mediterranean intensified and were strengthened as other multi-ethnic actors emerged, (from Asia Minor, Cyprus, Sardinia and possibly the Peninsula). From an archaeological point of view, their visibility, which extends to the western Atlantic, increased both in relation to the goods in circulation, namely the metals (featuring new items, styles and technology) and other materials (glass, ivory, amber), and the iconography on the "warrior stelae", clearly represented in the examples found in Telhado (Fundão) and Ervidel (Beja). It should be noted that these dynamics acted on the elites, without implying any process of "acculturation" for communities. As today, Europe was defined by numerous cultural, economic and social asymmetries, partly dictated by differential access to the key resources that constituted one of the bases of power, namely metals, raw and processed (gold, copper, tin, lead, bronze), which, metaphorically speaking, "make the world go round", in the words of Christopher Pare. Certain regions benefited from nature, while others were denied and left off the map.

Within these power relationships, Portuguese territory was favoured. In addition to its unique geostrategic position at the interface between these two worlds, it possessed all the minerals that would make it attractive (thus benefiting from new stimuli and contacts) and allow for independence and export capacity. Nevertheless, it also seems to have been an importer of metal, which reveals the existence of more complex dynamics with regard to the way in which communities interacted with each other and related to others. The centres of production and reception were not mutually exclusive and local resources were not always the first option: metal could travel long distances, as clearly illustrated in the case of certain bronzes from Southern Scandinavia produced with copper from the Alps and Slovakia, brought to light by recent research.

A vast bibliography has been dedicated to circulation models for goods in Prehistory, acknowledging the coexistence of different types of transactions (reciprocity, redistribution, gifting, trade). This perspective is well suited to the cultural mosaic of European societies during the Bronze Age.

The intensive circulation and amortisation of metal, in particular towards the end of this period, would have led to the creation of a process of "mercantilisation", with artefacts acquiring exchange value and even paleomonetary value, as in the case of certain types of axe. Systems were even adopted for inspecting some kinds of valuable goods (gold, possibly salt, drugs, etc.), apparently confirmed by the use of weights with multiples and submultiples based on a unit of 9.3 grams found in Pragança (Cadaval), Monte do Trigo (Idanha-a-Nova) and Baleizão (Beja), for example. Possibly corresponding to the 9.3-gram Syrian-Canaanite shekel or the 9.4-gram Egyptian qedet, these weights are a reflection of the Mediterranean in the far reaches of the globe. However, matter and material also constitute form, essence, exoticism and symbolism, extending beyond mere economic benefits. The strategic role of these materialities in social reproduction, within a framework still essentially governed by "global social benefits", should not be disregarded. Their value, which was not merely intrinsic but also conferred by the relationship and social distance between participants, was therefore mutable.

Amongst these materialities, the so-called "prestige goods" which conferred power and status became particularly important. They were essential to the establishment of pacts and networks of interregional alliances (control of territories, exogamy, etc.), whilst also creating dependencies and social asymmetries. They were the type of goods which normally circulated on a wide scale, meaning that they have the advantage of being easier for archaeologists to identify.

How is this determined? Firstly, "prestige goods" were rare and exotic, since the more common types of goods tended to circulate within local territories and were accessible to all. There was a preference within long-distance exchanges for these types of goods, which were also more likely to be imitated and passed on from one generation to the next. Later, they could be identified on the basis of morphological and stylistic comparisons, which has also allowed for the creation of maps showing the distribution of artefacts, configuring areas of contact or influence between regions. This was how certain artefacts from the important set of bronzes in Baiões (São Pedro do Sul) were assessed, such as the exotic carts used in rituals, displaying the distinctive Syrian-Cypriot style also found in the Alentejo piece from Pé do Castelo (Beja), which is very similar to another from Monte Sa Idda (Decimoputzu, Sardinia).

It was also by means of comparison that researchers such as Coffyn, Almagro Gorbea and Ruiz-Gálvez Priego began to perceive and establish the grounds for the existence of close connections between the Iberian Peninsula and the Mediterranean zone at the end of the Bronze Age.

In the face of these more dynamic areas, which included the centre of Portugal at the time – the "Groupe Lusitanien", according to Coffyn – and which boasted products, exports, imports and imitations double-ringed bifacial palstaves, unifacial palstaves, socketed axes, Porto de Mós daggers, Rocanes sickles, Alvaiázere spits), other centres emerged in step with them, such as Sardinia, "the Mediterranean market for the Atlantic bronze", as Lo Schiavo described it. Serving as a "pivotal point", this island built bridges and acted as an intermediary in the complex web forged between East and West on the eve of the arrival of the Phoenicians in the latter region.

The identification of goods which circulated on a large scale cannot be confined to parallelisms, which are very often debatable. The characterisation of objects from the perspective of their origins is a key line of research, as the study of metals based on the analysis of lead isotopes clearly demonstrates. According to studies by Armada, the isotopic match between some of the materials from Baiões and Monte do Trigo and the copper from Funtana Raminosa (Nuoro, Sardinia), whilst not providing proof, legitimizes the hypothesis that they were produced with metal from Sardinia, also reinforcing the interpretations of the aforementioned authors.

In other cases, it is possible to determine the origins of raw materials or objects with greater certainty, as revealed by analyses of Mycenaean pottery from Llanete de los Moros (Córdoba, Spain), which would have been produced at the Micenas-Berbati workshop (Argolis, Greece).

Determining the connecting points between the sources of materials and the use or amortisation of the artefacts also enables routes and paths to be configured, although they do not always overlap in terms of human mobility. It is important to consider the example of amber of Baltic origin or succinite, which experienced a veritable diaspora through Europe and the Mediterranean during the Bronze Age. Its presence is documented from at least the middle of the second millennium BC in Greece, Italy and Sicily and it had reached both the Iberian Peninsula, specifically the central southern region of Portuguese territory, and Syria by the beginning of the next millennium. Infrared spectroscopy analysis confirms that it is the source for the necklace beads from settlements in Moreirinha (Idanha-a-Nova), Baiões and Quinta do Marcelo (Almada), but does not prove the highly unlikely hypothesis that they came directly from there. In all these cases other exogenous evidence has also been found, namely the first iron blades and Mediterranean weights. It is the coherence of the contexts that points to the latter path and ascribes less importance to any direct relationship with the Baltics.

Finally, reference should be made to cutting-edge research in the field of bioarchaeology, based on the analysis of stable strontium isotopes in human and animal remains. Confirming paradigms formulated a long time ago, this "third scientific revolution", as Kristiansen calls it, has been demonstrating that human mobility was not infrequent and that hundreds of kilometres may have been travelled from place of residence to place of death. Therefore, throughout the Bronze Age people travelled, driven by specific activities such as long-distance trading or, more probably, a combination of different motives. These journeys had considerable consequences, leaving a trail in the form of shipwrecks loaded with goods, such as those found in Salcombe (Devon, England) and Langdon Bay (Dover, England) in the Atlantic, and in Uluburum (Kas, Turkey) and Gelidonya (Antalya, Turkey), in the Mediterranean. From the outset there were psychological consequences, with the discovery of new worlds, as they were experienced at the time, an awareness of difference and the actual notion of geographical distance itself. In addition, there were social consequences, since travellers, who acquired knowledge, also had power and prestige. In this sense, the goods that circulated and would also have included the less visible types, such as luxurious fabrics and wood, were not limited to their material dimensions: they were also the means of disseminating new codes of behaviour, technologies and ideas, fostering interaction between people from groups that had different forms of social organisation, diverse cultural models, and distinctive cosmologies.

Therefore, out of these convergences and divergences and their attendant acceptances and rejections, the Europe of "Atlantic and Mediterranean solidarities", according to Coffyn, was constructed, within a climate of latent tension which could only have led to confrontation and rivalry, clearly reflected in the panoply of offensive and defensive weapons for use in combat and display, which were invented, then imitated, at the time and have amortized by the thousands in dry land and wet environments throughout Europe.

The territory which is nowadays Portugal also mapped out this Atlantic-Mediterranean Europe which accelerated enormously throughout the second millennium BC, in an intense process of cultural transformation that was inseparable from the dynamics established between north and south and between east and west. If it is true that there are countless regional specificities, as Fokens and Harding claim, which emerge when we focus on a smaller scale, it is also certain that there are many indications that an unprecedented process of proto-globalization was unfolding on various levels and that this multiscale, far-reaching development may even have included Afro-Eurasia within what has been termed Bronzization, as proposed by Vandkilde.

RAQUEL VILAÇA
University of Coimbra

Bibliography

ARMADA, Xosé-Lois et al., "El impacto fenicio en el tráfico atlántico de metales: La aportación de los análisis de isótopos de plomo", *IX Congreso Internacional de Estudios Fenicios y Púnicos*, Mérida, Oct. 2018 (unpublished text).

COFFYN, André, *Le Bronze Final Atlantique dans la Péninsule Ibérique*, Paris, Diffusion de Boccard, 1985.

FOKENS, Harry, HARDING, Anthony (ed.), *The Oxford Handbook of the European Bronze Age*, Oxford, Oxford University Press, 2013.

VANDKILDE, Helle, "Bronzization: The Bronze Age as pre-modern globalization", *Praehistorische Zeitschrift*, vol. 91, no. 1, 2016, pp. 103–123.

VILAÇA, Raquel, "Late Bronze Age: Mediterranean impacts in the Western End of the Iberian Peninsula (actions and reactions)", in AUBET, Eugenia, SU-REDA, Pau (coord.), *Interacción Social y Comercio en la Antesala del Colonialismo: Los Metales como Protagonistas*, Barcelona, Universidad Pompeu Fabra de Barcelona, 2013, pp. 13–30.

Ninth to Fifth Centuries BC
The Phoenicians in Portugal

In the far west, the Tagus estuary was the earliest region to be affected by Phoenician colonisation. There is no evidence to show that the first contacts in other areas, some lying further south, were as old, which would appear to prove that the process was programmed in accordance with concrete predefined objectives, with clear intentions to head for specific territories.

Evidence of the presence of the Phoenicians in the territory that is nowadays Portugal dates from the end of the ninth century BC. It has materialized in various ways, concretely in the form of domestic and defensive architecture, construction techniques and archaeological materials, but also in the use of language and writing. It was essentially distributed along the coast but had a profound regional impact in social, economic, technological, religious and cultural terms, reaching inland territories with varying impacts and at differing rates during the seventh and sixth centuries BC

The arrival and settlement of eastern populations became part of a wider context, namely the establishment within the Iberian Peninsula of communities originating from the Near East, which had certainly been programmed and prepared. The western Phoenicians, installed in Huelva and the Gulf of Cádiz since the tenth century and the first half of the ninth century BC respectively, would have been responsible for planning this process, in collaboration with indigenous groups.

Neither their presence nor its relatively early timing are surprising. On the one hand, the wealth of metal resources such as tin and gold in western territories made them attractive. In addition, since the Late Bronze Age large areas of regions which are nowadays Portuguese formed part of Mediterranean-Atlantic networks which facilitated the circulation of artefacts of different origins from the end of the second millennium BC onwards.

The settlement of Phoenician groups is best recorded on the coast, in estuary environments. In the Tagus estuary, Lisbon and Santarém, on the right-hand bank, and Almaraz (Almada), on the left, were indigenous settlements with a Late Bronze Age occupation whose levels during the Iron Age reveal an early and deep-rooted oriental influence (from the beginning of the eighth century BC). Hence it can be argued that Phoenician communities established their own "neighbourhoods" within "urban" space.

This was also the time when profound changes were taking place in the landscape in the area, with a reduction in the amount of forest land, an increase in cultivated areas and the planting of vineyards. This data indicates demographic growth and changes in social and food habits, the latter also reflected in the introduction of poultry into the diet, as confirmed in Santarém.

In the oldest Iron Age levels for these sites, the local model is also significant. However, the discovery of two Phoenician inscriptions in Lisbon should be noted, both dating from the seventh century BC. One of them, a tombstone discovered in the riverside area, bears two indigenous anthroponyms. The adoption by the autochthonous community of writing and the language of the Phoenicians, prime elements of identity, is significant since it proves that there were very close links with populations from outside.

During the course of the seventh century BC, other sites in the Tagus estuary (Santa Sofia in Vila Franca de Xira, Castro do Amaral in Alenquer and Chões de Alpompé in Santarém on the right-hand bank, and Alto dos Cacos and Quinta da Alorna in Almeirim and Alto do Castelo and Cabeço da Bruxa in Alpiarça on the left-hand bank) became inhabited, with or without immediate prior occupation. They are all located on the riverside or in nearby areas and, as a whole, constitute a network of settlements which functioned in an organized manner. This network should be interpreted in relation to the river itself, which united the two banks and made them a single social space.

In the far west, the Tagus estuary was the earliest region to be affected by Phoenician colonisation. There is no evidence to show that the first contacts in other areas, some lying further south, were as old, which would appear to prove that the process was programmed in accordance with concrete predefined objectives, with clear intentions to head for specific territories.

Although they are later examples, there are many other significant elements that also enable us to assess the oriental influence in the Mondego and Sado estuaries. In the case of the latter, one site stands out for a number of different reasons. The unusual Abul structure, situated on a small, low elevation overlooking the Sado, was built from scratch in a place that had not been previously occupied. It is a small sanctuary founded by an exogenous population. However, the identity of the divine entity to which it was dedicated remains unknown.

The necropolis in Alcácer do Sal, a large indigenous settlement, is well-known. The oriental influence is strong and can be seen in the funerary area, residential spaces and places of worship.

In the first of these, the treatment of the corpse immediately stands out, as there is evidence of cremation. The funerary rituals and archaeological materials found in the

Alcácer do Sal necropolis, namely pottery, bronze items, a painted ostrich egg and adornments, in particular scarab rings, are associated with the Mediterranean culture.

The residential nucleus was established on a high hill, where evidence has been found of an occupation dating from the end of the Bronze Age, followed by one from the Iron Age with oriental characteristics, reflected in in the ceramic products, which include the Phoenician model. However, the local model is strong and can be seen in the use of hand-made vessels whose shapes and surface treatment follow the local tradition.

The oriental influence can also be seen at the foot of the hill on which the castle stands, in an area close to the river. The diverse set of materials recovered from Travessa do Rato suggests the existence of a Portuguese sanctuary. They include tools for furniture carving decorated with oriental iconography, a bronze lion's head which would have been part of a piece of furniture, possibly a throne, a Cypriot ladle and a set of items that would have been part of a set of goldsmith's tools (scales, cubic weights and anvils).

There is very little data for Setúbal, which lies at the mouth of the estuary. However, the presence of oriental-influenced pottery, still mainly produced by hand, in levels overlaying others from the Late Bronze Age attests to a situation which, although not identical to the one in Alcácer do Sal, is part of the same reality.

In the Mondego estuary, Santa Olaia is an important site, established on a small elongated hill on the right-hand bank of what was, during the Iron Age, a large estuary. As it had not been previously occupied, it corresponds to a Phoenician foundation *ex nihilo*, which explains the lack of hand-made pottery. The urban area was encircled by a wall and the walls of the rectangular dwellings were constructed from adobe. In the area adjoining the wall, a set of metallurgical furnaces have been identified.

Despite the existence of a Roman city in Conímbriga, an Iron Age occupation was also known to have existed early on in the area and included the rectangular dwellings found in the forum and the Trajan Baths esplanade. A vast hoard of pottery displays oriental characteristics, although the collection also includes hand-made vessels with shapes and decorations inspired by Late Bronze Age models. An ivory comb, indisputably oriental, completes the array of artefacts.

Along the southern coastline the Phoenician presence has been recorded above all in the eastern zone. Castro Marim, at the mouth of the Guadiana estuary, had an Iron Age occupation which overlapped with an earlier settlement dating from the Late Bronze Age. Relations with the western Phoenician world can be verified from the hoards and the defensive, residential and religious forms of architecture and it is certain that from the seventh century BC onwards the population was in contact with the Phoenicians who had settled in the area of the Strait of Gibraltar. A wall with casemates, floors made of shells, walls made from adobe and mud and an abundant hoard of pottery, in particular, but also metalware, all bear witness to this connection. It is also important to note what has been interpreted as a place of worship, consisting of rectangular compartments and a central altar. Studies of the fauna reveal the presence of poultry and donkeys from the initial phases, while carpological analysis shows that there was a clear dependence on barley.

Tavira, on the right-hand bank of the final stretch of the River Gilão, also contributes towards extending the Portuguese "Phoenician geography". Archaeological work in the historic centre of the present-day city has highlighted the importance of an Iron Age occupation whose beginnings date back to the seventh century BC, associated with the Phoenician expansion into the west. The wall with casemates and walkways has parallels with others in Phoenician colonies in the central and western Mediterranean area. With regard to the hoard, the existence of painted ceramic vessels with oriental decorations and shapes should be noted, in addition to the painted ostrich eggs and ivory artefacts. The pottery fragment with an inscription in Phoenician lettering is also significant; it is an ostracon, an intrinsically economical form of record, dating from the sixth century BC, which reveals a knowledge and use of writing and the Phoenician alphabet. The necropolis associated with this occupation used cremation, and the urns are also Mediterranean in style. In the western Algarve there is very little data for any occupation that shows signs of contact with the Semitic world, although related materials have recently been recovered from the Bay of Lagos.

In Mértola, which is only apparently interior, the existence of a necropolis with cremation urns has been confirmed, while other materials, in particular a Phoenician ceramic graffito, lend greater consistency to the Phoenician colonisation of the Iberian Peninsula. The traditional seventh-century BC chronology would appear to be most likely for the materials from the Alentejo town.

In Castro dos Ratinhos, an important Late Bronze Age settlement in Moura, a structure has been identified and interpreted as an oriental temple. The building has a layout that corresponds to an earlier architectural plan and the "Phoenician module" has been applied as the standard. It was built at the end of the ninth century BC with a "Syriac type" design originating from north Syria and south Anatolia. The exogenous nature of the construction is undeniable, confirming the existence of a cult dedicated to the oriental goddess Asherah, originating in Canaan.

The oriental-influenced hoards found in the Alentejo interior in necropolises in the Beja region and the area around Ourique date from much later (the sixth century BC). In this case, it must be remembered that the architecture appears to be interwoven with the indigenous culture, although certain funerary rituals and even the veneration of the dead may still have been associated with the Mediterranean model. Scarab necklace beads made from glass paste and Egyptian faience, and gold and silver jewellery are also present, revealing evident links with other oriental funerary spaces.

The presence and establishment of Phoenician groups on the Portuguese coast has been placed within a significantly early period of time. Nevertheless, it is several decades later than those in the regions of Huelva and Malaga, in Andalusia. This phase, which may be defined as the "third wave" of colonisation, corresponds to the founding of Carthage and other colonies on the coast of the Iberian Peninsula and can be attributed to the end of the ninth or the beginning of the eighth century BC.

These phenomena, which were initially mainly coastal, still reached inland territory in an early phase, as the so-called Ratinhos sanctuary in Moura confirms.

It was the western Phoenicians, established in the Strait of Gibraltar region and in Huelva since the tenth century BC, who were responsible for the expansion into the western Atlantic coast.

After what appears to have been the failure to settle in the Alentejo interior in the initial phase, identified in Castro dos Ratinhos, the oriental influence in the region only began at the end of the seventh century BC, originating on the coast. In this case, it has materialized in settings associated with death, particularly in votive hoards. Certain rituals were adopted and there is data to confirm the worship of entities associated with the Mediterranean divine couple Baal and Astarte.

Nevertheless, the funerary architecture remained linked to indigenous models, which may be explained by the need to legitimize land ownership in these territories, with funerary monuments serving as existential maps of the autochthonous community. Hence they may have functioned as spaces for memorialisation and resistance, ensuring that images of ancestors were preserved. It may therefore be concluded that penetrating the interior was a slow process that did not include the entire oriental cultural system.

ANA MARGARIDA ARRUDA
University of Lisbon

Bibliography

ARRUDA, Ana Margarida, *Los Phoenicians en Portugal*, Barcelona, Universitat Pompeu Fabra, 1999–2000.

Idem, "O 1.º millennium a.n.e. no centro e no sul de Portugal: leituras possíveis no início de um novo século", *O Arqueólogo Português*, series 4, vol. 23, 2005, pp. 9–156.

BERROCAL-RANGEL, Luis, SILVA, António Carlos, *O Castro dos Ratinhos (Barragem do Alqueva, Moura): Escavações Num Povoado Proto-Histórico no Guadiana*, Lisbon, Museu Nacional de Arqueologia, 2010.

NETO, Nuno M. et al., "Uma inscrição lapidar fenícia em Lisboa", *Revista Portuguesa de Arqueologia*, vol. 19, 2016, pp. 123–128.

PART
II

Antiquity

Introduction to Part II

From the Roman Empire to Gothic Iberia

CARLOS FABIÃO
University of Lisbon

Antiquity is the most obvious, yet most unusual chapter in a global history of Portugal. It is obvious because any approach to ancient history must contain some aspect of the global, given that it refers to geographical realities that bear no reference to the more recent nation states and draws on information from distant regions. However, it is unusual because it makes no mention of Portugal, hence the use of geographical boundaries such as the west of the Iberian Peninsula or the Iberian Peninsula itself.

Antiquity is also a distinctive period due to the nature of the sources that are used by scholars. From the outset, this includes the wide range of texts in Ancient Greek and Latin, read in versions established through the long tradition of textual exegesis which purged them of any modifications introduced into copies in the mediaeval *scriptoria*, up to the appearance of the first printed versions. The Graeco-Latin literature available today is different from the texts used by scholars in other times.

One good example of this is the vast *Geography* by the Greek author Strabo, which describes the territories of the Roman Empire at the beginning of the first century. It is important because of the time in which it was written and because it was the repository for a wide range of Greek and Roman authors whose works have since been lost. Strabo also produced a work of history in 47 volumes, of which practically nothing has survived, which would have followed on from the *Histories* written by Polybius, another Greek author from the second century BC.

Given the recognised limitations of these sources, the German historian Theodor Mommsen, the only historian to date to have been awarded the Nobel Prize in Literature (1902), founded the *Corpus Inscriptionum Latinarum* project with the aim of publishing a critical edition of Latin inscriptions recorded on solid surfaces (stone, metal, pottery), namely epigraphs. The objective was to build up another corpus of sources for the history of the Roman Empire to compensate for the irreparable gaps in the literary materials.

Moreover, the history of Antiquity is increasingly being produced on the basis of the archaeological record, thus bringing it closer to research in Prehistory but with the peculiarity that this data coexists with the other above-mentioned sources and it is not always easy to combine them. As British historian Moses Finley observed in *Ancient History: Evidence and Models* (1985), the archaeological record is indispensable: "The ancient historian nowadays has to accept that his armoury includes qualitatively different kinds of evidence which often appear mutually contradictory or at least unrelated".

Controversies aside, the archaeological record has been gaining authority within ancient history, not least because of the volume of information generated using this method, which is consistently growing at a much faster pace than the data derived from epigraphic or literary sources.

The archaeological record is also relevant in terms of interdisciplinarity, a key feature of archaeology. This cooperation between disciplinary areas is nowadays associated with a neologism that emerged in the Anglo-Saxon world in the 1960s, namely "archaeometry", also known as archaeological science. It involves the use of analytical procedures from chemistry, biology and other laboratory sciences to study materials from the past. Through analysis, it is possible to determine the Lusitanian origins of a fragment from an amphora, for example, and by applying techniques to analyse the residue adhering to the insides, identify the nature of the substance it contained. These studies have brought greater accuracy to our understanding of inter-regional contacts in the ancient world, based not only on artefact's morphology and typologies of objects, but also the use of such methods to provide independent validation of observations. The essays which follow deal with a variety of themes, selected on the basis of their relevance. They reveal how different authors have drawn on a variety of sources to present the current state of knowledge on the subjects which they cover.

They begin by explaining how the Mediterranean world constructed its understanding of the extreme west of Europe, the edge of the world or the western "land's end". The inhabitants of the so-called Old World were unaware of the existence of the American continent and their world therefore extended from faraway Asia, from whence spices and silk arrived via lengthy, centuries-old terrestrial routes to the *Promontorium Magnum*, the *finis terrae*: the most westerly point on Earth, beyond which lay only ocean. They knew that, having arrived there, they could travel north in search of The Cassiterides for supplies of tin for the copper alloys required to produce bronze, which was scarce in the Mediterranean. Literature provides references to these islands (usually describing their location off the coast of Galicia or Great Britain), whilst archaeology makes it possible to classify the artefacts, and archaeometric analysis can identify the origins of the raw materials.

Mediterranean characters such Pytheas, a Greek author from Marseille, also knew, apparently from experience, that further north lay the *Ultima Thule*, Iceland or the coast of Norway, where the sea froze. The archaeological record proves that the Greeks or Romans were not the first to sail into the Atlantic regions, which have been frequented since Prehistory. However, they were the first to describe them and thus introduce them into contemporary knowledge: the ability to name and describe spaces and places is a powerful way of endowing them with existence.

In the final centuries before Christ, the notion of areas that were continually visited without implying domination began to change, when Carthaginian and, above, all the later Roman expansion created a new reality. It was no longer a matter of contacts and exchanges, but territorial conquest. At the end of the third century BC, the Romans began to settle in the Iberian Peninsula and the first military campaigns in the far west began in the final third of the next century. The Iberian Peninsula became part of a vast empire that would eventually extend from Syria to Great Britain, with an extensive (from our perspective) eastern border defined by the River Rhine and River Danube. In this phase of greater expansion, the Peninsular *finis terrae*, whilst never losing its identity and mythical resonances, became the zone that entangled the Mediterranean and Atlantic worlds.

Conquering the Iberian Peninsula proved to be a difficult process. Firstly, it was necessary to confront stubborn resistance from the local populations. Afterwards, it became a province, experiencing frequent outbreaks of low-intensity conflicts, and an arena in the civil wars involving the different factions in Roman society, until it was finally conquered at the end of the first century BC. Paradoxically, it would have been during the time that the Peninsula served as the stage for conflicts between the Romans themselves that the most important steps were taken towards cultural assimilation, usually described as "Romanisation". This involved acquiring a new language to communicate with, namely Latin. In learning and using this language, the Hispanics also played a part in constructing Roman culture. Hence, it was the lost work of Cornelius Bocchus, a Lusitanian from the first century, which Pliny the Elder used in his encyclopaedic work for themes related to the Iberian Peninsula, as was also the case with the treatise on agriculture by the Gaditanian, Columella. Much later, Hydatius, the bishop of *Aquae Flaviae* (Chaves), described the vicissitudes faced by the German Barbarians in settling in the Peninsula. Nowadays, Latin is still the basis of the language spoken in Portugal.

A new provincial landscape began to develop, dotted with cities, in the Mediterranean style. The concept of *civitas* refers to a community which occupies a certain territory and sees the city as its main reference point. This was not entirely unknown in certain regions, but was totally new for most of the Iberian Peninsula. Through conquest and the organisation of territory, a new geography was established and consolidated along Roman lines and has become our legacy: the majority of historic Portuguese cities have been in existence since Roman times.

The political plan for the Roman provinces was no less important and made Lusitania an enduring reference for Portugal, even though there is no absolute physical overlap between them. In the Early Modern age, Lusitania still featured in erudite discourse as a synonym for Portugal. Obviously, those who study the history of the Roman province do not take the current Caia boundary into account and bypass the region north of the Douro, which belonged to another province at the time.

The new Roman landscape also implied a significant increase in the extraction of mineral resources which had an enormous impact on the environment, involving silver and lead from the mountains in Cartagena and Morena in the south of the Iberian Peninsula, copper and silver in the Iberian pyrite belt that extended from Andalusia to the Grândola mountains and passed through the entire Baixo Alentejo region, and primary deposits of gold in areas of Trás-os-Montes such as Jales and Tresminas but, above all, in river alluvium.

Nineteenth-century positivism and the cult of progress constructed the image of the human being as the ruler of nature. This epic vision of domination and exploitation suffered a major setback when nature began to answer back. Since then, the paradigm of the tamer of nature has been replaced by new concepts such as human ecology, and growing environmental concerns have alerted historians to a new set of issues. Research involving the polar ice caps and Alpine glaciers has revealed the huge environmental impact of the extraction of mineral resources in Antiquity. A significant part of this impact was due to mining activity in the Iberian Peninsula, with the records even registering a slowdown when the silver mines in the area were exhausted. A recent reassessment of the slag pile at the Vipasca mine in Aljustrel concluded that it had been one of the largest copper mining zones in the Roman world. It also became a landmark following the discovery in the nineteenth century of two bronze plaques on which part of the legislation governing the extraction and work routines in the mine is preserved. These epigraphic documents are unique in the Roman Empire and therefore highly important to the global history of humanity.

Roman Lusitania did not only live from its mineral resources or strategic location, as the area which linked two worlds. The ocean which bathed its shoreline had far richer fish resources than the Mediterranean, and its lengthy dry seasons and high temperatures provided favourable conditions for producing sea salt. Hence a flourishing fish preparations industry was established, which went on to supply the empire. This was more than a local phenomenon, given that traces of this activity have been found on the Peninsular and North African coasts west of the Strait of Gibraltar (known to the Romans as the Pillars of Hercules) and along the entire Atlantic front, combining the use of fish and salt, two important food resources for societies which had a plant-based diet.

The historical dynamics of the Roman Empire led to reforms in the fourth century, during the time when it was becoming Christian, firstly to accommodate one more religion that had come from the East, and then to make it the official religion. Provincial reorganisation redesigned the political and administrative geography and created new provinces, including *Gallaecia*, with its capital in Braga (*Bracara Augusta*), a city built from scratch by the Romans in the north-west of the Iberian Peninsula. This new political configuration was inscribed in the Peninsular landscape on a permanent basis and also influenced the Christian episcopal geography that was gradually being introduced. The notion of Christianity was the cement which bound communities together after the disintegration of the western half of the Roman Empire. When Romanity collapsed it was replaced by Christianity, which occupied the same spaces and preserved much of the Roman legacy.

Hard times followed the disintegration of imperial sovereignty, but did not result in chaos. New migrants arrived from the East but, rather than invasion by warriors, this was a matter of the settlement of new communities. Coexistence was not always peaceful, but new political entities were eventually created, governed by the secular and ecclesiastical elites.

Following the demise of the kingdom of the Suebi, which had existed for decades in the north-west of the Iberian Peninsula, and the end of the dream of reconstructing the old Roman Empire in the West initiated by Justinian I, the Emperor of the East, the Iberian Peninsula was unified under a new monarchy, the Visigoths. This was another ephemeral political entity which, although governed by people of Goth origin, had closer cultural affinities with the Roman model. Once again, the ecclesiastical authorities helped to ensure that continuity with adaptations would prove stronger than radical change.

Many of these traits did not begin then, or did they end when Visigoth rule collapsed. Continuity and perpetuity are the keywords in the pages which follow.

218–19 BC
The Romans in the Iberian Peninsula:
From Conquered Land to Imperial Province

After the Lusitanian War, the first great Roman military expedition in the west began in territory that is nowadays Portuguese. The campaign, led by Decimus Junius Brutus, set off from the Tagus Valley and advanced as far as the mouth of the River Minho via the coastal platform.

The Roman conquest of the Iberian Peninsula was not the outcome of any planned expansion project, but resulted from the clash between Rome and Carthage, the two hegemonic powers in the central Mediterranean area. It was a lengthy and troubled process that lasted around two hundred years. Caesar conquered the Gauls in ten years and, over short periods of time, the Hellenistic kingdoms in the eastern Mediterranean which had emerged from the disintegration of the Alexandrian Empire were also subdued. It was a process that transformed a very diverse territory, in terms of ethnicity, politics and landscape, within the provincial space of an empire that would extend from Syria to Great Britain. The urban model that already existed in some Peninsular regions was extended to the entire territory, also replicating a rural landscape based on a triad of rainfed crops – cereals, vines and olive trees – and there was a common language shared by various peoples and a single currency.

This process was closely linked to the profound changes affecting Roman society itself. The first military campaigns were carried out by a militia made up of citizens fulfilling their obligations, commanded by magistrates elected and appointed by the Senate of an aristocratic republic, but were concluded by a professional army commanded by the legates of a *princeps* who only superficially maintained the standards and dignities of the republican institutions. The closest antecedents to Roman expansion in the Iberian Peninsula date back to the third century BC and the conflicts between Rome and Carthage in the central Mediterranean, known as the Punic Wars. Following the first of these wars, which ended in 241 BC with Rome victorious, having seized Sicily, Corsica and Sardinia, and Carthage facing difficulties due to a rebellion by its mercenaries, the Carthaginians established themselves in the Iberian Peninsula, an area they had previously visited, creating concern in the Greek colonies allied to Rome on the coast of what is nowadays Catalonia.

Carthage justified settlement in the east of the Peninsula by the need to obtain valuable resources to pay the war tributes exacted by Rome. Tensions and suspicion led to the signing of the Ebro Treaty in 226 BC, which established the river as the boundary for Carthaginian rule (in areas south of the Ebro), committing them not to expand beyond this limit. In 220 BC the Roman Senate declared the city of *Saguntum*, which lay south of the Ebro or, in other words, clearly in the area conceded to Carthage under the Treaty, its protectorate. The Carthaginians reacted by taking *Saguntum* the following year and assembling a powerful army which set off for the Italian Peninsula, commanded by Hannibal Barca. In order to counter the Carthaginian threat and prevent the war from spreading to its territories, Rome then sent an army to the Iberian Peninsula, which landed in *Ampurias*, a Greek emporium on the coast of present-day Catalonia, in 218 BC.

The main Roman bid had failed, since the Carthaginian army was no longer in the

Iberian Peninsula, but marching on the Italian Peninsula. Nevertheless, there were other objectives: cutting off the sources of supplies and finance for the Carthaginian war effort – unlike the Roman army, the Carthaginian troops were made up of professional soldiers, usually described as mercenaries – and preventing reinforcements from setting out to join Hannibal's army.

While the war continued in Italy, another front was opening up in the Iberian Peninsula, which was not always favourable to the Romans. They entered into alliances with leaders of local tribes, with the aim of increasing their troops. In 209 BC, the Roman commander Publius Cornelius Scipio took *Carthago Nova* (nowadays Cartagena), a city founded by the Carthaginians and a centre for silver mining in the Peninsula. Eventually, Scipio defeated the Carthaginians at the Battle of Ilipa in 206 BC and managed to gain control of *Castulo* (in Sierra Morena, in what is nowadays Andalusia), another important silver mining centre in *Hispania*. Cádiz, a major southern port, agreed to surrender to Rome. Carthaginian rule in the Iberian Peninsula came to an end in 206 BC, although it appears clear that some Carthaginians and their allies engaged in low-intensity conflicts with the Romans in the decades which followed. However, these skirmishes did not form part of the Second Punic War, which was waged in Italy and North Africa and lasted for five years.

With every indication that it was not the outcome of any deliberately planned expansion and conquest, the installation of the Romans in the Iberian Peninsula emerged following the discovery that there were vast mineral resources, in particular silver, in the mountain ranges in Cartagena/Mazarrón in the south-east, and in Sierra Morena in the south. Hence, in 197 BC, the Roman Senate established two provinces, *Hispania Citerior* and *Hispania Ulterior*, literally, "the nearer one" and "the further one", from the perspective of Rome. The first controlled the resources in the Cartagena/Mazarrón mountain ranges and the second those in Sierra Morena, defining an initial axis of conquest extending from the north-east (nowadays Catalonia) to the south along the Mediterranean coastline. The provinces did not have clearly defined territories or borders and expanded according to the strength and ambitions of their governors, who were appointed by the Roman Senate. The settlement of groups from the Italian Peninsula introduced a new set of Roman habits and artefacts.

This was not a peaceful process. The first rebellion against Rome by indigenous Peninsular communities soon followed, in 197 BC. The areas controlled by the Roman governors were being expanded, often involving conflicts but also by means of pacts. There are interesting reports on the nature of these agreements. Unconditional surrender (*deditio*) to the new power was imposed and in exchange, if authorized by the Senate and the people of Rome, the local peoples were allowed to remain in their territories and keep their own forms of government, paying the necessary tributes and living in peace. This policy explains the success and longevity of Roman Empire, which imposed an inclusive form of rule compatible with that of the local powers.

Two other lines were added to the north-east to south-west axis of conquest, one along the Ebro Valley in the direction of the interior and the other along the coast to the west. They were associated with two important periods of intense conflict: the Numantine Wars (143–133 BC), centring on the Celtiberian city of *Numantia* (Soria) in the Spanish Meseta, and the Lusitanian War (155–138 BC). In both cases, the conflict only ended after the unconditional surrender of the enemies of Rome.

After the Lusitanian War, the first great Roman military expedition in the west began in territory that is nowadays Portuguese. The campaign, led by Decimus Junius Brutus, set off from the Tagus Valley and advanced as far as the mouth of the River Minho via the coastal platform. His success in such northerly regions earned him the cognomen Callaicus in honour of his victory over this people (or peoples), who were not particularly powerful but sufficiently exotic to justify the epithet. The geography of the campaign is revealing. The fact that he set off from the Lower Tagus is an acknowledgement that the territories to the south of the river basin were already, to some extent, under Roman rule. However, the occupation was not limited to the coastal strip. There is evidence for this in the form of an interesting document dated 104 BC inscribed on a bronze plaque that was found near Valença de Alcântara, establishing a surrender pact for a local population with the Roman governor as the agent. A legal document of this kind would only have been justified if there had been a Roman presence in the area. Moreover, the archaeological records corroborate this theory, providing evidence of a very significant Roman presence throughout the Tagus basin from the second half of the second century BC. The wealth of gold in the region would explain this, since the other previously mentioned metalliferous zones mainly contained silver, lead and copper deposits.

This focus on mineral resources was associated with news of a new Roman triumph. In 96–94 BC, the governor Publius Crassus had managed to identify the route to the Cassiterides, the tin-mining zones in the north-east of the Peninsula. This route, used for centuries to bring tin from the north-west to the Mediterranean region, was controlled by Gaditan merchants who zealously guarded their secret.

Roman rule was extended in the Iberian Peninsula, but not without opposition, although this tended to take the form of low-intensity conflicts that were never on the scale of previous wars. During the first century BC, more specifically from 80 to 45 BC, the Iberian Peninsula became the arena for various confrontations associated with the Roman civil wars in which local communities were involved. However, these disputes were not part of the process of conquest, but a reflection of the extent to which Peninsular populations were involved in Roman affairs.

During the period between the civil wars there was once again news of the west when Julius Caesar, governor of *Hispania Ulterior*, led successful campaigns against the tribes who lived in the mountainous regions of Entre Tejo e Douro, during the period 61–60 BC. It is assumed that it was only from this time onwards that Roman rule was finally established in the region. The wealth of alluvial gold in Lusitanian rivers, celebrated by the Greek author Strabo and by Pliny the Elder, may explain the Roman governor's efforts and, once again, this presence is confirmed by archaeological records.

Between 45 and 26 BC, the Iberian Peninsula does not feature in Latin literary sources. It is possible that there were minor skirmishes with local populations, but the ongoing civil wars were now based in the eastern half of the Mediterranean, meaning that there was no particular interest in the west.

The process that led to the conquest of Cantabria and Asturias, the last areas in the Peninsula to fall to the Romans, began in 26 BC. The war effort, which lasted until around 19 BC, was impressive in terms of the size of the army, given the small territory to be conquered and the reduced numbers and power of the local populations. Apparently, Augustus, the first emperor of Rome, who always ruled under the pretence of republicanism (during his lifetime he was "elected", in succession, to the consulate and the tribune of the people and as *pontifex maximus*), felt it necessary to establish an important military victory over a distant and supposedly hostile people, given that his military achievements had been associated with triumphs over other Romans in the final civil wars. There were also other factors, such as the need to establish control over the entire Iberian Peninsula and, once again, the significant amounts of gold in these northern regions.

The subsequent reorganisation of the province and the installation of numerous Roman settlers in Peninsular territory defined a new political geography for the whole of the Peninsula. This is how Augustus records it in his panegyric (*Res Gestae Divi Augusti*), composed as direct speech: "I extended the frontiers of all those provinces of the Roman people bordered by peoples not subject to our government. I brought peace to the Gallic and Spanish provinces as well as to Germany [...] without waging an unjust war on any population".

Carlos Fabião
Centre for Archaeology, Faculty of Arts and Humanities, University of Lisbon

Bibliography

BLÁZQUEZ, José María et al., *Historia de España Antigua*, vol. II, Madrid, Cátedra, 1985.

FABIÃO, Carlos, "The Roman army in Portugal", in MORILLO CERDÁN, Ángel, AURRECOECHEA, Joaquín (ed.), *The Roman Army in Hispania: An Archaeological Guide*, León, Universidad de León, 2006, pp. 107–126.

MORILLO CERDÁN, Ángel et al. (ed.), *Defensa y Territorio en Hispania de los Escipiones a Augusto*, Madrid/León, Universidad de León/Casa de Velázquez, 2003.

RICHARDSON, John S., *The Romans in Spain*, Oxford, Blackwell, 1996.

VV. AA., *Hispania Romana. Desde Tierra de Conquista a Provincia del Imperio, catálogo de exposição*, Rome, Electa, 1997.

155–139 BC
The Lusitanian Wars and the True Viriathus

There has been an insistence on separating Viriathus and the Lusitanians from the discussion on their relation to present-day nations, thus avoiding the nationalist tone that influenced Portuguese historiography in particular. Viriathus was simply a Lusitanian and any links to a Hispanic nationality no longer make sense.

In the traditional roll-call of glorious figures from Portuguese history, the first place is reserved for Viriathus, considered the vanquished hero of the Lusitanian Wars. This unique position has to do with his primordial status, but also a centuries-old historiographical tradition dating back to the classical Roman authors, which was continued by the Portuguese humanists in the sixteenth century. Hence he was considered worthy of special attention by the Portuguese education system, particularly during the *Estado Novo* regime (1933–1974).

The traditional historical paradigm for the Lusitanian Wars has been developed on the basis of presuppositions which are questioned by present-day historiography:

- the link between Lusitanian and Portuguese identity, in line with the different associations made between ethnic characteristics from the Roman period and nationalities in the modern world – identifying Gaul with France, Germania with Germany, Britannia with England, Lusitania with Portugal, etc. – whereas, although there may be some geographical approximation, none of these realities correspond exactly to one another;
- the link between Viriathus and his companions and the Serra da Estrela mountain region, which is not supported by any reliable data;
- the military supremacy of Viriathus and the Lusitanians, who were only defeated when they were betrayed by their fellow soldiers.

Throughout the third century BC Rome developed a markedly expansionist policy resulting in a series of conflicts with Carthage with a view to taking control of the western Mediterranean and the surrounding territories, leading to the so-called Punic Wars (264–146 BC) which extended as far as Iberia. In the south-west of *Hispania*, the military might and skilled and tested Roman diplomacy met with some initial difficulties, but later some successes, particularly with the Turdetani, who were gradually converted into allies. However, the problems caused by the Lusitanians, the main opponents of the Romans, were well-known.

The first report that refers to conflicts with the Lusitanians dates from 194 BC and was written by Livy:

> The same [Publius Cornelius Scipio Nasica] [...] fought [...] the Lusitanians when they were returning home with vast spoils after devastating the province of Hispania Ulterior [...]; the battle took place not far from the city of Ilipa, whither Publius Cornelius led his victorious army, enriched with the spoils.

Livy set the tone for Latin historiography, which justified the Roman strategy, condoned the tactic of spreading fear amongst Hispanic populations as a means of ensuring their surrender, assumed the legitimacy of intervention in this region and referred to the Lusitanians as *latrones* (bandits), a term used to describe those who adopted ethics and principles that differed from those of Rome.

Ilipa corresponds to the present-day Alcalá del Río in the Guadalquivir valley, the habitual arena for such conflicts, and had little to do with the province of *Lusitania* as defined by Augustus (16 BC). Livy himself may have missed this disparity and this may be the reason why the actions of the Lusitanians are wrongly considered, also in modern historiography, as incursions into distant territory over which they had no legitimate claim.

Later there were other confrontations, not always resulting in favourable outcomes for the Romans, such as the one in Lyco in 190 BC, when they lost 6,000 of their men. This was followed by Aemilius Paullus' victories over the Lusitanians in 189 BC and the events associated with the Battle of Hasta in the years which followed.

These episodes are linked to a document in which Aemilius Paullus "decreed that the slaves of the people of *Hasta* who lived in *Turris Lascutana* should be freed". His triumph over the inhabitants of *Hasta* entailed the liberation of the local surrendering populations, the city and the land they had owned. A comparison of different versions confirms that the Lusitanians, who were also defeated in this clash, supported Hasta against the Romans and the inhabitants of *Turris Lascutana*. It is this division –

between the Romans and their allies, generally identified as the Turdetani, on one side and the Lusitanians and the cities that had not surrendered to Rome on the other – which emerged during this phase and would continue.

The connection between the Lusitanians and *Hasta* (or *Hasta Regia*), nowadays Mesas de Asta (Jerez de la Frontera), is one of the most telling indications that in an early phase the Lusitanians controlled certain regions in the area which would become the province of *Baetica* and which sometimes lay vary far to the south.

This was followed by a period for which there is very little information. The narratives only become more detailed from 155 BC onwards, due in particular to Appian and Diodorus Siculus. This was the year in which responsibility for Lusitanian operations ceased to be anonymous and the name of Punicus emerged.

The name is more than an anthroponym and must refer to the Carthaginian origins of the individual, since it is natural that the Lusitanians would turn to the figure they considered had the best ability to command and the best understanding of strategy. It is logical that the interests of the Lusitanians would match those of the Punics and that they would be united by a common enemy and possibly old alliances. It was not by chance that Arsa, one of these Lusitanian cities, was a community heavily influenced by the Punics, as is clear from the coins produced there during the time of the Republic.

Appian tells the story of this Punicus, whose name reveals his origins, describing his victory over the *praetors* Manilius and Calpurnius Piso – with the loss of 6,000 Romans (the same round number once again), including the *quaestor* Terentius Varro – as well as his untimely death.

He was followed by Caesarus, whose army, according to Appian, wiped out 9,000 Romans who were pursuing them "in a disorderly way", recapturing their spoils and the camp and seizing Roman arms and standards which he then displayed "all over Celtiberia". Traditional historiography is still perplexed by the reference to this region, which makes no sense if interpreted in terms of its usual meaning (the territory to the west of the Middle Ebro), but must be linked to the presence of Celtic populations in the south-east of the Iberian Peninsula.

He was succeeded by Caucenus, who came from "the other side of the Tagus", an expression whose interpretation is controversial but must reflect the geography of events and the concept of *Lusitania* at the time. Caucenus' incursions extended to the territory of the Conii (traditionally associated with the Algarve) and northern Africa, in particular the city of Ocile (near Asilah), where he was defeated by Lucius Mummius. It was an action which was part of a global strategy that is difficult to understand but falls within the strategic and diplomatic manoeuvres of the Lusitanians, which also included North Africa.

The episodes which follow in Appian's narrative are illustrative of the Roman strategy of using all available means to conquer the enemy. Marcus Atilius, "having spread fear, celebrated pacts with all". Lucullus, who "had waged war with the *Vaccaei* without authority", headed for *Lusitania*, where he devastated part of the territory while Galba destroyed the rest. This policy of sowing fear and havoc was not exclusive to *Lusitania* and was therefore presented as a legitimate strategy in the context of conflict.

Galba was also the key figure behind one of the darkest episodes of the war, which led to him being brought to trial in Rome, only escaping a sentence because he was wealthy enough to offer bribes. Appian states that, with the promise of lands and peace, he persuaded Lusitanians to lay down their arms then took advantage of the situation to kill most of them. He also explains that "few escaped, among them Viriathus, who not long afterward became the leader of the Lusitanians, killed many Romans and performed great deeds".

The many episodes in the Lusitanian Wars which involve Viriathus extend from 150 to 139 BC. In recent decades, historiography has been critically examining the texts which contain reports of the conflicts and provide a very detailed portrait of the Lusitanian leader, punctuated by various accounts of his life that are still surprising in terms of their contents, describing his origins, youth, marriage, habits, wise sayings etc. The most significant aspects are those in which this new perspective contrasts with the traditional image, namely those referring to the construction of the figure of Viriathus, his origins and his fellow soldiers and the geography and historical interpretation of the conflicts.

In relation to the last of these points, a reading of the classical texts leaves no doubts as to the territorial context in which the conflicts took place. Even though it is difficult to match certain places (*Oxthraca, Tribola, Baikor*) to their present-day counterparts, in a significant number of other cases it is unquestionable. In addition to the afore-mentioned city of *Ilipa*, which was apparently allied to Rome, there is *Carmo* (Carmona, Seville), also on the same side and a refuge for Galba, where he was able to raise an army of 20,000 allies, according to Appian. *Urso* (Osuna) was the base for the army led by Q. Fabius Maximus but also the homeland of Viriathus' companions, since it was a divided city with wavering alliances, like *Tucci* (Martos, Jaén), which was the inspiration for a moral tale recounted by Viriathus. His side, at least at given moments, could count on cities such as *Escadia, Gemella* (possibly *Gemella Tucci*, nowadays Martos, Jáen), *Obulcola* (Castillo de Monclova, Fuentes de Andalucía, Seville), the aforementioned *Hasta/Asta* (Mesas de Hasta, Jerez de la Frontera), *Arsa* (in *Baeturia Turdulorum*, probably in the south-east of the province of Badajoz) and *Erisane*, described as "his city", which came to be considered equivalent to the former.

The general idea running through the episodes describing the Viriathan Wars and their various successes and failures is that the Lusitanian leader often had a clear advantage over the Romans, who did not always respect the terms of agreements and only ended up winning by means of corruption.

The heroic status of Viriathus seems to have been inspired in particular by a certain type of Greek literature. Posidonius is considered responsible for the model of the cynical hero: a man born in contact with nature and guided by its principles, who is not corrupted by the urban world and social conventions (a kind of early version of the Rousseauesque noble savage) and lives a sober life, speaks little but comes directly to the point, is in possession of a superior form of knowledge, etc. It seems clear that a large part of his portrait is based on a particular model taken from Greek philosophy and therefore some modern historiography has highlighted the artificial nature of this image.

There has been an insistence on separating Viriathus and the Lusitanians from the discussion on their relation to present-day nations, thus avoiding the nationalist tone that influenced Portuguese historiography in particular. Viriathus was simply a Lusitanian and any links to a Hispanic nationality, far less to any place that makes unfounded claims to hold the honour of being his birthplace, no longer make sense.

On a political and military level, the resistance of the western Hispanic populations altered significantly after his death, paving the way for Decimus Junius Brutus to advance as far as the River Minho in 138 BC and conquer the Gallaeci. Thus began a new cycle in the history of the Rome in the west.

AMÍLCAR GUERRA
Centre for Archaeology, Faculty of Arts and Humanities, University of Lisbon

Bibliography

FABIÃO, Carlos, GUERRA, Amílcar, "Viriato: em torno da iconografia de um mito", in *Mito e Símbolo na História de Portugal e do Brasil: Actas dos IV Cursos Internacionais de Verão de Cascais* (7–12 July 1997), Cascais, Câmara Municipal de Cascais, 1998, pp. 33–79.

GARCÍA MORENO, Luís A., *De Gerión a César. Estudios Históricos y Filológicos de la España Indígena y Romano-Republicana*, Alcalá de Henares, Universidad de Alcalá, 2001.

PÉREZ VILATELA, Luciano, *Lusitania. Historia y Etnología*, Madrid, Real Academia de la Historia, 2000.

RICHARDSON, J. S., *Hispaniae. Spain and the Development of Roman Imperialism, 218–82 B.C.*, Cambridge, Cambridge University Press, 1986.

SALINAS, M., "La jefatura de Viriato y las sociedades del occidente de la Península Ibérica", *Palaeohispanica*, no. 8, 2008, pp. 89–120.

Second Century BC to the Fourth Century AD
In the Marketplace of the Roman Empire

The trading of goods in this vast territory benefited from a road network that had been established and consolidated within the empire, although river and, above all, maritime trading proved more profitable. Shipwrecks bear witness to the inherently risky nature of this activity.

In an empire which at its height would include such different geographies as the Iberian Peninsula, North Africa and the central and eastern Mediterranean region, in addition to vast areas of Europe, including *Britannia*, it is easy to envisage it becoming a vast market for raw materials, food products and manufactured goods. Due to its location, the western area of the Iberian Peninsula was particularly receptive to these dynamics, especially from the reign of Claudius onwards, with the conquest of *Britannia* in AD 43 and more intensive use of the Atlantic route.

Production, trade, circulation, distribution and consumption were crucial to the economy during the Roman Empire. Yet although the literary sources provide information on the resources that were exploited in particular regions and how they were traded and consumed, they say little about the majority of the products that circulated within the territories under Roman rule and supplied citizens with their everyday needs. It is on this level that archaeology becomes particularly relevant.

The trading of goods in this vast territory benefited from a road network that had been established and consolidated within the empire, although river and, above all, maritime trading proved more profitable.

Shipwrecks bear witness to the inherently risky nature of this activity, creating authentic archives at the bottom of the sea which are nowadays essential to our understanding of the types of products that were traded and the amounts in circulation, calculated from the tonnage of the vessels or, for example, the number of amphoras used to transport them. On the other hand, in terms of consumption in urban, artisan or rural environments, archaeologists have recovered an enormous collection of materials, particularly ceramics, that enable us to at least partially reconstruct the framework for the main exchanges within the empire. It was a complex and sophisticated economic system, based in major cities which served as the main ports to which goods were sent that would later make up the shipments for vessels destined not only for Europe but the whole of the Mediterranean Basin. The main products in this intensive commercial activity would have been raw materials (particularly metals) and food products such as wine, olive oil, cereals and fish products, transported in amphoras.

In addition to the institutional trading organized by the state to supply its armies and the population of Rome, there is evidence of merchants engaging in free trade, made possible by agricultural surpluses, large-scale artisan production and extractive industries (mines, quarries, etc). Three cycles can be identified for markets in the empire: integration within the Roman world, corresponding to the Republican period (second to first centuries BC), the Roman Imperial period (first to third centuries) and the Late Roman period and Late Antiquity (fourth to sixth centuries). It is also important to note that long before the Romans arrived in the Iberian Peninsula, products manufactured in the Mediterranean region were already being exchanged and that this increased significantly after the conquest and developed new features.

Manufactured products from the Italian Peninsula are an essential reference for archaeologists identifying the stages and locations involved in the Roman conquest and consolidation of territory. The most important are the amphoras used to transport wine, together with the black glazed pottery used for tableware, namely the so-called Campanian ware which came mainly from Naples, Cales or Etruria. Other pottery can be associated with this, such as the drinking vessels that were intended as tableware, providing good evidence of the gradual cultural integration of the conquered populations within the Roman way of life, reflected in the adoption of new eating habits.

In the (military or civil) contexts in which these items were recovered, there were also remains of amphoras used to transport foodstuff from other regions, including imported fish products from *Hispania Ulterior*/the future province of *Baetica* (nowadays Andalusia) and the Gaditan coastal region, together with imports from the Guadalquivir valley, which would have supplied wine or olive oil to the recently Romanized populations. Imported olive oil from *Tripolitania* in North Africa was also a constant feature, albeit in smaller amounts.

Research aims to determine the contribution made by the products from each region to this market and the kind of interdependence generated between provinces in the different phases of the Roman period and Late Antiquity.

Following the conquest and pacification of the Iberian Peninsula and its effective integration into the economic network of the empire, its cities and territories became more exposed to medium and long distance trading. On the one hand, wealth was created through agriculture, the manufacture of fish products and mining, or even marble from Alentejo quarries, which provided the purchasing power to obtain food and manufactured products from a wide range of places. In addition, the road network, which provided links to different urban centres, ensured supplies when maritime and/or river transport was not viable. As the numismatic finds reveal, it was largely a monetarized economy, an important factor in integration and Romanisation.

In the early empire, the consumption of manufactured goods was dominated by a set of imported fine ware from the Italian Peninsula (*terra sigillata*). These were high quality vessels, sometimes with moulded decoration, which were intended to serve as tableware. They were followed by products from workshops in southern Gaul which flooded the markets from the first century onwards, later succeeded by products from the interior of *Hispania* (the Guadalquivir valley and *Tarraconensis*). Coarse wares destined for domestic use were also produced and traded in the local/regional markets or sometimes imported from the Italian Peninsula, the neighbouring province of *Baetica* or North Africa.

Completing the range of available items, there was also a wide variety of food products transported in amphoras. In the early empire, wines and their derivatives came mainly from the Guadalquivir valley, although some originating from Gaul, the eastern Mediterranean, Italian Peninsula, etc. have also been identified in cities on the western and southern coasts. This diversity is mainly found in urban environments such as Lisbon (*Olisipo*), Faro (*Ossonoba*) and Torre de Ares (*Balsa*) in Tavira, since they were important urban centres with affluent local elites and it may be assumed that this type of consumption became associated with the display of wealth.

The olive oil came from the Guadalquivir and Genil valleys. Intended for institutional supply (above all, for the armies and the population of Rome), it regularly circulated through territory that is nowadays Portuguese.

The local/regional Lusitanian fish products were manufactured in the Tagus and Sado valleys, Peniche and, on a smaller scale, the Algarve. In addition to being traded as an export, these types of fish preserves played an important role in supplying urban and rural centres throughout *Lusitania*. Together with these local products, there were also other fish-based items from the province of *Baetica* which were mainly imported from the Gaditan area.

Even in areas far away from the coast, the archaeological record shows evidence of a taste for and easy access to a wide variety of fish products. In addition to the sauces produced from macerated fish, viscera, salt and herbs (*garum*, *allec* and *muria*), salted fish (*salsamenta*) and possibly even dried fish would also have been brought to the inland regions, together with shellfish such as oysters, which have been recovered in large amounts during excavations of *villae* in the Alentejo and in cities in the interior.

Wine and olive oil was produced in the Lusitanian countryside, as confirmed by the remains of presses identified in rural *villae*, and the discovery of types of amphora destined for the transport of wine appears to be evidence that the surpluses were traded. However, it should be remembered that the fact that wine and olive oil was produced locally would not necessarily mean the end of imports of these products.

Cities were important consumption centres, but also production centres, in particular for artisanal items. Hence the provincial capital *Augusta Emerita* (Mérida), for example, supplied areas in the interior of Lusitanian territory with thin-walled pottery (cups and small pots used as drinking vessels) and lamps. In Lisbon, archaeological work has identified remains associated with the manufacture of fish products which far exceeded local needs and were certainly intended for more distant markets. From the end of the first and the beginning of second century, the North African markets gradually became the main suppliers of ceramic tableware (*sigillata*), with large-scale production confirmed in Northern Tunisia (in the Carthage and Oudhna regions) and later also in *Byzacena*, which was exported to places throughout the empire. In the more southern regions, these imports were accompanied by a significant amount of ceramic cooking ware (African cooking ware) and commodities transported in amphoras. Although olive oil was originally considered the main driving force for the North African economy, nowadays the data is more nuanced and other products, such as wine, fish products and, above all, wheat, are also regarded as important.

In Late Antiquity it was the African and eastern provinces that exported the largest amounts to the Iberian Peninsula, while local production of ceramic tableware increased. Although it is true that from the third century onwards the trading dynamics did not result in the same volumes recorded in previous periods, it is certain that the same exchange networks largely remained active until at least the fifth century and in some regions until the first half of the sixth century.

In short, the Roman world was responsible for creating a vast market which linked people and products from very diverse regions of Europe, North Africa and, broadly speaking, the entire Mediterranean Basin. Moreover, from at least the second century BC onwards, the region which is nowadays Portugal was active in these networks.

CATARINA VIEGAS
Centre for Archaeology, Faculty of Arts and Humanities, University of Lisbon

Bibliography

CARVALHO, António et al., *Lusitânia Romana: Origem de Dois Povos, catálogo de exposição*, Lisbon, Imprensa Nacional-Casa da Moeda, 2015.

FABIÃO, Carlos, "A dimensão atlântica da Lusitânia: periferia ou charneira no Império Romano?", in GORGES, Jean-Gérard et al. (ed.), *Lusitânia Romana entre o Mito e a Realidade: Actas da VI Mesa Redonda Internacional sobre a Lusitânia Romana*, Cascais, Câmara Municipal de Cascais, 2009, pp. 53–74.

Idem, "Centros oleiros da Lusitania: balanço dos conhecimentos e perspectivas de investigação", in BERNAL CASASOLA, Darío, LAGÓSTENA BARRIOS, Lázaro (eds.), *Actas del Congreso Internacional Figlinae Beticae. Talleres Alfareros y Producciones Cerámicas en la Baetica Romana (ss. II A.C. – VII A.D.)*, Oxford, Achaeopress, 2004, pp. 379–410.

FERNÁNDEZ OCHOA, Carmen, MORILLO CERDÁN, Ángel, "*Oceanus Hispanus*. Navegación y comercio a orillas del Atlántico en época romana", in MORAIS, Rui et al. (ed.), *O Irado Mar Atlântico: O Naufrágio Bético Augustano de Esposende (Norte de Portugal)*, Braga, Museu de Arqueologia D. Diogo de Sousa, 2016, pp. 57—97.

MANTAS, V. Gil, "Vias e portos na Lusitânia romana", in GORGES, Jean-Gérard et al. (ed.), *V Mesa Redonda Internacional sobre Lusitania Romana. Las Comunicaciones*, Madrid, Ministerio de Educación Cultura y Deporte, 2004, pp. 427–453.

139 BC–14 AD
Aligning with the Empire: Language

Linguistic integration led to the emergence of Hispanic figures who became established in the cultural and literary arena of Rome itself, particularly from the Augustan period onwards. With regard to Lusitania, the name of Cornelius Bocchus (first half of the first century AD) stands out, a member of an illustrious family from Salacia (Alcácer do Sal).

Although most Portuguese people do not know any Latin, everyone can see how close it is to their own language, since Portuguese, like other Romance languages, evolved from Latin in a historical context that began over two thousand, one hundred years ago. The difficulty in understanding Latin nowadays can be explained by the lengthy period that separates us from the Roman conquest of the territory that is nowadays Portugal, which has led to very substantial changes to a living and therefore constantly changing entity such as language. Yet, its origins reveal one of the many facets of the language of Rome, namely the provincial language, which is distinct from literary Latin. The different variations of Latin stem from the intrinsic conditions in the several regions of the empire, a situation which gave rise to the different Romance languages. This branching path began with the individual conditions in each region, motivated, from the outset, by the implantation of the language of Rome within an existing reality which determined the specific nature of each of these areas.

In the case of *Hispania* there was not one pre-Roman language, but several. Although there are still doubts concerning the general linguistic framework, at least three can be identified.

In the north-east of the Iberian Peninsula and in part of southern France, Iberian was spoken. Until the mid-twentieth century, it was believed that the only surviving trace of this language, which would have been spoken in almost the entire Peninsula, was the Basque language. However, it has also been argued that it is not possible to establish a link between present-day Basque and ancient Iberian and that the earlier linguistic features of the Basque Country and Aquitaine should not be related to the pre-Roman language known as Iberian. Although some authors have recently returned to the idea that Basque is descended from Iberian, the debate is far from over.

We are on safer ground when we turn to Celtiberian, a well-documented language discussed at length in certain texts and for which there is a firm consensus regarding its nature. It is an Indo-European language which definitely belongs to the Celtic group. The geographical range and possible variants of this language are more complex issues, but may vaguely indicate a region to the west of the Middle and Upper Ebro.

The linguistic landscape of western *Hispania* is still somewhat confused. However, it is clearer on the subject of the so-called Lusitanian language, spoken in a large part of the territory which is nowadays Portuguese and in neighbouring areas of Spain at the time when the Romans were making more consistent efforts to establish their rule there in the second half of the second century BC, after the death of Viriathus in 139 BC. A substantial set of names for people, deities and places taken from this language has survived, although very little is known about its everyday vocabulary and structure. It is definitely an Indo-European language and may belong to the Celtic group.

Nevertheless, there is no doubt that certain terms that have passed into Portuguese (such as "*arroio* – stream", "*lapa* – crag", "*lameiro* – marsh", "*veiga* – meadow") date back to this pre-Roman past about which still so little is known. Moreover, "Lusitanian" had a particular structure which left its mark on the locally spoken Latin.

The point at which the pre-Roman languages came to an end is a matter for debate. It was a complex process, particularly with regard to spoken language, for which there are no records and very little evidence to serve as guidelines in addressing the problem. Half a dozen inscriptions are known to exist which represent a phase in which the local language was still being used, at least in certain religious acts. However, there is no reliable data for the chronology of these monuments, although it is thought that they may date back to the first century AD. Religion was a conservative element in the life of these communities and the fact that something from this domain was preserved does not mean that it had remained in use in everyday language up to this point.

Latin was implanted within this linguistic context, a process which developed at very different speeds. It certainly happened much faster in urban or coastal habitats of a certain size, or places where contingents of Italic peoples or other Latin speakers settled, and more slowly in rural areas where there was less contact with the cultural universe of the conqueror. The Augustan period (27 BC–AD 14) must have been a time of profound change in the cultural and linguistic landscape of these communities. With its policy of founding a political and administrative structure based on the Roman model, urban structures were developed, civic and religious habits were installed, and production and trading were boosted. Naturally, these transformations had a strong impact on the spread of the Latin language. Although it was still little used, the dynamics of the Augustan era ensured that it took firm root throughout *Lusitania*.

In this phase, the most westerly province in the empire became part of a huge space in which the Roman matrix was established. Latin was one of the most important components in this process, particularly influencing the more westerly environments, whereas Greek remained the main means of communication in the Roman east. In this territorially vast world, with its diverse culture and economic, social and political development, Rome was introducing a uniform trend which extended to all provinces, profoundly changing their circumstances.

With regard to *Hispania*, the first contacts with the Latin language were the result, to a large extent, of Rome's diplomatic activities. It may be imagined that the treaties and agreements frequently referenced in the sources were based on relations between Rome and the local elites and materialized in the form of legal documents. The oldest document of this kind is a decree issued by Aemilius Paullus dated 189 BC which granted freedom to the slaves in the city of Hasta who lived in *Turris Lascutana*.

Roman historiography frequently alludes to pacts with local populations and the close relations they developed with the Romans, including their representatives. One of the most illustrative examples of these relations and their consequences concerns Sertorius, who developed a policy of promoting local elites with a view to integrating them into Roman culture. It refers in particular to an initiative known as the Huesca "school" which provided education for the sons of the Hispanic aristocracy. Although Plutarch's text emphasizes his concern to instil a solid understanding of Graeco-Roman culture in the young men, it also highlights their unusual situation as hostages of the rebel general. Nevertheless, in the context of the local communities the ability to speak Latin would certainly have been a distinction that was prized by the elites.

The Roman world gradually developed an urban culture in *Hispania*, sometimes associated with the promotion of a legal system, particularly in the colonies, the oldest of which was *Carteia*, proclaimed a Latin colony in 171 BC. In a transitional phase the phenomenon of bilingualism is understandable, evident in aspects such as the coins produced in certain cities. The use of inscriptions in other (Neo-Punic or Hispanic) sign systems, indicating a transitional stage at least during the Republican phase (II–I centuries BC), is clearly represented by certain local mints during the Roman period. Epigraphic documentation reveals that throughout the first century AD, "Lusitanian" was still used for inscriptions, especially in *Lusitania*, and that its specific features, particularly nominal inflections, stand out in many Latin texts.

However, the process of developing a legal culture and policies for territorial reorganisation such as those undertaken by Augustus in the province of *Lusitania*, were initiatives that consolidated Roman culture and led to the gradual disappearance of the language of the Lusitanians. Civic communities were developed whose political activities, administration and public life were dominated by the Latin language and culture. Latin was the only path for entering politics, contacting the administration and gaining access to the justice system. It was the language of local as well as Roman citizenship and of autonomous *civitates.*

Linguistic integration led to the emergence of Hispanic figures who became established in the cultural and literary arena of Rome itself, particularly from the Augustan period onwards. With regard to *Lusitania*, the name of Cornelius Bocchus (first half of the first century AD) stands out, a member of an illustrious family from *Salacia* (Alcácer do Sal) who became famous as the author of various works which gained a certain standing in illustrious circles in Rome but are nowadays only known through citations by other authors (especially Pliny the Elder), who gathered detailed information from them, in particular concerning the province. The learned Salacian mastered the language used in literary circles in the capital of the empire, which was different from the language spoken by ordinary people in the city where he was born. Although it was, in fact, the same language there were certain distinctive features which, in turn, differed from other versions used in this huge empire. There was no single form of Latin, but instead several models as diverse as the cultural panoply of peoples under Roman rule.

At the beginning of the twentieth century, based on epigraphic documentation, the Belgian linguist Albert Carnoy (1878–1961) defined certain particularities of the Latin used in *Hispania* in terms of its phonetics, morphology and syntax. Later, other authors returned to the subject, including A. Tovar, S. Mariner, M. Díaz y Díaz, M. Mayer, J. Velaza and even F. Beltrán Lloris, who produced a historical contextualisation.

Due to linguistic variety in the pre-Roman world, it is problematic to speak of Hispanic Latin as if it were uniform. It is possible to identify specific features in certain areas but in most cases this cannot be generalized to apply to the whole Peninsula. Nevertheless, it is legitimate to classify these features in order to create a list of characteristics that can enable us to define the specificities of the Latin used in *Hispania*. This also helps us to understand the different trajectories in each cultural area, which eventually converge as a linguistic mosaic similar to the present situation in Iberian Peninsula. In fact, there is no break in linguistic continuity between the Latin of *Hispania* and the Portuguese language, only a normal process of evolution that is common to all languages. To a certain extent, it may be argued that, in Portugal, almost two thousand years later, the Latin used by the inhabitants of the empire to communicate with each other is still spoken, not as the populations of Roman *Hispania* would have done (since languages are not frozen in time), yet incorporating the changes that have taken place over the centuries.

Amílcar Guerra

Centre for Archaeology, Faculty of Arts and Humanities, University of Lisbon

Bibliography

BELTRÁN LLORIS, Francisco, "El latín en la Hispania Roman una perspectiva histórica", in *Historia de la Lengua Española*, Madrid, Santillana, 2005, pp. 83–106.
CARNOY, Albert J., *Le Latin d'Espagne d'après les Inscriptions: Etude Linguistique*, Louvain, J.-B. Istas, 1902.

MARINER, Sebastian, "La latinidad hispánica y los contactos lingüísticos en la Hispania romana", in *Latin y Hispania Antigua. Scripta Minora,* Madrid, Editorial Complutense, 1999, pp. 479–506.

MAYER, Marc, "El latín de Hispania", in *Actas del VIII Congreso Español de Estudios Clásicos,* Madrid, Ediciones Clásicas, 1994, pp. 363–382.

TOVAR, Antonio, *El Latín de Hispania: Aspectos Léxicos de la Romanización, Discurso Leído el Día 31 de Marzo de 1968 por Don Antonio Tovar Llorente y Contestación Pública por el Excmo. Sr. Don Pedro Laín Entralgo,* Madrid, Real Academia Española, 1968.

First Century BC
Where Does the World End?

Regarding the Promontorium Sacrum, *Strabo clearly states that "This cape is the most westerly point, not only of Europe, but of the whole inhabited world". The coordinates in Ptolemy's* Geography *also show how this geographical accident extends much further than the others.*

Among the excerpts of poetry that defined a certain phase of school education for generations of Portuguese students, one extract from *The Lusiads* (III, 20) describing the position of Portugal has become emblematic: "See the head-crowning coronet is she / of general Europe, Lusitania's reign / where endeth land and where beginneth sea / and Phoebus sinks to rest upon the main". Fernando Pessoa reprised this theme in *Message,* presenting a Europe "staring with a sphinx-like, fatal gaze / the West, the future of the past / The face that stares is Portugal".

This image of the small kingdom as the head of Europe was developed under very specific conditions, particularly during the period in which Camões lived (1524–1580), and even today significant ideas can be drawn from this fact. The allegory is to a large extent rooted in the classical Graeco-Latin literary tradition and in its geographical vision of the universe in general and certain regions in particular, although not so much in terms of the visual image of a Europe that resembled the human body but the idea that one of the extremities of the terrestrial orb could be found there, thus giving rise to its configuration as the head of the continent. In the ancient world, this notion tended to crystallize as the "end of the Earth" (*finis Terrae*), the point where it converged with the other elements: the waters, the sky and the stars above.

Within this concept, the sea encircled the Earth and was known as the Exterior Sea, as opposed to the Mediterranean, and its western boundary was identified by a specific point in *Hispania.* The opinions of geographers in the ancient world were divided on this issue, attributing it to three different promontories: the Artabro, in the north-west of the Iberian Peninsula, the *Promontorium Magnum* or *Olisiponense,* and the *Promontorium Sacrum,* in the south-west of the Peninsula. Concepts with a religious perspective were developed around each of them which, having taken root in the pre-Roman world (eighth to second centuries BC), acquired particular political significance during the period of Roman rule (second century BC onwards).

The Artabro promontory was named after the Artabri, the people who inhabited the extreme north-west of *Hispania.* Strabo (64 BC–24 AD), however, associates this ethnic group with Cape Nerium, which may be the same place under a different name. It is known that the most westerly point of Galicia is Cape Finisterre, but it does not appear to be clear, according to current research, whether the name used in classical literature corresponds to this place. Nevertheless, in the Roman tradition this issue of the extremities of land acquired considerable symbolic importance and was therefore used to political advantage by certain figures from Roman history. During the time of Augustus (27 BC–AD 14), after conquering the north-east and establishing Roman rule throughout the Peninsula, his legate Lucius Sestius Quirinalis ordered altars to be built, the so-called "Sestian altars", religious monuments with a powerful political and ideological significance. The location of these monuments, also known as "Augustan altars", has been debated, since the information provided by the classical authors themselves is not always consistent. The Hispanic author Pomponius Mela situates them next to the city of Noega on the Asturian coast. The remaining ancient sources (Pliny, Ptolemy, Anonymous of Ravenna) opt for the opposite, locating them in the extreme north-west – in the territory of the Celtici Neri (Pliny) or Cape Nerium (Ptolemy). It is therefore more likely that these Sestian altars were situated in Galicia, given that they were meant for the extremities of inhabited land which were associated with a special symbolism in Roman politics, especially under Augustus.

Regarding the *Promontorium Sacrum*, Strabo clearly states that "This cape is the most westerly point, not only of Europe, but of the whole inhabited world". The coordinates in Ptolemy's *Geography* also show how this geographical feature extends much further than the others. Like other promontories, it is also associated with a complex sacred tradition, evident in its name, which appears to date back to before the Roman conquest. Concerning the rituals which took place there, Strabo notes "stones in many spots, lying in groups of three or four, which in accordance with a native custom are turned round by those who visit the place, and then, after the pouring of a libation, are moved back again. And it is not lawful to offer sacrifice there or even set foot in the place at night because people say the gods occupy it at that time; those who come to see the place spend the night in a neighbouring village then enter it by day, taking water with them for there is no water there".

Geographical tradition discusses the relationship between this sacred place and a cult dedicated to Heracles mentioned by Ephorus, a Greek historian from the fourth century BC, but denied by Strabo. Modern historiography has interpreted Ephorus' reference as a sign of a cult dedicated to Melqart, associated with Phoenician and Punic voyages in these regions at the ends of the Earth, and religious phenomena similar to examples documented in other promontories they visited.

However, many of the ancient authors considered that the *Promontorium Magnum* was the most westerly point on Earth. For Pliny the Elder (m. 79 AD), in his *Natural History*, it is "a promontory, by some called *Artabrum*, by others the Great Promontory, while many call it the Promontory of *Olisipo*, from the city near it, which separates the land, the sea, and the heavens". He notes that it is so named because it has a span of 60 or 90 miles, according to different opinions. This discrepancy was due to the fact that some authors calculated the distance from the mouth of the Tagus to Cape Carvoeiro, while others measured it from Cape Espichel, but not Cape Roca, as traditional Portuguese historiographical tradition often argues.

One place in which the archaeological evidence most clearly reveals the special symbolic nature of this promontory is located on a small elevation known as Alto da Vigia, overlooking the Maçãs beach, where very significant archaeological remains and epigraphs have been identified. The local Odrinhas Museum has organized excavations, led by José Cardim Ribeiro, that provide a better understanding of the unusual nature of the site within the context of the empire.

In the sixteenth century Roman remains were observed there, including some inscribed altars that became particularly well-known due to a drawing by Francisco de Holanda which was included in one of his manuscripts from 1571, accompanied by the following text:

> And we saw, at the mouth of the River Colares, revered in the past by the Romans, on a small hill overlooking the Ocean, a circle filled with many cippi and memorials to Roman emperors who had visited this place. Each one had placed there a cippus, bearing an inscription dedicated to the Eternal Sun and the Moon.

As is in other similar situations, Holanda's drawing is somewhat imaginative and it would be more realistic to accept that he would have seen something similar to what Valentim Fernandes, after a visit in 1505, described as: "under the ground, unexpectedly, three square stone columns with ancient Roman lettering engraved on one side only". In fact, the surviving epigraphic documentation indicates that it was not the emperors themselves who visited these remote places, but important agents of the imperial administration, their representatives in the province of *Lusitania*: one individual of name uncertain, another identifiable only by his cognomen, Coelianus, and C. Iulius Celsus, who states his position as "legate sent to *Lusitania* for the purpose of a census", a mission he would have carried out under Antoninus Pius, probably between AD 139 and 141.

Hence, the political designation of the place was preserved, together with the sacred nature of the site evident in the official invocations to the sun, the moon and the ocean, entities that clearly represented the natural elements which converged with the Earth at this point. The inclusion of the ocean in the list of divine entities is registered in one of the inscriptions and the association with the sun and moon in the dedication is a very eloquent expression of this union of elements. Finally, with regard to the lunar element in the dedications, it should be remembered that in Antiquity the toponym for the Sintra range was Moon Hill. One of the dedications from Alto da Vigia (dated AD 198–209), addressed to the Eternal Sun and the Moon, makes an interesting supplication for "the eternity of the empire and the health of the emperor", in this case Septimus Severus and members of the imperial family Caracalla, Geta and Julia Domna. It is an entreaty for those responsible for the empire, but above all for the endurance of this political reality and for its integrity, defined by concrete boundaries, one of which stood before the visitor.

It makes perfect sense that these entities would have been worshipped in this most unusual site, overlooking the vast ocean where the sun could be seen sinking into its depths. More than a matter of literary interest, the sunset itself became a matter for debate, inspired in particular by the commonly held belief that "in places close to the Ocean, the Sun is larger when it sets, and as it sinks it sounds as if the sea is sizzling as it falls into its depths", in the words of Strabo. The question of the size of the setting sun was subject to exaggeration, as in the case of Artemidorus (second to first centuries BC), who argued that the sun at that point was one hundred times larger and that night fell immediately, which Strabo contested, drawing on the authority of Posidonius.

In short, any one of these three promontories clearly represents a certain vision of this Atlantic façade overlooking the ocean. It was peopled with fantasy elements that were diffused by literary tradition and its myths and ghosts lingered on in the minds of certain authors during the imperial age. The ocean was inhabited by beings distinguished by their enormous size or exotic nature: giant octopuses, mermen who sank ships, tritons with horns made of shells, and sea nymphs whose mournful songs could be heard from far away.

These fabulous images, emerging particularly in earlier literature, would gradually alter as knowledge of the territory and the seas extended. Generally speaking, *Hispania* became well integrated within the Roman global universe, albeit at very varying speeds. Its extreme location at the end of the Earth was more of a geographical characteristic than a symbol of remoteness and marginal cultural status.

The epigraph which sums up the work of Augustus is *The Deeds of the Divine Augustus, by which he submitted the Terrestrial Orb to the Rule of the Roman People*. It is this universal sense of the Roman Empire that emerges in concrete spaces, in particular those which most effectively represent the true meaning of the expression, namely its extreme points. Hence, the inclusion of these symbolic places in the known universe within the territorial context of Rome has a special significance.

AMÍLCAR GUERRA
Centre for Archaeology, Faculty of Arts and Humanities, University of Lisbon

Bibliography

FERNÁNDEZ OCHOA, Carmen, MORILLO CERDÁN, Ángel, "El convento araugustano y las aras sestianas: Reflexiones sobre la primera organización administrativa del noroeste hispano", *Latomus*, vol. 61, no. 4, 2002, pp. 889–910.

GUERRA, Amílcar, "Promontório Magno: perspectivas da geografia antiga sobre o extremo ocidental da Hispânia", in *Actas do Congresso A Presença Romana na Região Oeste*, Bombarral, Câmara Municipal do Bombarral, 2005, pp. 119–129.

RIBEIRO, José Cardim, "*Ad antiquitates vestigandas*: destinos e itinerários antiquaristas nos campos olisiponenses ocidentais desde os inícios a meados do séc. XVI", in GONZÁLEZ GERMAIN, Gérard (coord.), *Peregrinationes ad Inscriptiones Colligendas. Estudios sobre Epigrafía de Tradición Manuscrita*, Bellaterra, Universidad Autònoma de Barcelona, 2016, pp. 135–250.

Idem, "*Soli aeterno lunae*: cultos astrais em época pré-romana e romana na área de influência da serra de Sintra: um caso complexo de sincretismo?", in RIBEIRO, José Cardim (ed.), *Diis Deabusque: Actas do II Colóquio Internacional de Epigrafia "Culto e Sociedade"*, Sintra, Museu Arqueológico de São Miguel de Odrinhas, 2011, pp. 595–624.

SALINAS DE FRIAS, Manuel, "El "Hieron Akroterion" y la geografía religiosa del extremo occidente según Estrabón", in *Actas del I Congreso Peninsular de Historia Antigua*, vol. II, Santiago de Compostela, Universidade de Santiago de Compostela, 1989, pp. 135–147.

First Century BC
The Emergence of Cities

Although settlements of considerable size already existed in pre-Roman times in the southern and central area of what is nowadays Portuguese territory, the construction of the province was due, for the most part, to the creation of a large network of urban centres linked by an extensive road system.

One important element in the process of creating the province of *Lusitania* was the emergence of urban centres with privileged legal status, which helped to diffuse the Roman way of life. Although settlements of considerable size already existed in pre-Roman times in the southern and central area of what is nowadays Portuguese territory, the construction of the province was due, for the most part, to the creation of a large network of urban centres linked by an extensive road system.

The political and administrative landscape that was consolidated during the reign of Augustus (27 BC–14 AD) saw the capital of the *civitas* as the focal point for controlling a territory whose boundaries are difficult to establish. Borders can only be identified when the boundary markers known as *termini Augustales* have been preserved and when it can be assumed that they were found in their original location.

Under Roman rule, cities acquired new roles and became the headquarters of political power and the administration of justice, as well as trading centres and platforms for the redistribution of food, raw materials and manufactured products. They were not only consumers, but also producers, noted for artisanal industries associated with ceramics and other manufactured goods and even the manufacture of fish products.

According to Pliny, the indigenous communities formed part of the *oppida foederata, libera* and *stipendiaria* and most cities were included in the third category, which required payment of an annual tax to the Roman state.

The written sources reveal that five cities in *Lusitania* were known to have colonial status in the Augustan period: *Augusta Emerita* (Mérida), *Metellinum* (Medellin), *Pax Iulia* (Beja), *Norba Caesarina* (Cáceres) and *Scallabis* (Santarém). However, the attribution of special status to certain urban centres may even have started under Caesar (49–44 BC), as the use of the cognomen *Iulium* in place names suggests. This has been confirmed by archaeological data and appears to be the case with *Scallabis Preasidium Iulium* (Santarém). Nevertheless, in the Algarve there is no known evidence of any existing colonial foundations or *oppida* which may have been promoted to municipalities during Caesar's dictatorship.

Cities such as *Ebora Liberalitas Iulia* (Évora), *Myrtilis* (Mértola) and *Salacia* (Alcácer do Sal) were granted the status of municipality under Augustus. Epigraphy is an important indicator of the different stages in the creation of colonies and municipalities and the integration of local populations within different Roman tribes (*tribos*) is considered, in this context, to be a valid chronological factor. Hence, inclusion within the Sergian tribe is attributed to Julius Caesar and inclusion within the Galerian tribe corresponds to the Augustan period. Finally, the extension of *ius Latii* to the whole of *Hispania*, under the Flavian dynasty (69–96 BC), led to integration within the Quirinal tribe.

Regardless of their status, most of the urban centres were small or medium-sized, covering approximately 10 acres or slightly more. However, the large variations that have been observed, coupled with the lack of consistent archaeological data in most cases, means that this information must be treated with caution.

Given that many of the remains of Roman cities are found in the subsoil of existing cities, the enormous difficulties which archaeology faces are understandable. In fact, most contemporary urban centres have been occupied throughout history since Antiquity and very few places have an integrated research project for the city. In addition to the material that was destroyed in the past when public policies did not ensure protection and appreciation of the archaeological heritage, the knowledge that is acquired nowadays is the result of various construction and/or urban rehabilitation projects in specific areas of historic city centres. Rarely do we have access to information on the whole city. What we do know can be envisaged as an uneven mosaic of data on the urban landscape, the different public buildings and the architecture – both domestic and artisanal.

The study of urban centres in Roman times has not developed continuously since the sixteenth century, a time when humanists such as André de Resende were involved in identifying the names of ancient cities and their contemporary toponyms. This research was based on ancient itineraries and literary sources, supported by some epigraphic and numismatic information. At a later stage, the results of archaeological excavations that were beginning to take place became significant, especially from the nineteenth century onwards.

With the development of scientific archaeology, research into cities initially focused on the monumental features of public buildings, highlighting the architectural and decorative models. Less attention was paid to domestic architecture, artisanal structures and water supply and distribution systems. Innovative approaches have only recently been developed to study infrastructures for the collection and storage of water and waste management. Efforts have also been made to study cities as populational centres within the framework of the provincial landscape, focussing on how they related to the surrounding territory.

The reception of new urban models varied, with different factors determining the solutions that were adopted. The existence of previous urban centres or their creation from scratch, together with the topography of the land, influenced the way in which cities developed in the early stages of the Imperial period. Moreover, this remodelling did not take place at the same pace in every city. The most frequently cited example is Conimbriga, due to the Luso-French research project based there in the 1960s and 1970s. The archaeological remains that were recovered were well-preserved, precisely because the site had not been occupied during the Modern era, which made this city the interpretative model for the whole of Portuguese territory in terms of the evolutionary dynamics of Roman cities. However, research has since revealed a richer and more complex scenario than the one originally proposed, as well as the unique nature of some of the urban development options that were adopted.

From the Augustan era onwards, architectural and artistic programmes were adopted in cities, a process which lasted throughout the entire Julio–Claudian dynasty (27 BC–69 AD). There are numerous examples of the creation and renovation of urban structures such as forums and baths during the Claudian era. However, it was only during the Flavian dynasty that *ius Latii* was attributed to all urban centres in *Hispania*, a phase defined by the reform of the legal models in all Lusitanian cities.

Very little is known about indigenous urban areas prior to their inclusion in the Roman Empire. Nevertheless, the profound changes brought about by integration are evident in the use of new materials and new construction techniques, with mortar made from lime and sand almost completely replacing the previous adobe structures. Together with the ceramics used in construction (the different types of roof tiles and bricks), they comprise the basic elements which, combined with the different types of stone available in each location, led to the construction of the great Roman projects.

The construction of the forum was one of the most important of these programmes, making use of architectural models based not only on the one used in the metropole (Rome), but also those in the capital of the province (Mérida), which were disseminated in different forms throughout *Lusitania*. The architecture of the political, administrative and religious centre was a reflection and a representation of the incorporation of the imperial ideology, in which the building of the temple to the imperial cult played a central role.

In addition, urban structures were transformed and standardized with the incorporation of models from Rome, which at first had a great influence on the construction and creation of the urban landscape of Mérida, then at a later stage spread from the provincial capital to the remaining urban centres in *Lusitania*. Following the same path, although the architectural programmes were initially based on granite, the use of marble later became widespread (especially from the second half of the first century onwards), as the stone quarries in the Estremoz region were developed.

The Roman public architecture of these emerging cities was also included bath buildings, varying in complexity and often featuring detailed decorative work. Just as relevant were the buildings dedicated to performance, such as the theatre, the circus and the amphitheatre, as well as the systems for collecting and channelling water (aqueducts, fountains and tanks, for example) and the sewage facilities. They all combined to provide urban centres with the necessary infrastructures to enable the inhabitants to "live the Roman way". It would appear that none of these efforts would have been possible without investment on the part of the imperial state and the local elites. It should be noted that in Roman society funds provided by the elite for the construction and renovation of public buildings were essential to the process of gaining access to public positions (euergetism).

In domestic architecture, layouts were developed for atrium houses and peristyles, involving the extensive use of decorative models, in particular mosaic floors often displaying geometric patterns but also figurative elements. The use of painted and moulded plaster or different types of marble (both local and imported) was also common, usually applied to various types of coatings, architectural elements or inlays. There are excellent examples of such techniques in the *domus* of Braga, Conimbriga and Miróbriga, amongst other cities, which demonstrate how the models from the capital of the empire had been fully absorbed within the various different regions of *Lusitania*.

Catarina Viegas
Centre for Archaeology, Faculty of Arts and Humanities, University of Lisbon

Bibliography

ALARCÃO, Jorge de, *A Lusitânia e a Galécia: Do Séc. II a.C. ao Séc. VI d.C.*, Coimbra, Imprensa da Universidade de Coimbra, 2018.

CORREIA, Virgílio Hipólito, *A Arquitectura do Ocidente da Lusitânia Romana: Entre o Público e o Privado*, Lisbon, Academia das Ciências de Lisboa, 2017.

Idem, *A Arquitectura Doméstica de Conimbriga e as Estruturas Económicas e Sociais da Cidade Romana*, Coimbra/Lisbon/Condeixa, Centro de Estudos Arqueológicos/Direcção-Geral do Património Cultural/Liga de Amigos de Conimbriga, 2013.
NOGALES BASARRATE, T. (ed.), *Ciudad y Foro en Lusitania Romana. Cidade e Foro na Lusitânia Romana*, Studia Lusitana 4, Mérida, Museu Nacional de Arte Romano, 2010.

80 BC
The Impact of the Roman Civil Wars

The clashes between the Roman elites had always been the central focus of the conflicts, yet in becoming an arena for the battles, the Iberian Peninsula witnessed an unusual concentration of Romans interacting closely with the indigenous elites, regardless of which side they supported.

Throughout the first century BC, the Iberian Peninsula encountered new dynamics in the interaction between indigenous societies and the Roman forces. Remaining a conquered territory, since it was still not fully controlled by Rome, it had to contend with a new situation as an arena in the Roman civil wars. The centre of the tensions was always Rome but the theatres of war were shifted to other areas to distance the military action from the city. The conflicts, emerging from disputes between Roman elites, often known as "factions" – the "Populares" and the "Optimates", even when their members came from the elites – can also be explained by clashes between certain personalities and their followers.

The first conflicts broke out when the consul L. Cornelius Sulla was fighting in Greece, which had rebelled against Rome, in particular against Mithridates, the king of Pontus (Asia Minor, nowadays Turkey). In his absence, the "Populares" led by G. Marius and Cinna took control of Rome. Following the death of Marius, the most prestigious leader of the group, Sulla made peace with Mithridates, the great enemy of Rome, and returned with his army to the Italian Peninsula. He marched on Rome with his troops, an unprecedented act, and defeated his enemies. Many decapitated heads of Roman citizens were displayed in the forum: Sulla assumed the office of dictator from 81 to 79 BC and began a violent phase of persecution.

One of the "Marianistas", Quintus Sertorius, who had served in *Hispania Citerior*, been forced into exile and fled to North Africa, was recalled to the Iberian Peninsula in 80 BC, where an army of Lusitanians was waiting near the Strait of Gibraltar, ready to follow him. This is the first controversial piece of information in the narrative, which is based on literary sources. It is not known why the Lusitanians wished to put themselves under the command of the Roman, far less what such an army would have been doing in the south of the Peninsula, a region that had surrendered to Rome more than a century ago. The reference must have been intended to emphasize the unlawful, or non-citizen, nature of these supporters of Sertorius, who may have already been Romanized and were keen to take part in the conflict.

Between 80 and 71 BC Quintus Sertorius fought successfully against the governors of the two Hispanic provinces. He gained important local support, both from communities that had not completely surrendered to Rome and from other Romanized populations who had taken up the cause of his "popular party". The Iberian Peninsula became the last refuge of the "Populares" and a wave of Romans headed for the area, where Sertorius had allegedly founded a "Senate" which was considered unlawful by the Roman authorities. He also established a school in *Osca* (nowadays Huesca) where he welcomed the sons of many powerful indigenous Hispanic subjects. Contradicting the contemporary narratives, it is said that the young men would have been hostages, to ensure the loyalty of the local chiefs. However, it should be noted that being a hostage was quite common in the ancient world and did not have the negative connotations it has assumed nowadays: the Greek historian Polybius, for example, an important author from the second century BC and a member of the close circle of Scipio Aemilianus, was a hostage in Rome. Whatever the case may be, the school helped foster the integration of the local Hispanic communities within the Roman way of life and the young men who studied there went on to become leaders in their communities.

Sertorius was eventually murdered by his followers, allegedly because he had become violent and intolerant. However, these narratives should be read with caution, given that the charge of tyranny was an acceptable justification for any homicide motivated by envy or a desire for power.

During the Sertorian rebellion, much of the Iberian Peninsula, particularly in the west, was quite literally beyond Roman rule. Several places where there had been a Roman presence were abandoned in this period and hoards of money were hidden and never recovered, indicating that these were troubled times. Archaeology has also been able to reveal another of Sertorius' intentions. Several lead bullets from slingshots (a weapon typically used by auxiliary troops in the Roman armies) bear the inscription Q.SERT.PROCOS, signifying Quintus Sertorius, Proconsul. The proconsulship constituted an extraordinary extension of the powers of the consulship, an elected office in Rome. In using these inscriptions on the bullets launched against the Roman soldiers, Sertorius was aiming to assert his claim to political legitimacy, as a Roman magistrate. The army of the governor of *Hispania Ulterior* had similar bullets bearing the inscription Quintus Metellus, Proconsul: battles were also fought with propaganda.

Sertorius made a pact with Mithridates, the king of Pontus and one of Rome's fiercest enemies, in the east, and with the Sicilian pirates, seeking to extend the conflict beyond the Peninsula even though this manoeuvre was pure propaganda. Reinforcements, commanded by Gnaeus Pompeius in the final phase of the war, were needed to achieve victory and the last of the Sertorians were defeated in 71 BC. In the final phase of the conflict Pompey complained repeatedly to the Senate about the lack of provisions for the army due to communication failures and support for Sertorius from communities in the provincial regions. There are signs of violent destruction in the aftermath of the conflict in various Roman archaeological sites, which can be attributed to Pompey's harsh treatment of those he defeated. One of the most striking examples is the forum in the city of Valencia, where several unburied corpses showing signs of violent death were discovered, evidence of the brutal devastation and abandonment of the area over a lengthy period. From the third quarter of the first century BC, there was a very significant increase in the amount of amphoras used to transport food products from the Peninsula, proof of the growing volume of agricultural surpluses which initially ensured that the army was less dependent on external supplies and later transformed *Hispania* into a centre for the export of food products to Rome and other parts of the empire.

In the first century BC, the 60s was a relatively peaceful decade. It was also the decade of Pompey, christened The Great, who triumphed over the slave rebellion led by Spartacus in Italy. Pompey served as consul together with Marcus Crassus and dismantled Sulla's laws, an indication of the volatility of each individual's position in these conflicts, since Pompey had fought in *Hispania* for the "Sullan faction".

Following this relative calm, the next decade was a time of great turmoil. Three prestigious Roman figures, Pompey the Great, Marcus Crassus and Julius Caesar, established an informal alliance for the government of Rome, usually known as the First Triumvirate (59 BC). Pompey governed the Hispanic provinces, Julius Caesar was responsible for independent Gaul and Crassus, the richest man in Rome but lacking military honours, travelled to Syria to fight the Parthians, who were the major obstacle to the eastward expansion of the Roman Empire.

The period which followed is well-documented, above all in the set of sophisticated literary texts produced by Caesar and his closest allies. Julius Caesar subdued the Gauls between 58 and 51 BC and also undertook naval expeditions to Great Britain, although he failed to establish permanent settlement there. Marcus Crassus led a disastrous campaign in the east and died in 53 BC, when he was serving jointly as consul with Pompey. The latter, although appointed governor of the *Hispanias*, did not leave Rome during this period and administered the western provinces by means of legates equipped with considerable military strength.

In 52 BC, after a new period of intense upheavals in Rome, including the assassination of the consul Clodius which once again left Pompey the only consul, Julius Caesar returned to the city without authorisation. Pompey was urged to organize the defence against Caesar's armies, who were powerful and well-trained after ten years of hard-fought campaigns, but preferred to abandon Italy and take refuge in the east.

Thus for six years, from 49 to 44 BC, there was a new period of civil war, covering a very wide geographical area. In Rome, Caesar decided not to pursue Pompey and headed for the Iberian Peninsula, stating that he preferred to confront an army without a leader than a leader without an army. In *Hispania*, his legions fought and defeated Pompey's three legates. He appointed Cassius Longinus, who had already served in the Peninsula under Pompey, governor of the *Hispanias*. Varro, one of Pompey's legates who was defeated in 49 BC, also joined Caesar's camp, clear evidence of the highly volatile nature of alliances within these Roman "factions". Caesar then went to the east in search of Pompey, whom he defeated in the Battle of Pharsalus in Macedonia, in 48 BC. Pompey fled to Egypt and was assassinated before Caesar arrived there.

After a famous sojourn in Egypt in the company of Queen Cleopatra, Caesar once again confronted his Roman adversaries in North Africa, finally returning to Rome in 46 BC to celebrate a quadruple triumph. This was also the time of the calendar reform, preserved for centuries in the European west as the Julian Calendar. However, his return was short-lived as the sons of Pompey were leading a new rebellion in the Iberian Peninsula. He went back to the *Hispanias* to confront and defeat them at the hard-fought Battle of Munda in the present-day south of Spain in 45 BC. After returning again to Rome, Caesar was assassinated in 44 BC, giving rise to a new period of civil war which lasted from 44 to 30 BC, started by Caesar's followers against his assassins, then waged between two members of the factions, Octavian and Mark Antony, until the former triumphed. This new phase in the Roman civil wars took place in the eastern half of the Mediterranean and there were no significant episodes in the *Hispanias*, although Sextus Pompeius, the younger son of Pompey the Great, who had escaped from the Battle of Munda with his life, was active there for around one year.

The Roman civil wars represented a period of relative stagnation in the territorial conquest of the Iberian Peninsula. The northern areas, usually known as Cantabria and Asturias, geographical names that should be understood in the broadest sense, were only finally brought under Roman rule in the final decades of the century after the civil wars had ended. However, this slowdown was accompanied by substantial progress in integrating the already subdued territories and their populations within the Roman world. For the populations in the Peninsula, it represented one of the major stages in the assimilation of Roman values and ways of life, memorably expressed in an extract from the work of the Greek author Strabo, written at the end of first century BC: "the Turdetani [the name of the inhabitants in the south of the Iberian Peninsula], and particularly those that live in the area around the Baetis [the River Guadalquivir], have fully adopted the Roman way of life and do not even remember their own language any more. Most of them have become Latins [in other words, communities granted Latin legal status] and have received the Romans as colonists, so they are almost entirely Roman [...] Moreover, all the Iberians who have adopted this model are known as *togati* [an allusion to the toga, the typical dress of Roman citizens] and they include the Celtiberians who were once regarded as the most savage of all". This is a particularly interesting description because it touches directly on identity issues (lifestyle, language, clothing), justifying the notion of the Romanisation of the Peninsula populations. The clashes between the Roman elites had always been the central focus of the conflicts, yet in becoming an arena for the battles, the Iberian Peninsula witnessed an unusual concentration of Romans interacting closely with the indigenous elites, regardless of which side they supported. This integration justifies the Greek geographer's observation that it would take little to make them entirely Roman.

CARLOS FABIÃO
Centre for Archaeology, Faculty of Arts and Humanities, University of Lisbon

Bibliography

BLÁZQUEZ, José María et al., *Historia de España Antigua*, vol. II, Madrid, Cátedra, 1985.

FABIÃO, Carlos, "O passado proto-histórico e Romano", in MATTOSO, José (dir.), *História de Portugal*, vol. I, Lisbon, Círculo de Leitores, 1992, pp. 79–299.

GARCÍA MORÁ, Félix, *Gayo Julio Caesar. Comentarios a la Guerra Civil*, trad., introd. and notes by J. A. Enríquez González, Madrid, Alianza, 1985.

Idem, *Un Episodio de la Hipania Republicana: A Guerra de Sertorio*, Granada, Universidad de Granada, 1991.

MANGAS MANJARRÉS, Julio (ed.), *Italia e Hispania en la Crisis de la República Romana*, Madrid, Universidade Complutense de Madrid, 1998.

16–15 BC
Founding of the Roman Province of Lusitania

Following the creation of the province, the period of conquest and territorial consolidation came to an end and integration within the Roman world began. It was a long and complex process which developed at different paces in different areas of the territory and was also uneven from a cultural point of view, given the mosaic of pre-existing indigenous cultures.

Having ensured peace in the Iberian Peninsula and maintaining military contingents in Cantabria, Octavian, who became Augustus in 27 BC, proceeded with a wide-ranging programme of administrative and territorial reorganisation which materialized in the creation of the province of *Citerior* (covering almost two thirds of *Hispania*, with its probable capital located in Cartagena) and the establishment of the provinces of *Ulterior Baetica* (corresponding to the present-day Andalusia, with its capital in Córdoba) and *Ulterior Lusitania* (occupying the western Peninsula as far as the Douro, with its capital in Mérida). The founding of the province of *Lusitania* occurred later, between 16 and 15 BC, in the aftermath of a war and was named after the people who had resisted the powerful Roman army for so long.

The boundaries of ancient *Lusitania* do not correspond to the borders of present-day Portuguese territory, since it included part of Spanish Extremadura. In Roman times, the region north of the Douro was part of the province of *Citerior* or *Tarraconensis*. For many years the current Portuguese and Spanish borders presented an obstacle to research into different aspects of *Lusitania*. More recently however, this has been replaced by open cooperation in the study of the shared Roman past of the two counties, allowing for a reassessment of the role of this province within the Roman Empire. Hence, Roman *Lusitania* has gradually become more relevant in the national and international research agenda, which focuses on different aspects of the transmision of models of classical culture, the economy, provincial interdependence and society.

Generally speaking, in the study of the province it is not only research based on incomplete and scant literary sources that stands out, but also research which seeks to combine a range of information resulting from archaeological work, epigraphic data and the study of materials preserved in museums and uses laboratory techniques for specialist analysis. In this apparently peripheral territory in the far west of the Iberian Peninsula, the Atlantic component of the empire, particularly after Claudius and the conquest of *Britannia* (43 AD), is being appraised, offering new perspectives on the role of navigation in supporting and supplying commodities for military contingents stationed on the northern border of the empire.

Following the creation of the province, the period of conquest and territorial consolidation came to an end and integration within the Roman world began. It was a long and complex process which developed at different paces in different areas of the territory and was also uneven from a cultural point of view, given the mosaic of pre-existing indigenous cultures. In the regions south of the Tagus – nowadays the Alentejo and the Algarve – this integration had begun in earlier phases during the Republican period (second century BC), facilitated by their exposure to Mediterranean culture.

Strabo provides an overview of the Iberian Peninsula in his *Geography*, which would have been based on geographical information, maps and descriptions of previous periods. Adopting an established descriptive method, the discourse on each region is organized around the course of the main rivers, enabling the different ethnic groups to be identified. The southernmost territories, corresponding to the central and southern regions of Portugal today, are described as fully urbanized areas with an abundance of natural resources (minerals and fish).

On the other hand, the creation of the province of *Lusitania* clearly indicates a knowledge of the territory in the extreme west of the Peninsula and the fact that the border with neighbouring *Baetica*, particularly in the south, was intended to separate an already known and conquered territory, centring on the Guadalquivir valley, from the far west, known as *Finisterrae*, which later attracted interest from Rome. With no landforms to define the borders clearly, they were united but also differentiated by cultural aspects.

The consolidation of control over the territory during the Republican period enabled an urban network to be developed, based on a road system that ensured communications within this vast region and its administration. The network began by serving the movement of troops in particular, but rapidly extended to the main urban centres, facilitating connections with the empire as a whole and strengthening the sense of belonging to the same political and cultural entity. Together with the rivers, this road system which, as Vasco Mantas confirms, would have had its origins in a network of older routes, became important as a means of providing military contingents with provisions and would be extended during the Imperial period (first to fourth centuries). The vast road network also facilitated trading and the administration of justice by delegates of the imperial powers, as well as tax administration.

In addition to designing roadways, bridges were constructed, some involving joint efforts by various cities, as would appear to be the case with the bridges in Mérida and Alcântara (Cáceres, in Spain) which spanned the Tagus. Given the extended coastline in *Lusitania* and the importance of rivers and estuaries, ports were equally important, although there is no detailed information about them.

In a process which had its own regional dynamics, urban centres began to develop through a remodelling process which meant that cities played a leading role in diffusing Roman culture, which also benefited from the road system. On one hand, some pre-existing cities were provided with civic structures and their urban structures and facilities were revitalized through initiatives which involved the combined efforts of the imperial state and the local elites, as was the case in Lisbon, Faro, Mértola and Alcácer do Sal. On the other hand, the creation of urban centres from scratch in strategic locations – in order to ensure control of inland regions close to certain rivers – was also common and they were sometimes granted privileged legal status. In other cases, regional dynamics and the evolution of urban centres led to the decline or even abandonment of sites that had previously been important urban settlements in the pre-Roman era.

In the north, the Romanisation of the *castros* is of particular interest, due to fact that they developed some elements of Roman urbanism and were included in the trade routes of the empire, whilst still retaining local features such as the circular layout. However, it is not known what their status was and how they would have been connected to cities in other regions.

For judicial purposes, three *conventus* were created: *Emeritensis*, with *Augusta*

Emerita (Mérida) as its capital; *Pacensis*, with *Pax Iulia* (Beja) as its capital; *Scallabitanus*, with *Scallabis* (Santarém) as its capital.

The demarcation of city territories (*civitates*) may not have been immediate but, regardless of the significance that may be attached to this, territories that belonged to the capital cities of the *civitates* may have included different types of rural establishments: the most typical was the *villa*, but there were also other categories such as estates or farm units. In addition, there would have been other smaller urban centres (*vicus*). This division of territories into *civitates* whose borders were identified by boundary markers (*termini Augustales*) led to a profound change in the mindset of the inhabitants. Combined with a road network supported by urban centres with municipal and judicial institutions, it would seem that the way in which the landscape was understood had been radically altered. This was the result of transformations to the indigenous economic and social structures and the process of Romanisation, also influenced by monetisation.

The farmhouse *villa*, excellent examples of which have been identified in the Alentejo and the Algarve as well as in the region of ancient *Olisipo* (Lisbon), allowed for the development of large territories, gradually transforming the countryside and the landscape. They became quite complex, including various buildings used for storing the food produced in the territory (*fundus*) belonging to the *villa* itself (such as granaries) or for processing it, such as wine and olive oil presses and artisanal infra-structures, as well as buildings to accommodate slaves and workers. Of all the elements which comprise these farm complexes, the one for which we have the most information, particularly in the later period, is the main house that belonged to the owners (the *domus*). Although these establishments were founded in the period between the end of the Republic and the mid-first century at a time when settlement in the countryside was being consolidated, the high point in their development occurred in Late Antiquity. Provided with all the amenities of urban houses, with sophisticated architectural programmes and decorative work including mosaics, painted and moulded plasterwork and marble features, it was not uncommon to find buildings with baths and different types of hydraulic systems required to access, store and channel water.

In addition to serving as production centres with facilities for processing food products (wine and olive oil and/or livestock) or artisanal units, these places are also excellent examples of how vast regions, even in the inland areas, were involved in the circulation of foodstuffs transported in amphoras, or manufactured goods (fine ceramic tableware), made possible by the highly monetized economy. As archaeology has revealed, these *villae* were one of the destinations for the various types of fish products made in the Tagus and Sado valleys. In addition to the Tagus and Sado estuaries, where the Roman site of Troia was particularly significant given the enormous output that can be envisaged from the salting vats, products made from fish, salt and seasonings would also have been prepared in Peniche, for example, and on the Algarve coast, due to the wealth of marine resources. The use of natural resources in the province would also have included the extraction of various minerals and stone quarrying, particularly marble from Estremoz, destined for decorative and architectural work in the civic centres of the main Lusitanian cities.

CATARINA VIEGAS
Centre for Archaeology, Faculty of Arts and Humanities, University of Lisbon

Bibliography

ALARCÃO, Jorge de, *O Domínio Romano em Portugal*, Mem Martins, Europa-América, 1988.

FABIÃO, Carlos, *Herança Romana em Portugal*, Lisbon, CTT, 2006.

Idem, "Mundo indígena, Romanos e sociedade provincial Romana: sobre a percepção arqueológica da mudança", *ERA – Arqueologia*, no. 3, 2001, pp. 108–131.

GORGES, J.-G., SALINAS FRÍAS, M. de (ed.), *Les Campagnes de Lusitanie Romaine. Occupation du Sol et Habitats*, Madrid/Salamanque, Casa de Velázquez/Universidad Salamanca, 1994.

MANTAS, Vasco Gil, *As Vias Romanas da Lusitania*, Mérida, Museo Nacional de Arte Romano, 2012.

First Century BC to the Second Century AD
Environmental Threats

Due to research by pluri-disciplinary teams which include physicists, chemists, historians and archaeologists, it has been possible to accurately verify that the phase which produced the highest level of environmental pollution, measured by suspended particles of lead and antimony, is the period between the final decades of the first century BC and the second century AD.

During the Roman period, a significant number of productive and even artisanal activities (especially between the first century BC and second century AD) had harmful effects on the environment in the form of air pollution.

Together with soil archives and samples gathered in lake environments or peatland, ice from Greenland or the Alps is a key source for identifying the highly pollutant activities developed in Ancient Rome, enabling researchers to measure the presence of heavy metals that would have existed in the atmosphere long ago. The available studies focus on samples taken from layers of ice and snow that have accumulated over the last millennia.

Due to research by pluri-disciplinary teams which include physicists, chemists, historians and archaeologists, it has been possible to accurately verify that the phase which produced the highest level of environmental pollution, measured by suspended particles of lead and antimony, is the period between the final decades of the first century BC and the second century AD and therefore during the end of the Republican period and the early empire. It has been confirmed that mining and metallurgy associated with the extraction and acquisition/processing of lead, silver and gold would have been responsible for the pollution. Even acknowledging that the chronological dates – obtained by the carbon-14 dating of small particles of organic material identified in the ice – may not be absolutely accurate, there appear to be no doubts in attributing the greatest growth in these activities to the end of the Republic and the beginning of the empire. It is not difficult to imagine the reason why these metals were in high demand. Lead, for example, was used in the Roman era in various household containers, weights, funerary urns and the different types of pipes used to supply and distribute water in Roman cities and *villae*. It was also used in the highly toxic process of gold metallurgy. Due to its harmful effects and the contamination it caused, the presence of lead in water pipes was even cited as one of the reasons for the downfall of the Roman Empire. However, analyses of the level of lead that might have affected the water and gradually poisoned the populations have shown that the toxic levels would have been minimal. As recently explained in a study of a plumbing system in Pompeii, the limestone in the water would have rapidly formed a coating that insulated the lead pipes and stopped them from coming into direct contact with the water, thus preventing contamination. According to Charlier, the amounts of antimony identified in this system appear to be more worrying and may have reached more significant levels of toxicity.

The need for silver in the context of a monetary economy such as the Roman one explains the importance of extracting this metal and the role it played as an indicator of economic growth during the Roman period. As for gold, in territory which is nowadays Portuguese there is evidence that it was mined in the River Tagus and in Vila Pouca de Aguiar (Jales and Tresminas).

Recent studies of lead isotopes analysed in samples of ice from Greenland also verify the association between these high levels of air pollution and regions in the southeast and southwest of Spain, since the lead that was detected had characteristics compatible with the lead mined in Rio Tinto (in the Huelva region). This mining complex, developed over a vast area of the present-day region of Huelva, would have been at least partly responsible, together with mines in the northwest and central Europe, for high levels of heavy metal emissions into the atmosphere, leading to significant pollution.

Another important conclusion is the synchrony recorded between peaks in the measurements of lead in ice samples from Greenland and the Alps and the greatest known phase of economic growth during the Roman Empire, which would have occurred between the end of the first century BC and the second century AD. McConnell has recently presented new data indicating a direct correspondence between oscillations in lead emissions in the atmosphere (at present measured with surprising accuracy on an annual basis) and phases of economic growth or periods of crisis, but also concrete historical events, wars and plagues.

There is also a growing record of emissions dating from the Phoenician expansion into the western Mediterranean onwards, together with records of intensive mining in the Punic context (fourth-second centuries BC). Lower levels have been identified during the Punic Wars, followed by an increase associated with the start of Roman rule in the south of Spain in 206 BC and consequently the transfer of mineral resources to the sphere of the Roman Empire, as well as a rise in pollutant emissions which coincides with the so-called *Pax Romana*, between 27 BC and AD 180.

The combination of geochemical and palaeobotanical techniques and methodologies used by F. Monna in the case of the Basque Country has made it possible for samples taken from peatland to be studied. Providing readings of the isotopic geochemistry of the lead, the data once again confirms that human interaction with the environment generated pollution peaks associated with mining and smelting industries in the Basque Country. In the Iberian Peninsula, the most important mining regions would have included Cantabria and Cartagena, in addition to Rio Tinto (Huelva). The Romans' interest in the territory that is nowadays Portugal would not have been unrelated to the fact that they knew it was rich in mineral resources, a fact also recognized by the classical authors. The gold deposits in Chaves, Castelo de Paiva and the Lousã mountains stand out, as well as the alluvial plains of the Minho and Tagus rivers. Lead mining has been identified in Aveiro and Meda. Silver, gold, lead and copper was already being extracted in the São Domingos mines pyrite belt (Mértola), before being extended to Aljustrel and the Caveira mountains (Grândola). Remarkable documents testify to the development of the Roman mines in Aljustrel (the Vipasca bronze plaques), providing an insight into how they were organized and the role of the mine administration (the Roman state) and its leaseholders.

In addition to measuring pollutants in the atmosphere such as lead and antimony extracted from the ice of Antarctica and the Alps, the content of methane gas in ice samples from Greenland has also been analysed. The results were surprising, showing that emissions of this gas did not begin with the Industrial Revolution in the eighteenth century. In fact, there was an increase in these emissions from 100 BC onwards, which was related to mining and livestock. Livestock raising in the Roman era, which included cattle, goats and sheep, may have been responsible for this. Moreover, although it is a recognized fact that the presence of this gas in the atmosphere may originate from various natural causes such as forest fires or volcanic eruptions, research has established that the increase in methane emissions was the consequence of burning forests down in the Roman era to increase agricultural land. These emissions also fell from AD 200 onwards, a time when instability began to increase in various regions of the empire.

Many other situations can be identified in which artisanal activities are associated with combustion and consequently the emission of polluting gases into the atmosphere on different scales. In addition to the mining and smelting industries, the manufacture of other products for domestic use, including ceramics and the containers used to transport food products, such as amphoras and, on a lesser scale, glassware, would have involved the use of kilns. It is not easy to determine the consequences of ceramic production. Although it is certain that in some cases the fuel that was used could have been sourced from shrubland that was easily renewed every year, as appears to have been the case with the fuel for the kilns used to produce Late Lusitanian amphoras in Martinhal, in Sagres, in other cases the impact of this use of the landscape may have been more significant. In the territory which is now Portugal, in addition to the Algarve, amphoras were produced in Antiquity in Peniche and above all in the Tagus and Sado valleys in response to the need to produce containers for the transport and export of the fish preparations that were made there.

In terms of the production and supply of olive oil to the city of Rome, archaeologists have documented more than 70 workshops engaged in producing amphoras in the valleys of the River Guadalquivir and River Genil (Baetica), in particular from the early empire period up to the third century. In this case, the possibility that at least part of the fuel for the amphora kilns would have consisted of remains from the pruning of olive trees and the waste from olive oil production (olive stones) should not be disregarded.

The enormous amount of materials that were needed to construct or remodel the extensive architectural layouts of cities all over the empire should also be taken into consideration, namely the ceramics used in construction, from the *tegulae* and *imbrices* used to cover roofs to a significant quantity of bricks and tiles (*lateres*), pipes, etc.

Environmental damage intensified with the use of lime kilns, which were essential for producing the resistant Roman mortars used in a wide range of constructions. A vast complex of lime kilns dating from the early empire was recently identified in Portugal in the Beja region, which may have been associated with the supply of these products to *Pax Iulia* (Beja), the capital of the *conventus*. Given the knowledge available on the huge network of urban centres that would have existed in *Lusitania*, several dozen more kilns would easily have been needed to supply the cities with lime and mortar.

The Romans had some awareness of the fact that these activities caused pollution and of the threat they presented, since the *figlinae* – workshops which supplied ceramics for domestic use in Roman households – tended to be located outside the city walls. In some places, such as *Urso* (Osuna, in the region of Seville), this was a legal obligation.

Nowadays, there can be no question that a dynamic which had an impact on the environment and was caused by human actions began during the Roman period and was linked to the growth of the urban world. Similar processes took place in other parts of the world and in later periods, intensifying dramatically in today's globalising world to truly disturbing levels.

Catarina Viegas
Centre for Archaeology, Faculty of Arts and Humanities, University of Lisbon

Bibliography
CHARLIER, P. et al., "Did the Romans die of antimony poisoning? The case of a Pompeii water pipe (79 CE)", *Toxicology Letters*, vol. 281, 2017, pp. 184–186.
MCCONNELL, Joseph R. et al., "Lead pollution recorded in Greenland ice indicates European emissions tracked plagues, wars and imperial expansion during Antiquity", *PNAS*, vol. 115, no. 22, 29 May 2018, pp. 5726–5731.
MONNA, F. et al., "Environmental impact of early Basque mining and smelting recorded in a high ash minerogenic peat deposit", *Science of the Total Environment*, vol. 327, nos. 1–3, 2004, pp. 197–214.
PREUNKERT, Susanne et al., "Lead and antimony in basal ice from Col du Dome (French Alps) dated with radiocarbon: A record of pollution during Antiquity", *Geophysical Research Letters*, vol. 46, 2019, pp. 4953–4961.
ROSMAN, Kevin J. R. et al., "Lead from Carthaginian and Roman Spanish mines isotopically identified in Greeland ice dated from 600 B.C. to 300 A.D.", *Environmental Science and Technology*, vol. 31, 1997, pp. 13–16.

17–23

The Tides According to Strabo

Strabo focuses on the phenomenon of the tides because they are related to the ocean, specifically the part which separates Europe from Africa. Hence they were important to the characterisation of the southern territory of Hispania and the western coastline.

The first image of the Hispanic world, including the territory which is nowadays Portugal, comes from ancient geography, in particular from certain Greek authors. Unlike the Phoenicians, who also explored the Mediterranean and the Atlantic coasts, the Greeks produced a vast amount of literature which described the different places they visited. It still offers some relevant information, sometimes from the very distant past, although it is very fragmentary. What would nowadays be called geography was presented in the form of routes, voyages, portolan charts and ethnographic or chorographic studies.

This literary genre drew on a vast experience of navigation and knowledge of the seas which revealed, as early as the second millennium BC and particularly during the Mycenaean period, a vast geographical spread, possibly even extending to the Peninsula, to judge from the ceramic remains that have been recovered and can be attributed to this phase, although they are rare. However, it was from the eighth century BC onwards that colonisation took on extraordinary dimensions, eventually covering many regions from the Black Sea to the western Mediterranean. The ancient voyages even went beyond the boundaries of this near-landlocked sea and extended to the Atlantic and Indian Oceans, wherever the spirit of adventure would take them.

One of the greatest examples of the geographical spread of the Greek explorations can be found in the figure of Pytheas, the author of *On the Ocean*. He was a mix of adventurer and scientist who was born in *Massalia* (nowadays Marseille) and lived in the fourth century BC. His greatest feats included a sea voyage to explore the North Atlantic, sailing beyond the British Isles and venturing deep into the North Sea. He was interested in the subject of the tides and is considered responsible for the observations presented by Strabo (64 BC–AD 24) in his *Geography*. In this essential text on the territory and ethnography of ancient *Hispania*, which is usually considered to date from between AD 17 and AD 23, he explains the unusual nature of the tides in *Hispania*: "Pytheas of Marseilles states that high tides occur in the first quarter of the moon and low tides in the last quarter". This same opinion is also attributed to his contemporary Euthymenes, who would have embarked on a similar ocean voyage, in this case to explore the African coast. Naturally, this sharing of ideas would have fitted well with the development of a tradition of studying the seas in the Phocaean Greek colony.

The Latin naturalist Pliny the Elder (first century AD) included Pytheas in the "foreign" authors who referred to matters associated with the universe and the stars which dealt with the ebb and flow of the tides. It is not known exactly which aspects in the text of the Latin encyclopaedist reveal his debt to Pytheas but it is clear that the explanation of what determines the tides, which was the cause of so many controversies in Ancient Rome, is resolved in his book in the same way. He states in his *Natural History* that, from among the many theories proposed to explain the phenomenon, the correct answer was that the ebb and flow of the sea is caused by the actions of the moon and the sun.

The main alternative to the explanation given by Pliny considers the cause of the phenomenon to be differences in wind direction. Hence, when the wind blew from the north the waters would be driven against the coast and the level would rise: whenever they blew in the opposite direction, they would ebb. This appears to be Strabo's position on the subject, particularly with regard to the stretch of the Atlantic between Africa and *Hispania*:

> The rises in sea level are greater here than in other places because the waters, forced from the great ocean into the narrow strait which Maurusia forms with Iberia, encounter resistance and rush towards those parts of the land that yield easily to them.

Strabo therefore disagrees with the explanation offered by Aristotle (384–322 BC), who believed that this phenomenon was characteristic of the Iberian and African coasts, in particular due to the rugged coastline in these regions:

The eastern side is high and craggy, but the land that lies below it is all flat, even up to the sea, except for a few mountains of no great magnitude. This, of course, is why Posidonius says that Aristotle is incorrect in attributing the cause of the high and low tides to the coastland (around Iberia and Maurusia), since he claims that the sea ebbs and flows since the coastland is high and rugged, resisting the waves and returning them with equal strength. Yet, on the contrary, the coastland is mainly sandy and low.

With regard to the tides and other matters that may be included in the field of geography, Strabo has a very different opinion to Pytheas. In a passage in which he analyses Turdetania, he is very critical of Artemidorus, who persisted in defending certain ideas that would have been taken from Pytheas. In particular, he maintained that no tides could be found after rounding the Sacred Cape (nowadays, Cape Saint Vincent). However, Strabo notes, tides are a widespread universal phenomenon and therefore cannot be absent from a substantial area of the Atlantic. A parallel and also highly controversial question, particularly in Greek science, concerned the oscillating levels of a famous spring in the Heracleium at Gades, whose waters dropped at high tide and rose at low tide. Strabo pays specific attention to this paradox, presenting the various theories, criticising some authors and accepting others, and re-examining certain aspects of Athenodorus' notion of the tides as a phenomenon comparable to the act of living beings inhaling and exhaling. The subject of the tides is undoubtedly very important in Strabo's text. Their greatest impact is associated with the southern Atlantic coast of *Hispania*, in particular the estuaries that lie between the Sacred Cape and the Pillars of Hercules (nowadays the Strait of Gibraltar). It is therefore closely linked to the concept of the estuary, which he defines as follows: "the name estuary is given to depressions that are covered by the sea at high tide and, like rivers, allow for navigation into the interior and to the cities on their shores".

Strabo's text gives a good explanation of how the estuary zone in Turdetani territory benefits greatly from the movement of the tides: "In fact, the whole region that lies inland between the Sacred Cape and the Pillars is flat for a considerable distance. Here, in several places, are inlets running from the sea to the interior, resembling moderate-sized ravines or river beds, extending for many stadia. When the sea level rises during high tide they are filled with water so that they are as easy to sail on as a river, in fact, they are even better because it is like sailing downstream with no obstacles and with the help of the sea, due to the flood tide which acts like a river current. [...] Some of these inlets are dry at low tide, while others are not completely empty of water; some of them even contain islands". Hence, there were certain economic consequences: "A rising tide like this offers a certain advantage to sailors, since it makes the estuaries more numerous and larger and they are often navigable for many stadia, so that the whole country is navigable to some extent and suitable for both exporting and importing goods".

Since the natural conditions there were identical to those in most of the rest of Hispanic territory, the Greek geographer also refers to the same conditions in other regions, particularly the Tagus, which had the same unusual features. The size of the river mouth and the depth of its waters enabled large ships to sail down it, namely those which embarked on sea voyages and were poorly equipped for river environments, unlike the situation in Rome where it was necessary to tranship the cargo at the port of Ostia. In the Lower Tagus, these ships could travel long distances, beyond Santarém. Strabo states:

The mouth of the Tagus is twenty stadia wide and very deep, so that cargo ships bearing ten thousand amphoras sail up it. When tides form, they create two estuaries in the flat land ahead, extending it like a sea by one hundred and fifty stadia and making the plain navigable; the upper estuary encircles a small island that is approximately thirty stadia long and a little less in width, which is fertile and has fine vines. This island faces Moron, a city well situated on an elevation near the river some five hundred stadia from the sea, also surrounded by fertile land. It is easy even for large vessels to sail a considerable distance up to it, although the rest of the journey can only be made by river boats (and beyond Moron, it is navigable for an even greater distance).

It is generally agreed that Moron, an island which was a striking feature of the Tagus at the time, would have been situated a little upstream of Santarém. It can therefore be concluded that sailing conditions on the Tagus have altered considerably, particularly since the nineteenth century when it was still common to make this journey by boat.

These observations on the tides emphasize two aspects in particular, namely their dimension and intensity, which would certainly have been astonishing for the Greeks and Romans who were used to much smaller fluctuations in sea levels in the Mediterranean, with virtually no perceptible results. This is why the effects of the ebb and flow of the sea observed on the coasts that would become Portuguese territory, whose negative consequences were highlighted by Strabo, made such an impression. The first of these negative effects was the risk to shipping, especially due to the force of the incoming tide; at low tide the most common problem was ships running aground. Animals were also affected, with Strabo referring to herds swept away by the waters, "but the cows, it is said, having observed what happens, wait for the sea level to go down and then head for the mainland".

Finally, Strabo focuses on the phenomenon of the tides because they are related to the ocean, specifically the part which separates Europe from Africa. Hence they were important to the characterisation of the southern territory of *Hispania* and the western coastline. It is in this region that this universal phenomenon becomes an important subject for geographical analysis and debate, due to its dimensions and effects. It would only be definitively resolved from a scientific perspective by the work of Isaac Newton in the seventeenth century. However, the reflections of Strabo and others who preceded him, based on the perspective afforded by the Portuguese coasts, were certainly a milestone in this journey.

AMÍLCAR GUERRA
Centre for Archaeology, Faculty of Arts and Humanities, University of Lisbon

Bibliography

BIANCHETTI, Serena, "Geografia e cartografia dell'estremo occidente. Da Eratostene a Tolomeo", *Mainake*, vol. 30, 2008, pp. 17–58.

Idem, *Pitea di Massalia, "L'Oceano". Introduzione, Testo, Traduzione e Commento*, Pisa, Istituti Editoriali e Poligrafici Internazionali, 1998.

CUNLIFFE, Barry, *The Extraordinary Voyage of Pytheas the Greek*, New York, Penguin Putnam, 2003.

CUTILLAS VICTORIA, Benjamín, "Mareas, puertos y canales en la región turdetana: Estrategias y dinámicas indígenas a partir de la *Géographiká* de Estrabón", in *Phicaria. IV*

Encuentros Internacionales del Mediterráneo, Mazarrón, Universidad Popular de Mazarrón, 2016, pp. 115–124.

MARTÍNEZ MARTIN, Leonor, "Teorías sobre las mareas según un manuscrito árabe del siglo XII", *Memorias de la Real Academia de Buenas Letras de Barcelona*, vol. 13, 1971, pp. 135–212.

First Century
Between Seas:
A Historical and Geographical Constant

The idea of the end point, or finis terrae, *persisted, together with its sacred significance. According to Pliny the Elder's description of the western coast of the Peninsula: "a promontory with an extended tip enters the sea; it has been called Artabrum by some and Promontorium Magnum by others, while many call it the Olisiponensis, after the nearby city, and it separates the land, the sea, and the heavens".*

"By weaving together the Mediterranean and Atlantic influences resulting from its geographical position, we arrive at an understanding of the duality of Portuguese territory". Thus Orlando Ribeiro began the conclusion to his classic work, highlighting the entanglement of Mediterranean and Atlantic influences as key aspects of the Portuguese reality. When referring to Antiquity, a period which predates the existence of Portugal, a broader designation may be used: the western Iberian Peninsula.

Orlando Ribeiro's historical approach did not focus specifically on Antiquity and the full richness of his thesis was limited by a certain bias in the historiographical perspective. This was mainly due to the fact that certain academic lines of research had identified the Mediterranean basin as an area in which great civilizations were forged and which served as a focal point for the diffusion of humanity's greatest achievements, such as the domestication of plants and animals, metallurgy, social complexification and, in parallel, the emergence of cities and written texts. Hence, the Atlantic Iberian *finis terrae* constituted a very peripheral area, in which these great creations would eventually arrive. The Mediterranean was understood as a creative hub and the Atlantic front as a place for merely receiving/assimilating what had been created in other regions.

Although it is not incorrect, this perspective disregards Orlando Ribeiro's notion of entanglement and the specific identity which the Atlantic world had developed since ancient times: in fact, "entanglement" should be the key word. Moreover, the location of the western Peninsula is particularly important in terms of the meeting of these two worlds, which were richer and more complex as a result of the clear advantages afforded by this duality. It is an accepted fact that both worlds had interacted since Prehistory. The tin available in the Atlantic region had been an essential resource since the Bronze Age (second millennium BC), given that it was a scarce commodity in the Mediterranean basin, but this is equally true of the copper and silver found in the Iberian Peninsula. Yet for a long time, the benefits of this contact were dismissed as an encounter between a literate world (the Mediterranean) and an illiterate one (the Atlantic), resulting in imbalances in information due to the nature of the narratives produced in the Mediterranean and, ultimately, the specific dynamics of research that was more inclined to concentrate on the focal points that created the *mare nostrum* (as the Romans called the Mediterranean) rather than the remote Atlantic. As an example, narratives of voyages to the great *Oceanus* – the name given to the Atlantic in Antiquity – were written in the style of heroic epics, including the Carthaginian *peripli* of Hanno the Navigator and Mago and the Massaliote *Periplus* which would later inspire the poem *Ora Maritima* by Rufus Festus Avienus, amongst other works known only from citations included in the work of other authors. The epic features of the narratives suggest that these voyages were rare and extraordinary, which is not entirely incorrect but does not reflect the richness of such interactions. Furthermore, questions have been raised since Antiquity, and amplified by modern scholarship, concerning the veracity of some of these narratives, and it is only recently that their probable accuracy has been redeemed by archaeological research.

Barry Cunliffe has produced a painstaking reconstruction of what is likely to have been the voyage of Pytheas, a fourth-century Greek adventurer from Marseille and the author of a body of work on the *Oceanus*, only known to us from references in the work of other writers. Pytheas travelled from his home town to the Ultima Thule, a remote place where the ocean would freeze and there was continuous daylight for six months, followed by uninterrupted nights for another six months, clearly a description of the Arctic Circle. Basing his opinion on archaeological records, the Oxford professor argues that Pytheas' work is both credible and plausible. His voyage probably took advantage of different communication networks, stopping off at various trading ports, evidence for the existence of which has been found in various archaeological sites on the Atlantic seaboard. These were places that offered favourable conditions for anchorage and shelter from the shifting moods of the "angry Atlantic sea", to use the powerful image created by Luis de Camões, which have now been clearly identified, together with the remains of imported products of Mediterranean origin found in local cultural contexts. Rather than simply locations occasionally visited during the course of extraordinary voyages, they were integral parts of small exchange networks that were used regularly.

As such, mythical sounding places such as The Cassiterides, a source of tin usually associated with the islands off the coast of Galicia or with Great Britain (not excluding the possibility that both identifications are correct, varying simply due to time and author), were both known and frequented, in addition to the Ultima Thule, which possibly referred to Iceland or the western coast of Scandinavia. According to the Greek author Strabo, these Atlantic routes were carefully protected in Antiquity by those who used and benefited from them. During the first century BC, the merchants of Cádiz headed for the Atlantic tin regions via private routes. The same author notes that a certain Gaditanian merchant, realising he was being followed by Roman ships, steered his vessel onto the rocky coast and was shipwrecked. When he returned to his home town, he was praised and offered compensation by the local Senate. However, this was a short-lived victory, since the Roman governor Publius Crassus later managed to identify the route. It was one of Julius Caesar's ambitions to conquer the *Oceanus*, beginning with a sea expedition to Brigantium (on the coast of Galicia) when he was governor of the province of Hispania Ulterior in the 60s BC, followed by expeditions to Great Britain after he defeated the Gauls in the following decade. These ventures were motivated by the potential economic benefits, since the regions were rich in tin. However, the known reports written by Caesar himself or others in his close circle emphasized his triumph over the mysterious sea more than the economic advantages.

Despite the longstanding relationship between the Mediterranean and the Atlantic, there is a reason for defining a milestone in this entanglement of the two worlds in the first century AD: the construction of the Roman Empire. In the middle of the century, following the conquest of Britannia (Great Britain) and the establishment of one of the frontiers of the empire in Germania Inferior (the present-day Netherlands), a broad Atlantic front was formed in the north which was in constant contact with the Mediterranean. This is celebrated in the grand panegyric which lists the many accomplishments of Augustus, the first emperor of Rome, and is narrated in direct speech: "I brought peace to the provinces of Gaul and Hispania, as well as to Germania, including the Ocean from Cádiz to the mouth of the River Elbe [...] My ships sailed on the Ocean from the mouth of the Rhine to the east, up to the coast of the Cimbri [the Jutland Peninsula, nowadays Denmark], where no Roman had ever gone before, by land or sea". It is also echoed by Pliny the Elder in his monumental encyclopaedic work, which included an account of a journey to Rome during the reign of Tiberius, the second Roman Emperor, by *Olisiponensis* ambassadors whose mission was to confirm the existence of tritons and nereids on the Lusitanian coast. Beyond the simple telling of a tale, the visit may also have been designed to enhance the attractions of the Atlantic front, a matter of obvious interest to the citizens of Olisipo (Lisbon), since they lived in a region with one of the best estuaries for navigation.

Following the conquest of Britannia by the emperor Claudius in 43 AD and the establishment of the vast northern Atlantic front of the Roman Empire, it became necessary to provide supplies of essential goods for the military forces based there. Hence, the new relationship with the great Ocean was consolidated through the construction of larger and more efficient ports, a fact deduced from archaeological records rather than from physical evidence, as well as a system of lighthouses and beacons for signalling and support for navigation.

Navigation itself was no longer a matter of cabotage, or small-scale coastal shipping which always remained in sight of the coastline and used anchorage areas to manage distance. It now involved deep-sea shipping using large cargo ships, transporting olive oil, for example, an essential element in the Mediterranean diet that did not exist in the north of Europe. The Romans delivered thousands of amphoras of olive oil produced in the Guadalquivir river basin to northern Europe to supply the troops stationed there. Each amphora of olive oil weighed around one hundred kilograms and had to be transported by sea in large ships to ensure efficient distribution.

Lighthouses therefore began to appear, the most impressive surviving example being the one in A Coruña (known as the Tower of Hercules), together with various others which are not so well preserved, such as the examples in the *sítio do Moinho* (Windmill site) in Berlenga and in Espigão das Ruivas close to Cape Roca. These lighthouses worked in conjunction with signalling equipment on the bars of the main estuaries that could serve as ports, including the one that existed in the Sado estuary where the Outão fortress now stands and another recently identified example in Figueira da Foz, signalling the Mondego bar. The crude toga-wearing granite statue recovered from the mouth of the River Douro in a context which remains unclear may have decorated another similar structure

Deep-sea navigation did not mean the end of cabotage, but merely added a new dimension and, most importantly, provided the old anchorages with new equipment. Evidence of Roman vessels frequenting the Atlantic can also be ascertained from the many anchors of distinctive sizes documented on the Portuguese and Galician coasts.

Nevertheless, the idea of the end point, or *finis terrae*, persisted, together with its sacred significance. According to Pliny the Elder's description of the western coast of the Peninsula: "a promontory with an extended tip enters the sea; it has been called Artabrum by some and Promontorium Magnum by others, while many call it the *Olisiponensis*, after the nearby city, and it separates the land, the sea, and the heavens". At the mouth of the River Colares near Cape Roca (the *Promontorium Magnum*), there was a sanctuary in the Alto da Vigia site dedicated to the sun, the moon and the ocean that had been known since the sixteenth century from references in the work of the humanists, but has only recently been recovered by archaeological research. Conquering and venturing out into the Ocean did not exclude the notion of the *finis terrae* or reverence for the place that was "land's end".

The close links developed in the Roman era never ceased to exist and in the Middle Ages a flow could be observed in the opposite direction, when the Vikings began their forays into the Mediterranean and crusaders from northern Europe heading for the Holy Land helped Portuguese kings to conquer the Islamic southern region.

CARLOS FABIÃO
Centre for Archaeology, Faculty of Arts and Humanities, University of Lisbon

Bibliography

CUNLIFFE, Barry, *Europe between the Oceans. Themes and Variations: 900 BC–AD 1000*, New Haven/London, Yale University Press, 2008.

FABIÃO, Carlos, "A dimensão atlântica da Lusitânia: Periferia ou charneira no Império Romano?", in GORGES, Jean-Gérard et al. (ed.), *Lusitânia Romana entre Mito e Realidade: Actas da VI Mesa-Redonda Internacional sobre a Lusitânia Romana (Cascais, 2004)*, Cascais, Câmara Municipal de Cascais, 2009, pp. 53–74.

GUERRA, Amílcar, *Plínio-o-Velho e a Lusitânia*, Lisbon, Colibri, 1995.

RIBEIRO, José Cardim, *Escrever sobre a Margem do "Oceanus". Epigrafia e "Religio" no Santuário do Sol Poente ("Provincia Lusitania")*, Sylloge Epigraphica Barcinonensis, Annexos III, Barcelona, Universidad Galerada, 2019.

RIBEIRO, Orlando, *Portugal, o Mediterrâneo e o Atlântico*, 4th ed., Lisbon, Sá da Costa, 1986.

Fourth Century
Administrative Reform of the Roman Empire

From the fourth century onwards, the administrative machinery was strengthened, bureaucracy increased and taxes were raised. In the following century, commenting on the Suebi invasion, Hydatius, the bishop of Chaves, and Orosius both refer to the heavy and abusive Roman tax system, citing it as the reason for the alleged Hispanic Roman support for the invaders.

Diocletian (284–305) carried out an administrative reorganization of the Roman Empire. In addition to restructuring the armed forces (to increase the military contingent) and the economy (including the reorganization of the monetary system and the pricing of goods and services) as part of a common political strategy, the most significant reform was the territorial reorganization which divided the existing provinces into smaller areas. Under Diocletian, between 284 and 288 or at the beginning of the final decade of the third century (before 298–297), the imperial provinces more than doubled, from 48 to 104. They were then integrated into larger territorial and administrative constituencies known as dioceses (*diocesis*). The more turbulent times which had weighed over the empire in previous decades had led Diocletian to carry out this administrative reform, seeking to reinforce Rome's authority through the tighter or more centralized administrative power of the provincial territories, thus facilitating tax collecting – which involved introducing a more effective and regular census. Certain documental sources such as the Verona List (Laterculus Veronensis, an authentic catalogue of the imperial provinces circa 340) and the Notitia Dignitatum, provide an overview of this provincial administrative division, specifically in the Iberian Peninsula.

Hispania now had six provinces: Baetica, Lusitania, Carthaginensis, Gallaecia, Tarraconensis and Balearica. The new province of Gallaecia (or Callaecia) which, together with Carthaginensis and Tarraconensis, occupied the land in the old province of Hispania Citerior, was added to the three existing provinces (Tarraconensis, Baetica and Lusitania) created from the provincial division of territory in the Augustan era (27 BC–14 DC). Not all of them had the same status: some were consular, presided over by a senator, and others merely praesidial, ruled by a *praeses* (governor) from the *equites* class. At a certain point, Baetica and Lusitania became consular provinces – in the case of Lusitania this would have been from 360 onwards, having previously been governed by members of the *equites* appointed by the emperor. Gallaecia was promoted from praesidial to consular status between 370 and 395. Tarraconensis, with its capital in Tarraco, Carthaginensis, with its capital in Córdoba, and Balearica, with its capital in Palma, always remained praesidial provinces.

Emerita (Mérida) was the headquarters of the provincial government of Lusitania and Bracara Augusta (Braga) was the capital of Gallaecia. This city, having until then been the capital of the Conventus Bracarensis, found its political and administrative authority strengthened when it was designated capital of the new province of Gallaecia. Hence, Braga became even more influential within the Peninsula during the fourth century and this was reflected in intensive construction and economic developments.

Doubts have been raised concerning the administrative or geographical boundaries of the new province of Gallaecia. It would certainly have included the territories of the *conventus* (an earlier monastic-based division which disappeared with this reform) of Bracara Augusta, as well as those of Lucus Augusti, Asturica Augusta and possibly part of Clunia. In other words, in the fourth century, the area belonging to the Bracarensis, Lucensis and Asturum *conventus* corresponded to the province of Gallaecia. Neither Lusitania nor Baetica were subdivided under this reform and there were no changes to their administrative boundaries, meaning that the old provincial demarcations dating from the end of the first century BC were preserved.

Each province was ruled by a governor (*praeses*) – a man of high status, belonging either to the *equites* class (the *vir perfectissimus*) or consular/senatorial class (the *vir clarissimus*), who would serve in Hispania (usually, governors were not Hispanic by birth) at a certain point in his illustrious career (*cursus honorum*). Epigraphy provides us with the names of some of these men. In Ossonoba (Faro), inscribed on a pedestal in honour of the emperor, the words "*Aurelius Ursinus, v[ir] p[erfectissimus] pr[aeses] provinc[iae] Lusitani[ae]"* are legible, probably referring to a *praeses* who served between the years 293 and 305. In Olisipo (Lisbon), Numerius Albanus, *vir claris-simus* (and therefore, unusually, a member of the senator class), gave orders for the renovation of the "Cassius Baths" in 336 AD. In Emerita, the capital of Lusitania, the governor G. Sulpicius Rufus was probably responsible for commissioning a large statue of an emperor (possibly Constantine) for the provincial forum, and Iulius Saturninus, who belonged to the *equites* class, was probably governor between 237 and 340, according to information inscribed on a commemorative plaque celebrating the renovation of the circus in the city, overseen by the provincial governor. In Callaecia, there is also epigraphic information referring to three other governors, one of whom, Aemilius Maximus, registered in Braga, would have held office at some point between 312 and 324.

These six provinces were integrated into the Diocese of Hispania, another political-administrative division on a larger scale created by Diocletian in 297 or 298, a few years after the division of the provinces. The Diocese of Hispania included a seventh province, Mauretania Tingitana (later known simply as Tingitana), situated outside Peninsular territory in North Africa, the most westerly region of the empire, and possibly added for strategic reasons as a better means of controlling what would later be known as the Strait of Gibraltar and preventing the Mauri (nomadic Berber peoples) from invading the Iberian Peninsula.

A diocese was governed by a *vicarius* (deputy) appointed by the emperor. The main residence of the Vicarius Hispaniarum was in Mérida, a city that had undergone urban renovation during the fourth century, as it was not the capital of the province of Lusitania but also the seat of the Diocese of Hispania. The names of seven of its *vicarii* are known, all apparently educated pagan men. The first to be identified was Aurelius Agricolanus, *agens vices praefecti praetorio*. However, there is also information on various others, namely Q. Aeclanius Hermias, *vir perfectissimus*, who ordered a statue of Constantine to be erected in Córdoba between 312 and 324, Septimus Acindyus, epigraphically registered in Tarraco and Mérida, who held office from around 324 to 326, and C. Annius Tiberianus, *vicarius Hispaniarum*, possibly in 335.

This reform created a heavier imperial administrative machinery. State bureaucracy was extended, the number of imperial and provincial officials increased, and provincial administrative positions also multiplied. Each position and function was clearly regulated. At the head of the administrative apparatus was the emperor. After him, in the case of Hispania, came the *praefactus praetorio Galliarum* (the empire had also been divided into various *praefacturae*, or prefectures). Serving as a delegate or deputy of the *praefactus praetorio* and directly answerable to him, was the *vicarius* Hispaniarum, who was responsible for the civil administration of the diocese. For a short period during the reign of Constantine, the role of the *vicarius* was reinforced by a *comes Hispaniarum* who assisted the *vicarius* in specific subjects. The provincial governors, both consular and praesidial, were supervized by the *vicarius* but had a considerable amount of autonomy and power, even under the administrative authority of the latter. In addition to general supervision of all matters concerning the diocese, the *vicarius* also managed the collection (*collatio*) of taxes (*annona*) and their transport (*transmissio*). He also had some authority over the army stationed in Hispania, and in some cases even functioned as a final court of appeal for those contesting decisions made by the provincial governors. He travelled throughout the diocese to carry out administrative and legal duties, which explains epigraphic evidence of the presence of the *vicarius* in other provincial capitals such as Córdoba and Tarraco. Provincial governors, in turn, were responsible for the payment of taxes in their territory and for ensuring the good functioning of roads and official mail (*cursus publicus*), in addition to managing the construction or repair of public buildings and serving as judges (*iudices ordinarii*). They also travelled regularly to the main cities in the province to take care of administrative and legal affairs. The most distinguished men were chosen for these positions: those belonging to the empire's elites, who had a recognized and extensive *cursus honorum* and experience of holding office in various regions of the empire, comprising a select bureaucratic-political group working in a variety of very different geographical contexts and anticipating by many centuries the governance models characteristic of the Iberian overseas empires. Serving as a *vicarius* or provincial governor meant having power, prestige and riches. Each *vicarius* had an *officium* (staff) composed of a large and diverse group of around 300 officials (*officiales*), each with specific duties and skills, mostly of an economic or fiscal nature. The *praeses* also had a large group of between 50 to 100 officials to serve him. It is therefore, estimated that a total of approximately 1,500 officials were working in the provinces of the Diocese of Hispania exclusively in civil administration.

From the fourth century onwards, the administrative machinery was strengthened, bureaucracy increased and taxes were raised. In the following century, commenting on the Suebi invasion, Hydatius, the bishop of Chaves, and Orosius both refer to the heavy and abusive Roman tax system, citing it as the reason for the alleged Hispanic Roman support for the invaders. According to Osorius "there are some Roman citizens who would prefer freedom in poverty with the Barbarians than endure taxes under the Romans".

The division of the provinces in the Iberian Peninsula in the fifth century, which created five ecclesiastical provinces (Tarraconensis, Carthaginensis, Baetica, Gallaecia and Lusitania), largely followed the (civil) Roman provincial division of the fourth century. In this context, the term "diocese" acquired the meaning of an ecclesiastical division under the authority of a metropolitan bishop, whose seat was also the provincial capital – Emerita, in the case of Lusitania. In the long term, this category of bishop would have an enormous impact on life in the areas which would eventually become Portugal.

Pedro C. Carvalho
Faculty of Arts and Humanities of University of Coimbra

Bibliography

ARCE, Javier, *El Último Siglo de la España Romana (284–409)*, Madrid, Alianza Editorial, 2009.

DÍAZ, Pablo et al., *Hispania Tardoantigua y Visigoda*, Madrid, Istmo, 2007.

EDMONSON, Jonathan, "The administration of Lusitania from the reforms of Diocletian to c. 340", in *A Lusitânia: Entre Romanos e Bárbaros: Atas da VIII Mesa-Redonda Internacional sobre a Lusitânia Romana*, Coimbra, Instituto de Arqueologia da Universidade de Coimbra, 2016, pp. 179–221.

TEJA, Ramón (ed.), *La Hispania del Siglo IV. Administración, Economía, Sociedad, Cristianización*, Bari, Edipuglia, 2002.

409–411
Arrivals of the Barbarians

At the beginning of the autumn of 409, the Suebi, Alans, and Vandals left Gaul where they had been roaming for three years, crossed the Pyrenees, entered Hispania and soon arrived in Lusitania and Gallaecia (or Callaecia), an invasion either permitted by the Romans or at least agreed with them.

The Roman Empire was first invaded by Barbarian peoples in the middle of the third century: in 260 or 261 the Franks and Alans crossed the borders of the Rhine and Danube, travelled through Gaul and in 262, having crossed the Pyrenees, spread into eastern Hispania. They did not continue west to the region nowadays known as Portugal but the impact of their presence would have been felt, particularly in Roman Lusitania. Although archaeology does not record a clear scenario of raids and devastation, even in the "invaded" areas, during the final decades of the third century some cities rushed to build defensive walls, even cutting off sections of the urban area, as was the case in Conimbriga, for example. On 31 December 406, the Suebi, Alans and Vandals, setting off from the borders of Pannonia (a Roman province located in the area which nowadays comprises Hungary, Austria and Slovenia), once again crossed the borders of the Rhine near Strasburg to enter an empire divided from within. The invasion benefited from the internal disputes that were weakening Roman authority and state organization in the western part of an empire that was rapidly coming to an end (476). At the beginning of the autumn of 409, the Suebi, Alans, and Vandals left Gaul where they had been roaming for three years, crossed the Pyrenees, entered Hispania and soon arrived in Lusitania and Gallaecia (or Callaecia), an invasion either permitted by the Romans or at least agreed with them. Despite their ethnic heterogeneity, they were all Germanic peoples, known as *barbarus*, a name used by the Romans to describe foreigners who did not speak Latin and therefore did not partake in the Roman culture and way of life.

In 411 the Suebi settled in the north-east of the Peninsula, in the western area of the old province of Gallaecia facing the sea and, most importantly, overlapping with the Roman territory of *Conventus Bracarensis*, as far as Lugo. In its early days, the "kingdom of the Suebi" extended north of the Douro to an area roughly comprising Porto, Braga and Astorga. The Alans settled in territory that was part of Lusitania (and also Carthaginensis). The Silingi Vandals were left with Baetica, which roughly coincides with present-day Andalusia, from which the name is derived. The Alans and Vandals did not stay long. Between 417 and 418, with the support of Visigoth troops, the Romans recovered part of the territories in which they had settled, and in 429–430, the Vandals, together with what remained of the Alans, abandoned the Iberian Peninsula and set sail for North Africa, crossing the Tarifa strait and settling in Mauritania.

Consequently, only the Suebi formed a Barbarian kingdom (411–585) – the first Roman-Germanic Christian kingdom in the empire. It was based on the existing Roman political system, even though this had been undermined, despite the administrative reform of the empire in the fourth century. Braga was chosen as the capital of the Suebi kingdom and a large part of the Suebi population, namely the elites, may have lived there, commanding what appears to have been an extremely hierarchical society. The walled mountain of Falperra which overlooks Braga seems to contain the ruins of the royal residence, including a large basilica. Porto (Portus Cale) would also have been an important permanent Suebi settlement. Other cities were also occupied by the Suebi, although never in large numbers, nor for any significant time. In the mid fifth century, the Suebi kingdom reached its maximum level of expansion, extending south as far as Cape Saint Vincent and the mouth of the River Guadalquivir. Hence it would have covered the entire western strip of the Iberian Peninsula from Lisbon to Mérida, the old Roman provincial capital that once again served as a capital and as the residence of the Suebi kings between 439 and 448.

The *Chronicle* of Hydatius (c. 395–469), Bishop of Chaves, offers a vision of this new age, superimposed on an older era that was fading away. It is an indispensable source of information for understanding the places which the Suebi inhabited and explored for most of the fifth century. Its perspective is catastrophic, documenting looting, kidnappings and ruthless killings against a backdrop of widespread hunger, plague and pestilence. However, this is a partial view of events – a story told to the Romans by a Roman belonging to the local Roman-Gallaecian elite. This Christian narrative (also observed in other parts of the empire) which, in proclaiming the end of time is almost apocalyptic in tone, must be compared with the archaeological records, even if they are not always complete.

The majority of the Suebi population lived in the area between Minho and Douro, mainly in cities along the Tui–Braga–Porto axis, cohabiting with the Hispanic Romans. This would have been the largest area in which the Suebi monarchy and the ecclesiastical administration became established. As they were a minority in relation to the population as a whole, and in order to maintain supremacy, they made strategic choices about the areas they would inhabit, concentrating on city locations that gave them the best opportunity to control the territory. During the fifth century, many of the Roman cities remained centres of power, even though some public buildings such as the forums and the areas reserved for entertainment were decaying rapidly and becoming abandoned, a well-known phenomenon in cities since the fourth century. News of devastation and flight due to Suebi attacks should be relativized. Conimbriga, for example, was taken by the Suebi in 465 and, probably because it remained a focal point for resistance, was attacked again and looted two or three years later. Part of its houses and defensive wall were destroyed and Cantaber, probably the leading figure in the city – its defender – saw his family taken captive by Remismund, king of the Suebi. However, this did not mean that the city was left in ruins. One hundred years later, in 561, it became the seat of the diocese before it was transferred shortly afterwards to Aeminium (Coimbra). However, during the Visigoth era it remained a parish.

Capital cities of other *civitates* preserved their central roles. In those which became capitals of dioceses, the bishops established themselves as leading figures in the urban landscapes which were being redeveloped. In Idanha-a-Velha a second baptistery was built in the early decades of the fifth century, possibly associated with the construction of a church located in the new central area of what was called Egitânia at the time.

The so-called *Parochiale Suevum* (Suebi Parish), probably written in 569, is a record of the dioceses and ecclesiastical organization in Suebi territory in the final phase of the kingdom, allowing for a possible reconstruction of the borders of the Suebi territory during the mid sixth century. To the east it would have coincided with the current border between Portugal and Spain and to the south it would have included territories belonging to the old Roman *civitates* established in Idanha-a-Velha and Tomar, thus extending to the Tagus (a river which served as the southern border of the Suebi kingdom from 465 onwards). The dioceses included in the Suebi kingdom (Lamego, Viseu, Idanha and Conimbriga) were at first dependent on the metropolitan church of Mérida (Emerita, the capital of the ecclesiastical province of Lusitania), but at a later stage were attached to the church of Braga (Bracara, the metropolitan head-quarters of the ecclesiastical province of Gallaecia), in a clear attempt to politically unite the religious structures under the territorial aegis of the Suebi.

During the fifth century and a considerable part of the sixth century, many of the cities which are part of present-day Portuguese territory were showing signs of commercial dynamism and openness to the rest of the old world, remaining active in the major trading networks. The discovery of fine ceramics, together with oriental and north African amphoras, are a clear indication of this. Oriental Mediterranean ceramics (such as amphoras or Phocaean and Cypriot sigillata) have been widely documented in important sites on the Atlantic coast (particularly coastal cities) but also in certain places (*villae*) in the rural interior in the south. These items, as well as others originating from North Africa (amphoras, sigillata and lamps), continued to arrive until at least the first half of the sixth century. In various parts of the old province of Lusitania (such as the city of Olysipona/Lisbon) production units also continued to work intensively to prepare fish sauce (garum) for export.

Conversely, in the rural areas these signs of dynamism became rare. The almost total absence of archeologically identifiable elements and lack of literary sources makes it impossible to identify any archaeological features specifically relating to the Suebi in rural settlements. It is likely that the Roman patterns of rural occupation remained largely untouched, although archaeology reveals a heterogeneous landscape, varying from region to region. Some *villae* were still inhabited, showing no signs of crisis, but instead evidence of renovation, mainly due to the construction of paleo-Christian basilicas. Others, however, were abandoned or reoccupied, revealing signs of environ-ments that were not in keeping with the sophisticated way of life characteristic of the previous period. Settlements could still be found on mountain tops which Hydatius, in his *Chronicle*, called *castrum, castella* and *castella tutiora*. Some of these *castra* and *castella*, which originated in Protohistory, may have been reoccupied during this period and perhaps even regained a certain importance.

The number of Suebi who arrived in Hispania and settled in Gallaecia would have been relatively small. It has been estimated at between 20,000 and 30,000, including approximately 6,000 to 9,000 warriors. In any event, it would have been a small group and the percentage of Suebi invaders negligible in comparison to the Hispanic Roman population (possibly no more than 5% of the total). Therefore, the impact of their arrival was not very significant in terms of many aspects which determine the material and non-material profiles of communities. Latin remained the official language (although some words of Germanic origin were adopted and some are still recognized today) and most of the customs and behaviour inherited from the Romans were preserved.

The fifth century, characterized by frequent conflicts, was followed by a century marked by greater stability, during which the Suebi kingdom became more peaceful and grew in strength, especially through its alliance with the Catholic Church, over-seen by Saint Martin of Braga, the "Apostle of the Suebi". In this context, the church gained authority. The kingdom was also reorganized in the search for religious unity.

The Suebi kings, who had adopted Arianism in 465, converted to Catholicism under Chararic in 550 and the alliance with the Gallaecian Catholic Church helped to consolidate the kingdom. The Suebi kingdom ended in 585 when it was conquered by Leovigild (567–586), who later integrated the old Roman Hispania into the Visigoth kingdom, which had its capital in Toledo. After him, Reccared I (586–601) established Catholicism as the official religion of the Visigoth Kingdom in 589, ending the division between Arians and Catholics. Bishop Isidore of Seville was one of the key figures of this time.

This final phase is clearly reflected in in certain forms of Visigoth art, in particular the remarkable pieces of jewellery occasionally found in rare funerary contexts in which the associated hoard (clothing and adornments) identifies individuals belonging to the elites, as in the recent case of the "Suebi princesses" of Mérida. Another outstanding feature is the distinctively decorated architectural elements often found in funerary contexts, in which Mediterranean, specifically Byzantine, influences can be detected.

The Visigoths first became allies of the Romans in the final decades of the fourth century when, faced with the threat of the Huns, they were fleeing the Balkans and the lands north of the Black Sea to seek refuge in imperial territories. They numbered no more than 100,000 individuals, most of whom settled in southern Gaul in the Goth kingdom of Tolosa (nowadays Toulouse) from 418 until 507, when they finally became established exclusively in Hispania after being defeated by the Franks. In the fifth century, Visigoth troops still roamed throughout Hispanic lands as allies of the Romans, occasionally even fighting the Suebi in present-day Portuguese territory when successive peace agreements collapsed. The *Chronicle* of Hydatius of Chaves documents the violent looting of Braga in 456 under the command of Theodoric II. Despite the internal fighting within the Visigoth monarchy, particularly in the final decades of the seventh century, the Iberian Peninsula remained stable and unified under Visigoth rule until the arrival of the Muslims, the new "invaders", in 711.

Pedro C. Carvalho
Faculty of Arts and Humanities of University of Coimbra

Bibliography

ALARCÃO, Jorge de, *A Lusitânia e a Galécia: Do Séc. II A.C. ao Séc. VI d.C.*, Coimbra, Imprensa da Universidade, 2018.

ARCE, Javier, *Barbaros y Romanos en Hispania (400–507 A.D.)*, Madrid, Marcial Pons-Ediciones de Historia, 2005.

Idem, *Esperando a los Árabes. Los Visigodos en Hispania (507–711)*, Madrid, Marcial Pons-Ediciones de Historia, 2011.

DÍAZ, Pablo, *El Reino Suevo (411–585)*, Madrid, Akal, 2011.

GARCÍA MORENO, Luis, *História da España Visigoda*, Madrid, Cátedra, 1998.

Second Half of the Sixth Century
A United Peninsula Under the Goths

The transition from Romanity to Christianity was a process involving stability and continuity. This Christianity was at least as extensive and vast as the old Roman Empire, with constant interaction evident in the mobility of its episcopal agents and the wide circulation of theological texts.

In the first half of the sixth century, the Iberian Peninsula was deeply divided. On the one hand, the majority "Hispanic Roman" communities continued to live in relative autonomy in terms of government, with the ecclesiastical authorities exercising powers inherited from their former rulers under the Roman Empire. In the southern and eastern coastal regions the Roman province of Spania was developing, the result of an attempt by emperor Justinian I – of the Eastern Roman Empire, usually referred to as the Byzantine Empire but also as Romanoi in Greek, its official language – to restore the lost section of the empire, although its extent and boundaries are difficult to determine. In the north-west, descending westwards to the Tagus basin, the kingdom of the Suebi had been established, following the settlement of one of the so-called Barbarian communities that had arrived in the area at the beginning of the fifth century. The kingdom, which had its seat in Braga, the former capital of the Roman province of Gallaecia, had existed for almost a century and the alliance between the Barbarians and the local elites, once again under the aegis of the ecclesiastical hierarchy, was becoming increasingly evident.

In the remaining territories, where there is less information about settlements, there were the Goths, said to be from the West, or Visigoths, now increasingly confined to the Iberian Peninsula after their virtual expulsion from the south of Gaul where they had first settled, due to the expansion of the Franks. Within this complex mosaic, the kingdom of the Visigoths remained unique in adhering to the Arian version of Christianity, named after Bishop Arius and considered heretical by the Catholic orthodoxy after the Council of Nicaea for denying the consubstantiality of the Holy Trinity. This specifically Goth religious tendency distinguished it from the Catholic universe of the Suebi and the imperials on the Mediterranean coasts.

For a long time, the Visigoths had been exercising a kind of protectorate over the Iberian Peninsula. In the fifth century they were involved in military campaigns in the service of the Roman emperors of the West, specifically against the Suebi and, according to an inscription in Mérida (now lost), in 466, during the reign of Euric (a monarch based in what is nowadays the south of France), a *dux* named Salla undertook to repair the bridge over the River Guadiana in the city, in collaboration with the local bishop, Zeno. The inscription is interesting, since it describes a Goth leader working with the local Christian hierarchy on a project that was important to the city. There is little other information of this kind, but what has survived helps us to understand how the military and ecclesiastical authorities joined forces to maintain essential facilities in cities.

Although contingents of Visigoths had settled in the large Hispanic cities, the process of constructing their kingdom would have been achieved more in opposition to the powerful "Hispanic Roman" communities than in collaboration with them. It was decided to base the court in Toledo, a smaller city in the interior. The choice of this central location has been interpreted as an attempt to claim and dominate the entire Iberian Peninsula, even though it would appear equally evident that the intention was to avoid the large cities that still existed there and were governed by the "Hispanic Roman" secular and ecclesiastical elites.

When Leovigild became king in 568, the process of creating an identity for the kingdom of the Goths began. He was the first monarch to mint coins that did not follow the iconographic models of the Roman Empire since, instead of displaying a realistic image of the bust of the emperor in profile, the new coins bore the face of the king. Previously, the new kingdoms that had emerged after the disintegration of the empire had produced coins that imitated the Roman models, as Leovigild had done at the beginning of his reign. He also founded Reccopolis, the first city built from scratch in the post-Roman period, near Zorita de los Canes in the province of Guadalajara, north-east of Toledo. It was named after Reccared, one of Leovigild's sons, who succeeded him after defeating and killing his brother Hermenegild, also a pretender to the throne and the leader of a rebellion in Seville, a clear indication of poor relations between the new kingdom and the elites in the surviving major cities.

Reccopolis, supposedly the palatial city of the Goths, seems not to have entirely lived up to expectations and never replaced Toledo in importance. Archaeological research shows how the Goth kingdom remained well connected to other political geographies during the second half of the sixth century. The decorative architectural work was inspired by Eastern (Byzantine) models, suggesting the migration of artisans from these areas. Products imported from different Mediterranean areas, ranging from the Orient to North Africa, also arrived there. The numismatic record is significant, including Byzantine, Merovingian and Roman coins from the fourth century, which continued to circulate in abundance in addition to the Gothic examples.

Throughout the sixth century, the Goth kingdom, now firmly established in the Iberian Peninsula, began to expand. At the end of his reign, in 585, Leovigild succeeded in annexing the kingdom of the Suebi and eliminating this political entity. On succeeding his father, Reccared converted to Nicene Christianity and the Goth elites followed during the III Council of Toledo in 589, thus helping to establish religious peace in the Iberian Peninsula, at least amongst Christians. However, the physical identification between the Iberian Peninsula and the kingdom of the Goths was only established later when the final imperials were expelled, following the conquest of Cartagena in 625.

Between the mid fourth century and the beginning of the eighth century, the high point in the rule of the Goths in the Peninsula, the overall scenario is somewhat contradictory. On the one hand, the kingdom had been strengthened by establishing its own identity, which involved intensive efforts to develop legislation inspired far more by Roman law than German traditions. The court and its ceremonies emulated those of the Eastern Empire, despite the many disputes resulting from an inability to ensure peaceful succession to the throne. In parallel, the episcopal geography was the clearest indication of continuity with the final years of the Roman Empire, with the episcopal seats serving as the main administrative centres and richest cities. It is known that the transition from Romanity to Christianity was a process involving stability and continuity. This Christianity was at least as extensive and vast as the old Roman Empire, with constant interaction evident in the mobility of its episcopal agents and the wide circulation of theological texts.

As the monarchy maintained close relations with the ecclesiastical hierarchy, conflicts were inevitable. Various episcopal "dynasties" can be identified in this period, with the office of bishop held by members of the same aristocratic family in succession. The councils began to meet regularly, always in Toledo, at the court and in the presence of the king, to deal with both religious and secular matters. During these years, in addition to the importation of products from different faraway places such as the Eastern (Byzantine) Roman Empire and North Africa which are documented in the archaeological records, there is also news of another, much more significant, form of exchange. The lives of certain figures are enlightening in this respect, including John of Biclaro (also known as João de Santarém, after the city where he was born), the author of a chronicle which is an important source for understanding the times. He had travelled to Constantinople, where he studied and graduated. Returning to the Iberian Peninsula, he was exiled to Barcelona by Leovigild for arguing with the Arians, at a time when religion in the kingdom of the Visigoths still followed this movement, which was considered heretical. Nor was this the only punishment Leovigild imposed on a clergyman for reasons associated with theological disputes, indicating how ecclesiastical and secular affairs were often interlinked.

It is also interesting to consider the situation of Paul and Fidelis, both Greek bishops of Mérida who had arrived in the city with merchants who were trading in the Iberian Peninsula, another significant example of mobility and interactions with distant regions. The case of these prelates is interesting due to the fact that they were both Greek and associated with Eastern trade. Since it is impossible to sail from Greece to Mérida, an inland city, the presence of merchants from destinations in the Hellenic world presupposes the existence of a complex network of connections that would have included maintaining a presence in port areas, possibly in Mértola, where there are several epigraphs in Greek, or in the great port of Lisbon, which remained in active contact with the Eastern Roman Empire. People and goods would have arrived in Mérida via one of these ports, using forms of overland or river transport which the Romans had established centuries earlier and which were still usable and used.

Hence, the Goth kingdom remained open to the exterior, although during the seventh century, this impetus began to die out, creating an increasingly rural, closed society. Imports of products from different Mediterranean areas, as well as other types of exchanges, became scarcer, even in coastal cities. There are no other known cases similar to those of John of Biclaro and the Mérida bishops, involving people travelling from one end of the Mediterranean to the other. The court was often a place for plots, conflict and political crises associated with difficulties in reaching a consensus on the succession. The church maintained all its power, not always fully cooperating with the monarch, but constantly involved in matters of the succession.

Isidore of Seville, the key author at the turn of the seventh century, epitomizes the age. The son of a senior Visigoth official, he was a bishop, like his two brothers. He was present at the III Council of Toledo, accompanied by his brother, the metropolitan bishop of Seville, whom he later succeeded. In 612, when his former pupil Sisebut ascended to the throne, he resided at the court in Toledo for lengthy periods of time, serving as counsellor to the king. In 633, almost an octogenarian, he attended the IV Council of Toledo during the reign of Sisenand. He bequeathed a vast collection of literary works to posterity which, in addition to theological treatises, included the greatest compilation of Ancient Greek and Latin learning. Thus, through

Isidore of Seville, Antiquity was handed down to the next generations: in other words, Christianity was able to fully absorb the Roman legacy.

Moreover, although direct contact between the Eastern Roman Empire and the western kingdom of the Goths had died out, the Roman legacy continued in the legal order and in erudite culture.

In political terms, the reign of the Visigoth kingdom eventually collapsed at the beginning of the eighth century, when the Berbers and Arabs arrived in the Peninsula. The divided kingdom was then subjected to further conflicts and a crisis over the succession. Given the speed at which it collapsed, it must have already been frail. Nevertheless, the most recent historiography tends to question this simplistic interpretation, although it has not found any alternative explanation. One thing is certain, however: by the beginning of the eighth century, the Iberian Peninsula was once again opening up to the outside world.

CARLOS FABIÃO
Centre for Archaeology, Faculty of Arts and Humanities, University of Lisbon

Bibliography

BODELÓN, Serafin, *Literatura Latina de la Edad Media en España*, Madrid, Akal/ Universitaria, 1989.

FERNANDES, A. de Almeida, *Paróquias Suevas e Dioceses Visigóticas*, Arouca, Associação para a Defesa do Património Arouquense, 1997.

GARCÍA MORENO, Luis A., *Historia de España Visigoda*, Madrid, Cátedra, 1989.

LEGUAY, Jean-Pierre, "O "Portugal" germânico", in SERRÃO, Joel, MARQUES, A. H. de Oliveira (dir.), *Nova História de Portugal*, vol. II, Lisbon, Presença, 1993, pp. 11–115.

WICKHAM, Chris, *The Inheritance of Rome: A History of Europe from 400 to 1000*, London, Penguin Books, 2010.

PART III

The Middle Ages

Introduction to Part III

From the Advent of Islam to
the Conquest of Ceuta

BERNARDO VASCONCELOS E SOUSA
Nova University Lisbon

The common sense view of the European Middle Ages is of an epoch of darkness, of stasis, of autocracy. Set between the splendour of Classical Graeco-Roman Antiquity and the brilliance of the Renaissance, it serves all too often, in current political discourse, as an example of backwardness, ignorance, intolerance and violence. These themes are taken up and diffused in the media, which adopt and lend resonance to dominant political and cultural platitudes. From this perspective, the Medieval era was simply a thousand years of history characterized by famine, pestilence and war.

European tradition and historiographical conventions usually establish the start of the Middle Ages in 476 with the fall of the Western Roman Empire, and the end in 1492 with the arrival of Christopher Columbus in America. This, a conventional as well as a Eurocentric vision, has only become global and managed to look beyond itself because the West has since then proceeded to 'conquer the world'.

What several authors have called the first globalization began with European expansion into other continents, in what is also known as the Modern Era, starting in the fifteenth century. But in the wider context, as well as within Portugal, the idea of a closed-in Middle Ages, composed of local cells of varying sizes, isolated from each other, producing and consuming locally, lacking their own dynamics, contacts or inter-relationships, is a highly compartmentalized view, taking the part for the whole and thus establishing hasty and unilateral generalizations.

Direct or indirect integration, seen in large-scale dynamics and in phenomena widespread over space and time, are clearly evident from times before the existence of Portugal as an independent political entity, constructed in the twelfth century. Despite its peripheral geographic position, at the *finis terrae* in the Latin representation of the known world or the *Gharb* (the West in Arabic), the territory which became Portugal was not immune to external influences. Nor did this position stop the kingdom of Portugal diffusing movements and actions which had repercussions outside Europe, even in the Medieval era.

It is thus that we can understand the meaning of a globalizing Middle Ages. There are two sides here: on the one hand, what came from the 'outside' and was reflected in Portugal, with consequences at the time of its appearance but also in future history; on the other hand, what was 'within' Portugal but with external repercussions, reaching beyond the territory of the kingdom. Whether in society, in the economy, culture and the arts, or in religion, results would have come from peaceful contacts, especially with other Christian entities, or from military confrontations, with Islam, with the Vikings, or even with other Christians. The phenomena might be long-lasting, or they might be single factors, or dependent on individual figures. The themes chosen in the present analysis are generally considered determinant, and are perhaps those that best capture the dimensions of globalizing Middle Ages. Any choice is always marked by subjectivity, and other topics might also merit attention. For example, the Jewish influence, the legacy of the Mozarabs – those communities which kept their religion under Islamic rule and were at the same time agents of the process of acculturation – or even the 'foreigner' King Afonso III, who lived for several years at the court of the French king Saint Louis and brought to Portugal many important influences from beyond the Pyrenees. This is merely to mention a few other topics which could appear in this volume: the options chosen are due to limits of space, and also to historiographic criteria, in an attempt to base the selection on the real impact of phenomena, facts and individuals.

This double dimension – what is received and what is transmitted – which more hasty analysts would reduce to the binomial inputs-outputs – is already detectable from 711 in the arrival and presence of Islam in the Iberian Peninsula, and to a much lesser extent in the Viking incursions of the ninth century. Even before the formation of Portugal as an independent political entity, the attribution to Henry of Burgundy of the government of the County of *Portucale* (1096), then part of the kingdom of León, accentuated the external influences felt at that date and later. It is useful to remember that the first king of the Portuguese was the child of an 'immigrant'.

Furthermore, the links nowadays known as international relations (although the present concept of nation is anachronistic for medieval times) were constantly established and strengthened, especially in political alliances celebrated through marriages between members of the Portuguese royal family and various other European ruling or aristocratic houses. After Henry of Burgundy and his son Afonso Henriques set the example (the latter marrying a lady from Savoy), this ample and profitable marriage market continued, from Castile and Aragon to the Holy Romano-Germanic Empire, including France, England and Denmark. The market lasted well beyond the Middle Ages.

The elements with wider dimensions and effects, local in origin or coming from outside, could be positive or negative in character. Without entering into convoluted value judgements, it is worth mentioning, on the positive side: the life and energy of cities, with Lisbon assuming its position at the head of the kingdom from the thirteenth century; art, with styles and aesthetic forms defined by strong trans-Pyrenean influences, but still incorporating native traces; and writing, and its use in documents and literary works, as elements of communication in politics, economics, culture and religion. And, connecting everything, language: at first, Latin – no longer classical, but medieval – and then Galician-Portuguese. This language, itself the expression of many external and internal influences, became an instrument of global communication, first within the kingdom and then spreading far and wide, until today it is one of the most widely spoken of the world's languages.

On the reverse of the coin are phenomena whose negative consequences were often generalized throughout medieval times: epidemics, reaching their peak in the paradigmatic Black Death, coming from Asia and spreading with stunning speed throughout most of Europe, and wreaking havoc in Portugal from 1348; and wars, for limited local motives but also set in wider contexts, such as the so-called Hundred Years War

(1337–1453), the lengthy conflict between France and England which extended to the Iberian Peninsula, through the political and military alliances of Castile with France and of Portugal with England. And it is not too much to claim that the Battle of Aljubarrota, in 1385, was of some importance in the context of this international conflict.

Dispelling the dark legend of a Middle Ages cloistered in itself, and of a Portuguese kingdom isolated within the bounds of an immobile world, we find networks of communication and movement on regional, inter-regional and also on 'international' scales. The commercial relations thus set up were some of the first on record: the formal support of the Portuguese Crown in forming a merchants' exchange in 1293 is evidence of this. These relationships, with emphasis on long-distance trade, were not the only ones: also important were the institutional networks created and strengthened in the context of the medieval Latin Church. Monasteries, dioceses, religious and religious-military orders formed centres and structures, connecting the networks through which their members and doctrines circulated, composing, integrating and framing western Christianity, of which the kingdom of Portugal was part. This Christianity, as a concept and a collective body, was a decisive unifying factor in what the great French medievalist Jacques Le Goff called the civilization of the medieval West.

In the same way, the foundation, in 1288–1290, of the General Studies (*Studium Generale*), first in Lisbon and then moving between there and Coimbra, was part of the movement that created and spread universities throughout Europe. Several Portuguese scholars moved in these religious and university networks: their actions and influence went beyond the frontiers of the kingdom. Among these is Saint Anthony, whose cult is still very much alive today, not only in Portugal and Italy but around the world, and John XXI, the only Portuguese pope in the history of the Catholic Church.

Even limiting this analysis to what might seem a strictly internal logic – the precocious fixation and stabilization of a political frontier with the neighbouring kingdom of Castile-León by the Treaty of Alcañices of 1297 – this is still an action with far wider consequences than the restricted context of Portugal. In fact, it not only solidified the physical limits of what was at the time the newest kingdom in the Iberian Peninsula, but also established a territorial base for the country whose Atlantic expansion, begun in the fifteenth century, was the origin of an extensive, discontinuous, pluricontinental and long-lasting empire. This construction, still disconnected, was to confer on the little Iberian kingdom, with few natural and human resources at the end of the Middle Ages, a reach and a global influence, clearly seen in international trade, in war and overseas conquests, in the colonization of diverse regions of the globe, in slavery, in the propagating of Catholicism, and in the spread of a language which would reach every continent. The first step of all this activity on a global scale – although this was not the intention of its protagonists at the time – was to the city of Ceuta, North Africa, in 1415: that is, in the middle of the second decade of the final century of the Middle Ages.

If there were still any doubts up to this point, it should now be clear that this is indeed a global history of Portugal.

711
Confrontation and Interaction:
Islam in the Iberian Peninsula

The history of the transformation of Hispania into al-Andalus – that is, from an old Roman diocese dating from the Diocletian provincial reorganization into a geographical, political and cultural entity within the Islamic world – is the result of a complex process of acculturation.

In the penultimate decade of the ninth century, a group of clergy from the south of Hispania created a historical narrative around King Alfonso III of Asturias which was also a program: the monarchy of Oviedo was to be the successor in Hispania of the Visigothic kingdom. This connected it to a familiar Christian religious continuity, with the Asturian royal line rooted in the Visigothic aristocracy. Its historical mission, therefore, was to return Iberia to Christian rule, forgetting almost two centuries of the presence and rule of Islam. This mission, outlined in texts from the 880s, gained more precise form when, in the *Prophetic Chronicle*, the end of al-Andalus was prophesied. This was to occur at a date which would come to coincide with what was to become a major event in its history: the rise to power of the young emir 'Abd al-Rahman, whose political abilities were to radically change the balance of power in Hispania in favour of Islam. Twenty years earlier, however, there could have been reasons to believe that the end of Islam in Iberia was close, since the emirate was in a deep internal crisis, with the power of the emir weakened to the advantage of independent powers operating at a regional level, still oblivious to the Asturian advances on the line of the Douro. The succession in the following century of the young emir, who proclaimed himself Caliph in 929, was to curb the ambitions of the Asturian royalty. For, despite the prophecy announcing the coming end of al-Andalus, its high point was yet to come. However, from the point of view of the Christian political entities to the north, especially the most structured one, Asturias, a narrative direction was found for the recent history of the Iberian Peninsula, and simultaneously a plan for the future: since Hispania was essentially Christian, the Arabic-Islamic presence constituted an intrusion which it was the duty of the Asturian monarchy to eliminate. The duration of this presence was an interval before the final restitution. This was the narrative, which, in various forms, served as the foundation for the construction of the various Hispanic monarchies, including the Portuguese, all sharing al-Andalus as memorialistic reference, and the reconquest of the territory as aim. Even though in a simplified and contradictory form, the argument still recognized the impact that the entry of Islam into Hispania in 711, as well as the three-quarters of a century of conquests which preceded it, had on the history of the Peninsula and of the Latin west which would be known as Europe. This impact resulted both from internal transformations and from connections with the eastern Mediterranean and the commercial and cultural flows, which united an Islamic world that, in entering Hispania, stretched from Samarkand to Lisbon.

In 711, the arrival in Hispania, then under Visigothic rule, of contingents of Berbers led by Tariq bin Ziyad – a *mawla* of Musa Ibn Nusayr, the Ummayad governor of the recently conquered province of Africa – followed in 712 by the Arab *djund* of the governor himself, was nothing extraordinary. It should be understood in the framework of a process of expansion begun in 636 with the defeat of the Roman and Persian empires, which ended thirty years of total war between two of the greatest global powers of the time. It led to the almost immediate destruction of the Sasanian Persian Empire, and the progressive splitting of the Roman Empire – as it was generally called, including by the Arabs – reducing it's area to the Balkans, Anatolia and, for some time, Italy.

The loss of the provinces of the southern Mediterranean, while allowing the Roman world to continue in the northern shore, would open up various possibilities for a new, Islamic, entity, directed by caliphs based, from 661, in Damascus. This would to some extent regain the geography – and the koiné spirit – of their Hellenistic predecessors, particularly of the short-lived Empire of Alexander, uniting the great areas of Persian and Mediterranean civilization. From the Roman (Byzantine) point of view, this meant losing power over Syria, Egypt, and at the end of the seventh century, over the province of Africa, from where the military forces would launch their attack on Visigothic Hispania. Their arrival and almost immediate victories in Hispania were part of a deliberate process of conquest, involving the Roman Empire and its western epigone kingdoms (Visigothic, Frankish), with the aim of replacing a Christian community, which, in one form or another, was reflected in the emperor, with the Islamic *ummah*. The failure of the various attacks on Constantinople, and the retreat from Gaulish lands, which lent strength and space to the formation of the Carolingian world, made the success in Hispania particularly significant, bringing the Peninsula ever closer to the east and the Mediterranean, and from the ninth century onwards, also to Persia, which, under the Abbasids, would make its influence felt in the Islamic world.

The history of the transformation of Hispania into al-Andalus, that is, from an old Roman diocese dating from the Diocletian provincial reorganization into a geographical, political and cultural entity within the Islamic world, is the result of a complex process of acculturation. Through it, Hispanic cultural unity, gained at the end of the sixth century by the conversion of Reccared to imperial Catholicism and by the absolute triumph of Latin and the late Roman model of royalty, was exposed to a new orientalising influence in terms of language and culture, and a new religion, even though monotheistic.

To measure the impact of the Arab-Berber conquest – through which the newly arrived minority came to dominate a weak tributary state structure – implies gauging the depth of the accompanying processes of assimilation. In question here is conversion to Islam, the triumph of Arabic as the political and increasingly culturally dominant language, and finally, contact between segmentary social structures where the tribal model was still very much alive – both among the subsidiary Berbers and the dominant Arabs, – and models of organization based on patriarchal rule, inherited from late imperial Roman society and maintained in the Visigothic kingdom. The depth of the transformation seen between the eighth and tenth centuries allows us to glimpse the multiple fractures, which threatened the society of al-Andalus in this first period. There was discord among Arabs, typical of intertribal and interfamily conflicts, and between Arabs and Berbers. Also, and, particularly from the ninth century, a new and increasingly socially influential segment, the *muwalladun* – converts to Islam, especially visible among elites – opposed other groups and the central power based in Córdoba.

The cohesion of this diversity of interests was assured, even before Islam became the religion of the majority in Hispania, by the creation of a political regime, charismatic in nature, able to set up, in the far west of the Islamic world, a bureaucratic state centred on the figure of local emir (*dawla*) – that he was a member of the Banu Ummaya, a branch of the family of the prophet Mohammed, justified the legitimacy and the duration of the dynasty (756–1031). The prestige of the court, initially on the Byzantine model, orientalised by 'Abd al-Rahman II (822–852) on Abbasid lines, was one of the fundamental elements in the construction of identity of al-Andalus, especially when, in 929, the emir 'Abd al-Rahman III assumed the title of Caliph. This marked a phase of intense economic growth, a reduction of regional division, and the high point of courtly culture – the best example would be the construction of a machine of government, the city of al-Zahra – growth and culture that both would survive the collapse of the regime during the great *Fitna* (1009–1031). For all these reasons, and especially through its intense urban dynamism (the largest cities in the West in these centuries were in al-Andalus), through the predominance of its Arabic literary culture, through the quality of its material culture and habits of consumption, and through its social organization and political system, this western extremity was connected more than ever to the eastern Mediterranean. This explains why the Caliph saw himself on a level with the Roman emperor in Constantinople and the Abbasid caliph in Baghdad, while also maintaining relations with the Holy Roman Emperor.

The moment when the Christian princes of northern Iberia became serious inter-locutors coincides with the fragmentation of the political space of the Caliphate into some three dozens of autonomous principalities, ruled by "kings of the factions" (*muluk al-tawa' if*), some becoming more powerful, such as those of Seville, Badajoz, Toledo and Zaragoza. None of them, however, despite their immense wealth and intellectual sophistication, had the capacity to maintain the integrity of al-Andalus in the face of the growth of the Christian kingdoms (León, Castille, Aragon, the Catalan counties and the emergent county of Portugal (*Condado Portucalense*), to the north, and the *jihad* of the proselytizing Almoravid Berber movement to the south. Undecided between the two, they finally supported Islamic continuity in Hispania by integrating for the first time with external political options, namely the Berber empires, first the Almoravid (Sunnites of the Malakite school) then the Almohad, centred on a new orthodoxy, prophetic in character. Al-Andalus survived for almost two further centuries thanks to this solution, until the final withdrawal of the Almohads, which was also the beginning of the end: in less than twenty years, the crown of Aragon occupied the kingdoms of Valencia and the Balearics, the crown of Castile, Murcia, Jaen, Córdoba and Seville, the kingdom of León, Badajoz, and the kingdom of Portugal, the Algarve.

All these kingdoms then became part of the Christian kings' royal titles, their territories being a decisive element in the claims of Iberian monarchs. However, parts of al-Andalus remained exclusively Islamic: the wealthy kingdom of Granada, along with the cities of Almeria and Malaga, with its silk industries. A situation that lasted until, in 1492, the Catholic monarchs decided to put an end to the last Islamic realm on this side of the Mediterranean, in a conquest which emulated, on an Iberian scale and in the opposite direction, that of Constantinople in 1453.

These fragmentary political presences in late al-Andalus, which the city-based *taifa* regimes had prefigured, were one of the longest-lasting traces of the Islamic period in Hispania, others being the strong eastern influence and the interdepen-dence of the European and the African sides of the Mediterranean. There was a constant tension between centralizing forces and the claims of potentially autonomous regional entities; these were more resilient in the frontier spaces of the periphery, such as the borders: the upper (the Ebro valley), the central (Toledo) and the lower (Gharb, the far West). In the last one, on the westernmost frontier of al-Andalus a first great political entity had risen from the ninth-century *Fitna*, that of Ibn Marwan in Badajoz and Ammaia, lacking territorial cohesion but maintained through cliental links among local lords.

However, we shall resist here to draw any necessary connection between these loosely organized lordships and the future kingdom of Portugal, unless perhaps in relation to the ability to construct autonomous political solutions in the space of the far West. The proximity of the *taifa* regimes of Badajoz and Seville, which had risen in the eleventh century, was greater, especially since the young Portuguese monarchy spent the entire first century of its history attempting to take control of its territorial and symbolic heritage. The failure of this enterprise, clearly demonstrated by the disaster of Badajoz (1169), defined a totally different direction for the Portuguese kingdom, whose Atlantic character was sealed by the conquest of the western part of the Algarve at Faro (1249). The legacy of al-Andalus survived, however, in material culture and institutional practices, long after the last king, Ibn Mahfud, abandoned Silves for the temporary protective vassalage of Ferdinand III of León and Castille.

HERMENEGILDO FERNANDES
Centre for History, Faculty of Arts and Humanities, University of Lisbon

Bibliography

COELHO, António Borges, *Portugal na Espanha Árabe*, 2nd ed., 2 vols., Lisbon, Caminho, 1989.
FIERRO, Maribel, *Abderramán III y el Califato Omeya de Córdoba*, San Sebastian, Nerea, 2011.
KENNEDY, Hugh, *Muslim Spain and Portugal: A Political History of Al-Andalus*, Abingdon, Routledge, 1996.
PICARD, Christophe, *Le Portugal Musulman (VIII–XIII Siècle). L'Occident d'Al-Andalus sous Domination Islamique*, Paris, Maisonneuve et Larose, 2000.
TORRES, Cláudio, MACIAS, Santiago, *O Legado Islâmico em Portugal*, Lisbon, Círculo de Leitores, 1998.

844
What Remained from the Time of the Vikings?

Some documentary evidence shows that there were Viking bases in what is now Portugal. The best example relates to the region between the rivers Douro and Ave, where, according to an account from the early eleventh century, Vikings stayed for nine months, from the summer of 1015 to the spring of 1016, taking prisoners which they then freed in exchange for ransoms.

In August 844, a group of Norsemen landed in the region of A Corunha, sacking it until they were defeated by a royal army. It was the first known attack by those people on north-western Iberia, marking the start of the Viking Age in the region. From northern Galicia, the attackers moved south, to what would later become Portugal.

They reached the region of Lisbon, where they arrived on August 20, leaving after thirteen days, during which time they fought local troops three times, though the exact place and the result are not known. Nor is it clear if the attack reached the city of Lisbon or only the outlying districts, where farms, small settlements and isolated buildings may have been sacked or temporarily occupied.

When the Vikings left – whether voluntarily or by force of arms is unclear – they sailed on to Seville, where they arrived about a month later. The duration of the voyage raises the possibility that additional attacks along the coast between the Tagus and the Guadalquivir may have occurred – of which no account has been made or survived. The possibility is also valid for much of the Viking Age in western Iberia, since the briefness of the sources and their fragmentary nature allow only for a partial view of the events. The voyage of the Vikings who sailed from A Corunha to Lisbon is no exception: in a coastline marked by the river-mouths of the Minho, Douro and Mondego, and which, if one takes away centuries of sedimentation, would have been more indented and with greater access to the interior than today, there would have been many places where pirates from the north could have sheltered, taken on supplies, repaired their ships, held religious ceremonies and pillaged small fishing or other communities. Note that the account of the arrival of the Vikings in Lisbon by Ahmad al-Razi, quoted by Ibn Hayyan in the *Al-Muqtabis*, indicates that the attacking fleet was comprised of an identical number of Norse ships and of *qaribs*. Were these boats stolen from native settlements attacked during the voyage south from A Corunha, perhaps in an attempt to make up for losses of ships in Galicia?

In 858 the Vikings returned to Lisbon, where, according to the so-called *Prophetic Chronicle*, probably written by a cleric, Mozarab or with knowledge of Arabic, there was great slaughter, though it is not clear if this was of local inhabitants, invaders or both. Once again, they sailed on to the Guadalquivir, but no further. However, there was a new assault in the following year, although it is not known exactly which places were attacked, since the Latin source only mentions the Iberian coast before moving on to the Vikings' entrance into the Mediterranean. The only point in what is now Portugal for which there is reference to a confrontation with the Vikings in 859 is the so-called 'coast of Beja', which must be the Alentejo seashore, where two Norse boats were captured by a naval force of the emirate of Córdoba. Gold, silver and slaves were found on board, certainly the result of pillaging carried out that same year, perhaps further along the later Portuguese coast.

The voyage of the Vikings through the Mediterranean was quite impressive: after passing through the straits of Gibraltar, they reached the Balearic Islands and continued along the Spanish coast until they reached southern France, where they wintered on an island in the Rhône, using it to pillage the surrounding area. According to the *Annals of Saint Bertin*, a Frankish source from the ninth century written by three individuals with connections to Carolingian power centres, they even reached northern Italy. But in 860, at least part of the group returned to the Atlantic, where it faced an Islamic fleet, and turning north, again sailed along the coast of what is now Portugal. Whether the Vikings made further attacks at this time is unclear, but the impressive nature of the Mediterranean odyssey has echoes in later legends concerning the sons of Ragnar Löðbrók, which, however, should not be taken too literally. Although they may be based on memories of real events, they have developed as legendary accounts, and so caution is needed regarding suggestions, sometimes seemingly convincing ones, on the supposed voyage through Portugal by figures such as

Björn Járnsíða, a semi-legendary Viking who was later credited with the Mediterranean adventure and a family connection with Ragnar Löðbrók.

It has also been claimed that the events of 858–860 were one great expedition, but the chronicles *Albeldense* and of *Alfonso III* mention only that the Vikings returned during the reign of Ordonho I (850–866), so this vague reference could include more than one incursion in successive years. In fact, considering the details of not only those two sources but also of the *Prophetic Chronicle*, and of Arab and Frankish accounts, it seems likelier that there were two separate waves, one in 858, which went no further than southern Spain, and another in 859, which reached the south of France.

The Mediterranean odyssey was the last known ninth-century attack in what is now Portugal. Raids continued during the next two centuries, apparently increasing in number or at least in intensity. At the beginning of the twelfth century they were succeeded by Norse crusading campaigns sailing towards the Holy Land. The best-known was led by the Norwegian king Sigurðr Jórsalafari, who attacked Sintra, Lisbon and perhaps Alcácer do Sal. Although the two processes are not necessarily related, the increase in Viking activity and the evolution from pagan to crusading pirates were accompanied by a change in the type of surviving sources: whereas for the ninth century there are mainly chronicles, for the tenth and eleventh centuries there are also small documents from the records of various monasteries, adding to the narratives of the kings' sagas and the skaldic poetry preserved in them, first for the legendary voyage of Saint Olaf along the western Iberian coast, then for the more historical expedition of King Sigurðr.

Obviously these are all written sources, since thus far no archaeological traces of Viking voyages along the later Portuguese coast have been found. There are no tombs, ships, buildings or portable objects in sufficient numbers to certify that they are related to Norse presence rather than to the chance acquisition of isolated pieces. However, there is some documentary evidence of Viking bases in modern-day Portuguese territory. The best example is from the region between the rivers Douro and Ave, where, according to an account from the early eleventh century, Vikings stayed for nine months, from the summer of 1015 to the spring of 1016, taking prisoners which they then freed in exchange for ransoms. It was a practice carried out in other parts of Western Europe, where, from the mid-ninth century on, they also set up bases where they wintered, allowing them to extend the looting season for the whole year, rather than only the milder months. In what later became Portuguese territory, it is known that they wintered in 1015–1016, but not where they set up their camp(s). Remains have never been found – or never interpreted as Norse – and the account from the eleventh century indicates nothing beyond the hypothetical suggestion that their base was somewhere on the banks of the Douro.

Similarly enigmatic, but with far less documentary substance, is the toponym Lordemão, on the northern outskirts of Coimbra. It dates from at least the twelfth century, when it is found in the form 'Lordomam' in an endowment made, according to Rui Pinto de Azevedo, between 1122 and 1125. The connection comes from the word 'lordemanos' and its variants, which in some Iberian sources were used for the Vikings. If there is in that an etymological link, it remains unexplained, since no surviving source mentions a Norse presence on the river Mondego or the outskirts of Coimbra, much less a base, colony or group of Scandinavian captives which might justify the toponym. This does not mean that such did not occur, since there are only brief fragments of information rather than a full record of the Viking Age in western Iberia, but the absence of sources means that one cannot present any concrete hypothesis.

A different matter, though, is the sometimes popular idea that traditional Portuguese boats owe some of their features to the presence of Vikings in what is now Portugal. The connection might seem obvious, given the close bond between those seafarers and their ships. But, on the one hand, there is no archaeological evidence and, on the other hand, there is a chronological hiatus – the Viking Age was not yesterday, a decade or a century ago, but about a thousand years in the past. Between then and now, there was enough time and opportunity, after the Viking Age, for Norse influences to have made themselves felt in Portuguese naval construction, but mediated by peoples who had been shaped by waves of Scandinavians. Specifically the English and French, with whom Portugal established commercial and diplomatic ties in the Middle Ages. The word 'quilha' (cognate with English keel) offers a good example of this: although its origin may be the Norse *kjölr*, it was introduced into Portuguese by way of French *quille*, a word which may be the result of Scandinavian settlement in Normandy.

What remains, then, of the Viking presence in what is now Portugal? Very little. Above all, memory is what is left, more written than living, and fortifications or their ruins may have survived, though it is not certain. The castle of Guimarães, for example, owes its construction in the 10th century to the fear of the 'gentiles', but it is not clear if the word refers to Vikings, Muslims or both. There is no evidence nor indication of any colonies, apart from the hypothetical case of Lordemão.

This lack of physical remains is the result of the dynamics of the Viking Age in western Iberia. While in France and the British Isles piracy became conquest, colonization and commerce, which naturally leave lasting traces in the landscape and culture, in Galicia and later Portuguese territories, Norse activity seems to have consisted generally of pillaging, the impact of which tends to disappear after the attackers leave. More so in the Iberian Peninsula, which in the ninth century and for the rest of the Viking Age was already a battleground between different kingdoms in the context of the so-called Reconquest. The arrival of the Vikings did not therefore introduce conflict into a peaceful region, or a religious split where none existed. For two hundred years, it merely added new forms of aggression to those already present in the region. Its impact dissolved in the following centuries of dispute, leaving behind the written memory preserved in the surviving documents.

HÉLIO PIRES
Institute of Medieval Studies, Faculty of Social Sciences, Nova University Lisbon

Bibliography

FERNÁNDEZ, Juan Gil et al. (ed.), *Cronicas Asturianas*, Oviedo, Universidad de Oviedo, 1985.

FERNÁNDEZ GONZÁLEZ, Francisco (ed.), *Ibn Idari al Marrakusi. Historia de Al-Andalus*, Málaga, Ediciones Aljaima, 1999.

JAMES, David (ed.), *Ibn al-Qutiya. Early Islamic Spain: The History of Ibn al-Qutiya*, London/ New York, Routledge, 2009.

MAKKI, Mahmud Ali, CORRIENTE, Frederico (ed.), *Cronica de los Emires Alhakam I y Abdarrahman II entre los Años 796 y 847 [Almuqtabis II-1]*, Zaragoza, La Aljafería, 2001.

PIRES, Hélio, *Os Vikings em Portugal e na Galiza: As Incursões Nórdicas Medievais no Ocidente Ibérico*, Sintra, Zéfiro, 2017.

882

Evolution of the Handwritten Text

In Portugal, the fourteenth and fifteenth centuries were the period when written texts established absolute primacy. The first will of King Afonso II (27 June 1214), written in Galician-Portuguese, is the oldest dated non-literary document.

The term 'writing' signifies creation, making, work or book, and also the technique or art of making letters and signs as the physical representation of a language. In the European Middle Ages, it was the main weapon against the weakness of orality and the ephemeral nature of knowledge: a tool of understanding, of creating history. As such, words had to be fixed on a support (stone, wood, gold, bronze, paper, parchment) which would keep alive the memory of man. But writing was also a means of juridical proof, a factor in the spread of laws, essential to structure institutions, to confer power and to support administration and politics in the government of territories. It was a long journey for it to become an ideal, a social necessity, and a force for defending rights, fighting oppression and abuses.

Between the fifth and tenth centuries, knowing how to write was a skill only of socio-cultural minorities: those who possessed it, almost as a monopoly, were certain members of the clergy, whether regular (monastic) – men, and in exceptional cases women – or secular. It was their task to write for public and private purposes, drawing up documents of endowment, judgment and emancipation, creating texts for epigraphic inscriptions, and transcribing and copying documents and books. Any such work could be carried out by one person, known as a notary-cleric, or, for one particular kind of work, a scribe – a copyist who knew how to read – could be employed. The diffusion of writing, in monasteries, colleges and churches, went through rapid changes in response to the political contexts of Western Europe, especially in the kingdom of Portugal in the fourteenth century. While the scribe, the diffuser of ancient and medieval culture, was asked to reproduce a missal, a psalter, a Bible or a law book, the notary-clerk was required to confer on a document the *fides publica* (public trust) essential to written laws. Without this, after the thirteenth century it would not survive the demands of jurisprudence, the desire of monarchs to have 'power over writing', or the increased worth of the written as against the oral. Allied to these were the resurgence of the cities, the growing circulation of goods, people and money, and the complexity of juridical, economic and governmental relationships. The use of writing was essential even for the illiterate, who at least once in their lives would require a deed of sale, a document, a will or an inventory.

At the beginning of the thirteenth century, particularly in the reign of King Afonso II (1211–1223), there was a revolution in the recruitment of scribes, in the organization of the centres of production of documents, and in the efficient management of the administration and validation of writing and of documents by the Crown. Writing kept its graphic refinements (elegant, cursive and semi-cursive), but the historic forms were slowly changing, coexisting in multiple varieties.

We shall consider first the Visigothic (882–1101); this script was only found in the Iberian Peninsula, arising in the line of graphic tradition from the Roman world. The oldest original evidence in Portugal, preserved in the Torre do Tombo, dates from 882. It is written in cursive Visigothic hand, which Millares Carlo considers as a rustic hand, the rough and negligent product of scribblers working in relatively uncultured centres, which can also be seen in the language they used, classified correctly as Vulgar Leonese Latin.

In fact, in "brass Latin", as Aquilino Ribeiro called it, the morphology of letters, the special signs, the intricate system of abbreviations and even the use of cryptography, make this style of handwriting one of the most difficult to read and transcribe. But when used in regular contexts, for example in books of liturgical music, it acquired an aesthetic sense, a harmony of elegant strokes. Such is the rounded Visigothic hand seen, though rarely, in sundry letters from centres such as Coimbra Cathedral.

However, a different script, the Caroline hand, was used in the eighth and ninth centuries in the Carolingian Empire. Beautiful and easy to read, it spread across the whole of Europe: the colours and illuminations in its parchment codices have become immortal. The introduction of this style of writing into the territory of what was to become Portugal is due to men and books: the reforms of Cluny (1085), the replacement of the Visigothic by the Roman liturgy, and the arrival in the Iberian Peninsula of French monks and nobility, acted as catalysts. The earliest influences, dating from 1054, are from the Monastery of Pendorada: the old cursive and rounded Visigothic hands are found together with the Visigothic in transition to the Caroline, in a hybrid mode with characteristics of the two styles of the High Middle Ages. The earliest example of Caroline script may date from 1103: it is a signature of Maurice Bourdin, the bishop of Coimbra; the oldest document entirely in Caroline script, dated 1108, is from Coimbra Cathedral.

Around 1131, the monastery of Santa Cruz in Coimbra began to use Gothic script, either 'pure' or with signs of the Caroline – the Caroline-Gothic or Proto-Gothic. Gothic script, known as 'University letters' (*letra das universidades)*, from the use made of it, has unmistakable characteristics, whether seen in books or documents. In the former, there is an almost complete lack of curves, and reduced use of abbreviations and of geometric and faceted forms, resembling cut gemstones. In documents, the Gothic becomes cursive and fast, the marks sometimes coarse and confused. The plurality of styles, 'Gothics' rather than Gothic, due partly to personalized forms of writing and accentuated by the influence of notaries and scribes, gave it a long life – almost five centuries, up to the early fifteenth century. The break in the evolutionary process produced humanistic script, born from the disparaging vision of medieval culture by the spirits of Renaissance Italy. Poggio Bracciolini (1380–1459) would create the model, inspired by the beauty of Caroline script allied to the values of classical Graeco-Latin culture. Examples of refined cursive calligraphy, Italic in style, existed, but in Portugal their diffusion was weak.

Visigothic styles were long-lasting, however. They survived from 882 to 1172, although the twelfth century was already marked by the transition to the Caroline. In this multi-graphism, however, they were gradually rejected in legal offices. The pioneer here was Coimbra Cathedral, where the final entry in transitional Visigothic is a letter from 1137, which reinforces the idea that by 1130–1140 this cathedral was no longer a Mozarabic religious and cultural centre. Others followed, despite notable resistance dictated by the mind-set, the culture and the age of the notary-clerics. It was the Monastery of Pedroso which, in 1172, closed the long and fertile cycle of multi-modal Visigothic script.

After around four decades, notary-clerics lost their exclusivity, their duties being transferred to lay notaries, connected to urban centres: created by King Afonso II, this was now a paid profession. Unlike notary-clerics, these lay notaries were usually nominated by kings, had *auctoritas* (authority), and, with an individual hand-drawn signet, conferred the essential *validatio* (validation). By a regulation of King Denis (1279–1325), the public notaries had a place or work, the *paço*, but they could travel to fairs, markets and manor houses, which added to their costs (for documents, animal transport and travel). Judicial notaries, particularly important and prestigious, dealt with the documents of law-courts.

Writing and documents played an important role in central administration with the organization of the royal chancellery. Monasteries, hospitals, churches and colleges too set up their own chancelleries, as a service for producing and diffusing legal documents. The production of single documents and of books increased, and with them, the problem of conservation. Single letters, being easy to lose, were copied and bound in books, kept in special stands or chests. Examples of these are collections such as the fifteenth-century *Livro Verde* (Portuguese University), the twelfth–thirteenth-century *Livro Santo* (Monastery of Santa Cruz, Coimbra), the thirteenth-century *Livro Preto* (Coimbra Cathedral) and *Liber Fidei* (Braga Cathedral), and the twelfth-century *Liber Testamentorum* (Monastery of Lorvão), all compiled with the clear intention of preserving the memory of people and their possessions.

The supporting material of writing in the medieval kingdom of Portugal was gener- ally parchment, although the earliest paper document, kept in the Torre do Tombo, dates from 1268. Parchment, as opposed to paper made from cloth, is sheep- or goat- skin, the hair removed; stretched on a frame, then dried and scraped, it offers two surfaces, inner and outer, for writing. A scriptorium, where manuscripts were copied, was the place to find superior quality material, such as vellum (calf-skin, from very young or stillborn animals). This is fine-grained, almost translucent, and was used for missals, books of hours and bibles. But there were also coarser parchments, yellowish in colour, showing defects of tension, or torn and stitched. These, since they were cheaper, went to notaries' offices, or were bought by poorer institutions. They were also used in the royal chancellery, for isolated documents or record books, since robust materials were preferred, to reinforce the documents; paper, whether of Portuguese or foreign origin, was cheaper and easier to acquire, but lacked robustness, as palaeog- raphy and codicology have proved.

As for the ink used, up to the nineteenth century it was mainly black or sepia iron- gall formula: the tannin was from oak galls, and the metal salts were iron sulphate. According to a fifteenth-century recipe, water, wine or vinegar was added to the galls (the best were from Aleppo, in present-day Syria) after grinding. Gum Arabic, from Sub-Saharan Africa, is also mentioned as a binding agent, essential for the quality of the ink. Finally everything was heated or exposed to the sun for several days. It was important to stir the mixture with a stick of fig wood split into four, since its sap would be good for the final product. Inks of several colours, vegetable or mineral in origin, were also used for books, capital letters, titles or paragraph marks. In medieval iconog- raphy they appear in inkwells of lead or glass or in inkhorns, since these were the best materials to avoid spoiling the precious liquid. The Chinese, for whom ink was an exquisite perfume, prepared it in the first century with soot, to which they added camphor, musk and cloves to create the finest fragrance. In fact, the whole dynamic of writing is evident in the circulation of the fundamental materials for making ink, in Europe, Africa and Asia.

Also essential for the act of writing by hand is the quill pen, defined as "a bird's feather, cut, and used for writing with ink". Books from the sixteenth century indicate the preferred birds for producing the best feathers: goose, duck and crow. After drying, naturally or by fire, and plunged into sand, the point was cut, symmetrically or asymmetrically to the left or right. There were nine rules for this process, as set out in a fifteenth-century manuscript in the chapter library of Leitz Cathedral in Germany. After removing the barbs of the feather, the quill was tested by making lines, letters or symbols, as can be seen in a codex from Santa Cruz, Coimbra. Quill pens were personal tools, prepared, like parchment and inks, in monasteries up to the eighteenth century. Later they could be bought cheaply, usually by the dozen. Their short life – due to damage to the tip – meant that they were not highly valued, in comparison with the dignity accorded by thinkers and writers to parchment and ink.

In Portugal, the fourteenth and fifteenth centuries witnessed the apotheosis of the written. The first will of King Afonso II, dated 27 June 1214, is the earliest non-literary document written in Galician-Portuguese. In this environment scribes flourished, rarely with *fides publica*, occupying an important place in medieval society. The second half of the fifteenth century was the beginning of the industrial era of writing, with the introduction of movable type and the printing press. Times would change, but writing by hand would always be one of the main methods that men and women used for remembering.

MARIA JOSÉ AZEVEDO SANTOS
University of Coimbra and Centre for the History of Society and Culture

Bibliography

ALTURO I PERUCHO, Jesús, *El Llibre Manuscrit a Catalunya. Origens i Esplendor*, Barcelona, Generalitat de Catalunya, 2001.
GOMES, Saul António, *In Limine Conscriptionis: Documentos, Chancelaria e Cultura no Mosteiro de Santa Cruz de Coimbra: Sécs. XII a XIV*, Viseu, Palimage, 2007.
SANTOS, Maria José Azevedo, *O Valor da Escrita em tempos de Inês de Castro*, pref. D. Manuel Díaz y Díaz, Montemor-o-Velho, Câmara Municipal de Montemor-o-Velho, 2005.
SIRAT, Colette, *Writing as Hand Work: A History of Handwriting in Mediterranean and Western Culture*, Turnhout, Brepols, 2006.
STIENNON, Jacques, *L'Écriture*, Turnhout, Brepols, 1995.

1089
From Romanesque to Gothic: Aesthetic Forms

The Saint Vincent Panels, now in the Museu Nacional de Arte Antiga in Lisbon, are attributed to Nuno Gonçalves, royal painter to King Afonso V. In their representation of a whole society arranged around Saint Vincent, the patron saint of Lisbon, they form a splendid group portrait, unusual in European art.

When Afonso Henriques was proclaimed the first king of Portugal in 1139, the predominant artistic forms of the new kingdom followed the Romanesque styles common in Europe at the time. In the innovations that followed the upheavals of around 1000, the Romanesque became what has been called the first great medieval

European style. Pilgrimages, and the new liturgy of the Gregorian reforms, help us to understand the spread of the new forms: they arose in France, and mobility of people and the role of Benedictine monks from the Abbey of Cluny in Burgundy, who used the new Roman liturgy, were the two most immediate reasons for the widespread acceptance of the Romanesque aesthetic.

Afonso Henriques's father, Count Henry, son of Henry of Burgundy and grand-nephew of Saint Hugh, Abbot of Cluny, was the first to encourage links with the French Benedictine world. This can be seen in the choice of Saint Gerald, a monk of Moissac, as Bishop of Braga, and Maurice Burdino, a monk of Limoges, as Bishop of Coimbra. It is also seen in the two earliest examples of Romanesque architecture in what would be the territory of Portugal: Braga Cathedral, begun before 1089 – the design of which resembles the Abbey of Sainte-Foy in Conques in France – and the monastery church of Saint Pedro de Rates, begun in 1096–1100. But together with these innovations, we can still see in both buildings some elements of the previously dominant Mozarabic style, about to be replaced by the Romanesque. In redesigning relatively small Mozarabic buildings, with their compartmentalized spaces, Romanesque architecture presented homogenous and continuous spaces, with a new sense of height and rhythm, necessary for the new Roman liturgy, along with a huge difference in architectonic organization.

The most impressive Romanesque buildings, both in their design and monumentality, are the cathedrals, such as those of Lisbon – begun shortly after the conquest of the city from the Muslims in 1147 – and of Coimbra, the present Old Cathedral, begun at the same time. Lisbon Cathedral, in the shape of a Latin cross, has three aisles of six spans and a prominent transept; the ceiling of the central aisle is a barrel vault, while the side aisles have groin vaulting, as was common in the European Romanesque. With its two towers defining the main façade, this design resembles Norman examples, which is understandable, given that the first Bishop of Lisbon, Gilbert of Hastings, and possibly the chief architect, Robert, were English. Robert also oversaw the building of Coimbra Cathedral; here, despite similarities with Lisbon, the central aisle has, instead of the triforium, a two-storey elevation with large galleries. This feature links Coimbra Cathedral to important European pilgrimage churches, such as Santiago de Compostela and Saint Sernin in Toulouse, even though it has no chancel with rotunda or radiating chapels.

Apart from cathedrals, Romanesque architecture in Portugal produced no other buildings on such a large scale. Although some Benedictine churches, such as Paço de Sousa, consecrated in 1088, or Travanca, from the mid-thirteenth century, have a Latin cross shape, three aisles with wooden ceilings, chancel with apse and vaulted semi-circular apse chapels, and even, as uniquely in Tomar, a Templar rotunda, Portugal is unusual in that almost 90 per cent of the churches are modest affairs, of a single aisle with wooden ceiling and a rectangular or more rarely polygonal or semi-circular chancel. Witnesses to an overwhelmingly rural landscape, they show the scarce resources of a region where the struggles of the so-called Reconquest and repopulation precluded more ambitious projects. Hence also the absence of large sculptural programs: apart from a few exceptions, such as the church at Bravães, in the north-east of the country, no sculptural portals have the grandeur and narrative complexity of nearby Santiago de Compostela. However, it is in the tympana, archivolts, capitals and modillions – the favoured sites for Romanesque sculpture – that the survival of earlier local sensibilities, along with the new iconographic and aesthetic forms, can best be seen. With the latter, anthropomorphic representations from Europe predominate, with biblical or secular figures, and zoomorphic images from Persian and Sassanid bestiaries. In the former, the designs are abstract and geometric, related to a Celtic world which survived in the north-east of the Peninsula, or non-figurative patterns based on a surviving Mozarabic aesthetic, maintaining the memory of the Muslim world which had come from North Africa.

This synthesis of influences, characteristic of the Romanesque in Portugal, is especially impressive in illumination, particularly in two manuscripts from the twelfth century, produced in the Monastery of Lorvão (Coimbra) – the Apocalypse and the Book of Birds (Livro das Aves). The former, the work of Egeias (1189), while influenced by French illumination, also adopted Mozarabic elements: its depiction of the beatitudes is one of the most original examples of this. The latter, a copy dated 1183 of *De avibus* by Hugh of Fouilloy, is an example of the movement of artists and works from France into the new Portuguese kingdom. This meeting of influences is also seen in the products of the Monastery of Santa Cruz, Coimbra, with around twenty manuscripts from the twelfth century and thirty-five from the thirteenth century showing clear connections to the south of France, by way of Saint Rufus of Avignon and the French pilgrimage abbeys such as Moissac and Limoges.

Another important site of production of illuminated manuscripts was the Cistercian Monastery of Alcobaça. Here, the ideals of austerity and simplicity in decoration propounded by Saint Bernard are visible in the almost total absence of figurative decoration, together with a predominantly abstract vocabulary: in a sometimes surprising way, this recalls Peninsula sensibilities, linked to the Celtic and Mozarabic worlds.

As throughout most of Europe, it was through Cistercian monks that the new Gothic architecture reached Portugal. In Alcobaça, the building of the monastery, begun in 1178, included a church with three long aisles of eight spans with ogival arches, a prominent transept and a rotunda with nine radiating chapels, a plan which, while replicating the Cistercian model of Clairvaux, is of a monumentality which Portuguese Romanesque cathedrals had not attained. Nevertheless, it was in two cathedrals that the first Gothic experiments on the model of the Île-de-France were put into practice: in Coimbra Old Cathedral, especially in the cloister, begun in 1218, and in Évora Cathedral, from the second half of the thirteenth century. The latter closely follows the model of Lisbon Cathedral, but ends by adopting shapes and proportions which make it a Gothic building. It is also in the cathedrals, throughout the fourteenth century, that some of the most impressive effects of International Gothic were created, such as the cloisters of the Cathedrals of Lisbon (which is similar to the contemporary Monastery of Alcobaça), of Porto and of Évora, and the new chancel of Lisbon's Romanesque cathedral – a rotunda with radiating chapels.

The greatest examples of Gothic architecture in Portugal, however, came from the new mendicant orders, especially Franciscans and Dominicans, who established themselves early. They transmitted important changes in the religious practice of lay people: they set up their establishments in cities as opposed to the rural roots of the monastic orders, their target being the marginal inhabitants of the largest urban centres. The ideal of simplicity and poverty practiced by Franciscans and Dominicans is mirrored in their buildings: churches with three aisles and a prominent transept and a chancel with from three to five graduated chapels. The rib vaulting was reserved for the chancel, with wood being used for the ceiling of the rest of the church. This mendicant architecture, which had its high point in the Graça Church in Santarém, is very simple and clear in its forms, as seen in the plan, the materials and the relative lack of sculpture. There is a large and imposing rose window in the main façade, with the lighting of the aisles increased by a row of small windows, resulting in a diffuse and homogenous light, creating ample, almost unified interior spaces. These characteristics link Portuguese Gothic architecture with a Mediterranean sensitivity which, in southern Europe (Italy, the south of France and eastern Spain), favoured similar solutions.

The fourteenth century ended with the architectural group that best exemplifies the evolution of the Gothic in Portugal: the Monastery of Batalha (Leiria), which was begun shortly before 1385, to fulfil a vow made by King John I. Both the plan of its church, a long Latin cross, with three aisles of eight spans, a transept and a chancel with five chapels, as well as its somewhat archaic aesthetic and constructive features, are typical of the work of the Portuguese architect Afonso Domingues, who was responsible for the project at the start. He was replaced in 1402 by Huguet, a Catalan: this involved the adoption of features of late International Gothic, thus aligning the building with contemporary European work. One of the most significant examples, apart from the innovative technical features such as the star vaulting in the chapter house and the Chapel of the Founder, is the elaborate decorative plan of the main door, similar to those of the great Gothic cathedrals, and first seen here in Portugal. In fact, the importance, both artistic and symbolic, of this whole monastery makes it the great workshop of the fifteenth century, with its innovative features spreading throughout the whole country. This synthesis of aesthetic forms characteristic of Portuguese Gothic art is seen particularly in funerary sculpture from the fourteenth and the fifteenth centuries. The former, which reaches its high point in the tombs of King Peter I (d. 1367) and Inês de Castro (d. 1355), in the Monastery of Alcobaça, has original features unique to Portugal, both in its iconography, featuring hunting scenes on the funerary chests, and in the representation of the deceased nobility. The second, on the contrary, as in the tombs of King John I (d. 1433) and Queen Philippa of Lancaster (d. 1415) in the Chapel of the Founder in the Monastery of Batalha, adopts an English and European formula, with the couple holding hands and the king in full armour, seen here for the first time in Portugal.

At the end of the Middle Ages, it was in the painting of altar-pieces that a golden age of Portuguese and European Gothic art came to fruition. The Saint Vincent Panels, attributed to Nuno Gonçalves, royal painter to King Afonso V, and now in Lisbon's Museu Nacional de Arte Antiga, represent a whole society arranged around Saint Vincent, the patron saint of Lisbon, thus forming a splendid group portrait, unusual in European art. It is a dense composition, focusing on various individuals, arranged in what seems to be a commissioned representation of the most typical strata of a Portuguese society totally immersed in the Discoveries, their faces individualized and highly expressive. While the influences of contemporary Flemish painting are obvious, the final work is one of the most successful expressions of the individualism and emergent humanism that Renaissance art was about to develop.

José Custódio Vieira da Silva
Nova University Lisbon

Bibliography

ALMEIDA, Carlos Alberto Ferreira de, *História da Arte em Portugal*, vol. 3, Lisbon, Alfa, 1986.

MIRANDA, Maria Adelaide, SILVA, José Custódio Vieira da, *História da Arte Portuguesa: Época Medieval*, Lisbon, Universidade Aberta, 1995.

REAL, Manuel Luís, "La sculpture figurative dans l'art roman du Portugal", in GRAF, Gerhard, *Portugal Roman*, vol. 1, Yonne, Zodiaque, 1986, pp. 33–75.

SILVA, José Custódio Vieira da, "Memória e imagem: reflexões sobre escultura tumular portuguesa (séculos XIII e XIV)", *Revista de História da Arte*, no. 1, 2005, pp. 46–81.

SILVA, José Custódio Vieira da, REDOL, Pedro, *The Monastery of Batalha*, London, Scala Books, 2007.

1128
Influences and External Relations in a County That Gave Birth to a Kingdom

The prestige and power of the knights and nobility, linked as always to the favour of prominent religious institutions, aided the processes of social organization in Terra Portucalense, making it a 'secure rear' to sustain the political ambitions of Count Henry within the monarchy.

The period succeeding the defeat in 1086 of Alfonso VI of León and Castile (1065–1109) by the Almoravids and their allies at Zalaca, proved to be difficult for this Christian king. Barely a year before, in 1085, he had achieved a remarkable victory with the conquest of Toledo. This was soon interpreted as the high point of a wider political, diplomatic and military enterprise, and an exceptional prize in symbolic terms, given the old city's status as the greatest memorial of the ancient kingdom of the Goths. At the end of 1086, however, the king had to continue his campaigns, attempting to limit the negative impact of his military failure and prevent a new reunification of Muslim Hispania. A significant act of Alfonso between late 1090 and early 1091 was to make Raymond of Burgundy (1090/1091–1107), husband of Urraca, Alfonso's daughter, the leader of Galicia and the counties of *Portucale* and Coimbra. In this, he aimed to continue the monarchy's political and ecclesiastical reorganization, and defend frontier territories from growing Almoravid pressure. By naming Raymond, now a member of the royal family, as ruler of Galicia, Alfonso VI aimed to take advantage of Frankish support.

The most important consequences of this restructuring, however, came from the nomination of Count Henry of Burgundy (1095/1096–1112) as governor of the territories between the rivers Minho and Tagus, that is, those same counties of *Portucale* and Coimbra, and of the recently-formed 'district' of Santarém. This measure was a response to the limited military results attained by Raymond. Henry was a member of the ducal house of Burgundy, and his family was linked to Raymond's by matrimony: he may have given signs of his talents before his marriage to Theresa, another daughter of the king. The 'renovated' county was the gift of a hereditary benefice, which implied that Henry paid homage to the ruler.

Equally important was the territorial configuration of the new political and administrative entity. The granting of a charter (*foral*) to Santarém, in 1095, was perhaps the first decision taken by Alfonso VI aiming to reinforce the southern boundary: there seems to have been a direct relation between this and the separation of the territories south of the river Minho from the county of Galicia. The two actions were linked, integrated in a wider vision seeking to establish a territorial unit to safeguard the frontier. The defence of Santarém and the line of the Mondego river would demand resources which could exceed the capacities of the two territories, showing the indispensable character of the association with the lands between the rivers Douro and Minho.

The evolution of Galicia and the lands south of Minho began now to diverge, particularly with regard to the ambitions of their respective political elites. This situation meant that the involvement in the anti-Islamic war of forces from Galicia and from the county of *Portucale* was not equal. In placing the counties of *Portucale* and Coimbra for the first time under the same authority, and associating them with Santarém, Alfonso VI precipitated the linking of these areas, promoting their ruling aristocracies, who were experienced in fighting wars against the Muslims. The course of events soon made the Lower Minho into an effective frontier, at the same time reducing the separation that the Douro river had represented for centuries. Henry must have seemed the right choice as lord of the county, and so he followed an identical course to that made by the lord of Galicia: he married a princess, joined the royal family, and received a great dominion and considerable ruling powers.

The first two charters granted by the 'chancellery' of the counties, those of Guimarães and of Constantim de Panoias, prove that Henry and Theresa rapidly exercised their wider authority. These documents show the priority given to the settlement of urban and rural communities within their domains. However, another fundamental line of the government soon appeared: the promotion of the regional aristocracy. It was with the help of these nobles that Henry organized and strengthened the administration of the *Terra Portucalense*, and it was from among them that he chose the major officials of his administration. He distributed benefits to them, and gave them political responsibilities, raising their prestige and reinforcing their roots in the territory and their investment in the war against the Muslims. In 1097 he and Theresa formally donated an important property situated south of river Ave to powerful Soeiro Mendes da Maia, which meant, in the words of José Mattoso, "an approval of the manorial regime, that is, the exercise of public authority over a territory removed from the jurisdiction of the king."

Henry also attended to ecclesiastical matters, such as trying to fill a vacancy in the Church of Braga dating from 1091. The diocese of Braga was fully restored by the appointment of Gerald (1097/1099–1108), a monk from Cluny, who, between 1099 and 1100, re-established the dignity of Braga as head of the ecclesiastical province of Galicia. After the death of the Bishop of Coimbra, Crescónio (1092–1098), another Frankish cleric, Maurice, was soon appointed to the diocese (1098–1108). He quickly established close links with Gerald, whom he succeeded at Braga between 1109 and 1118. This cycle of diocesan reconstruction ended, after the death of Count Henry, with the definitive restoration of the Church of Porto, signalled by the arrival of Bishop Hugh (1112/ 1114–1136), another Frank, the former archdeacon of Santiago de Compostela.

In replicating in his domains a set of powers similar to that of the monarchy, Count Henry needed the support of the great lords of *Portucale* and of the Church of Braga and other ecclesiastical institutions. Even though the boundaries of the ecclesiastical province were wider than those of the county, in fact it had come under the jurisdiction of the only established power in the interior of the Minho region. The government of

Henry and Theresa, like that of Raymond and Urraca in Galicia, had few if any parallels in León and Castile. The two sons-in-law of Alfonso VI received and used special powers, greater than those of other counts, ruling over large territories and acting as true representatives of the king.

These circumstances favoured the advancement of the manorial regime connected to the aristocracy. The prestige and power of the knights and nobility, linked as always to that of the most prominent ecclesiastical institutions, helped the processes of social organization in the *Terra Portucalense*, making it a 'secure rear' to support the political ambitions of Count Henry within the monarchy. Beyond the facts that testify to the Count's increasing part in the complex political chess game of the kingdom, this situation reflects the great questions of political reorganization which were affecting the Christian North of the Iberian Peninsula and indeed the whole of Western Europe in the final decades of the twelfth century and in the following century. A political system involving networks of communication was being established, although it varied considerably in intensity.

Evidence of this was the Pact of Succession between Raymond and Henry, involving the division of the kingdom after the death of the ruler, in mid-1105. At that time, the succession of Alfonso VI was already in need of clarifying. The Pact expressed the desire of various sectors of the aristocracy to find a solution to the problem, which would favour the Frankish party, and above all Counts Raymond and Henry. The terms outlined in the agreement, a true feudal pact, under the patronage of the powerful Abbot Hugh of Cluny, reveal the main factors that shaped the political and territorial structure of León and Castile.

After the death of Count Henry, Theresa took over the government of the County (1112–1128). The experience which she had gained beside her husband, and the autonomy of action she showed, for example in the intricate process of establishing the lands (*couto*) belonging to Braga Cathedral in 1109–1110, allowed her to follow previous policies. Like other prominent royal figures, she took part in political manoeuvres to build and demolish successive alliances and balances of power, most of them ephemeral and with limited consequences. She used the same instruments to maintain and strengthen her authority, favouring the great *Portucale* families, the dioceses and their bishops, and various monastic institutions and municipal communities, managing to strengthen a typically royal style of government within the territory of *Portucale*.

Based on this experience, Theresa was attracted to take part in questions of the monarchy, above all those in Galicia, reformulating alliances and redefining increasingly wider objectives. Events in 1116–1117, associating growing Muslim pressure in the southern territories with her intervention in Galicia, altered the scenario in northwestern Hispania. While the violence and the duration of the Almoravid offensive revealed the military weakness of the frontier, the operations that Theresa conducted north of the Minho river with the powerful Count of Trava, Pedro Froilaz, directed against her sister, Queen Urraca (1109–1126), make clear the role that the countess of *Portucale* was claiming for herself. This is also shown by the fact that Theresa was beginning to be called queen in letters produced in the county 'chancellery' from 1117 to 1128. This shows that she was certainly evoking her position as daughter of Alfonso VI, and as such the legitimate heir of a part of the imperial heritage.

The plan supported by Theresa, which sought to reconstruct the ancient and brief kingdom of Galicia (1065–1071), implied a close alliance with prominent groups of the Galician aristocracy. The presence and the manifestations of power by these lords beyond the river Minho, who had come to occupy important leadership positions, could hardly be compatible with the established rule of the *Portucalense* nobles, who had received so much from Count Henry. With the installation of the sons of Pedro Froilaz in the territory – especially Fernando Peres de Trava, documented in the county since 1121 and in the governance of Coimbra – it became clear, from a Galician point of view, how imperative was an alliance with Theresa. Fernando Peres married Theresa, with whom he had four daughters. In 1122 or earlier, his brother Bermudo Peres had married princess Urraca Henriques, daughter of Theresa and sister of Afonso Henriques. We can conclude that by 1121–1122, the lord of Trava had established his two most prominent sons in the *Terra Portucalense*, connecting them to the lineage of the counts and thus to the royal family. For Theresa these alliances were equally important, since the support of the Travas was an advantage in her conflict with her sister.

This new power relationship created unease among the *Portucalense* elites, threatened in their domains and their political and military interests. As José Mattoso has shown, the 'desertion' of the county government by the lords of the lands between the rivers Douro and Minho began in 1121, and in 1125 was almost total. A contributing factor was the confrontation between the Churches of Braga and Santiago de Compostela because of the definition of their ecclesiastical provinces and respective suffragan dioceses, accelerated by the election of Paio Mendes (1118–1137), a member of the Maia family, as Bishop of Braga.

The outcome of this extended imbroglio is well-known. On the 24th of June 1128, at São Mamede, near Guimarães, the troops of Theresa and Fernando Peres de Trava were defeated by the army of Afonso Henriques (1128–1185) and the *Portucalense* lords. The young prince, the son of Henry and Theresa, whose 'public life' had begun, symbolically, in the Cathedral of Zamora in 1125, when, in the presence of Archbishop Paio Mendes, he was made a knight, now became ruler of the County. From many points of view the internal conflicts of *Portucale* were nothing more than an extension, or a chapter, of the troubled political process which shaped the northern kingdoms of the Iberian Peninsula. However, from 1128 on, the question of *Portucale* developed in another direction. The period of the County ended and another history began, the History of Portugal.

Luís Carlos Amaral
CITCEM – Transdisciplinary Research Centre "Culture, Space and Memory",
University of Porto, and
CEHR – Centre of Religious History Studies, Catholic University of Portugal

Bibliography

AMARAL, Luís Carlos, *Formação e Desenvolvimento do Domínio da Diocese de Braga no Período da Reconquista (Século IX–1137)*, Porto, Faculdade de Letras da Universidade do Porto, 2007.

AMARAL, Luís Carlos, BARROCA, Mário Jorge, *A Condessa-Rainha Teresa*, Lisbon, Círculo de Leitores, 2012.

MATTOSO, José, "1096–1325", in MATTOSO, José (dir.), *História de Portugal*, vol. II, Lisbon, Círculo de Leitores, 1993, pp. 9–309.

Idem, *Identificação de Um País: Ensaio sobre as Origens de Portugal: 1096–1325*, 5th ed., 2 vols., Lisbon, Estampa, 1995.

SOARES, Torquato de Sousa, *Formação do Estado Português (1096–1179)*, Trofa, Sólivros de Portugal, 1989.

1128
Fighting in the Name of Faith:
Military Orders in Portugal

Not even a home-grown order such as Évora-Avis, escaped the trend, as is evident in its observation of the rule, customs and models of Calatrava and in the intervention of the Spanish master in Avis. The phenomenon was even more accentuated in Santiago, with the Convent of Alcácer subject to the master of Uclés. No less significant was the circulation of brethren between the Iberian kingdoms and the transfer of resources to other battle fronts.

On the 19th of March 1128, the Countess Theresa received, in Braga, Raymond Bernard, friar of the Temple. He was not one of those that had arrived from Jerusalem with the master, Hugues de Payns in 1127, but a knight recruited recently, perhaps in Perpignan, who had been entrusted with the mission of seeking support in Hispania. There he presented himself on behalf of the master, bringing with him recommendations from the king and the patriarch of Jerusalem, who had both ratified the Templars' religious vocation at the Council of Nablus (1120), and supported the Master's journey to the West. Despite the success of that trip, and the importance of those credentials (if Raymond in fact carried them with him), they would not have guaranteed him an interested audience. For various reasons, Alfonso VII of León and Castile was not very enthralled with the new militia, although in Zamora, he did confirm the donation of Soure made by his aunt, Theresa, in March 1128. For someone that was not a particularly illustrious visitor and who represented a small community that, till then, was not very well known, the welcome he received in Braga and the support that was offered will have come as a surprise. In addition to the castle of Soure and the territories it controlled (bequeathed by the countess in her will, though she was prepared to hand it over in life), we know of another collective donation, which was undated but from the period and analogous to others made to the Temple. In this case, the countess and around twenty or so magnates granted the Templars control of the Fonte Arcada in Penafiel and many other properties in the Minho and Galiza. Such general enthusiasm reveals the interest in what was going on in the Holy Land, and an appreciation of those that risked their religious life by bearing arms, although this lifestyle had not been formally recognized by the Church of Rome. Both donations were made to the knights of the Temple of Solomon in order to ensure the defence of the Holy Land.

Though there was a certain coherence in the patrimony (a castle on the border and holdings in the rearguard), it is not clear if Raymond took possession of it, whether for lack of manpower or because of the political tension in the county, on the eve of the Battle of São Mamede. By the autumn of 1128, he had already returned to France, without waiting for Afonso Henriques to make him a lay associate (*confrater*) of the order and secure the possession of Soure with a new donation.

We know little about the brothers' actions in these years, though it is probable that they were limited to the collection of rents to be sent abroad. The order only acquired fame with the first procurator of the Temple, Hugo de Martone, who in 1143 set up a community in Soure. This was when they became involved in the struggle against the Muslims in the unsuccessful defence of Soure in 1144, and in the conquest of Santarém. There is no reference to them in the context of the siege of Lisbon. Their war efforts attracted the attention of the faithful. In 1143, the Council of Valladolid put the knights of the Temple and their men under its protection, and the donations soon began to multiply. With the handing over of the castles of Longroiva, Mogadouro and Penas Roias in 1145, and a hospital in Braga the same year, the brothers' vocation became more clearly defined. After the conquest of Santarém, the king granted them the ecclesiastical rights over the town, which were later exchanged for the lands of Ceras-Tomar in 1159. There followed the fortresses of Idanha and Monsanto in 1165, and the lands controlled by the castle of Zêzere in 1169.

By this time, the Temple's territorial extent had become more or less established. In addition to the lands they controlled in the North (they had a house set up in Braga since 1148) and in the region structured by the towns of Soure, Ega and Pombal (fortified by the friars in 1156), their main centres were in the Tagus valley. These would later be reinforced following the exchange of the Douro castles for Idanha and Açafa, and the construction of another Castelo Branco, as a tribute to the fortress of the same name in the county of Tripoli, in present-day Syria. It was in that region that Gualdim Pais built the castles of Tomar, Almourol and Cardiga in 1171, and restored other fortresses. Together these were responsible for the defence of the Tagus frontier, put to the test during the Almohad incursions at the end of the twelfth century, when Tomar was besieged for six days.

The Order of the Temple was not the only witness to the local interest in the Holy Land. The Hospitallers, also placed under the protection of the Council of Valladolid, had been in the kingdom for a long time too. They had preceded the Templars, but we don't know exactly when they took possession of the Benedictine monastery of Leça, granted by the countess Theresa. There is no evidence that they were there in 1112, but the donation is unlikely to have been much later than that and probably occurred soon after the friars became established in Castile in 1113 (when Theresa's sister gave them a village in Salamanca). This is not completely certain, as we don't know the monastic affiliation of the superior of Leça between 1114 and 1122. However, his title on that second date (*servus pauperum*) and the fact that this diploma was kept in the Hospitallers' registry suggest that they had entered the monastery in the middle of the previous decade.

Based a long way from the Muslim border but not far from the coast, the brothers of the Hospital devoted themselves to collecting alms and resources for the Holy Land, and serving the poor and infirm (which was their primary mission). In the middle of the century, they were managing a hospital in Braga, with a church and cemetery attached, for the burial of the brothers and the faithful. In these years, their actions and their patrimony – acquired through alms and legacies bequeathed in wills or from fragmentary and dispersed donations – were concentrated in the regions north of the Douro and Mondego. A survey carried out in 1220 and 1258 reveal their importance and distribution, as well as the extent of the support given to the Order of the Hospital by the king, nobles and local communities from where many of the brethren were recruited. This was where the convent and some of the oldest commanderies were located, such as Aboim (1146), although there was also a house in Coimbra and another in Lisbon by the end of the 12th century.

As in the Holy Land, the Hospital only belatedly converted to military functions and became involved in border skirmishes. The change occurred in around 1150, but it was a long adaptation, without local repercussions, until the knight-brothers were cited in the statutes of 1182. It is possible that the process was accelerated by the end of the truce with the Almohads in 1178, as the Hospitallers had their first military operation in Silves in 1189, receiving from Sancho I a vast territory near the Tagus in 1194 to settle and defend. There they raised the castle of Belver, in memory of the Hospitaller castle in the Jordan valley. Contributing to the defence of the Tagus valley, they were involved in border fighting, in the conquest of Alcácer in 1217, and in the campaigns of the Provincial Prior Afonso Peres Farinha, which were decisive for the gaining control of the upper Guadiana valley. With the support of João Peres de Aboim, this prior founded there the Convent da Vera Cruz do Marmelar in 1268, where a relic of the Holy Cross was housed, which the Hospitallers took to the Battle of Salado in 1340.

The belated involvement of the Hospitallers in these combats, combined with the Templars' lack of interest in the lands south of the Tagus promised by the king in 1169, was conducive to the fixation of other military orders of Spanish origin. The Order of Santiago, organized in Cáceres under the patronage of the king of León in 1170, established itself in Portugal before Rome had approved its Rule in 1175. In 1172, it received from the king Arruda and the castle of Monsanto, and also the fortresses of Abrantes, Almada and Alcácer between 1173 and 1175. As in the neighbouring kingdoms, the militia was responsible for the defence of the Tagus border, but the lack of resources, or the fact that these were concentrated in León, meant that the castles of Abrantes and Monsanto could not be maintained. Suspicions about the militia's loyalties to León increased rapidly with the support of the Leonese king, who defeated Sancho I in Ciudad Rodrigo in 1179, and indeed it is likely that the Crown had confiscated all the property of the order in Portugal.

With a new donation from Sancho I in 1186, this time of the castles of Arruda, Almada, Palmela and Alcácer, on the condition of service and obedience, the brothers of Santiago were accommodated on the Setúbal peninsula, committing themselves to the defence of Lisbon, and moving away from the Leonese border. In Alcácer, they ordered their first house and, after the withdrawal from the border to the Tagus line, invested in the recovery of Palmela (1194) and Alcácer (1217), transferring from one to the other the convent associated with the kingdom's commandery. Later, they played a decisive role in the conquest of the South, along the valleys of the Sado and Guadiana in the direction of Aljustrel, Mértola, Seville and the Algarve. The success of these operations, in which other knights also participated, led Paio Peres Correia, Commander of Alcácer, to become Grand Commander of Castile and be elected Master of Santiago between 1242 and 1275. With this trajectory, he bore witness to the transfer of men and resources between kingdoms, but also to the tensions created by the affirmation of the authority of the kings in a military order that had its central structure outside the country.

The other order present in the kingdom, and the only one of Portuguese origin, was known as the Militia of Évora, and afterwards of Avis. It had its origins in a brotherhood of knights, perhaps organized after the conquest of the city, which converted into a religious order, adopting the Benedictine Rule, when it was placed under the patronage of the king and endowed with a Master chosen by him, in 1176. It was then given the castles of Évora and Coruche, and other belongings in Santarém, associating the defence of the city with the overseeing of the accesses to the Tagus and the protection of the southern and southeastern border. When pressured by the Holy See, which was hostile to the proliferation of religious rules, the Évora Militia joined up with the Order of Calatrava and adopted its rule in 1187, becoming subject to the powers of visit and correction of its masters and becoming one of the first affiliiates of that order.

Despite commitments with Estremadura, through the donations of Alpedriz and the castles of Mafra and Alcanede, and donations from the faithful in other places, the order did not leave Évora, which suffered two sieges, resisting, isolated south of the Tagus (1191). In it were installed the convent with a chapel, hostel and cemetery, which accepted the poor, prisoners and pilgrims. From there, it promoted the occupation of the territory, establishing in Coruche and Benavente its oldest commanderies and enlivening the village of Avis (1211), where the convent had moved to. Despite a presence in the conquests of Silves in 1189 and Alcácer in 1217, it was in that region that the brothers launched their most significant actions, making part of the cavalcade that devastated the Guadalquivir in the 1220s, and the confrontations organized in the Guadiana valley. Their military effort extended to the limits of the kingdom, as they took part in the Battle of Alarcos, in 1195, and in the conquest of Seville in 1248, as well as in the subjugation of the Algarve.

It was the ideal of service to Christ, the Church and the faithful that prevented the military orders from completely fulfilling their mission within the space of the kingdom. Our perception of this has been tainted by centuries of national history, and also by archives selected and transmitted by the Crown. Not even a home-grown order, like Évora-Avis, could escape the trend, as is clear in its observation of the rule, customs and models of Calatrava and in the intervention of the Castilian master in Avis. The phenomenon was accentuated even more in Santiago, with the Convent of Alcácer subject to the master of Uclés, who received the professions, supplied the commanderies represented the order and granted the charters. No less insignificant was the circulation of the brethren between the Iberian kingdoms, or the transfer of resources to other battle fronts, aspects that were only staunched by the opposition of the kings in the fourteenth century, when the Portuguese branch of the militia became autonomous.

This went even further in the case of the Templars and Hospitallers, whose houses in the kingdom were not autonomous but part of networks managed from Jerusalem. Various foreigners passed through them, from the provincial masters of the Temple (Richard, Bellomonte, Fouque), to the visitors of the two orders (Reimondo, Fulcher) and simple brothers (Iterio, Ravani, Gobert, Galcerand), following the example of Jaufré de Pierrevert, who professed in Castelo Branco and then left for Acre in 1275. There were also native Portuguese who went east (Gualdim Pais, Afonso de Portugal, Afonso Farinha and Gonçalo Pereira), not to mention the later journeys of João Fernandes, Vasco Fernandes and Lourenço Martins (the latter made two trips to Acre in 1282 and 1290). Money, horses and provisions were also dispatched, reconciling local commitments with the duty to provide assistance to the Holy Land. Of those consignments there is little evidence – the monies of the Templars and Hospital retained by Sancho I in 1188; the 500 silver marks given to Francon de Bort, Temple visitor, in 1272; but they were considerable, like the 40 mounts and burdens that Lourenço Martins took in 1282. In the 14th century, these dispatches lost importance because of the loss of Holy Land and suppression of the Temple, replaced by a national order, the Order of Christ, in 1319. In any case, these expeditions of men and resources did not disappear and remained in the Hospital in the following centuries, then destined for Rhodes and Malta.

Despite being the heir of the Temple, the Order of Christ brought some novelties. It arose as a national order, circumscribed by the frontiers of the kingdom and subject only to the visit and correction of the abbot of Alcobaça, with statutes (1319–1326) that left it at the mercy of the monarchs. Though the phenomenon dated from earlier, the creation of the order accentuated the Crown's control over the militias, in a process that extended to Avis and Santiago in 1327. It was also manifested in the Hospital, but at another pace, given that order's international structure and relations with the Mediterranean. Subjection to the Crown forced the orders to adapt to new missions, different from those foreseen by their founders. Amongst them, the most significant was the brothers' participation in combats between Christians, the first manifestations of which date from the end of the thirteenth century, but which multiplied over the course of the fourteenth, particularly in the context of the wars with Castile. In the same way, the masters of the orders began to be elected from amongst men that were trusted by the monarchs, which gave them greater influence at court and in service to the Crown. Royal interference soon started to intensify, with the election of two minors as masters of the Orders of Avis (in 1364) and of Christ (in 1372), both members of the royal family.

This did not mean that dedication to the service of God and the faithful, and the struggle against Islam, disappeared from the brothers' life horizon. This was in part because the wars between Christians sometimes began as struggles against heresy, but also because the king's service absorbed some of the functions and universality particular to the service of God. From the beginning of the fourteenth century, the kingdom's coastline became a frontier of Christendom, the defence and expansion of which were supported by Rome and financed by ecclesiastic tithes. There is little evidence of the collaboration of the orders in these undertakings, though in 1410, the master of the Order of Christ cultivated the memory of former combats against the Moors of Africa and Granada, and a text of this period associates the brothers of Santiago with attacks carried out by ships of the Crown off African coasts. In the 1380s, the Hospitallers had also reclaimed control of the vanguard of the faith, proposing to regenerate the Hispanic knighthood and with it free Christendom from the Muslim yoke. On the date of the conquest of Ceuta in 1415, the programme was not forgotten and was taken up again by the Crown, binding that city to the opening-up of a route to Jerusalem.

Despite the power that it exercised, and the handing over of the rank of Master to the princes of the realm, the Crown was unable to reform the orders and commit them to the defence of Ceuta and the war against the infidels. If masters and knight-brothers participated in the liberation of Ceuta, the attack on Tangiers and the later conquests, they did so in an individual capacity, without allowing the war in Africa to become their new mission. None of the projects to establish convents of the military orders in Ceuta (in 1456, 1462 and 1472, all on royal initiative and supported by Rome) ever came to fruition. Both the masters and the knight-brothers reacted against all of them, recalling that the militias had been founded to defend the realm and not to do battle in Morocco. The brothers' resistance was only challenged when King Manuel I resumed the measures already known from John I and Henry the Navigator and created new commanderies to reward the brothers that had done service in Africa. Thereafter, the orders' resources were associated to the developments of the Crown's overseas policies.

Luís Filipe Oliveira
University of Algarve and Institute of Medieval Studies,
Faculty of Social Sciences and Humanities, Nova University Lisbon

Bibliography

BÉRIOU, Nicole, JOSSERAND, Philippe (ed.), *Prier et Combattre. Dictionnaire Européen des Ordres Militaires au Moyen Âge*, Paris, Fayard, 2009.

BRONSTEIN, Judith, *The Hospitallers and the Holy Land: Financing the Latin East, 1187–1274*, Woodbridge, Boydell, 2005.

DEMURGER, Alain, *Chevaliers du Christ. Les Ordres Religieux-Militaires au Moyen Âge (XI–XVI Siècle)*, Paris, Seuil, 2002.

OLIVAL, Fernanda, *The Military Orders and the Portuguese Expansion (15th to 17th Centuries)*, Peterborough, Baywolf Press, 2018.

OLIVEIRA, Luís Filipe, "As ordens militares", in SOUSA, Bernardo Vasconcelos e (ed.), *Ordens Religiosas em Portugal. Das Origens a Trento: Guia Histórico*, 3rd ed. rev. and expanded, Lisbon, Livros Horizonte, 2016, pp. 453–502.

1140

Afonso Henriques, *Portugalensium Rex*, Son of Theresa of León and Henry of Burgundy

Foreign settlers, religious orders, military orders, tradesmen, scholars – all were multi-directional subjects and agents of trans-Pyrenean contacts; while the turn southwards to include spaces that had experienced a much longer and more entrenched Muslim presence contributed to the assimilation of an important legacy of Arab-Islamic civilization.

As the son of Henry of Burgundy and Theresa of León, Afonso Henriques brought together political traditions arising from the autonomization of the great fiefdoms of France and the claims to political power of the heirs of the Leonese monarch. He had only just been born when his father took advantage of the conflicts between Urraca and her husband Alfonso I, king of Aragon, to try enlarge the Portuguese fiefdom, something that was achieved when Urraca ceded the territories of Astorga and Zamora. Henry died shortly afterwards in Astorga, which meant that the government of the Portucalense County passed to Theresa. When Afonso was nearly eight years old, his mother began to title herself queen of that west Galician territory, which had been awarded to Garcia in 1067 following the division of the kingdom of León between the sons of Ferdinand the Great. While no one seemed to question the royal title, the chances of conquering Galicia were slim, even after the support of the Galician high nobility had been secured through the mediation of the Trava brothers and the seductive manoeuvring of the archbishop of Santiago. The result of Portuguese discontent, both ecclesiastical and nobiliarchic, acquired greater visibility in 1128, when the parties which by then had formed came face to face in the Battle of

São Mamede, in Guimarães. Theresa and the Trava were defeated by the Portuguese nobles, who had managed to attract the young Afonso Henriques over to their cause. He finally came to power at the age of nineteen. The following decade was possibly the most decisive of his life; for he had tried to forge his own path, not wishing to be so dependent on Leonese power games and claims to Galicia. This ultimately distanced him from the strategies of both Henry and Theresa, although, in the first instant, he seemed to be continuing his mother's policy in relation to Galicia. In fact, he was there in 1130, and perhaps in subsequent years, but definitely in 1136–1137, when he tried to conquer Tui. It was in this context, in the first years of the same decade, that he ordered the building of the castle of Celmes, north of the Galician stretch of the river Lima, near Xinzo de Limia.

Despite this presence in Galicia, or the north of Portugal, in the context of a confrontation with the Castilian-Leonese king, Afonso Henriques's attention had also started to move southward, and he was soon spending more time in Coimbra. The dynamism of that city, which was a receptor centre for religious and military transformations nature from the west and even from the east, was connected to the quality of its defensive structure, thanks to the city walls and the imposing Arab *alcáçova* – though this did not prevent him reinforcing some of the more sensitive zones (such as the area around the Sun Gate) with towers, and in this case, with a castle and keep. Till the beginning of the 1140s, these defensive concerns extended as far as some villages south of the Mondego, involving the reconstruction of castles, and political and administrative reorganization enshrined in respective charters of places like Miranda do Corvo and Penela. The Templars were involved in the process, following the confirmation in 1129 that Soure would pass into their control.

In 1135, repeating Celmes, but this time on the southern border, the future king established an advanced guard in Leiria, building there a first castle on an imposing spur which overlooked one of the main access roads to Coimbra. In other words, Afonso Henriques's initial efforts on the Galician border were subsequently enlarged by the expectation of a similar advance oriented towards the Almoravid lands to the south.

That advance took place in the second half of the decade, both from Leiria and by a more inland route, which followed the Rabaçal valley towards Tomar, a route that connected both the reconquered lands of Fernão Cativo, and the raided region of Ladeia. Irrespective of the precise date of these events, which are difficult to gauge, they marked the resumption of the offensive attitude that had led to the conquest of Coimbra in 1064, a course of action that was quickly confirmed with the victory in Ourique in 1139. Leaving aside the question of localizing this confrontation with the Moors, and their military relevance, it is clear that this combat was considered to be of great importance by both contemporary and later generations. In fact, it was from this moment on that Afonso Henriques began appearing in the documentation as the King of the Portuguese (*portugalensium rex*). It is this fact, full of future consequences, that should be retained. Claiming the royal title after a military victory against the Muslims, the prince Afonso connected it to territorial conquest from the boundary with the Muslim world, basing it, unlike his mother, on the possibility of Portugal's expansion in the direction of al-Andalus. This was the objective he sought and which started to define his image as someone that was less indecisive about which political strategy to follow and more focused on the task of drawing a new map for Iberian Portugal. Organizing military expeditions from Coimbra, Afonso Henriques gradually obtained significant victories in his expansion south. In 1147, he captured the cities of Santarém and Lisbon, amongst others. In the case of the latter, he was able to count on the decisive help of a contingent of crusaders, who had come by sea from northern Europe and were heading to the Holy Land in the context of the Second Crusade. By this time, Lisbon was already one of the most important cities on the far west of the Iberian Peninsula, and with its size, location and dynamism, it was soon to become the "head of the kingdom". The southward advance into Islamic dominions did not extinguish the new Portuguese king's desire to also incorporate territories from the kingdom of León. From 1157 onwards, when Alfonso VII died, and the kingdoms of Castile and León separated again, Afonso Henriques battened down in Galicia with plans of conquest, even managing to occupy Tui in 1159. Despite the truce celebrated with Ferdinand II of León, the Portuguese king resumed his attacks north of the River Minho in 1165. Salamanca also came into his sights in 1163. Looking in several directions at once, always with a view to incorporating new cities, he moved to Badajoz in 1169, to assist Gerald the Fearless (the leader of a guerrilla band that had taken Évora four years before and handed it over to him). However, this attempt to conquer Badajoz from the Muslims resulted in a resounding defeat. What is more, Afonso Henriques was seriously wounded and taken prisoner by Ferdinand II, who had allied himself with the Muslims in the hope of cutting off the Portuguese expansion into areas that would threaten the Leonese *reconquista* to the south. This "Badajoz disaster" put an end to the military actions of the Portuguese king, as he was probably unable to mount, or even walk, thereafter.

In any case, the balance of conquests marked the integration into the kingdom of important territories between the Mondego and the Tagus, as well as some extensions south of that river, as in the case of Évora. This expansion, incorporating differentiated regions in its physical and civilizational matrices, and above all, acquiring dynamic urban centres, proved fundamental for a composition that constituted the base on which to construct, make viable and guarantee the maintenance of the kingdom of Portugal. The Christian North, which was essentially rural and warfaring, was now joined with the Islamic south, which was more urban and commercial. The tension between the two gave rise to an independent political entity – a kingdom – which gradually cemented the aggregation of its parts, in what would become a global cohesion.

Although the legitimacy of the new Portuguese kingdom rested essentially on the abilities, victories and conquests of its warrior-in-chief, these did not guarantee immediate or unanimous recognition of his royal status. The founder of the monarchy would see his title formally recognised by Alfonso VII, king of León, in 1143, following a meeting at Zamora, at which a papal legate, Cardinal Guido de Vico, was also present. But this summit yielded a conveniently mutual ambiguity. Alfonso VII of León and Castile recognised his cousin as king of Portugal, but declared himself emperor, thereby positioning himself above the Portuguese king and increasing his own prestige (for as emperor, he would now count that king amongst his vassals). Afonso Henriques, for his part, at the same time as he saw himself recognised as king by his Leonese cousin, quietly made a deal with the papal representative to pay vassalage only to the pope, promising to pay the Holy See an annual tribute of four ounces of gold. By recognising the pope as his only lord, he thereby rejected any kind of subordination to Alfonso VII. But this was not enough to ensure the pope's immediate recognition of his royal title. In the long diplomatic battle that ensued, the figure of João Peculiar acquires particular protagonism, as the most important counsellor of the Portuguese king. João Peculiar had probably been educated in France, and was connected to the foundation of the Monastery of Santa Cruz in Coimbra. He also had extensive experience of contacts with the pontifical Curia. He was elected bishop of Porto in 1136 and appointed archbishop of Braga in 1139. Finally, he was present and active in many of the decisive moments for the international recognition of the royalty of Afonso Henriques: at the negotiations with Alfonso VII, in the affirmation of the provision of unique vassalage to the Holy See and also in the negotiations of Afonso Henriques's marriage in 1146 to Matilda of Maurienne, of the House of Savoy. When he died in 1175, João Peculiar's actions with the papacy had not yet borne fruit. But this came in 1179, when pope Alexander III recognised Afonso Henriques as king with the bull *Manifestis probatum.* Much of this political and diplomatic victory of the founder of the Portuguese monarchy was due to the intervention of the bishop of Braga. The content of the pontifical document extended the royal rights to Afonso I's successors, ensuring the recognition of the Portuguese sovereigns by the highest religious authority of Latin Christendom. The Crown of Portugal thus took its place amongst the monarchies of the medieval West.

During Afonso Henriques's governance, numerous foreign influences made themselves felt in Portugal, as an integral part of the West, and more particularly, of the Iberian Peninsula. In addition to those already mentioned, (such as the family background of founder of the kingdom, and others, such as religion, the arts, writing, the language, etc.), we should remember that many individuals and entities came here from abroad, playing an important role in the settlement of the country, application of farming techniques and in the activation of relations of various types with trans-Pyrenean Europe. Foreign settlers, religious orders, military orders, tradesmen, scholars – all were multidirectional subjects and agents of trans-Pyrenean contacts; while the turn southwards to include spaces that had experienced a much longer and more entrenched Muslim presence contributed to the assimilation of an important legacy of Arab-Islamic civilization. The royal claims of Afonso Henriques and the acquiescence of Alfonso VII gave shape to what became in the mid 12th century, the youngest Iberian Christiam Kingdom, a kingdom which was from the outset, part of the European west, and would continue to be so over the centuries, but which had, since the Middle Ages, arisen as a vital link between various points in a world that was becoming ever more global.

António Resende de Oliveira
Centre for the History of Society and Culture,
University of Coimbra
and
Bernardo Vasconcelos e Sousa
Institute of Medieval Studies, Faculty of Social Sciences and Humanities,
Nova University Lisbon

Bibliography

MATTOSO, José, *D. Afonso Henriques,* Lisbon, Círculo de Leitores, 2006.

Idem, "Entre oriente e ocidente: contactos de Portugal com o mundo nas origens da nacionalidade", in BARROCA, Mário Jorge (coord.), *No tempo de D. Afonso Henriques: Reflexões sobre o Primeiro Século Português,* Porto, Centro de Investigação Transdisciplinar Cultura, Espaço e Memória, 2017, pp. 11–25.

Idem, *Obras Completas,* vols. II–III, Lisbon, Círculo de Leitores, 2001.

OLIVEIRA, A. Resende de, "Do reino da Galiza ao reino de Portugal (1065–1143)", *Revista de História das Ideias*, vol. 28, 2007, pp. 17–37.

1146
Marrying for Love of the Crown

The need for alliances at times of crisis also led to rushed marriages, particularly when there was a need to resolve a conflict between two belligerent territories or to join the forces of two kingdoms against a third. For example, King John I of Portugal (1385–1433) married Phillippa of Lancaster, four years before the papal bull was issued that dispensed him from the ecclesiastical vows that he had made before.

It might seem strange to twenty-first century readers that, for centuries, any treaty Portugal entered into with another friendly kingdom would contain a clause establishing a matrimonial alliance between members of the two royal families. Associating a country's interests to a contractual social practice between two individuals does not form part of the framework of understanding underpinning most contemporary societies, or at least not those that are used to living within a republican political logic. But in fact, it is the very history of the evolution of monarchic thought that justifies this convergence between the interests of the kingdom and those of its incumbents.

From the sixth century onwards, Europe was divided into territorial circumscriptions ruled by kings, princes, dukes or counts, who considered the space over which they exercised jurisdiction to be their own property. In fact, the term kingdom was understood as the territory of a king, as postulated in the *Siete Partidas del Rey Don Alfonso el Sabio* (c. 1252–1265). When this was enlarged to include neighbouring regions, the king's jurisdiction was extended to the inhabitants of that zone, who were effectively transferred from one kingdom to another, obliged to become subjects of another lord.

But if this was the way the space was conceptualized by those that ruled those territories militarily and politically, it is natural that their actions in relation to other kingdoms should also reflect this personalized patrimonial thinking. The forging of relations of friendship and reciprocal assistance between different peoples (who were sometimes close and shared related languages, though at other times were separated by physical distance and different customs and tongues) only made sense if they were cemented by the creation of personal, even kinship, bonds between the families of the monarchs, dukes or counts.

It was within this political and mental framework that the dynastic alliances of the Portuguese monarchs began to take shape from the twelfth century onwards. The first king of Portugal – who had made himself king, according to some sources of the period – managed, in 1146, to arrange a marriage with Matilda, the daughter of Amadeus, count of Maurienne and Savoy, and niece of Louis VII, king of France, in the context of the Second Crusade, launched in reaction to the seizing of the city of Edessa in Syria in 1144. His successors, however, sought to espouse the daughters of other Iberian kings. It is in these early practices of establishing what would later be called international relations that we find the idea of a family, strongly anchored in the notion of the monarchy, which, in a concerted way, would collaborate to ensure the success of the lineage that ruled a territory. Such connections had not existed in the early days of the formation of the European kingdoms, when the king was chosen by his peers – as is shown by the Fuero Juzgo, of Visigoth inspiration (1241) – but had become essential when most monarchies had established themselves as hereditary regimes. With this, the same family would occupy power generation after generation, favouring kinship proximity to the person of the previous king, and opting (from a particular moment onwards) to place the deceased monarch's eldest son in the seat left vacant by him.

However, even when it was indeed the first-born son that inherited his father's place, the remaining sons still had roles to play for the sake of the monarchy to which all of them belonged. The boys formed a reserve in case something happened to the heir, and were his successors in turn, by order of birth. As for the girls, husbands were chosen for them who would enable them to retain their status as the daughters of a king (that is to say, men who were themselves kings, princes, or powerful dukes), which permitted their father's kingdom to make alliances with other kingdoms. After they were married, some were called to play a role of relative importance from the diplomatic perspective, since, with their knowledge of the language, and their personal and affective relations with whoever ruled their kingdom of origin (whether their father, brother, a cousin, etc), they were privileged interlocutors in sensitive matters. Sometimes, these ladies would use their family connections to confront their husbands if they felt that they had been shown a lack of consideration (or even been mistreated) by him, his family or their adopted kingdoms. The poet Luís de Camões, in the so-called "beautiful Mary" episode of the *Lusiads*, describes how Mary of Portugal, Queen of Castile, represented her husband Alfonso XI, before her father, Afonso IV of Portugal, in order to persuade him to participate in the Battle of Salado in 1340.

These matrimonial alliances, though constituting matters of international politics, were also forged in the conviction that, through a sense of duty on the part of the royal couple, they would produce many common descendants', able to maintain the communal interests of both parties. It is not surprising that one of the earliest collections of legislative documents theorizing about the exercise of royal power, the so-called *Siete Partidas*, drawn up on the orders of Alfonso X, king of Castile, (1252–1284), also includes a "mirror for princes", dedicated to advising the royal couple about the qualities, behaviour and harmony that they should display as an example to others, and their role in the education of their children. Thus, it was natural that special importance be given to the marriage and choice of a bride for the heir to the throne. The matrimonial process was normally longwinded and could suffer various setbacks from both sides until its final consummation. Chroniclers' narratives reveal the steps that had to be taken up to the wedding, with the presence of the betrothed couple. Messengers were sent (usually from the bridegroom's family to the kingdom of the intended bride), who would put forward the case – mostly in terms of the economic and/or territorial rewards to be enjoyed by the future queen or her kingdom of origin – after which a marriage contract was signed. Sometimes the marriage would take place immediately by proxy, in the presence of the bride, in which the betrothal was celebrated (the marriage of words or sponsalia). Despite the apparent seriousness of the act, this marriage of words could be repeated with various candidates, as indeed happened on a number of occasions. We might remember the various betrothals to which the only daughter of King Ferdinand (r. 1367–1383) was subjected, before she finally ended up marrying King Juan I of Castile, who was already a widower. The need for alliances at times of crisis also led to rushed marriages, particularly when there was a need to resolve a conflict between two belligerent territories or to join the forces of two kingdoms against a third. For example, King John I of Portugal (1385–1433) married Phillippa of Lancaster, daughter of the Duke of Lancaster (who was also a candidate for the throne of Castile via his second wife) four years before the papal bull was issued dispensing him from the ecclesiastical vows that he had made before. There were other occasions when future queens were unable to arrive in their husbands' kingdoms for a long time; one example was that of Constance Manuel, the wife of the future King Peter, who was sequestered and prevented from leaving Castile in a climate of war (1336–1340).

Even when the couple had already been married by words, the process was incomplete until carnal union had taken place, and could be still annulled. By then, various economic commitments would already have been signed, corresponding to property exchanged at the time of the marriage. Until Roman law became the dominant influence, at the end of the Middle Ages and in Early Modern period, it was very common for the husband to transfer some of his property to his wife upon marriage, apparently to safeguard her economic situation in case she was prematurely widowed. It was also natural that the father of the bride, wanting to help the young couple start out on their life together, should give them some property.

The monarchy and its protagonists seem to have been of little interest for twentieth century scholars because, for over a century, the only attempts to understand the Queens that were the consorts of the Portuguese monarchs were the nineteenth-century studies by Frederico Francisco de la Figanière and Francisco da Fonseca Benevides, with some contributions from J. P. Franco Monteiro. These authors had surveyed written and material documentation in order to gather information about the lives of these queens, and occasionally published documents relating to their assets and actions that had been lost in time. They realized early on that the status that these landowning ladies enjoyed in certain towns gave them jurisdictional rights, and allowed them to exercise a certain authority over their populations, particularly from the judicial perspective. The acknowledgement of the capacities of these Queen-consorts, in Portugal as in León and Castile, and the introduction of new parameters of analysis as regards the functioning of monarchies, has allowed scholars to approach this institution in a way that is less centred on the person of the king.

Thus, the relationship between kingdoms depended for centuries on marriages between members of the different European royal families. But the alliances that were sought, and obtained, by the Portuguese royal family did not always involve the same partners. While the first dynasty (till the end of the fourteenth century) always tried to marry the heir to the throne to princesses or aristocrats from Castile or Aragon, the problems of legitimacy at the beginning of the so-called Avis dynasty, combined with the need to affirm power within national borders, led to some marriages drawn from within the Portuguese royal family itself. The result of this matrimonial policy centred on Hispania would generate a sixty-year period of dual monarchy between Portugal and Spain. The trauma caused by this political situation could have been behind the tendency, in the so-called Braganza dynasty, to diversify the origin of various royal consorts.

MANUELA SANTOS SILVA
Faculty of Arts and Humanities, University of Lisbon

Bibliography

BENEVIDES, Francisco da Fonseca, *Rainhas de Portugal: Estudo Histórico*, Lisbon, Typographia Castro Irmão, 1878.

EARENFIGHT, Theresa (ed.), *Queenship and Political Power in Medieval and Early Modern Spain*, Aldershot/Burlington, Ashgate, 2005.

FIGANIÈRE, Frederico Francisco de la, *Memórias das Rainhas de Portugal (D. Theresa – Santa Isabel)*, Lisbon, Typographia Universal, 1859.

MONTEIRO, J. P. Franco, *As Donatarias de Alenquer. História das Rainhas de Portugal e da Sua Casa e Estado*, Lisbon, M. Gomes Editor, 1893.

RODRIGUES, Ana Maria S. A. et al., *Casamentos da Família Real Portuguesa*, 4 vols., Lisbon, Círculo de Leitores, 2017–2018.

1147
Lisbon: From Conquest to Head of the Realm

The conquest of Lisbon in 1147, a foundational moment in all respects, was achieved by a joint force comprising Portuguese warriors and a large contingent of crusaders including English, French, Flemish and Germanic divisions in transit to Jerusalem, who lent their support to King Afonso Henriques.

According to traditional historiography, Lisbon only began to play a global role once it had become the capital of an empire at the turn of the fifteenth/sixteenth centuries. However, this is best seen in the light of what is known today about Lisbon between the twelfth and fifteenth centuries, since this was a pivotal period when the city attained an undeniable centrality in terms of its relations with both the rest of Portugal and the broader world of West and East.

These centuries reveal a dynamic city that was comfortable with the protagonism that it had acquired in negotiating relations between North and South, connecting the Atlantic to the Mediterranean and reaping the benefits of having been an almost obligatory port of call for the various peoples, ideas, fashions, and trends that passed through it. Yet, prior to the Christian conquest of 1147, Lisbon had not played a particularly important role in the economy of maritime commerce, administration, or bureaucracy – a situation that was as true during the Roman Empire as it was later during the successive rules of the Suevi, Visigoths and Muslims.

As it was too far removed from the centres of power, administration, and commerce, which were located further to the south and east, Lisbon had existed until 1147 essentially to protect the mouth of the Tagus. The raids and attempts at conquest reported in the Lisbon and Sintra region were of no great consequence. Only after the Christian conquest was the city catapulted to an exceptional status.

The year 1147, which also marked the rise to power of the Almohad Caliph Abd al-Mumin in the Maghreb and al-Andalus, and the consequent disintegration of Almoravid rule in the Iberian Peninsula, witnessed new attempts in the remainder of the Medieval West at reunification of kingdoms plagued by internecine warfare and political dissension. These efforts were centred upon another call to Crusade (the Second Crusade) at a time when England was destabilised by "The Anarchy", Roger II of Sicily was attacking Greek and Cypriot lands, and the Scandinavian crusade was absorbing a great deal of Western Christendom's energy.

The conquest of Lisbon in 1147, a foundational moment in all respects, was achieved by a joint force comprising Portuguese warriors and a large contingent of crusaders including English, French, Flemish and Germanic divisions in transit to Jerusalem, who lent their support to King Afonso Henriques.

Nevertheless, the global importance of the conquest of Lisbon would far exceed the immediate reality. This was not just one more dazzling victory for the young Portuguese king. In fact, it was a fundamental moment in the birth of the kingdom, presenting an opportunity for the activation (and reactivation) of mechanisms that would promote Lisbon as the central protagonist in a cluster of narratives that began to circulate about the conquest both inside the kingdom and abroad and which included images of the restoration and reconsecration of its political, administrative and ecclesiastical structures, and of those involved in the campaign, as a strategy for the legitimisation of Portuguese royalty.

The involvement of crusading forces allowed the king not only to promote in Rome the notion that he shared of the objectives underlying the crusading movement as a whole, contributing to them with his efforts in the peninsular west and thereby reinforcing his image as an invincible *miles Christi*, but also to benefit symbolically from the fact that that this collaboration had taken place under the aegis of one of the crusade's most important promotors, Bernard of Clairvaux, an individual possessed of formidable influence in the spheres of power and in what today would be termed International Relations.

Certainly, Afonso Henriques appears to have sought to align his own trajectory with these global trends. If prior to the conquest of Lisbon he had granted a large territory above the Tagus to the Order of the Temple for it to defend and populate whenever the conquest of the city might be achieved, his founding of the monastery of Alcobaça, the largest Cistercian house in Portugal, shortly after the conquest, also appears to have fulfilled a similar design, putting Portugal firmly on the map of the contemporary West. Indeed, each piece of this puzzle seems to have served this dual purpose of reinforcing the image of the king and his ambitions *vis a vis* the most important powers of the period and simultaneously granting the European Far-West, and especially Lisbon, a central role within the events of the age. It was not by chance that the first bishop to be appointed to the Christian city was an Englishman, or that the majority of the city's chapter which could very well have included the author of the account of the conquest of Lisbon – was of Anglo-Norman origin. Certainly, it reflects an intention to captivate, fix, and honour a population that would then be likely to allow the king more influence in the busy world of the twelfth century.

The city's cathedral and chapter, and many of its monastic institutions display a "foreign" character from an early stage, a feature that would persist for a long time. The canons of Lisbon, who were often very influential in the royal Curia, moved with great dexterity within the intellectual and commercial circles of their times. Meanwhile, attempts to fix members of the crusader contingents or people from outside were a constant in Lisbon during the 1180s and 1190s where foreign merchants and crusaders in transit to the Holy Land were beginning to co-exist more closely with the Christian, Muslim and Jewish inhabitants of this multifaceted metropolis. Indeed, imbuing Lisbon with the quality of centrality within the most important events of the epoch was a calculated operation. Assuredly, the Bishop of Lisbon planned, and subsidised, the conquest of Alcacer in 1217, a project once again brought to fruition with the aid of crusaders.

By the middle of the thirteenth century, Lisbon was simmering with political, ecclesiastical, and commercial activity. The conquest of the Algarve, which established almost definitively the territorial configuration of the kingdom, not only distanced Lisbon from the war with Islam, but also granted it a privileged position in the Portuguese context. Its new centrality allied to its already important nexus of terrestrial and fluvial arteries, as well as ts possession of an exceptional port would, with Christian rule over Andalusia and the Strait of Gibraltar, transform it into a vital node in the maritime links between the Mediterranean and the Atlantic. This permitted the gradual inclusion of Lisbon into a network of far-flung ports which, in the fifteenth century, would span the South Atlantic generating exchanges of influences and building contacts with peoples, markets and sources of knowledge.

Thus emerged a city with a strong Mediterranean heritage accustomed to the ethnic and religious diversity of the populations that nourished its growth in the first century of its Christian occupation. Human contingents flocked to it from other parts of the kingdom, as did foreigners, including clerics, nobles and merchants, giving it a unique social identity within the kingdom and making it into a city of European scale.

These are all reasons which help explain why the city increasingly became a place of residence for the monarchs and their accompanying court, a presence made manifest in the palace of the Alcáçova, the royal seat in the city located on the castle hill, a space which in the Mediterranean tradition, had long been associated with the exercise of power. Especially from the fourteenth century onwards,, this was the venue for the reception of foreign ambassadors and other dignitaries, and where important ceremonies related to stages in the lives of the monarchs and the functions of royalty took place.

The sovereign's presence brought with it not only a panoply of courtiers and clerics but also a diversified and ever more voluminous body of royal officials serving those administrative and fiscal institutions that would gradually endow the kingdom with its political/governmental apparatus. Given their high office and qualifications, many of these royal officials (who especially in the thirteenth and fourteenth centuries, had attended renowned foreign universities) were sent on different missions which would sometimes take them far beyond the kingdom's borders.

The royal presence in the city also prompted a campaign of urban improvement beginning in the thirteenth century, under Afonso III and Denis, and intended to boost the prestige and the operation of the city, either because the city was an evident platform of power, or because the programme was intended to stimulate activities such as naval construction and port services. Particularly notable is the settlement of a Genoese population in the city, members of which would assist Micer Pessagna in the formation of the Portuguese royal naval fleet. The demands of so large and diverse a society turned Lisbon into a centre of production and consumption with characteristics that were unique in the kingdom. This sustained a great variety of trades in the city, and also called for the establishment of importation/exportation networks that would extend to the major ports in both the Mediterranean and the Atlantic, as is especially evident in the case of the trade in cereals.

During the fourteenth century, amid a succession of crises and armed conflicts, Lisbon was a coveted prize for invaders bent on conquest. Indeed, war was to overshadow Lisbon during the second half of the century as the city became embroiled in the broader context of the Hundred Years War, experiencing serious disruptions in its external relations.

Even so, at the end of the century, Lisbon was to emerge from dynastic crisis and conflict with Castile, as the beneficiary of a special relationship with the dynasty of Avis. As the city recovered from the war, it underwent a period of demographic and economic growth and became host to the establishment of numerous administrative structures. By the fifteenth century, it was unquestionably at the head of the kingdom, inhabited and frequented by a sophisticated and diversified society. On account of its size and wealth, an evident corollary of the vitality of its craftsmanship and mercantile activities, Lisbon became one of the principal sources of revenue for the Crown.

The cycle of expansion that had begun in 1415 with the conquest of Ceuta, opened up the way for an enlargement of Lisbon's role, as the Maghrebian coast was added to previously consolidated spaces of contact. A little later, it accrued the routes that were being pioneered into the South Atlantic including that serving sugar production in Madeira and those giving access to African gold.

It is hardly surprising, therefore, that the numbers of foreigners in Lisbon increased, their places of origin well illustrating the broad reaches of contacts facilitated by the city. Thus, from the North Atlantic, there arrived Galicians, Basques, Cantabrians, Englishmen, Bretons, Flemings, Germans, and Zealanders, while from the Mediterranean there came Prazentines, Florentines, Genoese, Catalans, Milanese, and Corsicans. Some of the more numerous, such as the Genoese, Germans, and English formed organized communities whose legal complaints allow us a glimpse of the difficulties and complex conflicts of interest arising between Portuguese and foreigners, the merits of which were adjudicated by the monarchs.

The importance that the maritime expansion was to attain from the second half of the fifteenth century and the consequent enlargement of Portuguese dominions and territories beyond Europe further elevated the role of Lisbon both as the head of the kingdom and as its main port. Indeed, it was precisely Lisbon's crucial relationship with the sea that the monarchs sought to highlight and celebrate when they vacated their palace on the castle hill in order to set up residence in the new Palace of the Ribeira (waterfront) adjacent to the bustling heart of the city at the edge of the Tagus, the river that medieval sources called "the sea" and which had always put the city into contact with other spaces and peoples.

AMÉLIA AGUIAR ANDRADE
Faculty of Social Sciences and Humanities, Institute of Medieval Studies,
Nova University Lisbon
and
MARIA JOÃO BRANCO
Faculty of Social Sciences and Humanities, Institute of Medieval Studies,
Nova University Lisbon

Bibliography

ANDRADE, Amélia Aguiar, MIRANDA, Flávio, "Lisbon. Trade, urban power and the king's visible hand", in BLOCKMANS, Wim et al. (ed.), *The Routledge Handbook of Maritime Trade around Europe, 1300–1600: Commercial Networks and Urban Autonomy*, London, Routledge, 2017, pp. 333–351.

BRANCO, Maria João, "A conquista de Lisboa na estratégia de um poder que se consolida", in *A Conquista de Lisboa aos Mouros: Relato de Um Cruzado*, translated and edited by Aires Augusto Nascimento, 2nd ed., Lisbon, Colibri, 2007, pp. 9–54.

FONTES, João Luís Inglês et al. (ed.), *Lisboa Medieval: Gentes, Espaços e Poderes*, Lisbon, Instituto de Estudos Medievais, 2016.

MAGALHÃES, Joaquim Romero de, "O enquadramento do espaço nacional", in MATTOSO, José (dir.), *História de Portugal*, vol. III, Lisbon, Estampa, 1993, pp. 13–60.

WILSON, Jonathan, "Tactics of attraction: Saints, pilgrims and warriors in the Portuguese Reconquista", *Portuguese Studies*, vol. 30, no. 2, 2014, pp. 204–222.

1153
A Religion without Borders: Religious Orders

All of these groups manifested another 'global' dimension of the orders, namely the trans-versality of these religious movements, which expanded across Europe, as a result of personal contacts, the circulation of texts, shared desires for the renewal of the religious life and new forms of participation on the part of the clergy and laity, both men and women.

On 8th April 1153, King Afonso I of Portugal and Queen Matilda signed a charter granting Alcobaça and its territories to the abbot Bernard of Clairveaux and the Cistercian monastery governed by him, with the obligation to house there the white monks that had come from France a year before and settled in Chiqueda on the right bank of the River Alcoa.

The document, which has long been known, bears witness to the multifaceted role played by the religious orders in the history of Portugal, and reveals how, despite different rules and different forms of organization (given the diverse objectives pursued by them), they rapidly exceeded their spatial frameworks of origin, expanding beyond political borders. These orders arose out of broader religious movements, sometimes contesting (with their radical lifestyles) the Church's disregard of the Gospel, and thereby impelling a profound renovation or reform, at other times proposing new solutions to old problems in historical contexts marked by new aspirations, whether social, political, economic, cultural or religious. Their history, and the dynamics of their expansion, are inseparable from the context in which they arose, and from the powers that supported and sponsored them, or against which they affirmed themselves (beginning with the papacy, involved from early on in a logic of affirmation of the Church of Rome on the whole of western Europe, and, overtly, from the 12th century, in the construction of an ideology of identification between the social body and the ecclesiastical body of Christendom).

The donation made to Bernard of Clairveaux is an example of all this. As José Mattoso has shown, it is only comprehensible within the broader strategies developed by the Holy See, and supported by Bernard, to promote Crusades to recover the Holy Land. It is also in this light that we should understand the support lent by the abbot of Clairveaux to the participation of Flemish and German crusaders in the conquest of Lisbon in 1147, and the choice of Matilda, from noble circles close to Saint Bernard and supporters of the Crusade project, to be the consort of the Portuguese king. The foundation of Alcobaça was also related to Afonso Henriques's strategy of affirming himself as a Christian king within the framework of European Christianity, victorious over his enemies and protector of the Church, to which he granted benefits and on which he wanted to be able to count in his efforts to order and populate the territory conquered from the Muslims.

The choice of the Cistercians to be the recipients of the new monastery is significant. Founded by Robert of Molesme in 1098, with the construction of the new monastery in Cîteaux (Bourgogne, France), in a desolate spot, marked by loneliness, poverty and penitence, the new order proposed a return to the primitive spirit of the Benedictine Rule, which in their view had been distorted by too much emphasis on the liturgical dimension, particularly connected to the cult of the dead, introduced by Cluny and which attracted generous donations from rich patrons, who also handed over of many of their children to swell the monastic ranks. The Cistercians aimed to recover the balance that Saint Benedict had proposed between prayer, work and rest, and refashioned the monk as a penitent, who, in the monastery and under the direction of the abbot, would expiate his sins, and in union with Christ, aspire to the plenitude of redeemed humanity and full communion with God.

In the territory that would become Portugal, this was a period of great change. In fact, the adhesion of many former Iberian monasteries to the customs of Cluny (which implied conformity exclusively to the Benedictine rule and the replacement of the former hispanic or Mozarab liturgy by the Roman one) had begun in the 1080s, through the intermediary of the Franks and with the support of the emperor Alfonso VI, the papacy and nobility. Many of the monasteries that resisted this Benedictization preferred the canonical model of the Rule of Saint Augustine, which was more adaptable to different organizational solutions, or sought solitude as a space of freedom. Thus, from 1140 onwards, many groups attracted by the Cistercian emphasis on separation from the world, penitence and poverty, were to be found in the wilderness. All these movements were protected by Afonso Henriques, especially the monastery of canons regular of Santa Cruz of Coimbra, founded in 1131.

The Cistercians also represented an attempt at a more centralized configuration. Its structure of governance gave jurisdiction over the whole order to the general chapter, and there was also a system of affiliation between abbeys, with the mother-houses having the right to visit the new houses related to them. Though each monastery had a level of autonomy under the government of the abbot, as prescribed by Saint Benedict, new forms of articulation and control were now initiated, aiming to maintain a unity as regarded monastic discipline and liturgy. The previous form of monasticism, in which each monastery had total autonomy, now gave way to more structured forms of organization, which placed the decision centres outside the spaces of the monasteries, and even outside the kingdoms in which they were established.

This solution was encouraged by the papacy as an opportunity to acquire more control over the orders and religious life in Christian kingdoms. New religious aspirations emerging from the urban world and the many movements that arose from them – some protagonized by the laity and even suspected of heterodoxy – provoked a pontifical reaction. In the 4th Lateran Council, held in 1215, a centralized structure of governance was proposed for the orders, placed, in the last instance, under papal authority. New monastic rules were prohibited, meaning that any new foundations had to be subject to pre-existing rules.

Cister was also a sign of the more extensive cluster of religious movements that arose, from the end of the 11th century, with the revitalization of the cities, and all that that entailed on the social, economic, cultural and religious levels. The potentials and paradoxes associated with the urban world brought new challenges and changes to spirituality, increasingly centred on Christ and his suffering humanity, and valuing the Gospel as a rule for life and source of authority, and sensitive to the poverty and deprivation voluntarily sought as an eloquent sign before an unjust society based on power and wealth. Reform became synonymous with returning to an exemplary mythical past, whether that of the founders of early monasticism or of the primitive Christian community, whose archetype could be found in the description of the Acts of the Apostles. Cister, with its desired return to the spirit of Benedictine life, joined the orders of canons, committed to study and pastoral work in cities, and to the more radical movements that rejected the world and its vices – hermits and anchorites, above all the female recluses that closed themselves off within cities or their surroundings.

It was in this context that the mendicant orders were born. Francis of Assisi (1181/1182–1226) founded an order that was open to the world, centred on a radical fraternity and an uncompromising commitment to individual and community poverty configured with Christ; while Dominic of Guzmán (c. 1175–1221), attentive to the importance of preparing friars for pastoral work and preaching, especially against heresies, gave particular importance to study. Both orders followed the dictates of Lateran IV, organizing convents in provinces and ensuring their submission to a general, under the authority of the Holy See. But while Dominic was content to follow the Rule of Saint Augustine, Francis wanted to have his own rule approved. The same happened with Clare, who, in the region of Assisi and under the guidance of Francis, founded a female order characterized by poverty, obedience and chastity. Other orders that appeared at around the same time, or shortly after (such as the Trinitarians, hermits of Saint Augustine, Carmelites) ended up following a similar scheme of centralized governance, sometimes with their own rules or adopting a rule that had already been approved by the Church, complemented by their own constitutions.

The mendicants' success in urban environments and the support granted to them by the papacy explain their rapid expansion, and their early arrival in Portugal by the second decade of the 13th century. They spread throughout the kingdom, firstly into the main towns and cities, usually supported by monarchs and welcomed by the populations, though often attracting opposition from the local clergy and established orders on issues such as the definition of jurisdictions, rights and privileges, and in the dispute over spaces of intervention and publics.

Tensions between the local and the global are clearly visible in the logic of Portuguese affirmation and opposition to Castile – particularly in the efforts to achieve autonomy made by the Portuguese branches of the military orders with their main headquarters in Castile or with monasteries based outside the kingdom but with territories within it. These tensions became more acute with the Western Schism (1378–1417), when the Christian European powers were divided between obedience to two popes, one in Rome and the other in Avignon. From the late fourteenth century onwards, this fact was exploited by the Portuguese kings of the Avis dynasty to achieve definitive autonomy for those Portuguese convents and monasteries still integrated into Castilian provinces, obtaining from the Holy See the creation of provinces with national circumscription for many of the orders present in the kingdom. The end of the fourteenth century and the following one were marked by the emergence of new religious movements, with a strong secular component, committed to the renewal of the religious life. Voluntary poverty and the quest for solitude were common to many of them, though the processes of institutionalization of their communities were different. Thus, there are hermitic groups documented in Serra de Ossa (near

Redondo in the Alentejo) from 1366, though they only became a congregation in 1482, despite professing a single vow (chastity) and having very simple rules. The Order of Saint Jerome, approved by the papacy in 1373, managed to get its first monasteries in Portugal in 1400, after a phase of hermetic living. As for the observant currents within the Franciscan and Dominican orders, these arrived in Portuguese territory in the last decade of the 14th century, proposing a more rigorous life of poverty and austerity, and for women, the strictest cloistering. The Congregation of the Secular Canons of Saint John the Evangelist (Loios) appeared in the 1420s as a clerical congregation, clearly different from previous ones, though also committed to an exemplary life for its members. Inside the towns and cities, various groups of women began a common life of poverty, without subjection to any rule already approved by the Church, but in obedience to the diocesan bishops. All of this diversity manifested another 'global' dimension of the orders, namely the transversality of these new religious movements, which expanded across Europe, as a result of personal contacts, the circulation of texts, shared desires for the renewal of the religious life and new forms of participation on the part of the clergy and laity, both men and women.

In short, this was a common quest for greater religious perfection, which was only consecrated by Catholicism into a 'universal call to holiness' much later on (Vatican II, 1962–1965), but which the orders and monasticism, in its origin, also embraced and developed.

João Luís Inglês Fontes
Institute of Medieval Studies of the Faculty of Social Sciences and Humanities, Nova University Lisbon, and
Centre for the Study of Religious History of the Catholic University of Portugal

Bibliography

AZEVEDO, Carlos Moreira (ed.), *História Religiosa de Portugal*, vol. I, Lisbon, Círculo de Leitores, 2000.
MATTOSO, José, *D. Afonso Henriques*, Rio de Mouro, Círculo de Leitores, 2006.
Idem, *Obras Completas*, 12 vols., Rio de Mouro, Círculo de Leitores, 2000–2002.
MOURÃO, José Augusto et al. (ed.), *Dicionário Histórico das Ordens e Instituições afins em Portugal*, Lisbon, Gradiva, 2010.
SOUSA, Bernardo Vasconcelos (ed.), *Ordens Religiosas em Portugal. Das Origens a Trento: Guia Histórico*, 3rd ed., Lisbon, Livros Horizonte, 2016.

1174
The Language Spoken and Written by the Portuguese

Latin documents reveal genuine Portuguese words, formed in the spirit of the language by traditional formation and derivation. These outcrops of Portuguese, revealed in legal Latin, are the earliest records of a language in the process of creation, searching for its independence.

Language, in its diachronic evolution as determined by human history, is subject to diverse historical, political and socio-cultural contexts which regulate the linguistic system of a community. Its progress over the centuries in the geographical area of

Portugal has been determined by migrations of peoples, by occupation of territories, by cultures imposed by conquerors, and by commercial contacts. If Galician-Portuguese originated in the eleventh and twelfth centuries, it had influential earlier antecedents. More than in the phonological and morpho-syntactic structures of the language, it is in lexis and semantics that historical traces are most clearly seen in all their diachronic heterogeneity. As Joseph Maria Piel remarked, "the lexical stream of the original heritage was augmented by successive waves of innumerable foreign elements from Europe and beyond, including practically all the languages with which the Portuguese had direct or indirect contact in the course of their history".

The Iberian Peninsula was inhabited by various peoples. In the southern zone, the Turdetani, related to the civilization of Tartessos, were, according to Strabo, the wisest people among the Iberians, since not only did they use writing, but also had ancient memories of chronicles, poems and versified laws dating back six thousand years, though historical proofs do not reach further than the seventh century BCE. Strabo also mentions that other Iberian peoples used different types of writing. In the southwest of the Peninsula, the Conii had lived in the Algarve and the southern Alentejo since the ninth century and had contact with Phoenician colonies from the seventh century BCE. These were non-Indo-European peoples, but in the centre and north of Portugal there were Indo-European groups, with successive waves of Celtic migrations from the fifth century BCE onwards. From this ethnic and cultural substrate there survive lexical vestiges of pre-Roman languages, both from non-Indo-European languages, such as *barro* (clay), *esquerdo* (left) and manteiga (butter) and from those of the Celts – *cabana* (hut), *camisa* (shirt), *carpinteiro* (carpenter) and *cerveja* (beer). Before the rise of a Romance language, Latin authors identified specific lexemes from other European languages and regions; it is therefore possible to recognise lexical vestiges from Iberian, Celtic, Gaulish or Germanic languages which have survived up to the present day. Greek, Phoenician and Carthaginian colonies had also been established in the Peninsula, leaving traces particularly in toponyms.

The Romanization of the Peninsula began in 218 BCE and proceeded from south to north; two centuries later, the whole Peninsula was under Roman rule. Military supremacy imposed administration, culture and language, which was absorbed without great difficulty, although there was a transitory period of bilingualism between Latin and pre-Roman languages. The north-west of the Peninsula was the last region to be Romanized. However, the Romanization of this zone was no less efficient and profound, if we are to judge by the lexical and semantic richness, by the archaisms and by the conservative Latin forms which clearly distinguish Portuguese from other Hispanic Romance languages.

The *pax romana* dictated the use of Latin, which progressively eliminated the languages of the original inhabitants. But the primitive and essential nucleus of any Romance language comes from Vulgar Latin, a predominantly oral variety of the language which coexisted in parallel from the end of the third century BCE until the Imperial period (first to second centuries CE). Despite traces of Vulgar Latin in Plautus and in the letters of Cicero, it is in the Imperial age that there are abundant written sources. Cicero spoke of *uulgaris sermo* or *plebeius sermo*; Quintilian mentioned *uerbis uulgaribus et cotidianis*. The concept was recovered in modern times, but its meaning was open to debate. József Herman proposed the best definition: Vulgar Latin refers to "set of all those innovations and trends that turned up in the usage, particularly but not exclusively spoken, of the Latin-speaking population who were little or not at all influenced by school education and by literary models". This definition includes no chronological limits, since variations in Vulgar Latin were diachronic. Diatopic, diastratic and diaphasic factors meant that it had no synchronic unity, varying from region to region according to the geographical, social and cultural specificities of its speakers in the diverse regions of the Empire. It was frequently called *sermo uulgaris, plebeius, rusticus, cotidianus humilis, castrensis, familia ris, uernaculus*, in contrast with *sermo nobilis, litterarius, urbanus*.

The expansion of Christianity brought with it the common language of a group with specific lexical and semantic characteristics: the Latin of the Christians, with its lexicological Christianisms, both direct (from Greek and Hebrew), indirect (neologisms created from Latin) and semantic (broadening of the meaning of already existing words). Latin was evolving: in the late period (third to fifth centuries CE), accent became intensive, losing its quantitative and tonal value, thus affecting the phonological value of vowels and the evolution of the vowel system; systems of inflection and syntax were also simplified.

The fall of the Western Roman Empire created the conditions for local varieties to emerge and gain status. In the fifth century, with the invasions of Suevi and Visigoths, the north-west of the Peninsula fell under Germanic influence, still seen in legal and military language and in personal names. This was followed in 711 by the arrival of Muslim peoples, speaking Arabic. In addition to their culture and technical innovations, their presence in the Peninsula for seven centuries left lexical traces in the various Iberian Romance languages, in the fields of administration, war, science and technology (mathematics, architecture, biology, geography) commerce and industry (units of measurement, professions) and culture (music and literature). Greek culture too was brought partly through the medium of Arabic, introducing some Greek terms to Hispanic languages.

Latin was no longer a language of common use: what people spoke were Romance languages derived from Latin. That is, two languages had come to co-exist: Latin, as the essentially written language of culture and knowledge, and Romance, the language of oral communication. Aware of this diglossia, the Council of Tours, in 813, recommended to bishops "that they should try to translate homilies *in rusticam Romanam linguam aut Thiotiscam*, so that all may more easily comprehend what is being said".

In the north-west of the Peninsula, there evolved from Vulgar Latin a group of dialects which formed a linguistic unit, developed in the literary language of troubadour songs of the thirteenth and fourteenth centuries, which has been called Galician-Portuguese. Works in prose from the fourteenth century (particularly chronicles) show more substantial differences between Galician and Portuguese, both in grammatical structure and orthography. This difference may have been related to the loss of political influence in comparison with Castile and therefore of the subordination of Galician to Castilian as a literary language. Although the *Cantiga da Guarvaia* was for long considered the first troubadour song in Galician-Portuguese poetry, today the first is considered to be the satirical *Ora Faz ost' o Senhor de Navarra*, by João Soares de Paiva, dated 1196.

As for documentary evidence of Galician-Portuguese, the first records date from the twelfth to thirteenth centuries. Here, in parallel with the use of Latin as the official language of diplomacy, Portuguese was emerging in less formal documents, relatively ephemeral texts such as two recently discovered documents which seem to be the earliest written in Portuguese. These are the pact between Gomes Pais and Ramiro

Pais (c. 1174) and the *Notícia de Fiadores* (1175), the last part of which, although certainly in Romance, is not considered sufficiently representative by some scholars, given that the rest of the text is closer to Latin. Previously the earliest were considered to be the will of King Afonso II (1214) and the *Notícia de Torto* (1211–1216).

Nevertheless, even before these texts, some earlier Latin documents show genuine Portuguese words, formed in the spirit of the language by traditional formation and derivation. These outcrops of Portuguese in legal Latin are the earliest records of a language in the process of creation, searching for its independence from its Latin roots.

It is usual to cite document 9 of the *Diplomata et Chartae*, on the foundation of the church of Lordosa, in 882, as the first original manuscript in Portuguese notarial documentation, but in the case of copied documents, document 16 (folios 9v-10r) of the *Liber fidei* from Braga Cathedral (873) shows the first flourishes of Portuguese. Apart from toponymic expressions such as "*et inde ad Petra Ficta et inde ad Monte Maior* (from there to Perafita and from there to Montemor)" and "*inde ad Castro Maximo*" or of syntax such as "*inter quos fuit [...] Leouerigo Boca Mala qui ierma nus fuit de ipso episcopus Fredosindus* (among whom was [...] L. B. M., who was brother of Bishop Fredosindo]", we find the toponym *Figeirola* (Figueirola), with the falling dipthong /ei/, one of the specific characteristics of Portuguese as a Romance language. This same dipthong is found in document 8 of the *Diplomata et Chartae* (875) in the Censual from the chapter-house of Porto Cathedral, the authenticity of which has never been questioned by critics. It appears in the word *leiga*, the earliest record of a Portuguese word with the dipthong /ei/ and sounding of the velar consonant, unless there had been contamination or anachronisms in the copy. From King Afonso III (1210–1279), onwards, especially under King Denis (1261–1325), Portuguese began to be used systematically in notarial documents, but Latin was still studied and practiced in monastery and cathedral schools and in the universities, in its turn influencing Romance, renewing its vocabulary with the introduction of cultured terms.

Due to pilgrimages to Santiago, the establishment of the Cluniac and Cistercian Orders, and the presence of the House of Burgundy in Portuguese territory, the northwest of the Peninsula was frequented by many French people, bringing their Provençal troubadour literature and Arthurian epics, introducing new vocabulary into the court, into chivalry, literature and religion. In the fifteenth century, cultural exchanges with Italy and the study of classical languages intensified. The princes of Avis now played a decisive role in the promotion of cultural and educational policy. With Renaissance humanism, Latin recovered its impetus, with its erudition infusing scientific terminology and influencing even the most popular language. Hundreds of Portuguese studied in France and Italy with grants from the Crown; Italian was making an appearance through the language of the arts. Overseas expansion in the fifteenth century not only enriched the Portuguese language with new words, but also contributed to other languages, and gave rise to pidgins and creoles, from Cape Verde in Africa to Malacca in Asia. Words from around the world became Portuguese: *canja* (soup) and *carambola* (starfruit), from Konkani; *manga* (mango) and *pagode* (pagoda) from Dravidian languages; *jangada* (raft) and *caril* (curry) from Tamil; *orangotango* (orangutan) and *bule* (teapot) from Malay; *junco* (junk) and *chá* (tea) from Chinese; *biombo* (screen) and *catana* (cutlass) from Japanese, among many others.

Aware of the intrinsic value of the language, Portuguese grammarians extolled the native tongue and encouraged linguistic standardization, although Luso-Castilian bilingualism dominated Portuguese literature in the sixteenth century. In subsequent centuries Portugal opened up to linguistic influences from dominant European cultures, first from France at the end of the seventeenth century, then from Britain in the twentieth century.

ANTÓNIO MANUEL RIBEIRO REBELO
Centre for Classical and Humanistic Studies, Faculty of Arts and Humanities,
University of Coimbra

Bibliography

CASTRO, Ivo, *Curso de História da Língua Portuguesa*, Lisbon, Universidade Aberta, 1991.
Idem, *Introdução à História do Português*, Lisbon, Colibri, 2006.
HERMAN, József, *Le Latin Vulgaire*, Paris, Presses Universitaires de France, 1975.
MAIA, Clarinda de Azevedo, *História do Galego-Português. Estado Linguístico da Galiza e do Noroeste de Portugal desde o século XIII ao século XVI (com Referência à Situação do Galego Moderno)*, Coimbra, Instituto Nacional de Investigação Científica, 1986.
TEYSSIER, Paul, *História da Língua Portuguesa*, Lisbon, Sá da Costa, 1982.

1196
From Latin Literature to Portuguese Literature

In the evolution of both the Latin and the Galician-Portuguese cultures, multiple currents connected Portuguese literary circles to institutions and figures from different regions of Western Europe and with the legacy of the ancient and contemporary Mediterranean.

In the Middle Ages, writing and reading were a privilege of the very few, mainly the clergy. In the twelfth century, writing began a slow process of diffusion among the laity, using the so-called vulgar tongues, but without altering significantly the previous situation, of a medium that barely reached one in a hundred of the population. With the liturgy, clerical preaching and troubadour performances, the cultural traditions of these elites reached a wider audience by way of words and music. Some minstrels, closer to popular oral culture, seem also to have been connected to troubadour circles, with some of their work preserved in song-books. The contributions of the more erudite Jewish and Muslim circles are still unclear and in need of research.

In 1143 the most active clerical centres in the emergent kingdom of Portugal were the monasteries, which preserved annals and narratives on their foundation and on the lives of their most prominent figures, presenting them as examples to be followed. In the second half of the twelfth century, the Monastery of Santa Cruz in Coimbra, while continuing to produce such literary genres, renewed and adapted them to a more urban society which was also closer to power, producing hagiographies and texts on the figure of Afonso Henriques.

With the thirteenth century came significant changes. Within this Latin culture, there is evidence of the cultural prominence of the urban clergy connected to episcopal sees; this is seen in cultural products, of course, but also in private libraries, in the operation of the *Estudo Geral* (that is, the University), and in the training of scholars in foreign countries and the roles that some of them played there. From this environment came hagiographies, legal literature, and works of philosophy, apologetics and medicine, broadening the scope of ecclesiastical writing and adapting it to new problems arising for the Church in its prominence in urban settings, its institutional diversification and the constant struggles between bishops and royal power. These last two areas directed the attention of clerics to legal subjects, which were the most constant element in their work.

At the same time, new monastic orders, known as mendicants (Franciscans and Dominicans), focusing on evangelizing in the cities, eagerly recovered the art of speaking, using it to promulgate a New Testament Christianity based on poverty; they were apparently confronting a Church which, after the Gregorian reforms (eleventh to thirteenth centuries), had emerged as the principal religious and political force in Western Europe. The profound cultural changes of the thirteenth century were not confined to clerical circles, however. In fact, the real cultural revolution was among the laity, from the moment when, around 1196, there was first heard, maybe near Navarre, but in Galician-Portuguese, the song *Ora Faz ost' o Senhor de Navarra*. The first sign that a circle which included Portuguese authors was attracted to troubadour ideals, this satirical piece, by João Soares de Paiva, was also the first sign of the return of the lay elite to the realm of writing, which conferred literary status on the spoken language of the north-west of the Peninsula.

After a faltering start, there followed a century of energetic cultural activity based in the principal courts of the Portuguese nobility, terminating in the middle of the fourteenth century at the court of the king's bastard son Peter, the Count of Barcelos. Married to Branca Peres de Portel, heiress of the houses of Sousa and Portel, and succeeding Riba de Vizela as Count – the three lineages that played a decisive part in supporting this culture – Count Peter ended a brilliant cultural period with three notable compilations. These summarized and extended the main groups of courtly texts, and also introduced to educated Portuguese circles the powerful chronicle tradition of the Castilian court. Among these varied aristocratic genres, we should mention troubadour songs; genealogical writing (including books of lineages); short narratives, often from family sources, especially those collected by Count Peter; the beginnings of Portuguese chronicle writing with the *Crónica Geral de Espanha de 1344*; and the translation of chivalric romances. All those works brought women and the family to the centre of aristocratic interests at a time when nobles were attempting to establish their political power. At the royal court culture was weaker, a sign that royalty were not interested in the literary culture of the aristocracy, apart from the presence of troubadours at the courts of King Afonso III (1248–1279) and King Denis (1279–1325), and especially the latter's composition of troubadour lyrics. Some more technical treatises survive from his court, as well as a short chronicle of the first Portuguese kings (the 'First Portuguese Chronicle'), genealogical in content apart from the section referring to Afonso Henriques, produced perhaps in the reign of Afonso III and later added up to the Battle of Salado (1340).

From the mid-fourteenth century, the change in the conditions of cultural production, together with developments in the Church and the internal political situation, created conditions for a profound transformation in the cultural world. With the disappearance of the lineages of the upper nobility who had supported aristocratic literature in the previous century, the military orders of the Hospitallers and of Santiago worked to preserve the memory of their part in the Reconquest (as in the *Chronicle of the Conquest of the Algarve* and the narrative of the Battle of Salado inserted in *Book of*

Lineages of Count Peter. From the end of the century the new court would speed up this effort, given the need to clear the clouds hanging over the legitimacy of the dynasty of Avis. The royal court thus quickly became the most important centre of culture in the country, centralizing such activities as production of narrative and didactic works, literary patronage, translation, and the creation of libraries. With chronicles becoming the main genre of a court in need of its own narrative of the troubled years of 1383–1385, a vast literary output came from royal circles, including some didactic and moral works aiming to influence the courtly environment, oratorical pieces connected to diplomacy, hagiographical biographies, technical treatises, poetry, and translations of classical authors such as Cicero's *De Officiis,* translated by Prince Peter. The vehicle was a Portuguese progressively distancing itself from Galician in the direction of modern Portuguese. In lordly circles little was left of thirteenth century culture. King Edward, in his *Book of Horsemanship,* shows an aristocracy concerned with conversing with ladies, song, dance, clothes, and other less literary arts, though poetry was not completely absent from some aristocratic circles.

In the sphere of Latin culture, in the context of a crisis in the Church and with the schools of the different institutions vegetating following the foundation of the University, only one sector produced anything worthy of note, taking on a role previously played by cathedral clergy. This was the mendicant orders, urban and close to the lay elite, who left a variety of writings, sometimes produced in conjunction with scholarly courtiers: sermons (given the importance of urban preaching to these orders), works of economics, philosophy, theology and apologetics, as well as religious poetry. In the evolution of both the Latin and the Galician-Portuguese cultures, multiple currents connected Portuguese literary circles to institutions and figures from different regions of Western Europe and with the legacy of the ancient and contemporary Mediterranean. From the beginning, clerical writing set its roots in the cultural model of the end of the classical Latin world, with erudition supported by the seven liberal arts, adapted by the Church of Rome to the needs of training priests and monks for their lives in the rural society of the time. This meant that the same Latin-Christian cultural substrate was present throughout Europe, as Christianity advanced north from Rome.

The north of the Iberian Peninsula in the High Middle Ages was to some degree absorbed in itself. However, at the end of the eleventh century there flowed into the Peninsula many liturgical and cultural novelties which challenged some aspects of the institutional and cultural evolution of the Hispanic Church. Instrumental in such changes were the presence of knights from beyond the Pyrenees in the reconquest of territories from North African Muslims, the establishment of firmer relationships with other European kingdoms and counties (Alfonso VI of León and Castile looked for queens in Aquitaine, Burgundy and Tuscany, and husbands for his daughters in Burgundy, Sicily and Toulouse, while his grandson married Matilda of Savoy) and the opening to Gregorian reforms and the ensuing uniformity of the Church. Modernizing forces turned to reforms in institutions, in knowledge, and in religion and liturgy. Beyond their privileged relationship with Rome, Portuguese monasteries and cathedrals renewed close relations with various institutions in Western Europe. This is seen in the case of Santa Cruz in Coimbra, with its contacts with the Monastery of Saint Rufus in Avignon, also a house of regular canons, and the presence of Portuguese monks and priests in European colleges. In the area of university education, the presence of Portuguese clergy in Bologna, some of them staying there to teach

Law after completing their studies, confirms the cultural reorientation of Portuguese clergy and the role they played beyond the Peninsula.

As for lay culture, João Soares de Paiva's song *Ora Faz ost' o Senhor de Navarra* mentioned above, a political satire in the Provençal style produced in an aristocratic circle frequented by Occitan troubadours, shows the influences at work in this cultural field. Courtly romances, this time from northern France, are relevant in this context, brought as a result of the stay in the French court of Prince Afonso, the future King Afonso III. Iberian links are seen in some works by Count Peter, such as his book of lineages, including narratives and genealogies of Navarre, Castile and Galicia but also some extra-Peninsula material, and his *Crónica Geral de Espanha de 1344*, which relied much on Castilian historiography. These texts are complemented by the later vogue for Latin classics in some circles at the court of Avis, with works that were then translated and included in the libraries of kings and princes.

A sign that some groups were also interested in Arab culture was the translation of the *Chronicle of the Moor Rasis* by a priest in the circle of Pero Anes de Portel at the end of the thirteenth or the early fourteenth century, and of the *Book on the Judgement of the Stars* by Abenragel, in the early fifteenth century. Further research in this field, and in that of Jewish culture, will expand our knowledge of the influences interacting in medieval Portuguese literature.

ANTÓNIO RESENDE DE OLIVEIRA
Centre for the History of Society and Culture, University of Coimbra

Bibliography

XVII Exposição Europeia de Arte, Ciência e Cultura. Os Antecedentes Medievais dos Descobrimentos: Convento da Madre de Deus, Lisbon, Imprensa Nacional-Casa da Moeda, 1983.

LANCIANI, Giulia, TAVANI, Giuseppe (coord.), *Dicionário da Literatura Medieval Galega e Portuguesa*, Lisbon, Caminho, 1993.

MATTOSO, José, *Portugal Medieval: Novas Interpretações*, Lisbon, Imprensa Nacional-Casa da Moeda, 1985.

MIRANDA, José Carlos Ribeiro, "Como o rei Artur e os cavaleiros da sua corte demandaram o reino de Portugal", *Colóquio Letras*, no. 142, Oct.–Dec. 1996, pp. 83–102.

NASCIMENTO, Aires Augusto, "A Igreja na história da cultura: percursos do livro em Portugal na Idade Média", *Igreja e Missão*, vol. 184, 2000, pp. 139–201.

1231

From Fernando Martins to Saint Anthony of Lisbon and Padua: A Saint for All the World

It was at the hermitage of Montepaolo, near Forlì, that the acclaimed and much-admired preacher began his career. He was immediately given pastoral duties that took him to preach in the north of Italy and the south of France, gaining esteem during his life and a reputation of sanctity throughout Europe.

The *Vita prima*, or *Assidua*, describes thus the death of Friar Anthony of Lisbon: "In the year one thousand two hundred and thirty-one of the Incarnation of the Lord, in the fourth indiction, on the thirteenth day of the month of June, on a Friday, near Arcella, in the residence of the friars, there passed away happily to the mansion of the heavenly spirits, taking the way of all flesh, our blessed father and brother Anthony, of Portuguese (Iberian) origin, in the city of Padua, where, through him, the Most High exalted His name." Thus, before the age of 40, ended the career of Fernando Martins, later surnamed Bulhões, who in his life captivated and aroused multitudes of the faithful, thanks to his powerful preaching, his example of an evangelical life, and his reputation as a man of miracles and virtues. His cult grew, making Anthony the most universal Portuguese, whose popular devotion still shines from the Basilica dedicated to him in Padua, where he was buried.

The fame of his sanctity and the prestige of having a holy and incorruptible body immediately gave rise to a struggle between the inhabitants of Capo di Ponte and the friars, the bishop and the citizens of Padua, until an act seen as miraculous occurred, which favoured the city. The miracles and prodigious events attributed to him were collected by representatives of the council and the bishop, and the call for his canonization was sent to the Pope. The process was resolved with unusual rapidity, partly due to the political needs of the papacy, in need of a saint as a bastion of Catholicism against the heresy represented by the emperor Frederick II Hohenstaufen and by his subject in the March of Treviso, Ezzelino III da Romano. Less than a year after his death, on 30 May 1232, by a bull of Gregory IX, the Portuguese Franciscan was declared a saint. His recognition as a saint and patron of Padua, a bulwark against heresy and a saint of popular miracles, guaranteed him over time the affection of believers from all social classes. His cult, highly popular and festive in its nature, has spread and survived throughout the Catholic world.

Friar Anthony's fame as a preacher began when, in Forlì, he preached to an audience of friars and clerics. To the surprise of all, he showed deep biblical knowledge applied to moral eloquence. His wisdom, reinforced by a meticulous memory – hence his name of 'Ark of the Testament' – was the fruit of study and meditation even in youth, before he entered the Order.

Born in Lisbon around 1190, according to tradition, into a wealthy family, Fernando was educated at the Cathedral school. As an adolescent, he joined the Augustinian Order of Regular Canons at the Monastery of Saint Vincent de Fora. Two years later he moved to the Monastery of Santa Cruz in Coimbra; here he studied in its library, deepening his knowledge of the Scriptures and exegetic works, which would later feed his moralizing oratory, full of rich biblical and naturalistic images. Around 1220 he witnessed the arrival in Coimbra of the mortal remains of five Franciscan friars, the martyrs of Morocco, which inspired him to imitate them in the conversion of Muslims. Presumably in 1221, with the authorization of his superiors, he joined the Order of Friars Minor, at the Chapel of Saint Anthony the Great at Olivais in Coimbra. Hence he took the name *Antonius*.

According to the *Vitae*, the beginning of the rise of the future saint dates from this time. On the voyage to Morocco, a storm caused the ship to divert to Messina, where he arrived deeply ill. After treatment, he headed for the General Chapter of the Order, taking place in Assisi. It was at the hermitage of Montepaolo, near Forlì, that the acclaimed and much-admired preacher began his career. He was immediately given pastoral duties that took him to preach in the north of Italy and the south of France, gaining esteem during his life, a reputation of sanctity throughout Europe, and fame as the 'hammer of heresies'.

It was the founder of the Order, Francis of Assisi, who, at an uncertain date, wrote Anthony a brief letter putting him in charge of teaching theology to the friars, which signalled a new opening of the Order to teaching. The prestige thus acquired explains Anthony's election as Provincial Minister for northern Italy, between 1227 and 1230. At this period, he went twice to Padua. On his first visit, he preached and wrote or finished sermons. The second coincided with the height of his fame during his life and his most successful preaching campaign, in Lent 1231. The hagiographers say that the crowds were so great that Anthony had to be protected from being crushed by the multitude trying to touch him or obtain some relic. The miracles attributed to him during his life include resurrections, cures and other prodigious events, mostly involving devout women who were not present where Anthony was speaking. Social and political effects have been ascribed to his words, leading to the freeing of insolvent debtors and the insertion of a written order safeguarding them into the city's statutes.

In the Spring of 1231, Anthony's health, already undermined by a latent illness, worsened as a result of excessive privations. He withdrew to a property belonging to the friars in Tiso da Camposampiero, where he spent the last years of his life, studying, praying and preaching. When he felt that his strength was leaving him, he asked his brothers to take him to Santa Maria Mater Domini, the chapel of the friars in Padua, so that he would die and be buried there. According to tradition, which is still echoed in annual local celebrations, he was taken there in an ox-cart. The *Vitae* say that when the cart approached the house of the Clarissan friaresses (now Arcella) outside the walls of Padua, he died, saying "I see my Lord". It was on 13 June 1231: Fernando, now Anthony, would have been under 40 years old. It was the beginning of a new phase in his fame.

The preaching which drew multitudes to the voice and doctrine of Anthony, and of which no transcript survives, was distinct from the surviving written sermons, which are rich, dense and literary, complex and interwoven with references and remissions. These were not sermons to be listened to, but rather models for training, a handbook for the study of a style of preaching based on the interpretation of a biblical text and on the example of evangelical life. Each sermon for the Sundays interpreted the four biblical readings of the Mass, forming a *quadriga* (a four-horse chariot), as he called it in the general prologue. If there are no doubts as to the authenticity of the sermons, where and when they were written is still undecided. A current hypothesis is that, in view of their biblical, literary and doctrinal content, they would have been written when he was a monk at Santa Cruz in Coimbra, and then taken to Italy, where he would have revised them. It is also possible that most of them, at least in their final version, were composed in Italy between 1221 and 1223. The book of sermons includes fifty-three texts for the Sundays of the year, introduced by a prologue, seven other short prologues which organize the Sunday sermons throughout the liturgical year, and an epilogue, as well as four Marian sermons and twenty sermons for the feasts of saints. The diffusion of the *Sermons* as a theological and moral work was linked to the expansion of the Franciscans, but it became weaker in the mid-fourteenth century with the arrival of new styles of preaching and new handbooks for the training of preachers.

The Friars Minor were quick to set up the cult of Anthony, first in their *studia* and Friaries, with reading of sermons, constant honouring of the virtues of the preacher saint and advice to emulate the simple life, and then among the laity, with stories of his miracle-working powers. Hagiographies of Anthony multiplied and became literary successes, while the iconography of the saint was becoming established, with the open book, the child Jesus, the white lily, the bread of the poor, etc. Sources relating to Saint Anthony are rich and diverse, including hagiographic narratives, liturgical texts, papal bulls, petitionary letters, vows of the faithful, accounts of miracles, chronicles and hundreds of sermons for the feast of the saint (especially on the anniversary of his death, the 13th June, and of the transfer of his relics, the 15th February). In 1263, the discovery by Saint Bonaventure of his incorruptible tongue was one of the most significant points in the diffusion of his cult among Franciscan and other clergy as well as lay people.

In the thirteenth and fourteenth centuries Anthony's cult spread by two sometimes divergent paths. The first, which could be called popular diffusion, linked to the veneration of the body and the relics of the saint – his fame as the saint of lost objects seems to have arisen later – was particularly strong in the areas where he lived: northern Italy, southern France and the Lisbon region. In Padua, he was rapidly promoted as *patronus civitatis*, with the cult also spreading strongly in neighbouring areas. Outside Italy, only Lisbon, Coimbra and the region of Limousin in France experienced a genuine dissemination of veneration for Anthony, even if in its popular form. The second path of devotion, which could be considered religious and ecclesiological, spread for a more limited time, mainly because it was probably the basis of the popular phenomenon. Promoted within the Order of Friars Minor, it was seen in sermons dedicated to the saint in the thirteenth and fourteenth centuries, as well as in the liturgy and in hagiographic narratives. Anthony became the model preacher and an example of virtue through which every friar should be inspired to reach Christian perfection. This is the message transmitted in the more than two hundred Latin sermons composed in his praise in the first century after his canonization. In them, the saint is the perfect preacher, the best son of Francis, the friar of friars, the example for every friar and monk wanting to preach or know the word of God. The fame of the saint, told in stirring words, the softness and sweetness of his human figure, and the growing iconography, which includes various areas of religious symbolism, are a sign of a long-lasting popular cult which has reached around the world.

The collection of his sermons was published in the nineteenth century; then, on 16 January 1946, Pope Pius XII declared Anthony a Doctor of the Church, the *Doctor evangelicus*. In more recent decades, Anthony has received renewed attention as author and theologian, with the critical edition of his *Sermons* and the study of his thought, marked as it was by encyclopedic interests and profound biblical culture.

ELEONORA LOMBARDO
Institute of Philosophy, University of Porto
and
JOSÉ FRANCISCO MEIRINHOS
Institute of Philosophy, University of Porto

Bibliography

Anthony of Padua, *Sermons for Sundays and Festivals*, 4 vols., transl. P. Spilsbury, Padua, Edizioni Messaggero, 2010–12. Latin critical edition: Antonius Patavinus, *Sermones Dominicales et Festivi*, ed. Beniamino Costa et al., 3 vols., Padua, Edizioni Messaggero, 1979.

CAEIRO, Francisco da Gama, *Santo António de Lisboa*, 2 vols., Lisbon, ed. author, 1967 & 1969; reed. Imprensa Nacional-Casa de Moeda, Lisbon, 1995.

Fonti Agiografiche Antoniane, 6 vols. ed. Vergilio Gamboso et al., Padua, Messaggero di S. Antonio, 1981–2001.

HARDICK, Lothar, *He Came To You So That You Might Come To Him: The Life and Teaching of St. Anthony of Padua*, Chicago, Franciscan Herald Pr., 1989.

SPILSBURY, Paul, *Saint Anthony of Padua: His Life and Writings*, Padua, Edizioni Messaggero, 2013.

Digital

'*Sermoni di sant'Antonio*', *Sant'Antonio di Padova*, s.d., http://www.santantonio.org/it/sermoni (accessed 10 March 2020).

1276

Pope John XXI, Portuguese Clergyman and Universal Pastor

His works weld the learning of European Christian, Judaic and Islamic cultures, thus connecting almost all the known world of his time. They reveal a global understanding of science, regardless of frontiers or even of faiths.

Pedro Julião, known in the intellectual circles of his time as Pedro Hispano and to the ecclesiastical world by the apostolic name of John XXI (1276–1277), lived a long life, most of it coinciding with the thirteenth century: typical of the emergent intellectuals of the period, he was forged within the intense atmosphere of the nascent universities. He began as a cleric, the essential condition of his existence and the basis of a remarkably long and convoluted career which took him from priesthood in the Portuguese Church to the pontifical Curia, where he occupied, for about eight months, the highest position in the Roman Catholic Apostolic Church, successor of Peter and spiritual leader of Christianity. He survives today as someone who is difficult to classify, only reconstructed unsatisfactorily and in fragments. From what we know there emerges a difficult, complex personality, who was an active protagonist in lively academic, political and religious circles.

Before his consecration as Pope John XXI, he had been a student, a university professor, a diplomat and politician, a doctor and a philosopher, a man of the Church and of the Court, a servant of kings and Popes. Furthermore, he was a prolific author in many fields of knowledge, his works circulating widely in Europe during the Middle Ages and the Renaissance.

The biographical data on Pedro Hispano has many lacunae, especially concerning when, where and into what family he was born. Following tradition, it is plausible to infer that he was born in Lisbon in the first or second decade of the thirteenth century; this agrees with calculations based on his age when he took up various posts. The connection with Lisbon can be conjectured from his career at the city's cathedral, first as an oblate at its school, then as a priest, canon and official of the cathedral. It is by no means certain, as has been suggested, that he was a member of the local bourgeoisie, possibly the son of the doctor Julião Rebolo and his wife Teresa Gil. His education too is still unclear, though there is ample historical evidence of his stay in Paris as a student, and possibly as a teacher of logic at the Faculty of Arts there, as he himself stated. We do not know how or where he studied medicine, although he was certainly a professor of medicine at the University of Siena during the first half of the 1240s. Other places where he studied or taught have also been suggested, based on current knowledge of medieval university networks and on the model of academic peregrination, which encouraged scholars to travel between universities, thus helping in the construction of a common European culture.

It was immersion in the scholarly environment of the medieval universities that allowed Pedro Hispano to build and strengthen the foundations of the vast knowledge and erudition admired by his contemporaries and successors. In view of their intrinsic pedagogic dimension, some of his attributed works would have come from this context: this is the case of two fundamental works in his canon. One, the *Sumullae logicales*, is a didactic treatise on logic which presents and synthesizes the most important philosophical teachings of his time, later adopted as a textbook in many European universities. Another, the *Thesaurus pauperum*, is a popular theoretical and practical book of prescriptions, including most known illnesses of the time and how they might be treated, arranged according to curious anatomical criteria and anchored in a broad knowledge of the main medical authorities – classical Greek and Latin, Arab and Christian.

The study of Pedro Hispano's scholarly works is not without controversy, however. The problems which complicate any definitive catalogue include authors' homonyms, medieval veneration of authority, the fragmentation of the works in the form of heterogeneous codices, and the great weight of anonymity in mediaeval textual production. Such problems have caused some scholars to question the identification of the philosopher and doctor Pedro Hispano with Pedro Julião, proclaimed as Pope John XXI. Seen from this perspective, the correspondence is ambiguous, admitting a possible confusion between distinct historical figures, a result of the similarity in names (Pedro was one of the most common names in the Middle Ages, Hispano was a common toponym for those from the Iberian Peninsula), allied to chronological coincidence and to parallels in career and in intellectual reputation. Nevertheless, this is a somewhat marginal historiographical position: in the absence of new data, the debate is still inconclusive. Long tradition, dating from shortly after the death of John XXI, still prevails, maintaining that the Portuguese Pedro Julião, who was Pope of the Roman Church for a short period in the thirteenth century, is identical with the intellectual Pedro Hispano, author of various treatises. In this perspective, it is still viable to impute to him a large corpus of works, mainly in medicine and philosophy, but also including alchemy and mystical theology, with some digressions into zoology and meteorology.

Although attributing works to Pedro Hispano is largely speculative, we are on much firmer ground in establishing his ecclesiastical trajectory. As his career was built and his posts accumulated, any gaps in his life have become smaller and better documented. During his ecclesiastical career, he passed through practically the whole of the *cursus honorum* of the Church. He held posts in Lisbon Cathedral as canon (c. 1250), schoolmaster (1260) and dean (1250–1272), and in the archdiocese of Braga as archdeacon (1250–1272) and later as archbishop elect (1272–1273), though never confirmed. His bishopric was only discontinued when he was made cardinal by Pope Gregory X, when he was allocated the suburbicarian church of Túsculo (1273–1276). Before this, in Portugal, he had been appointed Prior of the important Collegiate Church of Saint Mary of Guimarães (1273), after a contentious process which took sixteen years to settle, from the time when he was presented to this church by King Afonso III (r. 1248–1279) in 1257.

Pedro Julião's career in the Church was closely linked with the intricate system of relations between him and the king, which escalated from evident confidence to open conflict, a hostility which continued even after his elevation to the papacy. Their initial closeness is clear, for example, in his nomination as royal representative at the *Cortes* (assembly of the three estates) of Guimarães in 1250, and his appointment as prior of Saint Mary of Guimarães, mentioned above. The episode which led to the cooling of the relationship would have been the election, in 1258, of Master Mateus as Bishop of Lisbon, a post which Pedro Julião, supported by the Cathedral chapter, had been hoping for. However, his ambition was checked after the intervention of King Afonso III. The ill-feeling between the two extended to the question of the priorship of Guimarães, with the king withdrawing his initial support. After he was made pope, Pedro Julião maintained his predecessors' excommunication of the king, the result of a long dispute between him and the Portuguese clergy.

The coronation of Pedro Julião as pope took place sometime between 16 and 20 September 1276, after the successive deaths, in scarcely eight months, of Gregory X (pope 1271–1276), Innocent V (d. 1276) and Hadrian V (d. 1276). The final choice was in the hands of a small conclave of nine electors, meeting in Viterbo. His candidacy may have been facilitated by his being seen as a third way, an alternative to the clergy connected to the French and Italian factions. The decision was clearly unanimous. Anointed as John XXI, he governed the Catholic Church until late May 1277, his death being officially fixed as the 20th of that month. The cause of his death was the collapse of part of the papal palace of Viterbo, and he was buried in Saint Lawrence's Church there.

For his government he chose a motto taken from a prayer in the medieval books of devotions, inspired by a passage from the biblical psalter; translated freely, it reads "Guide me, Lord, in the ways of thy justice", and points to an ideological programme. In his brief time as pope, John XXI followed the directives and forms promulgated by the Second Council of Lyon (1274), presided by Gregory X, the guiding figure of his rule. Thus he reclaimed the role of champion of papal supremacy, he advocated the unification of the Latin and Eastern Churches, separated since the schism of 1054, and he was a staunch defender of the spirit of the crusades to liberate the Holy Land, presenting a challenge to Christian kings, to be materialized in the payment of tributes to finance an expedition which was, however, never carried out.

He was also active politically, participating in various areas of European Christianity. Among these was the war between Philip III of France and Alfonso X of Castile and León, in the struggle for the title of Holy Roman Emperor, disputed between Charles of Anjou and Rudolph I of Habsburg; the pacification of the Italian Peninsula, disturbed by tension between the communes of Perugia and Assisi; and the resolution of quarrels between Afonso III of Portugal and the Portuguese clergy. His plans came from an orthodox understanding of the faith, especially with regard to the greatest rival religion, Islam: a rigorous position which aimed to reconcile evangelization, the assimilation of pagans and heretics and the conversion of Jews and Arabs.

John XXI also devoted attention to the administration of the Curia, including the nomination and confirmation of priests in ecclesiastical roles, the granting and ratification of privileges and immunities to institutions and individuals, and the administration of justice, the pope being the highest resource of appeal in Christianity.

On the cultural field, he ratified the foundation of the Franciscan College of Raymond Lull in Mallorca, and he did not ignore the theological controversy which had broken out in the University of Paris, known as the "university crisis of 1277", supporting the conservative Augustinian faction, dominant in the Faculty of Theology, against the pro-Aristotelian currents, popular in the Faculty of Arts, in their more moderate (Thomism) or radical (Averroism) forms.

As pope, but above all as an intellectual, Pedro Hispano was an important cultural mediator, connecting different places and chronologies. The significant impact he had in his time lasted into subsequent centuries, at least until the definitive decline of scholasticism in the early sixteenth century. In particular, the medical and philosophical treatises attributed to him are a crucible of very different experiences, coming from diverse latitudes. His works weld the learning of European Christian, Judaic and Islamic cultures, thus connecting almost all the known world of his time. They reveal a global understanding of science, regardless of frontiers or even of faiths, a tolerant attitude not always visible during his papacy. This is a possible portrait of a man of the thirteenth century, a European scholar, product of the so-called 'first Renaissance', the circumstances of whose life are not always entirely clear, for whom Dante Alighieri reserved a place in the fourth of his nine spheres of Paradise – the reward of wise spirits. Here is someone who could have been condemned to obscurity, but who became the only Portuguese pope.

ARMANDO NORTE
Centre for the History of Society and Culture, University of Coimbra, and
Centre for History, Faculty of Arts and Humanities, University of Lisbon

Bibliography

MEIRINHOS, José Francisco, "Giovanni XXI", in *Enciclopedia dei Papi*, vol. II, Rome, Istituto della Enciclopedia Italiana, 2000, pp. 427–437.

NORTE, Armando, *João XXI, o Papa Português*, Lisbon, A Esfera dos Livros, 2016.

PEREIRA, Maria Helena da Rocha, *Obras Médicas de Pedro Hispano*, Coimbra, Universidade de Coimbra, 1973.

PONTES, J. M. da Cruz, "Para situar Pedro Hispano Portugalense na história da filosofia", *Revista Portuguesa de Filosofia*, no. 24, 1968, pp. 21–45.

POTTHAST, August (ed.), *Regesta Pontif cum Romanorum. Inde ab a. post Christum Natum MCXCVIII ad a. MCCCIV*, t. II, Berolini, Decker, 1875.

1290
A University That Would Develop a World Profile

Over many centuries, the University of Coimbra educated the elite – magistrates and officials of government, law and the Church, within the kingdom and in its multi-continental empire.

The university arose in Bologna in the Middle Ages as a corporate cultural institution of doctors, masters, scholars and students dedicated to study and knowledge. It was organized as an institution and had its own privileges, allowing it to award exclusive academic degrees and a licence or qualification for teaching and the practice of the specialized liberal professions to those who attended it. It was called *studium generale* (General Studies), 'studies' since it was a place for teaching, learning and training, and 'general' because it was universal and open to all.

The university served the Church. Protected under its guardianship, it benefitted from its associated privileges, especially the *licentia ubique docendi* (the right to teach at any university), and favoured the training of its jurists and theologians, a kind of clerical militia in the service of ecclesiastical orthodoxy and the fight against heresy. It also served political powers – of the cities where it grew up, such as Bologna, specializing in Civil and Canon Law, and Paris, famous for Philosophy and Theology. It served royal powers too, defended as they were not only by the sword of knights and crusaders, but by the pen of lawyers and jurists who shaped the ideological discourse of kings, contributing to the social legitimacy of imperial and royal authority; thus it formed the matrix of European nations.

Among the earliest *studia generalia* (though not all survived or functioned without a break), are, in Italy, Salerno, Bologna and Reggio Emilia, founded in the twelfth century, Arezzo (1215), Padua (1222) and Siena (1246); in France, Paris, Montpellier and Toulouse (first three decades of the thirteenth century); in England, Oxford and Cambridge (beginning of the thirteenth century); and in the Iberian Peninsula, Palencia (1208/1212), Salamanca (1215–1219), Valladolid (c. 1260), Lérida (1300), and the Portuguese university, officially founded in 1290. The growth in the number of towns and cities in Western Europe in the Middle Ages, commercial and financial development, and the increasing complexity of social relations and of legal guarantees concerned with property and the family created a need for more legal scholars, especially lawyers, judges, chancellors, notaries, advocates, procurators and many other public officials. Within the Church, there was a growth in the number of theologians and canon lawyers.

In Portugal, the University was founded by King Denis following an initial petition by a group of clergy; it benefited from privileges and funding given by the monarchy as well as by the Church. The kings liked it to be mentioned as theirs: "my college in Coimbra", "my university of my studies in the city of Coimbra", as we find in documents from the royal chancellery in the fourteenth century. The first document dates from 1309: here the king calls the institution a "university of scholars", and after this it was usually known as a "university".

A petition sent to Pope Nicholas IV in 1288 stated "Wisdom enlightens the world and leads subjects to obedience to God, better preparing his ministers and confirming the faith of the faithful and exalting the Church, defended by ecclesiastics". These were the words of the abbot of Alcobaça, the priors of Santa Cruz in Coimbra and of Saint Vincent de Fora in Lisbon, and twenty-four priors and rectors of collegiate and parish churches, meeting in Montemor-o-Novo, where King Denis was staying. These monasteries had long-standing cultural traditions and were provided with fine, up-to-date libraries, acting as training grounds for their members in spiritual, doctrinal, juridical, canonical, philosophical and theological matters. The Augustinian regular canons also encouraged medicine, which was practiced in the hospitals of their wealthy monasteries. In Alcobaça in 1269, abbot Estêvão Martins set up a *studium* for training monks, with its own income.

On 1st March 1290, in Leiria, King Denis granted his official protection to all those, whatever their provenance, who were studying or about to study in the General

Studies which he had founded in Lisbon, which was staffed by scholars in all the arts and provided with the necessary privileges. Wisdom, according to the king's document, was like a marvellous treasure: the more it grew, the more spiritual and temporal favours it would pour onto the world; its acquisition would help all believers better to know God and to embrace the Catholic faith. The king saw his foundation as conferring prestige on his native city, already embellished by the precious relics of the body of the martyr Saint Vincent, and as an act of piety, praying God that through his action, "we may dwell in Thy house" (Psalm 27, 4). Furthermore, Denis recognized that the General Studies would enrich the kingdom with "the precious treasure of knowledge", serving the Church as well as justice, which it was his duty to administer to his subjects. Pope Nicholas responded favourably to the king. By a bull of 9th August 1290, he praised the foundation of the General Studies in Lisbon, with its faculties of Arts, Canon Law, Civil Law and Medicine, but excluding the teaching of Theology, which was reserved for masters in the cloisters of the Dominican and Franciscan mendicant orders. He decreed that the rent of houses for students should be assessed by two clergy and by two laymen elected by students and by officials of the municipality. The masters of the university could keep the income from benefices and stipends that they held already. Masters, students and their servants were also eligible to be judged by ecclesiastical judges in legal premises. Finally, if masters considered a student to be promising and law-abiding, he could be awarded a degree by the bishop or, in his absence, by the diocesan vicar. With this set of privileges, the Portuguese university was on a par with the principal General Studies of Christendom of the time.

Although the university was a prestigious presence for any city, local authorities and oligarchs often viewed it as a source of conflict, costs and damage to their interests, rather than a body which would enrich municipal coffers. In this context, for political and financial motives, it was transferred in 1308 from Lisbon to Coimbra, where it remained until 1338. It went back to its place of origin until 1354, then returned to Coimbra until 1377, only transferring definitively from Lisbon to Coimbra in 1537.

As an organized seat of learning, officially recognized and supported, the General Studies governed itself, with officials elected by their peers and its own officers. Documents list the academic body, following the medieval lexicon: doctors and fellows, bachelors and licentiates, masters, experts and jurists, professors and sages. The tendency for the medieval clergy, especially in the Late Middle Ages, to move from one place to another, was felt in practically every Portuguese diocese, which received foreign bishops, canons and priests. In the University, too, there were masters such as the Italian Martino de Bosmarineto and Martin Rogido of Seville, both teachers of Medicine, Pedro de Botanego and Pedro de Corbinaco, professors of Law, Galhardo Eberardo, Guilherme de Cavanhaco and Elias Roberto; the majority of doctors and masters in the various faculties, however, were Portuguese, a tendency which, with certain exceptions, continues to this day. The majority of students, or scholars, were clerics, mostly from the minor orders, with a few from families of the new nobility. Despite the parity of scholastic knowledge taught in the Portuguese university with that of their equivalents elsewhere in Europe, in fact many Portuguese scholars still left the country to gain degrees and prestige in the General Studies of France, Italy, England and especially Salamanca.

Listed among the University's officials are curators and their scribes, a beadle, a porter and a proctor of studies. In 1344, the scholars of the General Studies in Lisbon asked the pope to give their rector Lourenço Eanes a canonship in Silves Cathedral. At this time, the rector was not yet the principal 'magistrate' of the University, as he would come to be later. It may be that it is this leadership function in the University that is referred to in 1354, mentioning Álvaro Pais as *escolar-mor* (principal scholar). In Coimbra, the General Studies students also had various tradespeople in their service, such as a butcher, a baker, fishermen and wine-growers, as well as inspectors of weights and measures.

In the medieval Portuguese university, students registered in one of the faculties (Canon Law, Civil Law, Medicine and Arts), following the curriculum for each area of training. The masters read (*lectio*) the texts of important authors (*auctoritates*), glossing and commenting on the content. In many cases, students might follow a more didactic method, that of *disputatio*, debating important questions within the scope of predominant scholastic and Aristotelian knowledge. The loss of the medieval University archives has made it impossible for us to know much about University culture and its contribution to humanistic trends in the thirteenth century, or to the maritime discoveries patronized by the Crown. It should be mentioned, however, that two of its most distinguished patrons at the time were Prince Henry (the Navigator, d. 1460) and King Afonso V (d. 1481).

Supporting the University, various colleges and institutions were set up, as pious acts of benevolence, to welcome and house students. Such was the one that the Bishop of Lisbon and the first chancellor, Domingos Jardo, founded in the city, dedicating it to Saints Paul, Eligius and Clement, and stating that it should maintain six students, two of Law and Theology and four of Grammar, Logic, Natural Philosophy and Medicine. In 1294, the king asked the Cistercians to set up a *studium*, probably in connection with the work of the University, which had been created at the beginning of the decade. There was also the attempt by Prince Pedro, duke of Coimbra, to found a second General Studies in Coimbra, with the support of Dominican masters, which was also supported in 1450 by King Afonso V.

In 1537 the University settled definitively in Coimbra, where some reforms were made: a Faculty of Theology was added, and some classes were now taught by Spanish, French and Scottish masters. New importance was given to the cultural relationship between Portuguese students and the University of Salamanca and its thinkers, such as the Dominican Francisco de Vitoria and, in the seventeenth century, Francisco Suarez.

Portuguese university teaching also included the Jesuits and their University of Évora, established in 1559 and closed in 1779: its school of philosophy included teachers from Coimbra . There was an emphasis on better-informed models of missionary evangelization, more in dialogue with other civilizations: an example of this is the Jesuit Matteo Ricci, who spent time in Coimbra and wrote the first Portuguese–Chinese dictionary.

Over many centuries, the University of Coimbra educated the elite – magistrates and officials of government, law and the Church, within the kingdom and across its multi-continental empire. The Discoveries inspired some of the masters of the modern university, such as the mathematician Pedro Nunes, contributing to scientific horizons which were then opening in the areas of the natural and medical sciences, in jurisprudence, and in the humanities in general.

The University of Coimbra was not immune to interference from the Inquisition, nor from periods of scientific conservatism, but it also experienced important reforms in pedagogy and learning, such as those instigated by the Marquis of Pombal, and historic changes in its organization in the twentieth century. The universal cultural significance of its material and immaterial heritage was recognized by the award of UNESCO's World Heritage status in 2013.

SAUL ANTÓNIO GOMES
Centre for the History of Society and Culture and Faculty of Arts and Humanities, University of Coimbra

Bibliography

Chartularium Universitatis Portugalensis (1288–1537), documents collected and published by A. Mokingra de Sá, vol. I, Lisbon, Instituto de Alta Cultura, 1966.
FERNANDES, Hermenegildo (coord.), *A Universidade Medieval em Lisboa. Séculos XII–XVI*, Lisbon, Tinta-da-China, 2013.
História da Universidade em Portugal, vol. I, t. I–II, Lisbon, Universidade de Coimbra/ Fundação Calouste Gulbenkian, 1997.
SERRÃO, Joaquim Veríssimo, *História das Universidades*, Porto, Lello, 1983.

1293
The Merchants' Guild: The Ports, the King and Portuguese Trade within European Networks

Arising in the context of growth in European trade, the Merchants' Exchange demonstrated Portuguese involvement in the process of European economic integration at the time.

The Merchants' Exchange was a medieval organization which brought together merchants and shipowners from Porto and Lisbon, who contributed capital to a common fund to defray the costs of accidents and of business dealings, in Portugal and abroad.

On 10 May 1293, King Denis ordered that there be entered in Chancellery record books the letter in which he recognized what would be known to posterity as the Merchants' Exchange. The document has been seen as the starting point of this commercial institution, and an expression of the monarchy's ability to invigorate maritime trade and shipping. This historiographical interpretation comes from centralist political contexts, however, and requires revision, since the King's document did not express this intention, nor did it found the so-called Exchange. What it did was to recognize, on the part of the Crown, the usefulness of a practice which had been carried on for some time by the most powerful agents of Portuguese ports. This does not diminish the importance of the document. Nevertheless, it makes us reflect on the commercial and maritime dynamics of the kingdom in the later Middle Ages, as well as on what would become, between the fifteenth and eighteenth centuries, a profound relationship – that of Portugal with the sea.

A general idea is worth emphasizing: for many years there was a tendency to stress the role of royal power in the historical narrative. Nowadays this is being re-evaluated. In the case of the Merchants' Exchange, the terms of the document show that the process happened in the opposite direction – from the agents of ports and commerce towards central power, which, objectively, used a framework of expansion in maritime trade to intervene actively in the sector, resulting in a dialogue (not always easy) between the Crown and the ports. This would continue in the following centuries, the era of the great sea voyages and the building of the overseas empire.

Arising at a time of growth in European trade, the Merchants' Exchange demonstrated Portuguese involvement in the process of European economic integration at the time. The similar associations which followed, after the so-called "crisis of the fourteenth century", guaranteed that this participation would continue, assured by the growing value of their maritime and commercial skills. The letter of King Denis shows certain facets of this evolution. Firstly, it does not differentiate merchants from shipowners, recognizing the social worth of the men who conducted foreign negotiations and their importance for the economy of the kingdom. The tendency from that point was a separation between capital and labour, with businessmen becoming sedentary and gaining in status, and shipowners increasingly dependent on them. However, they were never very far apart, and occasionally shared ownership of vessels. Secondly, it conveyed the new energy of voyages and maritime trade, and the awareness of the need for an entity that would protect and regulate them. Thirdly, it showed the weight of institutions in the progress of medieval and modern trade, a topic now much debated by historians internationally, although much less in Portugal.

Research indicates that exchanges, private trading companies, brotherhoods, professional bodies, guilds and confraternities, as well as the degree of involvement of central powers in these systems, are fundamental elements for understanding contemporary realities, and may explain the force and consistency, or the weakness and ephemerality, of maritime economies at this time. Studies are being made of merchants' associations in northern Europe, the Merchant Adventurers of London and their equivalents in Bristol and other British cities, the Hansa and the Italian companies in southern Europe, in an attempt to understand their origins, their organization, their relations with ports and cities, their degree of autonomy or dependence in relation to sources of power, and their ability to act in the organization or pre-capitalist economies; finally, considering the different forms of organization, there is discussion of the institutional framework of medieval (and modern) trade, assessing the mechanics of its operation and its efficiency. Points of contact might be found between these organizations and the Portuguese exchanges, raising the same questions, but such a study is yet to be made.

The Merchants' Exchange could be compared to the corporations of medieval trades. Arising in cities – in this case, in ports – on the initiative of those who shared the same profession and the same interests, the organizations of merchants and shipowners reached maturity when they were recognized by municipalities and kings, as happened with this Exchange. In generally requiring shipowners to agree to the Exchange's conditions, accepting common rules and identical benefits (on pain of those not doing so "paying ten pounds to this community" – here royal intervention was decisive), the Crown made trade a central concern of government, recognizing the existence of a body ever more fundamental for the prosperity of the kingdom.

The corporation was certainly not a business – rather, it was a structure designed to preserve economic advantages and social privileges. However, there was little in the Middle Ages that was fixed. Certain concepts and practices were adapted to circumstances, indicating certain paths: in this case, paths which businesses and trade networks in the Early Modern period followed and expanded without coercion of partners, despite the limits imposed by ever more assertive central powers. But the first steps had been taken, and there was no way back. Maritime trade had definitely entered the national political agenda, and turned to the outside world.

The Exchange shows a commercial geography which would continue between the fifteenth and eighteenth centuries, though the function of each place varied in line with the construction of the Portuguese maritime empire and the interests of the merchants involved in the Atlantic trade from the sixteenth century onwards. At the time it was set up, the dominant players were Flanders (in the fourteenth century, for the Portuguese this included Brabant), France, England, and in the background Genoa, whose influence was felt throughout Europe. It was best known for its characteristics of mutualism and insurance protection. In any work on the history of insurance, the letter of 10th May 1293 is seen as the foundation of this activity in Portugal. This is a reductive interpretation, however. In setting up funds for common use, overseas and within Portugal, it anticipated the use of money in the resolution of various difficulties, such as payment of licenses or special duties, or even of favours to facilitate the work of shipowners and merchants.

The document also details the type of vessels, an important though little studied topic. The contribution paid by members was estimated on the tonnage of ships, which was then rising to over 100 tons, showing that this was a period of technological progress. Ships were changing: those being used (like the Nordic cog in northern Portuguese ports) were becoming bigger, with more cargo space but still maintaining their manoeuvrability. A product of this evolution was the Portuguese *nau*. Resulting from the sharing of skills in shipyards, the process led to complex interpretations of the original use of ships and the design of new vessels.

This advance seems to be consolidated in the final third of the fourteenth century, when King Ferdinand renewed the privileges of the Exchange, even assisting in the expansion of the institution to function in both Lisbon and Porto. The document setting up the so-called *Companhia das Naus*, between 1375 and 1380, gave an incentive to further shipbuilding, broadening the concession of privileges to vessels over 50 tons, if fitted with decks, and inaugurating a policy to be followed in later centuries. As well as showing King Ferdinand (or his counsellors) as a ruler interested in maritime matters, this legislation shows increased concern with the question of insurance and protection against shipping accidents.

The *Companhia das Naus* also introduced the question of the evolution of the institution, which is not easy to analyze. In comparison with the Merchants' Exchange, in the forms described, it does not seem to have lasted long. The problems experienced by the Company after the death of the king, the interregnum (dynastic crisis) and the wars with Castile impeded it from functioning normally. The tendency, anyway, was for incentives to be included in royal legislation and converted into permanent, frequently adjusted subsidies for shipbuilding. But the unions of merchants and shipowners under the name "Exchange" continued. Though they were no longer mentioned in Lisbon, which was increasingly becoming a large-scale port, favoured particularly by the availability of ships from various Portuguese and foreign ports which had dealings there, in Porto this kind of association still continued until the mid-fifteenth century. In 1397, the City Council petitioned King John I to require restoration of payments due to the Merchants' Exchange, which had stopped during the Castilian wars – this request was repeated several times. How are we to explain such persistence? Perhaps because of the great investment that the city had made in shipbuilding, especially in freight vessels for the main economic centres of Europe. This meant that here too the nature of the Exchanges changed, now dealing more with chartering than with genuinely commercial subjects. This does not diminish the importance of these institutions and their role as regulatory bodies. From them came shipbrokers, with functions identical to those in the principal European ports, raising freight transport to the status of the "trade of the Kingdom", in the words of Themudo Barata.

For different motives, the medieval cities of Porto and Lisbon did not suffer feudal pressures crippling the development of their ports and the activity of their agents. In this sense, the emergence of Exchanges basically shows a will to improve commercial and maritime resources so that those agents could compete or at least be on a par with other businessmen in foreign markets. The way their functions were renewed and enlarged, regulating the load and the cargo of ships, shows that they fulfilled their role until new organizational practices emerged. This happened in the sixteenth century, when the capitalist spirit largely directed the rhythms of maritime trade, definitively separating traders from shipowners in the division of the work of ports. If up till then Exchanges had generally encouraged bilateral economic relationships, reinforced by the support of central power, from then on this ceased to make sense, since the merchants themselves organized their actions on the basis of multilateral relationships, relying on the strength of their networks and on well-defined practices of trust and reputation. The mutualist function of the Exchanges lost ground, too, until it disappeared with the rise of international insurance markets, which could act more cheaply and quickly in managing the risks that might threaten individual agents.

AMÂNDIO J. M. BARROS
School of Education, Polytechnic Institute of Porto and CITCEM –
Transdisciplinary Research Centre "Culture, Space and Memory",
University of Porto

Bibliography

BARATA, Filipe Themudo, *Navegação, Comércio e Relações Políticas. Os Portugueses no Mediterrâneo Ocidental (1385–1466)*, Lisbon, Fundação Calouste Gulbenkian/Junta Nacional de Investigação Científica e Tecnológica, 1998.

GELDERBLOM, Oscar, *Cities of Commerce: The Institutional Foundations of International Trade in the Low Countries, 1250–1650*, Princeton, Princeton University Press, 2013.

MARQUES, João Martins da Silva, *Descobrimentos Portugueses: Documentos para a Sua História*, Lisbon, Instituto de Alta Cultura, 1944–1945.

NORTH, Douglass C., *Institutions, Institutional Change, and Economic Performance: The Political Economy of Institutions and Decisions*, Cambridge, Cambridge University Press, 1990.

SILVA, Maria Fernanda Espinosa Gomes da, "Bolsas marítimas", in SERRÃO, Joel (dir.), *Dicionário de História de Portugal*, vol. I, Lisbon, Iniciativas Editoriais, 1971, pp. 355–356.

1297

The Treaty of Alcañices and the Establishment of a Border with Neighbouring Threats

As a peace treaty or a frontier treaty, for Portugal the Treaty of Alcañices defined the oldest border of a European state (even though Olivença became part of Spain in 1801). From the fifteenth century onwards, however, the Portuguese frontier would gain in dynamism in the process of expansion, both in the context of North Africa and in the Atlantic and the Indian Ocean.

The state of prolonged war in the Iberian Peninsula after the Muslim invasion of 711 turned the frontier into one of the most important and dynamic elements in the region. But in the Hispanic context it had different forms depending on the progress of the Reconquest. For if it initially divided adversaries which had always been and would continue irreconcilable – organized around the only two political structures in existence until the mid-ninth century, namely the kingdom of Asturias and the emirate of Córdoba – the gradual formation of other Christian political structures was delineating new frontiers, now not between enemies but between rivals.

This differentiation created dynamics of growth with varying directions. Thus, from the point of view of the Christian kingdoms, the southern border with the Islamic powers, whether they were centralized under the auspices of the Emirate, later Caliphate, of Córdoba or dispersed in the various *taifas* which resulted from its fragmentation in 1031, was a non-negotiable boundary. This border was seen simply as something that would disappear with the final expulsion of the Muslims from the Iberian Peninsula – which was only to happen with the definitive conquest of the kingdom of Granada by the Catholic Monarchs in 1492. On the other hand, the borders which divided the distinct Christian kingdoms of the Peninsula were being adjusted throughout the period, depending on their progress southwards and on pacts between neighbours, as happened at various times between León and Castile until their final union in 1230, and between Aragon and Navarre and later between Aragon and the Catalan principality, finally united in 1163 under the Crown of Aragon.

But the borders dividing the different Christian kingdoms had another aspect, which distinguished them in the European context, because the treaties which defined them had clauses applying not only to the time they were established, but also to the future. That is, the various agreements regulated the frontier as it existed at the moment of the treaty, but also as it would come be later. It was to be expected that thanks to the Reconquest, the border with al-Andalus would be advancing south: it was therefore necessary to define how to divide the future conquered territories among the neighbouring kingdoms. An excellent example is the Treaty of Cazorla, signed in 1179 by Alfonso VIII of Castile and Alfonso II of Aragon. It established how the southern territory that the two Crowns would later conquer would be divided, with the Islamic kingdom of Murcia going to Castile and that of Valencia to Aragon. Quite often, however, such definitions were not stipulated by treaties, but rather by tacit understanding as to the places where borders between the two rival Christian kingdoms could be drawn. And even with agreements, problems eventually arose.

The case of Portugal is very interesting. The northern frontier, fixed from the time of the foundation of the kingdom by the course of the River Minho – although the County of *Portucale* extended as far as the Ria of Vigo – was a barren zone which separated two of the three administrative centres of the ancient Roman province of Gallaecia: the northern part was dominated by Lugo, the southern part by Braga, and the eastern part by Astorga. The Roman administrative *Conventus bracarensis* practically coincided with present-day Portugal north of the Douro, with this river forming the border between Roman Gallaecia and Lusitania.

King Afonso Henriques (1128–1185) tried more than once to expand this frontier, going beyond the Minho to take control of the territories of Toronho and Límia, but he was always opposed by the rulers of León, both the emperor Alfonso VII (1126–1157) and his son and successor Ferdinand II (1157—1188). On the other hand, the Portuguese king's advance to the south never gave rise to serious opposition, and he soon reached the Tagus, seizing Santarém and Lisbon in 1147. What was missing was the eastern frontier with the kingdom of León, which followed the River Coa south of the Douro – this was the reason for important castles such as Penedono, Marialva, Trancoso and Pinhel. Here too Afonso Henriques tried to advance into the territory of León, encouraging the foundation of the Cistercian monastery of Saint Mary of Aguiar, near Figueira de Castelo Rodrigo. In fact there were many confrontations between him and his cousin and son-in-law, Ferdinand II of León.

Their most serious conflict developed much further south, however, and linked the two Portuguese borders – with León and with al-Andalus. After reaching the Tagus, Afonso Henriques began an aggressive policy of expansion into the lands across the river, supported mainly by local militias and by the mercenary armies led by Geraldo Geraldes (Gerald the Fearless). After a series of campaigns leading to the capture of Beja (1162), Trujillo, Évora and Cáceres (1165), Montánchez, Serpa and Juromenha (1166), and Moura and Alconchel (1167), he aimed for the Almohad fortress of Badajoz, key to the road to Seville. But Ferdinand II of León could not allow such an advance, invading territories which, in the context of the "future frontiers" mentioned above, would be for León to conquer. Hence, in 1169 at the attack on Badajoz, Ferdinand II joined forces with the Almohads to stop the fortress falling into Portuguese hands. Afonso Henriques' forces were surprised in the attack, and he himself was seriously wounded. Taken prisoner by Ferdinand, was forced to surrender several fortresses, particularly those north of the Minho.

The Reconquest of the Peninsula would only advance once again after the disintegration of the Almohad empire, particularly the defeat at the Battle of Navas de Tolosa in 1212, which led to the period of the greatest advances by the different Hispanic kingdoms: Aragon conquered the Balearic Islands and Valencia, Castile advanced into Andalusia, including Córdoba, Seville and other cities, while the kingdom of Portugal finished the process of Reconquest with the occupation of all of the Alentejo and the Algarve between 1217 and 1249.

The conquest of the Algarve, however, was contested by Castile, particularly by the crown prince, later Alfonso X, known as the Wise, who saw the region, since it was part of the *taifa* of Niebla, as an area to be won by León – that is, the old matter of "future frontiers" was still effective. The disagreement was only resolved several years later by the marriage of Alfonso's daughter Beatrice to King Afonso III of Portugal, and in 1267 by the signing of the Treaty of Badajoz, which strictly defined the border between Portugal and Castile and also resolved the problem of the Algarve.

By 1249 the kingdom of Portugal had completed the definition of its territory, thus becoming one of the earliest of the European monarchies. Apart from this, the stabilization of territory, consolidated even more by the Treaty of Alcañices, allowed the Portuguese kings to move forward with a highly ambitious programme to centralize power, which was also to be valuable in the context of European Christianity at that time and later, especially when compared with other Peninsular kingdoms.

The reign of King Denis (1279–1325) is notable in this context, since he succeeded in linking various areas of government which transformed Portugal into a well-defined political entity, with the Crown as the centre point of power and an increasingly specialized and active administration. Furthermore, the border was definitively fixed, the policy of settlement continued – with King Afonso III and King Denis granting more than a hundred and fifty local charters, especially in Trás-os-Montes and the Alentejo, often linked to the creation of markets – and finally the system of border defences was reinforced by work on over eighty defensive systems during Denis's reign, either strengthening existing structures or building new castles and walls.

Considering the first years of his reign, which included several conflicts with his brother Afonso of Portalegre, Denis's preoccupation with territorial defence comes as no surprise. Moreover, the conditions in the neighbouring kingdom of Castile since the death of Alfonso X were highly unstable. It is in this context that we can understand the agreement celebrated in Ciudad Rodrigo in 1291 between Sancho IV of Castile, his son and successor, and King Denis, by which Denis's daughter, Princess Constance, would marry Sancho's son, the future Ferdinand IV. However, Ferdinand's early death, in 1295, changed the good political relations between the two royal houses, since the queen-dowager Maria de Molina did not approve of the marriage that had been arranged for her son.

It was in this context that King Denis formed an alliance with his brother-in-law James II of Aragon, who did not have good relations with Castile, with both deciding to simultaneously attack the Castilian border in 1296, although King Denis had obtained an agreement in the previous year guaranteeing the return to Portugal of the Alentejan forts such as Moura, Serpa and Mourão. Despite this, James invaded and occupied the kingdom of Murcia from the border with Valencia, while Denis took the region of Ribacoa, then continuing to Simancas, less than a league from Valladolid, where he met Ferdinand IV of Castile, who was still a boy. Denis withdrew to Portugal, but not before occupying a series of forts which had belonged to León but which then became part of Portugal.

On the 12 September 1297, the kings Denis of Portugal and Ferdinand IV of Castile, in the presence of the queens, the princes, the wealthy and the bishops of both countries, signed the Treaty of Alcañices. They did this from different feelings and perspectives, since for Castile the treaty dealt mostly with peace, whereas for Portugal it was clearly about defining borders: places given to the king of Portugal were Olivença and Campo Maior, close to Badajoz, São Fins dos Galegos and also Ouguela, near Campo Maior, which had long been a source of contention. Also in the possession of Portugal were the settlements, castles and towns of Sabugal, Alfaiates, Castelo Rodrigo, Vilar Maior, Castelo Bom, Almeida, Castelo Melhor and Monforte, as well as other places in the region of the Ribacoa – thus moving the border from the River Coa to the Águeda. In his turn, King Denis ceded his rights to Aiamonte and to the settlements he held in Galicia and León.

As a peace treaty or a frontier treaty, for Portugal the Treaty of Alcañices defined the oldest border of a European state (even though Olivença became part of Spain in

1801). From the fifteenth century onwards, however, the Portuguese frontier would gain in dynamism in the process of expansion, both in the context of North Africa and in the Atlantic and the Indian Ocean. In these two maritime areas, the question of "future frontiers" would again become relevant, as shown by the treaties of Alcáçovas in 1479 and of Tordesilhas in 1494. That is, the medieval model of the frontier continued into modernity and even into present times.

J. A. DE SOTTOMAYOR-PIZARRO
Faculty of Arts and Humanities, University of Porto; Academy
of Sciences, Lisbon; Royal Academy of History, Madrid

Bibliography

GARCÍA FITZ, Francisco, JIMÉNEZ ALCÁCER, Juan Francisco (coord.), *La Historia Peninsular en los Espacios de Frontera: las "Extremaduras Históricas" y la "Transierra" (Siglos XI–XIV)*, Cáceres/ Murcia, Sociedad Española de Estudios Medievales, 2012.

MARQUES, Maria Alegria Fernandes, "A viabilização de um reino" & "As etapas de crescimento do reino", in SERRÃO, Joel, MARQUES, A. H. de Oliveira (ed.), *Nova História de Portugal*, vol. III, Lisbon, Presença, 1996, pp. 23–37 & 37–64.

RUIZ DE LA PEÑA, Juan Ignacio (coord.), "Cristianos y Musulmanes en la Península Ibérica la Guerra, la Frontera y la Convivencia", *XI Congreso de Estudios Medievales (2007)*, León, Fundación Sánchez-Albornoz, 2009.

SÁNCHEZ HERRERO, José (coord.), *"El Tratado de Alcañices". Ponencias y Comunicaciones de las Jornadas Conmemorativas del VII Centenario del Tratado de Alcañices (1297–1997)*, Zamora, Fundación D. Afonso Henriques, 1999.

SOTTOMAYOR-PIZARRO, José Augusto de, *D.Dinis (1261–1325)*, 2nd ed., Lisbon, Temas e Debates, 2008.

1348
The Black Death: The Near "Global" Plague

It seems to have originated in Asia, on the Tibetan plateau, and to have spread from there by way of various animals, from insects to mammals, crossing different climate zones until it reached from China to the Indian Ocean and the Mediterranean.

Sudden, invisible and fast, an epidemic swept through the entire known world in medieval times. Death travelled by land and sea, beside people and goods, along the trade routes which linked Asia, Africa and Europe. Where did it come from? What was it? How could it be fought?

Many contemporary Europeans saw it as God's punishment for man's sins. To drive it away, one needed to pray, particularly to the new protector saints, Saint Sebastian and Saint Roch, and do penance, often communally, such as in processions of flagellants. The more erudite claimed that there was a corruption of the air due to noxious, poisonous vapours caused by putrid matter spread by the wind, a miasmatic theory complemented by astrology, which declared that an inauspicious conjunction of planets caused these harmful exhalations. It was recommended that filth should be removed from houses and settlements, that air should be purified with aromatic herbs, and that preventive isolation and quarantine should be enforced. Certain groups were declared guilty of spreading the plague, but also wandering pilgrims and vagabonds: all should be banished and persecuted, especially Jews. People acquiesced or rebelled, giving themselves up to pleasures or to mortifications, wavering between order and disorder.

The disease had been called the Black Death since the sixteenth century; it was scientifically identified and its origins discovered at the end of the nineteenth century, when laboratory analyses by the Franco-Swiss bacteriologist Alexandre Yersin and the French doctor Paul-Louis Simond recognized the bacterium *Yersinia pestis* as the cause of the plague. In the first decades of the twenty-first century, microbiology revealed the evolution of the genome using techniques to reconstruct the genetic material of the pathogen on the basis of samples collected from bodies buried in medieval cemeteries. This research led to the reassessment of many of the hosts and vectors involved in the spread and virulence of the epidemic. It is known that the bacteria survive in favourable micro-environments, and that certain wild rodents would have played a large part in their maintenance and spread, although the exact roles of rat fleas and human beings in transmission of the plague is still being discussed. Nevertheless, it is certain that the Black Death is a kind of bubonic plague, with an incidence of mortality of about 80%, although occasionally the bacillus can enter the blood directly, or secondarily from the bubo, causing a septicemic or pulmonary variant which is always fatal. In this form there can be direct transmission between people, worse in winter, through spitting.

It seems to have originated in Asia, on the Tibetan plateau, and to have spread from there by way of various animals, from insects to mammals, crossing different climate zones until it reached from China to the Indian Ocean and the Mediterranean. The Mongol empire, which in the thirteenth and fourteenth centuries dominated a vast area of Eurasia, would have encouraged this mobility, both by trade along caravan routes, associated with that of the Italian merchants, and by military manoeuvres. From the Golden Horde, a khanate resulting from the breakup of the Mongol empire, which the epidemic reached in October-November 1346, it spread south by land, and by sea from the Black Sea to the Mediterranean. The Mongol army which attacked the Crimean city of Caffa would have infected Italians. Genoese ships transported the epidemic to Constantinople, where the disease was recognized in July 1347. This commercial metropolis, with its close relations with the Italian Peninsula and the Mameluke empire, caused it to spread to Alexandria (advancing from there through Egypt, Palestine, Syria and Arabia) and to the ports of the Mediterranean. The epidemic hit Messina, Sicily, in August 1347, and from that port, perhaps together with Alexandria, it spread through North Africa. But also from Messina, if not directly from Constantinople, in that year it reached as far as Marseilles and Mallorca. From there, sea traffic, together with the river and land routes of continental Europe, thronged as they were with traders, travellers and pilgrims, made the plague move in "metastatic leaps" from various urban epicentres. In only five years, between 1347 and 1352, it spread through southern Europe, passing to England, Norway, the ports of the Hanseatic League and Russia, as well as the interior of the continent. Only Iceland and Finland seem to have escaped the scourge. This was not the first pandemic in European history – that was the plague of Justinian (c. 541–c. 767) – but the Black Death (1346–1352, with outbreaks in Europe up till 1650–1722) was the most devastating and prolonged.

In Portugal, the chronicles of the *Livro das Eras* of the Monastery of Santa Cruz in

Coimbra recorded it at the feast of Saint Michael in September 1348, which, given the epidemiological developments in the disease up until death, and the extent that it was recognized by educated elites, can place its arrival there at the end of July or the beginning of August. Santiago de Compostela, the main centre of pilgrimage in the Peninsula, which had close relations with the Portuguese Church and clergy, and was struck by the epidemic in June 1348, may have been an important focus of diffusion from the north to the central-south of the country, though the disease may also have spread by other land routes or by sea. At Braga Cathedral at the end of December there were vacancies in the Chapter due to the deaths of dignities and canons: even the archbishop died and the plague also struck down the bishops of Viseu and Lamego. In Coimbra, the priors of the collegiate churches of Saint Justa, Saint Bartholomew and Saint Christopher died, as well as all the clergy of Saint Peter's within the space of a month. The priors of the churches of Saint Mary and Saint James in Óbidos, of Sacavém and of Torres Vedras also perished. In monastic communities the catastrophe was even greater, the majority of monks and nuns falling prey to the sickness: such was the case in Saint Torcato in Guimarães, in Lorvão, Seiça and Alcobaça. Lay people died too, as we can see from testaments and epitaphs of the urban aristocracy and of officials such as notaries. Names are rarely known, however – the speed and high mortality of the epidemic made death anonymous.

The chronicle from Santa Cruz, mentioned above, and another from Alcobaça, noting the spread of the slaughter throughout the world, declared that 67% of the population had perished, while a document from the collegiate church of Saint Peter in Coimbra suggested a 90% rate of death. The figures in the Portuguese chronicles are increasingly worth considering. Reliable demographic studies of Spain, Italy, France and England have raised the death rate, which had usually been estimated as between 25% and 33%, to around 60%. From this we can say that out of a European population of 80 million, the Black Death would have killed around 50 million. Demographic effects certainly varied according to degree of population density, and differed from region to region and from country to country, depending on hygiene and nutritional habits, whether the epidemic was at its most intense or was weakening when it arrived, and favourable or unfavourable climatic conditions. But it is certain that the Black Death rapidly accelerated the depression which had begun to be felt at the end of the thirteenth century, and caused a deep and long-lasting demographic crisis. In Portugal, the "great pestilence" or "first" (pestilence) was repeated in others of greater or lesser intensity throughout the fourteenth and fifteenth centuries. With the addition of wars and famines, which accompanied the epidemics, historians have estimated that a national population of at most 1.5 million, before the plague, had plummeted in a mere three months to a million, only reaching its former level a century and a half later.

Throughout the kingdom, in towns and villages, the passage of the epidemic left scars on people and possessions. Towns and cities complained of depopulation, and the death of house-owners led to buildings falling into ruin. In the country, many peasant holdings and villages were abandoned, and agricultural land of all kinds was left unworked, remaining so for years or decades through lack of farm workers. This was particularly evident in Church lands, partly because these had increased on account of bequests to the Church by plague victims.

Without hope in their lives, those who had any wealth invested it in the salvation of their souls, donating their goods, by written or oral wills, to the clergy, who would intercede with God on their behalf. This transferral of properties to the Church, which as a fiscally exempt institution neither repaid nor donated wealth, removed lands permanently from the property market, which was very harmful to royal power and to all those who had access to it. Even in these exceptional circumstances, the clergy were guilty of abuses, and King Afonso IV acted at once. On the 21st May 1349, he promulgated a law dealing with an irregular situation – priests were demanding, on pain of excommunication, that testaments be validated only by them, and were appropriating the goods of those who died intestate, without contacting their relatives. The king, defending the law of inheritance of the kingdmon, stated that the property of those who died without heirs would be considered abandoned, and therefore would become royal property. It would be a punishable offence to read testaments in the presence of a priest, rather than before a royal judge so that they could be legally executed, and he named external judges to carry out this legislation. There were many lengthy legal cases concerned with inheritance after the plague, which shows that the royal decree at least impeded ecclesiastical abuses and strengthened the power of litigants fighting for their family's property.

The death rate, and the uprooting and mobility of the remaining population, especially from the country to the city, caused or accelerated by the plague, also impacted on the world of work. King Afonso IV issued legislation on labour, as had happened in other countries, such as in England with Edward III's Ordinance of Labourers. Afonso's laws concerned a variety of situations. Some workers in agriculture, crafts and services refused to continue working, because thanks to inheritances they had become proprietors. The king required that the authorities should confirm this change of status, and, if genuine, they should oblige these newly enriched people to work. Furthermore, the lack of hands for agriculture, cattle-raising and crafts meant that waged workers could demand high pay and work only for short periods, rather than the whole year. The king decreed that such workers should be registered, and fixed a table of wages, favouring employers. However, although it was established that employees could not refuse to work a whole year, employers were obliged to pay wages on time. In the same way, he tried to solve the problem of the "false poor", who survived by begging, forcing them to take work on pain of heavy penalties. It is clear that the population decline caused by the plague was working in favour of free men who offered their services, and that wages were continually rising: landowners complained of this to the *Cortes* assembly in 1352, and Afonso IV renewed his order to fix wages. Nevertheless, there was still an imbalance between supply and demand, and the situation perisisted.

The demographic impact of the epidemic aggravated the many socioeconomic and cultural changes caused by the crisis. The rise of small and medium-level proprietors, and a golden age for waged workers, improved living conditions for a "middle class". An increased number of widows, orphans and the poor required assistance, while rising marginality and crime had to be watched and controlled. To increase administrative efficiency, governors relied on the support of professionals. New technologies compensated for the lack of manpower, intensifying the tendency to proto-industrialization. The lords, responding to falls in rent and production, oppressed the peasants, who protested and rebelled. As compensation, the landowners invested in cattle and commercial agriculture, turning it into an increasingly prominent economy of production and exchange. The reduction in income and land meant that kings and warrior aristocracies needed war to support them, but at the same time sea routes were opening, promising more commercial wealth. An intense religiosity and interior spirituality were a response to anxiety about salvation and the growing obsession with death, represented in art and literature by the implacable and ubiquitous dance macabre. But alongside this, new societal challenges opened the path to secularization and to rational and experimental thought as a way to better understand and confront the challenges of life.

The Black Death, long-lasting and unconfined by borders, involved all these strands, creating an unmistakably "global" history.

Maria Helena da Cruz Coelho
University of Coimbra and Centre for the History of Society and Culture

Bibliography

BENEDICTOW, Ole J., *The Black Death 1346–1353: The Complete History*, Woodbridge, The Boydell Press, 2004.

BIRABEN, Jean-Noël, *Les Hommes et la Peste en France et dans les Pays Européens et Méditerranéens*, 2 vols., Paris, Mouton, 1975–1976.

BOS, Kirsten I. et al., "A draft genome of *Yersinia pestis* from victims of the black death", *Nature*, no. 478, 27 Oct. 2011, pp. 506–510.

The Medieval Globe, vol. 1, no. 1, 2015.

ROQUE, Mário da Costa, *As Pestes Medievais Europeias e o "Regimento Proveytoso contra ha Pestenença"*, Paris, Fundação Calouste Gulbenkian-Centro Cultural Português, 1979.

1385

Aljubarrota: An Ancestral Enemy, an Old Alliance and Reinforcement of the Country's Identity

Aljubarrota was a brilliant adaptation of the tactics invented by the English and used by them in the earliest battles of the Hundred Years' War – Crécy in 1346 and Poitiers in 1356.

The Battle of Aljubarrota, fought on 14 August 1385 at São Jorge (Porto de Mós), is one of the most famous episodes in Portuguese history and figures in the short list of decisive battles in medieval European history. At the time, pitched battles were rare in Europe, since the weaker parties tended to take refuge in their fortresses: most military operations consisted of acts of plunder or siege. Military treatises recommended that commanders should resort to pitched battles only in highly advantageous circumstances, or when there was no alternative. Furthermore, it was unusual for kings to take part in a battle, since this made the action even more dangerous. Finally, in the European context, many medieval battles had no important political consequences, few precise locations of battlefields are known, and sometimes armies of only a few hundred men were involved.

Aljubarrota was a shining exception to all this: the battlefield is well-defined and has been the object of successive archaeological and paleobiological research. The battle was described by great medieval chroniclers (such as Pero López de Ayala, an eyewitness, Jean Froissart and Fernão Lopes); the kings themselves, John of Castile (Juan I) and John of Portugal (João I), commanded their large armies, (perhaps

20,000 on the Franco-Castilian side and 10,000 for the Anglo-Portuguese); and the final result (a resounding victory for João I) practically decided the fate of the Portuguese–Castilian war begun in 1384, ending the aspirations of the Trastámara kings of Castile to set one of their bloodline on the Portuguese throne. Aljubarrota was also a brilliant adaptation of the tactics invented by the English and used by them in the earliest battles of the Hundred Years' War – Crécy in 1346 and Poitiers in 1356.

All this shows that it is impossible to understand the event outside its international context. The distant history of the battle leads us to the upheavals among the Portuguese nobility in the reigns of Afonso IV and Peter I (between 1325 and 1367), and of the consequences of the civil war which spread in Castile from 1360, between the rightful king (Peter I) and his half-brother Henry, the Count of Trastámara. Portugal was a place of refuge for many of the participants, which increased the risk of Portuguese involvement in the internal affairs of Castile (Inês de Castro was murdered for this 1355) and caused changes among the high nobility at Court, culminating in the reign of Ferdinand I. By the time of his death, in 1383, the main titles of nobility were held by Castilian and Galician exiles in Portugal, thanks to the approval of Queen Leonor Teles, herself a member of one such family.

King Ferdinand, taking advantage of the crisis in Castile (King Peter was assassinated by his half-brother in 1369) and of being a great-grandson of King Sancho IV, launched three wars against Castile. These were in 1369–1371, 1372–1373 and 1381–1382, and showed his ambition to enlarge the national territory and to safeguard the Portuguese position in Iberia in the face of its powerful neighbour. These wars did not produce the desired effect, but they had two crucial consequences. Firstly, they brought to Portugal, in 1381–1382, an English army led by the Earl of Cambridge, as part of an alliance between Portugal and England. This convergence was a result of the fact that Europe was then involved in the Hundred Years' War (1337–1453) between France and England (and their respective allies). In this context, the English Crown would benefit from the removal of Juan I, heir of Henry of Trastâmara, from the throne of Castile (the main ally of France) and his replacement by someone loyal to English interests. The first Portuguese–English alliance could not defeat Juan I in 1382, but it was the germ of a coalition which would be renewed a few years later by the Master of Avis. Secondly, the end of Ferdinand's wars led, thanks to diplomatic strategy handled by Count João Andeiro, an exiled Galician who was Ferdinand and Leonor's most influential counsellor, to the Portuguese–Castilian treaty of Salvaterra de Magos (April 1383). This agreement not only confirmed the marriage of Juan I with Princess Beatrice (only daughter of Ferdinand and Leonor), but also stipulated that on Ferdinand's death the Portuguese throne would pass to the male firstborn of this union at the age of 14. Up to then, Queen Leonor Teles would be regent of Portugal.

With the (expected) death of King Ferdinand in October 1383, the breaches among the Portuguese aristocracy blew wide open, especially since the traditional nobility (families such as Cunha, Pacheco and Coutinho) did not feel integrated in the current establishment, which were to the benefit of Galician and Castilian families such as Castro, Teles, Meneses and Andeiro, and a small number of Portuguese families which had connections with them thanks to a strategy of matrimonial alliances crafted by Leonor Teles. It was in this context that Count Andeiro was assassinated in December 1383, as a result of a conspiracy led by John, the Master of Avis, bastard son of King Peter I of Portugal. The queen fled to Alenquer, and social agitation spread throughout the kingdom. It appeared at the time that the Master of Avis and his group were acting in the name of his half-brother, Prince John de Castro. But he, the son of Pedro and Inês, lived in exile in Castile, and King Juan I was astute enough to imprison him. So the cause of the Master of Avis could go forward alone.

1384 brought a series of important events: the victory of the Constable, Nuno Álvares Pereira, in Atoleiros in April; King Juan I's siege of Lisbon (defended by the Master of Avis) between May and the beginning of September – which failed due to an outbreak of plague – and the alliance with England. This allowed the Master to enlist a large number of troops with experience in the Hundred Years' War, who reached Portugal around Easter 1385. In March of that year, the Master and his allies summoned an assembly of the *Cortes* in Coimbra to discuss the war and find a suitable candidate for the throne. On 6 April, benefitting from the juridical subtlety of the lawyer João das Regras (John of the Rules) and the stubbornness of Nuno Álvares (who threatened the supporters of Prince John de Castro, particularly Martim Vasques da Cunha), the assembly chose the Master of Avis as king.

Juan I reacted with force and invaded Portugal again, in July 1385. Shortly before that, he had tried to seize Elvas, while a Castilian army attacked Beira, but was defeated on its return in Trancoso by a force assembled by the principal lords of the district (Cunha, Pacheco, Coutinho and Coelho). Regrouping his troops in Ciudad Rodrigo, Juan I advanced to Almeida and from there to Celorico da Beira, Coimbra and Leiria, where he arrived on the 12 August. Although he was suffering from seizures, similar to malaria, his aim was to reach Santarém and then to besiege Lisbon. King João and his supporters knew that it would be hard for the capital to resist a second siege, so they took the decision to give battle to the invaders. They assembled in Abrantes and advanced to Tomar and Porto de Mós, where they camped on 12 August. On the following day, the Constable and some of his English auxiliaries (there were at least 800, the majority of them archers) reconnoitred the terrain and chose the plateau of São Jorge for the battle. On 14 August, late in the morning, the Castilian army, which had come from Leiria and included between 800 and 1200 men-at-arms sent by Charles VI of France as part of the Franco-Castilian alliance against England, reached the hamlet of Jardoeira, to find the road blocked by the Anglo-Portuguese force. As this initial position could not be attacked, the Castilian column diverted seawards and marched across country until they eventually found the road further south, near the terrace of Chão da Feira.

In reply, the Anglo-Portuguese army inverted its disposition and moved two kilometres south. In doing so it lost several advantages, such as the position of the sun and the slope at the front, but on the other hand here the plateau was even narrower and still had a stream in a ravine on each side. Furthermore, after reaching their chosen position early, the army had time to organize a defensive system of abatises (tree-trunks set into the ground), ditches (a total of at least 180 metres), and pits (at least eight hundred have been found). All they had to do now was dismount and await the arrival of the enemy, hoping the Castilians and their allies would commit the error of attacking without reconnoitering the terrain.

And so it proved to be. Late in the afternoon, the Castilian council of war, dominated by young men who thought that victory would be easy, hastily started the attack on the Anglo-Portuguese position, even though they knew that many of the Castilian combatants were still in the marching column, and having been warned of the difficulties that the ravines would present to their flanks. All this shows an obvious lack of clear leadership, as well as the absence of the finest Castilian troops, killed in operations in the previous months.

The attack by the French cavalry was a failure, since the horses fell into traps and the riders were decimated by Portuguese crossbowmen and English archers. The Castilian royal battalion then joined the battle, but they also were overwhelmed, since the configuration of the land and the artificial obstacles obliged the men-at-arms to crowd together along the centre of the plateau, a "corridor of death" where they were slaughtered by fire from the wings commanded by the Constable Nuno Álvares. Even dismounted and with their long lances cut, only a few of Juan I's men managed to break through the Constable's vanguard. However, when this happened the wings turned towards the back, and the rearguard, led by João I, advanced and encircled the enemy in a pincer movement (commonly but wrongly called a square), overwhelming them. As night fell, what was left of the invading army, including the king, fled. Only their right wing, commanded by the Master of the Order of Alcántara, had managed to disturb the Portuguese supply lines. The massacre, in which thousands of Castilian and French troops must have perished, took less than an hour. Those who survived scattered into nearby fields, where they were slaughtered by local inhabitants, as recorded in the legend of the baker of Aljubarrota (said to have killed several Castilians hiding in her bakery oven). The Portuguese leaders halted the pursuit, fearing a Castilian regrouping: it was only the next day that they had a clear idea of their impressive victory.

After the battle, places that had still supported Princess Beatrice and King Juan I surrendered to João I. Nevertheless, the Castilian king had to be prevented from any further incursions, and this led João to strengthen the alliance with England. On 9 May 1386 in Windsor, a historic treaty of mutual help was signed, and in February 1387, in Porto, the Portuguese king married Philippa of Lancaster, daughter of the duke John of Gaunt, the English pretender to the throne of Castile. In the spring of 1387, an Anglo-Portuguese army attacked León, maintaining pressure on Juan I and stopping him from planning another invasion of Portugal. In 1390, Juan I died; this facilitated Portuguese–Castilian negotiations, which culminated in the signing in 1411 of a peace treaty, putting an end to the war. Portugal and its new dynasty, that of Avis, (which the chronicler Fernão Lopes and King Edward would work to legitimate and Luís de Camões to immortalize) could now think of other adventures. The conquest of Ceuta in 1415 was one of the first fruits of this new Iberian and international context.

João Gouveia Monteiro
University of Coimbra and Centre for the History of Society and Culture

Bibliography

DUARTE, Luís Miguel, *Guerra pela Independência, 1383–1389*, Lisbon, Academia Portuguesa da História/Quidnovi, 2006.

FROISSART, Jean, "Chroniques", in *Jean Froissart (Crónicas). Duas Passagens Relativas a Aljubarrota,* trans. Ana Sofia Laranjinha, coord. Mário Jorge Barroca, São Jorge, Fundação Batalha de Aljubarrota, 2008.

LOPES, Fernão, *Crónica de D. João I, Segunda Parte*, ed. William J. Entwistle, Lisbon, Imprensa Nacional-Casa da Moeda, 1977.

LÓPEZ DE AYALA, Pero, *Crónicas,* ed. José-Luis Martín, Barcelona, Planeta, 1991.

MONTEIRO, João Gouveia et al., *Aljubarrota Revisitada*, Coimbra, Imprensa da Universidade de Coimbra, 2001.

1415
New Horizons: The Conquest of Ceuta and the Sea

It was his position as defender and governor of Ceuta which allowed Prince Henry to demand colossal sums from the entire country, and to accumulate countless privileges and monopolies, which would later finance his African expeditions.

From a Portuguese viewpoint, the story of the conquest of Ceuta is not a long or difficult one. Although the struggle for independence from Castile, begun in 1383, had continued in skirmishes until 1400, the war concluded at dusk on 14 August 1385 with the end of the Royal Battle, later known as Aljubarrota. A quarter of a century later, the kingdom was enjoying a long period of peace and stable government under King John I, which continued for forty-eight years, since the succession to the throne was assured: Edward, Peter and Henry were next in line, followed by the young John and Ferdinand.

Despite this, the new dynasty of Avis had its problems. It had to keep busy an idle aristocracy, restless and with their incomes decreasing. Only by fighting for the king could they be granted more gifts and wealth. They were hoping for an opportunity to prove their military valour to the sons of the generation that fought at Aljubarrota, such as the three princes, Edward, Peter and Henry. King John also felt that he needed to reinforce his international prestige – the stigma of being a bastard, although diluted over time, could not entirely fade. Thus, almost three decades after his triumph at Aljubarrota, he needed to show his teeth to the kingdoms of western Christianity and to Rome. He had to show, first and as always to Castile, that his country might be small, peripheral, demographically weak and economically vulnerable, but on the battlefield it feared no-one.

The yer 1411 was the time to renew the truce negotiated in 1402 in Segovia, and Portugal did so. With the almost permanent Castilian threat contained for the next few years, King John would have thought the same as Guy of Lusignan, newly crowned king of Jerusalem, who in the film *Kingdom of Heaven* tells one of his supporters, "Give me a war!". But while in the film this was an easy task, since there was a designated enemy near at hand (Saladin and his army), King John had no such enemy. Now, once the truce with Castile was signed, or even before, the Crown began the complex, slow and costly stages – recruitment, arming, transport, provisioning, logistics in general – of a military operation, spectacular and intimidating for friends and enemies alike. For obvious reasons, it would be convenient if the targets of the attack were Muslims. – such a war would have the almost guaranteed support of the papacy. At the time of the Western Schism, the pope of Rome, weakened, would easily issue a Bull of Crusade in exchange for the political support which King John I had always given him. Such a Bull would be excellent for the morale of the troops and useful for the finances of the concern. And there were "infidels" near at hand, without leaving the Peninsula: the shrunken kingdom of Granada, a shadow of what it had been, but even so an impressive centre of culture. In fact the Portuguese Crown, or some Portuguese, particularly Prince Henry, had regularly suggested helping Castile in this final reconquest. Castile had expressed thanks, but declined the offer. If it needed any help, it would ask for it: Granada was well within its living-space.

This being so, attackable targets were few: the only other nearby Muslims were in Morocco, which, translated into cities, meant Asilah, Tangier and Ceuta. The first offered no special rewards, and disembarking there was highly dangerous (as seen in the hundreds of Portuguese who drowned in the capture of the city in 1471). In favour of Tangier was the huge prestige of the city, its obvious wealth and its excellent position on the Atlantic; against, that it would probably be difficult to capture (the Portuguese had proved this several times, at great cost), and even though strategically interesting, it would not make an outstanding base.

That left Ceuta, the ancient Islamic Sabta. Ceuta the invincible, as it was known due to the shape of its terrain and its mighty, intricate and overlapping systems of fortification. Favourable to Ceuta were its nearness, the relative ease of landing there and its strategic location – in many ways the best in the Mediterranean and well-situated for the Atlantic. And its riches: the splendour of the city and of its schools; its poets and sages; the brilliance of the caravans of gold from Timbuctu and Sijilmassa, and of silk and spices from Cairo; its granaries overflowing with wheat (particularly welcome to Lisbon, which seemed always to be in need of it) – were these advantages, or not? Surely any doubt would have appeared ridiculous: there were so many factors to arouse greed. And for many of the greatest Portuguese historians for many decades, some of these reasons – the search for gold and wheat for the mysterious "bourgeoisie" – were the main motives for the choice of Ceuta as the target. However, it is clear that the mythical Ceuta of the thirteenth century had long since ceased to exist. The population had shrunk, and intellectual life was a pale shadow of what it had once been, as the old houses and the semi-abandoned districts bore witness. Trade, once so enviable, hardly existed. A grief-stricken Muslim, describing with understandable exaggeration the city of his heart, just lost to the "barbarous infidels" (the Portuguese), did not hide the fact that the Ceuta of 1415 was far distant from what it had been. In addition, an outbreak of plague decimated the Moroccan population at the same time.

If the assault on the city had gone well, what would the Portuguese victors have done with it? If they planned to keep it as a commercial port, a point of arrival and departure for caravans of merchandise, whether from the interior of the Sahel, crossing the Sahara, or from the Middle East and Egypt by way of North Africa, as well as a centre for transhipment of wheat, there was only one way: take it without a fight, by a siege, for example, with no dead, or prisoners, or haphazard destruction. Then, establish a new politico-military regime and a new tax system, keep a garrison there, and above all guarantee that the inhabitants and the merchants do not leave. From the way that the city was attacked, taken and sacked, this scenario was clearly never on the agenda. Ceuta was therefore immediately empty and practically without trade and basic supplies. The Portuguese strategists were not stupid – they could not have expected any other result. A second possibility, which, according to the best and most "treasonous" chronicler of the expedition, Gomes Eanes de Zurara, was even seriously discussed after the victory, would have been to seize anything of value (which was in fact done), reduce the city to ashes and return to Portugal in time for the grain and grape harvests. A third solution was chosen, possibly the idea of King John: leave a garrison of 3000 men in the fortress, which was a lot at this time, and maintain Ceuta not as a commercial port, but as a point of strategic support for Christian shipping entering and leaving the Mediterranean (the north side of the Straits, Gibraltar and Algeciras, were under Castilian control). At the same time this would deal a severe blow to Muslim piracy that was tormenting the Algarve, and it would provide safety for the ships of Christian merchants, Portuguese included, which had to pass through the Straits, especially the galleys which travelled once or twice a year between Italy and Flanders.

The expedition to Ceuta is well-known: it was prepared in advance, carefully and efficiently. It mobilized a surprising number of soldiers (numbering probably around 20,000), who were transported, along with horses, weapons, supplies and engines of war, in more than two hundred ships, among them a splendid squadron of galleys, the aristocrats of the fleet, commanded by the king, and a flotilla of *naus*, captained by Prince Peter; the heir to the throne, Prince Edward, and Prince Henry, sailed in one of the galleys with their father. We know so much about the army and the fleet thanks to reports sent regularly to the king of Aragon by one of his spies. Winds and currents, which had so often fought for the soldiers of Christ, were this time allied with those of Mohammed: either the winds dropped and dozens of sailing ships were becalmed at Tavira (in the Algarve), or they let loose their fury, twice, on the Portuguese armada anchored in sight of Ceuta, threatening to sink it. The third time was lucky, and the indomitable Sabta fell in a few hours. All but deserted by its inhabitants, who had plenty of time to leave, badly commanded and even worse defended, the city made the mistake of opening one of its gates in an attempt to stop the Portuguese landing on the beach. The Portuguese vanguard, notably the three princes of Avis, who were waiting eagerly for the opportunity to be knighted (spilling enemy blood, as befitted the sons of kings, not attending festivities and sumptuous banquets, like rich bourgeois), easily routed their unprepared opponents and entered the besieged fortress through the open gate. Hand-to-hand, street-by-street, the fighting continued, breaking down doors, leaping over ditches, killing, sacking, destroying (and later lamenting what had been destroyed and could not now be stolen). The real castle, the *afraq*, which sat on the isthmus of the peninsula of Ceuta and isolated it from the mainland, and would have been very nearly impregnable, was abandoned by the inhabitants. Without diminishing what it was like to fight through the alleys of the medina, in the middle of August, in the heat of the sun, in a heavy, suffocating suit of armour, against people defending their land (Prince Henry, for example, determined to be noticed and having lost at least one early opportunity to create a good impression, made other highly suicidal attempts, ending up with serious wounds to his legs, having caused the death of a lord who sacrificed himself to save him), the capture of Ceuta proved to be surprisingly quick and easy. Why?

Knowing the history of Africa, we can see that the North had had a very wealthy past, before Islam, and afterwards became the most brilliant centre of this new religion. In the seventh century, despite the triumph of the armies of the Prophet, Islamization was neither quick nor easy: in some areas (among the Berbers, for example), it was never really profound. Under Islamic rule, various caliphates and cities vied for power, successively or simultaneously – Baghdad, Cairo, Granada – and after a certain point the ruling dynasties (Almohad and Almoravid) originated from western Europe. What now corresponds to Tunisia, Algeria and Morocco was divided into three kingdoms, each with its own dynasty; Ceuta belonged, in principle, to the kingdom of Fez. But whenever Fez became weaker, Ceuta rose up, proudly independent: it is no wonder that the rulers of Fez were slow to help when they were needed.

For the Portuguese Crown, or for the various social sectors, or for the kingdom, was Ceuta a good deal? Prince Peter, writing in 1426 from Bruges to his brother Prince Edward, told him that, thirteen years after the conquest, it was being said in European court circles that maintaining the garrison in Africa was a disaster for the country. Isolated, with no possibility of obtaining supplies from local Muslim traders, the city that was to solve Lisbon's wheat problem was importing it from Portugal. Wheat and everything else: wine, meat, dried fish, weapons, utensils, soldiers – it was a vast financial black hole. However, other factors have to be weighed in the balance: the Crown was ruining itself, but many merchants and lords, with Prince Henry in the lead, were rapidly becoming rich thanks to the "Ceuta line", this bridge of boats which came and went, taking out soldiers and food, bringing back soldiers and little else. It was his position as defender and governor of Ceuta which allowed Prince Henry to demand colossal sums from the entire country, and to accumulate countless privileges and monopolies, which would later finance his African expeditions. On the plus side, the *Casa de Ceuta* was founded to support the city, a company of blacksmiths was organized, and many ships made the necessary modifications for the new passage. Christian merchant shipping expanded in the Straits, and finally, Ceuta did not become a centre for piracy, like Tunis, Algiers and Oran.

Ceuta was not the beginning of Portuguese expansion (this began in the fourteenth century with the expeditions to the Canary Islands), nor did it do much to advance the future voyages of exploration along the West African coast. Rather, it was another success story in the Christian "Reconquest", and the first Portuguese possession on another continent (although the concept of a continent comes only from the sixteenth century). It helped to discredit the ruling dynasty of Fez, which collapsed in an orgy of blood, and to tip the balance of power, in the Mediterranean and the nearby Atlantic, in favour of Christians and to the detriment of Muslims. This imbalance would soon be reversed by the Ottomans, with interest.

A few years after the restoration of Portuguese autonomy in 1668, the inhabitants of Ceuta were asked if they wanted to return to being what they had been after 1415, Portuguese, or if they preferred to continue Spanish, as since 1580. They chose the latter.

Luís Miguel Duarte
University of Porto

Bibliography

BOUCHERON, Patrick (dir.), *Histoire du Monde au XVe Siècle*, Paris, Fayard, 2009.
CHERIF, Mohamed, *Ceuta aux Époques Almohade et Mérinide*, Paris, L'Harmattan, 1996.
DUARTE, Luís Miguel, *Ceuta, 1415. Seiscentos Anos depois*, Lisbon, Livros Horizonte, 2015.
FAUVELLE-AYMARD, François-Xavier, *Le Rhinocéros d'Or. Histoires du Moyen Âge Africain*, Paris, Alma Éditeur, 2013.
GRATALOUP, Christian, *L'Invention des Continentes*, Paris, Larousse, 2009.

PART IV

The Early Modern Period

Introduction to Part IV

Of Settlement and Slavery to Royal Exile

CÁTIA ANTUNES
Leiden University

In the fifteenth century, Portugal, in the West, like China, in the East, launched a series of maritime expeditions that resulted in increased mobility and in the acquisition of knowledge that became absolutely essential to the internal development of both countries and to their relationship with the rest of the world.

Portugal and China pioneered one of the first chapters in global history, although Portugal diverged from Ming China with regard to the extension and intensity of its explorations. Whereas Chinese fleets and sailors restricted themselves to the western-most shores of the Indian Ocean, rarely venturing into the Pacific and ignoring all the knowledge of Atlantic navigation, the Portuguese navigated, explored and established more or less lasting relationships in the three major oceanic regions in little more than one century. While the focus in the fifteenth century remained within the Atlantic, particularly in the South Atlantic, when the century came to a close, Portuguese fleets had reached the Indian Ocean, and by the sixteenth century the Portuguese were anchoring their ships in the Pacific. If the Portuguese were to be found in Ceuta in 1415, by 1543 they were a continuous presence in Japan. In just over a century, royal armadas and private fleets had mapped the Atlantic, Indian and Pacific Ocean regions, with symbolic arrivals and, at times, long term settlements, in Madeira, the Azores, Cape Verde, São Tomé, Angola, India, Brazil, Malacca, the Moluccas, China, Timor and Japan.

Portugal's early and significant involvement in the first globalization, dating from the fifteenth century and accelerating during the following century, justifies the emphasis on landmark information about the 1400s and the 1500s, whilst the seventeenth and eighteenth centuries figure less prominently. Nevertheless, we offer a balanced coverage of the three key centuries of the Early Modern period, focussing on certain moments when Portugal initiated global developments and on instances when it followed global dynamics.

The selection of dates herein are offered as starting points for global interpretations of the phenomena under analysis. The selection of these phenomenon followed a strict criteria that showcases historical moments that represent cycles in the history of Portugal, which have translated into transformative connectivity, rather than events taking place on a global level. At the same time, the selection emphasizes how Portuguese historical mobility manifested itself in various (positive and negative) impacts that extended beyond the Portuguese world, as it was defined at the time.

The positive outcomes include the nautical and cartographical developments best exemplified by the rounding of Cape Bojador (1434) and by Portuguese cartography

(1560). This production and reproduction of knowledge resulted in rapid technological progress, exported by the Portuguese to such distant regions as China. The use of the printing press to publish books, which could already be observed in India in 1563, is one of the many possible examples that could be listed here.

In addition to knowledge, the globality created by the Portuguese also included an intense exchange of products on a worldwide scale, leading to the transplantation of cultures and dietary habits. The arrival of American and Asian agricultural products in Europe and the circulation of many others between these continents, together with their various adaptations and reuse, are exemplified in the early cultivation of rice in Portugal, from 1509 onwards.

Material culture, including architectural developments in infrastructures for warfare, such as the fortress of Mazagan (1514), and the evolution of Baroque materiality immortalized in the construction of the Palace and Convent of Mafra (1717–1730) also provide vivid evidence of the international presence and influence of Portuguese landscapes.

Nevertheless, despite the circulation of technology and knowledge and the exchanges in a more general sense that were instigated by Portuguese exploration, the Portuguese presence and its intervention on a global level also devastated and destroyed existing worlds. The intensive cultivation of sugar cane, which began on the archipelago of Madeira (1425) and was transferred to São Tomé and later Brazil and the rest of the American continent, resulted in millions of human beings being transported from Africa to the New World. Deprived of their freedom and stripped of their humanity before the law, millions of Africans were taken from their towns and villages and forced to work on European plantations in the Atlantic islands, Brazil, the Caribbean and large parts of America. In addition to the plantations, enslaved Africans worked, and died, in mines as a result of the harsh conditions and hill treatment, while maintaining a continuous presence as cheap labour in most American ports and cities.

This systematic, inhumane exploitation of enslaved Africans and their subordination within the Portuguese colonies drove many to despair. Despair resulted in countless revolts and absconding from plantations, a movement that began in São Tomé (1517) and became a constant in all the European colonies in America during the course of the Early Modern period. Assisted by autochthonous American populations (often known as "Indians"), uprisings were organized against the European authorities, a collective act of rejection and refusal of the globalization initiated and imposed by the Portuguese.

Slaves and autochthonous Americans were not alone when rejecting the role allocated to them by the Portuguese and other Europeans in this chapter of global history. Colonial societies, often creolized and emerging from centuries of *métissage*, also tried to establish a place for themselves in this new order. Hence, they resisted attempts to create religious uniformity imposed by the Royal Patronage *(Padroado)* (1514) and later the Inquisition (1536) and claimed their autonomy, as in the example of the founding of the colony of Sacramento (1680), or even independence, as was the case in Brazil (1822).

The globalization launched by the Portuguese was therefore a conflicting process of gains and losses, engagement and rejection. These contradictions emerged in parallel with global processes initiated outside Portugal, yet received and adapted in the Portuguese worlds, more or less voluntarily. The inclusion of Portugal in the Iberian Union (1580–1640), the imposition of the Gregorian Calendar (from 1582 onwards), the new world order enforced by the Peace of Westphalia (1648) and the arrival of freemasonry, with the first lodge opening in 1723, are all examples of these dynamics.

These and other events selected for this section of the book are mainly associated with worldwide Portuguese mobility, colonial expansion and imposition, although they are not restricted only to these dynamics. They offer an overview and analysis of interconnections, circulations and social, political, economic, religious and cultural exchanges, highlighting various different courses of action and reaction to the globalization generated by the Portuguese.

Since part of the globalization shared and generated by the Portuguese resulted in an intensification of personal, institutional and governmental contacts in various parts of the world that extended to every continent and ocean, albeit at different times and levels of intensity with significant local, regional, continental and intercontinental impacts, the aim was to strive for a balanced analysis that would also highlight these different spatial interactions. Hence, at certain points the Portuguese influence in the world, as it was known and understood in the Early Modern period, is examined, whilst also considering the impacts and consequences of these processes for Portugal, as the seat of a kingdom forged from interrelationships between people with diverse origins and ways of life, which possessed long-established territorial borders.

It was therefore considered imperative to emphasize the difficulty faced by a small kingdom with a very low population density (at the dawn of the sixteenth century, the population of Portugal totalled 1,400,000) in initiating, engaging and changing global developments. However, since this implies a perspective based on an analytical approach to global history, the focus was not directed towards observing specifically Portuguese features, but rather the aptitude, obstacles, difficulties and adaptability of institutions and individuals within the overall process of globalization in the Early Modern era. As this complex process had considerable impacts on historical developments, moments of great success and profound maladjustment were identified, bearing in mind the specific contexts in which each event took place and the specialist and general knowledge of the protagonist(s), paying particular attention to the role of individuals within the dynamics of history in the light of the notion of agency. Hence, the actions of the São Tomé enslaved "rebels" (1517) and the Pernambuco autochthonous and enslaved "insurrectionists" (1645) are considered on an equal footing with the actors who completed the first voyages to India and Brazil and the individuals who defined the politics of memory by managing and curating the national archive after the 1755 earthquake.

The authors of the various texts come from different backgrounds and share a variety of academic and historiographical traditions. The deliberate choice of diverse perspectives and historical interpretations undoubtedly enriches the contents presented here and was also a means of ensuring that this would be a global history. In this collaboration between junior and senior researchers with links to university institutions and research centres in Portugal and abroad, the aim has been to offer the reader an up-to-date reconstruction of facts and specific conceptual analyses, as a means of stimulating knowledge in a broader sense and possibly deepening the understanding of the chosen themes. With the latter objective in mind, bibliographies are included, carefully prepared by the authors of the various texts, providing references to the most important studies on the subjects in question and also aiming to focus on the diversity of historiographical opinion.

In this context, the Early Modern history of Portugal, associated with a cycle in which the country undoubtedly had a major impact on world history, does not belong exclusively to the Portuguese, but to all who were involved in these dynamics, regardless of their place of birth. Refusing exclusions based on origin, social background, ethnicity, colour or religion, diverse historical actors are included here, equally and unequivocally as active participants in a shared history that should be, at all times, and unreservedly inclusive.

1425
Madeira: Settlement, Sugar and Enslaved Populations

After the mid sixteenth century, the enslaved population was almost exclusively of African origin. In the following centuries, the trade in enslaved Africans involved importing captives via the ports of Lisbon, Bahia and even Caribbean islands under British rule.

The arrival of the Portuguese in Madeira in 1419 took place against the background of the Christian conquest, territorial, trade and political disputes with the Muslim populations installed in the Iberian Peninsula and North Africa. Soon, the first settlers were experimenting with growing sugar cane, which resulted in the crop adapting to the new ecosystems. Portuguese settlers adopted the use of enslaved labour to increase production and profits. The cultivation of sugar cane and the trade in its derivatives (sugar and cane spirit) fuelled the expansion of the Portuguese Crown and its global contacts for more than four centuries, facilitating the circulation of goods and people. Although the monoculture system based on enslaved labour was established in Brazil and in the French and British colonies in the Caribbean in the eighteenth century, its origins date back to Portuguese overseas expansion in the fifteenth century, including occupation and settlement in the Atlantic islands of Madeira, the Azores and, later, São Tomé. The Portuguese overseas empire was the first to establish colonies in the Atlantic region and impose an economic model based on the commercial development and trading of spices and minerals, as well as the trade in human beings. Hence, in the fifteenth century, the Portuguese monarchy and merchants were the precursors of overseas colonial trade, firstly in sugar, and later in tobacco, silver, coffee, gold and diamonds.

The interest in sugar cane and its derivatives predates the founding of the kingdom of Portugal. The plant, originating in southern Asia, was cultivated in North Africa, the Levant and southern Europe before the turn of the first millennium and there are references to the trade and consumption of sugar during the Crusades (eleventh–thirteenth centuries). Muslim chroniclers described sugar cane plantations in Morocco in the ninth century, in Sicily in the tenth century, and in Tunisia in the eleventh century. In Andalusia, under the Islamic caliphates, populations consumed sugar and distributed it via trade networks that connected the Mediterranean world. There were attempts to introduce cultivation to the Algarve, although these were on a small scale, far removed from the plantation model that became established in the seventeenth and eighteenth centuries in the Americas. In these centuries of experimentation, free and enslaved farmers tested new techniques but the crops strug-gled to survive, faced with the dry terrain and a shortage of natural water sources. However, the climate in Madeira appeared to be ideal for cultivation. Its location, good soils and temperatures favoured the introduction of new crops at the beginning of the fifteenth century. Adventurers from different places settled there, occupied land and attracted investment from various European territories. Although it had been a dominion of the Portuguese Crown since 1425, traders of other origins settled there. Venetian, Genoan and Florentine merchants and bankers introduced new techniques and plants, such as sugar cane, which played a key role as an export product. This trade opened up new commercial routes, connecting the merchant elites in Funchal with Las Palmas, Santa Cruz de Tenerife, Lisbon and Cádiz. In order to facilitate their social and economic integration, foreign traders tended to marry the daughters of the local elite, which also guaranteed them rights in Portuguese controlled territories. In alliance with the local elite, they occupied the best agricultural land, took advantage of royal concessions and made their plantations the most productive. Meanwhile, Portuguese traders presented complaints to the Évora Courts (1481–1482) concerning the fact that Genoese and Jewish merchants had monopolized the trade in honey, orchil and sugar in Madeira, accusing them of controlling 78% of the exports of the latter product. Christopher Columbus was one of the Genoese traders who made his fortune in Madeira, before he set sail for America. Attracted by the oppor-tunities to make profits, Portuguese and Flemish merchants also settled in the island at the end of the fifteenth century, including João Esmeraldo, for example, who owned 14 enslaved individuals on his estate, Lombada de Ponta do Sol.

The arrival of more traders in the final decades of the fifteenth century fuelled the expansion of the sugar industry. In 1480, 100,000 arrobas of sugar were cultivated and processed in local mills and sent to Portugal. The growing demand for sugar in European markets meant that it became necessary to expand the cultivated area, resulting deforestation to make land available for cultivation, which required a large labour force. Free settlers began to acquire African captives, employed in the construc-tion of dykes, we well as in the cultivation and harvesting of sugar cane. Enslaved Africans were kidnapped or bought on the coast of West Africa and distributed among the cane fields in Calheta, Machico and Ribeira Brava, the three largest sugar producing regions in Madeira. In the mills, free and enslaved workers crushed the cane to extract and refine the juice to obtain the final product, sugar, which was then taken to the port and shipped to Lisbon. From there it was delivered to different urban centres in Europe. A small number of Genoese, Florentine, Flemish and Portuguese traders controlled the various stages of the production process, profiting not only from the sale of sugar but also the trade in enslaved human beings. The mills on the island of Madeira were small and operated with a reduced workforce, which made it difficult for them to meet consumer demand in Europe. The constant demand for labour favoured the expansion of Madeira's trade with the coast of Guinea, mainly the in the ports of Arguin, São Jorge da Mina and Cacheu. However, at the beginning of the sixteenth century, the mills in Madeira began to face competition from planters on the island of São Tomé, which received a larger supply of captive labourers from the kingdom of Kongo. In 1535, with the consolidation of the trade in enslaved Africans between Kongo and São Tomé, production in São Tomé increased to 200,000 arrobas of sugar, while the mill owners in Madeira exported no more than 68,000 arrobas. In the mid sixteenth century, several ships set sail for the coast of West Africa – a region which is usually known as Guinea in the Portuguese documents – to carry out raids to capture men, women and children who were then transported to the island of Madeira, where they lived in captivity. Although historiography traditionally downplays the importance of the trade in enslaved Africans during the fifteenth and sixteenth centuries, and even the role of enslaved labour in the mills in Madeira, it is undeniable that enslaved individuals helped to consolidate the Atlantic sugar industry.

Hence, during the second half of the fifteenth century and the first half of the sixteenth century, Madeira became the centre for sugar production, with a population of free Europeans and enslaved Africans. After 1560, however, the competition from sugar produced in Brazil created a number of difficulties which led to a decline in the status of Madeira as the main sugar producing hub for the European markets.

The presence of enslaved Africans in Madeira dates back to the mid fifteenth century, emerging in parallel with the first steps taken towards the occupation and settlement of the island. In 1441, the first African captives arrived in Lisbon, although it already had a large enslaved labour force of different origins, including Muslims from Granada, Morocco and Belgrade and even individuals from other parts of Portugal, such as enslaved *Mouriscos* born in Setúbal or the Algarve. In Madeira, Africans and Canarians represented most of the enslaved population. At a time when slavery was not yet associated with skin colour, anyone who was not a Christian was liable to be caught and taken captive, losing the right to earn their own living, and forced to do domestic, herding or agricultural work. In the fifteenth century, the Guanches, the inhabitants of the Canary Islands, made up the majority of the slave population in Madeira. Free residents of Madeira feared the Gaunches and associated them with social unrest. Muslim captives also formed part of the slave population in Madeira, largely due to Portuguese occupation of the African ports of Safi, Azemmour, Agadir and Mazagan (nowadays El Jadida). Portuguese soldiers and traders were actively involved in raids and incursions in these territories to capture and enslave free people. The enslaved captives arrived via trade routes which linked Madeira to Cape Verde and West Africa. However, following the decline of the Portuguese forts on the coast of Morocco at the end of the sixteenth century, the number of Maghribi captives in Madeira decreased.

From 1515 to 1520, Portuguese traders were responsible for the shipment of between 1,000 and 1,500 enslaved individuals from the *feitoria* (trading post) in Arguin, in present-day Mauritania, to Lisbon, an important domestic trade that supplied the cane fields of the Canary Islands and Madeira. Two decades later, in 1540, the flow had increased, with 6,000 enslaved Africans landing in Lisbon, some of whom were later sent to the Atlantic islands.

Despite the expansion of the sugar cane fields, Madeira landowners complained about the shortage of labour, which led to the issuing of an authorization for "*resgate*", a term used at the time to refer to the kidnapping and enslavement of free Africans in the rivers of Guinea. In Funchal, 3,000 enslaved individuals, classified as blacks or mixed-race, worked on the farms in 1552. In addition to the official documentation, some travellers, such as the Frenchman Jean Moquat, pointed out that Madeira settlers made extensive use of slave labour in their farmsteads. Madeira landowners invested in purchasing human beings to boost productivity, resulting in the constant arrival of captives of different origins. Isabel de Abreu, for example, owned two very large estates and one Muslim captive. After the mid sixteenth century, the enslaved population was almost exclusively of African origin. In the centuries which followed, the trade in enslaved Africans was carried out via the ports of Lisbon, Bahia and even Caribbean islands under British rule, as was the case in Barbados. Despite the decline in the Madeira mills, enslaved men and women continued to arrive on the island at the beginning of the eighteenth century, one example being Joana, from Saint Christopher Island, nowadays Saint Kitts.

The occupation, commercial development and colonization of Madeira served as a social laboratory, where new techniques, such as the mill and slavery, were systematically tested out for the first time. Settlement in Madeira was the start of the projection and establishment of the Portuguese Crown overseas. For the first time, it combined territorial occupation, colonization and the use of enslaved African labour in the name of the Portuguese Crown. This model defined the Portuguese empire for the next five centuries. In addition, the colonization of the archipelago served as a platform for the occupation of the Azores in 1431, and the Atlantic coast of the continent of Africa, and it was the driving force behind the construction of trading posts in Arguin (1445) and São Jorge da Mina (1482). However, attempts to colonize and found new towns on the African coast were only consolidated in the sixteenth century, with Luanda (1575) and Benguela (1617).

Moreover, the technological developments applied on the island of Madeira were essential to the introduction of sugar cane crops in Brazil, from the second half of the sixteenth century onwards. After 1580, the sugar produced in Brazil began to take over the European markets. Consequently, mill owners in Madeira began to acquire inferior quality sugar from the north-east of Brazil in order to refine it to suit European tastes, then re-export it. However, the quantities and final price of the sugar produced in Brazil did not allow the mill owners in Madeira to compete on the European market, and several opted to relocate to Portuguese America to invest their energies there.

Mariana P. Candido
Emory University

Bibliography

CALDEIRA, Arlindo M., *Escravos em Portugal. Das Origens ao Século XIX*, Lisbon, A Esfera dos Livros, 2017.

GALLOWAY, J. H., *The Sugar Cane Industry: An Historical Geography from Its Origins to 1914*, Cambridge, Cambridge University Press, 1989.

MENDES, António de Almeida, "Les réseaux de la traite ibérique dans l'Atlantique Nord (1440–1640)", *Annales. Histoire, Sciences Sociales*, vol. 63, no. 4, 2008, pp. 739–768.

RAU, Virgínia, MACEDO, Jorge de, *O Açúcar da Madeira nos Fins do Século XV: Problemas de Produção e Comércio*, Funchal, Junta Geral do Distrito Autónomo do Funchal, 1962.

VIEIRA, Alberto, *Canaviais, Açúcar e Aguardente na Madeira: Séculos XV a XX*, Funchal, Centro de Estudos de História do Atlântico, 2004.

1434
Rounding Cape Bojador: New Horizons

The rounding of Cape Bojador, in 1434, was a decisive step towards progress in the Atlantic region, after the many previous attempts that had been made since 1421. Due to its pivotal position on the coastline and as a passage to an area of Sub-Saharan African assumed, due to ignorance, to be torrid and uninhabitable, Cape Bojador was one of the barriers that featured in the geographical imaginary of the Late Middle Ages in Europe.

Like all capes, Bojador was seen by the medieval seafarers of the Atlantic as the "edge of the world", the *finis terrae*. It was only by rounding it that they would be able to catch sight of other lands and seas to explore. Hence, Cape Bojador, like the Cape of Storms (later known as the Cape of Good Hope) and, earlier in Antiquity, Cape Saint Vincent, acquired a mythical status which proved more difficult to overcome than any physical obstacle, whether geographic or cosmographic.

The name by which it was first known, Cape of Fear, suggests that the barriers for those who tried in succession to sail round it would also have been psychological. Current historiography gives due recognition to human factors: passions, emotions, fears and ambitions. Nevertheless, the interpretation of events of the past, as well as those of the present, cannot be reduced to these variables, otherwise we risk reproducing an interpretative model that defined and influenced analysis of the causality and motives for Portuguese maritime expansionism for decades. They would include courage, daring, the spirit of curiosity and the indomitable spirit of the Portuguese, which are difficult to observe, measure or refute and, ultimately, are all incompatible with the procedures required for any scientific method of constructing knowledge. Therefore, historians always aim to go back to the sources. However, unlike the positivists, the believers in complete "truth" and the probative value of sources, present-day historians insist on their limitations, allegiances and capacity to reveal information in terms of what is asked of them.

On the basis of this premise, the inquiry to be addressed here is based on two questions:

- Did the contemporaries have any idea that the rounding of Cape Bojador was essential to their plans, whatever they may have been?
- What did this event contribute, in the short and long term, to the phenomenon examined here (Portugal and globalization)?

It should be noted that in the fifteenth century the inhabitable world was understood as part of a larger reality, hitherto unexplored and unknown to Europeans, and the oceans were considered obstacles, often thought to be insurmountable. A simple examination of cartographic representations from the medieval period, from both the European and the Arab tradition, reveals this perception of the oceans as barriers rather than areas that linked and connected universes which were assumed, until then, to be closed off. The travellers and merchants from Asia who had been crossing the Indian Ocean since ancient times and the Chinese navigators who crossed the Pacific and Indian oceans before the fifteenth century, even reaching the east coast of Africa and the region of Kenya, would have disagreed with this "Western" view, which we will call "European" for convenience.

The geographic and cosmographic ideas of the leading West European authorities, from the geographers of Classical Antiquity such as Ptolemy in the second century, to medieval authors such as Sacrobosco in the twelfth century, fostered this notion of forbidden spaces, both in terms of physical geography and the mental representations of such geography.

This is the context in which the rounding of Cape Bojador should be understood, emerging during the fifteenth century as the first major obstacle that had to be overcome in order to progress down the Sub-Saharan African coast, which was still described as a torrid, uninhabitable zone. The rounding of the cape therefore features as a symbolic moment in the opening up of maritime routes that had never been navigated or known to Europeans before.

The papal bull *Romanus Pontifex* (1455) reflects this situation, referring to zones of Portuguese influence and dominion, taking Cape Bojador as a reference point. The same document associates the rounding of this cape and the areas that the Portuguese had reached by then with the work of Prince Henry, the son of King John I.

The comprehensive *Chronicle Of The Discovery And Conquest Of Guinea* by Gomes Eanes de Zurara does the same, claiming that one of the factors that would have led Prince Henry to encourage southbound Atlantic voyages along the coast of West Africa was the desire to know what lay beyond "a cape known as Bojador, for until then, neither in writings nor memories, no man knew with any certainty the nature of the land that lay beyond the said cape". It was understood that what men wanted to discover and explore were the lands, not necessarily the seas: exploring the seas was not a motive *per se*.

The rounding of Cape Bojador in 1434 was a decisive step towards progress in the Atlantic region, after the many previous attempts that had been made, according to the same chronicler, since 1421. Due to its pivotal position on the coastline, Cape Bojador was one of the barriers that featured in the geographical imaginary of the Late Middle Ages in Europe. It was considered dangerous, if not impossible, to sail beyond this latitude, largely due to the winds and currents which, combined with the shallow waters and cliffs, made coastal navigation dangerous. Added to this, and for lack of better knowledge, Sub-Saharan Africa, to which the Cape was the gateway, was assumed to be torrid and uninhabitable.

It is important to stress that it was not technical innovation that eventually made it possible to round the cape: this was accomplished in a simple ship, guided by traditional navigation instruments. Instead, the seemingly impossible was achieved by using practical knowledge based on the empiricism of an experienced navigator, who had already made a previous unsuccessful attempt in 1433.

This feat was accomplished by redirecting south-bound navigation. Hence, in taking a path that was further away from the coast, it was possible to avoid the greatest dangers and barriers that obstructed progress. However, this essentially simple fact involved abandoning the traditional method of navigating by keeping the land in sight.

Throughout the fifteenth and sixteenth centuries this change in the art of sailing, associated with improvements to vessels and navigational instruments that allowed for celestial navigation, or in other words, for ships to be guided by the stars, was the basis of a model that had evolved beyond the art of sailing to one that was supported by the techniques of navigation. It progressed to what would be conceptualized as nautical science, since it was guided by actual navigation routes and was based on information produced by academics or educated and experienced navigators, including Pedro Nunes and D. João de Castro, respectively. The model took root and, in small qualitative steps that eventually proved to be great leaps forward, became the basis for overriding the previous paradigm for the crossing of seas and oceans since Antiquity, namely cabotage navigation.

This expedient (attempting to overcome an obstacle by circumventing it, even if this involved entering into the deep seas in a careful and calculated way) not only removed the barriers to navigation beyond Cape Bojador, but also proved that the region to the south was not a scorching, uninhabitable world filled with monsters. Hence, the rounding of Cape Bojador was a fundamental step in the lengthy process of overcoming fears and prohibitions associated with the imaginary that had been inherited from Antiquity, using the knowledge acquired by Portuguese navigation. It became a milestone in the evolution of representations of the unknown and of terrestrial geography, gradually moving away from the mythical and the imaginary to operate on the basis of what could be observed and experienced. Moreover, the rounding of Cape Bojador enabled Portuguese voyages to continue along the West African coast, gaining ground in the decades which followed until they confronted another cape, known as the Cape of Storms, which quickly became the Cape of Good Hope. This event helped establish three milestones in the history of globalization:

- the so-called decompartmentalization of the real, the major contribution made by the Portuguese to the European understanding of a world that was beginning to be defined on a global scale;
- the overcoming of barriers by empiricism, based on eminently practical knowledge and experience accumulated during a number of previous attempts;
- the creation of a maritime area still unexplored by Europeans prior to the fifteenth century, namely the Atlantic.

The same ocean which featured in classic Western historiography as a "European creation", tailored to the interests and colonial projects of the Europeans, is the Atlantic of the geographical voyages of exploration which led to the mapping of a maritime route to India, forged by the West in the search for spices and gems. Voyages of exploration in this ocean also enabled the Europeans to identify a new continent: America. The same Atlantic facilitated global connections and the ongoing mobility of people, goods, knowledge, species, genes and pathogens, linking the Mediterranean to the Indian Ocean. However, it is also the area that will always be remembered as the arena for the most intensive slave trading, leading to forced migration, the basis for building a colonial economy managed by European powers but totally dependent on the continents linked by this ocean, which provided raw materials and trade routes that were resized in the interests of those who, for a long period of time, ruled the seas in order to conquer the lands.

In this context, another aspect can also be highlighted: the link between the individual and the global. Gil Eanes, the navigator who led this expedition, is one of the names most frequently cited in relation to Portuguese expansionism, usually associated with the initiatives of Prince Henry. Raised in the household of the latter as his squire, knighted in recognition of his achievement – according to Zurara – and resident in Lagos, his profile is similar to that of many other anonymous figures who collectively contributed, through their many successful or unsuccessful small achievements to the grand project of Portuguese maritime expansionism. This, however, did not exist *a priori*, but took shape progressively through a series of correlations between individual initiative and institutional support, a pathway forged by ships, men and women, established knowledge and ideas under construction, greatly enriched by an understanding of past experiences provided by an informal but select group bound by no institutional framework in the early days of Portuguese expansion.

These are the building blocks of a global age. However, this global world and the global history of Portugal can only be understood in the long term, centuries later, and can only be put into perspective by those who, like us, the authors and readers of the twenty-first century, question the world in the light of their own perceptions.

Globalization is a destination that has never been completely reached, the result of an elusive and endless number of combined and interconnecting contributions which produce systems, models, paradigms and trends that require hundreds of years to be fully understood. The rounding of Cape Bojador has remained, throughout centuries of history and successive historiographical revisions, one of the milestones in this journey: it is significant for the history of Portugal but it is also undeniably important in the construction of a global history.

AMÉLIA POLÓNIA
CITCEM – Transdisciplinary Research Centre "Culture, Space and Memory"
– Faculty of Arts and Humanities, University of Porto

Bibliography

ALBUQUERQUE, Luís de, "Gil Eanes", in *Memórias do Centro de Estudos de Marinha*, vol. XIII, Lisbon, Academia de Marinha, 1984.

BAILYN, Bernard, *Atlantic History: Concept and Contours*, Cambridge (Massachusetts), Harvard University Press, 2005.

DOMINGUES, Francisco Contente, "Cabo Bojador", in DOMINGUES, Francisco Contente (dir.), *Dicionário da Expansão Portuguesa: 1415–1600*, vol. 1, Lisbon, Círculo de Leitores, 2016, pp. 177–178.

RANDLES, W. G. L., "La signification cosmographique du passage du cap Bojador", *Studia*, no. 8, 1961, pp. 221–256.

WINCHESTER, Simon, *Atlântico*, Lisbon, Dom Quixote, 2013.

1468

The Guinea Monopoly: Pluricontinental Economic Development

The bull Romanus Pontifex, *issued on 8 January 1455, excluded all navigation in Guinea without the express authorization of the king of Portugal. In practice, this meant establishing a* mare clausum *regime on the ground of Portugal's priority of discovery and evangelical work, as well as the active pursuit of war against Islam.*

In November 1469, King Afonso V granted Fernão Gomes the exclusive right to trade on the coast of Guinea for a period of five years, on payment to the Crown of 200,000 *réis* per year. However, this monopoly excluded business or, in other words, commerce in the Arguin trading post (in present-day Mauritania), which the king had reserved for himself, as well as on the mainland nearest to the islands of Cape Verde, which had been granted to residents of the islands in 1466. As a further condition, Fernão Gomes may have been required to explore hundred leagues of the African coast per year beyond Sierra Leone, the southernmost limit of Henrican navigation. These are the main facts reported by João de Barros almost eighty years later, since the text of the agreement between the two parties has not survived. The date given by the chronicler has been questioned by historiography and it is nowadays considered more plausible that Fernão Gomes received the contract in June 1468. The agreement ended in 1474, after it had been extended for another year. While it was in place, caravels outfitted by Fernão Gomes explored approximately 3,000 kilometres of the coast, having discovered the entire northern coast of the Gulf of Guinea and part of its eastern coast as far as Cape St. Catherine (nowadays Gabon), including the islands of Fernando Pó, São Tomé, Príncipe and Ano Bom. One particularly important milestone was the identification of the stretch of the Gulf of Guinea where the auriferous regions lay – the Gold Coast – which confirmed the economic viability of the Guinean enterprise.

Within the framework of fifteenth-century Atlantic expansion, the contract for trade on the Guinea coast led to differing interpretations of the role played by the monarchy with regard to navigation in the South Atlantic. The agreement with Fernão Gomes was seen as an expression of a lack of interest on the part of the Crown in South Atlantic navigation at the time, an idea which can also be traced back to João de Barros himself. From this perspective, the monopoly allowed the Crown to concentrate its financial and human resources on pursuing conquests in Morocco, leaving voyages and trading activities on the coast of Guinea to private initiative. Whilst it is true that the Moroccan military campaigns claimed the attention of Afonso V, other interpretations contest the assumption that he was uninterested in South Atlantic navigation, citing the fact that the monarchy would never again grant exclusive rights to navigation and trade in Guinea, which remained part of the estate of Prince Henry until his death in 1460. Moreover, aware of the economic potential of such negotiations, Afonso V was responsible for founding the *Casa da Guiné,* the central agency administering the trade in Lisbon, in 1463. This institution had its origins in a small nucleus of royal officials who had been managing the interests of the Crown in the region since 1455, whose authority was linked to an early private trading post based in Lagos and founded by Prince Henry.

With regard to Fernão Gomes, the lack of information on his social status and activities prior to the agreement has also fuelled a historiographical debate on the involvement of social groups from outside the nobility in Atlantic expansion. Fernão Gomes would have been a prime example of mercantile interest in the western coast of Africa, as opposed to military conquests in Morocco, which was the main attraction for the nobility. This dichotomy, which defined traditional historiography, is now considered less important, since mercantile activities directly and indirectly mobilized various sectors of Portuguese society, ranging from the nobility, of whom Prince Henry is the best example, to the captains of fortresses, royal officials, sailors and soldiers. In the same way, the newly opened routes and the commercialization of new products attracted the interest of foreign trading communities. In this case, rather than discussing the social status of Fernão Gomes, it is more relevant to note that he had served as receiver of enslaved humans arriving from Guinea, having been appointed to this position in 1455. This office not only gave him privileged access to information on trade in the region, but would also have enabled him to become part of formal and informal business networks that were interested in these negotiations.

Fernão Gomes' experience may have been a relevant factor in the awarding of the contract. However, the circumstances surrounding the agreement are not known, nor has it been determined whether the initiative came from the monarch or from Fernão Gomes himself. Nevertheless, it is certain that the Guinea trade contract was put up to public tender and was awarded to the highest bidder, as Afonso V himself claimed at the 1472 Courts. The source of the capital used to manage the contract is also unknown, since the documents only mention the name of Fernão Gomes. Given the mercantile practice of sharing risks and costs, the contractor may have formed a trading partnership, thus involving Portuguese or even foreign capital. It is worth noting that, in addition to the monopoly, Fernão Gomes was also exempted from payment of customs duties on all goods which his ships transported from Guinea, with the exception of Melegueta pepper. This came under the royal monopoly, which signified the exclusion, within the terms of the contract, of certain trade items over which the monarchy had sole rights, unless expressly assigned to others. This was, in fact, the case with the trade in Melegueta pepper, which was eventually formally granted to Fernão Gomes on a date unknown but still within the term of his contract, on payment of 100,000 *réis* per year.

Regardless of the differing interpretations, discussing the importance of this episode and its implications for the building of the empire involves recognizing the early definition of an exclusive right to navigation and trade, which was understood to be a royal prerogative. The oldest example of this right dates back to 1443, when the regent D. Pedro implicitly assumed he had jurisdiction over the sea, in granting Prince Henry the exclusive right to navigation beyond Cape Bojador. It is worth emphasizing that this decision was probably based on texts written by jurists from the School of the Commentators, in particular Baldus de Ubaldis (1327–1400), who introduced jurisdiction over the sea as a royal prerogative for the first time. In the case of Portugal, this interpretation was recognized and extended by the the the bull *Romanus Pontifex*, issued on 8 January 1455, excluded all navigation in Guinea without the express authorization of the king of Portugal. In practice, this meant establishing a *mare clausum* regime on the ground of Portugal's priority of discovery and evangelical work, as well as the active pursuit of war against Islam.

Although the *mare clausum* would later be heavily contested from a legal point of view in the context of the emergence of international law, the path already opened up by Baldus de Ubaldis would be followed by all the European states, with the creation of "national" exclusive rights to trade in the Atlantic. Their administration was ceded to monopolistic companies, which were the most visible face of the European maritime empires, and lasted until the end of the Ancien Régime. In the case of Portugal, the national "exclusive" which began in the fifteenth century was consolidated in the centuries that followed, as the empire extended to other geographical areas. With regard to navigation to Asia, the Crown's exclusive right to the Cape route was a natural extension of the rights claimed and acquired during the fifteenth century, in particular by means of papal bulls, as well as the definition of areas of influence agreed with Castile under the Treaty of Tordesillas in 1494. The terms of the "national exclusive", which remained in place in the centuries which followed, were clarified in the law issued on 9 February 1591, included in the *Ordenações Filipinas* (Book 5, Section

107) and in the law of 18 March 1605. The latter encompassed all the overseas dominions – India, Brazil, Guinea, the Malagueta Coast, Mina, Angola, the islands of Cape
Verde and São Tomé – within the exclusive rights to navigation and trade, reserving
them for vassals of the Portuguese Crown.

However, the kings of Portugal dealt with their claims over navigation and trade
differently, depending on the geographical area within the empire. In the South
Atlantic, navigation and trade were ceded to vassals, creating a restricted area from
the end of the sixteenth century onwards since foreigners were excluded, although
they were open to private initiative and all subjects could operate in free competition.
The constraint introduced in 1649, when a compulsory convoy system for the trade
flows to the three main Brazilian ports was introduced, would restrict navigational
freedom but did not alter the premises of the model. In contrast, navigation via the
Cape route remained a royal shipping monopoly throughout the centuries, material-
izing in the *Carreira da Índia* maritime link organized by the Casa da India. Within
this "colonial exclusive", with regard to the Atlantic, the monarch claimed monopoly
rights over certain tradable items from the outset, including Melegueta pepper from
Africa, gold from Mina and brazilwood. Trade in enslaved Africans was also a royal
monopoly until 1669. In turn, within the *Carreira da Índia*, the king monopolized the
spice and pepper trade, although their importation into the kingdom would be liber-
alized in 1642. These alterations reveal the surprisingly mutable nature of monopoly
rights throughout the Ancien Régime.

Nevertheless, the private sector enjoyed many opportunities to participate in the
economic exploitation of the empire, whether within the "national exclusive" of navigation and trade or in the distribution of monopolized items. In the latter case and
depending on the situation, the king could either exploit them directly using royal
officials, or hand them over to merchants by way of short-term contracts. Hence, the
agreement established with Fernão Gomes was merely the first in a long series of
contract agreements with private individuals. Within the framework of the economic
development of the empire, this legal expedient proved crucial, not only to channelling
revenue for the monarchy but also to the alignment of interests with the private sector.

Susana Münch Miranda
CSG/GHES – Research Center of Economic and Social History,
Lisbon School of Economics and Management, University of Lisbon

Bibliography
BALLONG-WEN-MEWUDA, J. Bato'ora, *São Jorge da Mina, 1482–1637*, Lisbon, Fundação
    Calouste Gulbenkian, 1993.
GIALDRONI, Stefania, *East India Company. Una Storia Giuridica, 1600–1708*, Bologna, Il
    Mulino, 2011.
PEDREIRA, Jorge, "Mercadores e formas de mercantilização", in CURTO, Diogo Ramada
    (ed.), *O Tempo de Vasco da Gama*, Lisbon, Comissão Nacional para as Comemorações dos
    Descobrimentos Portugueses, 1998, pp. 157–178.
RILEY, Carlos, "Ilhas atlânticas e costa africana", in BETHENCOURT, Francisco, CHAUD-
    HURI, Kírti (dir.), *História da Expansão Portuguesa*, Lisbon, Círculo de Leitores, 1998,
    pp. 137–162.
THOMAZ, Luís Filipe, *A Questão da Pimenta em Meados do Século XVI. Um Debate Político do
    Governo de D. João de Castro*, Lisbon, Centro de Estudos dos Povos e Culturas de Expressão
    Portuguesa da Universidade Católica Portuguesa, 1998.

1494

The Treaty of Tordesillas: A New Vision of the Atlantic and Sharing of the Seas

Extending the Tordesillas line to the east universalized the global perception of the sea. The entire planet is represented in the maps, together with all the seas.

On 7 June 1494, the plenipotentiaries for the rulers of Portugal, and Castile and Aragon (John II, and Isabella and Ferdinand) – the two latter figures known as the Catholic Monarchs – assembled in Tordesillas to sign a treaty on the sovereignty of lands recently discovered by navigators in their service of their monarchs. In practical terms, the agreement established the division of the Atlantic "by a border or straight line running from pole to pole, that is, north to south from the Arctic pole to the Antarctic pole". The Portuguese mission consisted of the Lord of Sagres and Beringel, Rui de Sousa, his son João de Sousa, Chief Steward of the Royal Household, and Aires de Almada from the Crown Supreme Court, with Estêvão Vaz acting as secretary. The witnesses were João Soares de Siqueira, Rui Leme and Duarte Pacheco Pereira, already one of the most famous navigators of the time. Castile and Aragon were represented by the Lord Chamberlain, D. Henrique Henriquez, Commander-in-Chief D. Gutierre de Cárdenas, and Rodrigo Maldonado, with Fernando Alvarez de Toledo as their secretary. Their witnesses were Pero de León, Fernando de Torres and Fernando Gamarra.

While another treaty, signed on the same day, dealt with problems pertaining to borders and areas of expansion involving the Iberian kingdoms in the north of Africa, the document that became known as the first Treaty of Tordesillas sought to resolve problems that might result from potential clashes between the overseas projects of Portugal and Castile in the Atlantic (hence the frequent assertion that the document divided the world up between the Portuguese and the Spanish is clearly incorrect). This treaty contained an important new item: the concept of the Atlantic world as a vast space, an ocean stretching from the European and African coasts to Asia – as it was thought at the time, given that the American continent was still unknown – rather than a sea that was limited to the immediate coastline.

In fact, regulation of the Atlantic area had already been outlined in the treaty signed in Alcáçovas on 4 September 1479. After years of conflict (1475–1479) in which Afonso V defended the claim of his niece and wife, Joana de Transtâmara, to the throne of Castile against the faction supporting Isabella, the half-sister of Henry IV, who would later be crowned queen, the peace agreements contained in the 1479 treaty included the first definition of the areas of Atlantic influence of the Iberian kingdoms. An imaginary line was drawn, parallel to the Equator, for this purpose. The Canary Islands were recognized as belonging to the kingdom of Castile, and land discovered or to be discovered south of the archipelago belonged to Portugal.

The Treaty of Alcáçovas governed Iberian maritime expansion until 4 March 1493, when Christopher Columbus was forced to land in Lisbon on returning from America, due to adverse sailing conditions, as confirmed in a letter discovered very recently. In the letter, dated 3 May, John II informed his cousin Ferdinand, the Catholic King, of the arrival of Columbus ("Dom Cristóvão, your admiral, has arrived in the port of our city of Lisbon with a fortune from overseas").

The negotiations lasted fifteen months, from March 1493 to June 1494. John II immediately ordered preparations to be made for an armada, to be commanded by D. Francisco de Almeida, the future viceroy of India, on the understanding that the lands sighted by Columbus lay south of the Canary Islands parallel and therefore belonged to him. On the other hand, the Catholic Monarchs argued that the provision in the Treaty of Alcáçovas only applied to the coastal seas in Africa ("off Guinea", as the treaty stated). They did everything they could to extend the negotiations for as long as possible, sending a succession of ambassadors on inconclusive missions whilst seeking the support of the Roman Curia. Pope Alexander VI, a native of Aragon – whose election was paid for by Ferdinand, as Jerónimo de Zurita e Castro, the chronicler of the Aragonese monarch, later declared – issued five bulls in their favour (not in order to mediate but to intervene in favour of a petitioner), the so-called Alexandrine Bulls. The first, *Inter caetera*, dated 3 May 1493, assigned the lands discovered and to be discovered to the Catholic Monarchs. The second, known as *Inter caetera II*, was dated 4 March due to a clerical error by the papal chancellery and should have been dated 3 May to replace the previous one. It stated that the lands which lay west of a dividing line running from one pole to the other 100 leagues from the Azores and Cape Verde would henceforth belong to the monarchs of Castile and Aragon.

This bull overruled the initial proposal made by John II to the effect that sovereignty over lands discovered and to be discovered was defined, in the case of Castile, as north of a line parallel to the Equator plotted in relation to the Canary Islands and, in the case of Portugal, south of the same line, therefore replicating and, by implication, recognizing the initial interpretation of the Catholic Monarchs regarding the application of the Treaty of Alcáçovas to the coastal waters of Africa. Defining another parallel would hardly resolve the matter. The solution would have been found by Christopher Columbus, in the full knowledge that he had travelled south of the Canary Islands parallel, which implied that it should be replaced by a semi-meridian, as can be surmised from the wording of a letter from Ferdinand of Aragon to his admiral: "the line that you said should be included in the papal bull".

The geographical error of running a dividing line through the Azores and Cape Verde was resolved when it was stipulated in the treaty that the semi-meridian would be 370 leagues away from the latter, as proposed by the Portuguese king, thus ensuring the space necessary for Portuguese sailing ships to reach the Cape of Good Hope or lands that were known to exist "to the south", as Columbus testified that the king had told him personally, or both. Ferdinand and Isabella, in turn, were ensured possession of the new lands discovered by their admiral and others that would be found west of the Antilles, in America.

Four years after the treaty was signed, Vasco da Gama landed in India and the first maritime link between Europe and Asia was subsequently established. Since 1506, King Manuel I had been seeking to conquer Malacca and gain control of the strait of the same name, which was seen as a means of access to trade in the China seas. This was accomplished by Afonso de Albuquerque in 1511 and the Portuguese were then able to navigate and trade in ports and seas which extended as far as the Sea of Japan. In these distant waters, the aim was to reach the Moluccas, the only place which produced one of the most important spices traded by the Portuguese: cloves.

However, the problem of the location of the archipelago soon arose. The obvious solution was to extend the Tordesillas semi-meridian into a complete meridian but this entailed deciding whether the islands would stay within the dividing line (and belong to Portugal) or beyond it (and belong to Castile and Aragon). Cosmographers and other experts from both sides were inclined to position the Moluccas beyond the line and thus within the sphere of the monarchs of Castile and Aragon. The question was never resolved to the satisfaction of both parties and subsequently, under the 1529 Treaty of Zaragoza, John III agreed to pay Charles V an exorbitant amount for navigation and trading rights in the Moluccas. In fact, he paid for what was already his, since the islands were effectively within the meridian.

Hence, Luso-Castilian maritime rivalry was directly responsible for three events which affirmed, in writing, the radical changes in the way in which the world was perceived, since the ever-present desire for regulation to avoid serious confrontation indirectly obliged both parties to specify, on each occasion, what their understanding of the sea was and the possible extent to which it could be navigated.

On the first occasion, the sea was reduced to the African coastline. In effect, the Treaty of Alcáçovas resolved the warlike atmosphere in the Guinea seas caused by disputes over local trade. The Alcáçovas sea was a coastal sea.

In Tordesillas, on the other hand, it was lost on the horizon. There is no doubt that the Earth was understood to be round, but this was not the issue: the position of new lands in relation to the parallel was certainly important, as in Alcáçovas, and John II intended this should be applied again in 1494, although this time it would become a semi-meridian. However, the crucial change was that no limitations should be imposed on the wider maritime area. It was the open sea that was now being discussed, not the coastal one.

Extending the Tordesillas line to the east universalized the global perception of the sea. The entire planet is represented in the maps, together with all the seas. Essentially, there was a fundamental difference between the processes of commercial maritime expansion in countries in the south and those in the north-west of Europe. The former had to consider the total known area at any given moment in order to define their spheres of influence as accurately as possible, therefore acquiring a global notion of what the oceans were. In the case of England, the Netherlands and, even earlier, France, navigation had specific objectives and what was at stake was their specific success in each era, since the world view supporting the routes they followed was already reflected in Iberian nautical cartography, of which they made ample use.

The Treaty of Tordesillas ended up supporting the notion of the division of the world which, in its strictest sense, involved sharing the oceans and the Iberian conquests. This had never been an issue in 1494, but was affirmed when the Treaty of Zaragoza established the idea that the seas and lands discovered or to be discovered belonged to Portugal or Castile, which each had its own semi-hemisphere. However, recognizing that the seas were "reserved" for Iberian navigation was unacceptable to other European countries embarking on transoceanic navigation. From the perspective of the emerging international law, the Dutch jurist Hugo Grotius emphasized the freedom of the seas in an anonymous edition of an opuscule entitled *Mare liberum* (1609), which in fact consisted of the tenth chapter of a much larger work, *De jure belli ac pacis* (1625). The text served the interests of the European maritime powers, or those with ambitions to achieve this status, and was therefore an immediate success. However, this was not the case in Iberia, since its claims were being contested, leading Serafim de Freitas, a Portuguese professor of Canon Law at Valladolid, to challenge Grotius in his *Do Justo Império Asiático dos Portugueses* (1633). Ultimately, the right to navigate the oceans was defined, as might be expected, by what actually happened. To give one example, in the seventeenth century, the Portuguese sent 193 ships to the Indian Ocean, the English 811 and the Dutch 1,770: in the end, it was sailing power and cannons that decided the question of the freedom of the seas.

† Francisco Contente Domingues
Faculty of Arts and Humanities, University of Lisbon

Bibliography

ALBUQUERQUE, Luís de, "O Tratado de Tordesilhas e as dificuldades técnicas da sua aplicação rigorosa", *Revista da Universidade de Coimbra*, vol. XXIII, 1973, sep.

ALMEIDA, A. A. Marques de, "Ler o mundo e imaginar o possível: conhecimento e representação do mundo no tempo de Tordesilhas", *Revista da Universidade de São Paulo*, no. 45, 2006, pp. 6–15.

DOMINGUES, Francisco Contente (dir.), *Dicionário da Expansão Portuguesa, 1415–1600*, 2 vols., Lisbon, Círculo de Leitores, 2016.

FONSECA, Luís Adão da, *O Tratado de Tordesilhas e a Diplomacia Luso-Castelhana no Século XV*, Lisbon, Inapa, 1991.

PÉREZ EMBID, Florentino, *Los Descubrimientos en el Atlântico y la Rivalidad Castellano-Portuguesa hasta el Tratado de Tordesillas*, Seville, Escuela de Estudios Hispano-Americanos, 1948.

1496
Expulsion of the Jews: The Diaspora of the Diasporas

Those who reached North Africa, the Ottoman Empire, the Italian cities in which Jews were permitted to live and even India always remained immersed in their cultural and religious spectrum. They formed the classic picture of what was known, in the nineteenth and twentieth centuries, as the Sephardic world.

The decree issued at the beginning of December 1496, expelling the Jews and Moors from Portugal with practical effects until October of the following year – and describing those whom it targeted in negative terms as justification for the act – has a counterpoint in another surviving document and immediately reveals the intentions of its proponent, King Manuel I (1495–1521).

In the edict of expulsion, the discourse is coercive and should be read in the light of the alleged nefarious influence of those whom it targeted on Portuguese or Spanish Jews who had already converted to Christianity. Therefore, the text of the Manueline Ordinations states that the reason for the expulsion was that Jews and Moors were: "cursed sons, while in the hardness of their hearts they are cause for further condemnation; moreover, they make many Christians stray from their true path, which is the Holy Catholic Faith".

Another document contemporary with the edict of expulsion, preserved in the Loulé Municipal Archives, reveals royal considerations of a practical nature, designed to verify what was actually happening in various parts of the kingdom where Jews resided. According to this text, on 24 December 1496 a copy of a letter written by Manuel I in Coruche on 15 December 1496 concerning "the property of the Jews and their preaching" was presented in the public square in Loulé. Contrary to what might have been expected following the edict of expulsion, this document is indicative of the king's intention to immediately convert the Jews to Christianity. In the letter, the monarch obliged Christians who had acquired properties from Jews that had converted to return them at the purchase price. Only after this did Manuel I specify that there could be no more acts of worship amongst Jews in their synagogues or in any other place, on pain of losing their property and receiving a public whipping. Moreover, the king wished to determine whether synagogue properties had already been sold, to whom and how many there were, meaning that the Jews would have abandoned these places of worship as it was impossible to continue their religious practices. As it was a pragmatic document, there are no negative descriptions of the Jews, whom Manuel I intended to transform immediately into Christians. Any indication of ideological segregation would have been counterproductive.

This duality within Manueline policy had fundamental repercussions for the lives of Jews resident in Portugal, whose numbers included many who had been expelled from Castile in 1492. In Portugal, a growing number of measures were introduced up to Easter 1497, to prevent Jews from leaving the country. Minors were also seized so that they could be instructed by Christians and forced group baptisms took place all over the kingdom – the one at the Estaus Palace in Lisbon was a famous example – and even in the Portuguese stronghold of Asilah, in North Africa, conquered in 1471, where many Jews had gone in order to transfer to Islamic rule.

After 1496–1497, probably encouraged by opinions in Rome which did not always concur with the use of pressure to achieve conversion – which should have been a voluntary act – the king pursued a gentler policy which was, in fact, an extension of the strategy revealed in the Coruche document. This involved their gradual inclusion within the Christian community through the suppression of places used for religious gatherings, such as synagogues and the presumed influence of the majority in local society, including children and other relatives who had become Christian – the so-called New Christians, as opposed to the Old Christians, who were not of Jewish or Muslim origin. However, most of the population did not want to recognize these neighbours of theirs, the former Jews, as true Christians, knowing that in practice, contrary to the intentions of Manuel I, the pressure to convert had little to do with this influence, since they continued to live segregated lives and there was evidence that they still practised Judaic rituals. The entries in the Lisbon register of properties and rights in rem show that when the famous massacre of New Christians flared up in Lisbon in April 1506, there were still Jews living in the old Jewish quarters of the city who had maintained their Jewish identity but lived with relatives who had already converted. In fact, the records of the massacre reveal that the Old Christians still viewed the converts as Jews or, in other words, as "false" New Christians. Despite the repressive measures taken by Manuel I against those who led the carnage and the governors of the city of Lisbon, this dilemma was never resolved.

On 28 May 1536, during the reign of John III (1521–1557), the Tribunal of the Holy Office was finally established in Portugal, as an instrument for overseeing the orthodoxy of all Christians living in the kingdom, particularly in response to alleged evidence that New Christians were secretly adhering to their original faith.

This divide within the former Peninsular Jewish nation had structural repercussions for its evolution as a social group. The first generation of converts, namely those who had been born or had lived part of their lives as Jews, remained very close to those who, due to their wealth, influence or fortunate circumstances, managed to leave Portugal between the end of the fifteenth century and the beginning of the sixteenth century. Those who reached North Africa, the Ottoman Empire, the Italian cities in which Jews were permitted to live and even India always remained immersed in their cultural and religious spectrum. They formed the classic picture of what was known, in the nineteenth and twentieth centuries, as the Sephardic world, given their cultural heritage, religious practices (minhag [tradition]), and even their different (Judeo-Spanish) language which is linked to the vernacular languages of the Iberian Peninsula, with additions from Hebrew and local languages.

Many common cultural elements can also be found among the first generations of converts and these emigrant Jews, as well as a legacy of identity-based resistance which includes disregarding the figure of Jesus Christ as a divine entity, on the basis of the famous Toledot Yeshu (Life of Jesus) or extracts from it, which can be identified in both the testimonies of Jews in Morocco and in the Inquisition trials involving, for example, the relatives of Garcia de Orta. However, the growing isolation of those who remained in the Iberian Peninsula from their original culture, mainly due to inquisitional policing, and their immersion in the imposed religious culture led to the progressive distancing of New Christians from the original cluster who managed to emigrate. This led to divergence, such as the rejection of oral law, on the part of many of the converts who managed to flee persecution in Portugal during the seventeenth century, and a lingering suspicion of the authority of the rabbis descended from the first generation in the face of their ambivalent identity, evident in various rabbinical *responsa.*

In fact, the flight of many converts accused of heresy to economically thriving cities and territories during the seventeenth century, such as Amsterdam, Hamburg, Livorno, Bordeaux and other cities in the south-west of France, Izmir and London particularly in the eighteenth century, often ignoring the normative bases of Judaism, brought them closer to the Jews established in the Mediterranean basin, as the possessors of a rabbinic culture of Iberian origin who were also tempted by the economic possibilities and opportunities for promotion that they would provide. Yet it is also true that, even up to the eighteenth century, the New Christians who escaped persecution from the Inquisition and assumed a Jewish identity took pride in another aspect of their recognition: they were the "Portuguese nation", or the "Portuguese and Spanish nation". They used Portuguese or Spanish as a vernacular language, were immersed in the values of Peninsular Baroque culture and, as a way of attesting to their Peninsular difference, many used the patronymics of their famous Jewish ancestors, together with those of Peninsular Christians which had been given to them or their relatives as converts. The first official rabbi of Dutch Brazil, for example, was called Isaac Aboab da Fonseca (1605–1693).

This "nation" still included relatives who had assumed an "official" Catholic identity in Portugal and its empire. On the basis of Judaic yihus (lineage), the equivalent to Christian models of lineage, and the assumption that, ideally, Christian relatives would assume Jewish identity and join their relatives in the diaspora, the Iberian Jews who lived outside Portugal and Spain considered them an integral part of the "nation". This can be confirmed by the aid given to orphans who remained there, for example, or the wills of relatives in such faraway places as São João da Pesqueira. This strategy also contemplated their interests within the rival empires in which they circulated – Dutch, English and even French – since it was always necessary to have relatives in a business that might, sometimes simultaneously, extend to Dutch Brazil, the Caribbean, Suriname and the British colonies in North America, where the diaspora of the "nation" was expanding.

The dynamics of this group of Jews and converts which, in social, cultural and ideological terms, were related to a common Iberian origin, would have unavoidable repercussions up to the present day. Despite the dismantling of many of the business networks following the demise of the Ancien Régime, the establishment of active colonial policies by the European powers, or the independence of former colonies, the Iberian identity resulting from this diaspora remains with those who are aware of their place within the history of these truly epic events.

José Alberto Rodrigues da Silva Tavim
Centre for History of the University of Lisbon

Bibliography

ISRAEL, Jonathan, *Diasporas within a Diaspora: Jews, Crypto-Jews and the World Maritime Empires (1540–1740)*, Leiden, Brill, 2002.

TAVARES, Maria José Pimenta Ferro, *Judaísmo e Inquisição. Estudos*, Lisbon, Presença, 1987.

Idem, *Os Judeus em Portugal no Século XV*, 2 vols., Lisbon, Faculdade de Ciências Sociais e Humanas da Universidade Nova de Lisboa/Instituto Nacional de Investigação Científica, 1982 and 1984.

TAVIM, José Alberto Rodrigues da Silva, "A "fantastic" tale of the new Christians concerning the immigration of the Jews to Portugal", *Hispania Judaica Bulletin*, vol. 11, pt. 2, 2015, pp. 151–168.

Idem, "Judeus de Loulé nos séculos XIV e XV: no prolongamento do Al-Andaluz", in MOREIRA, Rita, VAQUINHAS, Nelson (coord.), *Atas do I Encontro de História de Loulé*, Loulé, Câmara Municipal de Loulé, 2018, pp. 91–110.

1498–1500
Calicut and Porto Seguro: The Birth of Pluricontinentalism

The ocean voyages and pluricontinental dispersion of the Portuguese paved the way for the establishment of connections that would prove transformative on an international scale. In certain cases, the economic, demographic and cultural interdependencies established after 1498 and 1500 had palpable short-term effects, while others were only felt later.

The arrival in Calicut of the fleet commanded by Vasco da Gama (1498), and Pedro Álvares Cabral's first voyage to Brazil (1500) were events that undoubtedly inscribed the history of Portugal within world history. Above all, they laid the foundations for the pluricontinental Portuguese empire. Extending from east to west, from Timor to the Brazilian hinterlands, this disjointed empire with its varying political and administrative configurations encompassed territories and circuits for people and goods that spanned two oceans and four continents. The transformations resulting from the establishment of the Portuguese beyond their domestic maritime border did not only affect a small peripheral kingdom situated in the extreme west of Eurasia. They were also felt in the autochthonous societies submitted to Portuguese authority, who dominated relations of production, and by non-European populations that interacted with the Portuguese in commercial, religious and cultural matters but were not politically subjugated.

The ocean voyages of exploration undertaken by the Portuguese and their commercial or colonial settlement outside Europe, together with the arrival of Columbus in the Antilles in 1492, were pivotal moments in global interconnectivity. These expeditions enabled all densely populated regions in the world to become linked and to interact economically, culturally and demographically on a continuous basis, with profound and lasting impacts for all involved. It may be considered that they were the beginning of a period in which the geographical reach of international trade was extended significantly and production centres and consumer markets that were oceans apart became linked. Flows of capital, forced or free labour, raw material, foodstuffs and manufactured goods started to circulate between continents, as different cultures made contact with each other for the first time or intensified previously tenuous relations. Emerging from these interactions, there were changes in patterns of consumption in communities, diversification in the production sectors of the different economies and an expansion of technologies and institutions. Together with their Iberian neighbours, the Portuguese were responsible for integrating the hitherto isolated continent of America into the network of people, products and micro-organisms that were circulating via the crossroads for continents and regions, namely Afro-Eurasia, the so-called "Old World".

Vasco da Gama's voyage led to the opening of a transcontinental artery which directly linked the two opposite end of Eurasia via the Cape of Good Hope, using the so-called "Cape Route". From then onwards, the dependence of the European Atlantic seaboard economies on intermediaries in the Mediterranean and the Levant for supplies of consumer goods from Asia was resolved. The merchant and state fleets, and later those of the monopoly companies, were no longer restricted to maritime corridors that followed the coastline or fishing routes on the high seas. They could now sail through non-European deep seas. Ships belonging to the line equipped by the Portuguese Crown were responsible for intercontinental shipments of spices, textiles, porcelain, ceramics, gemstones, shells and saltpetre. At the same time, ships supplied by the State of India or chartered by subjects of the king of Portugal were involved in transporting goods across the Indian Ocean.

In the South Atlantic, the Portuguese (and later the Luso-Brazilian) merchant fleet was responsible for the transport of people, goods and capital between Portugal, the west African coast and Ibero-America. Throughout the Early Modern period, ships chartered by Portuguese merchants ensured the importation of crops from plantations and later gold, which were then re-exported to areas outside the kingdom. Travelling in the opposite direction, certain types of food and manufactured goods were destined for consumer markets in Brazil.

In the Atlantic zone, the Portuguese also provided a new route and unprecedented volumes for a centuries-old form of commerce that had linked Sub-Saharan Africa to the Middle East, the Maghreb and the Mediterranean: the slave trade. The Portuguese pioneered transatlantic traffic, becoming the main suppliers of enslaved labour not only for the Brazilian sugar industry, but also for mining and the urban economy in Spanish America. Even after other European entrepreneurs joined them in the seventeenth century, merchants from Portuguese-speaking countries remained the leading suppliers of the American colonial markets, particularly in Brazil. Contrary to what might be expected, this trade was not restricted to the Atlantic coast, but acquired a transoceanic dimension with the use of shells from the Maldives and luxury fabrics from India to purchase captives on the west coast of Africa.

The Portuguese also actively contributed to what became known as the "Columbian exchange" or, in other words, the spread of animals and plants beyond their natural habitats and their introduction into distant territories. This transcontinental diffusion had significant impacts on ecosystems in the host areas and on food consumption patterns in their societies. Although the Portuguese did not unleash a bacteriological war in Brazil as deadly as that of their Spanish counterparts in the more urbanized and densely populated Spanish Indies, they also contributed to the devastation of native populations. The spread of very serious diseases to the Amerindian population resulted from the initial contact between two epidemiological regimes that had otherwise remained separate, prior to the sixteenth century.

However, what had proved to be a strategic advantage for the Portuguese in American territory worked against them in Africa, where tropical disease remained an almost insurmountable barrier to European penetration and territorial settlement until the nineteenth century.

In addition to germs, agricultural produce and luxury goods, it was precious metals in particular that were globalized throughout the sixteenth century. Since the latter were the only exchange currency used to purchase luxury imports from Asia, and gold and silver arbitrage transactions were immensely profitable, the Portuguese were involved in exporting metallic money far beyond the mining regions. From the end of the sixteenth to the second half of the seventeenth century they served as intermediaries in the intercontinental circulation of silver to China, the main consumer of precious metals in the world during this period. The Portuguese were engaged in this trade on two fronts, as they were responsible for the export of silver from Japan to China and also involved in the trans-Pacific flow of South American silver via the connection between Acapulco and Manila. However, despite the countess transformations generated by the Portuguese empire and pluricontinental diaspora, it is still necessary to account for the changes that did not take place in the three centuries that followed the voyages of Vasco da Gama and Cabral.

Neither Portugal nor its north European counterparts, who had launched their joint-stock companies in the seventeenth century, exercised hegemony over Asia, in particular the more robust states and economies in the continent, namely the Mughal and Chinese empires and Japan. In the African continent, despite the destabilizing effect of the transatlantic slave trade on local societies and the fact that Portuguese military incursions into western Central Africa had provided them with a tenuous hinterland and established a system of vassalage in Angola, in the three centuries after 1498 domination proved to be a mirage. Even with their naval superiority, the Portuguese, and later the North European trading companies, had no alternative other than to operate on the peripheries of the more robust Asian and African states, with scrupulous respect for the terms stipulated by the local powers. Any use of coercion had to be prudent and subordinate to trade priorities, meaning that maritime routes were favoured since they were less of a threat to the authority and economic interests of the local powers. Moreover, the violence exercised by the Europeans tended to be aimed towards small states and trading communities which lacked the support of any centralized authority and were therefore easier targets for naval artillery. On the other hand, it was not possible to control the "production" of African slaves and Asian luxury goods, nor establish authority over large swathes of territory and exercise sovereignty. It was only in America, where colonial rule facilitated the establishment of a plantation economy and, at the turn of the eighteenth century, gold mining, that they managed to dominate in political, economic and cultural terms.

Within international trade, the centuries-old pattern of Euro-Asian exchanges did not alter with the arrival of the Portuguese in the Indian Ocean. Valuable items, in particular, continued to arrive in the West from the Indian subcontinent, south-east Asia and China, reserved for a select clientele. Until the start of the Industrial Revolution, Europe, in turn, proved incapable of establishing its manufacturing production beyond the domestic markets and American colonies. In addition, the opening up of new maritime links and the incorporation of long-distance markets did not prevent transport and communications from remaining slow and unreliable and therefore expensive. Although the evidence points to a deflationary trend in imports of Asian luxury goods in Europe, imbalances in prices between the distant acquisition and consumption markets remained. These discrepancies would only be significantly reduced in the second quarter of the nineteenth century, in favour of European consumers and English-speaking America. Before the widespread use of railways and steamships in the nineteenth century, the natural barriers to trade and the movement of people and ideas were difficult to overcome, in addition to the political and institutional barriers.

Despite these limitations, there can be no doubt that the ocean voyages and pluricontinental dispersion of the Portuguese paved the way for the establishment of connections that would prove transformative on an international scale. In certain cases, the economic, demographic and cultural interdependencies established after 1498 and 1500 had palpable short-term effects, while others were only felt later, when the Portuguese were no more than secondary actors. In these cases, it may be considered that the pioneering voyages of Gama and Cabral sowed the seeds for historical processes that occurred much later, but which would not have been possible without the intercontinental connections forged in the sixteenth century. They include the Great Divergence and the colonial rule of the European West over vast areas of the world, industrial capitalism and the high-speed, high-impact globalization that characterizes the modern world today.

EDGAR CRAVO BERTRAND PEREIRA
Centre for the History of Society and Culture

Bibliography

BETHENCOURT, Francisco, "Political configurations and local powers", in BETHEN-COURT, Francisco, CURTO, Diogo Ramada (dir.), *Portuguese Oceanic Expansion, 1400–1800*, Cambridge, Cambridge University Press, 2007, pp. 197–229.

FLYNN, Dennis O., GIRÁLDEZ, Arturo, "Path dependence, time lags and the birth of globalisation. A critique of O'Rourke and Williamson", *European Review of Economic History*, vol. 8, 2004, pp. 81–108.

JERÓNIMO, Miguel Bandeira, "Imperial globalizations", in ANTUNES, Cátia, FATAH-BLACK, Karwan (ed.), *Explorations in History and Globalisation*, New York, Routledge, 2016, pp. 212–230.

O'ROURKE, Kevin H., WILLIAMSON, Jeffrey G., "After Columbus. Explaining Europe's overseas trade boom, 1500–1800", *The Journal of Economic History*, vol. 62, no. 2, June 2002, pp. 417–456.

VRIES, Jan de, "The limits of globalization in the early modern world", *Economic History Review*, vol. 63, no. 3, 2010, pp. 710–733.

1502
Asilah, Ceuta, Tangier and Ksar es-Seghir: The Global Phenomenon of the *Misericórdia* Brotherhoods

Wherever the Portuguese went, they ensured communications between the different parts of the empire, and between these areas and the metropole. In the State of India, the Misericórdias worked in conjunction with the Procuratorate for the Deceased, organizing the transfer to the kingdom of the estates of Portuguese subjects who had died in the East.

In 1502, only four years after the creation of the first Portuguese *Misericórdia* brotherhood in Lisbon, similar institutions existed in four Portuguese strongholds in North Africa: Asilah, Ceuta, Tangier and Ksar es-Seghir. In addition to the hundreds established in cities and towns throughout the kingdom, *Misericórdias* were created in territories resulting from Portuguese expansion up to the nineteenth century, even in areas that did not come under the political authority of the Crown, such as Salvador do Congo, Manila and Japan. Other regions, such as Ceuta and Olivença, kept their *Misericórdias* even after they were no longer Portuguese. The success of the *Misericórdias* can be explained by the many advantages they offered. They were brotherhoods under royal protection and, in legal terms, were not subordinate to episcopal authority but could operate autonomously. Although they functioned independently of each other, they were governed by certain common principles and quickly developed the capacity to operate as a network and, with the flexibility this offered, avoided a burdensome chain of command. The *Misericórdias* were useful to the Crown and the local elites: they symbolized the royal presence and protection in faraway territories or those less frequently visited by the central power, ensured that donations and bequests came under the aegis of the monarch, and brought the local elites together in charitable works on a voluntary basis, whilst also establishing divisions between different sectors of the population, essentially the poor and the elites, but also separating the latter group into the upper echelons of the brotherhood (the nobility) and the lower ranks (merchants, the higher levels of the artisan class, wealthy farmers, etc.). As organizations which included important local people, they acquired a trustworthiness which many did not feel for institutions and officials of the Crown.

The explicit aim of these brotherhoods was charitable work, as summarized, albeit not exhaustively, in the fourteen works of mercy. However, they could also serve other purposes. The accumulation of immovable assets and capital provided them with an income that enabled them to offer loans, mainly when investment capital was needed, for example in São Salvador da Bahia (for the sugar cane harvest and sugar production) or to ports in the State of India (for maritime trade).

The *Misericórdias* became consensual institutions, from which many, although not everyone, benefited. With few exceptions, women were not allowed to become directly involved and local people who had not converted to Catholicism were unlikely to be included in those who received aid, far less be admitted as members of the brotherhoods. Charitable work discriminated amongst the poor, dividing them according to social and moral criteria. The beneficiaries of more costly forms of assistance were carefully selected, as can be seen from the distribution of wedding dowries and admissions to residential institutions (hospitals for the elderly and infirm, and women's *recolhimentos*).

In addition, the *Misericórdias* in the overseas territories were involved in the transfer of capital, mainly from the State of India to Portugal, making use of the services of merchants and their respective networks of contacts. For the central power, this constituted a system of aid for the poor organized at low cost and anchored in the principles of the Catholic faith, since the brotherhoods accumulated assets through private donations and bequests. However, they also served as a source of liquid funds which the Crown could draw on if necessary, converting these forced loans into royal debt (*padrões de juro*).

In the East, the Jesuits formed part of these confraternities, in order to enhance their acceptance within local societies, as missionary epistolography confirms. Following Saint Francis Xavier's stay in the East (1542–1552), the Society of Jesus included charitable work in its programme and priests therefore cleaned jails, did voluntary work in hospitals and assisted with religious services, celebrating mass and preaching in churches that belonged to the brotherhoods. This strategy was also evident in Japan, where the Jesuits founded *Misericórdias* to support Catholic devotional practices in which, unlike those in other countries, the Japanese were the main actors.

The *Misericórdias* overshadowed all other brotherhoods, both within the kingdom and in the so-called overseas conquests, despite some exceptions. These institutions drew charitable bodies together, incorporating medieval hospitals founded by laymen and receiving donations from benefactors which enabled them to create and oversee new charitable services and institutions. After the Council of Trent ended in 1563, they also began to incorporate larger local hospitals. Their urban identity should be stressed: the larger the local population, the more capital and human resources they had, resulting in a greater number of poor in need of assistance and an increasing number of institutions under their administration. It should be noted that the larger *Misericórdias* were situated in sea ports, not only in Portugal but also in the empire.

One of the advantages of the system was that the *Misericórdias* functioned as a network whose nerve centres coincided with the political and administrative capitals or areas of greater economic vitality. Wherever the Portuguese went, they ensured communications between the different parts of the empire, and between these areas and the metropole. In the State of India, the *Misericórdias* worked in conjunction with the Procuratorate for the Deceased, organizing the transfer to the kingdom of the estates of Portuguese subjects who had died in the East, giving rise to a continuous exchange of correspondence, known as the "Letters from India" when it involved the Cape Route. This system of written communication functioned with very few central links: the Lisbon *Misericórdia*, for matters which involved the kingdom, and the Goa or Cochin *Misericórdias* for India. In Brazil, the role of transferring assets was organized on a less official basis than in the East, but the *Misericórdias* were also active in this sphere.

For many who had left Portugal and were unable to return, the *Misericórdias* provided a symbolic return home, transferring their estate to their birthplace where it would be converted into chaplaincies, often with their own buildings, masses on behalf of their souls or works of charity, the most common being the founding of wedding dowries. The name of the deceased thus remained alive in the memory of the living through the work of the *Misericórdias*. With regard to the Porto *Misericórdia* at least, the transfer of capital from the empire was the greatest means of enriching the brotherhood throughout the sixteenth and seventeenth centuries.

The withdrawal from the State of India during the seventeenth century, with the corresponding loss of many trading posts and fortresses, led to the disappearance of many *Misericórdias*. Yet, for as long as the East remained economically important to the kingdom, they not only continued to organize services such as the transfer of estates to Portugal, but also offered guarantees for capital transactions, providing cover for local traders. Like other institutions which accumulated liquid assets, they were used by the Crown to obtain money through forced loans in situations of urgent need, for military defence or to ensure overseas trade.

The Manila *Misericórdia*, also in Asia, deserves special mention, since this territory was never under Portuguese jurisdiction. Founded in 1594 by Portuguese men living in the city, it was governed by its own statutes, modelled on the *Compromissos* (statutes) of the *Misericórdia* of Lisbon (1577) and *Misericórdia* of Goa (1595), therefore structuring its activities according to the Portuguese tradition and also operating independently from the bishop and his curia. Initially, it restricted itself to providing credit in the form of private perpetuities (*censos consignativos*), but in 1668 introduced the *respondentia* system, consisting of loans at interest rates of 40% to 50% to finance trade with Mexico. Maritime interest rates were high, and also applied to sea loans by the *Misericórdia* of Macao, although the latter were lower. Overall, however, they were much higher than the usual rate for loans levied by the *Misericórdias* in the kingdom, which corresponded to 6.25%.

In Portuguese America, *Misericórdias* were not founded at the same rapid pace as in the East and most of the existing ones – with the exception of those in Rio de Janeiro and Salvador da Bahia – were not very significant before the nineteenth century. Third Orders and other brotherhoods were sometimes more important than the *Misericórdias* on a local level. The expansion of the brotherhoods unfolded in a different way from those in India, since, although Salvador da Bahia, until 1763, followed by Rio de Janeiro, served as administrative headquarters, *Misericórdias* in Brazil did not deploy the same interconnections between its different regions as Goa did with the Asian strongholds, which were all dependent on the sea route to Lisbon and the respective monsoon seasons. On the other hand, it was possible to make the journey to Portugal from various different points on the Brazilian coast and to ports other than Lisbon (such as Porto, Aveiro and Viana).

The *Misericórdias* were a marker of identity for the Portuguese communities on a global scale, although there were considerable limits to this form of globalization. On the one hand, many had an ephemeral existence, since they disappeared as soon as the Portuguese were expelled from the territories, as was the case with those in Japan and in many of the strongholds in the State of India (Hormuz, Malacca, the Moluccas and several in the Indian subcontinent). Moreover, they only operated in communities in which the influence of the Portuguese and the Catholic faith could be felt, whereas very few populations escape present-day globalization, which extends to a wide range of very different geographical areas and religious cultures.

Isabel dos Guimarães Sá
Department of History and Communication and Society Research Centre of the University of Minho

Bibliography

FRANCO, Renato, "O modelo luso de assistência e a dinâmica das santas casas de misericórdia na América Portuguesa", *Estudos Históricos*, vol. 27, no. 53, Jan.–June 2014, pp. 5–25.

MESQUIDA, Juan O., "Pious funds across the Pacific (1668–1823). Charitable bequests or credit source?", *The Americas*, vol. 75, no. 4, Oct. 2018, pp. 661–697.

PAIVA, José Pedro (dir.), *Portugaliae Monumenta Misericordiarum*, 10 vols., Lisbon, União das Misericórdias Portuguesas, 2002–2017.

SÁ, Isabel G., *O Regresso dos Mortos. Os Doadores da Misericórdia do Porto e a Expansão Ibérica (Séculos XVI–XVII)*, Lisbon, Imprensa de Ciências Sociais, 2018.

Idem, *Quando o Rico Se Faz Pobre: Misericórdias, Caridade e Poder no Império Português, 1500–1800*, Lisbon, Comissão Nacional para as Comemorações dos Descobrimentos Portugueses, 1997.

1502
The Cantino Planisphere: A Model of the World

The Cantino planisphere was valuable at the time when it was produced, due to its size and elaborate design, and also because it contained up-to-date geographical information in an age when knowledge of the world was increasing rapidly and access to this knowledge was strategically important.

The Cantino planisphere, preserved in the Estense University Library in Modena, in Italy, is one of the most precious monuments in the world cartographic heritage. Produced in 1502 by an unknown Portuguese cartographer and taken shortly afterwards to Italy by Alberto Cantino, an agent of the Duke of Ferrara, it is a representation of the known world after the Portuguese and Spanish exploratory voyages to America, Africa and India. Little remains of the traditional image of the *oecumene* described by Ptolemy fourteen centuries earlier in his *Geography* (first century). The Indian Ocean is no longer represented as a closed sea and hitherto unknown places, such as Newfoundland and Brazil, are in their correct geographical locations. Parts of the known world roughly depicted by Ptolemy, such as the western and eastern coast of Africa, are now drawn accurately and in detail. The author of the planisphere used a variety of sources as the basis for his work. In addition to the up-to-date geographical information resulting from recent voyages of exploration (Greenland, the Caribbean Sea, Newfoundland, Africa, India and Brazil), it also depicts representations collected by Vasco da Gama and other navigators from Arab sources (the Indian Ocean), copied from traditional portolan charts (the west coast of Europe, the Mediterranean and the Black Sea), inspired by the voyages of Marco Polo and Niccolo di Conti to the East (China) or even taken from Ptolemy's *Geography* (the Red Sea and Persian Gulf). In 1492, ten years before the planisphere was completed, Christopher Columbus arrived in the New World, convinced that he had reached China and Japan. The dividing line agreed under the Treaty of Tordesillas can be seen in the planisphere, marked as "the boundary between Castile and Portugal" and a note in red on the left states: "All of this land was discovered by order of the King of Castile", information which would have been compiled by an unknown Spanish source other than the planisphere produced by Juan de la Cosa (1500). The question of whether the Antilles were part of Asia would remain a matter of speculation for many years. However, the fact that the planisphere only represents approximately 250° of the equatorial perimeter of the Earth, together with the clear delimitation of Asia in the east, suggests that the existence of a large ocean separating Asia from the New World was already suspected. In fact, the planisphere contains two "*oceanus Orientalis*" legends, on the right and in the lower part, indicating the existence of a large ocean separating Asia from the New World. The Pacific Ocean was first sighted by Europeans in around 1513 by Vasco Núñez de Balboa, and was first crossed by the fleet commanded by Ferdinand Magellan in 1521.

As in the planisphere produced by Juan de la Cosa, the Equator (*linha equinocialis*) and the Tropics (*tropicus cancer* and *tropicus capricornii*) are represented, to which the Arctic Circle (*circulus articus*) was added. West of Newfoundland, which is represented as an island, and cutting through South America near the mouth of the Amazon, there is a line running north to south which represents the Treaty of Tordesillas dividing line.

Although it is not shown on the chart, a graphic latitude scale is implied by the representation of the Equator, Tropics and Arctic Circle. Six scales of distance, graduated in nautical leagues, are shown in the chart. When the length of the degree of latitude (determined from the implicit scale of latitudes) is expressed in leagues (measured using one of the distance scales), the figure of 18 leagues per degree is obtained. This was one of the three standard units, or *modules*, used by the Portuguese throughout the sixteenth century and everything indicates that it was expressly chosen y the author of the chart. The other two were 162/3 and 171/2 leagues per degree, with the latter being the most common amongst the Portuguese and Spanish in the sixteenth century. The value of the module was directly related to the value for the perimeter of the Earth. For example, the module of 18 leagues per degree results in a perimeter of 6,480 leagues (36,113 kilometres), which is approximately 10 percent less than the correct value. Two different cartographic models coexist in the planisphere: the traditional portolan chart model, in which places are represented according to the courses and the distances between them, and the latitude chart model, in which places are represented by their latitudes and the courses between them. The first was used to represent the Mediterranean, the Black Sea and western Europe, as well as Newfoundland and the Caribbean Sea; the second for the representation of the African coast, India and part of the coast of Brazil. For this reason, the Cantino planisphere is considered, together wih the anonymous Kunstmann III chart (c. 1501–6), one of the oldest known latitude chart.

The planisphere was not intended to be used for navigational purposes, even though it was certainly based on a nautical model. Its size, lavish decorative details and many annotations providing accounts of maritime discoveries and information on the various regions, indicate that this was a luxury item whose purpose was to glorify the king and the achievements of the Portuguese, and to be displayed in a library or the home of a nobleman. It is not clear how Alberto Cantino managed to acquire it, given that circulating charts and globes containing information about recently discovered lands was strictly prohibited by the Crown at the time. It is known from a letter written by Cantino to the Duke of Ferrara that the sum of twelve gold ducats was paid for the planisphere, a considerable amount of money at the time. An inscription in Venetian dialect written by Cantino himself which can be seen on the reverse reads, "navigation chart for the recently discovered islands . . . in the Indies, from Alberto Cantino to Duke Ercole".

The planisphere is drawn on six sheets of parchment mounted on canvas and measures 220 × 105 centimetres. Given the presence of incomplete Gothic lettering in capitals next to the northern end of the Tordesillas line and the fact that the legend for Greenland is truncated, it can be inferred that the top of the chart, where the title should be, has been cut off. The two central sheets are wider and the margins are not perfectly aligned with the north-south and east-west axes, suggesting that there would have been a border around the entire chart that was removed. On the left-hand side of this border there may have been a latitude scale, as in the Caverio planisphere (c. 1504), which was partially copied from Cantino. A brown bar has been painted around the current margins, perhaps to disguise the fact that it had been mutilated.

The chart has 39 annotations displaying various kinds of information, not only concerning the regions visited by the Portuguese but also other areas in the east. Five refer to the arrival of Portuguese navigators in different parts of the world, sent by King Manuel I, exemplifying eulogistic nature of the planisphere. Next to Greenland, for instance, it states: "This land was discovered by order of His Royal Highness King Manuel of Portugal and is believed to be the tip of Asia." Above Newfoundland ("Land of the King of Portugal"), represented as an island, there is an account of the disappearance of Gaspar Côrte-Real: "This land was discovered by order of His Royal Highness King Manuel of Portugal, by Gaspar de Côrte Real, a knight in the household of the said King who, having discovered it, ordered a ship to set sail with certain men and women he had found in the land, while he sailed in another vessel, but was never seen again and it is believed he was lost at sea." By the coast of Brazil, there is a reference to the arrival of Pedro Álvares Cabral: "Vera Cruz, discovered by Pedro Álvares Cabral, a nobleman in the household of the King of Portugal, the captain of fourteen ships which the said King had ordered to sail to Calicut: en route he came across this land, which is believed to be firm land [...] this land was discovered in the sixteenth century." According to Duarte Leite, the only place where the Portuguese disembarked would have been the stretch between the two flags; the remaining coastline is probably conjectural. Other notes provide information on the goods that could be found in the various different regions, such as the area around Sierra Leone: "In Sierra Leone there is a lot of gold, the best in the world, and it is brought to Portugal and many slaves, who are from the Wolof, the Mandinka and the Cape, and very fine mats and cotton cloth."

It is generally accepted that an official cartographer would have been commissioned to produce the planisphere and would have copied it from the official *Padrão Real* master map. However, there is no historical evidence to confirm this and the interpretation that the chart is a copy of the *Padrão Real* is not convincing. Although there can be no doubt that the author had access to up-to-date information on Portuguese maritime exploration, the problem lies in the existence of certain errors which would have been inadmissible in the official royal map. These include the distance between the Equator and the Tropics (24°, instead of 23.5°) and between the islands of Cape Verde and the dividing line defined by the Treaty of Tordesillas (385 leagues, instead of the 370 established in the Treaty). Rather than having been commissioned from an official cartographer, it appears more likely to be a planisphere commissioned for another client, possibly a nobleman or clergyman, which had been appropriated and exchanged for a large sum of money. The title would have been cut off to remove the name of the cartographer or the origin of the manuscript, bearing in mind the ban, by order of the Crown, on the circulation of charts or globes showing new discoveries.

However the history of the planisphere did not end, after it was delivered into the hands of Ercole d'Este, the Duke of Ferrara. In 1592, Pope Clement VII removed the Duchy of Ferrara from the House of Este and the map was transferred to the Palace of Modena, where it remained for almost three centuries. The building was ransacked in 1859 during an uprising and the planisphere was found some months later by the director of the Estense Library, hanging on the wall of a sausage shop. Perhaps because it had been taken out of Portugal, in defiance of the orders of the Crown, the planisphere would become the cartographic model for many other representations of the world that were produced in Europe during the sixteenth century, such as the planispheres by Nicolay de Caverio and Vesconti Maggiolo (c. 1504), the printed maps produced by Martin Waldseemüller (1506 and 1517) and, after the voyage made by Ferdinand Magellan and Sebastian Elcano, the planispheres drawn by Diogo Ribeiro and Nuño Garcia de Toreno at the *Casa de Contratación* in Seville (1525 to 1529). Cantino's cartographic model, based on latitudes and courses, would only be completely abandoned in the second half of the eighteenth century, after the problem of determining longitude at sea was solved and Mercator projection was fully adopted.

The Cantino planisphere was valuable at the time when it was produced, due to its size and elaborate design, and also because it contained up-to-date geographical information in an age when knowledge of the world was increasing rapidly and access to this knowledge was strategically important. It remains valuable today because it offers a unique vision of the maritime exploration and technological advances in Portuguese navigation and cartography between the end of the fifteenth and the beginning of the sixteenth centuries.

JOAQUIM ALVES GASPAR
Interuniversity Center for the History of Science and Technology,
University of Lisbon and PI of the ERC project *Medea-Chart*

Bibliography
Manuscript
Biblioteca Estense Universitaria (Modena), C.G.A.2, 1502.

Printed
CORTESÃO, Armando, MOTA, Avelino Teixeira da, *Portugaliae Monumenta Cartographica*, vol. I, Lisbon, Imprensa Nacional-Casa da Moeda, 1960.
GASPAR, Joaquim Alves, "Blunders, errors and entanglements: Scrutinizing the Cantino planisphere with a cartometric eye", *Imago Mundi*, vol. 64, no. 2, 2012, pp. 181–200.
Idem, *From the Portolan Chart of the Mediterranean to the Latitude Chart of the Atlantic: Cartometric Analysis and Modelling*, PhD thesis in Information Management submitted to the Nova University Lisbon, Lisbon, bound copy, 2010.

LEITE, Duarte, "O mais antigo mapa do Brasil", in *História da Colonização Portuguesa do Brasil*, vol. II, Porto, Litografia Nacional, 1923, pp. 223–281.
ROUKEMA, Edzer, "Brazil in the Cantino map", *Imago Mundi*, vol. 17, 1963, pp. 7–26.

1509
Santarém Rice and the Globalization of Food Products

Rice was originally cultivated in the Far East and arrived in the Iberian Peninsula via the Arabs, where it was known in Portugal but not necessarily cultivated, from around 1384. It would only be grown there from the sixteenth century onwards, albeit on a small scale, with production ceasing during certain periods.

Portugal, like Castile, functioned as a revolving platform, contributing to the globalization of various food products. These included spices, known and consumed in Europe even before the fifteenth century, and various fruits such as jackfruit, mango and coconut, originally from Asia but transported to America, in particular Brazil, and cassava, transported from Brazil to Africa and Asia. There was also sugar cane, originally from South and Southeast Asia, which the Portuguese attempted to cultivate first in the Algarve and later in Madeira, São Tomé and finally, Brazil, while the Castilians cultivated it in the Canary Islands and later in Spanish America (as the region was known at the time), initially in Hispaniola, nowadays Haiti and the Dominican Republic.

Tea arrived in Europe from China and although the Portuguese attempted to adapt it to the climate in Rio de Janeiro at the beginning of the nineteenth century, they had little success. Coffee arrived, possibly from Ethiopia, (via the Turkish Empire) and would become one of the most important industries in part of the American continent.

The most significant dietary legacy taken to Europe from what was known as the New World was the discovery and use of new foods, given that the inclusion of American produce in diets in the old continent constitutes the main difference between the medieval and the modern diet. Although not every type of food that was discovered became part of the European diet, some were adopted with success over different periods of time. This was the case with the potato, sweet potato, tomato, maize, cocoa bean and, in terms of meat, turkey. From the eighteenth century onwards, the potato was also responsible for ending cyclical hunger, replacing the cereals used to make bread when they were in short supply.

Rice, or *Oryza sativa L.,* known as white rice, which is the most common variety, is currently produced in over 100 countries throughout the world. However, it was originally cultivated in the Far East and arrived in the Iberian Peninsula via the Arabs, where it was known in Portugal but not necessarily cultivated, from around 1384. It would only be grown there from the sixteenth century onwards, albeit on a small scale, with production ceasing during certain periods. The hydrographic basins of the Tagus, Mondego and Sado rivers were, and remain, the best areas for cultivation. In the Tagus region, it was initially grown in the wetlands of Asseca, Ota and Muge in the sixteenth century; in the Mondego region, it was mainly cultivated in the fields around Coimbra, Montemor-o-Velho and Figueira da Foz, probably in the seventeenth century, since rice production is documented at the beginning of the eighteenth century in Quinta da Foja, which belonged to the monks of the Monastery of Santa Cruz. At a later stage, it was also cultivated in Sado, Alcácer do Sal and Setúbal.

At what point did such famous dishes as lamprey with rice (*arroz de lampreia*), duck risotto (*arroz de pato*) and rice broth (*canja de arroz*), or desserts such as rice pudding and rice cake, first become part of Portuguese cuisine? The answer is not straightforward, although it is possible to gain some insights from recipe books. These sources do not provide dates for dishes, which usually appeared before the books were printed, but do document their preparation and consumption.

The historian Maria Ângela Beirante discovered from the São Domingos das Donas convent archives that the term *paul do Arroz* (rice field) was first used in 1509, to describe a marshland area in Santarém. Given the relatively early cultivation of the land, during the final decades of the sixteenth century the nuns of the Santa Clara Convent were able to use rice in both sweet and savoury dishes. There is evidence of its use particularly during festive seasons. For Christmas, All Saint 's Day and Easter, they prepared butter rice (*arroz de manteiga*). At Christmas and on All Saint 's Day rice pudding was also served, while on 27th December, the feast day of Saint John the Evangelist, the preferred option was almond rice pudding. During Lent, supper included milk rice, a delicacy also consumed on Trinity Sunday. On 12 August, the feast day of Saint Clare of Assisi, the nuns offered the Franciscan priests blancmange made with rice flour. In convent culinary manuscripts from the eighteenth century it was common to find recipes for sweet and savoury dishes prepared with rice, especially rice pudding.

In the mid sixteenth century, João Brandão from Buarcos studied economic life in Lisbon, gathering information on the existing professions and respective incomes. He highlighted the large number of people who sold food on the streets, either choosing a specific location to sell from or walking around the city. Rice was sold daily, except on Sundays, by fifty women, black and white, both free and captive, who set out from the Ribeira with pans filled with rice pudding, peas and couscous. These foods were bought by manual workers, both black and white, and by children. The trade was worth more than 5,660 *cruzados* annually, although the price of each portion is unknown. However, it is clear that rice pudding was not consumed by wealthy people. Other sources of information, such as cookery books, confirm that rice was already in use by the time the *Livro de Cozinha da Infanta D. Maria,* an original work from the sixteenth century intended for members of the royal household, was compiled. It contained recipes for blancmange made from rice flour, and different types of custards (*tigeladas)* and fritters (*beilhós*), both made with rice grain. According to the first recipe book published in Portugal, the *Arte de Cozinha* (1680), written by Domingos Rodrigues, rice was available but not widely used in sweet or savoury dishes. Examples of recipes include rice pudding, rice flan, rice tart, lamb with rice, chicken with rice, hen with rice and turkey with rice, together with others in which rice, either as a grain or as flour, was one of the ingredients, such as sweet and savoury dishes, fish curry, yellow blancmange, blancmange with syrup and pear blancmange. Many more examples can be found up to the present day, in many other cookery books.

During the Early Modern period, (from the fifteenth to the eighteenth century), the cultivation of rice remained quite insignificant in relation to the production of other cereals. Changes only came in the mid nineteenth century, when the price rose due to greater consumption (particularly in urban environments) and productivity increased in comparison to other traditionally cultivated cereals. At the same time, there were ongoing protests, including riots, due to the problem of unhealthy conditions, frequently leading to cases of malaria, a disease caused by protozoans and transmitted by mosquitoes, which claimed many victims among those who lived or worked in areas where rice was cultivated.

During the Late Modern period, rice apparently began to be cultivated in Ribatejo at the beginning of the twentieth century by a farmer named Manuel de Oliveira in Casal do Outeiro, in Ulme in the municipality of Chamusca. During the dictatorship, the creation of the *Comissão Reguladora do Comércio do Arroz* (Regulatory Commission for the Rice Industry), which took care of the pricing and sale of the product, and the *Grémio dos Industriais Descascadores de Arroz* (Guild of Rice Huskers), made it possible to study the production of this grain in Portugal. The Santarém region became the largest producer in the country, which led to the construction of husking factories in various locations such as Cartaxo, Coruche, Ponte de Reguengo and Vila Franca de Xira, from 1930 onwards. One of the units, still preserved today although it has not functioned since 1987, is Casa Cadaval, an estate founded in 1960 which produced and husked rice.

The production and consumption of rice was not limited to Portugal, although in the overseas regions under Portuguese rule, the path which it followed is not very clear. Rice from the West African coast – it is not known whether it was already cultivated there before the arrival of the Portuguese – particularly from Guinea, or even from Portugal or the East, arrived in Cape Verde, although corn was the most important crop cultivated on the archipelago. In Brazil, various kinds of wild rice were known since the beginning of colonization. According to some historians, rice had already arrived in Brazil via Cape Verde in the sixteenth century. However, the first mill was only constructed in 1750, in the outskirts of Rio de Janeiro. Seeds were introduced via Portugal and were later taken to the north of Brazil by the *Companhia Geral do Grão-Pará e Maranhão*. Cultivation rapidly expanded to other captaincies and the yield was widely consumed in Brazil and exported to Portugal. Nowadays, Brazil is the largest producer and consumer of rice outside Asia. It is usually served with beans in everyday dishes and often used to make coconut rice pudding. It was also imported to the remaining overseas regions which did not cultivate rice, and thus established Portuguese cuisine, with various local adaptations, in these areas. The first settlers brought the eating habits of their own culture with them, which were gradually altered to accommodate specific local elements, thus creating new dietary habits and dishes in a dynamic process that responded to changes in different places and periods of time.

Isabel Drumond Braga
Centre for History of the University of Lisbon and Interdisciplinary Centre for History, Culture and Society of the University of Évora

Bibliography
BEIRANTE, Maria Ângela, *Santarém Quinhentista*, Lisbon, s.n., 1981.
BRAGA, Isabel Drumond, *A Herança das Américas em Portugal. Trópico das Cores e dos Sabores*, Lisbon, CTT Correios, 2007.
CUSTÓDIO, Jorge, "A fábrica de descasque de arroz da Casa Cadaval: património industrial de Muge", *Revista Cultural do Concelho de Salvaterra de Magos*, no. 3, 2016, pp. 167–220.

VAQUINHAS, Irene, "O "mal das sezões": Arrozais, malária e protesto popular nos campos do Mondego (séculos XIX e XX)", in CONDE, Manuel Silvio et al. (dir.), *Percursos de História. Estudos in Memoriam de Fátima Sequeira Dias*, Ponta Delgada, s.n., 2016, pp. 65–87.

VIEIRA, Alberto, "Plantas e frutos alimentares", in DOMINGUES, Francisco Contente (dir.), *Dicionário da Expansão Portuguesa*, vol. 2, Lisbon, Círculo de Leitores, 2016, pp. 848–853.

1514

A Religion for the World: Royal Patronage and a Pluricontinental Diocese

The royal patronage provided the framework for the organization of the Catholic Church in territories outside Europe, via missionaries from the religious orders and the work of the secular clergy, projecting a structure onto the world – the diocese – that had organized the life of Christian communities since the third century. Portugal shaped the design of world diocesan geography.

In 1999, when Macao transferred to China, the Portuguese state was no longer consulted on provisions for a bishop in the region. This marked the end of a cycle that had begun more than half a millennium before, during which the Portuguese monarchs had selected bishops and, after 1911, the Republic had been consulted before the Holy See appointed new bishops to dioceses in Africa, Asia and America. Following the conquest of Ceuta (1415), the arrival of the Portuguese in Madeira (1419) and the Azores (1431) and the rounding of Cape Bojador (1434), and with the construction of a fortress in Arguin (nowadays in Mauritania, 1445) underway, Pope Nicholas V issued the bull *Dum diversas* on 18 June, 1452. This granted King Afonso V and his successors authorization to take possession of lands ruled by "Muslims, pagans and infidels" and "reduce their peoples to perpetual slavery". With no specific spatial or temporal limits attached to this prerogative, it sanctioned rights of conquest to lands occupied by non-Christians, the expansion of Christianity and the legitimation of enslavement of free individuals, which became a central feature of the exploration of the African coast led by Prince Henry, Grand Master of the Order of Christ. Conquest, spreading the Christian faith and slavery were thus intertwined and the papacy supported a monarchy that was committed to expanding its territories and fighting the Muslims, just as it had done in the twelfth century when the kingdom of Portugal was founded.

The *Dum diversas* bull was not the only papal document which, on the basis of the thirteenth-century doctrine of the indirect power of the papacy, recognized the Portuguese conquests, regulated the activities of the Church and safeguarded Portuguese interests in territories outside Europe against other Christian powers. The first of these, in 1420, appointed Prince Henry administrator of the Order of Christ, thus authorizing a layman to use ecclesiastical methods to conquer land from the "infidels". The last, in 1551, granted the kings of Portugal the right, in perpetuity, to govern the three military orders (Christ, Avis and Santiago). In between, came the bulls which defined what would become known as the royal patronage. The *Romanus Pontifex* of 8 January 1455 authorized the king and Prince Henry to found churches and monasteries between Bojador and the "end" of Africa, reserving for them the right to choose and send clergymen to christianize the populations. The following year, the *Inter caetera* confirmed that spiritual jurisdiction over present and future conquered lands, from Bojador to India, lay with the Vicar of Tomar, the head of the Order of Christ, whose jurisdiction was equivalent to those of a bishop. Later, the *Dum fidei constantiam*, of 7 June 1514, the first to use the word "patronage", granted the Order of Christ full spiritual jurisdiction over churches constructed and to be constructed in territories conquered from the "infidels" but, amending the previous bull, granted King Manuel I and his successors the "right of patronage" and the "right to appoint (...) suitable individuals to hold office in all churches and ecclesiastical benefices".

Patronage consisted of a set of rights (honorary rights, the right to appoint clerics on behalf of the ecclesiastical authorities and the right to collect rates) and responsibilities (constructing and protecting churches, providing them with liturgical items and ensuring their maintenance and the upkeep of the clergy) which the Church attributed, in recognition of services rendered, to the founders, builders and benefactors of churches or ecclesiastical benefices. This institution was not invented by Portugal, nor did it first appear in the so-called Age of Discoveries: it had been used by the Church since the fifth century. It was mentioned for the first time in a document issued by Pope Nicholas II (1058–1061) and was established in the *Decretum Gratiani* (1140–1142) and the *Decretales* (1234). The kings of Portugal and Castile secured this privilege in the fifteenth and sixteenth centuries when they had divided up the sea, and consequently the world, between them in Tordesillas. At the time, the prevailing doctrines stated that the sea was reserved for them (*mare clausum*) and crises of various kinds had undermined papal authority. King Peter I of Aragon had already obtained the patronage in 1095 for areas conquered from the Muslims in the kingdom of Granada. Now it was introduced for the New World, and the king of Portugal held the monopoly until 1493.

Under this system, the papacy pursued the fight against the Muslims, protected its authority in the Christian world and provided for the worldwide expansion of Catholicism. Monarchs legitimized conquests and gained greater authority over the Church, acquiring influence, albeit indirect, in the organization and functioning of this power structure. Since 1505, Manuel I had been adopting similar measures within the kingdom. The royal patronage even authorized him to manage the income from tithes, which were later profitable in areas such as Brazil, although populations that had converted to Christianity were exempt from payment in order to encourage the process, following the example established by royal decree in 1570 which freed Christians in China, Japan and Malacca from this obligation for fifteen years.

The patronage did not grant unlimited powers to kings, nor did it encroach on the power of bishops or papal authority. The bishops enjoyed the same jurisdiction as their European counterparts and, due to the distances involved, even acquired privileges which the latter did not have, such as disregarding irregularities in applications for the priesthood or matrimonial impediments. The papacy sanctioned the choice of bishops, resolved issues concerning doubts related to sacramental and liturgical matters, responded to petitions from the faithful and granted special privileges. In Rome, particularly after the Council of Trent (1563), popes and various congregations made decisions which shaped the dynamics of evangelization and ecclesiastical governance in areas which came under the royal patronage.

The system in Portugal was not the same as the one which operated for the Hispanic monarchy. In the latter case, it was introduced later, in 1493, when Alexander VI granted the Catholic Monarchs privileges in America that were similar to those given to Portugal. However, in Castile, the 1508 bull that defined the right of patronage predated the Portuguese legislation. The Spanish *patronazgo real* was granted in full to the monarch, whereas in Portugal spiritual jurisdiction and the setting of tithes were conferred on the Order of Christ, although since the reign of Manuel I (which began in 1495) this also lay in the hands of the kings of Portugal. Moreover, this right was applied differently. The Portuguese patronage covered a larger area, particularly since in Asia it was not restricted to trading posts (*feitorias*) and fortresses controlled by the Portuguese. Clerics were sent by the king of Portugal and dioceses established in the present-day territories of Bangladesh, Myanmar, Thailand, Vietnam, Indonesia, China and Japan under the so-called patronage of the East. However, the application of the patronage by the Hispanic monarchs was already intensifying in the American territories. The best example of this difference was the application of the *pase regio* (*regium exequatur*) to all papal documents in Spanish America, which only came into force after a resolution by the Council of the Indies leading, in the second half of the seventeenth century, to the idea of the royal vicariate, which was condemned by Rome.

The royal patronage provided the framework for the organization of the Catholic Church in territories outside Europe, via missionaries from the religious orders and the work of the secular clergy, projecting a structure onto the world – the diocese – that had organized the life of Christian communities since the third century and whose creation, since the mid-eleventh century, had been the sole responsibility of the Holy See. Portugal shaped the design of world diocesan geography.

In 1420, the diocese of Ceuta (North Africa) was restored, its bishop having been appointed by King John I. The first diocese to be created at the request of a Portuguese king was the one in Tangier, in 1469, before Castile founded the ephemeral diocese of Hispaniola in 1504, in what is nowadays the Dominican Republic and Haiti, followed by the dioceses of São Domingos, Concepción de La Vega and Porto Rico in 1511. In the sixteenth to eighteenth centuries more dioceses were created in Spanish America than in the entire Portuguese world, due to the spatial configurations of the respective empires. The Spanish empire consisted of a large and continuous expanse of territory, whereas the Portuguese empire, excluding Brazil, was made up of small, disconnected territories linked by a network of maritime routes crossing the Atlantic and Indian Oceans.

The most important fact was the creation of the diocese of Funchal, under the bull issued on 12 June 1514, five days after King Manuel I had obtained the royal patronage for the empire and at a time when royal propaganda assumed that it was the divine mission of the king and kingdom to destroy Muslim power and evangelize the world. One of the reasons stipulated in the bull for founding the diocese was to ensure that divine worship would flourish and souls would be saved. The other aims were not so explicit, but included the construction of an imperial state that would begin to gain status in 1505, greater control for the Crown over the choice of bishops, and even emulation of the Castile monarchs. The creation of the diocese extended royal power at the expense of the Order of Christ, which lost its spiritual jurisdiction to the bishop. The king appointed the bishop, who in turn chose the members of the chapter, while the Order recruited the remaining clergy, including the parish priests, and collected the tithes which paid for the places of worship, liturgical items and the upkeep of the clergy.

It was an enormous diocese: never before had a bishopric encompassed such a vast expanse of land. It covered Madeira, the Azores, Cape Verde, São Tomé, Brazil, the western coast of Africa south of Safi (nowadays Morocco) including sites lying between the present-day Gambia and Angola, and even India. It therefore included places on the eastern coast of Africa (the present-day Mozambique, Tanzania and Kenya), in Hormuz (nowadays Iran) and territories in India, extending as far as Malacca and the Moluccas (nowadays Indonesia). Today it would be called a global diocese.

This presented considerable challenges: the distances that had to be covered, the provision of sufficient numbers of qualified clergymen and the construction of churches. There were also cultural and linguistic barriers to overcome, and the enormous task of making contact with populations who observed a variety of religions and animist faiths. This also explains why, following Funchal and even after it was dismantled, around fifty new dioceses were founded throughout the Portuguese empire up to the twentieth century, a process which began with the creation of bishoprics in the Azores, Cape Verde, São Tomé and Goa (1533–1534), followed by Salvador da Bahia (1551) and other places.

The dynamics of the patronage altered in the seventeenth century. The change which had the greatest impact was the creation of the Congregation for the Propagation of the Faith in 1622, as part of the centralization of the powers of the papacy, when relations between Rome and the Crown at the time of the union with Castile were weakening and doctrines originating in Holland (*mare liberum*) were challenging the Iberian monopoly over the seas. In 1674, the diocese of Quebec was created in New France (Canada), the first in North America, thus ending the Iberian monopoly. The prerogatives granted to Louis XIV of France concerning the diocese and choice of bishop were different from the Iberian patronages. Prior to this, the Iberian Union had already implied some reflection on the nature of the royal patronages of Portugal and Castile, which Rome considered were autonomous (1585). Nevertheless, new dioceses continued to appear, such as the one in Funai (1588), in Japan, where there were approximately 150,000 Christians, mainly due to the work of the Jesuits under the Portuguese patronage.

From 1622 onwards, despite strong resistance by the Portuguese after 1640, the interference from Rome intensified. Rome sent vicars Apostolic to various places in Asia, and there was also increasing French interest in the area, evident in the founding of the Seminary for Foreign Missions (Paris, 1663). In 1669 the apostolic vicariate of Siam (Thailand) was founded, with authority over the present-day Thailand, Cambodia, Laos, Korea, Vietnam and China, thus clashing with the jurisdiction of the bishops of Macao and Malacca. Even so, during the reign of Peter II it was still possible to create dioceses in China (Beijing and Nanjing, in 1690, which were only abolished in 1838), although the first bishops to be appointed were already vicars Apostolic. In 1745, King John V tried without success to appoint bishops to dioceses to be created in Tonkin and Cochinchina (in present-day Vietnam).

The expulsion of the Jesuits (1759) and the abolition of the religious orders (1834) severely curtailed Portugal's ability to preserve Christian life in the territories under its influence. In 1832, there was a shortage of clergymen in Asia, and Goa, Cranganore, Cochin and Mylapore did not even have a bishop. It was a time of bitter struggles with Rome following the establishment of liberalism in Portugal (1820), which led to Concordats (1857 and 1886) regulating the patronage of the East designed to limit Portugal's powers and spheres of influence, although it still continued to appoint bishops for Cochin, for example, even after the region came under Dutch, and then British, rule.

The Republican regime (1910) and the 1911 Law on the Separation of Church and State once again undermined the royal patronage, although it continued in Africa and Asia subject to revision during the *Estado Novo* period (in 1928 and 1940), when the government of Portugal, returning to centuries-old doctrines, deemed that the Catholic missions were an essential part of the civilizing work of Portugal in the world.

For six centuries this system resulted in the construction of multiple entangled histories which either brought distant places and different people closer, or isolated them. It was responsible for the spread of a religion that originated in Judea and had been consolidated in Rome and included behaviour that had profound implications for the lives of non-European populations, also generating resistance to the sometimes extremely violent methods used to impose the new faith. In addition, it yielded returns, some of which were spiritual. Countless liturgical items were designed outside Europe, as cross-cultural creations which circulated around the world, as well as beliefs and new forms of worship stemming from the cult of martyrs and saints that featured in the spread of Catholicism to lands under the Portuguese royal patronage.

José Pedro Paiva
University of Coimbra and Centre for the History of Society and Culture

Bibliography
FRANCO, José Eduardo, COSTA, João Paulo Oliveira e (dir.), *Diocese do Funchal. A Primeira Diocese Global: História, Cultura e Espiritualidades*, 2 vols., Funchal, Diocese do Funchal, 2015.
JACQUES, Roland, *De Castro Marim à Faifo. Naissance et Development du Padroado Portugais d'Orient des Origines à 1659*, Lisbon, Fundação Calouste Gulbenkian, 1999.
MARCOCCI, Giuseppe, *A Consciência de Um Império: Portugal e o Seu Mundo (Sécs. XV–XVII)*, Coimbra, Imprensa da Universidade de Coimbra, 2012.
WITTE, Charles Martial de, *Les Lettres Papales concernant l'Expansion Portuguaise au XVIe Siècle*, s.l., Nouvelle Revue de Science Missionaire, 1986.
XAVIER, Ângela Barreto, OLIVAL, Fernanda, "O padroado da Coroa de Portugal: funda-mentos e práticas", in XAVIER, Ângela Barreto, PALOMO, Federico, STUMPF, Roberta (org.), *Monarquias Ibéricas em Perspectiva Comparada (Sécs. XVI–XVIII). Dinâmicas Imperiais e Circulação de Modelos Administrativos*, Lisbon, Imprensa de Ciências Sociais, 2018, pp. 123–160.

1517
The Slave Revolt in São Tomé

In the sixteenth century, Portuguese merchants played a key role in the development of the transatlantic trafficking of enslaved people, supplying slave labour not only to the Portuguese imperial colonies, namely Brazil, but also to the Spanish West Indies, including the Caribbean and the viceroyalties in the Province of Tierra Firme.

The first documented revolt of enslaved individuals took place in São Tomé in 1517, associated with two specific but closely connected developments. The first was the introduction and spread of sugar cane mills throughout the island, leading to a substantial rise in the number of enslaved persons. This rapid increase then resulted in a lower standard of living for each individual (in terms of lodgings, food and water supplies), and many, driven to despair, decided to revolt. The 1517 revolt was the first of many rebellions by enslaved Africans in territories under Portuguese administration or within its sphere of influence. These uprisings were documented in the South Atlantic and Caribbean areas, which were dominated by a plantation economy based on sugar production that followed a near monoculture system.

As a global phenomenon, the revolts of the enslaved in the Early Modern world, particularly in the South Atlantic and Caribbean, should be considered historical events that can only be understood in the broad context of the intensive trafficking and exploitation of human beings within the world economy, particularly in areas on the coasts of the three largest oceans: the Atlantic, Pacific and Indian Oceans. In the case of the Atlantic, the intensification of trading and the exploitation of Africans played a central role in advancing the sugar, coffee, cacao, cotton and tobacco plantation-based economies, resulting in the development of the first supply chains of agro-industrial products operating on a transcontinental and intercontinental scale, which had a particular impact on supplies for the European and American manufacturing industries and the consumer markets in Europe and its overseas colonies.

Portugal played a fundamental role throughout this process, which can be summarized in terms of three developments. Firstly, Portuguese fleets and merchants, born in Europe or the Atlantic colonies, began to specialize in the acquisition and distribution of slave labour for this new Atlantic economy, supplying various different, geographically dispersed markets for a period of around four hundred years.

The Portuguese merchants were, in fact, the first Europeans to bring enslaved Sub-Saharan Africans to Europe, in particular to the south and the Mediterranean area, as well as the Atlantic islands. The first shipments date back to the initial contacts made with slave traders in Arguin, after 1443. Portuguese merchants were also essential to slave trafficking between the West African coast – especially in the areas between the Gambia River and Sierra Leone, nowadays known as the Bight of Benin and Bight of Biafra – and the Cape Verde and São Tomé archipelagos.

Moreover, throughout the course of the sixteenth century, following the transfer and development of the plantation economy to Brazil and the Spanish West Indies – and, at a later stage, to the Dutch, English and French imperial territories in the Americas – Portuguese merchants played a key role in the growth of transatlantic slave trafficking, supplying slave labour not only to the Portuguese imperial colonies, namely Brazil, but also to the Spanish West Indies, including the Caribbean and the viceroyalties in the Province of Tierra Firme. In fact, Portuguese and Brazilian merchants were responsible for trafficking over three million African enslaved populations to the Americas, making them the second most important group of traders after the English.

From the seventeenth to the nineteenth century this trade grew exponentially, stimulated not only by the development of the plantation economy but also the discovery of gold and silver mines and deposits of gemstones in both the Spanish West Indies and Brazil. During this process, the archipelagos of Cape Verde and São Tomé ceased to serve as re-export markets for slave labour sourced from the African continent. This operation was instead transferred, either to the coastal markets in Senegambia, Guinea-Bissau and Sierra Leone – by means of the various trading posts on the Grain Coast, Ivory Coast, Gold Coast, Mina Coast and Slave Coast – or mainly to the territories nowadays known as the Congo and Angola. Angola became the principal region involved in exporting slave labour to Brazil, the Spanish West Indies and, via interCaribbean trade, to other plantation colonies under Dutch, English and French rule.

At the same time, the planters and sugar mill owners on the islands of Madeira and São Tomé assisted in the transfer of the plantation model to Brazil and the Caribbean islands as a form of economic development. These were areas which, from an environmental and geographical point of view, offered more favourable conditions for the cultivation of the new products destined for mass consumption, especially in the European markets.

Finally, in the sphere of Portuguese influence and beyond, the interaction between the commercialization and exploitation of slave labour on the one hand, and the explosive advance in plantations contributed significantly to the development of slave-owning societies, in which the majority, the enslaved population, was exploited by a white and/or Creole minority. It was these particular forms of very violent human exploitation, extreme exclusion and inequality that led to the enslaved revolts and also explained their frequency. In addition to the revolts in São Tomé and other colonies, many enslaved humans escaped from the plantations and took refuge in the forests, founding communities of fugitive enslaved persons known in São Tomé as "mocambos". These communities frequently organized attacks on the plantations, their owners, and occasionally the main urban centres.

Identical phenomena took place in Brazil, for even longer periods of time and involving larger numbers of people. In Portuguese America these fugitive communities were known as "quilombos", the two best known and longest surviving being the Palmares quilombo (which was founded in around 1605 and had a population of 11,000 to 20,000 in the 1690s) and the Mato Grosso quilombo (dating from the second half of the eighteenth century). The first survived for around one century and the second for approximately twenty-five years. However, it is important to note that this was not a phenomenon exclusive to the Portuguese imperial territories. In the Spanish West Indies many enslaved Africans fled from the places where they were forced to work and organized themselves into their own communities, located in remote areas that were difficult for the colonial authorities to access, known as slave palenques. Fugitive enslaved communities were also relatively common in plantation colonies under Dutch rule (the Maroon communities), as well as those under English and French rule in the Americas (Marronage). Like the revolts in São Tomé, the quilombos in Brazil and the palenques in Spanish America, they should be understood as part of a global historical phenomenon and as a reaction against slave-owning societies and slavery, characterized by extreme physical and psychological violence that led to unimaginable human suffering and radical and permanent exclusion. It also signified a rejection of the abominable labour system at the heart of the development of a new capitalist system that relied on slave labour to produce the agro-industrial goods that fuelled international trade, the manufacturing sector and the highly profitable consumer markets. In short, the revolts and collective slave escapes in the Atlantic region were part of a much broader phenomenon of acts of resistance by the enslaved directed against their living and working conditions, reflecting a wider opposition and rejection of this facet of modern globalization in which many Portuguese subjects were actively engaged.

Filipa Ribeiro da Silva
International Institute of Social History, Royal Netherlands Academy of Arts and Sciences, The Netherlands

Bibliography

CALDEIRA, Arlindo, "Learning the Ropes in the Tropics: Slavery and the Plantation System on the Island of São Tomé", *African Economic History*, vol. 39, 2011, pp. 35–71.

CHENEY, Glenn A., *Quilombo dos Palmares. Brazil's Lost Nation of Fugitive Slaves*, New London, Librarium, 2014.

ELTIS, David, RICHARDSON, David (ed.), *Extending the Frontiers: Essays on the New Transatlantic Slave Trade Database*, New Haven, Yale University Press, 2008.

REDIKER, Marcus et al. (ed.), *A Global History of Runaways: Workers, Mobility and Capitalism, 1600–1850*, Los Angeles, University of California Press, 2019.

RICHARDSON, David, SILVA, Filipa Ribeiro da (ed.), *Networks and Trans-Cultural Exchange: Slave Trading in the South Atlantic, 1590–1867*, Leiden, Brill, 2014.

1519
Ferdinand Magellan and the First Voyage Around the World

The global circulation of men, goods, ideas, practices and knowledge between all continents had begun earlier, mainly due to the work of the Portuguese and Spanish navigators. Yet, with Magellan and with Elcano, who completed the circumnavigation, the world understood itself to be spherical for the first time

There is a misunderstanding associated with the name of Ferdinand Magellan, namely that this most famous of all Portuguese navigators would have been responsible for organizing and leading, although not in its entirety, the first circumnavigation of the Earth. This is an essentially erroneous notion which needs to be corrected and revised, since it is not possible to associate Magellan with any such project at any point in his life as we know it. In fact, his aim was to reach the Moluccas (nowadays Indonesia) by sailing west rather than using the so-called Cape Route which Vasco da Gama had opened up in 1498.

Throughout the fifteenth century, Iberian ships – particularly Portuguese vessels – regularly explored previously unknown regions of the Atlantic and the Portuguese Crown had been promoting the idea of reaching India by sea since the 1470s. In 1488 Bartolomeu Dias' voyage beyond the Cape of Good Hope proved that this was a feasible connection. The Genoese Christopher Columbus, who had attended the audience in Lisbon which King John II had granted to Dias on his return, went on to lead a Spanish expedition that attempted to find an alternative route to India. Heading westwards, in 1492 he unexpectedly came across some unknown islands in the central Atlantic which, it would be concluded a few years later, lay close to a large continental land mass.

The discovery of America led to a dispute between Portugal and Spain over maritime hegemony in the Atlantic and the right to develop new geographical areas. The matter was resolved in 1494 with the signing of the Treaty of Tordesillas. Portugal and Spain subsequently began an intensive exploration of areas beyond Europe, respecting, in essence, the Tordesillas agreement. The Spanish established regular routes to the New World and began to systematically occupy the Antilles and colonize increasingly larger areas of the so-called *Terra Firme*, whose exact contours were still unknown to the Europeans although it was soon suspected to be the size of a continent. In 1513, the Spaniard Vasco Núñez de Balboa crossed the Isthmus of Panama and sighted what was known at the time as the *Mar del Sur* (South Sea) which, it was speculated, extended to the coast of Asia. The spherical nature of the Earth was a concept that was fully accepted in Iberian nautical and cosmographical circles. Moreover, Columbus' expedition had been based on this assumption, albeit with estimations that fell far short of the true dimensions of the globe. However, in order to travel to the East via the West, it was necessary to find a viable passage somewhere along the coast of the New World that would enable the Spanish ships to sail to the South Sea, and this was proving difficult.

King Manuel I, who had ascended to the Portuguese throne in 1495, directed his voyages of exploration eastwards and, in 1498, an armada commanded by Vasco da Gama finally established a maritime link between Lisbon and the west coast of India. The Cape Route, which was controlled exclusively by the Portuguese for the next century, was opened. A new expedition followed in 1500, this time led by Pedro Álvares Cabral who, in attempting to reach India, landed in Brazil, a region of America that was immediately claimed for Portugal. The Portuguese quickly grasped the immense commercial potential of the eastern world, where regular routes between the main ports on the East African coast and the extensive Asian shores had existed for a long time. Many vessels used these routes, observing well-defined calendars based on the seasonal monsoons and transporting coveted oriental products.

Within fifteen years the Portuguese had decoded the mechanisms governing this vast trading world, having explored the whole of maritime Asia, from the Red Sea to faraway China, and established firm bases in various strategic locations such as Goa (1510), Malacca (1511) and Hormuz (1515). In general, the great oriental empires were continental, meaning that the coastal areas, overly peripheral in relation to the political centers and ruled by small autonomous potentates, permitted the intrusion of the newly arrived Europeans, whose naval and military technology was superior to that of their potential opponents. Hence what was later known as the State of India came into existence, a constellation of small, scattered coastal territories where the Portuguese, either by military force or diplomatic agreement, built their fortresses and trading posts and proceeded to trade in drugs and spices and other valuable goods, such as silk, porcelain, precious stones, and aromatic woods.

Ferdinand Magellan set off for India in 1505, with the armada of the first viceroy, D. Francisco de Almeida. For eight years he was involved in Portuguese naval and military campaigns in coastal regions of the Indian Ocean, including the conquest of Goa and Malacca. He remained in the latter port until 1513 but it is not known whether he took part in the expedition led by António de Abreu to the Moluccas, the easternmost islands in the Malay Archipelago, now part of Indonesia, where cloves and nutmeg were produced, two of the most valuable Asian spices. During his years in the East, Magellan gained experience of navigation by serving on Portuguese ships on long and medium-range expeditions, often engaged in military and command duties as part of the frequent warlike encounters in which he was involved, and also amassed a vast collection of geographical and cartographic information on the eastern world, either from first-hand experience or from the oral or written accounts of the many specialists and officers he encountered. In Malacca, for example, he would have been in contact not only with the apothecary Tomé Pires, who was working on his *Suma Oriental* at the time, an extensive and detailed geographical work on the East which included the most up-to-date information on the Malay Archipelago, but also Francisco Rodrigues, the pilot who had accompanied the expedition led by António de Abreu to the Moluccas and had prepared the first maps of this distant region.

Magellan returned to Portugal in 1513 and, after spending almost a year in the Moroccan port of Azemmour, settled in Lisbon. There he certainly established relations with Cristóbal de Haro, a leading Burgos merchant who was involved in overseas trading and had links with the Welsers, a German banking family. In 1517, Cristóbal de Haro and Ferdinand Magellan went to Spain, having both fallen out with Manuel I, the former over matters concerning the spice trade and the latter because he had been refused an increase in his royal pension. It is impossible not to detect a prior relationship in this joint departure to Spain, and possibly an agreement between Magellan and Haro, particularly given the fact that after Magellan had presented his project to seek a western route to the Moluccas to Charles I of Spain and it had been accepted, Cristóbal de Haro became the main financier of the planned expedition.

Magellan's idea was not new: in fact, it involved reprising Columbus' plan to reach the Indies by sailing westwards, but this time it was supported by first-hand experience of vast regions of the East and a more realistic estimate of the dimensions of the globe. However, Magellan's great innovation, based on the geographical and cartographic data he had been able to gather, was to claim that the Moluccas came under the sphere of Spanish influence as defined by the Treaty of Tordesillas. In order to convince the Spanish monarch that his project was viable, Magellan presented himself in Valladolid in 1518 with a technical report, a book and a map. The report, which he had written in collaboration with the Portuguese cosmographer Rui Faleiro (who had accompanied him from Portugal), claimed that the Moluccas were located within the area of Spanish influence and presented a plan to sail there via a passage that would exist somewhere in the southern regions of the New World or by making use of the Portuguese route via the Cape of Good Hope. The book was an edition of Ludovico di Varthema's *Itinerario*, an account of voyages in the East published in Rome in 1510 by an Italian he had met in Cannanore a few years earlier, who claimed to have visited the easternmost islands in the Malay Archipelago. The map was a planisphere drawn by the Portuguese cartographer Pedro Reinel (who had also arrived from Portugal at the same time), nowadays known as Kunstman IV, which represented the world in a very innovative way, featuring the American continent and the vast ocean which separated it from the eastern part of Asia and showing the Moluccas on the Spanish side of the dividing line.

Charles I accepted Magellan's proposal, since it offered Spain the opportunity to become involved in the lucrative trade with the East which was making Portugal's fortune at the time. In August 1519, an armada of five ships commanded by Magellan left Seville with 237 men on board, heading for the southern regions of the New World in search of a passage to the South Sea. The strait which would later be named after the Portuguese explorer was crossed in November 1520 by three ships, which then sailed across the entire Pacific to the most easterly islands of the archipelago that was later known as the Philippines. Magellan had managed to complete the impossible mission of sailing westwards to Asia but was killed in April 1521 during a skirmish with the inhabitants of Mactan. As far as we know, he was not intending to circumnavigate the globe, but had instead planned to return to America after reaching the Moluccas. The survivors from the fleet, left with two ships, arrived at the Island of Tidore in the Moluccas around six months later. However, only one of the ships, commanded by Juan Sebastián Elcano, returned to Seville in September 1522 with a cargo of spices and 18 men on board, having sailed via the Cape of Good Hope.

Meanwhile, the Portuguese had established a fortified base in Ternate, another island in the Moluccas. The return of Elcano, like the return of Columbus earlier, resulted in a new diplomatic issue for the Iberian Crowns, this time regarding rights to navigation and trade in the more easterly regions of Asia, which involved discussing the precise location of the Tordesillas antemeridian. To this end, bilateral talks were held in a meeting that took place in Elvas and Badajoz in 1524, attended by some of the most eminent Iberian mathematicians, cosmographers, cartographers, and pilots. The matter in question was the exact longitudinal location of the contested archipelago, an issue which the knowledge available at the time could not resolve. Given this impossible situation, Portugal eventually acquired rights of possession to an archipelago within its own area of influence in the Treaty of Zaragoza, signed in 1529.

Ferdinand Magellan's voyage had the extraordinary merits of locating the Atlantic passage to the South Sea and of exploring and crossing the Pacific for the first time, thus demonstrating the intercommunication between all the oceans in the world, an unprecedented achievement. The global circulation of men, goods, ideas, practices and knowledge between all continents – usually known as the first globalization – had begun earlier, mainly due to the work of the Portuguese and Spanish navigators. Yet, with Magellan and with Elcano, who completed the circumnavigation, the world understood itself to be spherical for first time. As the Portuguese chronicler Gaspar Frutuoso wrote at the end of the sixteenth century, "a feat never before recorded, nor heard of, nor seen: departing from the West and sailing round the world, they returned via the East to the same port from which they had left, which no one had ever accomplished since the world was first created".

RUI MANUEL LOUREIRO

Manuel Teixeira Gomes Higher Education Institute and CHAM – Centre for the Humanities from Nova University Lisbon

Bibliography

CASTRO, Xavier de et al. (ed.), *Le Voyage de Magellan (1519–1522). La Relation d'Antonio Pigafetta et Autres Témoignages*, Paris, Chandeigne, 2010.

GARCIA, José Manuel, *Fernão de Magalhães, Herói, Traidor ou Mito*, Lisbon, Manuscrito, 2019.

LOUREIRO, Rui Manuel, *Em demanda da Biblioteca de Fernão de Magalhães*, Lisbon, Biblioteca Nacional de Portugal, 2019.

MOTA, A. Teixeira da (ed.), *A Viagem de Fernão de Magalhães e a Questão das Molucas*, Lisbon, Junta de Investigações Científicas do Ultramar, 1975.

THOMAZ, Luís Filipe, *O Drama de Magalhães e a Volta ao Mundo sem Querer*, Lisbon, Gradiva, 2019.

1536
The Inquisition Arrives in Portugal

The Portuguese Inquisition became one of the most powerful disciplinary institutions in Europe and in the modern world. During the period 1536–1767 it was responsible for around 45,000 trials, approximately 10,000 of which were heard in the Lisbon tribunal, 10,000 in Coimbra, 11,000 in Évora and 14,000 in Goa.

In 1536, the bull *Cum ad nihil magis* established the Inquisition in Portugal, after more than ten years of royal diplomacy in Rome accompanied by a ban on New Christians leaving the kingdom which had been in force since 1532, a policy contested by their agents who were successful in obtaining various pardons and the annulment of an initial papal brief in 1531 appointing an inquisitor. The foundation process was a lengthy one, since the implementation of the Inquisition machinery, supported by the king, had been kept in check by papal interventions exempting New Christians from confiscation of assets and exempting the families of their representatives in Rome from prosecution.

The *Meditatio cordis* bull of 1547 granted the Portuguese courts powers similar to those of the Spanish Inquisition, although secrecy of proceedings was only authorized by the pope in 1560. The following year, the Supreme Pontiff granted the Inquisitor General, Cardinal Henry, the right to request cases of heresy from the ecclesiastical justice system, thus completing the legal framework for the functioning of the Inquisition in Portugal.

The jurisdiction of the Tribunal was later extended to cover the offences of sodomy (1562), bigamy (1612) and solicitation in the confessional (1608). The exemption of New Christians from confiscation of their assets was revoked by Cardinal Henry, as regent of the kingdom, in 1563. In 1606, Pope Paul V imposed inquisitorial jurisdiction to deal with cases of heresy within the religious orders, revoking previous exceptions. The Inquisition's authority to investigate offences involving heresy was therefore ensured, over private jurisdictions and all Church bodies.

The Portuguese Inquisition became one of the most powerful disciplinary institutions in Europe and in the Early Modern world. During the period 1536–1767 it was responsible for around 45,000 trials, approximately 10,000 of which were heard in the Lisbon tribunal, 10,000 in Coimbra, 11,000 in Évora and 14,000 in Goa. To this number should be added at least three times as many accusations. These figures reveal the extent of the surveillance and operations carried out by the Inquisition, given that the 45,000 trials and over 135,000 accusations refer to a population ranging from 1.5 to 3 million inhabitants in mainland Portugal and 50,000 to 1.7 million in the Atlantic colonies, together with several hundred thousand in the State of India during the period in question. In addition to the victims and the accused, there should also be added the 20,000 familiars (lay agents) of the Portuguese Inquisition, its 3,000 paid officials and 3,000 commissioners in the inland territories and ports. The Portuguese Inquisition mainly directed its work towards New Christians accused of Judaism. With the exception of the trials in Goa, which targeted Hindus and Muslim converts, the New Christians tried by the Lisbon tribunal represented around 70% of the total number of victims, 80% in Évora and 83% in Coimbra, which supports the estimate of over 24,000 New Christians brought to trial. Robert Rowland has proposed an average of 20% for mixed marriages in each generation, which challenges the commonly-held idea in historiography of endogamy amongst New Christians, while my latest research confirms a certain level of exogamy among New Christians within the financial and merchant elite. These estimates therefore raise a problem: how could a largely mixed population preserve its ethnic and religious identity? It recalls the old question posed by António José Saraiva concerning the accuracy of the accusations of Judaism made by the inquisitors, identifying New Christians with the persecuted bourgeoisie and therefore contesting the idea of widespread Crypto-Judaism claimed by I. S. Révah and many other authors. The well-known phenomenon of New Christian emigration to more tolerant places in Europe and the Eastern Mediterranean (such as Antwerp, Amsterdam, Hamburg, Ferrara, Livorno, Venice and Istanbul) rules out the idea that Judaism was completely invented by the Inquisition, while there is little basis for citing economic motives in a society in which merchants, financiers and bankers both supported and depended on the monarchy and nobility.

Nevertheless, there are reasons for questioning the dimensions of the phenomenon, since many trials lacked sufficient evidence and had clearly been fabricated on the basis of a single initial witness who only reported rumours, while others were stereotyped, following a standard pattern of accusation, denunciation and confession. Many *reconciliados* (those who confessed and were absolved of excommunication) appealed to Rome, claiming they had been forced to confess. Many others died at the stake, declaring that they had always been Catholics. There appears to have been a level of anti-New Christian obsession within the Inquisition that echoes the anti-witchcraft obsession in courts of law which swept through Europe between 1550 and 1650.

The methods used by the inquisitors complied with the norms for criminal prosecution codified in regulations published in 1552, 1613, 1640 and 1774. A series of interrogation forms were produced to guide the inquisitors when investigating the various types of crimes that came under their jurisdiction: Judaism, Islamism, Protestantism, heretical ideas, illuminism (understood in the sixteenth and seventeenth centuries to mean revelations and direct access to God), sorcery, witchcraft, blasphemy, soliciting in the confessional and bigamy. The edicts of faith and edicts of grace displayed in churches throughout the kingdom and empire called on the faithful to present themselves to the inquisitors and confess or denounce the said crimes. It was this checklist of heresies, detailed in the forms, which the witness accounts had to satisfy, which explains the repetitive nature of the accusations and confessions. The edicts of grace offered pardons for sins that were confessed but this was a trap, since a confession would not be accepted unless accomplices were denounced. The jails were the next place for extorting confessions and accusations. The method that was used involved leaving the prisoner in ignorance of the accusations for weeks or months. They would then be summoned and asked if they had any sins to declare: if they said they had nothing to confess, they would be sent back to their cell. This was a game which could last for years. When the Inquisition's legal representatives finally published the accusations, they did so without indicating the circumstances or the names of the witnesses.

The only way to refute accusations was to guess who had made them and allege enmity, which presupposed a list of witnesses. Yet even in these situations it was difficult to work out the names of all the accusers. Moreover, the accused could be considered *diminuto* and risked being excommunicated and handed over to the secular authorities to be burnt at the stake. The average detention period was three years, long enough to obtain any confession, although if this failed the inquisitors could resort to torture, which was used on men, women and adolescents.

My definition of racism as prejudice against ethnic descent combined with discriminatory acts applies perfectly to the persecution of New Christians by the Inquisition, which encouraged the implementation and extension of purity of blood statutes in the religious orders, military orders, universities, municipalities, brotherhoods and public offices in Portugal and also excluded convicts and their descendants from university education and access to honours.

Despite the apparatus of regulations, norms and forms, the Inquisition was not an impartial institution. There is clear evidence of persecution of members of the families of New Christian agents in Rome, as retribution. It could take years for this persecution to be carried out, with inquisitorial hatred passing from one generation to another.

An inspection which took place in 1627 revealed that assets confiscated during the course of the most important prosecutions in Coimbra had been appropriated by inquisitors and bailiffs and the houses of the condemned had been occupied by agents of the Inquisition. The involvement of the senior ranks of the hierarchy in this and other cases highlighted the corruption embedded in the institution, with inspections revealing inadmissible behaviour by inquisitors promoted to bishops who, naturally, were not punished.

The arrogance of the inquisitors, who took the place of God in judging supposedly heretical Christians, is evident in the staging of the auto-da-fé as an imitation of the Final Judgement, with the inquisitors seated by the high altar and the convicts on the opposite platform, rising to their feet to hear their sentences. The condemned exited to the left of the inquisitors and the absolved to the right. The auto-da-fé was prolonged by the public display of the *sambenitos* (penitential garments) of the condemned in the respective parish churches. The policy of defamation and exclusion was thus extended to the families of the condemned, with records kept of the *sambenitos* and regular checks carried out to ensure that they were exhibited in churches.

The distinctive feature of the Portuguese Inquisition, in comparison to its Spanish and Rome counterparts, was its focus on New Christians, the great majority of whom were artisans but also merchants and bankers with access to power, until a very late date. In the case of the Spanish Inquisition, this focus was evident initially but not in the long term, although important merchants and bankers were persecuted in the first half of the seventeenth century in Castile and in Spanish America. In Italy, the phenomenon of the New Christian did not exist, although Hispanic refugees who had returned to Judaism were persecuted, particularly in the mid sixteenth century.

The distinction between New and Old Christians was abolished by the Marquis of Pombal in 1773. In Spain, it remained until the 1860s. However, it was merely a matter of giving legal recognition to an established fact, namely the disappearance of the New Christians after centuries of persecution, simply because persecuting Judaism was no longer the order of the day, given the emergence of freemasons, illuminist ideas and atheism.

This silent disappearance suggests that the New Christian identity had been encouraged by inquisitorial persecution. Repression led many to become Jews abroad, taking their knowledge and capital with them. Many others were executed or saw their lives ruined by the vicious proceedings. Although some of the merchants and bankers who had been absolved after forced (or otherwise) confessions were able to reorganize their lives, most lost their reputation and ability to maintain their previous way of life and became destitute. The same fate befell many of the artisans, who were condemned to live from alms if they could not return to their former occupation.

The abolition of the Inquisition in 1821 was imposed by the Liberal Revolution, at a time when the institution no longer served any political or social purpose in an age of complete change and society therefore had to be controlled by other means than orthodoxy and religious intolerance. The parliamentary debate revealed the ageing face of an organization that had sworn allegiance to the French invaders and whose shadow of fear had been imposed on the country for more than two centuries. One of the inquisitors present in the parliament agreed that the institution was not necessary and the debate was quickly concluded, given the rumour that the Inquisition would be employing more officers to take advantage of the retirement pensions that would be their due after abolition.

FRANCISCO BETHENCOURT
King's College London

Bibliography

BETHENCOURT, Francisco, *The Inquisition: A Global History, 1478–1834*, Cambridge, Cambridge University Press, 2009.

COELHO, António Borges, *A Inquisição de Évora. Dos Primórdios a 1668*, Lisboa, Caminho, 1987.

LOPEZ-SALAZAR, Ana Isabel, *Inquisición y Política: el Gobierno del Santo Oficio en el Portugal de los Austrias, 1578–1653*, Lisbon, Universidade Católica Portuguesa, 2011.

MARCOCCI, Giuseppe, PAIVA, José Pedro, *História da Inquisição em Portugal, 1536–1821*, Lisbon, A Esfera dos Livros, 2013.

MEA, Elvira, *A Inquisição em Coimbra no Século XVI. A Instituição, os Homens e a Sociedade*, Porto, Fundação Eugénio de Almeida, 1997.

1540
The Jesuits and the First Global Knowledge Database

In their global missionary venture, the Jesuits understood like few others the diversity of human types and cultures since, in addition to the contacts they established, they endeavoured to study and review methods, languages, attitudes and concepts, always striving for greater effectiveness in evangelization.

The arrival of the Jesuits in Portugal in 1540, the same year in which the order was founded by the Basque priest Ignatius of Loyola with the approval of Pope Paul III, accelerated the worldwide projection of the Catholic mission, accompanied by the gathering of information on an unprecedented scale.

The creation of the Society of Jesus, together with the founding of other religious orders (such as the Theatines, in 1524), represented a modernization of the organizations dedicated to Christian monasticism, which were seeking to adapt to new historical contexts. Moreover, their development during the Middle Ages had prepared them for the dynamics of expansion which Europe was experiencing in the Early Modern age. The reforms and different branches of the orders, in particular the phenomenon of the mendicant orders in the twelfth century (such as Dominicans and

Franciscans), gave these institutions, which had been created in rural environments, the capacity to accompany population movements into the cities, which preceded overseas mobility.

Structured to operate as a network via the congregations of transnational monasteries and convent communities of very varying sizes, obeying a centralized power but with relative autonomy and elected offices, the religious orders discovered a global space for their projection and implantation in the age of maritime voyages and European empires. Missionaries were the agents of universal Christian proselytism, accompanying the naval fleets which crossed the seas and created new trade routes and, with them, the expansion of European powers.

The Iberian kingdoms' projects for political and economic expansion were closely linked to the plan to universalize the Christian faith, with missionaries from the religious orders serving as key figures in this process. Usually well prepared, in cultural terms, they were not only responsible for the first evangelization *ad gentes*, but also for establishing the practice of presenting information in writing, through correspondence, reports, treatises, chronicles, histories, text books and grammar books, which became tools for learning about people and cultures hitherto unknown in the European world and, naturally, for cultural exchanges and clashes.

The Society of Jesus, created with a structure which provided the necessary flexibility to enable it to act quickly, emerged during an advanced phase of Iberian expansion. It was soon noted for its ability to establish, within a few decades, a network of missions and colleges that extended from Japan to Peru, whilst also operating in Africa, Asia and America and later reaching Oceania.

The patronage of King John III (1521–1557), which was crucial to its initial reception and the opportunities afforded to young members of the new order, enabled Portugal to become the launch pad for the Society of Jesus in the wider world. Within two centuries, the Jesuits had built more than five dozen colleges and small schools and founded hundreds of missions within the framework of a very centralized structure, organized into provinces and regions spread over four continents.

The instructional efficiency of the Jesuits, which not infrequently led to controversies, was directed by the idea of universalizing the Christian message, formulated in documents which served as guidelines for its global practices. They included the *Ratio studiorum*, promulgated by the Superior General Cláudio Acquaviva in 1599, which regulated its educational activities throughout the world. At the College of the Arts in Coimbra (under Jesuit management since 1555), the teachers prepared a set of textbooks which were used in the Society of Jesus international network of colleges and included the famous *Latin Grammar* by Manuel Álvares (which ran to 52 translations and 530 editions in four centuries) and the *Conimbricenses*, commentaries on the philosophy of Aristotle, which were used by some students who later became famous, including René Descartes.

The Society of Jesus sought to combine spiritual ideas with effective methodology, tradition and innovation to respond to the challenges of their time. Its strong commitment to the education of its agents and neophytes who had converted to Christianity was one of the hallmarks of its modernity, together with the strategy of amassing resources for lasting achievements, focussing on populations concentrated in cities.

The Jesuits created a network of colleges in the main cities in the north and south of mainland Portugal, the Atlantic islands (Madeira, the Azores and Cape Verde) and the overseas territories where they were established (Angola, India, Japan, China, Brazil, etc.). To begin with, there was the College of Jesus in Coimbra (1542), where Jesuits from various countries studied and would go on to work in different parts of the world as missionaries, teachers and scientists. There was also the College of the Holy Spirit in Évora, which opened in 1553 and became a university in 1559. Colleges were later founded in Braga and Porto (1560), Braganza (1561), Funchal and Angra (1570), Ponta Delgada (1591), Faro (1599), Portalegre (1605), Santarém (1621), Elvas (1644), Faial (1652), Setúbal (1655), Portimão (1660), Beja (1670) and Gouveia (1738). Similar institutions were also opened in the missionary territories in the East and Far East, Africa and Brazil, including the colleges in Goa (1548), São Paulo (1554), Bahia (1560), Macao (1565), Rio de Janeiro (1573), Funai (1580) and Luanda (1607), where the curricula were adapted in terms of the teaching of languages and local cultures, bearing in mind the missionary work that stemmed from the colleges.

The largest schools could accommodate over 2,000 students. Until they were expelled by Pombal, the Jesuits had managed to build up a population of approximately 20,000 students in the kingdom of Portugal alone, defending the idea of general education, or inter-class and free education, as it would be described today, in some of the colleges, in opposition to the dominant trend which favoured education only for the elite.

These institutions, in which Jesuits from other European countries taught (particularly in the Classes on the Sphere, in Lisbon), produced individuals who were highly qualified, not only to serve the Society of Jesus, but also the church, state and society. The most famous of the students educated in Jesuit colleges throughout the world at different times include Egas Moniz, Fidel Castro, Gregório de Matos, Jorge Amado, Miguel de Cervantes and Voltaire.

The colleges and missions in various corners of the globe became ideal centres for observing a world which was becoming globalized, and for cultural, scientific and religious exchanges. The Jesuits who played a key role in missionary, pedagogical and scientific work and in mapping the lands beyond Europe, brought visibility to the Society of Jesus and recognition for its adaptive methods, which were not always clearly understood. Key figures included Adam Schall, Alessandro Valignano, António de Andrade (the first European to travel to and live in Tibet), António Vieira, Bento de Góis, Francis Xavier (who pioneered mass conversion in the East), João de Brito, Manuel da Nóbrega, Mateo Ricci, Roberto Nobili and Tomás Pereira.

Their investment in human resources and materials during the modern expansion of Christianity was accompanied by the development of the written culture as a means of communicating not only the religious message, but also knowledge. The Jesuits invested a great deal in the practice of writing, also imposed by their founder as an ascetic ideal, which to a large extent helps to explain their efficiency, together with other orders, in creating what may be called the first database of global knowledge. Its well-preserved archives are rich in useful sources for many disciplinary areas.

The link between the missionary ideal and investment in learning as strategic capital enabled the Society of Jesus to accumulate knowledge in all the continents in which it had a presence, founding missions and colleges and undertaking surveys and studies in the service of princes, kings and emperors.

The dissemination of its achievements in printed and manuscript form played a critical role in establishing the Jesuits. At a time when the written word was becoming widely adopted, together with the affirmation of the epistolary genre, in particular the letter-report, which was often printed, the Society of Jesus favoured writing as a form of management, communication, propaganda and knowledge. As Diogo Ramada Curto noted, in the "texts of the Jesuits, missionaries in Brazil, Africa or the East, it is possible to ascertain different links between the ethnographic perspective and the propaganda destined to affirm the virtues of the Society of Jesus itself".

In their global missionary venture, the Jesuits understood like few others the diversity of human types and cultures since, in addition to the contacts they established, they endeavoured to study and review methods, languages, attitudes and concepts, always striving for greater effectiveness in evangelization. The efforts to adapt made by members of the Society of Jesus were the precursor of contemporary inculturationist missionary methods.

The Jesuit missionaries stood out in promoting unprecedented cultural exchanges between the different civilizations and ethnic groups with whom they established relations. In this respect, the production of grammar books, dictionaries, catechisms and histories of languages and peoples who had no written culture should be noted. Drawing on Judeo-Christian theological and philosophical frameworks, a significant amount of historiographic work was also produced on peoples who did not share Western notions of time and history. The following provide some examples: in the second half of the sixteenth century Luís Fróis wrote a history of Japan (1584–1594), Baltazar Teles produced a history of Ethiopia (1660) and Fernão Cardim was the author of *Tratados da Terra e das Gentes do Brasil* (written between 1583 and 1601), in parallel with work on grammars and dictionaries for various languages spoken in Africa, Asia and America. In the same period, José Anchieta prepared the *Arte de Gramática das Línguas mais Usadas na Costa do Brasil* (1590), in line with other missionaries of the time who were developing similar studies of unknown languages. There were also examples of a deeper form of transmutation, for example in the missionary work in Cochinchina, nowadays Vietnam, in which Francisco de Pina and Alexandre de Rhodes played a leading role, Romanizing the local alphabet to produce a Vietnamese–Portuguese–Latin dictionary and catechism in 1651. Other works which helped to advance the natural sciences through the observation and classification of flora, fauna and physical and human geography in this region include the *Flora Cochinchinensis* (1790) written by João de Loureiro, a scientist who joined the Lisbon Academy of Sciences after Pombal expelled the Society of Jesus. The gathering of scientific data continued in the nineteenth and twentieth centuries when the Jesuits returned to Portugal after the pope restored the Society of Jesus: in this regard the journal *Brotéria*, founded in 1902, should be noted. While work of this kind in various fields was useful for communicating the Christian message, it also brought information on unknown peoples and cultures to Europe and the rest of the world, providing material for revising world views.

From the tenth to the fifteenth centuries, the religious orders had played a leading role in preserving and reproducing cultural and scientific disciplines from the classical world, whereas from the sixteenth century onwards the work of collecting and providing written information on territories unknown to Europe continued. In preparing, hosting and sending missionaries to every continent, Portugal proved to be a vital platform for such exchanges. It has maintained this status, despite difficult relations between politics and religion, up to the present day, having continued to host religious institutes with associated teaching projects in various missionary fields during the nineteenth and twentieth centuries, using old and new networks within and beyond the former territories under Portuguese governance.

José Eduardo Franco
CIPSH Chair for Global Studies of Aberta University and
CLEPUL – Research Centre of the Faculty of Letters of the University of Lisbon

Bibliography

ALDEN, Dauril, *The Making of An Enterprise: The Society of Jesus in Portugal, Its Empire and Beyond, 1540–1750*, Stanford, Stanford University Press, 1996.

BANCHOFF, Thomas, CASANOVA, José (ed.), *The Jesuits and Globalization: Historical Legacies and Contemporary Challenges*, Washington, Georgetown University Press, 2016.

CURTO, Diogo Ramada, "Cultura escrita e práticas de identidade", in BETHENCOURT, Francisco, CHAUDHURI, Kirti (dir.), *História da Expansão Portuguesa*, vol. 2, Lisbon, Círculo de Leitores, 1998, pp. 458–531.

FRANCO, José Eduardo, ABREU, Luís Machado (coord.), *Para a História das Ordens e Congregações Religiosas em Portugal, na Europa e no Mundo*, 2 vols., Lisbon, Paulinas, 2014.

FRANCO, José Eduardo, FIOLHAIS, Carlos, *Jesuítas, Construtores da Globalização. Uma História da Companhia de Jesus*, Lisbon, CTT Correios de Portugal, 2016.

1541
Mazagan: An Architectural Revolution

For reasons associated with the chronology, dynamics and preexisting civilizational features of each of the colonial processes, the Portuguese were precursors of the establishment of modern bastions systems outside Europe.

Mazagan is the original toponym of a site on the Moroccan Atlantic coast where the present-day city of El Jadida (*the New*, in Arabic) stands. This was the name originally used by the Portuguese and French and also later when the fortified city was included in the UNESCO World Heritage list in 2004. It has a strategic location: in front of the hill on which an existing population had been established, where the coastline forms a spur facing north, surrounded by shallow rocky waters and overlooking a wide bay open to the Atlantic in the north-west. In a letter written to the king on 30 September 1513, D. Jaime, the Duke of Braganza, summed up its qualities thus: "the best port in the world". It is not surprising that the Portuguese used it from early times for the flow of cereals from the fertile plains of Azemmour and that, in 1514, they build a fort on the spur, on the east, as the duke had proposed. Nor is it by chance that Mazagan was the only site in Morocco where the Portuguese maintained sovereignty for centuries.

Portuguese developments in North Africa began with the conquest of Ceuta in 1415, but only took shape after Tangier was taken for the second time in 1471. Along the approximately 800 kilometers of coastline ranging from Ceuta to Santa Cruz de Cabo de Aguer (Agadir), a dozen strongholds for trading or military support were either created or started in three decades, as the environment was becoming increasingly insecure. There were few successes in terms of numbers, duration and results and the idea of reform developed from the 1520s onwards. However, it was the fall of

Agadir, the southernmost stronghold, in March 1541, that proved to be the catalyst for a new strategy which included abandoning Azemmour and Safi. In the south, Mazagan remained and was subjected to major improvements which ensured sovereignty until it was abandoned in 1769. In the north, Ksar es-Seghir and Asilah fell in 1550, Ceuta lasted until 1640 and was later confirmed Spanish in 1668, and Tangier became part of the dowry of Catherine of Braganza when she married Charles II of England in 1662. In order to preserve these fortresses, as in the case of Mazagan it was decided to renovate the defensive system, in a paradigm shift that would prove to be an architectural revolution.

This change responded to the need to resist attacks using firearms, which had been introduced in the Late Middle Ages. The successes of this method, recorded from the second half of the fifteenth century onwards, meant that it was necessary to reconsider high, narrow medieval walls which offered little resistance to firearms and were also incapable of incorporating and positioning them at effective angles to counter-attack by sweeping across the surrounding area. It soon became clear that towers had to be replaced with bastions, straight walls with curtain walls and arrow slits with gun ports. However, the shapes and proportions still had to be decided.

The key to this question lay in the design of the bastion, a feature which eventually gave its name to the defence system and affirmed military engineering. Many experiments were carried out in Europe but as the main Portuguese theatre of war was North Africa, this was where the master masons of King John II, King Manuel I and King John III tested out the new architectural feature. Among other cases, the closest to what would become the archetype, namely the bastions of Porta de Ceuta in Ksar es-Seghir, Pata de Aranha in Asilah and Raio in Azemmour, are surviving examples of these old Portuguese experiments. However, the most important of all predates them: the Belém Tower in Lisbon, where the old system was merged with what was to come, namely a tower with a low bastion. Work began on its construction in the same year (1514) and under the same direction (Diogo and Francisco de Arruda) as the original Mazagan fort.

There was a heated debate on what to do and how to accomplish it. The documentation is far more substantial for the Mazagan process in 1541 than for the previous preparatory phase, which highlights the role of the master mason and architect João de Castilho and Duarte Coelho, who is only known for this episode. In 1529 they were sent to the fortresses in Morocco to carry out assessments and propose solutions, but the contents of their report to the king are unknown. Yet, whatever it may have recommended, it would not have been very different from what was constructed shortly afterwards, given that Duarte Coelho had travelled extensively in Italy and observed various fortresses and walls in different cities. In other words, he was aware that the most successful experiments had been in the Italian Peninsula, where the prototypes for the polygonal, pentagonal or orillon bastions represented the way forward.

This would have been one of the main reasons why a very young Francisco de Holanda, the painter, draughtsman and (future) author of key texts on the artistic culture of the Renaissance, set off for a study trip or spy mission to Italy in 1538. In April 1541, he returned, coincidentally or not, with a set of designs drawn from first-hand observation of fortresses, including some which were French and Spanish, showing details and variations in features. Some were still being secretly constructed, such as the one in Fano (Pesaro), whose representation may have been particularly helpful for the Mazagan project. He wrote in *Da Ciência do Desenho* (1571) that the fortress of Mazagan was "built from my design and model, being the first well-fortified defence to be constructed in Africa, which I designed on my return from Italy and France, having drawn by my own hand and measured the principal fortresses in the world".

This clear statement has been interpreted in various ways, since the large amount of the documentation on Mazagan also suggests other possible authors, from Benedetto da Ravena, an Italian in the service of Charles V, to whom the project is usually attributed, to the young Miguel de Arruda and the experienced Diogo de Torralva and João de Castilho (all four worked on the site) and even the king and his brother, Prince Louis, who headed the decision-making process on an equal footing, not to mention the military leaders in the field. Rather than a single author, an intense debate can be identified at the heart of the experimental "laboratory" for the project.

The new fortress was built in around six years, facing east, partly on land and partly on rocks surrounded by a navigable moat. Essentially it involved the construction of a fortified perimeter that encircled a small city, offering it protection and the services of a small garrison, so that it could support the commercial operations of the port. Between the original Mazagan and the 1514 fort a new neighbourhood had sprung up, enclosed by the new wall and the moat. This urban development continued in the free space within the walls. Occasionally it was guided by correspondences between the fort and the new perimeter, but it is evident that the already difficult exercise of constructing the new system did not contemplate urban design.

The models that were used were for forts, not cities, which entailed adjustments, namely to the slope of the curtain walls, allowing for a wider space between the bastions set in each of the four corners. The general profile was low and the space between the curtain walls ample and flat, providing a broad walkway for rounding and moving artillery during a counter attack. To the east, at the sea front, lay the trickily shaped but well-protected dock where, at the worst moments, all the port traffic seemed to be moving at the same time. There were still many atavisms, above all in the details, since a revolution always needs assimilation time.

It was, in fact, an innovative step in the design of defensive structures, which had an enormous impact on landscapes. This was evident from the outset in the massive low, compact areas within which cities were enclosed and the considerable increase, in area and skills, in the *non ædificandi* border area that was crucial to crossfire operations between besieged and besiegers, in addition to the newly styled substantial moats, revelins and glacis.

Inevitably, at a time when architects became autonomous, gained social status and began to construct their own collections of theoretical and subject-specific material, military architecture followed the same process, in solidarity. Yet none of this was an exclusively Portuguese invention or concern. In Mazagan, the innovative features were the evolution of the bastion system to an urban scale and the construction of the first polygonal bastions in a colonial context. For reasons associated with the chronology, dynamics and preexisting civilizational features of each of the colonial processes, the Portuguese were precursors of the establishment of modern bastion systems outside Europe.

In the mid sixteenth century, Portugal faced problems on various fronts associated with the enormity of its potential area of conquest, as it was described at the time. The success of the "laboratory" that was Mazagan and the training it provided for those involved resulted in immediate loyalty to the bastion system. This rapidly materialized in the reform of defensive structures in places as diverse as Ceuta and Tangier, Diu and Ormus, and in the renovation or construction of new forts, on the Island of Mozambique and in São Jorge da Mina and São Julião da Barra (Lisbon) for example, or new urban perimeters such those in Chaul, Vasai and Daman (in the 1570s), or even Salvador, the city founded in 1547 as the capital of Brazil. Moreover, as was the case with Mazagan, Ceuta and Tangier (in Morocco), all the strongholds in Asia which did not introduce this innovation were eventually conquered by the Dutch during the Iberian Union and subsequent Restoration period (1580–1668). The choice of locations in which to apply scarce cutting-edge technical and constructional resources corresponded to decisions concerning the areas in which there were intentions to maintain control. Moreover, although the new system was not adequate in the Persian Gulf, in Ormus for example, it played a crucial role in restoring the border between the two Iberian kingdoms after 1640. On the other hand, the militarization of the empire, the chronic shortage of means, in particular demographic resources, and the necessary specialization meant that, with rare exceptions, military engineers were potential architects, which had repercussions for various forms of Portuguese architecture up to the beginning of the nineteenth century, including in the metropole. For organizational and methodological reasons, the system of shared options that had been used in Mazagan in 1541 remained standard practice. The creation of the office of Chief Engineer, attributed to Miguel de Arruda (the youngest participant in the "Mazagan laboratory"), signified general co-ordination, not universal authority. In fact, he would be the technical and strategic driving force behind almost all the immediate works, with the assistance of others who accompanied the projects and made decisions in the field.

The laboratory which emerged in Mazagan in the summer of 1541 was, in various ways, a revolution for architecture and the construction of Portuguese landscapes or those influenced by the Portuguese, and had an impact on many features which still structure territories and inspire imaginaries of different regions of the world today.

WALTER ROSSA
University of Coimbra

Bibliography

AMARAL, Augusto Ferreira do, *Mazagão, a Epopeia dos Portugueses em Marrocos*, Lisbon, Tribuna da História, 2007.

CONCEIÇÃO, Margarida Tavares da, *Da Cidade e Fortificação em Textos Portugueses (1540–1640)*, Lisbon, Nota de Rodapé, 2015.

CORREIA, Jorge, "Mazagão: a última praça portuguesa no Norte de África", *Revista de História da Arte*, no. 4, 2007, pp. 184–211.

MOREIRA, Rafael (ed.), *A Construção de Mazagão. Cartas Inéditas 1541–1542*, Lisbon, Instituto Português do Património Arquitectónico, 2001.

ROSSA, Walter, TRINDADE, Luísa, "1514 El Jadida 1541: Le vicende della fondazione di una città marocchina", in CASAMENTO, Aldo, *Il Cantiere della Città. Strumenti, Maestranze e Tecniche dal Medioevo al Novecento*, Rome, Edizioni Kappa, 2014, pp. 103–120.

1563

Colóquios dos Simples, or the Globalization of the Printing Press and Knowledge

Due to the efforts of the Flemish doctor and naturalist Charles de l'Écluse, Orta's work soon proved appealing and interesting to Europeans. L'Écluse not only recognized and appreciated the importance of the new medical and botanical knowledge it provided, but also Orta's fearless and fierce criticism of statements made by various ancient authors concerning medicinal products from Asia.

Throughout the sixteenth century, Portuguese territorial expansion led to increasing mobility and the exchange of goods, cultures and knowledge on a global scale. Printed in Goa on 10 April 1563, the *Colóquios dos Simples e Drogas he Cousas Mediçinais da India* (Colloquies on the Simples, Drugs and Materia Medica of India), by Garcia de Orta, is one of the most remarkable testimonies to this dynamic. It has also served as a very significant example of the importance of the printing press in redefining and broadening knowledge of the world since it first appeared in Europe in the mid fifteenth century. Together with this favourable context, the study written by a Portuguese doctor and naturalist was the result of a lengthy and ambitious programme dedicated to amassing knowledge and may be considered exceptional on several levels.

One of the distinctive features of the *Colloquies* is the fact that it was the first work on medicine and botany to be printed in the East. In fact, it was the only Portuguese book on this theme published in Asia in the entire sixteenth century. During this period, some Portuguese based in India wrote books and reports on the natural world in Asia based on first-hand experience. A very small amount of this literature was published in 1550 in the first volume of *Della Navigationi et Viaggi* by the Italian author Giovanni Battista Ramusio, but the vast majority remained in manuscript form. This situation was linked to the policy of secrecy associated with the Portuguese voyages of discovery. In fact, there is evidence that in the sixteenth century the Portuguese Crown developed strategies to restrict access to news of discoveries and trading in Africa and Asia. The printed format of the *Colloquies* was particularly significant, since this made it possible for multiple identical copies of the information to be produced.

It was the Society of Jesus that decided to introduce the printing press to India for the purposes of evangelization, initially in Goa, in September 1556, and later in other areas of Asia where there was a Portuguese presence. The first press with Portuguese fonts was brought from Lisbon and assembled in Saint Paul's College, where it was managed by the Valencian printer Juan de Bustamante, assisted by João Gonçalves and a Goan man. In the same year, the *Conclusiones Philosophicas* by Crisóstomo Fernandes first appeared, followed by three other religious works. The *Colloquies* was the fifth volume to be published by the Saint Paul's College press, now managed by the German printer Johannes de Emden. It was a modest edition containing many transcription, printing and pagination errors. After this, several religious treatises, catechisms and prayer books were published, some in Asian languages. In view of this list of publications, Orta's work on the natural world in Asia appears odd. What would have led to its appearance and what was the significance of this?

By the time Garcia de Orta published his book, he was elderly and infirm. Born in Castelo de Vide to a New Christian family in around 1500, his Jewish origins defined his path in life. From 1515 to 1523 he studied medicine at the universities of Salamanca and Alcalá. A few years later, in 1530, he was appointed Lecturer in Natural Philosophy at the University of Lisbon. However, as New Christians were facing increasing pressure he decided to leave for India in 1534, serving as physician to Martim Afonso de Sousa, Commander-in Chief of the Indian Ocean.

Orta took part in military campaigns and witnessed the expansion of the Portuguese empire in the territory. Having established an extensive network of fortresses and trading posts along the coast of the Indian Ocean, the Portuguese consolidated their presence in Asia by conquering geopolitically and commercially strategic cities. Goa, conquered in 1510, rankest highest, as the capital of the Portuguese empire in the East and the centre for commercial and cultural exchanges. It was here that Orta decided to settle in 1538 and where he remained for the rest of his life (1568). During this lengthy period of time, he practised as a doctor with great success and pursued his studies in natural history. He also traded in precious stones and worked at the Goa Military Hospital. The centrality of Goa ensured that he was able to associate with Luís de Camões and Gaspar Correia and make the acquaintance of influential aristocrats and officials of the empire. To a great extent, it would have been their protection that allowed for the publication of the *Colloquies*, which was authorized by the inquisitor and censor Aleixo Dias Falcão. Goa was also an important waypoint for merchants and individuals from many other different places. Their knowledge of the benefits and origins of medicinal plants, drugs and spices was key to Orta's work.

An appreciation of local medicine is one of the striking features of the *Colloquies*. The author was aware that the heat and humidity of the Tropics made the body more prone to infection, debilitation and decay. For this reason, it offered a range of information on specific treatments in the region, in particular procedures used by local doctors. It also draws on other medical traditions, providing a critical assessment of the opinions of ancient and modern authors on the simples and drugs of India. This is yet another innovative feature of the *Colloquies* which links the author to the European naturalists who were his peers, such as the Spaniard Andrés Laguna and the Italian Pietro Andrea Mattioli.

At the time It was not common for a book on medicine and natural history to be written in dialogue form. Unlike the treatise, this genre is more dynamic and can capture the reader's interest more effectively through its communicative and persuasive style. Throughout the 59 colloquies between the author and the other characters in the book, some historical and others fictional, Orta presents 75 botanical and other medicinal products. In each case, he considers their versatility and provides information on the names in several languages, price, place of origin, morphological and sensory characteristics and use according to specific physical conditions. A significant desire to provide uniform information underpins the presentation, since there were many different appraisals of the natural resources of India and neighbouring territories.

This scheme presupposed broad geographical and knowledge-based coverage which Orta could not have acquired alone. To some extent, many of the observations and considerations in the *Colloquies* were the result of the author's direct experience, written over a period of thirty years. Nevertheless, even this considerable length of time would not have been sufficient to gather observations on natural products that existed in territories Orta had never visited, including parts of Hindustan and certain regions of Africa and Asia. The author of the *Colloquies* therefore depended on information provided by witnesses from various countries, with different social backgrounds, occupations and levels of credibility. His network of informants included doctors and pharmacists but also merchants, soldiers, missionaries, administrators, travellers and interpreters.

Hence, Garcia de Orta's work is the result of a massive and protracted process of accumulating knowledge which focussed on first-hand local observation but also required the inclusion of information from more distant territories.

In addition to its comprehensive coverage of the subject matter, the *Colloquies* was also written for a wider audience. While it may have been useful to Portuguese doctors and pharmacists resident in India and institutions such as the *Misericórdia* brotherhoods and the Goa Military Hospital, the contents could also have provided valuable information for traders, prospectors in search of natural products in the territory and officials of the empire. Moreover, its potential to attract readers along the coast of the Indian Ocean, where Portuguese was an influential language, should not be forgotten. In addition to these readers, Orta clearly demonstrates that his book would be of interest to European doctors and naturalists. The *Colloquies* was designed by the author to circulate in an increasingly wider world.

The print culture which produced the *Colloquies* quickly proved to be very advantageous. Due to the efforts of the Flemish doctor and naturalist Charles de l'Écluse (Carolus Clusius), Orta's work soon proved appealing and interesting to Europeans. Clusius not only recognized and appreciated the importance of the new medical and botanical knowledge it provided, but also Orta's fearless and fierce criticism of statements made by various ancient authors concerning medicinal products from Asia. By means of careful appropriation he was soon able to publish an annotated summary in Antwerp, in 1567. This was followed by a series of revised and improved editions in 1574, 1579, 1593 and 1605, and the version produced by Clusius also served as the basis for the French and Italian translations. In addition, the *Colloquies* influenced works produced by other authors, including the *Tractado de las Drogas*, by Cristóvão da Costa, published in Burgos in 1578. This Portuguese-born doctor and naturalist stayed in India from 1568 to 1571 and therefore not only had the opportunity to discover Orta's *Colloquies*, but also the flora of various regions and their medicinal uses.

Despite the numerous typographical errors in the original edition, the *Colloquies* soon generated a flow of knowledge on a global scale and may be considered one of the most influential products of Portuguese geographical expansion. Hence, it is a little strange that the second edition only appeared in Portugal at the end of the nineteenth century. However, this situation was not unrelated to the author's origins and his posthumous conviction for Judaism by the Inquisition in 1580. Silenced for so long, the history of the *Colloquies* also represents a form of resistance to religious and political censorship, reflecting the power of the printed book.

PALMIRA FONTES DA COSTA
Nova University Lisbon

Bibliography

CARDOSO, Adelino, COSTA, Palmira Fontes da (dir.), *Botânica, Medicina e Cultura nos "Colloquies" de Garcia de Orta*, Lisbon, Colibri, 2015.

CARVALHO, Teresa Nobre de, *Os Desafios de Garcia de Orta. "Colóquios dos Simples e Drogas da Índia"*, Lisbon, A Esfera do Caos, 2015.

COSTA, Palmira Fontes da (dir.), *Medicine, Trade and Empire: Garcia de Orta's "Colloquies on the Simples and Drugs of India" (1563) in Context*, Aldershot, Ashgate, 2015.

FRANCO, José Eduardo, FIOLHAIS, Carlos (dir.), *Obras Pioneiras da Cultura Portuguesa*, vol. 15, Lisbon, Círculo de Leitores, 2019.

LOUREIRO, Rui, "Information networks in the Estado da Índia, a case study: Was Garcia de Orta the organizer of the Codex Casanatense 1889?", *Anais de História de Além-Mar*, no. 13, 2012, pp. 41–73.

ŽUPANOV, Ines G., "Drugs, health, bodies and souls in the tropics: Medical experiments in sixteenth-century Portuguese India", *The Indian Economic and Social History Review*, no. 39, 2002, pp. 1–43.

1572
Camões: Arms, Letters and the Clash of Civilizations

The Lusiads tells the story of a voyage and a people who did not cultivate a knowledge of letters and the sciences. Moreover, instead of being guided by the values of Christianity and Antiquity, understood to be civilized values, they engaged in warfare and were violent in spirit, destroying and killing their enemies.

The antithesis between arms and letters has the merit of serving as a recurring, if not main, argument in *The Lusiads*, the first edition of which was published in 1572. Luís de Camões announced in the opening stanza that he would sing the glory "of arms and matchless men", of those who had set sail from the "Lusitanian shore", and of "the memories /of kings who spread / both Faith and Empire". The poem is therefore written as a celebration of war, its heroes and great deeds. Yet, from the outset there is also a preoccupation with the role of letters, both in the sense of exploring how this poem on the Lusitanians relates to similar works within the same epic genre that celebrated the heroes of Greece and Rome, together with the links established on different levels between the voyage, history and mythology, whilst also recalling that letters serve to designate the culture of the word or the book, which can provide the foundations of law and order. Moreover, it is through this latter interpretation of letters that one of the most extreme expressions of opposition to arms and war can be found, beginning with the opening canto.

It should be remembered that in the initial stanzas of Canto I, Camões aims to extol the king and his imperial might, as well as the Lusitanian people, recalling their "valiant deeds" inspired by "love of country". The broader framework within which this exaltation is presented is conceived of as a clash between Christianity and the rest of the world, and the hope that the king and the Lusitanian people would become the "yoke and chastiser / Of the ignoble Ishmaelite knight, / The Turk from the East and the Heathen / Who drink the waters of the sacred River". In other words, the rest of the world was conceived of as divided between Muslim empires and Hindu kingdoms.

Thus, when the armada commanded by Vasco da Gama reaches the Indian Ocean in 1498, stopping first at the Island of Mozambique, the "Regent of the islands" is portrayed as a "Moor" who asks whether the new arrivals had come "from Turkey's fertile shores". Then he asks Gama for the "books of their law, precept or faith" to determine whether they accorded with his own or belonged to those of Christ. At the same time, he asks the noble captain to show him his weapons. Gama shows him the suits of armour, with harnesses, gleaming habergeons, fine chain mail and protective plates, and the shields, ammunition, steel muskets, bows and arrows, sharp pikes and spears. He speaks of his God, who descended to Earth as a man, but is forced to admit that "Of this Man-God most high and infinite, / The books you ask for, I carry not".

Gama could display his weapons but had not even brought the books of his law or, in other words, his religion with him. This is a significant omission, particularly for the reasons explained a few stanzas later by the Regent. According to him, Gama and those who had arrived with him already have a reputation as "robbers", "bloodthirsty Christians / Who, on their course, have harried all the sea / With fire and sword" and whose main objective is killing, looting and seizing women and children. The weapons were used for amphibious attacks that made populations flee and, even worse, after their victory, the Portuguese "strike and kill / The exposed, defenceless people / Whom they bombard, burn and rout". Then, as if it were an act of chivalry, the same valiant people collect their "rich prize", the spoils of war.

From the very beginning of his epic poem, Camões celebrated the glorious deeds of the sailors and captains, but did so whilst criticizing the violence of war, the values of soldiery and how the empire was built. In many other sections of *The Lusiads* the reader encounters the same opposition to warlike expansionism. The speech by Velho do Restelo is one of the best-known examples: Why did Gama chase after Fame? Why was he seeking out an enemy so far away, so that the king could call himself Lord of India, Persia, Arabia and Ethiopia? Why depopulate the kingdom, a complaint also made by the poets Sá de Miranda after 1530, and António Ferreira, in 1557 or 1558? Finally, in a clear repudiation of expansionist and imperial ideas applied on a global scale he asks whether it would not be preferable to fight the enemy closer to home, in North Africa, the "Ishmaelite" who also needed to be confronted since he followed the "cursed law".

The same tension between, on the one hand, Gama's voyage, arms and the plan for imperial expansion and, on the other hand, this critical, or rather, educated aware-ness reappears at the end of Canto V. This is a passage that has received less attention from scholars, yet it is one in which Camões once again comments on the way in which "the glorious deeds" of noble captains such as Gama, were not recorded in writing to ensure that they would remain in the memory of families and the homeland. The coarseness, lack of skills, science and education and the predominance of ignorant barbarians were all typical of the Lusitanian people. Moreover, this was in striking contrast to Greece and Rome, where "there never was a strong Captain / Who was not also wise and learned".

In this and other episodes, *The Lusiads* tells the story of a voyage and a people who did not cultivate a knowledge of letters and the sciences. Moreover, instead of being guided by the values of Christianity and Antiquity, understood to be civilized values, they engaged in warfare and were violent in spirit, destroying and killing their enemies. If the main battle was against Islam, paradoxically it was through the interpellation of a Muslim "Regent" that Camões chose to present his criticisms of imperial expansion and the right to conquer and oppress other peoples. What was the cost of building an empire? Chasing greedily after riches, building an empire that was too large when it would have been more important to fight the enemy at the door, and engaging in acts which, given the coarseness of the people involved and their lack of education, would not inspire any response consistent with what were considered to be fundamental values, whether Christian or humanist.

This critical, anti-war conscience, aligned with the values of Christianity and educated, textual humanist philology, may be explained by Erasmus of Rotterdam and his direct or indirect influence. Yet regardless of this, *The Lusiads* also stems from a literary and intellectual tradition that ranges from the Dominican priest from Seville, Bartolomé de Las Casas, to Miguel de Cervantes, via the essays and scepticism of the French author Michel de Montaigne. In all these authors and their works, a critical stance can be identified with regard to the right to expansion and conquest, as well as a denunciation of the archaic nature of soldiery and crude, aggressive warmongering. Modernism, to use the language of today, was rooted in this critical awareness, not in expansionism or violence, which contradicted the main cultural and religious frames of reference.

In demonstrating the same critical awareness in relation to the glorious deeds that took place during the voyage, the history of the Lusitanians and the ambitious project to build an empire, Camões is not an isolated case in Portuguese literature, even though he chose the epic genre. He was preceded or followed in this endeavour by the aforementioned poets Sá de Miranda and António Ferreira, the playwrights Gil Vicente and Jorge Ferreira de Vasconcelos and, in what would nowadays be called travel literature, by the reports that form the *História Trágico-Marítima* and *Peregrinação* by Fernão Mendes Pinto. However, it is in the different versions of the dialogue entitled *Soldado Prático* (1570, 1612) that Diogo do Couto explored criticisms similar to those of Camões in greater depth. For example, the main character, the Soldier himself, in discussing the military organization of the State of India, argues that "if the soldiers band together, they will ransack the cities, rob the people and commit other atrocities: and I do not know which is worse – whether the king should lose everything or there should be such chaos".

Certain conclusions can be drawn from an analysis of some episodes in *The Lusiads*. Firstly, the antithesis between arms and letters enabled Camões to praise the former, but with a heightened critical awareness of any wrongful use that may have been open to moral and political condemnation in the light of the values of Christianity and classical humanism. Secondly, the poet draws closer to a vision of a world envisaged as a clash between at least two or three civilizations. Primarily this involves the confrontation between Christianity and Islam, but also includes the comparison drawn between the crude, ignorant Lusitanians and their cultured, well-educated counterparts from Antiquity, and finally the shocking deviance in the homeland, involving warrior heroes whose barbaric behaviour was not fit to serve as a model for civilization, as it is understood in Christian terms.

A third and final conclusion is necessary: using *The Lusiads* to justify historiographical agendas inspired by the creation of global connections may not only appear anachronistic, but is also a forced exercise in which the meaning of the epic poem becomes difficult to understand or loses perspective, as a whole or in terms of its different parts. The same doubts regarding the forced use of the global extend to other institutions and social configurations dating from the second half of the sixteenth century, when there were many other examples of disavowal that were not only related to the size of the empire. I refer here to institutions affected by the Council of Trent, such as the Society of Jesus and the city of Lisbon, two examples to which the title "global" has been added, with very little reflection. Finally, from a methodological point of view, instead of the forced application of present-day concepts to periods and events which scarcely reflect them, it would be more valuable to take inspiration from the more sophisticated literary works of the past to develop our critical awareness and challenge our own way of studying history.

DIOGO RAMADA CURTO
Portuguese Institute for International Relations and Faculty of Social Sciences
and Humanities of the Nova University Lisbon

Bibliography

ALBUQUERQUE, Martim de, *A Expressão do Poder em Luís de Camões*, Lisbon, Imprensa Nacional-Casa da Moeda, 1988.

ALVES, Hélio J. S., *Camões, Corte-Real e o Sistema da Epopeia Quinhentista*, Coimbra, Centro Interuniversitário de Estudos Camonianos, 2001.

ASENSIO, Eugénio, MARTINS, José V. de Pina, *Luís de Camões: el Humanismo en Su Obra Poética: los "Lusíadas" y las "Rimas" en la Poesia Española (1580–1640)*, Paris, Fundação Calouste Gulbenkian, Centro Cultural Português, 1982.

SARAIVA, António José, *Camões*, Lisbon, Jornal do Fôro, 1963.

SENA, Jorge de, *Trinta Anos de Camões, 1948–1978 (Estudos Camonianos e Correlatos)*, Lisbon, Edições 70, 1980.

1580
Union of Crowns, Union of the World

Francesco Carletti described the significance of the 1580 Union from the perspective of a planet that had finally been discovered and dominated, in his Raggionamenti, published in 1701: Portugal, "sailing East, reached China and Japan", while Castile, "heading West, arrived at the Philippine Islands [...]. Together, these two Crowns encircled the entire world, a feat most worthy of praise".

The dynastic crisis in the House of Avis, which culminated in the death of King Henry in January 1580 leaving no direct heir, unleashed a process that extended beyond the incorporation of Portugal within the Hispanic Monarchy of King Philip II. The Union of Crowns – an expression which is to some extent a euphemism – did not envisage the merging of Castile and Portugal, but rather the inclusion of the latter within the composite monarchy of the House of Habsburg, meaning that, at least in principle and as guaranteed by the Courts of Tomar in 1581 at the time when the new king was crowned, Portugal would be governed separately, according to its own laws and institutions. After 1580, the first two global empires would come under the rule of the same king, but their administrations would remain autonomous.

This vision of the future was not shared by all the protagonists of the time, whether within the monarchy of King Philip II or in Portugal. For the subjects of *The Prudent*, as he was known, there was the justifiable fear that the union would make their monarch an excessively powerful ruler and possibly a tyrant. For the Portuguese, particularly the popular sector, there was a belief that the elite within the kingdom – the bishops, nobility and lords of the cities – had delivered Portugal into the hands of a foreign monarch in exchange for bribes and favours, neglecting the morally more serious obligation to defend the political community, which included the sovereignty of the kingdom. On the other hand, the supporters of King Philip – both in the Hispanic Monarchy and in Portugal – cited the advantages of a union that would help preserve the Portuguese empire, weakened after the death of King Sebastian in 1578, and provide new opportunities for expansion, wealth and prestige. Despite the negotiations between Philip and the heads of the kingdom, the two opposing attitudes eventually led to a very serious unification crisis, only resolved by the Spanish king with the dispatch of an army commanded by the Duke of Alba to Portugal and the expulsion of the self-proclaimed king, D. António, Prior do Crato, a member of the House of Avis unable to claim the throne due to his status as an illegitimate son. D. António had become the leader of a large, primarily popular, resistance movement which was defeated at the Battle of Alcântara in August 1580, but remained active in the Azores until the summer of 1583.

Hence, it is easy to see why, after the triumph of *The Prudent* and for almost the entire duration of the Union of Crowns, "globalist" arguments played a key role in the Hispanic propaganda designed to legitimize the incorporation of Portugal. In extolling dominion over the world which God had granted to the Spanish – in the sense of the sons of Hispania – the aim was to encourage the Portuguese to join the House of Habsburg, since Portugal would then become part of an undeniably powerful world-wide monarchy. The choice of global images to celebrate the arrival of King Philip in Lisbon in 1581, after he had proclaimed himself King Philip I of Portugal, says a great deal about the reaction of others at the time to this phenomenon. In fact, Portugal was already an imperial monarchy prior to 1580, due to its conquests in Africa, Asia and America. It is true that from a Castilian point of view, with the exception of Brazil, the Portuguese empire that extended to all four corners of the world consisted of a series of trading posts which were particularly important in Asian regions, rather than large territories like the ones Castile possessed in America. Nevertheless, the qualitative impact of the Portuguese presence in the world implied a respected and established reality at the time when King Philip was recognized as king of Portugal, a situation which the new dynasty did not hesitate to use it to its advantage. There are numerous examples of this: in 1581, according to Isidro Velázquez in *La Entrada Que en el Reino de Portugal Hizo la Sacra, Católica y Real Majestad de Don Philippe*, the new monarch was greeted in Lisbon with a triumphal arch dedicated to the *Universi Globus* (World Globe) in which the forefathers of *The Prudent*, King Manuel I of Portugal and Ferdinand, the Catholic Monarch, were portrayed as the owners of the world, divided at the time but reunited under the power of King Philip II, who had become "Lord of all East and West". In 1618, the Castilian playwright Lope de Vega boasted, in the words of one of his characters from *La Octava Maravilla* (set in Bengal, in present-day India and Bangladesh), that "the world can be traversed through the lands of Philip". One year later, the city of Lisbon received King Philip III and his son, aged 14 and the future King Philip IV, with another magnificent arch featuring a statue of King Philip II, accompanied by two figures representing Castile and Portugal bearing the world. At the ceremony, the king said to his heir: "Son, take these two crowns which I give you and strive to preserve them, for if one should be lost, your empire will fall." In 1634, Gonzalo de Céspedes y Menezes recorded in his *Historia de Don Felipe IV, Rey de las Españas* that this monarch reigned "over all the terrestrial orb", due to the vast Portuguese–Castilian legacy bequeathed to him by his father and grandfather.

Beyond the Hispanic Monarchy there were also testimonies extolling the global grandeur of the Philippine dynasty. In his work *I Capitani* dating from 1607, the Piedmontese Giovanni Botero, who was a supporter of Spain, celebrated the 1580 Union of Crowns, which united "the incomparable grandeur of the Catholic King with the most fortunate kingdom of Portugal and all the states which it possesses, so that Christianity has received one of the greatest monarchies that has ever existed and the Catholic faith a firm shelter, not only in Europe and America, but also in Asia and Africa". Between 1610 and 1616, the Florentine trader Francesco Carletti described the significance of the 1580 Union from the perspective of a planet that had finally been discovered and dominated, in his *Raggionamenti*, published in 1701: Portugal, "sailing East, reached China and Japan", while Castile, "heading West, arrived at the Philippine Islands [...]. Together, these two Crowns encircled the entire world, a feat most worthy of praise".

Hence, celebrating the Portuguese presence throughout the world was an intelligent means of demonstrating that the House of Habsburg recognized and respected the uniqueness and autonomy of this legacy. However, the message could also be interpreted as an invitation from the king for all his subjects to share their respective empires, an incentive to enjoy the redoubled glory under the same monarch. As the facts demonstrate, as the Union progressed, this joint celebration of the planetary achievements of each of the Crowns was quick to present itself as an integrated political project.

The reason for this movement towards centripetalism is similar to what is nowadays termed globalization. Between the discovery of America in 1492 and the first circumnavigation of the world led by Ferdinand Magellan as far as the Moluccas and completed by Sebastián Elcano (1519–1522), humanity entered into an era characterized by global connectivity, economic interdependence and cultural interchange. In the areas under Spanish and Portuguese rule this process was more intensive, challenging the agreement between King Philip I and the Portuguese established by the Courts of Tomar in 1581, in which both Crowns would have the same king but would be governed separately. It became increasingly clear that this was not a realistic solution, since the migratory, financial, commercial and cultural dynamics of the final decades of the sixteenth century and the beginning of the seventeenth century made it necessary to redefine the zones globalized by each Crown in such a way that both Portuguese and Spanish internationalization were altered and, depending on circumstances, forced to collaborate, if not integrate.

There were certain elements of complementarity between both empires which functioned as magnets. This was the case with Spanish silver, which the Portuguese needed in order to trade in Asia, above all in China (where it was worth more than gold), which they acquired by supplying African enslaved populations to the colonies of Mexico and Peru, and in exchange for silks and Chinese porcelain in Manila. In this way, even though the Portuguese route to India and Portuguese trade with Brazil remained officially separate from the Castilian circuits for America and the Philippines, there was a general tendency towards convergence. While thousands of Portuguese subjects emigrated to the Spanish Indies (Mexico City, Acapulco, Lima,

Cartagena or Buenos Aires), São Paulo was filled with Castilians and the borders between Brazil and Paraguay, and between Macao and Manila, virtually disappeared.

In the Iberian Peninsula, the Lisbon–Seville–Madrid triangle created an area that was becoming increasingly open and accessible to financial groups, many of whom were Portuguese New Christians also involved in Portuguese–Castilian economic ventures in the most dynamic centres in the rest of Europe, such as Amsterdam, Hamburg and London. There were even plans to offer a more effective functional response to these developments, whether economic, political or military. In Asia, for example, the idea of establishing a new viceroyalty was considered, which would unite the Portuguese Far East – separating it from the State of India – with the Philippines to help provide better defences for the area against the attacks from the Dutch that had begun at the start of the seventeenth century. In America, the possibility of incorporating the south of Brazil into the Castilian Río de la Plata region was contemplated, thus limiting the governmental autonomy of the São Paulo residents – considered excessive in Madrid – whilst ensuring administrative continuity in a region that had a measure of populational and economic unity.

Undoubtedly, these proposals only represented the interests of a certain section of the population, but clearly reflect the extent to which the subjects of the Philippine dynasty – whether Castilian or Portuguese – were considering drawing their respective empires closer together on a worldwide level in order to benefit more from globalization, given that they were aware of its vast potential. Therefore, this first, mainly Iberian, globalization was not restricted to the usual practices of colonial expansion, such as the occupation of territories, imposition of a certain culture and exploitation of human and natural resources, but was also characterized by the ability of its leaders to identify the opportunities afforded by worldwide connections, based on approaches which would nowadays be described as modern. These included the establishment of international navigation routes, the creation of extensive trading and financial networks, the adoption of a single currency as an international means of payment (the Castilian silver *real*), reflections on anthropological alterity based on parameters that were not always Eurocentric, and the adoption of foreign cultural habits which included learning and using non-Western languages.

From this perspective, the collapse of the Union of Crowns in 1640 can be relativized. Even though, in political terms, the Restoration under the House of Braganza signified the end of the link between Portugal and the Hispanic Monarchy, the process of globalization to which the two courts had made an enormous contribution, remained unstoppable. In this sense, internationalization proved more decisive in the long term than the political crisis that ended with the presence of the House of Habsburg in Portugal. Whilst it is true that the epiphany of the Hispanic *Universi Globus* lasted only three generations, from 1580 to 1640, its legacy has remained in the history of the world as a key contribution towards understanding the process which is nowadays known as globalization.

RAFAEL VALLADARES
EEHAR – Spanish Institute of Roman Archeology, and
Spanish National Research Council

Bibliography
BOUZA, Fernando, *D. Filipe I*, Lisbon, Círculo de Leitores, 2005.
ELLIOTT, John H., "Reflexiones sobre una unión fracasada", *Espacio, Tiempo y Forma. Serie IV Historia Moderna*, no. 25, 2012, pp. 21–36.
GODINHO, Vitorino Magalhães, *Ensaios*, 2 vols., Lisbon, Sá da Costa, 1968.
GRUZINSKI, Serge, *As Quatro Partes do Mundo. História de Uma Mundialização*, São Paulo, Editora da Universidade de São Paulo, 2014.
LEVENSON, Jay A. et al., *Autour du Globe: le Portugal dans le Monde aux XVIe e XVIIe Siècles*, Brussels, Imprimerie National, 2007.

1582
The Gregorian Calendar: Globalizing the Measurement of Time

Portugal was one of the first countries to adopt the Gregorian calendar and consequently the first to introduce it to Brazil and to Christian communities in Asia.

The Gregorian reform of the calendar was the culmination of a complex process that involved correcting the secular and ecclesiastical calendar that had been developed over several centuries, a process which reached its high point with the publication of the papal bull *Inter gravissimas*, issued by Pope Gregory XIII on 24 February, 1582. The Gregorian reform was, without doubt, the most ambitious and successful operation to regularize time and the calendar in the history of humanity. From the outset, it was intended to be used both within and outside Europe and, over the course of time, was extended to the entire world. Portugal was one of the first countries to adopt the Gregorian calendar and consequently the first to introduce it to Brazil and to Christian communities in Asia.

The Julian calendar, introduced by Julius Cesar in 45 BC, was adequate for everyday purposes and later, particularly after the First Council of Nicaea in 325, also served the needs of the Christian liturgy. However, it was soon realized that its principles and approximations – unavoidable in any calendar – would eventually result in significant errors with the passing of the centuries. Between the fourth and fourteenth centuries various studies highlighted these problems, suggesting procedures to rectify them and from the fourteenth century onwards, the need to correct the calendar had become an important issue for the papacy. By the fifteenth century, the matter was being addressed in the councils of the Catholic Church. It was discussed at the Council of Rome (1412), in which Cardinal Pierre d'Ailly's proposal *Exhortatio super kalendarii correctione* (1411) was analyzed, and the Council of Basel (1434–1440), when the *De correction Kalendarii* (c. 1436) by Nicholas of Cusa was debated, as well as the *Phaselexis* (1437) by Hermann Zoest. At the Fifth Council of the Lateran (1512–1517), the Catholic Church took more concrete measures, appointing a committee to study the question, headed by Paul of Middelburg, Bishop of Fossombrone, who published the very complete and influential study *Paulina de recta Paschae celebratione* in 1513. The committee prepared a proposal for the reform of the calendar which Pope Leo X sent to the most important Christian monarchs in the autumn of 1514, requesting opinions and comments from specialists. It was a process that involved mathematicians from various European kingdoms, although these efforts never resulted in any concrete restructuring. The matter was not forgotten by the Council of Trent (1545–1563), but once again no definitive measures were adopted. However, during the final session, on 4 December 1563, it was decided that the Pope would be responsible for correcting the current breviary, which therefore implied the revision of the calendar.

The ruling by the Council of Trent was the starting point for adopting measures to resolve the problem. Shortly after being elected in 1572, Pope Gregory XIII appointed a committee to reform the calendar, in which the German Jesuit Christopher Clavius, who had studied in Coimbra, played an important role. The committee adopted the procedure developed by the Calabrian doctor Luigi Giglio (Lilio) (1510–1574/1576) which focused on using a cycle of epacts to substitute the traditional golden numbers (epacts and golden numbers are used to calculate the dates of the new moon, which are essential for defining the date of Easter). Giglio's proposal was not only highly ingenious, but also complied with the wishes of the Holy See, which intended to carry out a technically advanced reform of the calendar while maintaining the ancient traditions of the Church and causing the least possible disruption to everyday life. The committee prepared a summary of the new proposal, the *Compendium novae rationis restituendi calendarium*, which was sent to mathematicians, astronomers and leading Christian academies for comment and opinions in 1577. In the years which followed, after the documents had been received and analyzed, a decision was finally made.

On 24 February 1582 the *Inter gravissimas* papal bull was proclaimed, stipulating the nature of the reform to be undertaken and the necessary steps for its implementation. The most immediate effect of this restructuring was the removal of ten days from the month of October of that year: those who went to sleep on the night of Thursday 4 October 1582 awoke the next day on Friday 15th October. This was merely the most obvious facet of a very complex reform which also stipulated a new rule for the intercalation of leap years and new rules (using epact cycles) for determining Easter. The official documents and technical explanations were compiled in the *Kalendarium Gregorianum perpetuum*, published in 1582, which ran to many subsequent editions.

There were mixed reactions to the reform: almost all Catholic territories accepted it, while almost all Protestants opposed it. It was implemented almost immediately (in 1582) without protest in France, Italy, Portugal and Spain. Belgium, the Catholic states of Germany and the Catholic region of the Netherlands adopted it in 1584 and Hungary followed in 1587. Despite the obvious technical superiority of the new calendar, it took much longer for it to be accepted in Protestant countries because, as a famous (apocryphal) dictum attributed to Kepler explains, "the Protestants would rather disagree with the sun, than agree with the Pope". However, reality finally intervened and almost all European countries eventually adopted the Gregorian calendar during the course of the next two centuries.

The first indication that a Portuguese author was involved in the technical discussions concerning the correction of the calendar is a brief statement sent to Rome by Diogo Mendes Vizinho on 30 November 1515, bearing the title *De certa ratione inveniendi festa mobilia* (On the correct method for determining moveable feasts). This document was written in the context of the ongoing attempts to revise the calendar during the V Council of the Lateran, in response to a request sent by Leo X to Manuel

I of Portugal. The Portuguese only became involved once again in the matter of the calendar during the pontificate of Gregory XIII, in response to the *Compendium* of 1577. This document reached Roberto Fontana, Collector of the Apostolic Nunciature in Lisbon, at the beginning of April 1578. The individual whose opinion was sought was Pedro Nunes and the request for his evaluation of the calendar was delivered to him a few weeks later. Nunes was elderly and ill and several months elapsed without the mathematician responding, until he passed away on 10 August 1578. Rome, expecting an answer within a few months, was showing signs of impatience and two other mathematicians, Tomás da Orta and Manuel Mendes Vizinho, were therefore appointed to reply. In the weeks which followed both prepared their reviews and, on 27th February 1579, Cardinal-King Henry of Portugal signed a letter addressed to Gregory XIII, forwarding them to Rome.

Following the publication of the papal bull *Inter gravissimas* in February 1582, the calendar reform began to take shape. The first copies of the *Kalendarium Gregorianum perpetuum* arrived in Portugal in the summer of 1582. The administrative procedures for its implementation were officially set in motion with a series of dispatches addressed to the clergy which Philip I of Portugal (Philip II of Spain) issued between 4th and 9th of September of the same year in Lisbon. The second step involved advising the secular authorities by means of the *Lei do Rei de Portugal Filipe I sobre os 10 Dias do Calendário* (The Law of King Philip I of Portugal on the 10 Days of the Calendar), enacted on 20 September 1582. The implementation of the Gregorian calendar ran smoothly in Portuguese territory. As in other Catholic countries, there was no opposition or disapproval. The documents of the time simply note some natural concerns during the months of October and November 1582. The Portuguese response was prompt: in 1583 three different editions of the *Kalendarium Gregorianum perpetuum* were published, providing an abundant supply of all the information required to understand and use the new calendar.

The Portuguese authorities were also responsible for introducing the new calendar to all regions outside Europe under its dominion. The date on which it came into effect in Madeira and Brazil appears to be connected with a fleet which set sail from Lisbon on 5 March 1583 and arrived in Madeira on the 14th of the same month, bearing the new Governor of Brazil and various members of the Society of Jesus. It is likely that the new calendar officially came into effect in the archipelago of Madeira in 1583, meaning that the day after Friday 4 October (in the Julian calendar) became Saturday 15 October (in the Gregorian calendar). The voyage to Brazil from Funchal lasted another fifty days, reaching the bay of Todos-os-Santos on 9 May 1583. There, the local authority was informed of the decision made by the Pope and the King and the new calendar was officially adopted in October 1583.

In Asia, the process was associated with the departure from Lisbon on 8 April 1583 of a fleet sailing on the "India Run". Among the correspondence transported by the ships were instructions from the king, addressed to the Viceroy of India, ordering the implementation of the new calendar, as well as a letter from the king to the Provincial Superior of the Jesuits, written on 16 March 1583 and containing similar orders. The ships docked in Goa in September 1583, an arrival date which did not allow for the introduction of the calendar in October of that year and it was therefore postponed to the same month the following year. Although it had been impossible to implement the calendar in 1583, the matter was addressed in the months which followed. The letter from Philip I of Portugal ordering the Jesuits to introduce the Gregorian calendar was read at the Provincial Congregation of the Jesuits held on 14 November 1583 (according to the Julian calendar) in Goa, headed by Alessandro Valignano. This information was then circulated to Malacca, Macao and other areas. The need for a new calendar was one of the most important points in the complex discussions with the Saint Thomas Christians in the south of India.

Documentary sources reveal that the Julian calendar was still in use in Christian communities in Japan until 1584 and the first reliable indication that the Gregorian calendar had been adopted dates from 4 December 1586. The Jesuit historian Joseph Wicki, editor of the *History of Japan* and possessed of a thorough understanding of contemporary sources stated, without revealing his source, that the Julian calendar was still in use in Japan during the first months of 1585, which suggests that it would been revised in October 1585 or 1586.

The Gregorian calendar, introduced by papal initiative in the sixteenth century, is nowadays established as the most common measurement of time in all countries on Earth. The long, complex process that led to its widespread acceptance was a remarkable episode that can only truly be understood from the perspective of global history.

HENRIQUE LEITÃO
Interuniversity Center for the History of Science and Technology,
Faculty of Sciences, University of Lisbon
JOSÉ MADRUGA CARVALHO
Independent researcher

Bibliography

BOURDON, Léon, "Avis des astronomes portugais sur le projet gregorien de réforme du calendrier", *Revista Filosófica*, no. 7, 1953, pp. 5–46.

COYNE, G. V. et al. (ed.), *Gregorian Reform of the Calendar: Proceedings of the Vatican Conference to Commemorate Its 400th Anniversary, 1582–1982*, Città del Vaticano, Pontificia Academia Scientiarum/Specola Vaticana, 1983.

KALTENBRUNNER, Ferdinand, "Beiträge zur Geschichte der Gregorianischen Kalenderreform", *Sitzungsberichte der Philosophisch-Historischen Classe der Kaiserlichen Akademie der Wissenschaften*, vol. 97, 1881, pp. 7–54.

LEITÃO, Henrique, CARVALHO, José Madruga, *A Questão do Calendário em Portugal no Séc. XVI* (due for publication in 2021).

NOTHAFT, C. Philipp E., *Scandalous Error: Calendar Reform and Calendrical Astronomy in Medieval Europe*, Oxford, Oxford University Press, 2018.

1614
The Scientific Revolution Reaches Asia

It was a Portuguese Jesuit, Manuel Dias, who first informed China, in 1614, of Galileo's ground-breaking telescopic observations in Italy in 1609. Using a telescope he had made himself, Galileo discovered the existence of mountains and craters on the moon, spots on the sun, the phases of Venus and the moons closest to Jupiter.

When Jorge Álvares arrived as a trader in Canton, China, in 1513, from Malacca, becoming the first European to reach the Middle Kingdom by sea, and when the first

Portuguese arrived on the island of Tanegashima from China in 1543, also for the purpose of trading, they were both engaged in establishing relations between Europe and the Far East that would prove lasting. One of the high points of this relationship was the transmission of the European Scientific Revolution to Asia. Since Lisbon was the only official departure point in Europe for harbours such as Macao and Nagasaki for many decades, Portugal played a significant role in the globalization of science. Jesuit missionaries, both Portuguese and foreign subjects based in Portugal, were especially important in this dynamic.

It was a Portuguese Jesuit, Manuel Dias, who first informed China, in 1614, of Galileo's ground-breaking telescopic observations in Italy in 1609. Using a telescope he had made himself, Galileo discovered the existence of mountains and craters on the moon, spots on the sun, the phases of Venus and the moons closest to Jupiter, which supported the audacious heliocentric theory proposed by the Polish scholar Copernicus, who had opposed Ptolemy's geocentric model in 1543. These new discoveries were published in 1610 in the *Sidereus Nuncius* ("Sidereal Messenger"). The Jesuits validated the observations and enthusiastically welcomed Galileo to the Rome College in 1611 – the school where Christopher Clavius (1538–1612) taught – although they did not agree with his opinions on heliocentrism. Clavius, who had studied at the College of the Arts in Coimbra in 1555–1560 and was responsible for the international projection of Pedro Nunes' work, simply stated that if Galileo's observations were correct, they would be adopted by the astronomers as yet another refinement to the Ptolemaic model.

Although it had been run by the Society of Jesus since 1555, the College of the Arts in Coimbra was not the first Jesuit college in Portugal. Jesuit priests had established their first institutions in the kingdom in 1542, namely the College of Jesus in Coimbra and the College of Saint Anthony (of the Desert) in Lisbon. It was the Jesuit college in Lisbon that offered the *Aula da Esfera* (Class on the Sphere), which was mainly responsible for the reception of Galileo's ideas in Portugal. In fact, some of the Jesuits who taught there built telescopes and observed the sky, shortly after the Pisan scientist's announcement. The most important figures among the Jesuits who arrived in Portugal from Italy were the Austrian Christoph Grienberger (1561–1636) and the Italians Giovanni Lembo (1570–1618) and Cristoforo Borri (1583–1632). The first two were part of the group which confirmed Galileo's findings in 1611. The first observations carried out Portugal using a telescope were probably undertaken by Lembo as part of the *Aula da Esfera*, in 1614. The notes from his classes in 1615 confirm that he taught his students how to build telescopes. The Jesuit contribution to the *Aula da Esfera* was not only fundamental to the reception of the Scientific Revolution in Portugal, but also to global history, given its re-transmission to China and Japan. After a short stay in Lisbon, Borri, whose support for heliocentrism had aroused hostility within the Church, headed to Macao, later leaving for Cochinchina (the central and southern region of present-day Vietnam), where he remained for four years, becoming one of the first missionaries in the area. When he returned to Portugal, he taught mathematics at the University of Coimbra, where he carried out public astronomical observations using a telescope and other instruments. In 1627 he observed the moon. His book, *Collecta Astronomica*, published in 1631 in Lisbon, where he taught on the *Aula da Esfera* course, contains an engraving of the moon seen from Coimbra which is the oldest representation of our satellite observed in Portugal with a telescope, and the second to be published after Galileo in the entire world. From the classes he gave in Coimbra and Lisbon, his aim to advance beyond Aristotle, following in Galileo's footsteps, is clear. His fame earned him an invitation from King Philip IV (Philip III of Portugal) to visit Madrid.

Science, in particular mathematics and astronomy, proved extremely important to the introduction of Christianity in China. In the words of the great English sinologist John Needham, "in the history of relationships between civilizations, nothing appears to parallel the arrival in China in the sixteenth century of a group of Europeans so inspired by religious fervour as the Jesuits, and simultaneously so learned in most of the sciences that were developed during the Renaissance and at the dawn of capitalism".

In this context, the Italian Matteo Ricci (1552–1610), who learnt Portuguese in Coimbra in 1571 before leaving for China, where he would spend the rest of his life, was an important figure. Having entered the Society of Jesus in 1571 and studied at the Rome College under Clavius, he set sail for Goa in 1578 (and was only ordained a priest in India). In 1582 he entered China via Macao where he learned Mandarin. From Macao he went to Zhaoqing in 1583, where he began preparing his famous world map which represented China in a global context and provided Chinese translations for Western place names. In 1589, while in Shaoguan, he introduced the Gregorian Calendar, which Clavius had helped to devise and which had been decreed by papal bull in 1581, to China. In 1599 he arrived in Beijing. However, he was only received at court in 1601, which gave him the opportunity to present the Wanli Emperor with his world map, a copy of the Ortelius atlas, a mechanical clock and some optical instruments. In a departure from the usual climate of isolation from the outside world, the emperor gave him permission to reside in China and practice his faith. Ricci was not only the main driving force behind Catholic missionary work in China, but, in learning Mandarin and Confucian philosophy and adopting Chinese clothing and habits, was also responsible for developing links between European and Chinese culture. He showed great curiosity and respect for both ancient Chinese culture and everyday life, which he recorded. In addition to his missionary work, he contributed towards the globalization of science by preparing the first Portuguese–Chinese dictionary (1583–1588), in collaboration with his Jesuit compatriot Michele Ruggieri, and translating the *Treatise on the Sphere* by Sacrobosco into Chinese, as well as the first six books of Euclid's *Elements* and works by Clavius. Ricci, like other Jesuits, requested astronomers from Rome when he realized that the matter of preparing calendars was crucial to good relations with the imperial court. He died in Beijing, a famous man. The Millennium Museum in the city includes only two foreigners in the great figures of Chinese history: Marco Polo and Matteo Ricci. After Ricci had paved the way, for more than two centuries many Jesuit astronomers were actively engaged in working for the imperial court, including in senior positions on the Mathematical Board, an institution dedicated to the preparation of calendars, and the Astronomical Observatory in Beijing, for the simple reason that the astronomy developed during the Scientific Revolution allowed for more accurate astronomical predictions than ancient Chinese astronomy. Certain challenges associated with the prediction of eclipses clearly demonstrated the superiority of European science. The Jesuits built scientific instruments, carried out astronomical observations and established a comprehensive programme for the translation of scientific works.

Ricci's work was continued by the Portuguese Jesuit Manuel Dias (1574–1659), who published the *Tian wen lue* (Summary of Questions on the Heavens) in Chinese in 1615, a description of the Ptolemaic system which would be followed by Chinese astronomers (Copernicus theory arrived much later in the East). In this book, he explained the discoveries made by Galileo with the use of a telescope. In India, in 1612, the Italian Jesuit Giovanni Rubino wrote a letter requesting further information about the latest astronomical discoveries from Italy. The first globe in China, dating from 1623, was made by Manuel Dias and the Italian Niccolò Longobardi to explain the spherical nature of the Earth in a region where this notion did not exist. One high point of the exploration of Asian lands was the arrival of the Portuguese Jesuit Antonio de Andrade (1580–1643) in Tibet in 1624.

In 1619 two other Jesuit astronomers, who had been students of Clavius in Rome and would play an important role in the imperial court, arrived in Macao, namely the German Johannes Schreck (1576–1630) (in Latin, Terrentius), who introduced the first telescope to China and presented it to the emperor, and Johann Adam Schall (1591–1666), who started working on the calendar in 1630 and became the first Jesuit to be appointed president of the Mathematical Board in 1644. The Jesuits occupied this position from 1644 to 1805, apart from a short interval between 1665 and 1668. Schall had great influence in the imperial court. The Portuguese Jesuit Gabriel de Magalhães (1610–1677), from the family of Ferdinand Magellan (Fernão de Magalhães), collaborated with him and constructed a series of mechanical devices, including a carillon tower clock that played Chinese music every hour. However, his main assistant and follower was the Flemish scientist Ferdinand Verbiest (1623–1688). Appointed director of the Observatory in 1669, Verbiest was responsible for the modernization of its instruments, in addition to serving as president of the Mathematical Board. Like Schall, he had a Portuguese collaborator, the Jesuit Tomás Pereira (1645–1708), who had arrived in Beijing in 1673 and succeeded him in the Observatory, although only temporarily. Pereira introduced Western music to China and also assisted the Chinese authorities with cartography issues at the time of the Treaty of Nerchinsk in 1689, which established the borders between China and Russia, and in matters concerning engineering.

Following the famous Chinese Rites controversy, in 1721 the Chinese Kangxi emperor banned Christian missions in China. Interestingly, however, there was tolerance for the "priests of the Court", the members of the Society of Jesus associated with mathematics and astronomy. The last four Jesuits – in fact, ex-Jesuits as the order had been abolished by papal bull in 1773 – who headed the Mathematical Board were all Portuguese: Félix da Rocha (1713–1781), José da Espinha (1722–1788), André Rodrigues (1729–1796) and José Bernardo de Almeida (1728–1895). Rodrigues and Almeida founded an astronomy academy in Beijing in 1792.

In Japan, these flows, although significant, were not as intense as those in China due, on the one hand, to the different civilizational background, but also the lack of political unity in the archipelago at the time when the Portuguese arrived (the introduction of firearms by the Portuguese became a new factor in internal disputes). However, as in China, the Jesuit Francis Xavier, who arrived in Japan 1549, requested missionaries from Rome who had a knowledge of astronomy, given the Japanese interest in the subject. The first known telescope in Japan, which dates from 1613, was presented to Shogun Tokugawa Ieyasu by an English captain. The first mechanical clocks in Japan also came from Europe. In the *Outline Theory of Terrestrial and Celestial Globes*, written by the Japanese astronomer Kobayashi Yoshinobu and dating from the mid seventeenth century, there are references to astronomical observations carried out in Japan. Towards the end of his life, the Jesuit Cristóvão Ferreira (c. 1580–1650), who became known for his apostasy, wrote works on astronomy and medicine. The Portuguese Jesuit Luis de Almeida (1525–1583) merits recognition for establishing the first European hospital in Japan in 1557, in Oita, previously known as Funai. To this day there is a hospital in the city which bears his name.

Various inventions, such as paper and gunpowder, arrived in Europe from China, but the new approach to science – based on observation, experimentation and mathematical reasoning – arrived in China, and in Japan, from Europe, with the help of the Portuguese.

CARLOS FIOLHAIS
Department and Centre for Physics, Faculty of Sciences and Technology,
University of Coimbra

Bibliography

BOXER, Charles, "Some aspects of Portuguese influence in Japan, 1542–1640", *Review of Culture*, series 2, no. 17, Oct-Dec 1993, pp. 35–62.

LEITÃO, Henrique, *A Ciência na "Aula da Esfera" no Colégio de Santo Antão, 1590–1759*, Lisbon, Comissariado Geral das Comemorações do V Centenário do Nascimento de São Francisco Xavier, 2007.

Idem, "The contents and context of Manuel Dias' Tianwenlüe", in SARAIVA, Luís, JAMI, Catherine (eds.), *History of Mathematical Sciences: Portugal and the East III. The Jesuits, the Padroado and East Asian Science (1552–1773)*, Singapore, World Scientific, 2008, pp. 99–12.

RODRIGUES, Francisco, *Jesuítas, Portugueses Astrónomos na China 1583–1805*, Macao, Instituto Cultural de Macau, 1990.

UDÍAS, Agustín, "Jesuit astronomers in Beijing, 1601–1805", *The Quarterly Journal of the Royal Astronomical Society*, vol. 35, 1994, pp. 463–478.

1640–1648
The Luso-Spanish Split and the Westphalia Treaties: A Changed World Order?

The regulatory mechanisms of the two Habsburg conglomerates were being replaced by a system of relationships based on political and juridical equality between all the states, as well as parity of religious rights.

The dates 1 December 1640 and 24 October 1648 were decisive in the history of Portugal and of Europe respectively. What were the main changes that were let loose at the time, and to what extent did they determine the subsequent path of history?

December 1, 1640 was the start of the process of breaking with the Spanish monarchy. This revolt for independence was the result of certain factors combining, almost by accident: discord between the various factions which were ruling Habsburg Portugal; discontent of sectors of Portuguese society on seeing their space of influence invaded by people from other parts of the monarchy; social unease caused by the increasing cost of living and rising taxation; problems inherent in the composite structure of the Spanish monarchy; interference by France in Portuguese affairs, with the aim of destabilizing the rule of Phillip IV; as well as a series of totally fortuitous circumstances which not only set off the rebellion, but also led to its final triumph in 1668, after almost thirty years of war.

The rupture between the two Iberian monarchies opened a visible fissure within the group of European Catholic kingdoms. Portugal and the Spanish monarchy had for decades formed a cohesive Catholic block against Protestantism. While making Catholicism the most powerful element of their identity, they severely restricted contact with the Protestant world. But after 1640 this situation changed. Both Portuguese and Spanish authorities established diplomatic relations with Protestant powers, something that would have been difficult to foresee only a short time before. It was only possible because a new system of foreign relations was appearing, one in which religion had less weight.

The year 1640 also marked the end of a particular geography of personal movement, defined by the borders of the Spanish monarchy. Since the fourteenth century, the Crowns of Aragon and Castile had built social, political, cultural, intellectual and commercial links with Southern and Mediterranean Europe. Portugal too had developed strong links with this region, which were reinforced when it came into the House of Austria's conglomerate of countries. However, after the split of 1640, these links became weaker, and a new geography of relations and intellectual contacts took over. The Mediterranean was losing its importance as a space for Portuguese traffic, and 1640 marked the end of a long period when links flourished between the overseas territories of Portugal and of Castile. Despite rivalry and conflict, the two Iberian imperial projects had developed in a fairly connected and articulated way, with intense movement of people and goods. Interaction was so strong that the Iberians could fight together against northern Europeans who were crossing the Atlantic and the Indian Ocean in the sixteenth century. After 1580 this synergy intensified, especially in the Atlantic. The authorities in Madrid and Lisbon saw the initiatives of the English, Dutch and French as unacceptable incursions into what they considered their own exclusive sphere. This overseas space, marked as it was by Iberian power, began to collapse in the 1620s with the great Dutch offensive against Portuguese America and the State of India. The rift of 1640 intensified this process, since the need for support in the fight against Phillip IV made a rebellious Portugal open its overseas space to northern European powers. The same happened after 1648 to the Spanish monarchy, conceding to the Dutch the right to participate in transatlantic traffic in enslaved Africans, up until then very much dominated by the Portuguese. In parallel, both the Iberian monarchies were accepting as a given fact northern European sovereignty over certain regions of America, Asia and Africa.

Some of these changes intersected with the impact of the two agreements sworn in Westphalia on 24 October 1648. Negotiated over more than four years in Münster and Osnabrück, these treaties put an end to the long and bloody conflict known as the Thirty Years' War. The aim of the Westphalia negotiations was indeed to end this devastating war and establish a *"pax generalis"*. Around 230 representatives of various states, mostly from the area of the Empire, took part in these multilateral talks. Although each participant would have had a different understanding of the expression *"pax generalis"* and even of "Europe", the priority was to achieve a secure, lasting and honourable peace for all parties. Furthermore, it attempted to break with the ancestral hierarchy among political units, adopting instead a more equitable arrangement. Expressions such as *"repos de la Chrestienté"* and *"reposo de la Christiandad"* were used in the instructions to French and Spanish diplomats to indicate the principal objective of negotiations. However, despite these religious references, the Westphalia negotiations differed from earlier ones in that they rejected the role of the pope as mediator or promoter of peace. It is also significant that, once initial distrust was overcome, Protestants and Catholics mingled freely during the talks, thereby reducing their differences.

From these marathon negotiations two main treaties emerged, one signed in Osnabrück by the representatives of the Emperor, of the states of the Empire and of Sweden, and the other signed in Münster by the Emperor and by France. Both were formally sworn on 24 October 1648; thousands of copies were made, so that the agreements could be widely circulated.

Scholars of Political Science and International Relations usually praise the modernity of these treaties, declaring that Westphalia created the modern international order, based on sovereign states. Historians tend to be more cautious. Some question the application of the category "international" to an era when protagonists in external relations did not define themselves as "nations". Others claim that the treaties had a limited impact on external relations, given that peace did not include the whole of Europe, that many wars continued after 1648, that many protested against the treaties, and also that the Spanish monarchy did not allow the Portuguese and the Catalans to participate in the talks.

However, despite these divergent views, there is no doubt that the agreements played a part in the process of creating a new understanding of external relations in Western Europe. The regulatory mechanisms of the two Habsburg conglomerates were being replaced by a system of relations based on political and juridical equality between all the states, as well as parity of religious rights. The treaties also show that the subscribers considered it advantageous to have a structure which would permanently regulate interactions between diverse European political entities. One of the principal characteristics of this structure was its religious neutrality. The treaties still used Christian terms, but they were conceived as neutral concerning faiths, and were important in discrediting the use of force as a way of achieving religious aims. Symptomatically, the Pope was among those who rejected the treaties.

The transforming effects of the 1648 agreements, and of the Portuguese–Spanish split of 1640, should not be exaggerated. Above all, the majority of the changes were basically concerned with the ruling dynasties and elites of each territory: the processes set in motion in 1640 and 1648 had very little effect on the lives of most inhabitants of Western Europe. In both cases, nothing was done to alter the order – profoundly patriarchal, inequitable, and discriminatory in terms of race, jurisdiction and religion – prevalent in Europe and its colonial territories, or to widen political participation. It is even possible that most of the population was not aware of these events.

For many Portuguese, the geography of personal movement altered after 1640. The lands of southern Europe and of Spanish America were no longer the main destination for emigration, intellectual contacts or trade, since traffic with northern Europe once again became possible. On the other hand, a new type of restriction was developing: "natural". Over time, to be a "natural" of a certain territory (a category which already existed before 1640) came to be one of the main indicators of belonging to a determined political community, replacing religious identity.

As for the treaties, the situation in Europe after 1648 shows that the ambition to establish a "general peace" had yet to be realized. Respect for sovereignty was observed only occasionally, and the notions of equality and religious neutrality were not always respected. While it is true that the pacts ended a war which had caused massive mortality and devastation, "regional" conflicts continued, showing that Westphalia did not result in an efficient system of collective security. Taking all this into account, it is hard to discern in the 1648 agreements a step towards European modernity.

Regarding the internal structure of political alignments, 1640 and 1648 point in different directions. The Empire managed to adapt to the changes introduced by Westphalia, maintaining its power in Central Europe as a successful territorial conglomerate based on political and jurisdictional diversity. In this it contrasted with the compact and centralized model which was gaining ground elsewhere in Europe, a direction indicated by the revolt of 1640. In reality, Portugal's secession was partly the result of the structural problems of the composite monarchy of the House of Austria, and its success contributed not only to break up this conglomerate, but also to foster the conviction, among some, that the future belonged to more compact political formations, more uniform in terms of their policy making and jurisdictional framework. For the majority of African, Asiatic and Amerindian societies and cultures, however, these events had little impact. The rupture in 1640 between Portugal and Spain had some reverberations in other parts of the globe, but meant little or nothing of significance for most of the world. Political changes in China in this same decade (the Manchu conquest, the end of the Ming and the rise of the Qing dynasties) certainly had a much larger impact on the lives of far more people than the return of Portugal to political independence.

The treaties of Westphalia had little or no effect on the major empires of the time, whether Chinese, Mughal, Ottoman, Safavid or Russian: all these continued to be much more important to much larger sections of the world's population. Nor did any of these huge conglomerates appear to seek inspiration from the Westphalia mode of negotiations, so as to deal better with their own problems. Their internal politics were barely affected by treaties, neither is there any indication that these agreements served as a model for relations between these empires and other potentates. The emperors of the Qing dynasty, for example, never changed their way of conducting foreign relations, always seeing other rulers, including Europeans, as inferior to the Chinese. In the seventeenth century, the leaders of China and other empires were aware that their conglomerates were much larger and more powerful than most European political formations. And they knew, too, that the Europeans, in their scanty colonial possessions, depended far more on the support of Asian and African rulers than these did on Europeans.

PEDRO CARDIM
Nova University Lisbon

Bibliography

CARDIM, Pedro, "Portuguese rebels" at Münster: The diplomatic self-fashioning in the mid-17th century European politics", in DUCHHARDT, Heinz (org.), *Der Westfälische Friede. Diplomatie, Politische Zäsur, Kulturelles Umfeld, Rezeptionsgeschichte*, München, R. Oldenbourg, 1988, pp. 293—333.

CROXTON, Derek, *Westphalia: The Last Christian Peace*, New York, Palgrave Macmillan, 2013.

PAQUETTE, Gabriel, *The European Seaborne Empires: From the Thirty Years' War to the Age of Revolutions*, New Haven, Yale University Press, 2019.

SCHAUB, Jean-Frédéric, "The union between Portugal and the Spanish monarchy (1581–1640)", in BOUZA, Fernando et al. (ed.), *The Iberian World, 1450–1820*, London, Routledge, 2019, pp. 126–141.

VALLADARES RAMÍREZ, Rafael, *La Rebelión de Portugal. Guerra, Conflicto y Poderes en la Monarquía Hispánica*, Valladolid, Junta de Castilla y León, 1998.

1645

The Pernambucan Insurrection and the Rejection of Globalism

The construction of Portuguese globalism after the demise of the Philippine dynasty encountered obstacles from the powers that vied for rule over the oceans. In the case of Pernambuco, it was also obstructed by the faction which had gained strength in the foreign war and which, after the defeat of the Dutch in Brazil, was reluctant to transfer the re-conquered power to the king.

Between 1630 and 1654, the Dutch West India Company occupied part of the northeast of Brazil. Created as a weapon against the Habsburg monarchy, the long-term enemy of the Republic of the United Provinces from 1568 to 1648, the Company's central aim was to undermine the Iberian overseas economy which sustained the Spanish Empire, and to open its ports, from America to Asia, to Dutch shipping.

Incorporated under the Spanish Crown as a result of the Portuguese dynastic crisis of 1580, Brazil became a focus of Dutch interest when its trade with the Netherlands was embargoed by the Spanish monarchy. After an early attempt in 1624, it was in February 1630 that an armada of the Dutch West India Company arrived at the Captaincy of Pernambuco, at the time the world's major sugar producer. Despite resistance by the settlers, the capital and its port were captured. The Dutch then endured a long siege, the settlers only being defeated in 1632. Gradually the Dutch captured important positions in Brazil, including in the interior of the country.

The total collapse of Hispanic-Portuguese resistance to this offensive was seen in 1635, after the capture of Cape of Santo Agostinho and Arraial do Bom Jesus. The cape was the main port of the resistance, important because of its proximity to Recife. At Arraial, a encampment on the outskirts of Recife, forces were gathered to besiege the Dutch and stop them moving inland, where some of the inhabitants had fled, together with the resistance forces, who were attempting to hold the south of Pernambuco while awaiting reinforcements. The destruction of the region and the flight of the inhabitants were only halted in 1637 with the arrival in Recife of a new governor of the Company, John Maurice of Nassau-Siegen. Nassau managed to push the resistance beyond the São Francisco river and also expanded the colony to the north, annexing Ceará in 1637 and capturing the factory of São Jorge da Mina (now located in West Africa at Elmina, Ghana), the following year.

The war only abated in the 1640s, when the Portuguese rebelled against the Spanish, acknowledged the Duke of Braganza as King John IV, and agreed an armistice with the Republic of the United Provinces. Nevertheless, the Dutch West India

Company took advantage of the situation to enlarge its possessions in Brazil, annexing Sergipe and Maranhão; it also captured Luanda and São Tomé in 1641. Nassau had to face many challenges, among them how to revive the sugar trade, which had been destroyed in the conquest of the territory. Sugar-mill equipment was confiscated, sold, and rebuilt with Company finance, mostly to Dutch and Portuguese. As the colony grew, many mills began working again, despite attacks in 1640 by local troops attempting to regain the territory, and, perhaps more seriously, despite the fall in the price of sugar in Holland due to its increased availability in Europe. Conflicting interests of the various groups also increased discord among the colony's inhabitants, which continued with the departure of Nassau in 1644 and the formation of a new government, unable to understand and solve the problems of Dutch Brazil, as it was called by the Portuguese, or New Holland, in its Dutch version.

The Company also committed strategic errors, not correctly interpreting Portuguese developments after the so-called Restoration of 1640. Facing financial difficulties, it reduced its armed forces in Brazil, dismissing veteran officers who knew the territory well. It lost Angola and São Tomé – re-conquered in 1648 by Salvador Correia de Sá e Benevides, who used Rio de Janeiro as a base to mount the coup – and dismissed Nassau, replacing him by a council which, against Nassau's advice, began to reclaim inhabitants' debts. Rather than calming ongoing hostility in the colony, this policy exacerbated friction with local people. An insurrection had been planned ever since the installation of the Duke of Braganza as king, although in Portugal there were doubts as to his support for the plan. In fact, it was only in 1644, after all diplomatic possibilities for the return of Brazil to Portugal had been exhausted, that the Crown participated actively in the plan for a rebellion.

The revolt against the Dutch started in May 1645, uniting Portuguese, and Brazilians, including the Portuguese sugar-mill owner João Fernandes Vieira; the governor André Vidal de Negreiros, native of Paraíba and son of Portuguese parents; António Felipe Camarão, the native commander of a regiment of Brazilian Indians; and Henrique Dias, commander of the Black troops of the territory, comprising enslaved individuals, emancipated slaves, and freemen. Despite the initial success of the revolt, the Portuguese could not recapture Pernambuco. Nevertheless, the situation of Dutch Brazil in the second year of the rebellion was calamitous, with the colony suffering the effects of war and famine. A possible change only appeared in 1648 with the arrival of a fleet bringing soldiers from the Netherlands. The Dutch tried to break the Portuguese siege but were lured to ground more favourable to the besieging Portuguese, where they were defeated: this was the first stage of the Battle of Guararapes (present Jaboatão dos Guararapes). In February 1649, in the second stage of the battle, the Dutch West India Company tried again to break the siege but was again defeated. These debacles sealed the fate of the colony, and in 1654 the Dutch agreed to surrender their capital and their other forts in Brazil.

The Portuguese monarchy, although it had encouraged the Pernambuco rebellion only discreetly and behind the scenes, now found itself at a crossroads. Should it support the rebellion, which would lead to wars, not only with Castile but also with the Netherlands? Or, respecting the truce signed in 1641, should it repudiate and reprimand the rebels, at the risk of the rich sugar-producing region paying homage to another European king, or even, like a new Holland, declaring itself a republic? Portugal, under great pressure and particularly fragile at the time, with the succession of the first Braganza kings, chose a double game: to publicly condemn the rebellion, thus calming Dutch hostilities, but fostering it discreetly behind the scenes. This it did through secret orders addressed to the governor-general in Bahia and by appointing a new general to command the rebel forces, Francisco Barreto de Menezes, later to be governor of Pernambuco and governor-general of Brazil.

On the horizon, Lisbon's aim went beyond regaining Pernambuco. What were the basic intentions of the house of Braganza after 1640? Firstly, to secure the sovereignty of the kingdom; secondly, to restore the geography of the Portuguese empire. Not simply to save Portuguese territory in the Peninsula from integration into the Spanish Crown, but to rebuild the overseas globalism founded in the fifteenth and sixteenth centuries under Afonso V (1438–1481), John II (1481–1495), Emanuel I (1495–1521) and John III (1521–1557), and now under threat. In the current delicate context, with the reigns of John IV (1640–1656) and Afonso VI (1662–1667) and the regency of Louisa of Gusmão (1656–1662), this agenda of restoration was completely successful in its first aim but only partially in its second, in recapturing former possessions in Africa and Brazil from the Dutch. Under the regency and in the reign of Peter II (1667—1706), these successes were enough to link the House of Braganza with the "kings of the Discoveries" of the Avis dynasty, as seen in internationally-known works by authors close to the monarchy, such as the *Historia de Portugal Restaurado* (1675) by the Count of Ericeira, and the *Istoria delle Guerre del Regno del Brazile* (1698), by the Carmelite friar João José de Santa Teresa.

This policy of the Portuguese Crown, however, clashed with another restoration, that of Pernambuco, which was triumphant after the Dutch surrender at Recife. It was not that anti-Portuguese feeling was strong there, nor that political separation from Portugal or adoption of a republican model was seriously suggested (not only was Flemish Calvinism a repugnant heresy, but the republican political system of the United Provinces obviously lacked the figure of a monarch). Those supporting "restoration" for Pernambuco repeated their claims of fidelity, but simply as vassals who had, of their own accord, restored a lost province to its king. The sugar-growing elite, enriched in the period of prosperity under the Albuquerque family of donataries (1534–1630) – absentees for long periods – were used to a considerable degree of autonomy. After the Dutch surrender in 1654, with the Captaincy of Pernambuco transferred to royal jurisdiction, tension grew between its capital, Olinda, and Lisbon. Claiming that they had won victory over the Dutch Company at the cost of their "blood, lives and lands", supporters of restoration in the tropics – led by figures such as Fernandes Vieira, Vidal de Negreiros and João de Souza – were expecting ample rewards from the king, the greatest of which would be power over the re-conquered region. Independence, for them, was to consist in local control of fiscal and military authority, especially of the governor de Pernambuco, and reduced interference by the governor-general in business north of the São Francisco River, an area which the Chamber of Olinda aimed to control.

In the 1650s, the Crown agreed to most of the demands, appointing Vidal de Negreiros as governor and granting wider powers to Olinda. However, conflicts in jurisdiction between Pernambuco and Bahia soon surfaced, with the governor-general Barreto de Menezes sending troops to punish the "insolence" of Vidal de Negreiros. After 1661, the Crown frustrated the plans of the local nobility, appointing governors with no connection to the territory, and restricting the power of Olinda in comparison with other Captaincies in the North and with Salvador, to which it was finally subordinated. The appointment of the Count of Óbidos as viceroy of Brazil in 1663 was a clear sign of centralizing intentions. In this clash of restorations, the Kingdom imposed its plan on the Captaincy. But not without costs.

The resentment of the local elite was interpreted by historians as the seed of Pernambucan nativist ideology, which would later ripen into anti-Portuguese feelings. Their grievance as a group nurtured ideas of belonging to a "nobility of the land", meritorious but treated unjustly by Lisbon, which led in the late seventeenth century to riots against royal governors, to the War of the Mascates (1711–1715) and to the cycle of revolutionary events between 1817 and 1848. Pernambuco was certainly not the only focus of opposition in the seventeenth century to the restoration under the House of Braganza. In Rio de Janeiro, the Sá e Benevides family had guaranteed greater autonomy for the city, a situation which the Count of Óbidos tried to control.

Thus, the construction of Portuguese globalism after the demise of the Philippine dynasty encountered obstacles from the powers that vied for rule over the oceans. In the case of Pernambuco, it was also obstructed by the faction which had gained strength in the foreign war and which, after the defeat of the Dutch in Brazil, was reluctant, on the basis of a contractual political tradition, to transfer the re-conquered power to the king. The tension was seen in the narratives and histories of the Dutch war produced under the patronage of the local sugar-growing elite, where their deeds are exalted, and their names inscribed in the history of a global Portugal.

BRUNO MIRANDA and KLEBER CLEMENTINO
Federal Rural University of Pernambuco

Bibliography

BOXER, Charles R., *The Dutch in Brazil (1624–1654)*, Oxford, Clarendon Press, 1957.

CLEMENTINO, Kleber, *Política e Historiografia nas Narrativas Lusocastelhanas Seiscentistas da Guerra Holandesa no Atlântico Sul*, doctoral thesis in History, Federal University of Pernambuco, Recife (photopy), 2016.

MELLO, Evaldo Cabral de, *A Fronda dos Mazombos. Nobres contra Mascates: Pernambuco, 1666–1715*, 2nd ed., São Paulo, Editora 34, 2003.

Idem, *O Negócio do Brasil. Portugal, os Países Baixos e o Nordeste, 1641–1669*, 3rd ed., Rio de Janeiro, Topbooks, 2003.

MELLO, J. A. Gonsalves de, *João Fernandes Vieira, Mestre-de-Campo do Terço de Infantaria de Pernambuco*, Lisbon, Comissão Nacional para as Comemorações dos Descobrimentos Portugueses, 2000.

1680
The Founding of Colonia de Sacramento

Instability, precariousness, and provisionally were thus typical of Colonia, but they were also common in many other colonial situations. In many cases, the territories Europeans claimed were contested among the various European powers, as well as among them and the native groups that pre-dated their arrival.

In 1680, the Portuguese established Colonia de Sacramento (in present-day Uruguay) to lay claim to a territory, which they argued belonged to them according to the Treaty of Tordesillas, signed between the monarchs of Portugal and Spain in 1494. This move was immediately criticized by Spaniards who confirmed on the contrary that the territory was theirs according to the treaty. At stake were legal, as well as political and economic questions, as the location of Colonia, overlooking Buenos Aires across the River Plate, placed it in a perfect position to facilitate contraband trade between Portuguese and Spanish domains as well as to accelerate penetration into the still barely dominated South American interior. Disagreement led to conflict and conflict to war. Eight months after it was established, Colonia was taken by Spanish forces. In 1682 it was returned to Portugal (provisionally, as agreed between both powers in 1681), in 1701 Spain recognized Portugal's claims to the territory but, in 1704, its forces conquered Colonia yet again, returning it to Portugal in 1715, and blockading it for two years between 1735 and 1737 (with the apparent aim of bringing about its capitulation and demise). In the Treaty of Madrid (1750) Colonia was recognized as a Spanish territory in return for a Spanish recognition that several missions established by Spanish Jesuits were located on Portuguese soil. Although, thereafter, Colonia was to be Spanish, nonetheless, before the transfer of the territory took place, the 1750 treaty was annulled. Spanish forces took Colonia again in 1761, returning it to Portugal in 1763, and conquering it yet again in 1777. Subsequently, it remained in Spanish hands, yet its continuously undetermined status became apparent during the wars of independence, when some locals claimed an autonomy vis-à-vis both Buenos Aires and Brazil, while others, encouraged and supported by these now-portrayed-as-outside powers, strove to bring their settlement and the future Uruguay under the hegemony of one of these forces.

This great volatility was not only political and military but also involved heated juridical disagreements. While Colonia was built, destroyed, rebuilt, and destroyed yet again, the parties continued to debate whose was its territory according to the Treaty of Tordesillas, but also who penetrated and took possession of it first. Negotiators representing the Spanish and Portuguese courts performed certainty, arguing that they knew and were certain that their country and only their country had rightful dominion over the territory. Negotiators also implied that what was conquered, destroyed, and rebuilt, namely Colonia, was a clear unit that required no definition. They thus ordered locals to conquer "it", destroy "it," or return "it." Yet, this clarity dissipated as it crossed the Atlantic. In the heartland of South America, local actors confessed that they were unsure and that they were uncertain. Each time they received orders to surrender, conquer, or return Colonia they asked what exactly were they supposed to do and what Colonia consisted of. Spaniards wondered whether they were instructed to return to the Portuguese the territory of the fort. In this case, should they consider as territory of the fort the parts where fortifications were located or perhaps the area protected by the canons? Or was Colonia, as the Portuguese argued, a proper settlement that included not only a fort but also an agricultural hinterland? If such was the case, how big was this hinterland and should it be returned to the Portuguese along-side the fort? Did this hinterland include only the terrains where crops were planted, or also the larger area where the inhabitants collected wood or fruits and let their animals pasture? Could it be that Colonia controlled not only an agricultural hinter-land but also an entire region that extended from the River Plate to the nearest Spanish enclave in Paraguay (which was enormously far away), as some Portuguese pretended?

While kings constantly ignored pleas to define what Colonia was, locals got involved in discussions that sought to distinguish what was occupied from what was not and by whom. Their interpretation depended on medieval Roman law doctrines as understood and implemented in the Americas, but it was also contingent on what was at stake. Paradoxically, both sides insisted on their rights according to their reading of the Treaty of Tordesillas, but they were mostly concerned with political and economic interests according to which the presence of Colonia was either beneficial and necessary or highly detrimental and dangerous. And, although discussions purportedly confronted the Spanish with the Portuguese, in reality local actors instigated most of these conflicts and their interests did not necessarily align with those of their states. The governors of Buenos Aires, for example, were charged on occasions with blockading or conquering Colonia, but contemporaries suspected that many locals, including several governors, were content with the presence of the Portuguese across the Plate estuary, because it allowed intense contacts with the Portuguese maritime network. These contacts were frequent during the union of the crowns of Spain and Portugal (1580–1640) but they were partially disrupted after the union was dissolved (officially in 1668, when the Spanish king recognized the independence of Portugal). Other sectors within Buenos Aires might have opposed Colonia not because it was Portuguese, but because they desired to use the territory it occupied as pastureland for their growing herds or they were afraid that the Portuguese of Colonia would treat these free roaming cattle as their own. The cabildo of Buenos Aires wanted its inhabitants to remain nearby rather than release their animals to pasture on the other side of the river and might have therefore considered the foundation of Colonia a good thing because it hindered the penetration, followed by the immigration, of Bonarenses (and their animals) across the estuary.

Tensions among European actors did not mask the difficulties they faced in controlling a territory mostly populated by indigenous peoples. In the late seventeenth- and in the eighteenth century, Colonia was attacked on various occasions by native forces, sometimes allied with and working for Spain, sometimes not. Natives also attacked the Spanish forces stationed in the area, and laid claims to the herds pasturing nearby. Both the Spanish and the Portuguese attempted to control the native population mostly by reducing it to missions or by ensuring its pacification in other ways. Natives, of course, had their own agenda. Among other things, they treated both sides of the river as a single territory, which they constantly roamed and whose resources – including cattle – they wished to exploit, and they alternated as allies of one power or the other. The omnipresence of the religious orders, mainly the Jesuits, in the territory did not facilitate things either, as Jesuits could be considered both allies and enemies, both facilitators and obstructers of European domination.

Instability, precariousness, and provisionally were thus typical of Colonia, but they were also common in many other colonial situations. In many cases, the territories Europeans claimed were contested among the various European powers, as well as among them and the native groups that pre-dated their arrival or had immigrated to that region because of colonial presence. Because in the Early Modern period most actors claimed usage rights (including jurisdiction) rather than abstract entitlements, what all parties sought to achieve was a recognition that they could settle, trade, pasture, convert, or collect. The territory they imagined and constructed acquired as a result the shape of an archipelago, with islands that were occupied in a sea of unoccupied land. Fault lines did not necessarily follow ethnic or political divisions, but instead could easily confront Spaniards against Spaniards, Portuguese against Portuguese, and natives (and sometimes religious orders) against one another.

It is thus fair to say that, while the courts debated the rights of kings, in the colonial territories that they coveted in Asia, Africa, and the Americas, locals formed different coalitions that were constantly reconfigured as well as modified. Ambiguity and chaos were more typical of these situations than certainty and clarity. The outcome of these processes was not the construction of an uninterrupted colonial territory, but instead the emergence of a fragmented space that constantly changed shapes. In other words, rather than having a clear purpose and advancing progressively into "no man's land" as European expansion overseas was once portrayed, what existed was a struggle over the use of land, as well as over securing the allegiance of local inhabitants and their alignment with the interests of states. This struggle required to define what a legitimate use (that would grant rights) was and who were legitimate users (who belonged to the community that purportedly had or was about to acquire rights). This was true in the Americas as elsewhere. In Gujarat (India), for example, Mughals contested Portuguese claims to hegemony over certain ports and sea routes through allowing or not certain individuals to trade, by adopting or rejecting conversion, and by playing with what the court wanted versus what local officials and residents did. Pretense to possess certain areas by virtue of occupation led to claims for jurisdiction and claims for jurisdiction produced the hope to control both territory and its people.

This discontinuous and contingent nature of space, which was typical of the Early Modern period, was called into question in the nineteenth and twentieth centuries by state makers. State makers wanted to delineate the territory and its people, clearly distinguishing what and whom they were. Nonetheless, in most cases, their efforts at imagining and consolidating borders that encompassed a clear group of citizens and a clear territory took over one hundred years to complete and, in many areas, it succeeded only partially. As late as the 1980s, the authorities of Ecuador and Peru could thus disagree over whether certain indigenous groups were Ecuadorian or Peruvian and, as a result, whether their territory belonged to one country or the other.

TAMAR HERZOG
Harvard University

Bibliography

CORTESÃO, Jaime, *Tratado de Madri: antecedentes; Colonia do Sacramento, 1669–1749*, Rio de Janeiro, Biblioteca Nacional, 1954.

GARCIA, Elisa Frühauf, *As diversas formas de ser índio. Políticas indígenas e políticas indigenistas no extremo sul da América portuguesa*, Rio de Janeiro, Arquivo Nacional, 2009.

HERZOG, Tamar, "The Meaning of Territory: Colonial Standards and Modern Questions in Ecuador", in RONIGER, Luis, WAISMAN, Carlos H. (eds.), *Globality and Multiple Modernities: Comparative North American and Latin American Perspectives*, Brighton, Sussex Academic Press, 2002, pp.162–182.

Idem, *Frontiers of Possession: Spain and Portugal in Europe and the Americas*, Cambridge MA, Harvard University Press, 2015.

POSSAMAI, Paulo César, *A vida Quotidiana na Colónia do Sacramento. Um bastião Português em terras do futuro Uruguai*, Lisbon, Livros do Brasil, 2006.

PRADO, Fabrício, *Colônia do Sacramento. O Extremo Sul da América Portuguesa*, Porto Alegre, F. P. Prado, 2002.

1703
The Methuen Treaty

The Methuen Treaty symbolizes the strategic alliance between Portugal and England and it is considered as the reason for the opening of the domestic and the colonial markets to the English merchant communities of Lisbon and Porto, giving them a decisive role in the economic development of Portugal and its empire.

The Methuen Treaty was a commercial treaty signed between Portugal and England in 1703, in the context of the War of Spanish Succession (1701–1714) and the diplomatic realignment of Portugal with the maritime powers (England and the United Provinces). The treaty included two articles on the commercial relationship between both parties: Portugal agreed to readmit English woollen textiles, which required the lifting of restrictions imposed by a series of sumptuary laws issued between 1668 and 1702. In exchange, England guaranteed the import of Portuguese wines for two-thirds of the tariffs imposed on French wine.

By mid-eighteenth century, the treaty began to be perceived negatively. Contemporary authors blamed it for the failure of industrial and agricultural development in Portugal and for the deficit in the balance of trade. In the international context, the treaty served as a positive example to emphasise the competitive advantages that productive specialization could bring to both countries. In the twentieth century, Marxist analyses insisted in the unfavourable nature of the treaty, stressing Portugal's dependence on England caused by the imbalance of exchanges and resulting in restricted economic development. Recently Portuguese historiography has re-examined the effects of the treaty seeing structural limitations and other events as contributors to the dominant position of England in the trade with Portugal.

An evaluation of the Methuen Treaty needs to include an analysis of the historical context of the early eighteenth century. The dynastic crisis in Spain and the subsequent war in Europe resulted in Spain and France confronting the Holy Roman Empire, England and the United Provinces. Allied at first with the Franco-Spanish block, Portugal changed sides on 16 May 1703, with the signing of a double treaty of alliance with England, the Holy Roman Empire, the United Provinces and Savoy. Events between July and October 1702 had contributed to this change of heart. The siege of Cádiz, the defeat of the French navy, and the capture of the Spanish Atlantic fleet in the Bay of Vigo by the Anglo-Dutch navy combined, highlighted the vulnerability of Portuguese ports and overseas trading routes, vulnerabilities that the Franco-Spanish alliance was in no position to defend. These developments, associated with a diplomatic offensive by the maritime powers drove King Peter II to join the Great Alliance.

In this diplomatic realignment, John Methuen, special envoy of Queen Anne, played a decisive role. In contrast with the representatives of the United Provinces and the Holy Roman Empire, Methuen established a good personal relationship with Peter II, a relationship that turned out to be decisive in the signing of the treaty on 27 December 1703. The pact between both countries aligned the British mercantile interests in Iberia with the economic interests of the Portuguese monarchy.

British historians argue that Methuen took the initiative in the negotiations with the king. His family connections to cloth production and trade made him aware of the many complaints among English traders concerning the restrictions caused by the sumptuary laws and their negative effect on the import of woollen cloth into the Portuguese markets. These laws had long been a problem, but the interruption of direct trade between Spain and England after 1702 only exasperated further the English cloth traders. For them, it became imperative the accessibility to the port of Lisbon to serve as a distribution centre for imports and exports to Iberia, particularly Spain, and the Mediterranean. As the third largest market for English woollen cloth, Spain guaranteed the English access to raw wool and silver, essential to maintain the global circulation of other goods. In Lisbon, Methuen became the spokesman for the various trading groups importing and exporting, via Lisbon into Spain.

Portuguese interests in the framework of the treaty have also been amply discussed in the literature, with an emphasis on wine production for export. However, there is no evidence of an organized group of wine-growers having lobbied the court for an advantageous agreement. At the same time, there is no evidence that the Duke of Cadaval and the Marquis of Alegrete, representing King Peter II in the negotiations, hoped to profit from the treaty, since the income from their estates did not depend on the production of wine. Notwithstanding, among the Portuguese products that could counterbalance the import of English woollen cloth, wine was perhaps the obvious choice. Not only did wine exports show encouraging signs of growth, but the English embargo on French wine was an opportunity to increase the Portuguese quota in the English market. In light of the developments of 1703, it seems that the economic interests of the monarchy justified accepting the treaty. In a time of war, with the defence of the country and its empire at stake, customs restrictions included in the sumptuary laws were incompatible with the financial needs of a monarchy, whose income depended overwhelmingly on customs revenues. In this sense, the signing of the treaty signalled the end of the industrial protectionism of the 1670s and 1680s and symbolizes a renewed policy of openness to foreign trade.

In order to discuss the impact of the Methuen Treaty, one needs to consider the two sectors specified in its clauses.

While it certainly contributed to the internationalization of Portuguese wines, it is hard to blame the treaty for the failure in development of the woollen industry. At the time, the Portuguese textile industry was evidently unable to compete with English woollen cloths, and the terms of the treaty only precipitated the suspension of the Count of Ericeira's policy of industrial stimulus. The growth in English imports was but one of the reasons for the trade deficit between Portugal and England. More importantly, the Brazilian gold boom stood at the core of the widening of the Portuguese domestic and colonial markets, aggravating thus the trade deficit with England.

The Methuen Treaty is often perceived as the culprit for the opening of domestic and colonial markets to the English merchant communities of Lisbon and Porto, affording them a decisive role in the economic development of Portugal and its empire. Notwithstanding the benefits English trading communities enjoyed after the treaty, they were not alone in their penetration of the Portuguese markets.

From the mid-fifteenth century, Lisbon was commercially attractive to various foreign communities. The role of the Genoese and the Flemish in the Portuguese overseas expansion is well-known, as are the investments of large German banking houses, who played an important part in the country's financial and commercial activities.

The Italian community, on the other hand, arrived in Lisbon in the late Middle Ages and remained well into the Early Modern period. Italian traders prospered in the leather trade that they held under a royal monopoly. They also profited from a royal monopoly in Brazilian sugar that was consequently channelled to the Mediterranean ports, after this had been replaced by sugar from the West Indies in the Northern European markets. Furthermore, the Italians financed various exploratory ventures throughout the Portuguese world, linking these investments with short-term loans to the Crown and to the purchase of public debt.

Contemporary with the Italians, and also long-term residents in Lisbon, were the Germans. Coming from several states in the Holy Roman Empire and divided between Catholics and Protestants since 1517, they remained close to royal circles. They were attracted to Lisbon because of its role as a redistribution market for exotic goods from colonial markets, but during the eighteenth century members of the German community also became contractors of royal rents, connecting their commercial activities with financial services to the Crown, to private institutions and businesses.

The Italians and the Germans had long competed with the Flemish, who had played an important part, since the fifteenth century, in the settling and development of the Azores. Their community in Lisbon was dominated by agents of textile traders from Bruges, to be replaced in the sixteenth century by the great commercial houses of Antwerp. While investing in colonial products traded via Lisbon, the Flemish from Antwerp, either as permanent residents or as commercial travellers, competed fiercely with their northern counterparts.

After the revolt of the Low Countries (1568–1648), the Flemish community divided between Protestants (Holland and Zealand) and Catholics (Flanders). The latter group concentrated their efforts on buying and transporting goods from the South Atlantic to Antwerp. The former community, although enemies of the Habsburg kings during the Union of the Crowns (1580–1640), were essentially concerned with trade in grain from the Baltic in exchange for salt, fruit and wine, and serving as agents for the commercial houses of Amsterdam that bought and carried sugar and brazilwood directly from the colony to the Northern European markets.

There are two key differences between these groups. Firstly, the Flemish never traded with their own fleets, depending instead on Hanseatic or Portuguese shipping. The Dutch, on the other hand, always had their own fleets, with low freight costs and the ability to attract foreign crews, to make use of different flags during embargoes on Portuguese ports. Secondly, disposing of a large, cheap merchant fleet gave the Dutch the chance to organize illegal trade with the Portuguese colonies, especially in the South Atlantic, eliminating Lisbon as port of call. This is what transformed the Dutch community from agents of northern European trade into independent entrepreneurs, particularly interested in the financial sector. It was in this sector that they distinguished themselves as Crown rentiers and bankers, especially in the second half of the seventeenth century and throughout the eighteenth century. The prominence of the Dutch community is reflected in the signing of a trade agreement identical to that of Methuen in 1704 (ratified in 1705). Nevertheless, this treaty with the Dutch did not result in the predominance of Dutch textiles in exchange for Portuguese wine.

All foreign communities in Portugal coexisted with the British, despite the Methuen Treaty. The beginning of the Brazilian gold boom contributed to the vigorous growth and socio-economic activities of these communities, consolidating the status of Lisbon as a cosmopolitan and global city up to the 1760s.

CÁTIA ANTUNES
Leiden University
JOÃO PAULO SALVADO
Interdisciplinary Centre of History, Cultures and Societies, University of Évora

Bibliography

ANTUNES, Cátia, *Globalisation in the Early Modern Period: The Economic Relationship between Amsterdam and Lisbon, 1640–1705*, Amsterdam, Aksant, 2004.

CARDOSO, José Luís et al., *O Tratado de Methuen (1703). Diplomacia, Guerra, Política e Economia*, Lisbon, Livros Horizonte, 2003.

COSTA, Leonor Freire et al., *An Economic History of Portugal, 1143–2010*, Cambridge, Cambridge University Press, 2016.

FISHER, H. E. S., *The Portugal Trade: A Study of Anglo-Portuguese Commerce, 1700–1770*, London, Methuen and Company, 1971.

FRANCIS, A. D., *The Methuens and Portugal, 1691–1708*, Cambridge, Cambridge University Press, 1966.

1717
The Palace of Mafra, or a Global Vision of the Baroque

The monumental complex of Mafra is a majestic symbol of the reign of King John V and a paradigm of royal taste, linking the ceremonial splendour of papal court festivities with the prestigious French model of Louis XIV. Its principal architect, Johan Friedrich Ludwig, was a German trained in Rome, and from Rome, too, came materials, works and artists.

The time when the Palace of Mafra was built – the foundation stone was laid in 1717, and the basilica was consecrated in 1730 – was one of notable dynamism in architecture and the visual arts in Portugal and its overseas empire, particularly in the Atlantic. The forces at work here arose from different origins, and brought different meanings. Benefitting from an exceptional set of circumstances, particularly the flow of mineral wealth from Brazil, King John V (1707–1750) launched an ambitious cultural, artistic and building programme, aiming to raise his court to the level of its main European counterparts. Furthermore, due to developments in traditional techniques and aesthetics, new artistic forms or syntheses came into use. Curiously enough, it was the latter that most contributed to define, in the Atlantic area, a distinctly Portuguese visual universe.

The monumental complex of Mafra (palace, convent and basilica, totalling 40,000 square metres, with a 220-metre long façade), is a majestic symbol of the reign of King John V and a paradigm of royal taste, linking the ceremonial splendour of papal court festivities with the prestigious French model of Louis XIV. Its principal architect, Johan Friedrich Ludwig, known in Portugal as Ludovice (c. 1670–1752), was a German trained in Rome, and from Rome, too, came materials, works and artists to decorate and furnish the church and other royal institutions. Later, Alessandro Giusti (1715–1799) headed a school of sculpture there, which reinforced Portugal's taste for marble statuary. In 2019, Mafra was added to UNESCO's list of World Heritage sites.

It is not easy to trace the influence of Mafra's architecture within Portugal, although its workshop acted as a school for architects and specialized craftsmen. However, in Évora, the chancel of the cathedral (1718–1729), the work of Ludovice and associated with John V, is a major example of the new taste for the international Baroque, imposed by the central power. The role of the king in modernizing and developing the country's arts and culture can also be seen in other areas. He founded the Royal Academy of History in 1720, fitting it with workshops for typography and for engraving (the latter being the first of its kind in Portugal), with artists and craftspeople coming from abroad to work there. Also in the 1720s, he ordered from the famous Parisian merchant, publisher and engraver Jean Mariette an extraordinary collection of prints, bound in over a hundred large-format volumes. These formed a systematic and exhaustive history of European prints; they were kept in the Royal Library in the Ribeira Palace (destroyed in the 1755 earthquake), and were constantly augmented by acquisitions of printed books and manuscripts.

Other libraries were founded under John V's patronage: in Mafra, in the Necessidades Palace in Lisbon, and in the University of Coimbra (the Joanine Library). The Coimbra library, built between 1717 and 1728, is divided into three rooms, their ceilings decorated with *quadratura*, illusionistic or trompe-l'oeil paintings by António Simões Ribeiro in 1723–1724. This demanding artistic form had been introduced into the country by the Florentine Vincenzo Bacherelli (1672–1745), who lived in Portugal from 1701 to 1721. Ceilings by him can still be seen in the Alvor Palace in Lisbon (the Museu Nacional de Arte Antiga) and in the entrance hall of São Vicente de Fora Convent (Lisbon). Simões Ribeiro *quadratura* paintings in the Joanine Library are the most important of this kind in Portugal. They follow an allegorical programme centred on three main personifications, one in each room: the Library, the University and the Encyclopaedia. As in most other European countries, the use of allegory was becoming common in visual arts in Portugal, both in graphic arts and in monumental decoration.

These innovations – *quadratura*, allegories – went with Simões Ribeiro to Brazil, where he settled in 1735. In Bahia, apart from works now lost, he painted the *quadratura* decoration in the Library of the Company of Jesus, now Bahia Cathedral, and other smaller works, besides ceiling *cassoni* in the Church and the Convent of Saint Francis and in the meeting-room of the Misericórdia. Simões Ribeiro was the originator of the so-called "Bahia school of painting"; in Rio de Janeiro, architectural painting had already been introduced by another Portuguese painter, Caetano da Costa Coelho, as seen in the church of the Third Order of Saint Francis (1732).

In northern Portugal, architecture followed a different path with its own characteristics, thanks to the Tuscan painter, decorator and architect Niccolò Nasoni (1691–1773). Nasoni's main works in Porto (Clérigos Church, 1731–1750; Misericórdia Church, 1749–1753; Freixo Palace, 1749–1754), with their profusely decorated façades, bear witness to his remarkable sense of scenography. Certain elements of his decorative vocabulary were used in unexpected ways: for example, a fragment of a pediment (inverted or included in the mouldings of openings) reappears, transformed and much enlarged, in the Misericórdia Church in Viseu

(1775) by António da Costa Faro, and in frontispieces in churches in Minas Gerais in Brazil (Terceiros do Carmo in São João del Rei, Bom Jesus in Congonhas do Campo, etc.) The Clérigos Church, on the other hand, fits into a typology which extends throughout the eighteenth-century Portuguese cultural space: symmetrical plan, deep chancel, side corridors leading to the sacristy (Clérigos Church in Recife, 1728–1759; Glória do Outeiro Church, Rio de Janeiro, 1714–1739; Rosário Church in Ouro Preto, 1757–1784, etc.).

Like the sculptors and the *quadratura* artists, the Italian painters who worked in Portugal also taught students, thus helping to modernize local aesthetic sensibilities. Other artists, painters and sculptors received training in Rome in the Portuguese Academy there, set up in the 1720s under government patronage. This school did not last long, however, so only a very few artists, mostly close to Court circles, were able to attend it. For various reasons (fragility of the art market, general lack of aesthetic education), Portuguese painting had long been in a situation of crisis, worsened by the deregulation of the profession. This had resulted from a royal decision in 1689, perhaps superficially "modern" but with disastrous effects. Declaring painting to be "noble and liberal", the regulation abolished the administrative and legal prescriptions that governed its practice, without providing anything to replace the ancient structure of craft guilds. This opened the gates to self-taught, inadequately trained artists, later to be denounced by some painters. As Félix da Costa explained in 1696, to correct this situation, dignify the practice of art and train competent professionals, in touch with current cultural trends – in other words to transform the craftsman of medieval tradition into a modern artist – an academy of painting was needed. The obvious example was the *Académie royale de peinture et de sculpture*, created by Louis XIV in 1648 (together with academies dedicated to dance, music and architecture). The French Academy was the paradigm of such institutions and the model for most of those founded in the eighteenth century both in Europe and the Americas. In Portugal, however, the academy was not created, and the absence of a coherent and structured policy of artistic training, such as that founded by Louis XIV, is one of the most notorious failings of King John's cultural programme.

Nevertheless, other art forms with strong narrative content expanded considerably in this period, such as woodwork or wood sculpture and *azulejos*, large-scale tile painting. In 1717, the year that building started on the Convent of Mafra and the Joanine Library, work began on the choir-stalls of Monastery of São Bento da Vitória in Porto, one of the masterpieces of its kind. The structure in gilded wood that covers the walls behind the seats includes thirty-six relief carvings in wood showing episodes of the life of Saint Benedict, the work of Marceliano de Araújo of Braga (c. 1690–1769). Despite the large number of panels, the work is memorable more for its visual impact than for its narrative and hagiographic content.

It was in this period, too, that there appeared interiors completely covered with carved and gilded wood, the "golden churches", as they were called. Superlative examples of these are Santa Clara in Porto (by Miguel Francisco da Silva, after 1730), the chancel of the Convent of Jesus in Aveiro (by António Gomes and José Correia, 1725–1729), and in Brazil, the church of the Third Order of Saint Francis in Rio de Janeiro (by the Lisbon architects Manuel de Brito and Francisco Manuel de Brito, 1726–1740).

The art of altarpieces, the main focus of post-Tridentine Catholic liturgy, went through an important evolution at this time. Two examples from Porto illustrate the passage from the so-called national style to the "Joanine" style, both of them in fact variants of a Solomonic Baroque, generalized in Europe and in Iberian America. The first, in São Bento da Vitória (1716–1719), attributed to Gabriel Rodrigues, occupies the rear of the chancel, a static and self-contained composition with Solomonic columns and round arches. The second, by Miguel Francisco da Silva, at the high altar of Porto Cathedral (1727–1729), is also Solomonic in design, crowned with a broken pediment and pelmet, with four statues; the elements of the design advance and retreat at various levels, showing awareness of the work of Andrea Pozzo (*Perspectiva pictorum*, 1693). Both stylistic modes can be found on São Miguel Island in the Azores (in São Pedro in Ponta Delgada and in the parish church of Vila Franca do Campo) and in Brazil (Monastery of São Bento in Rio de Janeiro; Salvador Cathedral in Bahia, etc.).

The use of *azulejos* (painted tiles), common in Portuguese architecture since the late fifteenth century, was particularly profuse in this period. *Azulejos* were used for various purposes, and were often the main narrative element in large-scale decoration at this time. Exclusively in blue and white in the first half of the eighteenth century, the panels were usually arranged in series, adapted to the surface of the walls. In no other region of Europe were tiles used in this way and on such a large scale. In the Convent of Loios, in Évora, the panels by António de Oliveira Bernardes, dated 1711, individually framed by simple bands, show episodes from the life of Saint Lawrence Justinian; they are to be read sequentially, one after the other. Increasingly the frames become complex scenographic structures, with fantastic composite pilasters, spiral shells, atlases, medallions etc. (see the *azulejos* by Valentim de Almeida in the cloister of Porto Cathedral, from 1729–1731). In the organization of the decorative sets, there are cases where the *azulejos* are divided into several series, a main narrative sequence and a secondary one serving as a basis. Sometimes *azulejos* are combined with a series of oil paintings, suggesting varied or multidirectional readings. This is what happens in the Misericórdia Church in Évora, with narrative *azulejos* panels by António de Oliveira Bernardes (1715–1716), combined with emblems and oil paintings, and in São Gonçalo in Angra do Heroísmo (Terceira Island, Azores), with paintings and *azulejos* attributed to Teotónio dos Santos, c. 1720–1730).

With the Oliveira Bernardes family – António and his son Policarpo – we find a phenomenon which might be seen as the culmination of this form of decoration. In Nossa Senhora dos Remédios, in Peniche (1720s), in São Lourenço in Almancil (1730) and in São Filipe in Setúbal (1736), the entire wall cladding is in *azulejos*. Everything was drawn in blue and white on a flat ceramic surface: narrative and emblematic pictures, allegorical figures, borders and frames, as well as all the architectonic elements dividing the space and structuring the decoration (entablatures, cornices, pediments, arches, columns, pilasters, atlantes etc.). The general effect is surprising and overwhelming, and it almost hides the contradictions of the implied system of representation. Unable to prioritize or differentiate the levels of reality depicted (a story presents the same consistency as its frame) and thus to establish a convincing fictional pact with the beholder, the *azulejos* of Almancil, Peniche and Setúbal are Baroque mimicries, and perhaps just for this they are the most tangible symbols of the century of John V. And yet, the *azulejos* of the Joanine period are more than this. Exported on a large scale to the overseas colonies, they are a form of monumental Baroque decoration that gives buildings a specifically Portuguese identity. Particularly significant examples of this situation can be seen in Luanda (Angola), in the Atlantic islands, and in the coastal regions of Brazil, such as Olinda and Recife (Pernambuco), Salvador (Bahia) and Rio de Janeiro.

LUÍS DE MOURA SOBRAL
University of Montreal

Bibliography

DELAFORCE, Angela, *Art and Patronage in Eighteenth-Century Portugal*, Cambridge, Cambridge University Press, 2002.

MANDROUX-FRANÇA, Marie-Thérèse, PRÉAUD, Maxime (dir.), *Catalogues de la Collection d'Estampes de Jean V, Roi de Portugal par Pierre-Jean Mariette*, 3 vols., Lisbon/Paris, Fundação Calouste Gulbenkian/Bibliothèque Nationale de France/Fundação da Casa de Bragança, 2003.

PEREIRA, José Fernandes (dir.), *Dicionário da Arte Barroca em Portugal*, Lisbon, Presença, 1989.

PIMENTEL, António Filipe, *Arquitectura e Poder. O Real Edifício de Mafra*, Lisbon, Livros Horizonte, 2002.

SALDANHA, Nuno (dir.), *Joanni V Magnifico. A Pintura em Portugal ao tempo de D. João V, 1706–1750*, Lisbon, Instituto Português do Património Arquitectónico e Arqueológico, 1994.

1727
The Arrival of Freemasonry in Portugal

With a history of almost three hundred years in Portugal, freemasonry was an organization that always had an important presence in political, social and cultural life, extending beyond national borders and also profoundly affected by outside influences.

Freemasonry arrived in Portugal ten years after the founding of the Grand Lodge of London and Westminster. By 1727, a lodge had been founded in Lisbon by British merchants, classified by the Inquisition as "heretical traders" since almost all the members were Protestants. It was officially recognized by the Grand Lodge of London in 1735. In 1733, a second lodge appeared, the Royal House of the Free-Masons of Lusitania, with English, Irish and Scottish members who were mainly Catholic and included merchants, soldiers, seamen, doctors and friars. None of them were Portuguese except for the Hungarian military engineer Carlos Mardel, a naturalized Portuguese subject. A third lodge was mentioned in 1741, founded in Lisbon by the Swiss diamond cutter John Coustos, the son of French Protestants but a naturalized British subject, who had already been active as a freemason in London and Paris. It had 30 foreign members – French, English, Dutch and Italian – all resident in Portugal and mainly merchants, as well as one Portuguese member. Denounced to the Inquisition in 1743, Coustos and two other masons were sentenced to deportation and forced labour on the galleys.

The repression of freemasonry began to ease from 1755 onwards due to Sebastião José de Carvalho e Melo, known as the Marquis of Pombal, who had a more tolerant attitude towards the organization, although Madeira remained an exception and masons were still persecuted there by the local authorities. The arrival in Portugal of the Count of Lippe, in 1762, and many foreign soldiers who were masons helped promote the order, particularly among military circles. In Lisbon, in 1763, there was an English and a French lodge and another lodge composed of soldiers and civilians.

After the death of King Joseph I in 1777, the persecution intensified and would be aggravated by the French Revolution. However, in 1797, following the arrival of English troops in Portugal to help combat potential Spanish and French aggression, a measure of tolerance was restored, inspired or imposed by the influence of free-masonry in England.

Portuguese lodges were organized and a liaison committee was created, which functioned as an embryonic federative structure. In 1802, the Grand Orient of Portugal was founded – the first Portuguese Obedience – and Sebastião José de São Paio de Melo e Castro Lusignan, the grandson of the Marquis of Pombal, was elected Grand Master. Treaties were signed with the United Grand Lodge of England and the Grande Orient of France. In July 1806, the first Portuguese Masonic Constitution, which adopted the French rite, was approved.

The French Invasions (1807–1811) and the presence of the English disrupted the activities of the freemasons, whose sympathies were divided between the two influences. At the time of the Second and Third French Invasions (in 1809 and 1810), masons or alleged masons were arrested, particularly those associated with the events of September 1810 (the *Setembrizada*), and dozens of suspects were deported to the Azores.

Despite these adversities, freemasonry survived in Brazil and was reorganized in Portugal after 1814, following the return of expatriates such as Gomes Freire de Andrade, a former general in the Portuguese Legion serving under Napoleon, who was elected Grand Master in 1815 or 1816. His arrest and execution in 1817, together with other companions accused of sedition, cast another shadow over the activities of the masons in a hostile climate aggravated by the Pernambucan Revolt, which took place the same year.

In 1818, King John VI issued an order banning secret societies, whose members could be charged with the crime of lèse-majesté and receive harsh sentences ranging from the death penalty to confiscation of assets. Many lodges suspended their activities, although there were some indications of an opposite trend. Several masons were members of the *Sinédrio*, a secret political organization founded in 1818 that supported the uprising of 24 August 1820 in Porto which marked the beginning of the Liberal Revolution.

Until 1823, many masons were involved in political life, in the *Cortes* and the governments, but after the counter-revolution that year – known as the *Vilafrancada* – their interest waned, faced with the threat of interrogations, arrests and repressive legislation which was only curbed in 1824, following the defeat of the attempted Absolutist coup. In 1828, when King Michael ascended to the throne, freemasonry was banned and members or suspected members were imprisoned, while others sought salvation in exile. Persecuted in Portugal, they reorganized abroad, but the political differences that divided the Liberal camp spread to an organization that should have been immune to factional struggles. Many exiled Portuguese masons joined French and English lodges.

Political and personal issues resulted in the creation of rival Obediences, a situation that worsened in 1834 following the Liberal victory. The masons elected two Grand Masters in exile, José da Silva Carvalho and João Carlos Saldanha. On their return to

Portugal, two Orients coexisted, each with its own Grand Master, and a third was created in Porto, headed by Passos Manuel. It was the age of the consolidation of liberalism and the triumph of the Portuguese freemasons, but also a time of contradictions. Each Obedience was used as an extension of the political factions to help them influence society: Costa Cabral was the best example of this practice.

Until 1869, there was a succession of parallel and rival masonic structures, all interrelated in complicated ways, interrupted by many disagreements. One of the most important organizations was the Grand Orient of Portugal, which adopted a new constitution in 1840. In 1843, there were 80 active lodges, 34 belonging to the Grand Orient of Portugal, 17 to the Freemasons of the North, 15 to the Grande Orient of Silva Carvalho and 11 to the Freemasons of the South, in addition to three or four lodges that were affiliated to the Provincial Lodge of the Grand Orient of Ireland.

A decisive step was taken towards unification in 1869 when several Obediences were merged into the United Grand Orient of Portugal (GOLU), the Supreme Council of Portuguese Freemasons, whose first Grand Master was the Count of Paraty. For half a century it remained relatively united, despite the existence of independent lodges or others affiliated to foreign Orients. However, it was also moving in the opposite direction, with the GOLU joining dozens of Spanish, Romanian and Bulgarian lodges and extending its presence throughout the Portuguese colonial territories, particularly in Cape Verde, Angola and Mozambique. Slowly, from the end of the nineteenth century onwards, Republicanism began to influence the GOLU. Although freemasonry itself did not participate in the Republican revolutionary movement, many masons played a key role in the revolution of 5 October 1910.

During the First Republic, the number of lodges and triangles increased and freemasonry had a profound effect on political, social, economic and cultural life in the country. In this period, almost half of the ministers and members of parliament were masons, including three presidents of the Republic: Bernardino Machado, Sidónio Pais and António José de Almeida. The first and third were also elected Grand Masters of the GOLU. However, internal disputes within the Republican Party led to division, as had been the case under the Liberal monarchy.

Masonic unity, preserved for decades, was challenged in 1914. The reasons cited for the crisis, which apparently concerned matters of jurisdiction and autonomous rites, masked those that were of a political nature. Disagreements emerged between the executive and legislative powers, on the one hand, and the Supreme Council of the 33rd Level of the Ancient Scottish Rite and Acceptance regarding the new Masonic constitution, which was considered a violation of the 1869 agreements that permitted the unification of various Orients and representation of the different rites. The Supreme Council eventually broke away from the GOLU, claiming it had the exclusive right to the Scottish rite and subsequently formed the Luso-Scottish Guild, electing General Augusto Ferreira de Castro to serve as its sovereign Grand Commander. Most of the lodges and triangles associated with this rite joined the new Obedience, representing one third of the Portuguese masons. The confusion between freemasonry and the political struggle discouraged and alienated many members and the number of GOLU members fell to 1,807 in 1919, distributed among 88 lodges. This decrease was due to the departure of those who supported the split and the discontent generated by the division. The Luso-Scottish Guild also resented the demobilization, which affected the 30 lodges under its jurisdiction. Nevertheless, discussions were held between the two Obediences concerning reunification, a difficult process finally accomplished on the eve of 28 May 1926 and the establishment of the military dictatorship, the precursor to the *Estado Novo*. Some refused to compromise and were left out of the merger between the GOLU and the Luso-Scottish Guild. At the end of 1926, there were 3,000 masons in Portugal, organized into 115 lodges and triangles.

Once the dictatorship had been installed in May 1926, restrictions on freedoms began to affect the activities of the freemasons. On 16 April 1929, the headquarters of the GOLU was stormed by police officers and the masons inside were arrested.

From May 1929 until the following year, the Masonic Palace remained closed to prevent further violence. Although no ban had been issued, the GOLU ordered the "triangulation" of all lodges or, in other words, their division into triangles to avoid larger meetings that could easily be discovered by the new authorities. At the end of 1929 the GOLU elected General Norton de Matos its Grand Master, at a time when many masons were imprisoned, in exile or had been deported for opposing the military dictatorship. Due to a lack of members or the impossibility of carrying out their work, dozens of lodges and triangles suspended their activities, even though new offices were founded in the years 1931–1935.

On 19 January 1935, the deputy José Cabral presented a draft bill to the National Assembly which proposed to ban Portuguese citizens from joining secret associations, on pain of sentences that could include imprisonment and exile. Candidates for public office and public sector employees were obliged to swear that they did not, and would not, belong to any secret society.

Fernando Pessoa published an article at the time contesting the ban on free-masonry, but the bill was unanimously approved on 6 April 1935. The Grand Master Norton de Matos resigned and transferred his powers to the Council of the Order and its president, Maurício Costa, who died in 1937.

Luís Gonçalves Rebordão presided over the clandestine GOLU until 1974. On 21 January 1937, the Lusitanian Guild – the public face of the GOLU – was officially dissolved and its assets handed over to the Portuguese Legion. Insignias, possessions and documents were held by the PIDE (International and State Defence Police), but a substantial amount of archive material was saved by masons. During the period of clandestinity, most of the offices disappeared, although others were founded, some-times only for very brief periods of time. In 1974, the Sympathy and Unity, Liberty and José Estêvão lodges in Lisbon, and the Revolt lodge in Coimbra were operational.

The National Salvation Junta, which came to power after 1974, returned the Palace, books and confiscated assets to the freemasons during the period when the government was led by Adelino da Palma Carlos, himself a mason initiated in 1928 at the Dawn Lodge in Lisbon. At the time there were approximately 100 masons and new offices were founded. Luís Gonçalves Rebordão resigned as Grand Master and was replaced by the Grand Master adjunct Dias Amado, who was elected Grand Master in 1975.

GOLU activities continued and a change of name was registered in 1984, when it returned to using its original title of Grand Orient of Portugal. New Obediences emerged later. A split in 1984 removed those who supported closer relations with the United Grand Lodge of England, and the short-lived Grand Lodge of Portugal was founded, without international recognition. This group was established in an official district of the Grand National French Lodge in Portugal and became independent as the Grand Regular Lodge of Portugal in June 1991. Following a split in the latter, the Grand Legal Lodge of Portugal emerged in 1996 and both were reunited in 2012. Other male, female and mixed Obediences with a variety of international links then appeared, sometimes as the result of divisions within other existing organizations.

With a history of almost three hundred years in Portugal, freemasonry was an organization that always had an important presence in political, social and cultural life, extending beyond national borders and also profoundly affected by outside influences.

ANTÓNIO VENTURA
Centre of History, Faculty of Arts and Humanities, University of Lisbon

Bibliography

DIAS, Graça da Silva, DIAS, J. S. da Silva, *Os Primórdios da Maçonaria em Portugal*, 4 vols., Lisbon, Instituto Nacional de Investigação Científica, 1980.

MARQUES, A. H. de Oliveira, *Dicionário da Maçonaria Portuguesa*, 2 vols., Lisbon, Editorial Delta, 1986.

Idem, *História da Maçonaria em Portugal*, 3 vols., Lisbon, Presença, 1990–1997.

VENTURA, António, *Uma História da Maçonaria em Portugal, 1727–1986*, Lisbon, Círculo de Leitores, 2013.

1732

Preoccupations of the Overseas Council: Decline of the Portuguese Diaspora in the World

Portuguese overseas expansion had, from the onset, been driven and sustained by the emigration of millions of Portuguese in three distinct waves between 1400 and 1974 to the overseas imperial territories in the Atlantic Islands, Brazil, Africa and Asia. However, the dispersal of the Portuguese global diaspora was not just limited to these territories but extended to geographical regions that straddled, lay between, and beyond the formal boundaries of the Portuguese empire.

With the exception of its American colonies, the general weakness of the Portuguese economy during the eighteenth century, owing to recurrent crises in the agricultural sectors coupled with a relative lack of industrial development, resulted in unemployment, destitution and poverty in both rural and urban areas, increasing the attractiveness amongst broad sectors of the population to emigrate in search of better prospects. This period represented an unprecedented and identifiable stream of emigration shaped by the movement of family members seeking to join with earlier settled relatives in the various localities of Portuguese America, leading to the creation of extended familial network consolidating a Portuguese diaspora in provinces such as Minas Gerais. Such a significant movement of metropolitan Portuguese sparked by the fame of Brazil's riches fuelled preoccupations on the part of the *Conselho Ultramarino* (Overseas Council) concerned that such a haemorrhaging of people would lead to the general impoverishment of the kingdom. The departure of able-bodied men and entire families resulted in decreased fertility rates, labour shortages, and threatened the agricultural sector that constituted the backbone of the Portuguese economy in regions of the north such as Minho and Douro, and led to an upheaval of village communities. Consequently, legislative measures such as the imposition of a system of passports decreed on the 20th of March 1720 were enforced that sought, albeit with little success, to limit the emigration of "valid men" and control the free movement of metropolitan Portuguese overseas.

The question at hand, however, is whether such efforts on the part of an alarmed metropole were successful in stemming the flow of emigrants and at effectively ending the presence of a global Portuguese diaspora that had decisively departed in the dawn of the sixteenth century. Once the legislation of 1720 revealed itself to be incapable of stemming emigration from Portugal to the empire and within the various colonies, the Overseas Council instituted an additional consultation in 1732, that sought to reinforce and substantiate the reasons for maintaining the existing legislation. Despite these efforts however, simply put, the continued existence of a Portuguese diaspora today would lead us to conclude that these efforts were not wholly successful. However, the difficulty in ascertaining the exact contours and identity of a "Portuguese" diaspora, which is it itself internally variegated by a host of diverse subgroups and identities claiming an imagined or real link to a "Portuguese" identity, thus requires a more complex reckoning with the question at hand.

Portuguese overseas expansion had, from the onset, been driven and sustained by the emigration of millions of Portuguese in three distinct waves between 1400 and 1974 to the overseas imperial territories in the Atlantic Islands, Brazil, Africa and Asia. However, the dispersal of the Portuguese global diaspora was not just limited to these territories but extended to geographical regions that straddled, lay between, and beyond the formal boundaries of the Portuguese empire. Metropolitan anxieties fluctuated between balancing the exigencies of empire that required stimulating (and also forcing) the emigration of metropolitan Portuguese to the colonies, with retaining the demographic integrity and development of an already weakly populated homeland. Frequent implorations from the governors and viceroys of the territories of the State of India, Mozambique, Luanda and the archipelagos of Cape Verde and Guiné, as well as the islands of São Tomé and Príncipe where levels of emigration did not match that to Brazil, provoked attempts by the Crown to promote emigration. However, in the twentieth century, the Portuguese state, fearing uncontrolled migration, was opposed to mass emigration to the colonies prior to World War II thus reflecting earlier anxieties expressed by the Overseas Council two centuries earlier. Nevertheless, the encouragement of the Salazarian regime for mass immigration to the African colonies from the mid-twentieth century onwards, in order to protect and continue the development of the colonies, overrode trepidations as to the potential impact on the metropole. Historically, however, emigration was not solely spurred by the official interests of the Crown. Merchants, artisans, labourers and others emigrated on their own accord in seek of greater opportunities and a better quality of life. The global emigration of Portuguese between 1950 and 1974, for example, was internally driven and stimulated by an externally directed economy. Once again, attitudes on the part of the metropole in response to this wave reflected earlier anxieties regarding the extent to which emigration exacerbated Portuguese underdevelopment.

Importantly, the *longue dureé* of six centuries of Portuguese emigration and patterns of settlement did not result in one homogenous diaspora. In the Portuguese context, therefore, one must in fact talk of *multiple* diasporas. Even in regards to a diaspora very broadly defined, there was no one "Portuguese" community of *estrangeirados* bound together by a single identity that shared a similar sense of collective myth regarding the homeland, or memory of the metropole as the point of reference. The Portuguese diaspora that gradually emerged was itself internally fragmented and "chameleonic", assimilating and resulting into communities able to invoke only a weak biological, ethnic, or cultural link to metropolitan Portugal. Furthermore, the existence of an informal "Shadow Empire" and the movement of so-called Portuguese "tribes" – a designation used to identify groups who maintained a distant link to the Portuguese empire but who lived under the sovereignty of other states or polities, within and outside areas of Portuguese control, adds to a further degree of uncertainty in ascertaining the shape, numbers and persistence of other potential Portuguese diasporas. In Siam, modern day Thailand, from the early sixteenth century onwards, Portuguese diasporas or *bandéis* as they were known, arrived primarily as free trading merchants and mercenaries, reaching their peak between the period of the 1640s and 1660s and managed to survive as a community until the nineteenth century.

The settlement, movement and heterogeneous character of the descendents of Portuguese emigrants who settled in and between the margins of the formal and informal empire, and the emergence of *mestiço* communities especially in Africa, Brazil and Asia, who considered themselves Portuguese variegates this global diaspora even further. High rates of miscegenation, the "creolisation" of many parts of Portuguese world and the multiple identities ("*mestiço*", "*criolo*", "*lusodescendente*", "*filhos da terra*") claiming origins from a Portuguese ethnic identity also reflect the difficulty in conclusively delineating the boundaries of a Portuguese global diaspora.

Diasporas require historicity, i.e. time to form and consolidate and the persistent efforts of subsequent generations of community to retain a sense of communality shaped by cultural or even ideological affinity, by invoking a sense of memory or myth of the homeland and what it meant to be "Portuguese". Do we apply the analytical category of diaspora to the flexible, vast and internally differentiated Lusophone world, and the communities of people who claimed and claim a remote, imagined or actual connection to Portugal? Do we consider colonial and postcolonial elites who self-identify and self-ascribe as Portuguese, and who in their own global diasporas, claim a common link as Portuguese, as a sub-category of a Portuguese global diaspora? Theoretically speaking, true diasporas are said to retain a strong attachment to the homeland and seek to retain an identity and cultural separateness which prevents assimilation within their host society. *Mestiço* or creole descendents of Portuguese settlers often claimed and sought to perpetuate markers of Portuguese identity, be it dress, religion or a way of life, to set them apart from the rest of society, which would indeed constitute them as part of a "true" diaspora. However, would the pluriethnic and hybrid forms of identity of such communities exclude them from the "Portuguese" global diaspora in the strictest sense? The difficulty of unequivocally classifying the heterogeneous world of "Portuguese" communities and individuals who emerged within the body and shadow of the empire as "Portuguese" challenges the notion of a diaspora even further. After the constitutional reforms of 1951, the colonies became "overseas provinces" and thus merely territorial extensions of a now pluricontinental Portugal, rendering subjects into citizens. Did those Portuguese who emigrated to the colonies prior to these reforms, and those who settled after, thus cease to become a diaspora? Would the movement of peoples from the metropole to any territory of the empire then constitute a diaspora or simply a relocation of citizens?

The global movement(s) of the Portuguese is said to have been the first to have taken a people from their homeland to settle in almost every part of the world with the exception of Russia and Central Asia. This continued movement of people continues to question the finality of the decision of the Overseas Council in 1732, considered to the beginning of the end of the Portuguese global diaspora. This doubt is consolidated by the need for a more nuance and complex discussion regarding the movement of a "complex constellation" of communities of people who consider themselves to be Portuguese, and who have settled within, between and beyond the boundaries of the overseas empire, and the construction and survival of a global Portuguese diaspora. Diasporic or "expatriate" Portuguese communities were and are still found in the former territories of the empire, scattered in various countries around Europe particularly France and the United Kingdom, and after unprecedented levels of migration in the twentieth century, North and South America, South Africa, and the Caribbean. The importance of this diaspora for the metropole persisted and remittances by Portuguese emigrants back to families were considerable sources of revenue and support, thus maintaining links of Portuguese diasporic workers to the homeland. Nevertheless, many returned to the homeland as *retornados,* though some went to South Africa, Brazil, Australia and elsewhere, but this happened only because the empire had ceased to exist, and they returned "home". Far beyond the period of 1732, pockets of diasporic "Portuguese" communities continued to emigrate, settle and move between the spaces overseas empire. The remarkable and durable presence of the Portuguese in the world at the beginning of the twenty-first century thus forcefully challenges any notion of the end of Portuguese global diasporas.

NOELLE RICHARDSON
Utrecht University

Bibliography

HAVIK, Philip J., NEWITT, Malynn (eds.), *Creole Societies in the Portuguese Colonial Empire,* Newcastle upon Tyne, Cambridge Scholars Publishing, 2015.

HESPANHA, António Manuel, *Filhos da Terra. Identidades Mestiças nos Confins da Expansão Portuguesa,* Lisbon, Tinta-da-China, 2019.

MORIER-GENOUD, Eric, CAHEN, Michel, "Introduction: Portugal, empire, and migrations – Was there ever an autonomous social imperial space?", in MORIER-GENOUD, Eric, CAHEN, Michel (eds.), *Imperial Migrations: Colonial Communities and Diaspora in the Portuguese World,* Basingstoke, Palgrave Macmillan, 2013, pp. 1–28.

PEREIRA, Miriam Halpern, *A Política Portuguesa de Emigração, 1850–1930,* Lisbon, A Regra do Jogo, 1981.

RUSSELL-WOOD, A. J. R., "A emigração. Fluxos e destinos", in BETHENCOURT, Francisco, CHAUDHURI, Kirti (coords.), *História da Expansão Portuguesa,* vol. 3, Lisbon, Temas e Debates, 1998, pp. 158–168.

1755
History and the Great Lisbon Earthquake

The consequences of the earthquake for Portuguese history and heritage were devastating. The Royal Library, the repository and therefore the greatest symbol of knowledge gathered and administrated by the empire, had almost completely disappeared

On the morning of Saturday 1 November 1755, Lisbon was preparing to celebrate All Saints' Day. The inhabitants of the city were leaving their houses or had already arrived in the churches for the first masses of the day. Little did they know that at around ten o'clock a tremendous earthquake would strike the capital of Portugal, leaving such a massive trail of destruction in its wake that the history of the city would henceforth be divided into two periods: before and after the quake. There were three successive shocks, each several minutes long, lasting until midday. This was followed by a fire which rapidly consumed much of what the earthquake had spared. Finally, as if this were not horrifying enough, the city then saw the waters of the River Tagus begin to rise due to what would nowadays be called a tsunami, which claimed the lives of those who had fled to the port and riverside to escape the tremors. The fire raged for six days and was fiercest in the centre of Lisbon, destroying roads, the port, churches, convents, hospitals, houses and public buildings. The royal palace itself and all its treasures lay in ruins. It is estimated that 30,000 people died.

Periodicals from all over Europe provided reports of the catastrophe in the months which followed. The news circulated in the form of newspaper articles, but also inexpensive treatises, sermons, verses and engravings. From the outset, the devastation of Lisbon – one of the main ports on the Atlantic route and therefore vital to global trade – was met with shock, perplexity and even fear amongst readers. Within a few years, a huge amount of texts had accumulated, including historical narratives, diaries and memoirs published in several languages in different European cities, offering dramatic descriptions of the event and speculating on its causes and moral implications. Some even cited the wrath of God as the explanation for the disaster.

The earthquake also had a strong impact on philosophical thinking. At a time when Enlightenment philosophers were contemplating progress and modernity in the world, it provided an opportune moment for various thinkers to reflect on the limitations of the concept of linear progress advocated by the Enlightenment. Voltaire's *Candide* presented a harsh critique of current ideas on the causes of physical and moral corruption in the world, thus removing the debate on the origins of the earthquake from the sphere of religion – the focus of the more popular publications – and instead proposing a discussion of the nature of good and evil on Earth. In reply, Jean-Jacques Rousseau claimed that it was necessary to examine human guilt and understand the earthquake in relation to the social and cultural context in which it had taken place. Sebastião José de Carvalho e Melo, the Secretary of State and later Marquis of Pombal, not only took responsibility for planning and coordinating the reconstruction of the ruined urban centre, but also commissioned an inquiry into the earthquake. By means of a questionnaire sent to all the parishes in Portugal, he investigated the occurrence and the consequences of the earthquake. The replies provided support for the beginnings of seismology as a modern science. Immanuel Kant then used the report and other information on the Lisbon earthquake to develop a theory of earthquakes as phenomena resulting solely from natural causes.

The consequences of the earthquake for Portuguese history and heritage were devastating. The Royal Library, the repository and therefore the greatest symbol of knowledge gathered and administrated by the empire, had almost completely disappeared. Anything that remained was salvaged and added to new collections, providing the impetus for the creation of a new royal library. Ironically, Lisbon was fated to lose this too, little more than half a century later. When the royal family and court transferred to Rio de Janeiro in 1807–1808, a large portion of the collection was shipped to Brazil in batches between 1810 and 1811, where it nowadays forms part of the National Library collection.

The Royal Archive was also part of the heritage destroyed by the earthquake. Housed at the time in one of the towers of the Lisbon Castle, it stored official documents pertaining to the monarchy, its vassals, the administration of the kingdom, the overseas possessions and relations with other countries. Also known as the Torre do Tombo Archive, it served the royal administration, storing and organizing the documents deposited there. Its purpose was to support the administration, but also preserve the memory of the Crown, its patrimony and activities, in addition to issuing certificates on request. Given the volume and range of its collections, by the first half of the eighteenth century indexes had been created to provide descriptions and locations for the documents.

This wealth of material disappeared when the tower of the castle collapsed. Documents and books were crushed or ripped, bindings destroyed, loose pages and papers scattered and eventually lost. A few thousand documents were retrieved from the rubble – a small fraction of the original collection – and stored temporarily in wooden huts before they were transferred to the south wing of the São Bento Monastery in 1757. There they remained, with new documents later added and, over the course of time, collections transferred there from other institutions. In 1825, for example, the Inquisition archives were transported to the Torre do Tombo. The documents were only rehoused in 1990, in a new building specifically designed to serve as the National Archive, based in the *Cidade Universitária* (University campus) area of Lisbon.

Returning to the earthquake and its consequences, by 2 November 1755 the Archive of the Crown and the Royal Library, whose collections dated back to the fourteenth and fifteenth centuries respectively and documented much of the history of Portugal and its overseas possessions, lay in ruins. However, this loss, which was to a certain extent irreplaceable, did not signify the end of historiography. Although the earthquake had seriously damaged and partially destroyed the material and documentary traces of the empire that were preserved in Lisbon, an enormous number of institutions both within and outside the country still preserved the historical memory of Portugal and its former colonial dominions – starting, naturally, with the *Arquivo Histórico Ultramarino* (Overseas Historical Archive) in Lisbon. These institutions not only house copies of documents originally stored in Portuguese archives, but principally original documentation relating to the colonies which, up to the eighteenth century, were usually known as the "conquests". In terms of the documents referring to the Portuguese overseas possessions that were stored in the Torre do Tombo until 1755, this means that there was another corresponding set of documents and books produced by the administrations of the colonies *in loco*. This was the work of various government centres in each territory and their administrative institutions in America, Africa and Asia.

In fact, ever since they first appeared in Classical Antiquity, archives have served as premises for administrative centralization. During the Roman Empire (27 BC–476 AD), they were an instrument used by its administration. Between the sixteenth and eighteenth centuries, central archives were introduced, established by states which were also in the process of establishing themselves. The emergence of institutions such as the General Archive of Simancas (1540) in Spain, founded and developed as a central archive during the reigns of Charles V and Philip II and, later, the creation of the National Archive of France, a product of the French Revolution (1790), reinforced the notion of the archive as an institution which held the official documentation of the state. Later, the idea of openness and the citizen's right to access archives was also consolidated. During the course of the nineteenth century, standards and rules were created for the work and functioning of archives, establishing archival science as a profession and field of knowledge.

In brief, this is the traditional background to archives, which are still used today to research and write about history. As state institutions and institutions in the service of the state they influence the view of the past according to the libraries, assets and collections which they create and make available, but also through what is not available for consultation. Archives are therefore not only repositories for documents that are intended to be preserved for posterity: they are, first and foremost, places where knowledge is stored and produced. Hence, the location, form and context of archives are just as important for historiography as their contents. From a modern point of view, reflecting the so-called "archival turn", it is understood that archives are cultural artefacts and are themselves producers of facts or, in other words, influence history by making certain types and amounts of documentation available, as well as organizing collections according to classifications that refer to the administrative machinery of the state, or other categorizations. Access to archive material and therefore the histories that can be written on this basis is subject to the contexts determining the existence, maintenance and access to each archive.

The royal archive of Portugal contains the official histories of a centralized and centralizing state, incorporating the administrative apparatus of a government which, in addition to archives, included an official communications system (mail), official press, at a certain point, a National Library and, later, national museums. The history written on the basis of these archives is therefore defined by the question of the nation and its interests, as understood from the nineteenth century onwards. Thus, focussing on the creation and the conditions that determine the existence of archives and libraries broadens the perspective and allows for observation of how the founding of national centralized repositories of information corresponds to the formation of the same institutions and apparatus in the colonies.

The National Archive in Brazil, for example, although founded in Rio de Janeiro in 1838 as the Imperial Archive of Brazil, preserves documentation relative to earlier times, including correspondence on the overseas empire and the archives of King John VI, which were transported from Portugal when the royal court transferred to Rio de Janeiro. Moreover, the state archives of Brazil contain documents such as regulations, charters, decrees and letters from Lisbon, Rio de Janeiro and residents in the former captaincies established in the sixteenth century. The same applies to the archives of Angola, Mozambique, Sri Lanka, Goa, East Timor and Macao, among others.

In addition to the actual archives and libraries, museums can and should be included in efforts to write a more complete and interconnected history of the Portuguese overseas empire. The National Museum in Rio de Janeiro, for example, contained an item known as the Throne of Dahomey (a region in present-day Benin). This carved wooden throne was a replica of the throne of King Kpengla and had been presented by the ambassadors of his grandson, King Adandozan, to the Prince Regent John in 1811. Rather than merely displaying illustrative items, museum collections evoke relations between different kingdoms, potentates and individuals. Those who produce, consume, modify and preserve such items are part of a vast network of interconnected social actors. Their histories can be rediscovered by studying the documentation for the collections, but also the items themselves, taking factors such as materials, style, manufacturing techniques and signs of use into consideration.

The fire which damaged the National Museum in Rio de Janeiro in 2018 destroyed the Throne of Dahomey, demonstrating that, unfortunately, catastrophes such as the earthquake, fire and tsunami that devastated Lisbon in 1755 do not belong to the distant past alone. The current practice of digitalizing museum, library and archive collections is an important initiative designed to avoid the risk of losing historical heritage. In addition, open-access publication of this type of material – exemplified by the Europeana.eu site which offers a digital presentation of almost 60 million items from European archives, libraries, galleries and museums – makes it easier to visualize the historical and thematic links between various collections.

The lost collections from the Torre do Tombo are one of the many interconnected parts of a global history that can be reconstructed and told from a series of different perspectives. Therefore, in order to write a (global) history of Portugal, it is necessary to consult the various archives produced by Portuguese and Luso-American, Luso-African and Luso-Asian communities around the world, which were spared by the 1755 earthquake. The catastrophe conditioned history but did not invalidate it.

MARIANA FRANÇOZO
University of Leiden

Bibliography

ARAÚJO, Ana Cristina et al. (org.), *O Terramoto de 1755: Impactos Históricos*, Lisbon, Livros Horizonte, 2007.

MURTEIRA, Helena, "The Lisbon earthquake of 1755: The catastrophe and its European repercussions", *Economia Global e Gestão*, vol. 10, 2004, pp. 79–99.

SCHWARCZ, Lilia et al., *A Longa Viagem da Biblioteca dos Reis: do Terremoto de Lisboa à Independência do Brasil*, São Paulo, Companhia das Letras, 2002.

STOLER, Ann Laura, "Colonial archives and the art of governance", *Archival Science*, vol. 2, nos. 1–2, 2002, pp. 87–109.

TAVARES, Rui, *O Pequeno Livro do Grande Terramoto: Ensaio sobre 1755*, Lisbon, Tinta-da-China, 2005.

1756
The Demarcation of the Port Wine Region

In the vast amount of literature on the Douro demarcated region, most authors consider it the first wine demarcation in the world, a claim which is only partially true since other European winegrowing regions producing quality wines that were recognized by the market had also been the subject of earlier demarcations.

The first demarcation of the Alto Douro, the region which produces Port wine, was undeniably a pioneering initiative, serving as an instrument for regulating and guaranteeing the quality and authenticity of a variety of wine that had already achieved market recognition, and introducing key notions which were only adopted by the main designations of origin for wine in the twentieth century.

This "primordial demarcation" was, from the outset, associated with other instruments used to regulate the production, transport and trade in fine wines from the Douro region, as well as the creation of an organization with disciplinary powers delegated by the state to oversee the sector, namely the General Company for the Agriculture of the Vineyards of the Upper Douro. As stipulated in Article 29 of the royal license issued on 10 September 1756, it would define the demarcation and the Company would be responsible for producing "a map and general Inventory of the Northern and Southern coasts of the River Douro, defining all the land which produces the genuine shipping wines" or, in other words, the better quality fine wines destined for export which had to be separated from "all other wine from lands where it is only produced to be drunk locally". Hence, it was not only a matter of defining the boundaries of the region which produced "Factory wines", "fine wines" or "shipping wines", as the wines destined to receive the designation "Port" were called at the time. The concept of a register was already being developed, for which it was necessary to specify "each of the large and small estates of this kind, and declare a general estimate or average, calculated on the basis of production over the last five years, of how much each estate usually produces", in order to control the current output of the properties. Given the complex nature of the regional land, Articles 31, 33 and 34 ordered the classification of plots and the quality of the respective wines – including the first- and second-class wines destined for shipping and the "*de ramo*" or table wines, whose maximum prices were set by the document – as well as a system for consignment notes and fire marks which certified the quality and origin of the wine. The founding license, signed by King Joseph and Sebastião José de Carvalho e Melo, the Secretary of State of the Kingdom, endorsed the Company's statutes presented by the "main farmers of *Cima do Douro* (the Upper Douro) and eminent men of the city of Porto" on 31 August 1756, which were elaborated with royal consent, but also with the collaboration – if not guidance and formulation – of Carvalho e Melo. The license would later be supplemented with a large amount of further legislation.

State intervention in the Port wine sector, involving various protectionist measures – most notably the demarcation of the winegrowing region controlled by the Company, which was provided with ample fiscal and jurisdictional powers and also served as a commercial body enjoying certain privileges, monopolies and exemptions – was part of the redefinition of the economic policies identified with Pombaline government. It was mercantilist, in favour of nationalization, and centralist, and aimed to control strategic places and products in the economy of the kingdom while also protecting and subordinating the dominant groups. Since the end of the seventeenth century Port wine had conquered the British market, defeating rival French and Spanish wines, and become the main Portuguese export product, apart from products re-exported from its colony in Brazil. Throughout the early decades of the eighteenth century, an increase in exports and the price of Port wine resulted in the expansion of viticulture in the Douro region to meet the growing demand.

The profits from the wine trade also boosted the number of national and foreign merchants involved in the business, particularly British exporters based in the city of Porto. They not only had more capital and privileged relationships with English importers, but also a headquarters, the British Factory House, which allowed them to defend their interests with regard to the Douro winegrowers from whom they bought the wine, specifically by establishing purchasing prices. At the same time, the exporters valued the wines preferred by the consumer market, thus contributing towards reinforcing or even transforming certain characteristics of the Douro fine wines, such as their strength, colour, sweetness and aroma, which greatly influenced winemaking practices. On the other hand, the reputation these wines enjoyed in the British market and the rise in prices prompted imitations and counterfeits using cheap wines from other regions, which merchants attempted to pass off as Port wines. The Douro fine wine became popular with British consumers in the first half of the eighteenth century. Initially a drink for the upper classes, enjoyed in the most prestigious colleges and at the tables of the aristocracy, it later spread to the lower and less demanding classes and became popular in the pubs of London and other cities.

The commercial crisis during the mid-eighteenth century, which is still poorly defined in many aspects, led to a fall in exports and the price of wine, a situation which worsened during the first half of the 1750s. It was in this context that the interests, not only of the great Douro winegrowers but also the merchants, began to shift. Having founded the Company, this now served as a pretext for Sebastião José de Carvalho e Melo to control this strategic sector of the economy. It is true that state intervention had been preceded by various projects – such as the one launched by the Biscay trader Bartolomeu Pancorbo, who made an unsuccessful attempt to create a joint stock company in order to negotiate, essentially, with the Baltic States – and the court had come under pressure from the leading Douro winegrowers, headed by Luís Beleza de Andrade and Friar João de Mansilha. Nevertheless, the process and final result of the establishment of the General Company for the Agriculture of the Vineyards of the Upper Douro reinforced the state's power over the Porto wine producing region.

The task of demarcating the various winegrowing areas of the Douro, especially those which produced the "Factory wines", only began in September 1757. Undoubtedly, the process was delayed by problems associated with establishing the Company and, above all, the difficulties surrounding the first shipment of wine to Brazil, for which the Company held the exclusive right, as well as the Porto innkeepers' riot in February 1757 in protest against the Company's monopoly on the sale of "*vinho de ramo*" and the brutal interrogations which followed. However, on 28 July 1757, Sebastião de Carvalho e Melo sent the Company director, Beleza de Andrade, detailed instructions, together with a map which included 105 points between Arnelas and Castanheiro do Douro with indications of the categories and prices of the wine, as guidance for the demarcation committee. In little more than three months, between the middle of September 1757 and the beginning of January 1758, the first demarcation was defined for the territory. However, in September 1758, considering that the committee had not followed his instructions to the letter, Carvalho e Melo annulled the demarcation and ordered it to be replaced it with another, to be carried out "with as much haste as possible, before the current wines are blended". The new demarcation was executed in October and November of the same year by positioning granite markers, usually bearing the inscription "FACTORY", along the borders of the vineyards, paid for by the owners. After considering claims and petitions submitted to the king by various farmers in the region whose vineyards had been excluded from the Factory area, additions were made to the 1758 demarcations in 1761, resulting in the inclusion of a few more vineyards. After these additions, the "Factory wines" zone was defined by 335 landmarks. In the vast amount of literature on the Douro demarcated region, most authors consider it the first wine demarcation in the world, a claim which is only partially true since other European winegrowing regions producing quality wines that were recognized by the market had also been the subject of earlier demarcations. They include the winegrowing regions of Chianti, Pomino, Carmignano and Val d'Arno di Sopra in Tuscany, which were defined in an edict issued by the Grand Duke Cosimo III de' Medici on 24 September 1716. The Tokaj-Hegyalja region of Hungary was also demarcated by Emperor Charles VI in a decree issued on 11 March 1737 which defined the lands that could produce wine with "the value and quality of Tokay wines"

Notwithstanding these earlier initiatives – which sought to control the production and transport of some of the most prestigious wines at a time when the international wine trade was expanding, in order to protect their quality and reputation from imitations and ensure advantages for their regions of origin and respective winegrowers – the importance of the Pombaline demarcation of the Port wine region lies in the fact that it was linked to other regulatory instruments, and thus was the pioneer for various features which are characteristic of the present-day controlled appellations of origin. Therefore, in addition to simply defining the boundaries of a winegrowing region, the creation of a register and a classification system for the plots and their respective wines, as well as the introduction of institutional quality control and product certification mechanisms supported by ample legislation, allow the Douro region to be considered the first demarcated and regulated winegrowing region in the world.

The historic continuity of the Pombal demarcation system is equally important, despite the profound transformations which the Douro region and its wines have undergone. In a territory with no political or administrative unity, regional identity was founded on its status as a demarcated territory producing quality wines, regardless of changes in the area and the regional borders – the Demarcated Region of the Douro has expanded from around 40,000 hectares in the Pombaline era to 250,000 since the beginning of the twentieth century, while its eastern borders have been extended from the River Pinhão valley area to the border with Spain – or in the size of vineyards and the amounts produced, winegrowing methods, winemaking processes, varieties of wines, and institutional organization models for this economic sector.

Yet at the same time, from 1756 up to the present day, Port wine has maintained its prestige amongst the great wines of the world, initially by conquering the British market, which became responsible for practically all of its export trade. However, in the last two centuries the consumption of Port wine has spread to an increasing number of countries in all continents. Although Great Britain ceased to be the leading consumer of Port wine in the 1960s, having been overtaken by France and more recently by Belgium, Holland and the Portuguese market itself, it still remains a reference for exceptional quality in certain special categories, in particular vintages and late bottled vintages. Moreover, in the most prestigious international oenophile magazines such as *American Wine Spectator*, and in the most expensive luxury wine auctions, major wine exhibitions and other international wine events, Port wines often rank highest, reinforcing the image of Portugal as one of the leading quality wine producing countries.

GASPAR MARTINS PEREIRA
CITCEM – Transdisciplinary Research Centre "Culture, Space and Memory",
Faculty of Arts and Humanities, University of Porto

Bibliography

FAUVRELLE, Natália (coord.), *Marcos da Demarcação*, Peso da Régua, Museu do Douro, 2007.

FONSECA, Álvaro Baltasar Moreira da, *As Demarcações Pombalinas no Douro Vinhateiro*, 3 vols., Porto, Instituto do Vinho do Porto, 1949–1951.

Instituição da Companhia Geral da Agricultura das Vinhas do Alto Douro, Lisbon, Oficina de Miguel Rodrigues, 1756.

MACEDO, Jorge Borges de, *A Situação Económica no Tempo de Pombal*, 2nd ed., Lisbon, Moraes, 1982.

MARTINS, Conceição Andrade, *Vinha, Vinho e Política Vinícola em Portugal: Do Pombalismo à Regeneração*, 3 vols., PhD History thesis submitted to the University of Évora, Évora, bound copy, 1998.

PEREIRA, Gaspar Martins, "A região do vinho do Porto: origem e evolução de uma demarcação pioneira", *Douro: Estudos & Documentos*, vol. 1, no. 1, Spring 1996, pp. 177–194.

1759–1773
The Suppression of the Society of Jesus

The suppression of the Society of Jesus – a political process that was transnational in nature and global in its effects – began in Portugal and was led by the powerful Marquis of Pombal, chief minister of King Joseph I.

In 1773, the Society of Jesus was declared extinct in the papal brief *Dominus ac Redemptor* issued by Pope Clement XIV. This was the culmination of concerted international action that had started in Portugal some fifteen years earlier, involving several European governments, a great deal of diplomacy and a persistent anti-Jesuit propaganda campaign which had already led to the suppression of the Society of Jesus in Portugal (1759), France (1762–1764), Spain (1767), the Kingdom of Naples (1767) and the Duchy of Parma (1768). It was a political process that was transnational in nature and global in its effects, since the Jesuits were active in various parts of the world.

Founded by Ignatius of Loyola in 1540, the Society of Jesus soon stood out for its solid internal organization, the militancy of its members and its ability to maintain close ties with the papacy. It was therefore possible for the Society to achieve a rapid exponential growth in its membership and social, cultural and political power. By the eighteenth century, it was already overseeing the main network of colleges, seminaries, universities and private teachers in the Catholic states, guaranteeing that it became highly influential among the people and, above all, the elites. Many Jesuits also became confessors to monarchs, political dignitaries and the high nobility, which ensured they had powerful political influence. Moreover, the institution invested a great deal in spreading the Catholic faith in the overseas empires of Portugal, Spain and France, where it became known for its role in the resettlement, administration and religious instruction of indigenous peoples, in addition to its presence in territories that were not ruled by the European empires (e.g. Japan, Mughal India, Ethiopia and the Congo). Meanwhile, on the pretext of financing this system, the Society of Jesus was always very actively engaged in securing economic resources by means of donations and its own investments, thus accumulating an enormous patrimony in terms of properties and rents.

All this power, influence and wealth made the Society of Jesus the target for increasing criticism and hostility, particularly from within the Church and from political and intellectual spheres. The other religious orders and the secular clergy envied its success and the privileges it received from the Roman Curia. Some influential theological and doctrinal currents – namely Gallicanism and Jansenism – considered the Jesuits one of their main adversaries. So did the reformist rulers and statesmen identified with Catholic Enlightenment, who accused the Jesuits of opposing their reformist agenda and political goal of total subordination of the Church to the absolute power of the monarchy. Even the emerging and influential Enlightenment movement itself soon represented the Jesuits as symbols of the backward politics and ideology of the Ancien Régime. In addition to other factors which were specific to each country, these various sources of anti-Jesuit feelings, which were largely independent of each other, converged from the mid eighteenth century onwards to create an environment that was conducive to taking measures against the Jesuits and their acceptance by public opinion.

The process that culminated in the suppression of the Society of Jesus began in Portugal and was led by the powerful Marquis of Pombal (Sebastião José de Carvalho e Melo, 1698–1782), the chief minister of King Joseph I. The reasons why Portugal and Pombal assumed this role are still not entirely clear. Although it is likely that Carvalho e Melo became aware of criticism of the Jesuits during his diplomatic missions to London and Vienna in the years 1738–1749. There is no evidence to suggest that he had conceived of an anti-Jesuit agenda before entering the government in 1750, or that his first measures were part of a concerted international plan to attack the Society of Jesus. His anti-Jesuitism only became consistent, systematic and even obsessive during the time he served as a minister and would have begun in reaction to Jesuit opposition to his political rise to power. Over time, however, anti-Jesuitism became a useful and powerful political expedient, serving either to legitimize successes and failures of the government, or to be used as a propaganda weapon, an instrument of foreign policy, or even one of the main elements that forged political and ideological cohesion within Pombalism.

As the sequence of events has already been explored extensively, a brief description will suffice here. It all began in South America, where the Society of Jesus was developing active resistance, at first to the 1750 Treaty of Madrid, even organizing a mass uprising of the Guaraní people of Uruguay, and later against certain measures decreed for Brazil between 1755 and 1757, namely those intended to ensure the freedom of the indigenous peoples and the civil administration of their settlements, as well as others intended to reorganize the economic development of Amazonia. Pombal considered this opposition intolerable, in the case of the former because it created a diplomatic problem and constituted a challenge to the sovereignty of the two Iberian monarchies, and in the latter case because it was in direct defiance of the new colonial policy devised for Brazil. However, the crucial factor that led Pombal to launch a systematic attack on the Jesuits concerned their role in the intense political struggle in the metropole that aimed to halt his rise to power. In retaliation, the Jesuits were accused, with varying degrees of evidence, of being involved in almost all forms of resistance to the new power, including the protests against the newly created Grão-Pará Company (1755); the campaign of criticism and defamation of the government which included sermons preached in churches, the spread of false news and, in particular, their political activities behind the scenes; the riots in Porto against the new Douro Wine Company (1757) and, above all, the attempted regicide in September 1758. These accusations were followed by actual punitive measures. In Brazil various members of the Society of Jesus were deported back to the kingdom, while in Portugal the backlash included the trial of the priest Gabriele Malagrida, the expulsion from the palace of the Jesuit confessors to the king and the royal family and the establishment of an investigation and reform procedures for the Society of Jesus, in April 1758. Although lacking sufficient evidence, the allegation that the Society of Jesus had been involved in the attack on the king served as justification to deliver the final blow. The verdict delivered on 12 January 1759, sentencing several defendants to the death penalty, had declared the Jesuits the moral authors of the attack and was followed by the royal charter of 19 January, reaffirming that the Society of Jesus as a whole was responsible for the crime, thus broadening the accusations and blaming it for the crimes of "lèse-majesté, rebellion, high treason and parricide". Hence, it ordered the seizure of its assets and income and placed all its members under house arrest. Finally, the decree issued on 3 September 1759 banished the Society of Jesus from the kingdom and its overseas dominions, transferred its assets to the Crown and ordered all Jesuits to be rounded up in Lisbon for deportation to the Papal States or imprisonment.

From the beginning of the offensive, the Portuguese government and Pombal's inner circle were particularly concerned to justify their measures on the basis of political, theological, legal and historical arguments. The ongoing task of producing an anti-Jesuit discourse – which Pombal himself took charge of, together with some of his closest associates such as José de Seabra da Silva and António Pereira de Figueiredo – systematically took shape in the form of documents with restricted circulation, the wording of legislation and, above all, books, opuscules and pamphlets, many of which were translated – mainly into French, Italian, Spanish and German – and circulated throughout Europe. In addition to news frequently published in the gazettes of various countries and the production of a substantial amount of iconography, this material was not only designed to legitimate the decisions that had been taken, but was also clearly intended to create a media campaign to influence enlightened public opinion and decision makers in other countries. This mediatization and mobilization of public opinion, on an unprecedented scale within European culture, is important evidence of the transnational nature of the process.

It is not only the media and diplomatic initiatives of the Portuguese government that should be credited with the broad international projection of the measures taken by Portugal against the Jesuits. It was also fuelled and magnified by intellectual, ecclesiastical and political circles in Europe, including the Roman Curia itself, that were committed to attacking the Society of Jesus and would eventually link up to generate of wave of anti-Jesuitism. It is from this perspective that the initiatives introduced in France by various parliaments and the courts from 1761 onwards should be understood. In Spain, faced with the major accusation of having been the force behind the violent popular riots of 1766, the institution was abolished in 1767, its assets seized by the Crown and its members imprisoned and expelled, following procedures that were very similar to those used in Portugal. The same procedures were then deployed in the Kingdom of Naples and the Duchy of Parma. From then on, all the said governments intensified their combined diplomatic efforts with a view to obtaining a statement from the pope on the total abolition of the Society of Jesus, which was issued in 1773.

It is not easy to provide an overview of the effects of the suppression of the Society of Jesus, a complex matter surrounded by controversy from the outset. From the Jesuit perspective, the results were disastrous, destroying its work, political influence and economic power worldwide for several decades. From the opposite perspective, the consequences varied according to the country and the subject at stake. Politically, it served the reformist and regalist purposes of enlightened absolutism and helped reinforce the authority of the metropolitan governments in the colonial world. Moreover, the anti-Jesuit campaign fuelled the rise of the Enlightenment and some authors would argue that the eradication of the Jesuits was crucial to paving the way for the French Revolution and the establishment of Liberalism. Within the Catholic Church, it created a new balance, ultimately reinforcing the secular clergy and other congregations, as was the case in Portugal with the Oratorians. In terms of education, the sudden departure of the Jesuits disrupted the entire system and made it necessary for various reforms to be introduced, including a trend towards secularization, the results of which were slow to emerge.

Virtually the same can be said of scientific knowledge and experimentation, an area in which, despite the criticisms levelled against them, the Jesuits had made some remarkable contributions. With regard to the economic effects, in general they fell short of expectations. A portion of the Jesuit revenue and assets was transferred to other ecclesiastical or public institutions; another portion, particularly the rural and urban estates, ended up in private hands, often through donations or sales at below market prices, while those that remained with the Crown did not swell the public coffers due to various difficulties and the costs involved in their direct administration. Hence, with few exceptions, the public finances of the various states involved in the process did not benefit particularly from the seizure of the assets, revenue and net wealth of the Society of Jesus, nor did the redistribution of Jesuit property lead to any significant change in the social or economic model in the countries and regions affected by this measure.

José Vicente Serrão
ISCTE – University Institute of Lisbon

Bibliography

BURSON, Jeffrey D., WRIGHT, Jonathan (eds.), *The Jesuit Suppression in Global Context: Causes, Events, and Consequences*, Cambridge, Cambridge University Press, 2015.

FRANCO, José Eduardo, *O Mito dos Jesuítas em Portugal, no Brasil, no Oriente e na Europa*, 2 vols., Lisbon, Gradiva, 2006.

LEITE, Edgard, *Notórios Rebeldes: A Expulsão da Companhia de Jesus da América Portuguesa*, Madrid, Fundación Histórica Tavera, 2000.

VAN KLEY, Dale K., *Reform Catholicism and the International Suppression of the Jesuits in Enlightenment Europe*, New Haven/London, Yale University Press, 2018.

VOGEL, Christine, *Guerra aos Jesuítas: A Propaganda Antijesuítica do Marquês de Pombal em Portugal e na Europa*, Lisbon, Círculo de Leitores/Temas e Debates, 2017.

1807
The Transfer of the Portuguese Royal Court to Brazil

Around 10,000 people left Lisbon on 27 November of 1807, accompanying the regent and the royal family. They disembarked at different points on the Brazilian coast between Paraíba and Rio de Janeiro, while the regent himself arrived in Salvador on 22nd January 1808 and reached Rio on 7 March. Many more set sail for Brazil in the years which followed.

The transfer of the Portuguese royal family and court to Brazil is a difficult subject to address with impartiality. The Brazilian perspective is rarely free of a certain teleological bias, viewing the episode as the founding of Brazil. The metropolis was "interiorized", according to an interesting interpretation presented by the Brazilian historian Maria Odila Leite da Silva Dias, the colonial status was profoundly altered with the opening up of ports to friendly nations (given the advantages conceded to the English under the 1810 treaties), foreign travellers could circulate within the interior of the territory and the Bank of Brazil, Royal Mint and Press were created. Hence there is a positive aspect to the event, which is often highlighted: the arrival of the court paved the way for independence, and what could have been seen as a shameful act became dignified in association with the birth of the nation. In a classic study published in 1907, the Brazilian diplomat and historian Manoel de Oliveira Lima considered the transfer proof of the competence and ability to compromise displayed by Prince John, who was regent at the time as his mother, Queen Mary I, suffered from dementia, arguing that he had performed better than other contemporary deposed European sovereigns who ruled over second- and third-rate monarchies. From the Portuguese perspective, there was a wide-ranging debate on the faint-heartedness of a ruler who hastily abandoned his kingdom to its fate, with the French about to enter Lisbon, and took the entire royal family with him – including the heir, Prince Peter, thus violating the law of the land according to expert opinions at the time. This was followed by critical and defamatory epithets from the anti-monarchist, liberal and socialist authors of the late nineteenth and early twentieth centuries, including Oliveira Martins and António Sérgio, who viewed Prince John as a coward as well as a poor ruler. On the other hand, for the historians of the Portuguese *Estado Novo*, Prince-Regent John was a magnificent figure who had planned everything with great astuteness and managed to keep the project a secret.

At the end of the twentieth century, more "structural" analyses examined the event in the context of the general crisis in the old colonial system, as can be seen in the studies by the Brazilian authors Caio Prado Jr. and Fernando Novais, which were discussed and even contested with regard to certain points by Portuguese historians such as Valentim Alexandre. In considering the long term, the general outlines of phenomena which had much in common were highlighted while disregarding their unique aspects, and the ideas behind the structures were foregrounded, virtually obscuring those associated with the events. On the other hand, when the scholars turned their attention to events, they essentially emphasized their originality and lost sight of the whole. Hence, the long-term perspective was neglected in favour of selecting a singular manifestation of short-term events – the years 1807–1808, the removal of the court to a part of its empire, the first European monarch to set foot on American soil – represented as an isolated episode, floating like a bubble over other comparable contemporary experiences. Since anecdotal, unusual and bizarre stories were widespread, this was an example, even if unconscious, of a long tradition of prejudice and defamation typical of north European countries whenever they voiced their opinions of southern Europeans, from at least the seventeenth century onwards.

In eighteenth-century Europe, the Iberian kingdoms were to a large extent disparaged. Referring to the "disdainful superiority typical of the Iberian people", Giacomo Leopardi asks, in his *Zibaldone*: "but who considers the Portuguese and the Spanish, when referring to civilized nations?" In the late 1720s, the French traveller Silhouette claimed, in a brief memoir, that Portuguese was a Spanish dialect, the Portuguese government imitated the Spanish one and the Portuguese court copied the Madrid court in all aspects, in order to not seem inferior. Accounts of the transfer of the court were adversely influenced by this pre-existing and deep-rooted censorious tradition: the court was depicted as ridiculous and backward, and Prince John as obese, obtuse and obsessed with eating chicken. These images circulated on both sides of the Atlantic, reaching educated elites and ordinary people alike, and found their way into films and books that became best sellers, including Laurentino Gomes' highly successful *How a mad Queen, a fearful King and a corrupt court tricked Napoleon and changed the History of Portugal and Brazil* (2007). Hence the true meaning of the transfer of the Lisbon government to Rio de Janeiro was simplified and old prejudices such as those expressed by Silhouette were reformulated and reabsorbed.

Oliveira Lima revealed the impasse facing the smaller powers in a world dominated by titans, whilst also highlighting the importance which these apparently subaltern players then acquired, which Great Britain, after Utrecht, understood very well. Ingeniously, the British power almost always succeeded in maintaining close relations with the most important kingdoms of the south: Portugal, its old ally, with whom it had strengthened ties after the Restoration; Sardinia, with its capital in Turin; the Kingdom of Naples, later known as the Two Sicilies.

On the basis of Oliveira Lima's work, the transfer of the Portuguese court to Rio de Janeiro can be considered from an international perspective and associated with other analogous phenomena. Thus, Portugal's downfall as a result of the French Invasion is undoubtedly related to the earlier abdication of King Charles Emmanuel IV of Savoy in December 1798, as well as the flight of Ferdinand I of Naples under the same circumstances, when both monarchs settled in their Mediterranean possessions, namely Sicily – where the court was established in Palermo – and Sardinia – where it took refuge in Cagliari. Subsequently, Portuguese diplomats sent to these two Italian courts incessantly warned the regent and his ministers about what could happen to Portugal. The Italian kings soon returned to the continent, following the short-lived victories of their allies, and remained there until 1806. However, between the end of January and the beginning of February they took refuge in their respective islands for the second time, as Portuguese diplomats and politicians became increasingly fearful of the fate of their own kingdom. At the end of the year, when Napoleon ordered the Continental Blockade of English ships on 21 November, the situation worsened and pressure to define Portuguese alignment intensified. In 1807, Russia and Prussia surrendered to France in Tilsitt on 7 and 9 July, respectively. On 27 October, following the Treaty of Fontainebleau, it was the turn of Spain which, by means of secret clauses, opened its territory to the French troops to enable them to invade Portugal.

Although well documented, the period leading up to the escape is unclear and has been subject to various different and even contradictory interpretations. Amid a climate of extreme tension and conflicting reports and under constant pressure from the great powers, Portugal sought to preserve an impossible neutrality, wavering between a French alliance and alignment with England. Among the factions that formed, the two most significant were led by António de Araújo Azevedo, the future Count of Barca and French sympathizer, and Rodrigo de Sousa Coutinho, later Count of Linhares, who aligned with the English. This rivalry continued in Rio de Janeiro, where the two great figures of the time opposed each other until Linhares' death in 1812.

The nature of the transfer is also subject to debate. Had it been carefully planned in advance or was it a chaotic escape, carried out in a disorderly and hasty manner? Although there are specific examples from the sixteenth century onwards which indicate that the transfer of the head of the kingdom to America may have been contemplated – invoked by Tomé de Sousa, the Prior of Crato and António Vieira – the idea only took shape in the eighteenth century, mainly due to Portugal's frailty in the face of the intensifying political struggle in Europe. A range of documentary evidence indicates that this possibility had been part of the political horizon since at least the early 1790s, when the English were already pressurizing the court to move to Rio de Janeiro and facilitate British access to the Southern Atlantic. In the second half of the decade the idea was reinforced in some of the best known texts by Rodrigo de Sousa Coutinho and in dispatches sent by his brother, Domingos de Sousa Coutinho, the future Marquis of Funchal, when he was serving as diplomatic envoy to the Sardinian court. In these documents, as well as in conversations attributed to leading figures in the court, there are echoes of a much older idea that the riches of Brazil would tip the scales in its favour to the detriment of the small kingdom: in the eighteenth century, when the revenue from the slave trade was largely responsible for shifting the axis of the Portuguese empire to the Southern Atlantic, the ambassador Luís da Cunha predicted that the future of the Portuguese empire would lie in Portuguese America. At the end of the century, the idea of a Luso-Brazilian empire was strengthened on the basis of erudite concepts presented by men such as Rodrigo de Sousa Coutinho and the Brazilian Hipólito da Costa. This tradition considerably relativizes the interpretation of the transfer as a disorderly stampede and the same may be said of the discussions between ministers concerning the possibility of sending Prince Peter, the regent's heir, to Brazil, thereby protecting, in America, the dynasty that was being threatened in Europe.

In conclusion, the transfer of the Portuguese royal court to Brazil should be analyzed from two perspectives. From a long-term point of view, it is necessary to recall the evolution of the notion of a possible change in the political axis of the empire, which could be virtually relocated from Lisbon to one of the coastal towns of Brazil. However, the short-term perspective of the actual events implies that they should be considered in relation to similar phenomena, such as the collapse of the lower-ranking royal houses and monarchies which, nevertheless, still played a significant role in the European context.

Around 10,000 people left Lisbon on 27 November of 1807, accompanying the regent and the royal family. They disembarked at different points on the Brazilian coast between Paraíba and Rio de Janeiro, while the regent himself arrived in Salvador on 22nd January 1808 and reached Rio on 7 March. Many more set sail for Brazil in the years which followed, resulting in a considerable population shift which should also be compared with others, such as the anti-Revolution immigrants who left France in 1789 and moved around various European and even American cities.

The transfer of the court was therefore a complex but not entirely original phenomenon. Its historical significance was, however, unique, due to the overseas status of the Portuguese empire. Although both the Italian courts cited here as comparisons took refuge in two of their dominions which did not border on their country – the islands of Sardinia and Sicily – the Portuguese court settled in an enormous and extremely wealthy region. Interestingly, after the crisis which swept through Europe at the turn of the nineteenth century, the ruling houses of Savoy, Bourbon-Naples and Braganza returned to their capitals and were able to restore the monarchies that had seemed irredeemably lost in 1807.

Laura de Mello e Souza
Sorbonne University

Bibliography

LIGHT, Kenneth, *A Viagem Marítima da Família Real: A Transferência da Corte Portuguesa para o Brasil*, Rio de Janeiro, Jorge Zahar, 2008.

LIMA, Manuel de Oliveira, *Dom João VI no Brasil*, 4th ed., Rio de Janeiro, Topbooks, 2006.

PEDREIRA, Jorge, COSTA, Fernando Dores, *Dom João VI: Um Príncipe entre Dois Continentes*, São Paulo, Companhia das Letras, 2008.

PEREIRA, Angelo, *Os Filhos d'el Rei Dom João VI: Reconstituição Histórica com Documentos Inéditos Que, na Sua Maioria, Pertenceram ao Real Gabinete*, Lisbon, Empresa Nacional de Publicidade, 1946.

PART V | The Modern Period

Introduction to Part V

From the Independence of Brazil to Portuguese Global Emigration

ANTÓNIO COSTA PINTO

Instituto de Ciências Sociais, Universidade de Lisboa

At the beginning of this period, Portugal found herself embroiled in the crises of the ancien régimes and liberal revolutions that were sweeping across Europe between the end of the eighteenth and beginning of the nineteenth centuries. The flight of the Portuguese Crown to Brazil, the Napoleonic wars and the cycle of liberal revolutions, civil wars and consolidation of liberalism put Portugal into tune with broader European dynamics. The great waves of revolutions and the consolidation of liberalism (1820, 1830 and 1848), the crisis of democracies in the "Era of Fascism" (1918–1945) and finally, its participation in the "Era of Decolonization" (1945–1974) meant that Portugal was well integrated into the great processes of political and social change to the point of becoming a pioneer of the so-called third wave of democratizations that occurred in Southern Europe in the 1970s.

When we observe the dynamic of change in Portugal in the Modern period in interaction with global history, we can see that the Conference of Berlin at the end of the nineteenth century, with its great impact on Portugal and her African colonies, was a decisive factor in the emergence of republican nationalism and its persistence until decolonization in the 1970s.

The Republican revolution of 5th October 1910 was an early example of such political phenomena in the European context, one of a cycle of "democratic revolutions" that stretched from Russia in 1905 to Mexico in 1911. Though most of those that Charles Kurzman called "positivist revolutions" were ultimately defeated, in Portugal the republican regime survived triumphantly, despite the participation of Portuguese troops in the First World War. With its African colonies threatened by some of the European powers recently arrived at the carving-up of Africa (such as Germany), the young republican regime forced its intervention in the war also to legitimize itself domestically. Its entrance into that conflict on the initiative of the republican elite provoked an almost immediate reaction from their conservative counterparts with the coup d'état commanded by Sidónio Pais. This short dictatorship (1917–1918), with its charismatic leader and attempt to create a single party and corporative representation, launched the cycle of dictatorships in Europe. Supported by the Catholic Church in marked reaction to the anticlericalism of the republic, this event coincided with the apparitions of Fatima in 1917, a phenomenon which profoundly touched the religiosity of the Portuguese and rapidly assumed international proportions within the framework of the expanded Marian cult.

Although the "*Estado Novo*" of Oliveira Salazar was part of the "Era of Fascism",

with some of its institutions directly inspired by Italian fascism, the regime's consolidation during the 1930s gave it an external image that was considerably more powerful
than its propaganda services could have imagined. In fact, from the Baltic republics
to Latin America, Salazarism was considered by some to be a third (authoritarian and
anticommunist) way between fascism and democracy, perceived as a model to be
followed by many segments of the conservative elite, who supported its catholicism
and corporativism.

After the Second World War, with the onset of the Cold War, Salazarism tended
to be considered as a lesser evil by the western powers, led by the USA. To a large
extent, this attitude explains how a country with a dictatorial regime could be so swiftly
integrated into NATO and the new international order. However, in contrast, it did
have one dissonant element that would prove to be its most decisive challenge after
1945: its resistance to decolonization. In this scenario, Portugal ended up assuming a
fundamental role in the establishment of a new postcolonial and post-imperial global
order, for decades opposing a process that seemed unstoppable and which, to a certain
extent, had begun with the Independence of the US from England in the last quarter
of the eighteenth century. Although it had not yet become a relatively isolated state,
Portugal was on the margins of the international community. Despite this, Salazarism
managed to resist strong international pressure for various decades, even earning
political, economic and military support for its resistance to decolonization on the part
of countries like France, the Federal Republic of Germany, and even, from time to
time, from the United States. In the 1960s, right in the middle of the Colonial War,
Portugal managed to join the European Free Trade Association (EFTA) on the initiative of the United Kingdom, and experienced mass emigration to Europe, an
important factor in the economic growth associated also to the increase in European
investment in the country. There was social and also cultural modernization, despite
this being stigmatized with the triad of "Fatima, football and fado", which associated
Fatima to the massification of sport (symbolised by the outstanding performance of
Eusébio in the 1966 World Cup) and the internationalization of fado that consolidated
as the "Portuguese song form".

The capacity for survival of this authoritarian and colonial regime was thus an
example of resistance to global dynamics, which explains, if only partially, the unique
nature of its downfall – though a military coup d'état, led by sectors of the armed forces
that doubted the regime's abilit to win the wars being waged in the African colonies.

In the new phase that then opened in the life of Portugal and its relationship with
the world, the country became an involuntary pioneer of the third wave of democratizations, followed shortly after by Greece (1975) and its neighbour Spain (1977). In
mid Cold War, to the surprise of many in the international community, the rupture
of 25th April 1974 and above all the crisis of state that followed, with a simultaneous
process of decolonization and democratization marked by a "pre-revolutionary'
context, thrust Portugal onto the international stage. Political radicalization, manifested with particularly intensity in 1975, motivated an important international
intervention on the part of the main countries of Western Europe, the United States
and the eastern bloc led by the Soviet Union, putting the country at the crossroads of
the last "revolutionary crisis" associated to the radical left of twentieth century Europe.
As yet unrecovered from the crises of 1968 and 1969 that had rocked France and Italy,
it was with some distrust that the European democracies observed and monitored a
rupture which, though presented in the official version as a split between democracy

and pro-Soviet communism, found new political and social agents with strongly transgressive social movements protagonizing the political conflict in Portugal. The dynamic of land occupation, nationalizations, and the radicalization of social conflict, with military actors and civilians of the extreme left, rapidly antagonized by forms of conservative mobilization, transformed the country into a stage for global intervention. Both the United States and the European democracies used models like those that had been applied in Italy after the Second World War to support the consolidation of democracy in Portugal, infiltrating parties, organizations of interest and the media, and animating some more violent structures in order to offset what was viewed as a dangerous communist and revolutionary threat.

It was in this short period that power was transferred to the liberation movements in the Portuguese colonies, and countries like Cape Verde, Guiné-Bissau, São Tomé and Príncipe, Angola and Mozambique experienced the rapid transition to Independence. This almost simultaneous withdrawal of Portugal from its colonies thus ended late colonialism and resistance to decolonization. One of the consequences of this process, in the case of Angola, was a contribution to the localized radicalization of the Cold War, with the direct military intervention from Cuba and South Africa, and indirect intervention from the Soviet Union and United States, prolonging the fighting in that territory until the twenty-first century.

Once democracy had been achieved and decolonization consummated, the conditions were in place for Portugal to join the European Union in 1986. This quickly became an important driver of profound economic and social change in the country, including the creation of a market economy, which became a determining agent of globalization, as well as providing the gradual synchronization of Portugal with the framework of Western Europe from the 1980s.

All of these issues are developed in more detail in the pages that follow.

1822
Brazilian Independence: The Global and the Specific

It was Europe, the hub of world domination, that lay at the heart of this global conflict. The Portuguese and Spanish empires were part of a network over which the British empire was exerting its hegemony: by the early nineteenth century it was beginning to overcome the negative effects of USA independence and to enjoy the benefits of its industrial revolution.

There can be no doubt that the date on which Brazil emerged as an independent political state should be 7 September 1822, during the "age of revolutions" and clashes between modern empires. However, this cannot be considered the only possible perspective. It was the intensification of the old rivalry between France and England that formed the background to the American Revolution of 1776, and the momentous Haitian Slave Revolt (1789–1804) took place under the influence of the French Revolution. These are experiences that must be taken into consideration in order to understand what happened in other American colonies: in 1811 in Colombia, Ecuador and Venezuela; in 1813 in Paraguay; in 1815 in Uruguay;

in 1816 in Argentina; in 1818 in Chile; in 1821 in Mexico and Peru; in 1822 in Brazil; in 1825 in Bolivia.

However, it was Europe, the hub of world domination, that lay at the heart of this global conflict. The Portuguese and Spanish empires were part of a network over which the British empire was exerting its hegemony: by the early nineteenth century it was beginning to overcome the negative effects of USA independence and enjoy the benefits of its industrial revolution and a political system based on naval supremacy and the defence of free trade.

In this context, the role played by Portugal was not insignificant due, above all, to the importance of Brazil as a source of raw materials (cotton and sugar) and as a consumer market for finished products. Moreover, with the destruction of part of the French fleet at Trafalgar in October 1805, the Lusitanian fleet, like that of Denmark, was envied.

This increasing importance would put the traditional neutrality of Lisbon foreign policy to the test. In launching the Continental Blockade on 21 November 1806, France anticipated occupation of the Portuguese colonies if Prince Regent John opted to become pro-British. England did the same. Between 1805 and 1806, it drew up a secret plan which involved sending two fleets – one to Rio de Janeiro and the other to Lisbon, to collect the Portuguese royal family – if the regent weakened before Paris. Under this plan, the main ports in Brazil would always be occupied. In response to the Portuguese negotiations with London, the French, in alliance with the Spanish, proceeded to sign the Treaty of Fontainebleau in October 1807, under which Portugal, when conquered, would be divided between the families of Napoleon and the Spanish politician Godoy, and the empire would be shared between France and Spain, whose monarch would be promoted to Emperor of the Two Americas.

A few days later, in November 1807, an English fleet with almost 7,000 men on board blockaded the Tagus estuary. Prince Regent John had still not publicly breached his neutrality but, given the imminent arrival of the French in Lisbon, set sail for "his" "States of Brazil" on the 29th of the same month, taking 36 vessels with him (18 warships and 25 merchant vessels), personal and public property, a precious library and a sizeable retinue (12,000 to 15,000 staff), which included a large part of the Portuguese elite. This was not a makeshift solution: it had been shielded by the Secret Convention of 22 October 1807, designed and executed by Canning, Strangford and Sydney Smith and negotiated, on behalf of Portugal, by the Anglophile ambassador Domingos de Sousa Coutinho. It contained the promise that if Prince John had to "transfer to Brazil", the king of England, George III, would offer assistance, including naval support. The idea was rooted in the old practice of the itinerant court and, in the light of the values of the Ancien Régime, could not be described as escape, abandonment or exile, but as the transfer of the seat of power to another location within the dominions of the monarch. The possibility of this practice re-emerged at the end of the eighteenth century, contemplated by, amongst others, figures such as Pombal, Luís da Cunha and Rodrigo de Sousa Coutinho. The latter – an Anglophile and the brother of Domingos, who would become one of the regent's main counsellors – recalled the practice once again in 1803, emphasizing that for Portugal, even if it was "devastated by a long and bloody war", there would still remain "its Sovereign and its peoples, to create a powerful empire in Brazil from whence it could return to reconquer what may have been lost in Europe and to wage an eternal war against the savage enemy that refused to recognize the Neutrality of a Power that had expressed its desire to preserve it".

This was the period in which, following the Pombaline Reforms (which included the University) and a rise in exports, the role of Brazil within the economy of the empire was further consolidated and its educated elites were integrated into the political, administrative and religious cadres within the empire.

In going to Brazil, Prince John avoided the fate which Napoleon reserved for Charles IV and Ferdinand VII of Spain, namely abdication, and ensured that he remained in possession of his territories and coveted navy. Yet the main victor was Great Britain, which saw its political and military supremacy strengthened during the Peninsular War, and the Foreign Office strategy of dismantling Portuguese "mercantilist" protectionism justified.

Fulfilling his promise under the Secret Convention, the regent opened Brazilian ports to foreign trade on 28 January 1808 and revoked "all bans on the establishment of factories in the State of Brazil" on 1 April 1808, a provision reaffirmed by the Strangford Treaty of 18 January 1810 and by decree on 15 October 1810. Whereas, at the beginning of the nineteenth century, Portugal's balance of trade with Great Britain (including the contribution from Brazil) showed unprecedented surpluses, which had troubled the British, the new legislation displeased the Brazilian sectors and led to a decline in trade and industry in Portugal, particularly in Lisbon and Porto. On the other hand, it reinforced British influence in the South Atlantic, and therefore those who argue that the 1807 Convention was more an attempt to take over the Brazilian market than to save the Portuguese monarchy are to some extent justified.

Prince John based his court in Rio. In Europe (and in Portugal), popular and Anglo-Portuguese resistance to the French legitimized his prolonged absence – in the Iberian Peninsula, the conflict ended on 10 April 1814. Having defeated Napoleon, the victors endeavoured to rebalance the international political order to restore the borders that had existed before the conflict. This was the task allotted to the Congress of Vienna between 1814 and 1815, resulting in the Holy Alliance, celebrated on 26 September 1815, originally composed of the anti-Liberal nucleus of victorious empires (Austria, Prussia and Russia), but transformed into the Quadruple Alliance when England joined later in the year. In Vienna, Portugal proved unsuccessful in its diplomatic struggle for the restitution of Guiana and Olivença, and in its mission to revise the onerous 1810 trade and navigation treaty. However, even though the information was not fully documented, it would not have been indifferent to the debate on the advantages of maintaining the Portuguese court in Rio. One faction close to the English saw a return to the metropole as a means of strengthening a movement opposed to the possible re-emergence of alliances between the French and the Spanish, and of allowing the British greater freedom to dominate trading in South America. Another French-influenced faction proposed restructuring Portuguese imperial ambitions in the Tropics as a means of fighting more effectively against the wave of decolonization, whilst also hindering the advance of English imperialism.

The decision of the Prince Regent to create the United Kingdom of Portugal, Brazil and the Algarves in December 1815 would not have been unconnected with the French proposal presented by Talleyrand to the Count of Palmela. Brazil was therefore changed from a colonial viceroyalty to an autonomous kingdom, although this did not have any major impact. In the metropole, however, it was seen as yet another sign that the man who was still regent would not return. Moreover, events such as the adoption of the new symbology of power, the marriage of Prince Peter and the coronation of King John – which had led to widespread discontent – appeared to point in the same direction.

The dissatisfaction with the cost of the Rio "court society" and the burden of the centralism of absolutist government, growing inequalities between the provinces with regard to taxation, and revolts in the Spanish colonies radicalized protests, which included the Pernambucan Revolt of 7 March 1817, an anti-centralist, Republican, nativist and anti-Portuguese revolt that was violently suppressed after more than seventy days of struggle.

A few months later, certain sectors of Lisbon public opinion became aware of what had happened. The prolonged absence of the monarch was questioned, as well as the economic opportunities conceded to the British, the authoritarianism of Luso-British governance of the metropole – a protectorate under the command of Marshal Beresford since May 1810 – the very weak economic and financial situation of Portugal and the mobilization of military forces for the Cisplatine War (1817), in which the United Kingdom of Portugal (re)took Montevideo and Uruguay. Describing the dream of the House of Braganza of creating a "glorious empire" extending from Amazonas to the La Plata River as a "fantasy" and placing their hopes of regeneration in the leadership of the renowned general Gomes Freire de Andrade, twelve individuals plotted to install a constitutional monarchy, even if this required a change of dynasty. Denounced in May 1817, they were shown no mercy and hanged on 16 December. In August 1820, a new movement erupted in Porto, aiming to constitutionalize and reverse the imperial structure enshrined in the founding of the United Kingdom of Portugal. Like the previous conspiracy, this revolution was also "not opposed to the king of Portugal, but the king of Brazil, and Brazil's rule over Portugal. Therefore, Portugal had not conspired against the authority, but the lack of a king".

After Prince John had sworn allegiance to the Constitution and the Brazilian elites in the capital and the provinces had shown significant support for the Vintist movement, representatives from the provinces of Brazil were elected to the Constituent Assembly convened by Lisbon (1821–1822). However, they did not all share the same ideological positions and loyalties. Many were inspired by a powerful local patriotism and sense of identity based on belonging to a common Portuguese nation, in which the figure of the king was very important.

Meanwhile, in the Central-Southern epicentre, under the influence of José Bonifácio, the requirements for Brazil to adhere to a new social pact were clarified. This involved the creation of an autonomous legislative centre in Rio and the refusal to remove Brazil's status as a kingdom, together with the loss of state and parastatal institutions based there, which were threatened by the monarch's return to the metropole – having appointed his eldest son regent, he had departed for Lisbon in April 1821 – and the possibility that Prince Peter would follow. The growing desire for separation advised that the ties should be stretched to the limit, since the Lusocentric premises of the Porto Revolution and the unification-based approach of its leaders regarding the concept of national sovereignty to re-establish the legitimacy of the United Kingdom of Portugal clashed with the dual and confederal basis of the Brazilian proposal.

In the opinion of many of its key mentors, the Revolution could be justified by the natural right to resist despotism and tyranny embodied in the figure of Beresford: the metropole was subjugated to the despotism of the king's courtiers and the military representative of British imperialism. Believing that Portugal had been transformed into a "colony of its colony", Vintism also intended to serve as a decolonizing movement. However, from Brazil's perspective, this approach was dictated by plans for recolonization.

The new constitution of the United Kingdom of Portugal was approved on 24 September 1822, before news had been received of events taking place on the other side of the Atlantic and with votes cast in favour by some Brazilian deputies who followed the project to its conclusion. However, many others had already left Lisbon and begun to support the calls for immediate independence, which was proclaimed in Ipiranga on 7 September 1822 under the command of Prince Regent Peter, soon to become Emperor and finally persuaded to disobey the Lisbon Courts by heading the rupture. His closest advisors – many of whom held monarchist and Catholic-Illuminist sympathies and had come from the University of Coimbra – were convinced that, due to the transfer of the court to the Tropics, and given the spectre of events such as the massacre of white people in Tahiti in 1804 or the Republican *caudilhismo* rife in South America, it would be advisable to resort to a monarchist solution, since both the confederation solution chosen by Bolívar and the federal solution in the USA favoured fragmentation.

The mystical body of imperial power, with its symbology, rituals and tradition of paternalism (enhanced by the old alliance and the subordination of the Church to the throne), and the royal command of the armed forces were more solid reasons for a transition that also intended to preserve slavery and the monarchy, since for the most part the split with Portugal was not the work of the colonized (Indians and Blacks), but primarily the wish of the colonizers.

Moreover, the power of local patriotism in this country-continent, as well as an awareness of the weakness of "civil society" and the existing bureaucratic state demanded that the latter should be given sufficient power to create a national identity for the elites and the multi-ethnic and multicultural population scattered throughout the country, for whom it should, ideally, provide universal care. A commitment was made to the centripetalism of the institution of empire to cement the legacy of a unified Brazilian territory, inscribing it within the plan to construct and internalize the single and indivisible imperial nation state, in which the presence of a model that was more French than North American can be detected. Hence, the first test was the repressive response to the attempt by the Confederation of the Equator (July 1824), a movement which, in the context of the approval of the conservative and doctrinaire Constitutional Charter (25 March 1824), dared to fight for an "American" system, rather than one from "old Europe". This explains how the deep-rooted Brazilian "national" consciousness emerged from the gradual integration of the different provinces under the new court and the image of a strong state which the empire appeared to offer. After all, the throne had been in Rio since the beginning of 1808.

Fernando Catroga
Centre for the History of Society and Culture,
University of Coimbra

Bibliography

ALEXANDRE, Valentim, *Os Sentidos do Império: Questão Nacional e Questão Colonial na Crise do Antigo Regime Português*, Porto, Afrontamento, 1993.

ARRUDA, Jobson, *Uma Colônia entre Dois Impérios: A Abertura dos Portos Brasileiros: 1800–1810*, Bauru, Edusc, 2008.

DIAS, Maria Odília Leite da Silva, *A Interiorização da Metrópole e Outros Estudos*, São Paulo, Alameda, 1980.

JANCSÒ, István, *Independência: História e Historiografia*, São Paulo, Hucitec, 2005.

PAQUETTE, Gabriel, *Imperial Portugal in the Age of Atlantique Revolutions. The Luso-Brasilian World, c. 1770–1850*, Cambridge, Cambridge University Press, 2013.

1823
King Miguel and Miguelism

The revolutionary and counter-revolutionary events in the Iberian Peninsula are closely connected and inseparable from the imperial dispute between Great Britain and France, and the crisis in the Atlantic empires.

Miguelism was a Portuguese political phenomenon synonymous with counter-revolution, anti-liberalism, royalism and legitimism. The term refers to the role played by Prince Miguel from 1823 onwards in the resistance to the constitutional regime.

The revolutionary and counter-revolutionary events in the Iberian Peninsula are closely connected and inseparable from the imperial dispute between Great Britain and France, and the crisis in the Atlantic empires. The Napoleonic Wars, the English alliance, the situation in Spain and the pluricontinental nature of the Portuguese empire forced the court to leave for Brazil in 1807. Prince Miguel, aged five at the time and the son of the Prince Regent John (the future King John VI) and Carlota Joaquina, lived there until the royal family returned to Lisbon in July 1821.

In the meantime, the world had changed. In 1820, a wave of revolutions had swept through the south of Europe, affecting Portugal, Spain, Piedmont, Naples, Sicily and Greece. Opposition to the Portuguese Liberal governments was led by Queen Carlota Joaquina who, in December 1822, refused to swear an oath of allegiance to the Constitution and in 1826 advised her son to do the same with regard to the Constitutional Charter. Other counter-revolutionary leaders were military noblemen from the provinces, including the Silveira family from the Douro region who headed an armed revolt in February 1823. Defeated by troops loyal to the constitutional government, they retreated to Spain, giving rise to the first wave of counter-revolutionary exiles. In April 1823, in response to requests sent by Ferdinand VII of Spain to Louis XVIII of France, a French military expedition commanded by the Duke of Angoulême invaded Spain, ending the *Triénio Liberal* ("Liberal Triennium") and restoring Ferdinand VII as an absolute monarch.

In Portugal, less than three years later, the military coup led by Prince Miguel, known as the *Vilafrancada* (May 1823), put an end to three years of Vintist Liberal government in Portugal. Whereas until then the counter-revolution had been personified by the figure of Carlota Joaquina, the *Vilafrancada* marked the beginning of the process by which Miguel became identified with the counter-revolution, making him its figurehead. The counter-revolutionary press helped transform him into a hero: "and if the Portuguese hero, his Most Serene Lord Prince Miguel does not respond [...] Miguel is our Liberator, say millions of Portuguese today". The counter-revolutionaries did not fail to point out that in Spain, Naples and Piedmont the revolution had been overthrown with the aid of foreign intervention, whereas this had not been the case in Portugal.

The moderate regime over which King John VI ruled after 1823 did not satisfy the counter-revolutionaries. With the support of his mother, Prince Miguel led a new coup in April 1824: the mass arrests, verbal and physical violence and persecution were a foretaste of his own reign. The *Abrilada* (April Revolt) failed due to the interference of foreign diplomats, in particular the French ambassador Hyde de Neuville, but revealed the relative isolation of Prince Miguel within the royal court. Taking refuge in a British ship on the Tagus, John VI dismissed Miguel as commander of the army, ordered him to release the prisoners and sent him into exile. In May 1824, he left for Vienna, via Paris, and lived there until 6 December 1827. Influenced by Metternich and the Austrian emperor, he completed his education and led a worldly existence, only resuming his political activities after receiving the news of the death of his father in March 1826.

The death of John VI raised the issue of the regime once again and also the new question of the succession. Prince Peter, the emperor of Brazil and the legitimate heir to the throne, granted the Constitutional Charter of 29 April 1826, then abdicated on 2 May in favour of his daughter Princess Maria da Glória (the future Queen Maria II) on two conditions: firstly, that she should swear an oath of allegiance to the Charter and, secondly, that she should marry Prince Miguel. With the latter in Vienna, an intensive round of diplomatic activity began in the main European courts, involving the governments of England and France, the Austrian chancellor Metternich, the Brazilian representative, the Viscount of Resende, and the Spanish government. The installation of a new Liberal government, the rights of succession and the independence of Brazil were discussed. Meanwhile, in Portugal, the counter-revolutionaries were plotting. At the end of July 1826, Carlota Joaquina wrote to her son advising him not to swear allegiance to the Charter, and to her daughters, who were living in Spain, urging them to work for the "cause". At the same time, popular counter-revolutionary uprisings broke out in the North, joining forces with the Absolutist troops who, with the collaboration of the Spanish government, invaded the country in November. Cheers for Prince Miguel mingled with cries of "Death to the Charter!".

With the regime under threat, the regency government asked England for assistance and the prime minister George Canning sent troops commanded by General Clinton (1826, December). After they were defeated, around 6,000 Miguelists took refuge in Spain. However, in Vienna, in October 1826 Prince Miguel, advised by Metternich, who had been pressurized by Canning, swore allegiance to the Charter and became betrothed. On 3 July 1827, Prince Peter appointed him his lieutenant in Portugal, to govern in compliance with the Charter. The conditions for the return of Prince Miguel were defined by Austria and England. Lord Dudley told Prince Esterhazy: "As England liked the Charter but not the Prince, and Austria liked him but not the Charter, it was an easy business to negotiate: Austria got the Prince returning with the Charter and England got the Charter, with the Prince". In October 1827, Metternich, the British ambassador Henry Wellesley, and the Baron of Vila Seca and Count of Vila Real, representing Portugal, signed the Vienna protocols resulting from the involvement of Austria and Britain, the relegation of France and the undermining of Spain. As a whole, they expressed the approval of the powers with regard to the regency of Prince Miguel, the consolidation of the separation between Portugal and Brazil and support for the principles of legitimacy.

Prince Miguel arrived in Lisbon on 22 February 1828. Two days later he swore allegiance to the Charter, Prince Peter and Princess Maria, as Regent, while the people in the streets shouted "The king has arrived!". Believing that the prince was the solution to the situation in Portugal, since he would abide by the Vienna agreement, and now more concerned with the Eastern Question, the English, French and Austrian executives would have considered not intervening in appointments to the new government, new military governors and magistrates and the dissolution of the Chamber of Deputies by Prince Miguel. In April, Clinton's troops withdrew on the orders of Wellington, the British prime minister.

However, the convening of the *Cortes* in "the manner of the ancient régime", in May 1828, changed the position of the powers and the attitude of the constitutional forces. Official diplomatic representatives in Lisbon suspended their activities and the regiments loyal to the Charter began a revolt in the north of the country (the *Belfastada*) on 16 May, which was defeated at the beginning of July. The agreement negotiated in Vienna was jeopardized and the rupture was completed on 7 July 1828, when Miguel was proclaimed king by the traditional *Cortes*. There had been an important change in the tactics used by the counter-revolutionaries: accession to the throne had been secured by controlling the traditional institutions, rather than by a military coup. A *de facto* reign began, recognized only by Spain (1829), the United States (1829) and the Vatican (1831). The way in which Miguel had seized power, the actions of his government and the popular violence would influence the attitude of the powers and the image of Miguelism. However, they were no obstacle to the policy of non-interference which England had decided to adopt and which the other powers followed. Between 1830 and 1831, the political swing in Europe (the July Revolution in France, the Whig government in England) and Brazil (the abdication of Peter) altered domestic and foreign affairs for the government of King Miguel. Diplomatic and propaganda efforts – such as the Manifesto of King Miguel (1832), distributed in Portugal and abroad – failed to convince European governments to accept the Miguelist regime. A financial loan negotiated with France shortly after 1830 was cancelled and the government only managed to obtain another foreign loan, on unfavourable terms, at the end of 1832. The repression, thousands of arrests and, above all, refusal to grant any amnesty rekindled the debate on the legitimate claim of King Miguel and spread the image of a tyrant king and a reign of terror throughout Europe. Balzac described King Miguel as the Portuguese Nero: others called him the crowned tiger, Caligula or tyrant.

On 8 July 1832, Liberal troops commanded by the Emperor Peter landed in the north of Portugal to begin a long and difficult civil war which only ended in May 1834. It was not only a national dispute, since foreign volunteers served in both armies. The political changes in France had resulted in the emigration of many Legitimists, which helps to explain their presence in the Miguelist army during the civil war. In 1833, the Miguelist António Ribeiro Saraiva contracted Marshal Count Louis de Bourmont, in London, to activate the European network of exiled royalists. Those who responded included French veterans from the War in the Vendée but also other nationalities, such as the Scottish Jacobite MacDonnell. After the Miguelists were defeated, some went on to fight for the Carlists. Mobilization was added to the principles of counter-revolutionary internationalism.

In 1833, the refusal of Prince Charles Maria Isidro to swear allegiance to Isabel II as heir to the throne of Spain, and the death of Ferdinand VII in September of the same year strengthened the ties between the Portuguese and Spanish counter-revolutions, changing the position of the Iberian kingdoms within the Concert of Nations. In Spain, as in Portugal, the question of the dynasty developed into a political issue. In March 1833, in the midst of the civil war, Prince Charles went to Portugal. There, in early October, he declared himself the legitimate sovereign of Spain (in the Abrantes Manifesto) and signed decrees as Charles V. In Spain, proclamations and uprisings began in support of his claim. The Portuguese royalists ceased to rely on the collaboration of the Spanish government – whose objective was to capture Prince Charles – and began to support the Liberals. After prolonged negotiations, the Quadruple Alliance between England, France, Spain and Portugal (or rather, Emperor Peter) was signed in London on 22 April 1834. It concerned the question of the succession in both Portugal and Spain and decided to expel King Miguel and Prince Charles from the Iberian Peninsula. In May 1834, the Convention of Évoramonte confirmed the defeat of King Miguel and stipulated that he had to renounce his right to the Portuguese Crown and never return to "any part of the Iberian Peninsula or the Portuguese dominions". In June 1834, Prince Miguel left Sines for Genova and Prince Charles departed from Montijo heading for London. Hence, a new period of exile began. Some of the supports of Prince Miguel and Prince Charles accompanied their respective kings, while others fled to Italy, France, Austria and England, where they established small groups of exiled Carlists and Miguelists which would form the basis of the European Legitimist network. In London, Princess Maria Teresa, the sister of Prince Miguel and the second wife of Prince Charles, became the head of the Carlist group which lived there in exile.

During his long second exile Prince Miguel lived in Italy (Genova and Rome) from 1834 to 1847, the year in which he travelled clandestinely to London, where he resided until 1851. Finally, he went to Germany, where he died in 1866. In 1967, his mortal remains were transferred to Portugal and laid to rest in the Pantheon of the House of Braganza.

Following the Liberal victory in 1834 and the exile of Prince Miguel, the influence of the counter-revolutionaries and their anti-Liberal ideology began to wane. Unlike Carlism, which remained part of political life in Spain from 1833 until at least the end of the 1936–1939 Spanish Civil War, after a final attempt at insurrection in 1846–1847 during the Maria da Fonte uprising, Miguelism ceased to be a threat. Although revived by the Integralists at the beginning of the twentieth century as a movement opposed to Liberal society, it was never adopted by any political force again. Moreover, although the presence of exiled Portuguese, Spanish and French royalists in the European monarchies helped to construct Legitimism as one of the European political identities, the contribution of the Miguelists was the least significant.

Maria Alexandre Lousada
University of Lisbon

Bibliography

CARDOSO, António Monteiro, *A Revolução Liberal em Trás-os-Montes (1820–1834): O Povo e as Elites*, Porto, Afrontamento, 2007.

LOUSADA, Maria Alexandre, FERREIRA, Maria de Fátima de Sá e Melo, *D. Miguel*, Lisbon, Temas e Debates, 2009.

MÓNICA, Maria Teresa, *Errâncias Miguelistas*, Lisbon, Cosmos, 1997.

PAQUETTE, Gabriel, *Imperial Portugal in the Age of Atlantic Revolutions: The Luso-Brazilian World, c. 1770–1850*, Cambridge, Cambridge University Press, 2013.

TORGAL, Luís Reis, VARGUES, Isabel Nobre, "Da revolução à contra-revolução: vintismo, cartismo, absolutismo: o exílio político", in MATTOSO, José (dir.), *História de Portugal*, vol. V, Lisbon, Estampa, 1993, pp. 65–87.

1834
The Institutionalization of Protestantism in Portugal

It was Vicente Gomez y Tojar (1796?–1878), born in Granada and one of the pioneers of the Protestant movement, who was responsible for founding a Protestant church in Portuguese territory.

The year 1834 marks the beginning of Protestant activity in Portugal, with the emergence, in Lisbon, of evidence of its first forms of social organization. The end of the civil war solved the immediate problem of national political leadership but not the deep wounds that had opened in Portuguese society in the previous decades. The disturbing episodes involving Roman Catholicism were also an expression of the unease that had been developing throughout the fraternal conflict, aggravating mistrust between the secular and regular clergy and the fraught relations between regalists and those who supported Ultramontanism. During this period, the salient features of religious reform, that was extensive both in terms of depth and range, were the almost total functionalization of the secular clergy and the abolition of the religious orders, decreed on 30 May 1834. In a society that was very dependent on relations between the population and the clergy, this offered opportunities for other religious groups to claim their own territories.

Over three hundred years had elapsed since Martin Luther's Ninety-Five Theses (1517) had been presented in Wittenberg, the symbolic founding moment in a movement which would lead to the creation of new Christian faiths that were not subordinated to the authority of the pope, the supreme head of the Catholic Church. The establishment of the first Protestant church in Portugal signalled the beginning of the contemporary process of religious differentiation within the country. Although the Portuguese nation was the result of a process of recomposing the religious identity of a people who had lived in the territory since early times, this had never been achieved by amalgamation, but instead by segregation. Therefore, since the second quarter of the nineteenth century, when Protestant communities began to emerge in Portuguese territory, specifically in Lisbon, Funchal and Porto, it was not the existence of this religious ideology that was new, but the fact that Portuguese citizens belonged to these groups. The religious diversity which the Portuguese had always embraced had previously only envisaged coexistence with groups with strong ethnic and cultural traits, who could be contained and isolated and had established themselves in separate areas, such as the Moorish and Jewish quarters.

When Luther's ideas began to take root, King Manuel I tried to prevent them from circulating within Portugal. Shortly after the *Exsurge Domine* bull was issued in 1520, threatening Luther with excommunication, but before the Diet of Worms in 1521, which banned him from the Holy Empire, Portuguese diplomacy was already inclined to keep a close watch over any religious episodes that would disturb the fragile status of Europe at the time. In Portugal, despite resistance to the ideas of Luther and other reformers who followed him, mainly stemming from the work of the Inquisition, several religious communities were established by foreigners belonging to the Protestant and Reformed churches, both in the metropole, including the examples in Lisbon – Dutch Calvinist (1641) and English Episcopalian (1642) – and in more distant regions, namely Brazil – French Huguenot (1557) and Dutch Calvinist (1624) – and the Far East – Dutch Calvinist (1641) and Danish Lutheran (1706). Nevertheless, there is no evidence of any strong support amongst the Portuguese for Protestant ideas or practices during the three centuries which followed. There were some "Protestants in exile", including João Ferreira de Almeida (c. 1628–1691), the first person to translate the entire Bible into Portuguese and a pastor in the Dutch Reformed Church, who spent most of his life in the Far East (Malacca, Tranquebar, Ceylon and Java). His translation of the Bible, which ran to several editions, circulated widely.

However, it was Vicente Gomez y Tojar (1796?–1878), born in Granada and one of the pioneers of the Protestant movement, who was responsible for founding a Protestant church in Portuguese territory. There is little information on his family background and early life, but he is known to have studied medicine, as well as theology and philosophy. While still a young man, he became a parish priest in the diocese of Malaga and later a member of the cathedral chapter. By the time he was ordained as a canon, he had become interested in the Liberal ideas which attracted certain intellectuals of the time with whom he associated. Persecuted by the forces of King Ferdinand VII, Gomez took refuge in Gibraltar, enjoying British protection. He then moved to Tangier and finally to Brazil, which was now independent, remaining there until 1830. The exact time at which he became associated with the Protestant faith is not known, but this change of faith was certainly linked to his Liberal ideas and connections with the British. In 1831, he travelled to England where he married Ann Pratt, a Protestant woman from London, and associated with other Portuguese Liberals. In 1833, he decided to sail for Lisbon to practice as a doctor and become involved in religious activities, aligning his evangelical mission with the political and religious upheaval he believed was necessary for Portugal. By July 1834, without the declared support of any church or missionary institution, he had settled in the Portuguese capital and was working as a correspondent for the British and Foreign Bible Society, known in Portugal as the *Sociedade Bíblica*.

His religious work included distributing the Bible and establishing a community which held meetings in the Calçada do Sacramento district in Lisbon. On 10 November 1839, now based in Rua Nova do Almada, probably in a private family residence, the *Capela da Promulgação do Santo Evangelho de Nosso Senhor Jesus Cristo* was inaugurated and its first service was attended by 110 individuals, 31 of whom had signed the deeds authorizing its constitution. On 8 April 1841, Gomez abjured the "errors of Roman Catholicism" in the presence of the Bishop of London at the Chapel Royal in Whitehall, and his orders were canonically accepted by the Church of England.

In its early years this Protestant community in Lisbon would have been received with lenience and tolerance, given that there is no evidence of any unrest in response to its presence or activities, or any objections to it pursuing its work, which included holding religious services, baptizing children, administering Holy Communion and assisting its members. However, the effects of the 1852 Penal Code had a major impact on the newly-emerging Portuguese Anglicanism. The vague and ambiguous concept of freedom of religion enshrined in the 1826 Constitutional Charter was undermined by the clarification and classification of crimes resulting from any departure from the Roman Catholic faith. Hence, its religious services were banned and the religious community dispersed, although it managed to survived until 6 December 1870, when it performed its final religious service, the baptism of a child. Vicente Gomez y Tojar died in 1874 in the city where he had spent the last four decades of his life.

In this early phase of the Protestant presence in Portugal as a church, other initiatives similar to those of Gomez were introduced by foreigners, mainly British subjects, including Robert Kalley (1809–1888) in Funchal, Ellen Roughton (1802–1883) in Lisbon, James Cassels (1844–1923) in Porto and George Robinson (1815–1895) in Portalegre, as well as the Spaniard Ângel Herreros de Mora (1815–1876), also in Lisbon. They therefore comprised a series of disconnected private initiatives, interrupted only by the arrival in Portugal of Robert Hawkey Moreton (1844–1917) in 1871. Moreton received financial support from the Wesleyan Methodist Missionary Society, an institution created in London in 1818 to respond to the enormous increase in missionary work within this branch of Protestantism since its foundation at the end of the eighteenth century. Nevertheless, Moreton arrived only in response to persistent requests from James Cassels. From the 1870s onwards, Protestantism began to develop a lasting form of social organization and would become established in Portuguese society in the decades which followed.

Although small in number and inadequately distributed within the territory, the structures required for the functioning of Protestant churches were gradually established, with human and financial assistance essentially provided by Great Britain. Various buildings were acquired or constructed, most adapted to the liturgical and pastoral needs of the communities and also suitable for use as Sunday schools (religious instruction) and day schools (basic literacy for children and adults). In addition, they offered a strong component of social activities, particularly for young people, with the creation of Christian youth organizations in 1894, later renamed Young Men's Christian Associations, dedicated to spiritual reflection, but also to encouraging intellectual development and care of the body through physical exercise and healthy habits. The provision of Bibles, the basic instrument for the spiritual training of the faithful who joined these communities and also for teaching literacy, was ensured by the steady work of the Bible Society, a presence in Portugal since the beginning of the nineteenth century and officially established in 1864.

The forces which saw Protestantism as a movement opposed to nationalism and therefore damaging to Portuguese society, as well as to the idiosyncratic plurality of the Reformed universe, which tended to be schismatic, were stumbling blocks that appear to have been overcome, from an official point of view, with the creation of the Portuguese Protestant Association in 1909, replaced by the Portuguese Evangelical Alliance in 1921, which has since united the main branches of Portuguese Protestantism.

The first century in the life of Protestant communities in Portugal was defined by a gradual increase in the number of believers, reflecting the regional imbalances which affected the Portuguese population in general. The first advance occurred during the second half of the 1970s, following the influx of Portuguese populations from the African nations where Portugal had maintained a presence and where Protestantism had penetrated and evolved to a proportionally greater extent than in the metropole. The second development, since the 1990s, stemmed from migration, which saw the arrival in Portugal of many believers from the various different branches of the Protestant faith, in particular from Brazil. However, one hundred and eighty years after it was first established in Portugal, there is clear evidence that Protestantism is still, to a certain extent, invisible within Portuguese society, even though it is the largest religious minority group in the country (representing approximately 3 percent of the population).

Timóteo Cavaco
Institute of Contemporary History from Nova University Lisbon

Bibliography

ASPEY, Albert, *Por Este Caminho: Origem e Progresso do Metodismo em Portugal no Século XIX: Umas Páginas da História da Procura da Liberdade Religiosa*, Porto, Igreja Evangélica Metodista Portuguesa, 1971.

[CASSELS, James], *A Reforma em Portugal: A História Resumida já Publicada na "Igreja Lusitana" nos Anos de 1897 e 1898, Revista, Aumentada e Dividida em Cinco Capítulos*, Porto, Tipografia a Vapor de José da Silva Mendonça, 1908.

LEITE, Rita Mendonça, *Representações do Protestantismo na Sociedade Portuguesa Contemporânea: Da Exclusão à Liberdade de Culto (1852–1911)*, Lisbon, Centro de Estudos de História Religiosa, 2009.

MOREIRA, Eduardo, *Vidas Convergentes: História Breve dos Movimentos de Reforma Cristã em Portugal, a partir do Século XVIII*, Lisbon, Junta Presbiteriana de Cooperação em Portugal, 1958.

SANTOS, Luís Aguiar, "Pluralidade religiosa: correntes cristãs e não-cristãs no universo religioso português", in AZEVEDO, Carlos Moreira (dir.), *História Religiosa de Portugal*, vol. 3, Lisbon, Círculo de Leitores, 2001, pp. 401–501.

1867
Abolition of the Death Penalty

The death penalty was abandoned in 1846. Portugal ensured that its legal abolition was preceded by its de facto disappearance. It did not make the mistake of hasty abolition only to run the risk, recalled by Goethe, of seeing it restored shortly afterwards.

On 1 July 1867, during the reign of King Louis, two new laws were passed that would define the path of Portuguese legal institutions. One approved the first Portuguese Civil Code, inspired by the wisdom of the Viscount of Seabra. The other, following a proposal presented by Augusto César Barjona de Freitas, a professor at the University of Coimbra Faculty of Law and the Minister for Justice at the time, sanctioned penal and prison reform. The first article of the latter stated that the death penalty had been abolished in Portugal for civil crimes.

The publicizing of the right to punish and the centralization of royal power, promoted intensively in Portugal in the thirteenth century, had created a repressive system in which the death penalty played a key role. From the mid fifteenth century and the first Ordinations, penal law was known for its harshness. The sentences were, at times, shockingly disproportionate, cruel, unjust, transmissible and shameful.

The Ordinations of King Afonso (1445–1446) created a punitive legacy that was passed on to the later Manueline (1512–1513) and Philippine (1603) Ordinations, which prescribed the death penalty for many offences, ranging from crimes de lèse-majesté to counterfeiting currency, crimes of passion to serious offences, and theft to willful murder.

In the second half of the eighteenth century, Sebastião José de Carvalho e Melo, usually known as the Marquis of Pombal, made widespread use of the death penalty, instituting a brutal reign of terror and intimidation. Criminal trials had to proceed swiftly and without great formalities. Society need to triumph over the effects of sentencing in the emotive context of the defence of the community. Hence the extraordinary importance attributed to the public nature of criminal justice following the earthquake of 1755, when individuals found guilty of robbery were ordered to be hanged from the highest gallows possible, with their bodies remaining on display until they rotted. Pombaline politics formed no part of the movement for the abolition of the death penalty that was beginning to emerge in Europe at the time. Nor was it guided by penal law associated with reasons of state, as can be seen from the torture inflicted on the Távora family who were convicted following an attack on King Joseph in 1758. By decree, there was no appeal against the sentence, which had to be executed on the same day, in contravention of the legal period of three days which would normally elapse between the issuing of a sentence and the execution of the death penalty. At the time, this was extended to the use of the death penalty for new crimes.

In essence, the key recommendation of the Pombaline legislator regarding the death penalty can be summarized as follows: the guilty should die, and die quickly if there were no royal pardon, but with due Christian obedience and forbearance. This is evident in the decree issued on 6 July 1752 and in various laws which address the subject of the death penalty in the third quarter of the eighteenth century.

Drawing on humanitarian ideas derived from the Enlightenment, of which Montesquieu and Voltaire in France, and Beccaria and Filangieri in Italy were the most famous advocates, a reinterpretation of penal law emerged: in the light of an understanding of law and the state based on the notion of a social contract, penal law should separate itself from all religious premises and confine itself to the exterior function of defending the general values or interests essential for collective life.

The idea of common need or utility was affirmed as the defining criterion for penal law, rather than a predominantly ethical and religious axiology.

In the history of the objectives of sentencing, the change in perspective was clear. As far as criminal sanctions were concerned, the most important argument was now simply prevention and the protection of society, rather than any ethical imperative. The sentence was justified not as a punishment for a past fact, but as a means of preventing future violations of criminal law, although preventive measures had to be confined to the limits of justice and the dignity of the human person. Punitive measures had been radically transformed. Considering human liberty a *res inestimabilis*, the most important of all assets, the criminal sanction par excellence was therefore a sentence that deprived the individual of their liberty: in other words, a prison sentence.

The humanitarian outcry met with some tentative echoes in various different parts of Europe. In 1767, Beccaria's ideas resonated in the instructions for the Code in Russia, but were never enshrined in law. In 1786 Leopold II of Tuscany, influenced by a commission headed by Beccaria himself, banned the death penalty in his dominions. King Joseph II did the same for the new Austrian Code. However, these measures were short-lived. Tuscany re-established capital punishment in 1790, while Austria re-introduced it in 1796 and extended its application in the Penal Code of 1803. As Goethe observed, "if it is difficult to abolish capital punishment, when this happens it is only to restore it at the first opportunity".

In the nineteenth century there was a clear downturn in the progress of the abolitionist movement. The French Penal Code of 1810 prescribed the use of capital punishment in over thirty different situations. The Bavarian Code of 1813 also enabled it to be applied widely, and England, undaunted, remained generous in its acceptance of the death penalty in over two hundred cases, a situation that would remain unchanged until 1860.

It fell to France to signal a turning point. The penal reform of 1832 reduced the use of the death penalty and in 1848, influenced by Liberal ideas, it was abolished for political crimes. Some inspired and emboldened local governments turned to abolition, in the canton of Fribourg, for example, and the Republic of San Marino, in 1848. However, these were very localized cases: the great European powers hesitated to commit to total abolition, extending to ordinary offences.

However, Portugal managed to overcome the old preconception. Little by little, professors at the University of Coimbra, who comprised the doctrinal elite, began to support the abolitionist movement. The founder of the history of Portuguese law, Mello Freire, stated that he was familiar with the ideas of the Marquis of Beccaria. However, he deliberately restrained himself, not concealing his own thoughts. He wrote: "I am of the opinion that, for now, there can be no public safety in Portugal without capital punishment: everyone knows that the genius and character of the nation is the main measure of any rise or fall in sentencing". In his *Institutiones iuris criminalis Lusitani*, published in 1794, he explained that there could be three kinds of death penalty: simple, ruthless or cruel. The ruthless death emerged at the extreme limits of humanity and justice, for example, by arrest. The cruel death was brought about slowly, by means of torture. Mello Freire repudiated both but declared himself in favour of the simple death penalty. Hence, the criminal code he drafted at the behest of Queen Maria I banned any form of torture in the execution of the death penalty. It also went further, abolishing its use in many other cases and reserving it only for what were defined as very serious crimes.

Souza e Sampaio, one of Mello Freire's colleagues in Coimbra, stressed that the death penalty did not fulfill two of the main objectives of sentencing: it did not correct the criminal and it did not improve him. However, pure vengeance was unacceptable, since it was not legitimate to compensate the victim by killing the offender: in fact, the momentaneous nature of the death penalty itself recommended a more prolonged form of punishment. Nevertheless, in praising the idea of a general deterrent, he showed himself to be opposed to abolitionist arguments. After Mello Freire, the canonist António Ribeiro dos Santos analyzed the subject in a study published in 1815, focussing, like Beccaria, on two aspects: if, and to what extent, capital punishment was lawful, and whether it was appropriate for society. Unlike Beccaria, he maintained that capital punishment was admissible. Society could put a criminal to death when it could not safeguard its political existence or maintain the peace in any other way. On this legitimate basis, whenever the country was threatened, the highest penalty was justified. For Ribeiro dos Santos, death was not a true punishment, but simply a means of defence.

Concerning the second strand of his enquiry, the canonist proved to be extremely progressive, stating that in a peaceful society, the death penalty was neither necessary nor useful. In affirming that the death penalty was unnecessary and inappropriate, Ribeiro dos Santos became the first convinced abolitionist in Portuguese legal thinking.

The abolitionist arguments extended beyond scholarly books. Jurisprudential practice had already been sending out significant signals: it will suffice to recall the abandonment of torture, which was considered revoked due to disuse. The legal practice of mitigating the severity of sentences, clear opposition to torture and the gradual withdrawal of capital punishment resonated from the reign of Queen Maria I onwards and were also evident in individual responses. I will cite just one example, taken from a law approved during the regency of Prince John, the son of Queen Maria I. It concerns the decree of 11 March 1797 which reduced the death penalty to perpetual exile in Mozambique for convicts under the age of forty imprisoned in the Limoeiro jail and awaiting execution, except for those who had received sentences for "the most hideous crimes".

With the advent of liberalism came a growing desire to reform penal law. Some effective advances came from the Constitutionalist movement, prompted by the 1822 Constitution, sanctioning the principles of equality and proportionality. Moreover, through a precept that had clearly utilitarian leanings, it also established the principle that no law, far less penal law, would be enshrined unless absolutely necessary. A silence fell over the death penalty, which was maintained in the Constitutional Charter of 1826 and the 1838 Constitution. Nevertheless, the 1832 judicial reform, which included mandatory recourse to royal clemency in the case of death sentences issued by the courts, was an important advance. The provision resulted in a wave of commutations of death sentences, granted by monarchs, during the reigns of Maria II, Peter V and Louis I from 1846 onwards, the year in which the last execution took place in Portugal.

This meant that the death penalty was allowed to die 1846. In other words, Portugal ensured that its legal abolition was preceded by its *de facto* disappearance. It did not make the mistake of hasty abolition only to run the risk, recalled by Goethe, of seeing it restored shortly afterwards

A new chapter began in 1852. On the initiative of the Chamber of Deputies, the Amendment to the Constitutional Charter announced the abolition of the death penalty for political crimes, as in France. With regard to civil crimes, the Penal Code, also approved in 1852, restricted itself to prescribing the death penalty for the extreme cases of treason, lèse-majesté and second-degree willful murder. This was all that remained of a death penalty which, in practice, no longer existed.

Portuguese legal literature was not satisfied and continued to campaign throughout the 1850s and 1860s. There were major contributions from the judge of the Supreme Court of Justice, António Fernandes da Silva Ferrão, and the Coimbra professors Aires de Gouveia and Levy Maria Jordão. In 1863, in his capacity as member of parliament, Aires de Gouveia delivered a fiery speech in defence of the abolition of the office and salary of the hangman, finding this item of expenditure shameful and unworthy of a civilized society. Despite the hearty applause from the audience, the outcome proved farcical, since the salary was abolished but not the office.

It was time to reap the precious harvest, namely the abolition of the death penalty, which King Louis announced in parliament in 1864. However, after various difficulties emerged, it was necessary to wait for the prison reforms of 1867 to ensure that the prime objective of abolition covered civil crimes. The inclusion of abolition in a law on the reform of prisons was justified by the intention to prevent further delays, since it was a measure which, if interpreted correctly, extended to the overseas dominions of the Portuguese empire.

Even when faced with the taxing problem of replacing capital punishment, the Portuguese legislator did not feel obliged, except briefly, to rule that the equivalent should be life imprisonment. In fact, in 1884, it was converted into a term of imprisonment and, from 1893 onwards, conditional release was also admitted.

The author of the abolitionist motion, the minister Barjona de Freitas, was a learned man. He showed that he understood the arguments, from Beccaria to Mittermaier, the latter being the author of a famous study published in 1862 which argued that the death penalty was ineffective. Deploying powerful rhetorical skills, the minister did not hesitate, in his well-argued report, to interpret the death penalty as "the penalty that pays for blood with blood, that kills but does not correct, that avenges but does not improve and, usurping God's prerogative over life and closing the door to repentance, erases all hope of redemption in the heart of the condemned and confronts the fallibility of human justice with the darkness of an irreparable punishment".

In 1867, the time had come for the death penalty to die in Portugal, thus ensuring that every citizen had "the right to die his own death", in the words of the twentieth-century author Miguel Torga.

Rui de Figueiredo Marcos
Faculty of Law, University of Coimbra

Bibliography

CORREIA, Eduardo, "La peine de mort. Réflexions sur sa problématique et sur le sens de son abolition au Portugal", in *Pena de Morte: Colóquio Internacional Comemorativo do Centenário da Abolição da Pena de Morte em Portugal*, vol. I, Coimbra, Faculdade de Direito da Universidade de Coimbra, 1967, pp. 23–37.

COSTA, Mário Júlio de Almeida, *História do Direito Português*, colab. Rui Manuel de Figueiredo Marcos, Coimbra, Almedina, 2017.

CRUZ, Guilherme Braga da, *Obras Esparsas*, vol. II, pt. 2, Coimbra, Universidade de Coimbra, 1981.

PINTO, Basílio Alberto de Sousa, *Lições de Direito Criminal Portuguez*, Coimbra, Imprensa da Universidade, 1861.

SILVA, Henriques, *Elementos de Sociologia Criminal e Direito Penal*, Coimbra, Imprensa da Universidade, 1906.

1884
Portugal at the Berlin Conference

The initial agenda for the conference contained three items for discussion: Recognition of free trade in the Congo Basin, the application of the principles of free navigation to the Congo and Niger rivers, and a definition of the principles to be adopted for future occupations on the African coast.

On 14 November 1884, the German chancellor Otto von Bismarck inaugurated the Berlin Conference on West Africa, attended by representatives from 14 countries: Austria-Hungary, Belgium, Denmark, France, Germany, Great Britain, Italy, the Netherlands, the Ottoman Empire, Portugal, Russia, Spain, Sweden-Norway and the United States. The main objectives of the international meeting were to regulate free trade and navigation in the region and define the principles for future occupations of the African coast.

Due to the subsequent process of division and occupation of Africa and the popular imagination fuelled by misinterpretations of its conclusions, the Berlin meeting is still largely seen as the moment when the European powers carved up the African continent between themselves. However, the conference did not divide Africa. When the German and French diplomats drew up its agenda, they deliberately decided to omit any discussion of territorial claims. This option ran contrary to the main aim of the Portuguese government, that the assembled powers should recognize their stated "historical rights" to the Lower Congo region. Rather than discussing claims that were not, from the Portuguese perspective, at issue, they were anxious to obtain formal and unequivocal acceptance of their political rule. The question of sovereignty had led to the decision to bring the major powers together to resolve the impasse created by the international challenge to the Anglo-Portuguese Treaty of 26 February 1884, also known as the Zaire Treaty or Congo Treaty.

This agreement was yet another attempt to settle the dispute over political and economic rights in the region of the River Congo estuary, ongoing since the mid-1830s, in which Portugal's plans for political and economic expansion on the African coast (the tentative "new Brazils" in Africa) clashed with the commercial interests of other nations, in particular Great Britain. Associated with the defence of the free trade system and the fight against the slave trade which flourished in the region in collusion, to a greater or lesser extent, with the Portuguese authorities, these interests forced the governments in Lisbon to accept the conditions imposed by the British in the hope that the latter would recognize Portuguese political sovereignty in the region. However, fears of an unfavourable protectionist trade regime and the continuation of slave trading made this difficult for London to accept and it threatened any territorial expansion with armed intervention on several occasions.

Moreover, international pressure over the Congo region had intensified since the late 1870s. The Brussels Geographic Conference (1876), the founding of the International Association of the Congo (IAC) (by King Leopold II of Belgium), the expeditions led by Stanley and Brazza, the French advance, and the beginning of the German colonial enterprise threatened the existing status quo in the Congo. For Great Britain, it was no longer only a matter of curbing Portuguese ambitions, but also preventing the region from falling into the hands of a rival power, especially France.

The British were therefore willing to recognize Portuguese political sovereignty between latitudes 5° 12' and 8° south. In exchange, they reiterated their demands: allowing free navigation of the Congo and Zambezi rivers, regulating favourable customs tariffs for the British in all Portuguese territories in Africa, and limiting Portuguese sovereignty in the African hinterland.

However, the 1884 Zaire Treaty met with strong opposition, both domestic and foreign, from various commercial and religious sectors as well as from within certain political circles, fuelled simply by opportunism. In Portugal, colonial interests were alarmed by the guarantees conceded to the British and the risks they would entail in terms of the country's colonial revenues. In Britain, the commercial sectors doubted the concessions granted by the Portuguese, and the humanitarian and missionary sectors who had long protested about the Portuguese colonial administration, particularly with regard to slave trading, mistrusted their professed good faith – and had many reasons for doing so. These groups were influenced by officials from the International Association of the Congo and Leopold II, who emerged as the champions of the "civilizing" movement in Africa and strong opponents of Portugal's claims to the region. Their influence on public opinion in various countries incited arguments against Portugal's colonial activities: Portugal was a protectionist country that did not favour free trade and was incapable of opposing slavery and slave trading. The remaining European powers swiftly aligned with these views, displeased at being excluded from the potential economic benefits that the Congo appeared to offer.

Given the objections to the Treaty, Barbosa du Bocage, the Portuguese Minister of Foreign Affairs, considered holding an international conference to resolve the issue, an approach typical, to a great extent, of nineteenth-century international politics in the wake of the Congress of Vienna (1815). His proposal, presented to various European governments, was accepted by Bismarck, who saw it as a way to become involved in colonial affairs and offset British colonial ascendency. In London, growing pressure at home and abroad led the government to abandon the Treaty and accept the proposed conference. The main concern for the British was to guarantee the existence of a system of free navigation and trade in the region, as demanded by opponents of the agreement such as Bismarck. Leopold II, in turn, asserted that if the International Association of the Congo constituted an independent state, this system would be applied there. Hence, abandoning the treaty was far from harmful to British plans. For the Portuguese, for whom the main issue was their political sovereignty over the Congo, the purpose of the conference was to obtain this formal recognition from the other powers. Hence, Portugal was willing, from the outset, to grant some commercial benefits. Nevertheless, Bismarck and Jules Ferry, the head of the French government, agreed to exclude any debate on the "historical rights" claimed by the Portuguese.

The initial agenda for the conference contained three items for discussion: recognition of free trade in the Congo Basin, the application of the principles of free navigation to the Congo and Niger rivers, and a definition of the principles to be adopted for future occupations on the African coast. Unmoved by German and French resolutions regarding the conference programme, the Portuguese government planned to discuss its political claims on the fringes of the meeting. The choice of the delegation itself demonstrated a national commitment to achieve positive results: the Marquis de Penafiel (the Minister of Portugal in Berlin), António de Serpa Pimentel (a leading member of the government party, the Regenerator Party), Luciano

Cordeiro (one of the founders of Lisbon Geographic Society, acting as scientific advisor), Carlos Roma du Bocage (military attaché in Berlin and the son of Barbosa du Bocage), the Count of Penafiel (the son of the Marquis de Penafiel) and the Count of São Mamede, the latter both attachés.

According to Barbosa du Bocage's instructions to the Portuguese delegation, the primary objectives were to ensure recognition of the "historical rights" in exchange for trade guarantees (with restrictions) and, most importantly, to oppose the political ambitions of the International Association of the Congo. Leopold II, in turn, sought to obtain recognition of the IAC as an independent state, gaining the support of Bismarck on the eve of the conference. Hence, even though territorial issues were not part of the working agenda, political recognition of the International Association of the Congo became a central topic during the conference. Other items on the agenda, such as the free trade system and the principle of effective occupation, did not lead to significant disagreements between the delegates in the plenary sessions since, in one way or another, they all had similar objectives and positions concerning these matters.

Above all, Bismarck wanted to resolve the problem of the International Association of the Congo before the conference ended, pressuring the other countries to follow his example. For Portugal, this was a vital matter that needed to be settled. At the end of November, the Portuguese delegation realized that Germany and the United States supported the International Association of the Congo and that the British were willing to accept the claims of Leopold II once free trade was guaranteed. For a while, only France, serving as an intermediary in the strenuous negotiations between Portugal and the IAC, seemed to offer potential support, due to its own disputes with the association. However, the French managed to resolve the territorial quarrel, therefore siding with the British and the Germans on the founding of the future Congo Free State.

The coalition between Germany, France, and Great Britain left Portugal isolated. Under pressure from the powers and fearing that its intransigence over the territorial concessions that the International Association of the Congo had agreed to offer would further complicate its position, the Portuguese delegation ended up signing the agreement that recognised the association as an independent state. Consequently, Portugal renounced its claims to the Congo Basin but safeguarded its rights over the left bank of the river and the enclave of Cabinda. Despite this apparent defeat for Portuguese "historical rights," the delegation secured substantial, albeit partial, international recognition for its territories, which the previous half century of diplomatic efforts with the British had failed to achieve. Nevertheless, in a final push to enhance further territorial demands, the Portuguese delegates tried to guarantee Portugal's rule over the territories that lay between Angola and Mozambique (anticipating the future Rose-Coloured Map) but were unsuccessful.

Once the agreement between Portugal and the International Association of the Congo had been finalized, the conference could be closed. The main terms settled during the meeting were included in the General Act signed on 26 February 1885, exactly one year after the Zaire Treaty had been signed. The Act guaranteed freedom of trade and navigation on the Congo and Niger rivers, free exercise of missionary activities, and the principle of "effective occupation" along the African coast (but not in the interior). The two latter points became a matter of serious concern for Portuguese governments, leading to the 1890 British Ultimatum.

The conclusions of the Berlin Conference would be immediately challenged in Portugal, namely by the Progressive Party (the opposition), which contested the international "plunder" accepted by the Regenerator government under Fontes Pereira de Melo, and within colonial circles such as the Lisbon Geographic Society. However, as was the case in the aftermath of the 1890 Ultimatum, and despite the protests and public opinion voicing accusations of national humiliation, the conditions negotiated by Portuguese diplomacy helped consolidate the effective Portuguese colonial presence in Africa rather than jeopardize it. Portugal left Berlin having secured international recognition for its political rule in the Congo and in the expectation that its claims to Central Africa (eventually endorsed by Germany and France in 1886, but disputed overall by Britain) would be accepted. Moreover, the internationalization of imperial and colonial issues, which had important antecedents and lasting historical impacts, some on a global scale, gained significant momentum as a result of the Berlin Conference, intensifying in the decades which followed with the Brussels Anti-Slavery Conference (1889–1890), successive treaties for the division of the African continent between the imperial powers and, thirty years later, the founding of the League of Nations. Portugal would play a leading role in this process, but not always for the most respectable of reasons.

HUGO GONÇALVES DORES
Center for Social Studies, University of Coimbra

MIGUEL BANDEIRA JERÓNIMO
University of Coimbra, Faculty of Arts and Humanities,
Department of History, European Studies, Archaeology and Arts

Bibliography

AXELSON, Eric, *Portugal and the Scramble for Africa 1875–1891*, Johannesburg, Witwatersrand University Press, 1967.

FÖRSTER, Stig et al., *Bismarck, Europe and Africa. The Berlin Africa Conference 1885–1885 and the Onset of Partition*, Oxford/London, Oxford University Press/The German Historical Institute of London, 1988.

JERÓNIMO, Miguel Bandeira, *A Diplomacia do Império: Política e Religião na Partilha de África (1820–1890)*, Lisbon, Edições 70, 2012.

PINTO, Françoise Latour da Veiga, *Le Portugal et le Congo au XIXe Siècle. Étude d'Histoire des Relations Internationales*, Paris, Presses Universitaires de France, 1972.

1908
The International Impact of the Regicide of Charles the First

News of the regicide had spread throughout the world: at the time, information was already circulating rapidly. Telegraph networks served by undersea cables, railway lines and steam navigation routes now covered the entire planet, enabling news to travel faster than ever to a much wider audience.

Nowadays, almost everything is known about the assassination of King Charles: who killed the king and his son D. Luís Filipe; where, when and who decided to eliminate the royal family; who could have prevented the shots being fired from the Terreiro do Paço on Saturday 1st February 1908; the assassins' motives; the weapons used in the massacre; who sold them and who bought them; who financed the operation and how and where the crime was committed. It is also known which group of the *Carbonari* Manuel Buíça and Alfredo Costa belonged to, and that they did not act alone. They were, in fact, part of a much bigger operation, divided into three teams stationed in different areas of the Baixa district of Lisbon. The regicide brigade was made up of 18 people, including three foreigners.

The regime was facing a crisis due to its lack of credibility in the eyes of the public and was surrounded by escalating electoral violence and the threat of bombings, carried out by anarchists, *Carbonari* and Republican radicals. The system of rotating parties was also running out of political solutions and a succession of financial scandals were rapidly accumulating.

This pre-revolutionary environment was far from exclusively Portuguese. Throughout Europe, but also in the United States of America and other parts of the world, the end of the nineteenth century and the beginning of the twentieth century were characterized by political violence directed against the ruling elites and the established social order. It was no longer a matter of the territorial debates, questions of sovereignty or dynastic conflicts of the past, but the emergence of a new phenomenon which differed in its intensity and internationalism. Kings and their heirs, emperors, presidents of republics, prime ministers and heads of government were ambushed and slaughtered by anarchists intent on using violence to bring about a social revolution in Europe. In railway stations, cafes, restaurants, parliaments or on the streets, the ruling classes were targets for terrorist attacks carried out, in most cases, by lone assassins. Monarchs and Republican leaders alike faced stabbings, shootings and bombs. King Charles himself, with prescient wit, often remarked that as well as catching common illnesses such as flu, kings could also suffer from other "attacks", a joke attributed to his uncle, King Umberto I of Italy, who survived two previous assassination attempts before dying at the hands of an anarchist in July 1900.

The social unrest and bombings in Portugal were insignificant in comparison to what was happening in Spain, France, Italy, or Russia. In Barcelona alone, for example, 140 attacks took place between 1888 and 1909. In Portugal, almost all the apprentice bombers had connections with the *Carbonari*, the armed wing of the Freemasons. Fuelled by a hatred of the institutions of monarchy and the king, they made themselves known mainly at gatherings in cafes in the Baixa district of Lisbon and, less frequently, by acts involving rudimentary explosive devices on the streets of the capital, which often caused more damage to the perpetrators than the intended victims.

The planning of the regicide began outside the country, a few weeks before it took place. In September 1907, Sebastião de Magalhães Lima, Grand Master of the Grand Orient of Portugal, travelled to Bordeaux for an international publishing congress. In November, while in Paris, he was photographed with a group of other members of the Grand Orient of Portugal who were involved in meetings with representatives of the Grand Orient of France and revolutionaries from Barcelona. He was seeking support to carry out a coup in Portugal, develop revolutionary propaganda and organize an attack on the prime minister João Franco and King Charles. Some French anti-Masonic organizations published reports on the meetings in the local newspapers. The minister in Paris, Sousa Rosa, warned the authorities in Lisbon that something was being planned. In the weeks that followed, while still in France, Magalhães Lima spoke at various Masonic lodges, repeating his threats.

The Elevator Coup, carried out on 28 January 1908 by Progressive and Republican dissidents failed to overthrow the government of João Franco and strike a blow against the regime, but the operation led by Alfredo Costa and Manuel Buíça did not make the same mistakes. Four days later, the king and his heir were killed. News of the assassinations spread rapidly throughout a frightened Lisbon. In the afternoon alone, 3,200 telegraphs were sent from the capital, the greatest communication flow since the telegraph had been introduced to Portugal. In the days which followed, the newspapers were busy reporting the details of the assassinations, offering different interpretations of the event. The press was responsible for broadcasting the events that had taken place in the Terreiro do Paço, and for giving it added international significance. Europe had already discovered that its monarchs and political leaders could be slaughtered in broad daylight and journalists from various countries rushed to Lisbon to report on the regicide.

There is no photographic record of the assassination. The group accompanying King Charles included the photographer from the *Illustração Portugueza*, who had been in Vila Viçosa reporting on the royal family's winter holidays and photographing a royal hunting party. Joshua Benoliel photographed official receptions and scenes from everyday life or strikes and riots with the same ease and aesthetic expertise. Although he was at the scene, he did not manage to capture any images. In order to compensate the readers of the *Illustração Portugueza*, he went to the morgue two days later to photograph the corpses. The cover of the magazine published that day offered a different time perspective on the story – a typical Benoliel photograph entitled "A hundred metres from the throne" in which the future king greeted the dignitaries awaiting his father's arrival in Lisbon, moments before he disembarked – while the inside pages featured predictable images of the area where the assassination had taken place, together with photographs of the corpses of the assassins.

Having missed the opportunity to capture the fatal moment, from then onwards everything would be photographed, reported and published: the murder weapons, the vigils and funerals, the funeral procession, the crowds on the streets, the ranks of soldiers, the condolences from national and foreign figures, and João Franco heading into exile.

In the weeks which followed, the headquarters of the *O Século* newspaper, which owned the magazine, would be flooded with articles on the assassinations that had been published in foreign newspapers, since Spanish, French, English, Brazilian, German, Italian, Austrian and other newspapers had all reported it. This chain reaction added a new dimension to the regicide. Starting on 2 March, the *Illustração Portugueza* itself decided to publish a series of drawings of the scene, thus creating an iconography of the attack. It then became a matter of making the facts visible through the imagined gaze of the press in various countries, presenting the regicide as an international event. These reconstructions were full of dramatic details that were often incorrect or even imagined: whereas photography was supposed to capture the instant, drawing offered any artist and publisher the opportunity to interpret it and add their own understanding of the facts. Having failed to do justice to the moment, this was how the *Illustração Portugueza* chose to record what had taken place.

The publication of graphic reconstructions of the attack in the foreign press continued. Three months later, illustrations of the regicide were still appearing in the international press. In total, more than two dozen images from very different places were circulating, ranging from Paris to Belém do Pará in Brazil. The most remarkable of all, due to its creativity, came from a Canton newspaper in China, which reproduced the scene in an imaginary Terreiro do Paço. News of the regicide had spread throughout the world: at the time, information was already circulating rapidly. Telegraph networks served by undersea cables, railway lines and steam navigation routes now covered the entire planet, enabling news to travel faster than ever to a much wider audience. The attention given to the Portuguese regicide beyond its own borders was not due to its tragic or sensationalist aspects, but primarily because it was a sign of an era dominated by the popular press. The explosive growth and industrialization of news from the second half of the nineteenth century onwards may be explained by a combination of different factors: the arrival of the telephone; the invention of the rotary press, which enabled 60,000 copies of an eight-page newspaper to be printed per hour; the introduction of the linotype machine, with a keyboard that made it possible to assemble the lead typographic matrices mechanically, thus increasing the number of characters that a typographer could set from 1,200 to 6,000 per hour; the growing number of news agencies, of which the European *Havas*, *Wolff* and *Reuters* and the American *Associated Press* are the best examples.

The subject became attractive. Monarchs featured frequently in the news and were still at the centre of political life. The Constitution in force at the time – the Constitutional Charter- maintained the king's role as arbiter in domestic politics. The journalists who arrived in Lisbon realized what had taken place: rather than simply an "anarchist" coup, this was a coup d'état. The regicide was the precursor to the Republic, which arrived thirty-one months later. Once the figurehead of the regime had been removed, the regime itself was left fighting for its survival, thus magnifying the impact of the news abroad. Furthermore, King Charles was a well-travelled monarch. He had stayed in Madrid, Paris and London, received heads of state from various countries and given interviews to foreign newspapers. Portugal was part of the international relations itinerary. Hence, the regicide pushed a small, peripheral European country onto the front pages of the world's newspapers, making it the first truly global event of the Portuguese twentieth century. As the journalist for the *Kreuz-Zeitung* in Berlin wrote on 5 February 1908, "the dramatic end to King Charles of Portugal and the Crown Prince relegates all other current events to second place". The day before, the *New York Times* had published a text which claimed "Portugal is so small and of so little importance to the development of modern civilization that the political crimes which have brought this kingdom to the centre of international affairs become even more sinister." On 4 February, *Le Journal des Débats* in Paris confronted its readers with "this drama which demands universal attention that is, even today, still somewhat unusual for Portuguese affairs". The ambush in Terreiro do Paço made the headlines and was the subject of reports, analysis, commentaries, caricature and illustrated reconstructions. There was huge interest in the event. The *Correio da Manhã* from Rio de Janeiro reported, also on the 4th of February: "A dense crowd gathered outside the entrance to our building, eager to read the bulletins we posted on the unfortunate events that had taken place in Lisbon. Our first edition sold out completely, and in many places was sold by the page for exorbitant prices". Another sign of the global impact of the events of 1 February 1908 can be examined in terms of references in contemporary literature. The Czech writer Jaroslav Hašek mentioned the crime in Lisbon in the first chapter of *The Good Soldier Švejk*, one of the best and most famous satirical novels of the time, written in around 1916. In addition to King Charles' assassination – the assassination of the Crown Prince was omitted – the opening pages include references to the assassination of the Empress Sissi of Austria-Hungary ten years earlier. The memory of the political violence of this era was reproduced in numerous ways: the Portuguese case was no exception.

PAULO JORGE FERNANDES
Institute of Contemporary History, Nova University Lisbon

Bibliography

BAÊNA, Miguel Sanches de, *Diário de D. Manuel e Estudo sobre o Regicídio*, Lisbon, Alfa, 1990.
EVANS, David, CANAVEIRA, Manuel Filipe (coord.), *Regicídio e República: Olhares Britânicos e Norte-Americanos*, Casal de Cambra, Caleidoscópio, 2010.
RAMOS, Rui, *D. Carlos*, Lisbon, Círculo de Leitores, 2006.
SAMARA, Maria Alice, TAVARES, Rui, *O Regicídio*, Lisbon, Tinta-da-China, 2008.
VIEIRA, Joaquim, MONICO, Reto, *Mataram o Rei! O Regicídio na Imprensa Internacional*, Almoçageme, Pedra da Lua, 2006.

1910
The Republican Revolution

The most important event in Portugal in 1910 was the downfall of a monarchy that had existed for over seven hundred years and its replacement by a regime – the Republic – of a kind that was still a rarity in the continent. At the time, Europe was composed of four empires, eleven monarchies and only two republics.

Despite material progress and the sociopolitical consolidation of liberalism under the nineteenth-century monarchy, when the Republican revolution triumphed in Lisbon on 5 October 1910 Portugal was largely a poor, rural and illiterate country. In the globalizing context of the *Belle Époque*, defined by the acceleration of industrialization, social massification and political pressure for democratization, the country was backward, lagging behind the Anglo-Germanic driving force in Europe and the French, Belgian, Dutch, Swiss and Nordic economies and societies; it was on a level with Spain or southern Italy, only ranking higher than the Slavic and Balkan autocracies of the East.

A small, peripheral country in the old continent, Portugal compensated for its inferior status by the fact that it possessed a vast colonial empire amounting to two million square kilometres, twenty times larger than the metropole, divided by three ocean coastlines that were very distant from each other. It was this empire – in the process of being restructured at the time, albeit hampered by a lack of resources and the territorial ambitions of its neighbours – together with the fact that its constitutional monarchy had European-style laws and institutions which ensured Lisbon remained aligned with the other major capitals, sharing their cosmopolitan fashions, values and expectations within an increasingly competitive international environment defined by new diplomatic alliances and tensions that would result in the Great War of 1914–1918.

Studying the establishment of the Republic in Portugal entails, from the outset, recognizing that it emerged within a European and world context which, in the early years of the twentieth century, witnessed a resurgence of revolutionary ideas and violence on an international level: there was an attempted revolution in Russia in 1905, the Persian Revolution in 1906, the rebellion of the "Young Turks" in 1908, the Greek military coup and the Tragic Week in Barcelona in 1909; insurrections in Mexico and the fall of the Chinese empire in 1910–1911 and, finally, the Balkan War of 1912–1913. Even in countries which did not experience such dramatic events, social and political upheavals intensified: urban uprisings and strikes, government instability, political radicalism and institutional challenges were evident in Berlin, London, Madrid, Paris and Vienna. The regicide of King Charles in 1908 may have given Portugal a bad reputation, but the wave of assassinations of high-ranking dignitaries was transnational, claiming the lives of the American president William McKinley in 1901, King Umberto of Italy and King Alexander of Serbia in 1900 and 1903 respectively, and the Empress Elizabeth of Austria in 1898. In 1906, King Alfonso XIII of Spain barely escaped an assassination attempt.

The most important event in Portugal in 1910 was the downfall of a monarchy that had existed for over seven hundred years and its replacement by a regime – the Republic – of a kind that was still a rarity in the continent. At the time, Europe was composed of four empires, eleven monarchies and only two republics, namely the French, which had been in existence since 1870, and the Swiss, based on a system of cantons that dated back to the Middle Ages. Republicanism was primarily an American model, which would triumph in China in 1911 but only arrive in force in Europe after 1918, extending from Germany to Russia and from Austria to Turkey and including the new states created when the European map was redrawn at the Versailles Peace Conference. The Portuguese Republic was therefore original in two aspects: it was the only major change of political regime in Western Europe that took place prior to the Great War and also the pioneer for the wave of Republicanization in the continent that defined the post-war era.

Even in an atmosphere conducive to change, acceleration and dizzying progress, the events in Lisbon were still viewed as highly irregular by many European governments. The Third French Republic and the short-lived Spanish Republic (1873–1874) had been the result of concrete events: the resignation of Napoleon III after the triumph of German unification in the case of the former, and the abdication of King Amadeu I, in the latter. The barricades in Lisbon, manned by civilians and Machado Santos' *Carbonária*, the surrender, almost without a struggle, of the monarchists, and the exile of King Manuel II and the royal family recalled the Springtime of the Peoples in 1848 or the earlier outbreak of anti-monarchism and anti-conservativism in 1789 – an interpretation later reinforced when the Republican government began to resemble a sectarian and liberticidal repetition of the Jacobinism of the past, in the eyes of monarchist Europe. There was, in fact, an entrenched "Frenchism" in the Portuguese Republican movement and ideology, particularly during the propaganda phase and the assault on power, but also afterwards in much of the legislation produced by the new regime. From the 1870s to the final radicalization of the struggle against King Manuel II, the Portuguese Republican ideology – which intended to carry out a broad modernizing, emancipatory and messianic revolution destined to restore the glory of Portugal – was heavily influenced by the imaginary, achievements and heroes of the French Third Republic, also popularized by the Masonic networks and social circles which united the leading figures in the anti-monarchist cause. In the European roll call of left-wing movements, other sources of inspiration may have been Spanish socialism or anarchism, the British trade unionist labour movement or German social democracy. Yet none of these alternatives had the force of ideological Francophilia as a model for Republicanism. The key elements in the Portuguese Republican world view came from Paris: the revolutionary methodology, the rhetoric of liberties and the secular programme for removing the Church from education and the state. With regard to this latter – defining – aspect, the 1911 law on the separation of church and state was modelled on the French law of 1905, just as the Portuguese legislation on divorce in 1910 and part of the Constitution in 1911 echoed the work of the French revolutionaries of 1791–1792, while the post-1910 education reforms closely followed the pedagogy of Jules Ferry.

Concerning the major options for foreign policy within the Republican doctrine, until the end of the nineteenth century a certain closeness to France coexisted with plans for Iberian federalism, envisaged as the future for the Iberian Peninsula, finally liberated from the "reactionary" rule of the Braganzas and the Bourbons, in Madrid. Due to the British Ultimatum and the Republicanization of nationalism and of the colonial cause, Francophilia and the Iberian dream were the reverse side of the Anglophobia of the revolutionary left and its desire for Portugal to escape the stranglehold of the English by diversifying international relations. However, in 1898, after Spain's colonial losses to the United States of America and the weakness demonstrated by the Republicans in its neighbouring country, the Portuguese Republican movement became convinced that the Iberian project was a fantasy and that the viability of any future regime in a country in need of support from the major powers, both in Europe and Africa, would have to involve reconciliation with Great Britain. Despite the Ultimatum, or because of it, King Charles had never lost sight of this question. With King Manuel II already on the verge of assuming power, the Portuguese Republican Party embarked on a course of political realism, pledging to honour all the international commitments (political, financial and diplomatic) of the Portuguese state and reaffirming the old alliance with London.

Despite its Francophile sympathies, the Republican regime needed to be pragmatically Anglophile, adopting a system of dual affinities that would define the position of the Republic on the complex and changing international political chessboard of 1910 and which was, in fact, facilitated by the existing *Entente Cordiale* between Paris and London. In the summer of 1910, just a few weeks before seizing power in Lisbon, the leaders of the Portuguese Republican Party sent a delegation to France and to England to sound out European acceptance of the Republic. It was composed of José Relvas, Magalhães Lima (the Grand Master of the Freemasons) and Alves da Veiga (the civilian leader of the failed Republican revolt of 31 January 1891). In preparation for the trip, the three published a Republican manifesto in leading newspapers in London, Madrid, New York, Paris, Rio de Janeiro and Rome.

The main concern was England, the old ally of the Braganzas and head of the *Entente Cordiale*. The Portuguese delegation promised the Foreign Office that the Portuguese Republic would be a government of law and order at home and abroad, in order to convince London to treat the future regime change as a matter of domestic politics, and argued that the alliance, which still existed and always would, served to unite peoples, not dynasties. Rather than expressing active support, Great Britain declared its neutrality.

The English position encouraged French endorsement. France welcomed the Portuguese anticlerical programme and saw the future Republic as a "sister" in Europe that would help undermine any threats from the Spanish: the monarchy under Alfonso XIII, known to be hostile to the prospect of a Republic on its borders, would not intervene without British approval. Moreover, the English government had been making approaches to Madrid since 1906–1907, with certain voices (such as Winston Churchill) claiming that Spain was a more important partner than Portugal in the Iberian Peninsula and, by extension, the western Mediterranean, where the British had interests. Hence, it was vital for the Republican revolution to court London and obtain (some) recognition, not only as an international endorsement, but also to temper any political alignment between Edward VII (and later George V) and Alfonso XIII.

The Republican delegation returned satisfied and hastened preparations for the revolution, which triumphed in October. The new Republic, however, was received with some coldness and hostility by the more conservative countries (particularly Spain) and with a certain reserve, mistrust or caution by other governments. Hence, international recognition was somewhat delayed, instilling fears in Lisbon that a part of Europe might take advantage of the downfall of King Manuel II to destroy Portuguese independence and divide up the colonial assets of a small state with insufficient military resources, that was financially dependent on foreign support and was developing an (overly) radical political agenda. Initially, at the end of 1910, only the South American republics inspired by Brazil (a post-Braganza republic since 1889), recognized the Portuguese Republic. The United States of America did so in 1911, following the opening of the Constituent Assembly. French recognition came in August, shortly after the Constitution was approved and President Manuel de Arriaga was elected. London only acknowledged it at the beginning of September, eleven months after 5 October when it felt that the new institutional order had been established in Lisbon, thus paving the way for its recognition by other countries – Germany, Austria, Spain and Italy, the latter diverging form the Holy See which was in open opposition to Portuguese secularism. The First Republic of Portugal, which had finally broken with almost all aspects of the monarchy (except the Africanist mission), established itself as a regime that would continue to pursue the major foreign policy options, maintaining and relaunching the alliance with England and seeking acceptance and friendship among the nations closest to it in Europe and Africa. The leaders of the Portuguese Republican Party were aware that they had created a new regime which was revolutionary and radical in many aspects – and which would appear even more sectarian in the eyes of its many enemies and critics as a result of the practical politics involved in the everyday management of the country. They also knew that Portugal was sailing through troubled international waters. In Europe the position of the new Republic remained weak and Lisbon attempted to circumvent this by reviving the Africanist option, embracing the patriotic task of building up a "new Brazil" in Africa, planned to be much greater than the original Brazil. The Ministry of the Colonies was therefore created in 1911 and, following the new Constitution, a policy of decentralization and development was established for the overseas territories, destined to mitigate the policies of war and conquest of previous years.

As history would later record, in order to safeguard the colonial empire, remove the "Spanish threat" and enhance the reputation of the Republic within the European order of great democratic powers, the Republican government decided to become involved in the Great War of 1914–1918, sending troops to the African hinterlands in

Angola and Mozambique and a Portuguese Expeditionary Force to Flanders. However, this voluntary internationalist commitment – perhaps the most important and risky foreign policy option in the whole of the First Republic – had drastic consequences, chiefly the crisis and overthrow of the regime itself by the military in May 1926.

José Miguel Sardica
Faculty of Human Sciences from Catholic University of Portugal

Bibliography

CATROGA, Fernando, *O Republicanismo em Portugal da Formação ao 5 de Outubro de 1910*, 2 vols., Coimbra, Faculdade de Letras da Universidade de Coimbra, 1991.

FERREIRA, José Medeiros, *A República Corrigida e Aumentada*, Lisbon, Edições 70, 2015.

RAMOS, Rui, "A revolução republicana de 1910 e a política externa portuguesa", in ALMEIDA, João Marques, RAMOS, Rui (coord.), *Revoluções, Política Externa e Política de Defesa em Portugal: Séc. XIX–XX*, Lisbon, Cosmos/Instituto da Defesa Nacional, 2008, pp. 55–94.

SARDICA, José Miguel, *Da Monarquia à República: Pequena História Política, Social e Militar*, Lisbon, Alêtheia, 2011.

TEIXEIRA, Nuno Severiano, "A República e a política externa", in MENESES, Filipe Ribeiro de, OLIVEIRA, Pedro Aires de (coord.), *A Primeira República Portuguesa: Diplomacia, Guerra e Império*, Lisbon, Tinta-da-China, 2011, pp. 23–33.

1911
Resorts and Tourism: From Madeira to the Algarve

From the eighteenth century onwards, the grand tour *was linked to the holiday resorts visited by European invalids. In spas, patients sought treatment for a variety of ailments and, in the winter, they looked for the mild climate of the Mediterranean to cure respiratory illnesses. Spas were an early part of tourism, and the search for a cure was one of the main reasons for visiting holiday resorts.*

The year 1911 was decisive for tourism in Portugal. From 12 to 19 May, Lisbon welcomed around four hundred delegates at the 4th Tourism Conference, three hundred of whom took a cruise to the Portuguese islands. At the same time, on the mainland, the Republican government endorsed the sector by an official statement by the Ministry of Development and by the creation of the Madeira Agricultural Board (1911–1919), whose support of development was based on tourism. In 1914, a plan for Estoril included beaches, spas and gambling. Gradually, over the twentieth century, touristification and national awareness of tourism were gaining ground, partly as a result of writers from the previous and the current century, such Almeida Garrett (1799–1854), with *Viagens na Minha Terra* [Travels in my Country] (1846), Ramalho Ortigão (1836–1915), with *As Praias de Portugal: Guia do Banhista e do Viajante* [Beaches of Portugal: a Guide for Bathers and Visitors] (1876), Raul Proença (1884–1941), with his excellent *Guia de Portugal* [Guide to Portugal] (1924), and José Saramago (1922–2010), with *Viagem a Portugal* [Trip to Portugal] (1981).

England played an important part in the early development of tourism worldwide. A doctor, Richard Russell (1687–1759), who settled in Brighton in 1747, started the idea of sea-water bathing, which was the basis of therapeutic spa tourism and led to the creation of other resorts. In Portugal, the appreciation of the coast and the beach came later, led by Ramalho Ortigão's study, which mentions the benefits of sea bathing to provide "calcium phosphate for your bones, iodine for your tissues, bromide for your nerves, [and] vital heat for your cold and pallid blood". He also gave an itinerary of beaches, from the Lisbon region to the Minho, selecting "elegant beaches" (Cascais, Foz, Granja), "cosmopolitan beaches" (Figueira da Foz, Espinho, Póvoa de Varzim) and "obscure beaches" (Nazaré, Santa Cruz, Ericeira, Foz do Arelho, São Martinho do Porto). He considered São Pedro de Moel "the most delightful, friendliest and most intimate of Portuguese beaches". The south, including the Algarve, was not mentioned, since it only began to be appreciated many decades later, although some of its beaches were visited. José Malhoa's painting *À Beira-Mar* [At the Seaside], from 1918, symbolises a new approach, a new conquest of the sea.

Madeira, the gateway to the Atlantic, had a dominant position in the sector, thanks to British influence and to its historical ties with England from the early seventeenth century. In the eighteenth century the island developed as an upper-class resort, but its occupation by British troops in 1801–1802 and 1807–1814 led to a recession in leisure trips. At the same time, as a consequence of the loss of British visitors, in 1815, to French and Italian resorts, the role of Madeira as a fashionable resort in the style of the Alps grew in importance. The presence of a British community on the island led to changes in patterns of socialization, as seen in the conversion of manors and farm-houses for rent. Such families, who spent the winter enjoying the mild climate, laid the foundations of the present hotel businesses and tourist guides. The innovative project created by the Reid family is a paradigm, with echoes that subsist today. The growing number of steamships on the Cape route and the needs of their passengers gave rise to new services, which in turn promoted the islands economy.

From the eighteenth century onwards, the *grand tour* was linked to the holiday resorts visited by European invalids. In spas, patients sought treatment for a variety of ailments, and, in the winter, they looked for the mild climate of the Mediterranean to cure respiratory illnesses. Spas were an early part of tourism, and the search for a cure was one of the main reasons for visiting holiday resorts. Portugal has a long tradition of thermal waters, from Roman times up to the present day, offering many and various forms of treatment. In Madeira, as in Mediterranean Europe, patients travelling in search of treatment for conditions such as tuberculosis and depression led to two trends: tourism, and climate-based resorts. The latter implied lengthy stays, temporary residence permits, often the displacement of whole families or of patients and their servants, and help from local doctors. Many doctors from the United Kingdom and other European countries accompanied these patients, using their stay to study the best places for climate-based treatment. Today, health tourism still includes these motivations related to physical health and well-being.

The development of transport and communication networks was a response not only to the need for improved personal mobility, but also to a growing interest in travel, mainly by European elites. The railway and later the motor car enabled increased flows of people throughout the country, while the modernization of sea traffic led to increased transatlantic and leisure travel, finally reaching the impressive number of tourists now travelling by plane, one of the dynamics which most clearly shows the shortening of distances, the speed of personal movement and the globalization of tastes.

The growth of spa tourism, in Portugal and in the rest of Europe, was closely related to the development of railways. Between 1888 and 1940, the Portuguese *Railway Gazette* played a fundamental part in the general promotion of tourism in Portugal. From the mid-nineteenth century, the rail network brought people to the coast and the beaches. In Madeira, from 1893 to 1943, it spurred tourism in the hill resort of Monte, and later helped to develop the famous wicker toboggan rides down from Monte as a one of the island's permanent tourist attractions.

The history of tourism is related to that of leisure, relaxation and the legitimization of rights, which were spreading throughout society, including the working classes, in the 1930s. Cruises from Germany, organized by *Kraft durch Freude* [Strength through Joy], which brought to Lisbon and Funchal over six thousand German holidaymakers between 1935 and 1939, are clear evidence of this phenomenon. Social tourism from Italy and Germany influenced the creation in Portugal, in June 1935, of the *Fundação Nacional para a Alegria no Trabalho* [National Foundation for Joy in Work], today well-known as INATEL. After the Second World War, tourism became increasingly important: in 1948, the Universal Declaration of Human Rights included the right to rest and leisure, a defined work timetable and breaks for holidays. Nowadays, tourism is directly related to the political management of a society's leisure culture. Its impressive energy and development, which was still growing in the twenty-first century, is predicated on paid holidays, leisure time, appropriate facilities and lower transport costs.

Beaches, the most popular sites for mass tourism, have added to the attraction of destinations such as the Algarve. This region – which has experienced a continuous and vertiginous growth in tourist numbers, first of Portuguese in the 1960s and then opening gradually to a mass influx from all over Europe, especially the United Kingdom and Germany – has finally become one of the brand images of the country, as well as an important source of income. The phenomenon of the Algarve and of Portugal as a tourist destination has resulted in many changes, in urban lifestyles as well as in landscapes, in recent years.

Currently, though Madeira and the Algarve continue to be attractive destinations, Portugal is facing other trends, which result from a desire for contact with and observation of Nature; this first arose around 1965, thanks to Claus-Dieter Hetzer, but gained impetus in the 1980s. This segment of nature tourism relies on sustainability, rejecting more aggressive and/or undisciplined approaches. Nature tourism is often confused with rural, adventure or sport tourism. On Madeira, where beach resorts are almost impossible, most effort has always been directed to mountain tourism. With their mild climate and unequalled landscape, the *levadas* (irrigation channels which cross the island from north to south) present a unique natural experience for visitors to enjoy.

† Alberto Vieira
Centre for Studies of Atlantic History

Bibliography

BARTON, Susan, *Working-Class Organisations and Popular Tourism, 1840–1970*, Manchester, Manchester University Press, 2005.

BERGHOFF, Hartmut et al. (coord.), *The Making of Modern Tourism: The Cultural History of the British Experience, 1600–2000*, London, Palgrave, 2002.

GOMES, Luís Francisco Valentim, *O Caminho do Comboio e as Alterações Urbanísticas do Funchal*, Funchal, Centro de Estudos de História do Atlântico, 2005.

ORTIGÃO, Ramalho, *As Praias de Portugal: Guia do Banhista e do Viajante*, Porto, Magalhães e Moniz, 1876.

PIMLOTT, J. A. R., *The Englishman's Holiday. A Social History*, London, Faber and Faber, 1947.

SILVA, Raquel Henriques da, "Estoril, estação marítima, climática, thermal e sportiva: As etapas de um projecto 1914–1932", *Arquivo de Cascais: Boletim Cultural do Município*, no. 10, pp. 41–60.

1914
Amadeo, the Delaunays and Modernism

In interaction with the Delaunays, especially with the perspective of Sonia Delaunay, Amadeo de Souza Cardoso constructed a dialogue between Portuguese popular motifs and an internationally-driven modernism. Far from being exceptional, this confluence is part of a global phenomenon – the relationship between the vernacular and the modern.

On 20 April 2016, the largest retrospective of the work of Amadeo de Souza Cardoso since 1958 opened in the Grand Palais in Paris. In the press release and in various communication media, the phrase of the respected American art historian Robert Loescher, published in *Art in America* in 2000, following the exhibition dedicated to the artist in Washington DC and Chicago, served as a summary and a motto: Amadeo was for a long time "one of early modernism's best-kept secrets". The subtitle of the documentary by Christophe Fonseca, released in conjunction with the Paris exhibition, went further, presenting Souza Cardoso as "the last secret of modern art". The geographical and cultural peripheral origins, the involvement in the Parisian art scene (1906–1914), the personal take on the canonical avant-gardes, the early death (1918) and late recognition (delayed until the 1950s) explain the continuous articulation and re-elaboration of the idea of revelation as related to Amadeo's work. In 1916, on the basis of the only two, and badly received, solo exhibitions held in Portugal while he was alive, Amadeo was described by the artist Almada Negreiros as "the first discovery of Portugal in twentieth-century Europe". The idea reappeared in the title of the exhibition dedicated to Amadeo at the Modern Art Centre of the Calouste Gulbenkian Foundation in Lisbon in 1983, at the time when Portugal was becoming closer to the rest of Europe through the negotiations for its membership of the European Economic Community (1986).

Over a hundred years after Souza Cardoso's death, his (re)discovery continues to fascinate, and not only because more of his works have come to light in the twenty-first century. The clear links of his art with the avant-gardes of Europe's "centre" have become recognized not only, or not necessarily, as a proof of closeness or belonging. Gradually, they have also been re-appreciated for their critical distance – for the difference which still allows acknowledgment. Following the impact of the global turn in art history, Amadeo grew to be a seductive and "corrective" "other". In line with the present challenges and agendas of the discipline, his work, both local and global, not only enriches the cartography of modernism, rescuing marginalized geographies and contexts, but also expands the conceptual definition of modernism itself, showing circuits and networks, appropriations and fusions which defy orthodox definitions and reductive methodologies. However, despite some changes, the continuous "discovery" of Amadeo's work up until today still carries on the impulse of discovery that had such a structural role in the art developed in generic terms from the end of the nineteenth century up to the mid-twentieth century. Modernism, in its multi-faceted reaction to the process of modernization – urbanization, secularization, the spread of liberalism, general belief in scientific and technological evolution, globaliza-tion of capitalism and the development of a mass consumer society – was seeking, in art as in other fields, routes to regeneration. The other, distant in space and/or time – "primitive", "naive" and/or "exotic" – was a particularly fertile creative stimulus. But it also acted to reinforce supposed hierarchies and evolutionary gradations. From the mid-1980s, art history tried to deconstruct or overcome such evaluative assumptions, but in fact sometimes succeeded in reanimating them. While not being the last secret of modern art – a subject whose global history remains largely unwritten – Amadeo is crucial for placing Portuguese art in a global context and for reflecting on the epistemological profile of this endeavour.

Born in 1887 in Manhufe, in the district of Amarante, Amadeo moved to Paris in 1906, living and working in Montparnasse, the exuberant artistic heart of the city. His journey was far from unique: it was part of an international transit which, since the mid-nineteenth century, had brought artists from many countries to the French capital for further training, and in particular to the influential École des Beaux-Arts, either privately funded (by relatives or others) or on government scholarships. He travelled to Paris with the Lisbon-born painter Francis Smith, and early in his stay he socialized with Portuguese artists such as Eduardo Viana, Manuel Bentes, Domingos Rebelo and Emmerico Nunes. Paris was a magnet for many artists from all over the world – from Latin America to Japan, from United States to Russia. Increasingly an artistic centre of gravity, this imperial metropolis was one of the focal points of modern art, whose development was based on transnational intersections and exchanges.

It was here, a dynamic crossroads of ideas and people, that Souza Cardoso constructed his personal and artistic path. The window of time when he did this is also significant. The chromatic ferocity of fauvism had just been recognized and labelled (1905), and expressionism was unfolding. Henri Matisse had his second solo exhibition at the Galerie Druet (1906). The post-Impressionism legacy was given its first major single artists retrospectives (Paul Gauguin in 1906 and Paul Cézanne in 1907, both in the Salon d'Automne). The Germans Daniel-Henry Kahnweiler and Wilhelm Uhde opened their galleries in Paris and positioned themselves as influential dealers in the emerging art. Pablo Picasso painted *Les Demoiselles d'Avignon* (1906–1907), and the critic Louis Vauxcelles commented on the reduction of reality to cubes in the work of Georges Braque (1908). The French newspaper *Le Figaro* published Marinetti's futurist manifesto, and Diaghilev's Ballets Russes performed in the capital for the first time (1909). The Salon des Indépendants in 1911 officially recognized cubism as a movement, and hosted Henri Rousseau's first posthumous retrospective, which would add other sources to the fascination with "primitivism", beyond African art and French Polynesian landscapes. Sonia and Robert Delaunay were developing a strand of abstract painting around 1912, called "orphism" by the critic Guillaume Apollinaire and "simultanism" by the Delaunays themselves. The influential American artist, critic and art historian Walter Pach, living in Paris since 1907, was a member of the circle surrounding Gertrude and Leo Stein and played a crucial role in the choice of artists for the 1913 Armory Show, the significant international exhibition of modern art which toured in New York, Chicago and Boston.

Souza Cardoso was able to critically absorb this fertile and creative context, outlined briefly above, through observation and interaction, including possible but not always verifiable contacts. Distancing himself from his earliest intention to study architecture, which he had begun in Lisbon, Amadeo soon dedicated himself to drawing and painting. From 1910, he attended classes given by Hermen Anglada-Camarasa (Academia Vitti), an internationally-exhibited Catalan painter with a particular approach within post-impressionism. In 1908, he met Lucie Pecetto, his future wife, and gradually distanced himself from the group of Portuguese artists, broadening his sphere of international contacts and becoming involved in the inter-cultural energy of Paris. He became friends with Amedeo Modigliani, the Jewish Italian painter and sculptor who had settled in Paris in 1906, exhibiting with him in 1911. They shared an interest in African sculpture and in the work of pre-Renaissance and early Renaissance painters, which Souza Cardoso had seen when he was in Brussels. He knew many modernist artists living in Paris: the Italians Gino Severini and Umberto Brunelleschi, the Spaniard Juan Gris, the Romanian Constantin Brancusi, the Russian Alexander Archipenko, the Mexican Diego Rivera, and the French Max Jacob, Robert Delaunay, and Delaunay's wife Sonia, Ukrainian-born and later naturalized French. Through the Delaunays, Souza Cardoso was introduced to figures immortalized in the history of modern art, such as Guillaume Apollinaire, Paul Klee, Francis Picabia, Marc Chagall, Umberto Boccioni and Albert Gleizes. His friendship with the Delaunays from 1911 led to changes in his painting, from then on alluding to their "simultaneous discs" and using a more vibrant and luminous palette; it also contributed to his international recognition beyond Paris. Also decisive for this was the publication of his album *XX Dessins*, which he sent to the most important art critics. After exhibiting alongside some of these artists in major Paris exhibitions (Salon des Indépendants in 1911 and 1912; Salon d'Automne in 1912), Amadeo was invited to participate in the Armory Show (1913) by Walter Pach, who helped him choose eight paintings. That year he also exhibited in the Galerie Der Sturm in Berlin and in other collective exhibitions, such as in Hamburg (1913), Milwaukee and London (both in 1914).

Returning to Portugal in August 1914 for his customary summer holidays, he stopped first in Spain, where he met Antoni Gaudí. Taken unawares by the start of the First World War, his visit home, meant to be brief, became final. Aged only 30, he died suddenly from the 1918 influenza pandemic in Espinho. His isolation in Manhufe had been alleviated by occasional visits and regular contact, especially with Eduardo Viana and the Delaunays. Between 1915 and 1917 Sonia and Robert took refuge from the war, first in Vila do Conde, where they stayed with Viana, and later in Monção and in Valença do Minho. The correspondence between them and Amadeo is evidence of the collective initiative *Corporation Nouvelle*, which, though frustrated, speaks of the desire to bring together geographically separated artists, to establish a dialogue between artistic disciplines, to join forces for international touring exhibitions (*Expositions Mouvantes*) and to publish art albums. Amadeo's network included a connection with the short-lived group of Portuguese futurists, among which the friendship and projects with Almada Negreiros stand out. Negreiros was also involved in the *Expositions Mouvantes* project, conceived from Portugal but with international ambitions. Within this collective enterprise, Delaunays' experiments with light effects were linked to the themes of the popular art and daily life that the couple encountered in northern Portugal.

In line with the independence which Souza Cardoso always maintained in relation to any kind of artistic orthodoxy, his work shows how reductive the practice of stylistic compartmentalization can be. He explored the visual, rather than theoretical, potential of the various avant-gardes that he met first-hand. He developed a formal and chromatic approach to painting which never abandoned representation; rather, he explored the possibilities of fragmentation and montage, commenting, sometimes humorously, on the avant-gardes closest to him, namely the Delaunays themselves. The last four years of his life were a phase of artistic maturation. In interaction with the Delaunays, especially with the perspective of Sonia Delaunay, Souza Cardoso constructed a dialogue between Portuguese popular motifs and an internationally-driven modernism. Far from being exceptional, this confluence is part of a global phenomenon – the relationship between the vernacular and the modern, gradually recognized by the historiography of modernism. The apparently random montages of elements and techniques (including collages of mirrors, hair-clips and mixtures of paint with sand) seen in his later works, completed in 1917, led some to hastily recognize a Dadaist sensibility, being developed at the time in Switzerland and New York. More important than claiming this label is the recognition that in Manhufe, shortly before he died, Amadeo was questioning the very limits of painting, while never relaxing his focus on contemporary reality.

JOANA BRITES
Faculty of Arts and Humanities, and Centre for Twentieth-Century
Interdisciplinary Studies, University of Coimbra

Bibliography

CASTRO, Lourdes Simões de (dir.), *At the Edge. A Portuguese Futurist. Amadeo de Souza Cardoso*, Lisbon, Ministério da Cultura, Gabinete de Relações Internacionais, 1999.

FREITAS, Helena de (coord.), *Amadeo de Souza-Cardoso: 1887–1918 [Catálogo Raisonné]*, 2 vols., Lisbon, Centro de Arte Moderna, Fundação Calouste Gulbenkian, 2007–2008.

HAYOT, Eric, WALKOWITZ, Rebecca (ed.), *A New Vocabulary for Global Modernism*, New York, Columbia University Press, 2016.

LEAL, Joana Cunha, "Trapped bugs, rotten fruits and faked collages: Amadeo Souza Cardoso's troublesome modernism", *Konsthistorisk Tidskrift/Journal of Art History*, vol. 82, no. 2, 2013, pp. 99–114.

VASCONCELOS, Ana (ed.), *O Círculo Delaunay/The Delaunay Circle*, Lisbon, Fundação Calouste Gulbenkian, 2015.

1916
Portugal and the Great War:
Victory with a Taste of Defeat

At the outset of the First World War, this was the international situation of the Portuguese Republic: threatened in Europe by Spain and in its colonies by Germany and weakened in both scenarios by the British policy of compromise with Spain regarding the Peninsular question, and with Germany in relation to the colonies.

In the final decades of the constitutional monarchy, before its abolition in 1910, Portuguese foreign policy and diplomatic action were conducted on two fronts: the European, dominated by the Anglo-Portuguese Alliance, and the colonial, directed towards the African empire. Within the international context at the turn of the century, their purpose was the same: to include Portugal in the foreign policy dynamics and plans of the great powers, whose interests and goals intersected with those of Portugal in Europe and Africa. The implantation of the Republic did not change the direction of the government's foreign policy or its strategic options, which were centred on the British alliance and on the African colonial enterprise. It also did not alter the threats and challenges which the monarchy had faced. Despite its international isolation, the Republic was still part of the ongoing developments in the international scene, both in Europe and in the colonies.

In the Mediterranean and the Atlantic, the interests of Portugal and the European powers continued to intersect. In the Atlantic, the Azores was still the focus of sustained interest, and the change of regime made no difference to Britain's position. Despite a report from the Admiralty, in 1912, questioning the strategic value of the Portuguese territory in the context of the Iberian Peninsula, Britain's interest in Portugal's Atlantic islands never wavered, and the request for guarantees on the exclusivity of the "facilities" was renewed by London whenever a new Foreign Minister took office in Lisbon.

In the Mediterranean, the Portuguese presence found expression in Portugal's accession to the Franco-German agreement of 1911, which ended the Agadir crisis. The Portuguese position, which was supportive of the powers of the Entente Cordiale, could not directly antagonise Spain, whose issues with France were still unresolved. The difficult relationship between the two Iberian states required an exercise in diplomacy on the part of Portugal, leading it to defer its accession until after the signing of the Franco-Spanish agreement in May 1912.

The Portuguese diplomatic adroitness in the process notwithstanding, Spain's growing rapprochement to the powers of the Entente, particularly Britain, resurrected the spectre of the Cartagena Agreement and renewed the central question of Portuguese foreign policy: the geopolitical balance between Spain's continental pressure and the overseas compensation of the Anglo-Portuguese alliance. The Spanish lobby in favour of the annexation of its neighbour was powerful, and although it was not the official position of Spain's foreign policy, the idea had not been totally rejected by King Alfonso XIII. The hypothesis was indeed encouraged by the atmosphere of political instability experienced in Portugal. Under such conditions, would the alliance with Britain prove to be sufficient, diplomatically and militarily, to guarantee Portuguese security?

This was a sensitive issue, and the British Foreign Office chose not to interfere directly in the Iberian question, favouring bilateral understandings between the protagonists. In the most critical moments, however, it was forced to step in. It never went so far as to accept military intervention and the annexation of Portugal, but consistently showed a degree of leniency towards Spain during the royalist incursions. Twice in 1911 and 1912, with the knowledge and consent of the Spanish government, monarchist troops marched from Spain into Portugal with the intent of restoring the monarchy. The raids were unsuccessful, but they had the immediate outcome of heightening the fear of the "Spanish threat".

In the face of this, in 1912 and 1913, Lisbon repeatedly asked the British Foreign Office to give formal guarantees regarding the alliance. To no avail – it never obtained more than an oral guarantee. The reason for this concerns the other dimension of Portuguese foreign policy: the colonial question.

As in 1898, a second Anglo-German agreement on the sharing of Portuguese colonies was signed between 1912 – 1913. Like the first, this was also a result of two distinct dynamics: first, the atmosphere of international tension, the arms race, and Anglo-German pre-war rivalry; second, the difficult situation in Portugal after the revolution, marked by international isolation and the internal political instability of the Republic. After the absolute fiasco of the Haldane mission (1912), the only way for Britain and Germany to keep dialogue open was the colonial question. Overseas compensation for Germany would be a final chance for Britain to uphold the fragile balance in Europe and to avoid conflict.

The internal and external vulnerability of the Portuguese Republic favoured this Anglo-German rapprochement. In 1912, on the basis of 1898 agreement – never put into practice, but also never terminated – the two powers signed a new treaty, renewing the terms of the first: it renegotiated the zones of influence, and, above all, expanded the legal grounds for intervention in Portuguese territories. This agreement also failed, under separate but simultaneous diplomatic pressure from the Portuguese and the French, who had been excluded from the division. The onset of the Great War would render it ultimately impracticable. But this instrument for international stability, which British foreign policy did not hesitate to use whenever it was deemed useful for British aims and interests, represented a real concrete threat to the colonies and to the Portuguese imperial project. At the start of the First World War, this was the international situation of the Portuguese Republic: threatened in Europe by Spain and in its colonies by Germany and weakened in both scenarios by the British policy of compromise with Spain in the Iberian question, and with Germany in relation to the colonial question. These two factors, together with the political situation at home, were at the root of Portugal's decision to enter the Great War.

Portuguese historiography has so far based its explanations for the country's entry into the 1914 – 1918 war on two distinct theories. The first is essentially based on the colonial thesis: Portugal joined the war to safeguard its colonies. This is beyond dispute. The Portuguese colonies, as we have seen, were the object of economic and strategic interest on the part of the great powers and, prior to the war, had twice functioned as a compensatory mechanism and exchange currency in the European balance of power. During the war, interest in the Portuguese colonies increased. Germany made them the target of military attacks and stirred their inhabitants up against Portuguese rule. Britain used them strategically for logistic support in its war operations. Above all, there was nothing to guarantee that, after the war, should its outcome require it, Britain would not once again play the hand of the Portuguese colonies at the negotiating table. The threat was real – the future of Portuguese sovereignty over its colonies was at stake. The colonial question was a heavy constraint and a mobilising factor for the country's foreign policy, indeed the only one that gathered consensus in Portuguese society.

However, the colonies on their own are insufficient to justify joining the war, and certainly do not account for active belligerence and military intervention in the European theatre of war. Future sovereignty and the integrity of the empire might have been ensured by means of a different strategy and a different choice of a theatre of operations – that is, by the maintenance of undeclared neutrality and by the concentration of war efforts in Africa.

The second theory is based on the European–Iberian thesis. Portugal entered the war to ensure its place in the "concert of Europe", and basically to keep the Spanish threat at bay. This is also beyond dispute. The international situation of the country was difficult prior to the war and did not become any easier during the course of the conflict. The "Spanish threat" was something palpable, and the fear was well-founded, the more so when Britain warned Portugal, on more than one occasion, that the Anglo-Portuguese Alliance would guarantee the security of the colonies and of the Portuguese coast but not of its land border. In this context, the diversification of the international status of the Iberian states was important for Portugal: in the face of Spanish neutrality, Portugal's belligerence on the side of the Allies and under the English alliance was a double guarantee, weakening Anglo-Spanish relations and strengthening the Anglo-Portuguese Alliance. It was a way of diversifying Portugal's international status, and of affirming Portugal's preponderance in the context of the Iberian Peninsula – in short, of dispelling the Spanish threat. This second theory explains why Portugal became belligerent, but still does not account for its military intervention in the European theatre.

To understand Portugal's participation in the European war these two theories have to be considered together with a third one: the internal political question – the republican regime's lack of political consolidation and national legitimacy. The interventionist strategy has to be considered in the following framework: in the face of social divisions and the political instability of the Republic, only an external threat and military intervention in the central theatre, alongside the great and among the great, could sustain national unity around the regime and achieve not only the external goals but also democratic consolidation and legitimation of the Republic.

And so Portugal entered the war, on the side of the Allies and under the Anglo-Portuguese Alliance, on 9 March 1916.

This strategy of opting for active belligerence and military intervention in the European war was clearly the surest way to attain the country's objectives: to safeguard the colonies, dispel the Spanish threat and consolidate the Republic. But despite being surer it was also the most difficult, since it required better conditions and more resources. And it was a realistic assessment of the strategic situation, that Portuguese foreign policy was betrayed by its own voluntaristic strategy. Firstly, because it failed to achieve national unity, aggravated internal divisions and led to a new change intended to alter the war policy: Sidónio Pais came to power in December 1917. Secondly, because it made a strategic mistake: its aims were too ambitious for the means available (economic and financial resources, military power and political consensus itself).

The results were seen in the Treaty of Versailles, signed in 1919. Portugal marched side by side with the victors, under the Arc de Triomphe, at the victory parade. However, it was far from having achieved its war goals at the Peace Conference.

The colonial question, which was the initial goal of the war, never really became a peace goal. Sovereignty over colonial territories ensued almost directly from Portugal's participation in the war. Even the restitution of Kionga, a small territory on the eastern coast of Africa, occupied by Germany since the late nineteenth century, cannot be seen as war reparation: it was only a reinstatement of international law. In terms of its colonies, Portugal claimed nothing more, but maintained the integrity of its empire.

The goals of peace were different from those of war, the most urgent need being the economic reconstruction of the country. Portuguese foreign policy would now concentrate its diplomatic efforts on financial matters: non-payment of war debts and the right to reparation and compensation from Germany.

However, there still remained the fundamental political question: Portugal's place in the "concert of nations" and the resolution of the Iberian question. While the economic and financial aims were in general attained, the same cannot be said of the country's international situation, which now involved participation in the reorganisation of the new world order and in the Executive Council of the League of Nations. This was the major failure of Portugal's foreign policy. A failure in absolute terms, because Portugal's application was not even considered; even worse, a failure in comparative terms, because neutral Spain achieved what belligerent Portugal could not.

Does it mean that Portugal lost the war? Yes and no. It did not, in the sense that it was a belligerent country that had fought beside the Allies and taken its seat as a victorious power at the Peace Conference. Moreover, because it managed to fully secure its colonial objectives and, to an extent, also its economic objectives. Yes, because it did not achieve its major political goal. The thwarted international objective, together with the never fulfilled domestic objectives, was the unarguable sign of a negative balance. By the end of the war, it was clear: the economic and financial situation, social instability, splits in the party system and the crisis of institutions had not only hampered the implementation of the Republic's modernising project, but also, in the end, precluded the regime's political consolidation and nationwide legitimation. Moreover, it had opened the door to the authoritarian drift that largely emerged from the rubble of the First War.

Nuno Severiano Teixeira
Portuguese Institute of International Relations, Nova University Lisbon

Bibliography

CORREIA, Sílvia, *Entre a Morte e o Mito: Políticas da Memória da I Guerra Mundial (1918–1933)*, Lisbon, Temas e Debates/Círculo de Leitores, 2015.

LOUSADA, Abílio Pires, ROCHA, Jorge da Silva (coord.), *Portugal na 1ª Guerra Mundial: Uma História Militar Concisa*, Lisbon, Comissão Portuguesa de História Militar, 2018.

MARQUES, Isabel Pestana, *Das Trincheiras com Saudade: A Vida Quotidiana dos Militares Portugueses na Primeira Guerra Mundial*, Lisbon, A Esfera dos Livros, 2008.

MENESES, Filipe Ribeiro de, *União Sagrada e Sidonismo: Portugal em Guerra (1916–1918)*, Lisbon, Cosmos, 2000.

TEIXEIRA, Nuno Severiano, *O Poder e a Guerra: Objectivos Nacionais e Estratégias Políticas na Entrada de Portugal na Grande Guerra (1914–1918)*, Lisbon, Estampa, 1996.

1917
Fatima, the Global Shrine

Fatima shares with other pilgrimage sites several characteristics seen in shrines that attract millions, for either religious or touristic reasons. What is less common in global terms is Fatima as a place of centrifugal movement, particularly in the journeys of the 'pilgrim' images of Our Lady of Fatima.

Up to 1917, Fatima, a civil parish in the municipality of Ourém, district of Santarém, and integrated in the patriarchate of Lisbon, was hardly worth including on maps of the country. But various newspapers, especially since July of that year, reported the beginning of a continuous flow of people who, for religious reasons, headed to the Cova da Iria in Fatima, drawn by the news that three children from the parish claimed to have seen the Mother of the Christian God there. This episode, known as "the apparitions of Fatima", has since becme a highly significant event.

A century later, we can see that the Fatima phenomen soon grew beyond the local scale; in fact, it became of international interest from the first months of the apparitions (the mariophanies, as they are known in theological terms). Due to the political and ideological context of religion in the First Portuguese Republic (1910–1926), to the international framework (when for the first time a world war was being waged), and to the intrinsic content which Catholic epistemology designated as the message of Fatima, these events were already known in France before the cycle of Marian apparitions had reached its end.

The different scenarios where Fatima was important for humanity can be defined as follows: first, between 13 and 27 May 1917, the events attracted the attention of local people; then, from August onwwards, they reached Ourém (seat of the municipality), Santarém (capital of the district, following instructions from the civil governor) and the rest of the country, including the most important platforms of discussion, such as the Parliament in Lisbon; from September onwards, they spread across Europe, especially into the battlefields where the Portuguese Expeditionary Force was engaged. During the 1930s, the site of the apparitions developed rapidly as a national centre of pilgrimage. Although it was only in 1930 that the devotion was formally approved, after the Bishop of Leiria had concluded the work of the canonical commission which he had set up to analyse the process, the numbers published in the press at the time showed a growing number of pilgrims during the 1920s. Throughout that decade the site was progressively equipped to welcome multitudes, and on the anniversary of the apparitions (13 May) records show 40,000 people in 1922, 100,000 in 1923 and in 1924, 200,000 in 1925, 240,000 in 1926, 200,000 in 1927, 500,000 in 1928, and 300,000 in 1929 and in 1930.

Fatima shares with other pilgrimage sites several characteristics seen in shrines that attract millions, for either religious or touristic reasons. What is less common in global terms is Fatima as a place of centrifugal movement, particularly in the journeys of the 'pilgrim' images of Our Lady of Fatima, which since 1947 have regularly travelled the world to spread the message of Fatima. The entity of the devotion, through its figurative representation, not only receives its devotees but also travels out to them, making a pilgrimage in reverse, travelling beyond its shrine. The first image, which went to the Netherlands in that year, crossed post-war Europe; by 2019, in all its journeys, it had travelled a distance equivalent to over sixteen times around the word measured at the Equator. Its itineraries, yet to be thoroughly studied, show the extent of the phenomenon on a global scale.

The representation of Fatima in the Catholic world, while it can be explained on a chronological basis, as showing particular actions related to the cult of the Virgin Mary, is also due to the fact that the community of believers understand the content witnessed by Jacinta Marto (1910–1920), Francisco Marto (1908–1919) and Lúcia de Jesus (1907–2005) as forming a theologically structured *corpus* of ideas. This *corpus*, known as the Message of Fatima, is based on axes such as prayer, penitence, conversion, reparation and peace. For this reason, and especially through the means mentioned above (power of place, and the pastoral strategy of the journeys of the Fatima pilgrim image), many places, in Portugal and in the wider world, are points on a map that show how Fatima has attained a universal dimension.

The databases of the Department of Studies of the Shrine of Fatima show ample evidence of the spread of the phenomenon on a global scale, allowing us to see the different features of this devotion and the typologies with which it is honoured and recalled. There are numerous Catholic territorial areas dedicated to the Virgin of Fatima: 17 dioceses (such as Nampula in Mozambique, Jardim in Brazil, Leiria-Fátima in Portugal, Zacapa in Guatemala, Warangal in India, and Alexandria-Cornwall in Canada), 1132 parishes (such as Acacia Ridge in Australia, Buenos Aires in Argentina, Heule in Belgium, Uíje in Angola, Kingston in Canada and Fatimapura Ankihalli in India) and 75 missions (Winston-Salem and Coldwater in the United States, Guayanilla Macana Rio in Puerto Rico, and Nyimba in Zambia).

The spirituality of Fatima has also originated several religious life congregations (there are 525 references to these, such as Sisters of the Immaculate Heart of Mary in Baltimore, USA, the Suore Oblate di Maria Vergine di Fatima in Italy, and the Sisters of Charity of the Convent of Our Lady of Fatima in Trichur, India), the associations of the faithful, brotherhoods, fraternities and other apostolate movements (475 references, among them the World Apostolate of Fatima, an international movement of pontifical right). The globalization of Fatima has other dimensions too, such as schools (400 references, such as the Altoona Central Catholic School of Our Lady of Fatima and the Immaculate Heart of Mary Seminary, in Santa Fé, USA, the Escola de Nossa Senhora de Fátima in Mazucana, Mozambique, the Scuola Materna Madonna di Fatima in Annone Veneto, Italy, and the Escola de 1.º e 2.º Grau Nossa Senhora de Fátima in Areia, Paraíba, Brazil). Health institutions are also represented (100 references, such as the Maternidade-Escola Nossa Senhora de Fátima in Dili, East Timor, the Farmácia de Nossa Senhora de Fátima in Belo Horizonte, Brazil, the Nossa Senhora de Fátima Physiotherapy Clinic in Ilhéus, Brazil, and the Our Lady of Fatima Hospital in North Providence, USA), as well as social welfare institutions (125 references, such as the Lar do Sagrado Coração de Maria in Quelimane, Mozambique, the Orphanage of the Immaculate Heart of Mary in Hyderabad, India, and the Boystown of Our Lady of Fatima in Yokohama, Japan). There are also many toponyms (375 references, such as the Fátima neighbourhood in Asunción, Paraguay, Villa Fátima in Puno, Peru, the Praça de Nossa Senhora de Fátima in Suai, East Timor, and Fatima Avenue in Laton, California), and even commercial businesses (425 references, such as the Fábrica de Bolsas Nossa Senhora de Fátima in Belo Horizonte, Brazil, and the Perfumeria Nuestra Señora de Fátima in Moguer, near Huelva, Spain). Finally, we may mention 75 media outlets across the world, such as the newspaper

Bote von Fatima and the publishing house FatimaVerlag, both in Germany, the *Ediciones La Voz de Fátima* in San Martín, Argentina, and the *Fatima Crusader* in Ontario, Canada.

It is not surprising, therefore, that the richness of the phenomenon should have attracted a range of interpretations, expressed in thousands of works, some of them published as books. The library of the Shrine of Fatima has records of 6370 publications in over 30 different languages, including 4700 monographs and 1670 chapters in areas of knowledge such as Anthropology, Political Science, Information Science, Sport, Economics, Ethnography, Geography, History and Theology. It is also not surprising, given the political-ideological circumstances of their authors, that these interpretations provide different meanings. Academic approaches to the phenomenon, whether they are closer or further from the archival sources that gave rise to them, also vary in their interpretations.

The historical events in which the phenomenon arose led to its interpretation as a revival of Catholicism within the religious controversy of the First Republic. However, the decades of the Shrine's growth show even more clearly the development of a political reading of Fatima as part of anti-atheistic ideas during the twentieth century, going so far as to relate it it to the fall of the Berlin Wall in 1989. Sources and authors who interpreted the Fatima message therefore positioned it in the public debate not only about the presence of God in human history, but also about the consequences of legislation in different countries that promoted or contradicted Catholicism. The most remarkable example of this is the discourse which traditionally opposed the Kremlin's Red Square with Fatima's white square.

The crowds of Fatima cannot be counted, for that would require that all the assemblies gathered around the world, in each shrine, church, altar or niche dedicated to the Virgin Mary with that title would have to be counted. It is however possible to give an approximate estimate of the total number of the faithful, from the most diverse points of Portugal and the world, who gather in the prayer area of Fatima on the thirteenth day of each month, especially in the months from May to October, and on the days of the Catholic calendar especially devoted to the Virgin Mary (15 August and 8 December). These figures, always high, often number more than 500,000 people, reaching one million on 13 May 1967, on the occasion of the visit of Pope Paul VI, 800,000 on the 13 May 1982, at the first visit of Pope John Paul II, and 500, 000 on 13 May 2017, during the visit of Pope Francis. Even if we ignore the data referring to papal visits, the numbers remain significant for a shrine of the Contemporary era, when indicators of religious practice in Europe show a fall in religious observance.

The global scale of Fatima has made it an object of study for analysts of culture and religious thought. The religious tension in Portugal during the First Republic lasted in the minds of the elites throughout the twentieth century, nurtured by interpretations of contemporary political history which saw the apparitions of Fatima as one of the pillars of the *Estado Novo*, a period popularly summarised by the motto of the three Fs: Fatima, Football and Fado. Interpretations suggesting that Fatima could be detached from the discourse of António de Oliveira Salazar (who in fact did not attend services at the Cova da Iria), and that, during the Colonial War, it could even have been a place which showed the symptoms of an empire about to fall, are not yet common in academic circles.

The fact that Fatima has always been a mass event has been seen by some Portuguese intellectuals as a merely a popular phenomenon, and thus unworthy of sympathy from those who dismiss narratives associated with the people. Literature and the other arts have had an ambiguous relationship with Fatima, using it for material, but with caricatured or heroic characters, first on a Portuguese scale and then, during its first century, more globally.

Marco Daniel Duarte
Department of Studies of the Shrine of Fatima, and Centre for Lusophone and European Literatures and Cultures, Faculty of Arts and Humanities, University of Lisbon

Bibliography

AZEVEDO, Carlos Moreira, CRISTINO, Luciano Coelho (coord.), *Enciclopédia de Fátima*, 2nd ed., Estoril, Princípia, 2008.

Documentação Crítica de Fátima, 15 vols., Fatima, Santuário de Fátima, 1992–2013.

DUARTE, Marco Daniel Carrola, *Fátima e a Criação Artística (1917–2007): O Santuário e a Iconografia: A Arte como Cenário e como Protagonista de Uma Específica Mensagem*, 4 vols., unpublished doctoral thesis in History of Art presented to the University of Coimbra, Coimbra, 2012.

FRANCO, José Eduardo, REIS, Bruno Cardoso, *Fátima: Lugar Sagrado Global*, Lisbon, Círculo de Leitores, 2017.

TORGAL, Luís Filipe, *O Sol Bailou ao Meio-Dia: A Criação de Fátima*, Lisbon, Tinta-da-China, 2017.

1933
Salazarism and the Interwar Dictatorships

Every authoritarian and totalitarian dictatorship of the interwar period claimed it would save the international social order from Moscow's "Red Menace". The global threat of communism had to be opposed by an equally global anticommunism. This meant declaring for "order against disorder".

In 1933, Hitler was named Chancellor of the Reich, thus initiating a policy of racism, imperialism and militarism which led to one of the darkest periods in the history of Germany and the world. His contemporaries could not have known the extent of the evil which would be unleashed. Salazar, for example, considered the German "a madman", but despite this, more tolerable than Stalin and communism – it was these that were the real threat to the social order. Salazar, a former professor of the University of Coimbra who had also become head of the Portuguese government in 1933, blamed *demoliberalismo* (liberal democracy) for the crisis which had overtaken Western civilization, and considered that only vigorous action by men such as himself could save the "civilized" world from the communist abyss. For this, he proposed the creation of a social, economic and political organization which would allow his people to "live by habit". With the help of God and the traditional family, he himself would take responsibility for implementing his plan for social order. Was his regime original, or a replica of other interwar dictatorships?

In 1931, when the *Estado Novo* (New State) had not yet been set up, and Salazar was Minister of Finance in the Military Dictatorship (1926–1932), the nationalist João Ameal described a conversation he had had with an Italian professor "totally devoted to fascism", who told him, "with a touch of envy": "What Mussolini and Italy lack is a man like your Salazar!". This admiration of Italians for the future President of the Council has no support in existing historical sources. On the contrary, it is the fascination of Portuguese nationalists for the Italian solution, as well as for other foreign doctrines, that is indisputable. Salazar, for example, had long had in his library many works by Italian fascists, such Alfredo Rocco, Carlo Costamagna and Giovanni Gentile, and important figures from the radical French right, such as Maurice Barrès, Charles Maurras and Georges Valois. The future dictator also read Gustave Le Bon, a critic of democracy and socialism who had studied crowd psychology. Salazar's library illustrates the efficacy of the circulation of ideas in the interwar period, which transformed these figures into global phenomena; this was true even in Portugal, where there were many declarations of originality on the part of the ideologues and politicians of the new regime.

António Ferro, director of the Secretariat of National Propaganda from 1933, claimed that some of Salazar's admirers would have preferred him to be "more theatrical, more of a disciple of Mussolini or Hitler, more revolutionary in the outward sense." Such was the case of Rolão Preto, chief of the National Syndicalist Movement, who doubted that Salazar, unlike Mussolini and Hitler, would be capable of arousing in the Portuguese the passion and the military virtues which the country needed to escape the ruin in which liberal democracy had left it. For Ferro, however, Salazar was no disciple, but rather a "master".

In fact, many nationalists from Latin America to Eastern Europe came to be inspired by Salazarism, attracted by the conservatism of this Catholic regime (its description of itself as a "national revolution" was the only revolutionary thing about it) and by its political and social actions. Essentially what they were looking for in the Portuguese dictatorship was a formula to keep politicians in power indefinitely, with (limited) recourse to physical violence and (unlimited) use of complementary repressive means, such as the elimination of freedom of expression and association, supported by the police and censorship, both under the control of the President of the Council. Salazar's admirers were particularly interested in how he demobilized the population by the use of a shrewd "economy of terror", to use Hermínio Martins' term.

Ferro also claimed that Salazar governed without the "exuberant, Mediterranean gestures of the great Mussolini" and the "theatrical, carefully orchestrated speeches of Hitler". While the Italian and German dictators attracted supporters by appealing to the "courage of the crowd" and their instincts, both "good and bad", in Portugal people were attracted by the "intelligence" and the "character" of the President of the Council), virtues which the dictator cultivated to please his admirers. In reality, the majority of the population was caught up in the daily struggle for survival, or dependent on jobs in public administration, nationally or locally. Only a few opposed him, protesting against fraudulent elections or other self-legitimizing manoeuvres by the regime – which few people paid much attention to anyway.

Despite statements such as Ferro's, the *Estado Novo* as a political regime was simultaneously original and a copy of its European counterparts. It did not spring from an irrational reaction against ethnic minorities. Nor did it result from a party seizing power, from involvement in territorial disputes at the end of the First World War, or from having to deal with a vast number of demobilized and demoralized troops after the conflict, as happened in Germany and Italy. The Portuguese regime could therefore distance itself from the more radical aspects of fascism. Its basic affinities with these regimes, and with other contemporary dictatorships, were a result of reactions to "common evils". Every right-wing authoritarian and totalitarian dictatorship of the interwar period claimed it would save the social order from Moscow's "Red Menace". The global threat of communism had to be opposed by an equally global anti-communism: this meant declaring for "order against disorder".

Apart from these global connections, which united the diverse nationalist regimes of the 1930s, there were other affinities, of a more specific nature. In the case of Portugal, the institutional design of Salazarism owed much to Italian fascism. Soon after the 1933 plebiscite on the Political Constitution, which inaugurated the *Estado Novo*, the *Estatuto do Trabalho Nacional* (National Labour Statute) was instituted as a legal instrument. Published on 23 September that year, and inspired by its Italian counterpart, the fascist *Carta del Lavoro*, it was nevertheless tempered, to quote José Barreto, "by criticism – appropriately conservative, Lusitanian and Catholic (traditionalist) – of the more nationalizing aspects of fascism". There was little originality in this. Indeed the same process was replicated in Francoist Spain, which published the *Fuero del Trabajo* in 1938, and in Vichy France, which established the *Charte du Travail* in 1941. Thus, freely constituted professional associations were replaced by unions and guilds dominated by the State – as had happened in Nazi Germany, individual interests were subordinated to the interest of the "Nation", workers were expected to act "in the spirit of social peace", and both employers and workers were controlled by collective labour contracts, approved by the government. The idea of class struggle was in theory abolished by ministerial decree.

In the same way, the pillars of corporatism in Portugal were established in August 1933. Based initially on the doctrine of the Catholic Church, corporatism was presented as a third way between socialism and economic and social liberalism. Grounded on a romantic view of medieval European guilds, it was a system that was supposed to allow for the representation of various interests but was in fact promoted and dominated by the State. As a mode of political representation, it was also to act as an alternative to Parliament. In the Corporative Chamber various forms of social organization were represented, such as the family, municipality, and professional and economic associations. In practice, the main benefit of corporatism was the suppression of the class struggle, which antagonized economic and labour interests.

1933 was also the year in which the *Estado Novo*'s political police, the *Polícia de Vigilância e Defesa do Estado* (PVDE, or Surveillance and State Defence Police), was set up, a fusion of the Political and Social Police (overseeing domestic political activity) and the Portuguese International Police (in charge of border control). Since both were heirs of the First Republic and the Military Dictatorship, it is not surprising that historians reject the idea that the PVDE originated in its Nazi and fascist counterparts. The Gestapo, for example, was actually created after the PVDE. Whilst Douglas Wheeler has pointedly highlighted the similarities between the structures of the Portuguese political police and Britain's MI5, there were nevertheless evident similarities also between the political policing entities in dictatorial regimes. All were forces of social and political control, punishing their opponents as they saw fit, through torture and incarceration, both "preventive" and indefinite. Nevertheless, such similarities were due more to adopting the same responses to similar threats, rather than to any supposed external inspiration.

Internationally, there were significant links between the different European secret services, especially after the start of the Spanish War Civil (1936–1939). They increased during the Second World War, when agents of the *Policia de Vigilância e Defesa do Estado* regularly supplied information to the Nazi regime. In this context, too, an agreement of cooperation was signed in 1937 with fascist Italy, as a result of which a high-ranking official of the Italian police, Leone Santoro, stayed in Lisbon for two years with the aim of teaching the Portuguese how to fight communism. His activities are still little known, but he produced a report advising the Portuguese government to unite the various police forces under a general directorate of public security, as had been done in Italy, though this advice was ignored.

When identifying connections between dictatorships in 1933, an important element was the creation of the Secretariat of National Propaganda, with Ferro as its first director. This body was to "integrate the Portuguese in the moral thought which should direct a Nation" and to promote the image of Portugal abroad, particularly "our civilizing activities and especially [...] activities in the colonies and the progress of our Overseas Empire". Like propaganda organizations in Italy and Germany, the Secretariat was important in reinforcing the legitimacy and prestige of the regime. To this end, Ferro invited radical right-wing French intellectuals to visit the country and testify to its achievements. Abel Bonnard, Jacques de Lacretelle, Jacques Maritain, Maurice Martin du Gard and Wladimir d'Ormesson all came to Portugal and gave their blessing to the novel regime.

Also common to Nazism and Italian fascism was the role of propaganda in the invention and promotion of a popular culture, and an attempt at standardization of taste. Here too there are similarities, rather than connections.

Finally, the relation between the interwar dictatorships and the papacy was also a common theme. Mussolini agreed a concordat with the Holy See in 1929, as did Hitler in 1933: both dictators thus benefited from their apparent good will towards the Church. Salazar also attempted to establish a concordat in 1933, but the Vatican refused. As a Catholic and a friend of Cardinal Cerejeira, the highest authority of the Portuguese Church, Salazar on this occasion tried to arrange a "minimal programme" with the Church, a vague declaration of principles that would not go against "the prevalent secular mentality", thus avoiding any political unrest against the regime. However, the Cardinal Secretary of State Eugénio Pacelli made it clear to Salazar that such an agreement should always include matters such as education and marriage, including the legal prohibition of divorce. Concerned with the reaction of his secular-minded opponents, Salazar did not consider such a concession to be possible at that time. A concordat on the terms agreed by other regimes, including fascist and Nazi governments, therefore had to wait until 1940. With the *Estado Novo* now firmly intrenched, a government ban on religious matrimonies no longer threatened the regime's stability. Furthermore, in an exemplary example of propaganda, the regime arranged for the signing of the accord with the Holy See to coincide with Lisbon's Portuguese World Exhibition, a nationalist exercise in propaganda which displayed the "marvels" that Portugal had brought to the world – the same world which was then at war. It was only then, seven years after the dictatorship's first attempt, that Portugal joined the extensive group of countries that had celebrated concordats with the Holy See – each of these concordats was a response to the global phenomena of anticlericalism and secularization which were threatening the long-established status of the Church.

To conclude, interwar right-wing dictatorships are global phenomena in the sense that they responded to the crisis of demo-liberalism and to the communist threat. As a means of overcoming this crisis, they borrowed and recycled each other's useful resources and instruments – such as corporatism, the single party, and youth organisations, to mention but a few. But each of them had to cope with particular social and economic circumstances that transformed every single case into a singular one.

RITA ALMEIDA DE CARVALHO
Instituto de Ciências Sociais, Universidade de Lisboa

Bibliography

ADINOLFI, Goffredo, "The institutionalization of propaganda in the fascist era. The cases of Germany, Portugal and Italy", *European Legacy, toward New Paradigms*, vol. 17, no. 5, 2012, pp. 607–621.

PINTO, António Costa, FINCHELSTEIN, Frederico, *Authoritarianism and Corporatism in Europe and Latin America: Crossing Borders*, London/New York, Routledge, 2019.

RIBEIRO, Maria da Conceição, *A Polícia Política no Estado Novo, 1926–1945*, Lisbon, Estampa, 1995.

ROSAS, Fernando, GARRIDO, Álvaro, *Corporativismo. Fascismos. Estado Novo*, Coimbra, Almedina, 2012.

WHEELER, Douglas L., "In the service of order. The Portuguese political police and the British, German and Spanish intelligence, 1932–1945", *Journal of Contemporary History*, vol. 18, no. 1, 1983, pp. 1–25.

1934

Cod: Global Connections within the National Myth

Historically, Lisbon was the world's largest consumer market for Atlantic cod, closely followed by Porto. In the second half of the eighteenth century, both cities were part of a global cod trade, mediated by British brokers based in London.

What is there in common between the Canadian economist Harold Innis's study of the role of cod in the economy of the American Atlantic provinces (1940), the historian David Alexander's work on the international networks of the Newfoundland cod trade (1977), and the American journalist Mark Kurlansky's imaginative book on the Atlantic cod, "the fish that changed the world" (1999)? Although their registers are very different – more academic and documented in the first two, less rigorous in Kurlansky's bestseller – these three books treat cod as a transatlantic product which acted in global exchanges, especially between the New World and southern Europe. There is a clear common denominator here: cod as a commercial product and also as a cultural construct, since it combines technical elements (modes of fishing and preserving) and cultural factors (from religions, pagan traditions and daily socialization).

Despite the common elements and the invariable historical aspects which these authors, and others, identify in the cod phenomenon, any Portuguese reader comparing these three books would notice a troubling omission in Kurlansky's work – *Portuguese cod*.

"Portuguese cod"? The expression is meaningless in terms of the biological and oceanographic sciences, but finds a place in the fields of cultural anthropology and history. The identification of this food product with a national tradition means that, for a historical understanding of the relationship of hyper-identity which Portugal established with cod, we need to take account of processes of acculturation or even the nationalization of an ancient habitus of consumption. The extraordinary relationship of Portugal and the Portuguese with cod, a food loaded with symbolism and social practices reflecting the nation's cultural topography, can also be explained on a multicultural level. The tradition associated with cod is the result of commercial and immaterial flows, of mutual influences between distant peoples, and adaptive responses to the needs of subsistence. Two transatlantic economic activities, strongly capitalist in nature, drove these global flows and created lifestyles around the seasonal exploitation of cod: firstly, the equipping of ships for line fishing in the seas of Newfoundland and the coast of Labrador, based on commercial ports in Portugal, the Basque country and Brittany, a business which always contended with the risk of the voyages and the return on the invested capital; secondly, the trade in the import and transport of dried salt fish from Newfoundland, dominated by British merchants and always fiercely competitive. This British involvement in the trade pre-dates the Modern period, but grew considerably in the seventeenth century, after Portuguese ships had left Newfoundland.

Some cod-producing regions were practically outside these global geo-economic complexes for centuries: Norway and the Norwegian Arctic archipelagos, where the Portuguese only began fishing in 1978, and Iceland, where Portuguese-flagged ships never fished, but where French vessels had operated since the end of the eighteenth century, a saga on which Pierre Loti based his popular novel *Pêcheur d'Islande* (1886). It is assumed that Portugal had always imported cod from Norway, especially dried salt *bacalhau*. As for Iceland, it became the main supplier of fresh salt cod from the 1930s, when the export business formed a cartel.

The memory of the legendary "white fleet" and the saga of the Portuguese sailor-fishermen in their dories – small boats launched from schooners, crewed by one or two fishermen left to their fate – are the central ideas of national and international mythology built on the Portuguese cod fishery. These images include epic, dramatic elements which *Estado Novo* propaganda diffused beyond Portugal, a strategy which was part of its economic diplomacy and its reproduction of the social order.

Independently of its contemporary aspects and of the social memory it left in many European countries and regions, the fishing and eating of Atlantic cod (dried or dried and salted) in the countries of southern and Mediterranean Europe were a mercantile invention of the Modern period. Since the discovery and exploration of the Grand Banks of Newfoundland by southern Europeans and the British at the end of the fifteenth century, great fleets, including whalers, left from European ports for the north-west Atlantic, some 1800 nautical miles away, to fish for cod. Evidence and stories of abundant catches, the ease of preserving the fish and the efficiency of business networks led to an unprecedented revolution in food habits. Catholic rules on fasting and on abstinence from meat, the scarcity of fresh sea fish, and the low-protein content of a basically medieval diet, explain the adoption of cod as a common foodstuff in Mediterranean Christian Europe. When these factors lost their significance, tastes and traditions were enough to maintain high levels of consumption of dried salt cod, which tended to increase in Portugal when per capita income also rose.

More than a biological resource, cod is a preserved food and a highly efficient concentrate of animal protein. It is no accident that the semantic diversity of the expressions used for the fish in various languages is related far more to processing and preservation processes than to its natural history and morphology. *Bacalhau* (Portuguese*)*, *morue* (French), *baccalà* or *stoccafisso* (Italian), *kabeljau* or *stockfisch* (German) and *bakailaoa* (Basque) are eloquent reminders both of fishing techniques and of types of curing. In both cases, the words also reflect the processes of trade, the forms of consumption and the tastes of the respective societies.

The North Atlantic cod fishery from Portuguese ports had irregular cycles. Historically, since records began, it is estimated that cod fished by Portuguese ships made up no more than 10% of what was consumed. Cod's identity and cultural status in Portuguese society is based above all on food habits and social practices of consumption.

From the early sixteenth century, the cod trade was always a long-distance and global business. The Atlantic cod fishery, initiated by the Spanish (Basques), Portuguese and French in Newfoundland and Labrador, created international economic flows, maritime careers and schools of seamanship. For hundreds of years, the migratory fleets of southern European countries left port in April or May for the Grand Banks of Newfoundland to fill their holds and carry the fish back to European city markets. Caught by baited hand lines, the cod was salted on board in the holds (fresh salted), and after unloading it was wind-dried at moderate temperature (dried salted), or re-salted and then dried. From the seventeenth century, French and English used their American coastal colonies for exporting dried salt cod to Europe and the Caribbean. All the conflicts and efforts to colonize Newfoundland and Nova Scotia were related to this need, and to the comparative advantages to trade that could result from it. The use of long lines and of the dory technique came from New England and was initiated by Portuguese ship-owners in 1835. The experience of Azorean fishermen in the Gloucester schooners, later evoked in the film *Captains Courageous* (1937), and the role of the Bensaúde family (Moroccan-born Jewish ship-owners) in the revitalization of the fishery from Portuguese ports consolidated these methods, making Portuguese dorymen an international legend.

A simple exercise in geo-economy shows the main countries and regions of the world which historically depended on the Atlantic cod fishery and trade, and how Portugal fitted into these global subsets:

- The group of countries which pioneered the trans-oceanic cod fishery from the beginning of the Modern period, forming migratory fleets protected by the naval powers, and contesting control over the trade routes of the product between the sixteenth and eighteenth centuries: Spain, France, England and Portugal;
- The countries which led the primary production and the global trade of dried salt cod as direct exporters or intermediaries in trade destined for the major markets of southern Europe and the Mediterranean – Lisbon, Porto, Alicante, Bilbau, Le Havre, Marseille, Genoa, Naples and Pireus (Athens). The vast

majority of the agents of this small group of countries were British, and for some time, also French;

- Finally, the colonial peripheries involved in the global economy of cod through trade with the European empires and their slave-trading oligarchs. For these Caribbean islands (the Antilles), cod was a form of animal protein supporting the plantation economy in a triangular trade between America, Europe and Africa.

Historically, Lisbon was always the world's largest consumer market for cod, closely followed by Porto. In the second half of the eighteenth century, both cities were part of a global cod trade, mediated by British brokers based in London. The firm of Hawes & Company, particularly active in Lisbon during the Marquês de Pombal period (1755–1777) and the early nineteenth century, shows this trading network. The tradition of trade and sale of "English cod" in the groceries of Lisbon and Porto, where it is still popular today, recalls the role of British dealers, particularly in wholesale importing and distribution. Competition in supply, and the practice of dumping by exporters, were enough to hinder the growth of Portuguese production up until the 1930s, when the Salazar regime formed an import cartel and initiated an unprecedented programme for economic autarky.

What distinguishes Portuguese cod from other forms of curing and preparation around the world? The writers Eça de Queirós, Oliveira Martins and Ramalho Ortigão posed the question in literary and cultural terms, and the politicians Afonso Costa, Basílio Teles, and Oliveira Salazar himself, posed it at the level of political economy. Although the myth of cod and the socialization of the popular parable of the "loyal friend" (*fiel amigo*) were nineteenth-century inventions, the tendency continued during the First Republic, from 1910 to 1926, and especially in the First World War. The social and political centrality of the "cod question" – the scarcity of Portuguese production compared to consumer demand and the state's inability to correct the balance – account for its importance in popular art and culture, well before the *Estado Novo* launched its cod campaign in 1934.

In the twentieth century the Portuguese cod industry went through three distinct phases: state reorganization of supply and production, imposed by the *Estado Novo* in 1934, when a powerful corporatist administration was created to regulate the sector; the high point in the 50s and 60s, based on fixing of prices, state credit and other protectionist mechanisms supervised by the corporatist fisheries organization; and the decline of the last quarter of the century, linked to the end of the fisheries administration in 1974 and to basic changes in the law of the sea, which culminated in unilateral adoption by many coastal nations of the concept of exclusive economic zones. This last, current phase, influenced by the common fisheries policy of the European Union, is defined by multilateral management of biological resources, which has led Portugal to act as a coastal state and to drastically reduce the primary production of cod, since it is impossible to gain access to supply.

Nowadays, Portugal has ten long-distance fishing vessels, operating under the quotas for the fishing of cod and other gadoids as attributed by the European Union. This "national production" does not even reach 2% of annual consumption in the Portuguese internal market. The import of this raw material is now more important than ever, with dozens of businesses and thousands of jobs depending on a product whose competitive advantage is based on the quality of the "traditional Portuguese cure". Added to this is the human dimension of the economic activities linked to cod production and trade. It is a cultural heritage of the whole of Portugal, and especially strong in the imagery of maritime and emigrant communities around the world and in countries whose official language is Portuguese, which are now important export markets for the dried salt cod produced by Portuguese companies. The gastronomic variety of cod recipes in Portugal, and the permanent reinvention of this tradition, is unique on an international level.

ÁLVARO GARRIDO
Faculty of Economics, University of Coimbra

Bibliography

ALEXANDER, David, *The Decay of Trade: An Economic History of the Newfoundland Saltfish Trade, 1935–1965*, Saint John's, Institute of Social and Economic Research, Memorial University of Newfoundland, 1977.

GARRIDO, Álvaro, *O Estado Novo e a Campanha do Bacalhau*, 2nd ed., Lisbon, Círculo de Leitores/Temas e Debates, 2010.

INNIS, Harold A., *The Cod Fisheries: The History of an International Economy*, New Haven, Yale University Press, 1940.

KURLANSKY, Mark, *Cod: A Biography of the Fish that Changed the World*, London, Vintage, 1999.

SOBRAL, José Manuel, RODRIGUES, Patrícia, "O "fiel amigo": O bacalhau e a identidade portuguesa", *Etnográfica*, vol. 17, no. 3, 2013, pp. 619–649.

1940
A Portuguese World on Display

An authentic "city of dreams" was constructed on the northern bank of the River Tagus, where the past intermingled with the present and even the aroma of coffee was part of the spectacle.

Conferences, pilgrimages, pageants, sporting events and reproductions of popular and colonial life entertained the whole country. The year 1940 was the year that celebrated the "footprints and traces of Portugal in the world", whilst Europe finally entered the long tunnel of the Second World War.

In March 1938 António de Oliveira Salazar announced, in a statement from the Presidency of the Council of Ministers, that in 1940 the country would celebrate the two centenaries of its founding in 1140 and the restoration of its independence in 1640, evoking "eight centuries of its history, which are also eight centuries in the history of the world". A few months later, the *Diário de Notícias* newspaper published an open letter in which António Ferro, the director of the Secretariat of National Propaganda, explained to the Portuguese people the importance of the year 1940 in the life of the nation. The years 1140, 1640 and 1940, he emphasized, "are three sacred years in our history: the year of the birth of the nation, the year of its rebirth, and the year which marks the apotheosis of its resurgence". Therefore, he continued, it was "not only the Portugal of yesterday, but also of today, not only the Portugal of

King Afonso Henriques and King John IV, but the Portugal of Carmona and Salazar" that would be celebrated. The past, present and future would be combined in a rich and varied calendar of commemorative events, duly divided into three key periods: the medieval age, the imperial age and the age of the Braganzas. Festivals, historical and folk pageants, pilgrimages, solemn masses, popular parades, conferences, exhibitions and even sporting events would feature in the life of the whole country, from Guimarães – revered as the "cradle" of Portugal – to the Algarve, from May to December 1940. The celebrations were described by Salazar as a "grand family festival", involving not only mainland Portugal, but also "the islands and all the colonial dominions".

Headed by Júlio Dantas, the National Commission for the Centenary Commemorations planned the celebrations to ensure that they would play an important role in the general and civic education of the population. The events, in fact, were intended to reflect the grandeur of leading figures from Portuguese history, celebrate the nation and empire and, indirectly, enable the *Estado Novo* to represent itself as heir to a great patriotic legacy and the guarantor of a glittering future, endeavours best expressed, in visual terms, by the Monument to the Discoveries created by José Ângelo Cottinelli Telmo and Leopoldo de Almeida. The monument features navigators, poets, kings, clerics and saints, led by Prince Henry, standing on a caravel designed in the "historicist-modernist style" – or national historicism, according to Artur Portela – which was a specific feature of artistic representation during the regime. In addition to serving as the third pillar of the celebrations, 1940 was also an important year for Portugal with regard to international relations and domestic politics. In May and June, two important documents were signed. The first was the Concordat with the Holy See which – after long and complex negotiations and the creation of a well-defined, stable system of regulations – finally restored relations between church and state and re-established the diplomatic channel with the Vatican which had fallen into disuse after the establishment of the First Republic. In June the signing of an additional protocol to the Iberian Pact celebrated the previous year reinforced the new path for relations between Portugal and Spain, finally leading to the creation of a neutral Iberian bloc within a Europe that had just become involved in a war. The agreement was the most important demonstration of the government's policy of neutrality. Salazar, who had graduated as an academic and political thinker in the turbulent years after the Great War (1914–1918) and, as President of the Council of Ministers, had followed the events of the bloody civil war in neighbouring Spain (1936–1939), was well aware of the disruptive and subversive effects that could result from Portugal's involvement in the Second World War (1939–1945), from the perspective of the economy, preservation of the regime and the overseas territories, and national unity (and even independence). In a Europe which, after Italy joined the conflict and the Second Armistice of Compiègne had been signed, formally establishing the Nazi occupation of France, was unquestionably becoming involved in a full-scale war, the Salazar government endeavoured to create a narrative that would present his country as an oasis of peace and harmony in the eyes of the Portuguese and foreigners. Whereas most other nations in the continent were obliged to adapt their economies and industries to the demands of warfare, despite some minor difficulties with maritime transport and supplies of fuel and raw materials, Portugal managed to continue on its path of economic development, evident in the fact that in 1940 the annual growth rate for industrial production was 7.6 percent.

While other nations were dealing with the concrete threat of destruction, invasion and loss of territories, the *Estado Novo* was engaging in a propaganda drive to publicize its restoration of Portugal's historical heritage, its new projects and completed urban developments, and its colonial territories which, by means of specific legislation, had allowed for a steady increase in import/export activities. The Lisbon of 1940 is the clearest example of this narrative. It was the year in which, following the demolition of a number of buildings that were disfiguring the area, structural consolidation and the partial reconstruction of its wall, the Directorate-General for National Buildings and Monuments completed the renovation of the São Jorge Castle which, in the words of Salazar, should "spiritually overlook the country, as the sacred acropolis, the chosen site for patriotic pilgrimages". The process of recovering the historical heritage was accompanied by a profound change in urban planning in the capital. By 1940, the construction of the Portela airport was in its later stages and work had begun on the Monumental Fountain that would provide the architectural and sculptural finishing touches to the Alameda D. Afonso Henriques and, at the same time, the site for a view-point. Designed by the brothers Carlos and Guilherme Rebelo de Andrade, the fountain was also intended to symbolically commemorate the impressive engineering project which channelled water from the Tagus valley to Lisbon, thus increasing the supply available for consumption.

In addition to the work on the Alameda-Portela axis, the urban regeneration project for the new riverside area in Belém captured the attention of the nation in 1940. Until the end of the 1930s, Belém was known for its lively and diverse urban fabric, composed of small traditional shopping areas, a local market, a mixture of working class and middle class housing and large industrial areas, many of which had been abandoned, comprising old factories, shipyards, docks and some buildings that belonged to the gas industry, including a large gasometer. Within a short period of time, thanks to continuous demolition work overseen by the energetic Minister for Public Works Duarte Pacheco, the *Estado Novo* had completely transformed the area, covering over 560,000 square meters. Designed as a space for leisure, cultural and other urban activities, it included new roads, docks, ferry terminals and stations, with the Empire Square serving as its hub. The new development convincingly combined the innovative features introduced by the *Novo Estado* with the most iconic areas associated with the nation's past, specifically with the Maritime saga – the Jeronimos Monastery, Afonso de Albuquerque Square, River Tagus and Belém Tower– thus converting the Belém waterfront into a site for the public display of power and endorsing the historicist discourse underpinning the celebrations for the double centenary.

It was this "new Belém" that was chosen as the site for the imposing temporary pavilions for the Exhibition of the Portuguese World, perhaps the high point in the representation of the Portuguese nation as a rural paradise prepared by history for a civilizing mission and imperial grandeur. In little over a year, the chief architect, Cottinelli Telmo, and the General Commissioner, Augusto de Castro, assisted by members of the organizing committee, 17 architects, 43 painters and 24 sculptors, planned and created a "city of dreams" divided into four thematic areas: the historical section, commercial area, centre for popular life and colonial section. Initially the exhibition had been envisaged as international, but the escalation of the war meant that eventually the only non-Portuguese countries represented were Spain, which hosted a cartography exhibition inside the Jeronimos Monastery, and Brazil, which had its own pavilion, as a reflection of the close link between the two countries. Nevertheless, the organizers planned the event to replicate some of the characteristics of the major international exhibitions that had enlivened cultural and political life in the western world since the nineteenth century: the use of spectacle, spatial-temporal illusion and ephemerality. This was, in fact, the most distinctive feature of the 1940 Exhibition: although it had a national theme, the intention was not only to display one nation, but the hypernationalist idea of *Portugueseness* ("the Portuguese spirit"). Hence, an entire world, the "Portuguese world", would be condensed into Belém. Although aware of the ephemeral and illusory nature of the exhibition, visitors were invited to journey through eight hundred years and four continents. In a short space of time they could appreciate the majesty of medieval Portugal in the pavilion dedicated to the founding of the Nation, walk through a typical small square in a Beira Alta village where figures in traditional dress were seated around the pillory talking, take a look inside an artisan's workshop, visit a street in Macao and even smell the aroma of coffee from São Tomé and Príncipe. As Augusto de Castro stressed on the opening day, despite taking one nation as its subject, the exhibition was global in nature, since it displayed "the enormous amount of evidence of Portuguese universality". The *Estado Novo* used the 1940 exhibition to reinforce the idea that "Portugal is not a small country".

The event was the last of great political exhibitions from the age of fascisms. In the year in which the *Estado Novo* affirmed its neutrality, definitively turned its back on the continent of Europe and cast its eyes towards the Atlantic, the political significance of the Exhibition of the Portuguese World was of the utmost importance. Although it reproduced an aesthetic style and form of representation typical of the interwar European dictatorships to showcase various aspects of the "Portuguese world", it unequivocally emphasized the Portuguese tendency to "look inwards" and seek its strength primarily in its overseas empire, which in the coming years would play a key role in the survival – and downfall – of the regime from the point of view of politics, economics and prestige. Eighty years after the exhibition, traces of the event have survived in Belém: the Espaço Espelho d'Água, designed by António Lino, the Tropical Gardens which was the setting for the colonial section, the Museum of Popular Art created in the former Popular Life Pavilion, and the Monument to the Discoveries. This monument, which was rebuilt as a permanent structure in 1960 on the occasion of the Henrician commemorations, is nowadays one of the symbols of the city of Lisbon and one of the most popular attractions for global tourism. Yet, in general, the whole area still retains its identity as the main stage for cultural and political life in the country. It was in Belém that Mário Soares signed the protocols for Portugal's membership of the European Economic Community in 1985. A few years later, when Portugal held the European Community Presidency, the Belém Cultural Centre was created as a definitive break with the aesthetics of the *Estado Novo*, marking the complete transformation of the symbolic space of Belém as the centre for culture and life in democratic Portugal.

ANNARITA GORI
Instituto de Ciências Sociais, Universidade de Lisboa

Bibliography

ACCIAUOLI, Margarida, *Exposições do Estado Novo, 1934–1940*, Lisbon, Livros Horizonte, 1998.

CARVALHO, Rita Almeida de, *A Concordata de Salazar*, Lisbon, Temas e Debates, 2013.

GORI, Annarita, "Celebrate nation, commemorate history, embody the Estado Novo: The Exhibition of the Portuguese World (1940)", *Cultural and Social History*, 15 (5), 2018, pp. 699–722.

Revista dos Centenários, 1939–1940.

SAPEGA, Ellen W., *Consensus and Debate in Salazar's Portugal: Visual and Literary Negotiations of the National Text*, University Park, Penn State University Press, 2008.

1949
Egas Moniz, a Nobel Prizewinner Who Founded a School

For most of the twentieth century, and particularly in the early years, scientific activity in Portugal was quite inferior, meaning that Egas Moniz's prize was an extraordinary achievement.

The most internationally famous Portuguese scientist of the twentieth century is unquestionably António Egas Moniz (1874–1955), a professor at the University of Lisbon Faculty of Medicine. This is largely due to the fact that the Swedish Academy awarded him the Nobel Prize in Physiology or Medicine in 1949, for "his discovery of the therapeutic value of leucotomy in certain psychoses" (according to the statement released by the Swedish Academy), a prize which he shared with Walter Rudolf Hess, a Swiss professor of Medicine at the University of Zürich "for his discovery of the functional organization of the interbrain as a coordinator of the activities of the internal organs". Egas Moniz was the only Portuguese Nobel prizewinner in the sciences and one of only two nationals to receive the award. The other was the writer José Saramago, who received the Nobel Prize in Literature in 1998.

The fact that Portugal can only claim one Nobel prizewinner in the sciences may seem a humble achievement. However, when compared to Spain, which has a population that is five times larger, one concludes that the neighbouring country has only succeeded in winning two Nobel prizes in this field, both for medicine: one awarded in 1906 to Santiago Ramón y Cajal, a medical doctor specialist in neurology like Egas Moniz, and the other in 1959 to Severo Ochoa, a biochemist who worked in the United States. In literature the Spanish are clearly in the lead, as six authors from the land of Cervantes have been awarded a Nobel Prize. Yet, considering all the fields – which, in the case of the Iberian Peninsula, are restricted to medicine and literature – in a ranking provided by Wikipedia based on the ratio of prizewinners per current population of the respective countries, Portugal lies in 40th place, far below Switzerland (3rd), but nevertheless above Spain (43rd) and Russia (44th).

For most of the twentieth century, and particularly in the early years, scientific activity in Portugal was quite inferior, meaning that Egas Moniz's prize was an extraordinary achievement. The Web of Science database of indexed scientific journals shows only 33 scientific articles published by authors with an address in Portugal between 1900 and 1944. Obviously this is far less than the amount published nowadays (over 21,000 articles in 2018). Once again, however, it should be considered in comparison with the figures for other countries. During this period, only 45 articles are registered for Spain. Between 1900 and 1910, no Portuguese author appears in the database, only a British writer who was working at the Hospital Britânico in Porto. Moreover, during the sixteen-year existence of the First Republic (1910–1926) only 14 articles were registered. From 1925 to 1944, when Egas Moniz was at the peak of his scientific career, there were 19 articles. The author who produced the most was Abel Salazar, a doctor from Porto who published eight texts, but the most frequently cited article, written by Egas Moniz for the *American Journal of Psychiatry* in 1937, has 78 citations and led to the award of the Nobel Prize.

How did Egas Moniz become an international name working in a country which, during his lifetime, had such low levels of scientific culture, not to mention general education? In fact, his career path was highly unusual. Born in Avanca, near Aveiro, in the place where the Egas Moniz House-Museum now stands, António Caetano de Abreu Freire de Resende became known as Egas Moniz due to the fact that the Resende family were apparently directly descended from Egas Moniz, the tutor to King Afonso Henriques. Supported by a priest who was also his paternal uncle and godfather, he completed his secondary education at the Jesuit college of São Fiel in Castelo Branco.

After graduating in Medicine from the University of Coimbra (with a Bachelor's degree in 1899 and a Licentiate degree in 1900), he was awarded a PhD in 1901 for his thesis *A Vida Sexual: Fisiologia (Sexual Life: Physiology)*, a work which ran to several editions and was considered daring at the time. In 1902, he became a substitute lecturer at the university in Coimbra, teaching courses in physiology and neurology. In a call for applications for five academic positions, the two vacancies for full professorships were filled by José Sobral Cid and Ângelo da Fonseca. He was promoted, following another call for applications, to full professor in 1910, but the next year transferred to the University of Lisbon, which had been created by the Republic from existing schools, where he held the Chair of Neurology and was involved in clinical work at the city's Santa Marta Hospital.

One of his reasons for transferring to the capital was the political work he had been involved in for some time, which required him to be present in Lisbon. As a Member of the Constituent Assembly, Egas Moniz was the founder of the Centrist Party and an Evolutionist Party dissident. He supported the short-lived regime of Sidónio Pais (who was a professor of Mathematics in Coimbra and therefore his colleague), serving as the Portuguese ambassador in Madrid (1917) and Minister for Foreign Affairs (1918). In this latter capacity, he was present for the Versailles Armistice which ended the First World War. However, even before the First Republic came to an end, he had abandoned politics to dedicate himself entirely to science. His path to the Nobel Prize had begun.

His scientific career, established in middle age, was centered in two main areas: cerebral angiography, in 1927, a technique used to visualize the arteries in the brain, and prefrontal leucotomy, in 1935, which involved the ablation of part of the brain in cases involving certain psychotic disorders. Cerebral angiography, which was developed using injections of a chemical substance which served as a marker, revealed certain types of brain diseases, opening up new possibilities for surgery. This innovation was recognized by the leading neurologists of the time, who did not hesitate to express their admiration for the Portuguese doctor's great powers of observation. Egas Moniz established scientific links mainly with France, strengthened by periods he spent in Bordeaux and Paris. In 1931 he published *Diagnostic des Tumeurs Cérébrales et Épreuve de l'Encéphalographie Artérielle* and in 1934,

L'Angiographie Cérébrale, Ses Applications et Résultats en Anatomie, Physiologie et Clinique, both in Paris.

Moniz was nominated three times for the Nobel Prize in Physiology or Medicine for his work in angiography (in 1928, 1933 and 1937). The last nomination also referred to leucotomy, but the Academy assessor ignored this. The first was submitted a few months after he had published his article on angiography and subsequently demonstrated the technique at the Necker Hospital in Paris. However, the specialists consulted by the Academy in Stockholm refused to recognize the methodology developed by the Portuguese doctor which, having first been applied to the head, was then extended to the internal organs and limbs of the human body. Internal reports from the Nobel Academy which are now available refer to the small number of clinical cases and the need for further confirmation.

In the 1930s, Egas Moniz concentrated on developing prefrontal leucotomy. He had become interested in this form of psychosurgery (the name he had given to surgery carried out on patients with mental illnesses, specifically schizophrenics) at a conference on neurology held in London in 1935, also attended by the Russian 1904 Nobel Prizewinner Ivan Pavlov. There he learned about experiments in psychosurgery performed on apes, carried out by the English-born but naturalized American John Fulton, which significantly altered their behaviour by reducing aggressive acts. He soon considered applying this technique to human beings and proceeded to carry out dozens of experiments which produced good results. After yet another nomination had been rejected in 1944, he finally saw his work recognized by the Swedish Academy. His main studies in the field of prefrontal leucotomy are *Tentatives Opératoires dans le Traitement de Certaines Psychoses* (1936) and *La Leucotomie Préfrontale. Traitement Chirurgical de Certaines Psychoses* (1937), published in Paris and Turin respectively.

In 1948 he chaired an international conference on psychosurgery held in Lisbon, at which the North American doctor Walter Freeman served as secretary. Freeman, a friend he had met at the London conference, became the master of this procedure (which he adapted into the technique that became known as lobotomy), carrying out thousands of operations. At the end of the conference, a motion recommending that Moniz should be awarded the Nobel Prize was unanimously approved by acclamation, with an influential group of Brazilian participants playing a relevant part in the process.

The technique developed by Egas Moniz, which was abandoned in the 1960s when new drugs appeared that could reduce the problems leucotomy proposed to treat, has been a highly controversial subject for many years. The relatives of some patients who had been subjected to this type of surgery demanded that the Nobel prize awarded to the Portuguese doctor should be annulled on ethical grounds, a claim which was not accepted, following a statement from the Nobel committee to the effect that the award could never be withdrawn. Despite this response, the award remains a contentious issue in some circles who have proved very active on the internet. João Lobo Antunes, the distinguished Portuguese neurologist and biographer of Egas Moniz, has defended the relevance of psychosurgery at the time. Famous names in Portugal who underwent lobotomies include the writer Raul Proença and Teresa Caetano, the wife of Marcelo Caetano, President of the Council of Ministers. The truth is that the past cannot be viewed only through the eyes of the present.

Like his colleague Miguel Bombarda, a convert to Republicanism who was attacked by a patient on the eve of 5 October 1910, Egas Moniz was shot in 1939 by a psychiatric patient but was able to make a partial recovery from his very serious injuries. He retired in 1944, physically weakened. He was awarded the Nobel Prize when he was 75 years old and his state of health prevented him from travelling to Stockholm to receive it. Moniz not only wrote scientific works but was also the author of autobiographical books such as *A Minha Casa*, an account of his childhood and youth in Avanca, and *Confidências de Um Investigador Científico*, which tells the story of his dazzling career and was published the same year he received the Nobel Prize. He was also awarded numerous national and international honours, including the Oslo Prize in 1945 for his work on angiography, and was a member of several international scientific societies. It has been said that his fame is greater abroad than in Portugal, which may perhaps be explained by the fact that he was an opponent, albeit moderate, of the *Estado Novo*. In fact, for political reasons the regime did not take full advantage of the award of the Nobel Prize to the Portuguese doctor.

The medical opinion of Egas Moniz was sought by individuals who are nowadays famous, including the writers Mário de Sá-Carneiro and Fernando Pessoa. Within higher education institutions, he may be considered the recipient in Portugal of Freud's ideas on psychanalysis, revealing in this and other aspects of his professional development, as well as in the circulation of his works, a clearly international dimension. Abel Salazar once said that "a doctor who only knows about medicine does not really know medicine". Egas Moniz knew about much more than medicine: he was interested in literature and art, revealing very conservative tastes.

He also founded a school at the Faculty of Medicine in Lisbon, a rare achievement in Portugal. The Lisbon School of Angiography was headed by Pedro de Almeida Lima, his main collaborator and, quite literally, his right-hand man, given that Moniz suffered from gout which affected his hands particularly badly and was therefore unable to perform surgery. Reynaldo dos Santos and his son João Cid dos Santos, among others, were associated with this School. Mário Corino de Andrade, who discovered what is commonly known as the *doença dos pezinhos* (Corino de Andrade's disease), worked in the Egas Moniz hospital and António Damásio, the Portuguese neurologist based in the United States, may be considered an heir of the School.

CARLOS FIOLHAIS
Department and Centre for Physics, Faculty of Sciences and Technology,
University of Coimbra

Bibliography
ANTUNES, João Lobo, *Egas Moniz: Uma Biografia*, Lisbon, Gradiva, 2010.
CORREIA, Manuel, *Egas Moniz no Seu Labirinto*, Coimbra, Imprensa da Universidade, 2013.
FERNANDES, Henrique Barahona, *Egas Moniz: Pioneiro dos Descobrimentos Médicos*, Lisbon, Instituto de Cultura e Língua Portuguesa, 1983.
OLIVEIRA, Victor, *Egas Moniz: Legados da Sua Vida e Obra*, Lisbon, By the Book, 2019.
PEREIRA, Ana Leonor, PITA, João Rui (coord.), *Egas Moniz em Livre Exame*, Coimbra, Minerva, 2000.

1949

Portugal and NATO: Rediscovering the Atlantic Option

In an Atlantic security system based on two pillars, one European and the other North American, the Azores bases in the middle of the Atlantic became essential to connecting both and to Europe's so-called rapid reinforcement.

Once the Second World War was over, Portugal, a neutral country, did not play a part in the diplomatic efforts to restore peace and reorganize the new international system. Even though the authoritarian regime managed not to succumb to the wave of democratisations the post-war period, Portugal experienced a period of international marginalisation and uncertainty in its foreign policy between 1945 and 1949. However, this does not mean that it remained on the fringes of international developments. The signing of the Washington Treaty and its accession to NATO as a founder member are proof of its involvement in the international dynamics of the second post-war period.

The first sign of its international marginalisation can be traced to April 1945, when Portugal was not invited to the San Francisco Conference which led to the establishment of the new post-war international order. Unlike its status with regard to the League of Nations, not only did Portugal fail to become a founding member of the United Nations (UN), but its first application for membership, in 1946, was vetoed by the USSR in the Security Council.

A degree of political indecisiveness and uncertainty in foreign policy were added to Portugal's international isolation during this period, reflecting an inability to adapt to the new world order. Salazar appeared not to understand, or rather accept, the deep changes in the second post-war international scene. To begin with, he did not accept the bipolar order and the emergence of the two superpowers and, in particular, England's decline and the rise of the United States as a great naval power in the Atlantic. Only the signing of the Lajes Agreement, in February 1948, began to change this perception, which the Washington Treaty and the founding of the North Atlantic Treaty Organisation (NATO) would confirm. Secondly, he appeared not to realise the importance of the UN as the new world organisation. As in the case of the League of Nations, Salazar also reacted against the return of multilateralism and the "international *assembliarism*" that the UN stood for. Thirdly, Salazar rejected the end of old Europe and of European powers as protagonists in the international scene. Moreover, he failed to understand, that the rebuilding of Europe could no longer be tackled individually by each state but had to be carried out within a framework of international cooperation. Finally, he failed to accept that the two new superpowers – albeit for different reasons – were both anti-colonial. What is more, he neither understood nor accepted that the right of peoples to self-determination was the UN's cardinal principle, and that the contribution of many colonised peoples to the allied war effort had made the process of decolonisation all the more inexorable. Salazar's perspective had a decisive effect on the evolution of Portuguese foreign policy, particularly with regard to European integration and the colonial question.

The first signs of reluctance towards the new post-war reality became evident in Portugal's position regarding the Marshall Plan, in June 1947. Salazar's inability to understand the international conjuncture, and his traditional mistrust of the

Americans led him to decline the North American offer, thus excluding Portugal from the first phase of the Marshall Plan in 1947–1948. The beginning of the Cold War and the deterioration in Portugal's finances and exchange rate eventually changed this initial position on American assistance, leading to Portugal's application for the second phase of the Marshall Plan in 1948–1949.

As the Cold War intensified, the new Soviet threat, the new framework for Atlantic security, and consequently American leadership in this context became clearly defined. Despite Salazar's misgivings, the first sign of this new reality in Portuguese foreign policy was the bilateral agreement on military cooperation signed by Portugal and the United States in February 1948. Unlike the 1943 agreement, and reflecting the new post-war strategic order, this new agreement officially made the North American air base a permanent fixture in the Azores archipelago.

To some extent, the hesitations regarding the Marshall Plan and the signing of the Lajes Agreement indicated two opposite approaches to Portuguese foreign policy: disengagement from the process of European integration, and integration in the Atlantic security system. When the defence, at all costs, of the colonial territories, is added to these orientations, the strategic options of Portuguese foreign policy until practically the end of the authoritarian regime become clear.

In June 1948, faced with the spectre of the Soviet threat and the newly defined framework for Atlantic security, the United States, Canada and the European countries that had been signatories to the Treaty of Brussels entered into negotiations with a view to creating a security system in the North Atlantic: the future Atlantic Alliance. In December of the same year, initial contacts were established with Lisbon with a view to exploring Portugal's possible integration. This marked the beginning of complicated diplomatic proceedings, leading to Portugal signing the North Atlantic Treaty on 4 April 1949. Portugal's NATO membership immediately raises three key questions: firstly, from the point of view of the powers involved in the negotiations, what might have been the reason for inviting Portugal, which was governed by an authoritarian regime, had been neutral in the Second World War, did not belong to the UN and remained on the fringes of international post-war reorganization? Secondly, from Portugal's perspective, why should it have accepted the invitation when it meant such a radical change to Portuguese foreign policy, requiring it to relinquish the hard-won neutrality it had established during the war, which was the crowning glory of the regime's propaganda? Finally, what were the consequences and the significance of Portugal's NATO membership for Portuguese foreign policy?

The answer to the first question is simple and of a geostrategic nature: rather than the political authoritarianism of the regime or its international position, the Cold War highlighted the strategic importance of Portuguese territory, in which the Azores archipelago was an added asset. With an Atlantic security system based on two pillars, one European and the other North American, the Azores bases in the middle of the Atlantic became essential to connecting both, and to Europe's so-called rapid reinforcement. It confirmed the strategic value of the Azores and the Lajes Agreement, now strengthened within a multilateral framework.

The answer to the second question is more complicated and essentially concerns the reduced room for diplomatic manoeuvre for Portuguese foreign policy within the context of the Cold War. When Portugal was formally invited to sign the treaty, Salazar, adopting his customary stance towards the Americans, viewed the proposal with mistrust. Following familiar negotiating tactics, he expressed diplomatic reservations in order to gain some negotiating power that would allow time for the decision-making process. He began by presenting two formal observations on the proposed wording of the treaty: the reference to democracy, which did not apply to Portugal, and the reference to the UN Charter, which Portugal had not signed. He then submitted three reservations concerning its content: firstly, the duration of the treaty (the period of twenty years appeared to be too long); secondly, the question of Spain, affirming the strategic unity of the Iberian Peninsula and the importance of Spain in the defence of the West, demanding the inclusion of both Portugal and Spain in the Alliance. Finally, he tried to include the colonies in the area covered by the treaty which, in the event of foreign aggression, would guarantee Portugal's security and sovereignty in the colonial territories under Article 5. All of Portugal's claims were rejected since none of them actually affected the great powers. Subsequently, Portugal came under pressure from two opposite sides: invoking the Iberian Pact, Spain urged Portugal not to join or, preferably, to set the terms for its own accession, while the United States and England insisted that it should join, with the British prime minister and the North American secretary of state both applying personal pressure. Despite Salazar's reservations and the fact that the executive itself was divided, Portugal had very little alternative: in a polarized world in which various memberships were being negotiated, Portugal's rejection might have influenced others to do the same, thus creating a fracture in the West which could only benefit the USSR. It was too great a responsibility to bear and one which, ultimately, Salazar did not want to take. Under international pressure and with no room for diplomatic manoeuvre, Portugal decided to join as a matter of obligation rather than conviction, thus becoming a founder member of the Atlantic Alliance.

What were the consequences of Portugal's accession to NATO? Despite Salazar's mistrust and reservations – an irony of history – the country's NATO membership represented a victory for Portuguese foreign policy. First of all, on a global level, once Portugal had joined the Alliance it enabled the regime to re-explore its traditional diplomatic orientation: the "Atlantic vocation" and preferential alliance with naval power. The novelty lay in the centre of reference for the naval power: the decline of the old English alliance and the emergence of a new axis on the other side of the Atlantic – the United States of America. Secondly, this triumph was even more visible on a Peninsular level. Despite affirming the strategic unity of the Iberian Peninsula and the Portuguese diplomatic claims for Spain to be included in the Alliance, the refusal by the Western powers proved advantageous for Portugal. Portugal's admission and Spain's exclusion from the Treaty reinforced Lisbon's status within the Iberian context and made it the favoured interlocutor in negotiations with third countries. Thirdly, in terms of domestic politics, although Portugal's NATO membership undoubtedly led to divisions within the regime, it divided the opposition even more, for a longer period of time and more profoundly. The Portuguese Communist Party, following the Soviet thesis, considered the Alliance the military instrument of American imperialism. The democratic opposition, on the other hand, seeing allusions to the UN Charter and the principles of democracy in the Treaty, supported Portuguese membership in the hope that it might signify implicit condemnation of the authoritarian regime and the possibility of a political opening up in the future. The result, however, was the opposite: the fact that the dictatorship was accepted in an alliance of democratic countries conferred a certain international legitimacy on the regime and led to a crisis within the opposition which lasted throughout almost the entire 1950s, until General Humberto Delgado stood as a candidate in the 1958 presidential elections.

Hence, when Portugal joined NATO in 1949, this was the beginning of one of the most positive periods for foreign policy under the *Estado Novo*, which only came to an end when it joined the UN in 1955.

The Atlantic option remained a basic reference in Portuguese foreign policy and, despite periods of greater tension during the decolonisation conflicts of the 1960s and the presence of communists in the government during the transition period between 1974 and 1976, Portugal's NATO membership was reaffirmed with the consolidation of democracy and strengthened by the reinforcement of its military commitments in the form of peacekeeping operations under the democratic regime.

NUNO SEVERIANO TEIXEIRA
Portuguese Institute of International Relations, Nova University Lisbon

Bibliography
Nação e Defesa, no. 123, 2009.
TEIXEIRA, Nuno Severiano, "Da neutralidade ao alinhamento: Portugal na fundação do Pacto do Atlântico", *Análise Social*, vol. XXVII, no. 120, 1993, pp. 55–80.
Idem, "Portugal e a NATO 1949–1999", *Nação e Defesa*, series 2, no. 89, 1999, pp. 15–41.
TELO, António José, *Portugal e a NATO: O Reencontro da Tradição Atlântica*, Lisbon, Cosmos, 1996.

1955
Portugal in the "World Parliament"

The ability of an authoritarian and colonial political regime to survive for almost thirty years after the end of the Second World War is clear evidence of how, in an increasingly globalized context, the results of such a process may be unexpected, since local, regional, or national identities may possess a vitality which global history must address

"The spirit of men is more important to world peace than the words of the Charter [of the United Nations] and its parts". Appearing in a speech, this judgement of what the United Nations was and could be is the first reference by Oliveira Salazar, the head of the Portuguese government, to an international organization created to oversee and guarantee peace and progress for humanity and regulate the functioning of a new world order. There were essentially two reasons for the evident skepticism in his words. Firstly, Portugal had not been asked to take part in the San Francisco Conference which ran from 25 April to 26 June 1945, attended by delegates from 45 of the 46 governments that had been invited. The participants were countries that had been involved in the Second World War and were signatories to the Declaration by United Nations of 1 January 1942. Therefore, unlike the League of Nations (1919), of which it remained a member until the organization was abolished in April 1946, Portugal did not become one of the founder members of the United Nations. Secondly, Salazar's words reflected the fact that a large part of the political elite in the *Estado Novo*, beginning with the President of the Council himself, did not believe in the principles or the proposals that had led to the creation of the United Nations, even though this elite recognized that Portugal could hardly avoid belonging to the organization, particularly if it consolidated its role, although at the beginning of 1946 this was something that could not be taken for granted.

The difficulties experienced by Portugal in gaining admission to the United Nations, and their causes, are well-known. The immediate reason was the fact that Portugal had remained a neutral country throughout the Second World War and did not have, and refused to establish, diplomatic relations with the Soviet Union. However, the main reason was that after 1946 Portuguese neutrality was considered pro-Axis (Germany, Italy, and Japan) by both the Soviet Union and its partners in the United Nations (Ukraine, Belarus, and Poland), who did not respond favorably to Portugal's request for membership. The proto-Cold War and Cold War climate affecting the Soviet and Atlantic blocs, which defined the years 1946 and 1947 in the case of the former, and 1948 onwards in the latter, is crucial to understanding the veto systematically used by the Soviets to block Portugal's entry to the United Nations, at a time when the country was, for example, involved in the Marshall Plan under the European Recovery Program and had become a founder member of the Organization for European Economic Co-operation and the North Atlantic Treaty Organization.

From 1946, the year in which Portugal, urged by the governments of the United States and United Kingdom, formally requested entry, until 1954, the United Nations Security Council not only opposed its admission but also that of several new member states. This was achieved with vetoes by Soviet Union, the United States and, in some cases, the United Kingdom and France. The threat of the direct use of the veto by at least one of the permanent members of Security Council also blocked the submission of various applications for admission, creating difficulties for former neutral states such as Spain, Portugal, the Republic of Ireland (all admitted on 14 December 1955) and Switzerland (which never applied for entry), but not Sweden (admitted on 19 November 1946) or the reluctant Japanese ally Thailand (accepted on 16 December 1946).

Moreover, several belligerent powers such as Austria, Albania, Bulgaria, Finland, Hungary, Italy, and Romania who had been enemies of the allied countries were only admitted on 14 December 1955. Japan was the last state from this group to become a member of the United Nations, on 16 December 1956. The delay on admitting these countries, which in most cases had persisted since 1946–1948, was the result of a moral and political judgement made by a group of countries headed by the Soviet Union, on one hand, and the United States, on the other hand, concerning their role during the Second World War – aggression within the Axis camp and real or alleged pro-Axis neutrality – and an assessment of the current political system or regime in countries such as Portugal and Spain or Albania, Bulgaria, Hungary and Romania. In reality, since its foundation, the United Nations had included various states with authoritarian regimes or states whose neutrality during the Second World War had been questionable from the perspective of Allied interests, in the case of Sweden and Turkey (in fact Ankara government declared war on the Axis powers in February 1945, but no Turkish soldier fought on the war).

Finally, the United Nations Charter stipulated the organization's respect for the political and constitutional model of each of its member states. Under Article 4 of the Charter, new countries would be accepted by decision of the United Nations General Assembly: however, any recommendation for admission was issued by the Security Council. Hence, the real obstacle to various countries joining the United Nations, which was only removed in 1955 and 1956, was the formation and consolidation of a strategy of confrontation between two blocs with different and irreconcilable models of political and social organization. Although this did not prevent the number of United Nations member states rising from 51 to 76 during the period 1946–1955, it left out a dozen European states, in addition to Japan, which were almost all former members of the League of Nations. These states had, in some cases since 1946, sought and been refused admission to a structure which claimed to be universal and which, in principle, all states should have been able to join if they wished, due to the hostility between the two increasingly antagonistic political and military blocs.

The circumstances in which the new countries were admitted, in December 1955, were not the result of the diplomatic skills of these states or their willingness to belong to the organization, but the outcome of new developments taking place in international politics after the death of Stalin on 5 March 1953. This brought changes to Soviet Union foreign policy, creating an atmosphere of detente in so-called "East–West relations" during the second half of the 1950s. The end of Soviet and North American vetoes on new states joining the United Nations is just one sign of this new reality, which was defined by a less marked antagonism.

However, between March 1953 and December 1955 there was no straightforward development towards a detente in "East–West relations", nor was this the case after-wards. Nevertheless, the new Soviet government – both before and after Khrushchev triumphed in the internal power struggle – strived to effect a qualitative change in Soviet relations with the "Western" bloc led by the United States and this had results that would have been unthinkable at the beginning of 1953. Three events will serve as examples. Firstly, Moscow pledged to find a political solution that would put an end to the Korean War. Subsequently, the Soviet authorities indicated that they were willing to negotiate with the other occupying powers to achieve a military withdrawal from Austria and a definition of its neutral status, which took place in 1955. Finally, the Soviets were responsible for setting up, preparing, and presenting the first summit after the Potsdam Conference (in July–August 1945), which was held in Geneva, attended by the heads of state of the United States (Eisenhower) and the Soviet Union (Khrushchev).

When Portugal acquired the status of a member state of the United Nations this had political consequences, not because it could have forced the almost immediate abandonment of the colonial territories, as a certain Portuguese elite determined to defend the integrity of its "overseas" territories feared, but because Portuguese diplomacy and foreign policy began to operate, scrutinize and be scrutinized on a multilateral and global level in a way that had never happened when the country had been involved in the work of the League of Nations. Questions raised by the United Nations and its agencies or discussed individually or collectively by member states very often had a global dimension and profile, even though, in the vast majority of cases, this was not known or acknowledged by public opinion worldwide.

Faced with this new reality, both on the level of foreign and international politics and in various areas of domestic politics, specifically colonial affairs, the reaction, and behavior of the Portuguese authorities was ambivalent. On the one hand, they let themselves be carried along by the "internationalizing" and "globalizing" trend implied by the existence of institutions such as the United Nations, the North Atlantic Treaty Organization, the Organization for European Economic Co-operation (which later became the Organization for Economic Co-operation and Development) and the

European Free Trade Association (in only one case, namely the United Nations, Portugal did not have the status of founder member). Between 1946 and 1974, the country was therefore actively and passively subjected to a process of globalization and could not remain isolated from a phenomenon which was not, in fact, entirely new and was creating increasingly uniform societies with fewer distinguishing features. At the same time, however, Portugal's involvement (as a state and as a society) in this process of globalization and internationalization emphasized and reformulated some aspects of its differences and uniqueness. The ability of an authoritarian and colonial political regime to survive for almost thirty years after the end of the Second World War is clear evidence of how, in an increasingly globalized context, the results of such a process may be unexpected, since local, regional, or national identities may possess a vitality which global history must address. In other words, it raises the question of why identical global or international circumstances produce different results on a local, regional and/or national level.

FERNANDO MARTINS
Interdisciplinary Centre for History, Culture, and Societies,
University of Évora

Bibliography

MARTINS, Fernando, ""A crise da paz": Portugal e a Organização das Nações Unidas: das origens à admissão (1945–1955)", *Relações Internacionais*, no. 47, Sept. 2015, pp. 39–73.

MASTNY, Vojtech, "Soviet foreign policy, 1953–1962", in LEFFLER, Melvyn P., WESTAD, Odd Arne (ed.), *The Cambridge History of the Cold War*, vol. I, Cambridge, Cambridge University Press, 2010, pp. 312–333.

MAZOWER, Mark, *Governing the World: The History of an Idea, 1815 to the Present*, London, Penguin Books, 2013.

SALAZAR, Oliveira, "Ideias falsas e palavras vãs (reflexões sobre o último acto eleitoral)", in *Discursos e Notas Políticas*, vol. 4, Coimbra, Coimbra Editora, 1951, pp. 195–213.

ZUBOK, Vladislav, PLESHAKOV, Constantine, *Inside the Kremlin's Cold War: From Stalin to Khrushchev*, Cambridge (Massachusetts)/London, Harvard University Press, 1996.

1961
Portugal as Pariah State During the Late Colonial Wars

Portugal played a key role in the creation of this new post-imperial global order, since it not only resisted it for decades but did so as a colonial empire in denial, forcing a clarification of these new norms.

In order to analyze the role played by Portugal in the global history of the period after the Second World War, dominated by decolonization and the Cold War, it is necessary to look beyond Salazar's rhetoric and that of the opposition, which exaggerated the international isolation of the *Estado Novo* for propaganda purposes. The regime invested in a discourse of heroic isolationism, the opposition in showing that the authoritarian regime had never been accepted by the European democracies. However, there are certain international connections which are indispensable for a fuller understanding of the origins, dynamics and outcome of the last great armed conflict waged by the Portuguese state from 1961–1974. Moreover, Portugal also had some global influence during this period, both in terms of contributing to the establishment of irregular warfare as the prevalent type of conflict in the world today, and to the creation of a new international post-colonial and post-imperial world order.

These international connections were crucial in initiating the anti-colonial armed uprising in Angola, in February–March 1961. Nevertheless, the importance of internal factors should not be forgotten, first and foremost grievances arising from the more abusive aspects of Portuguese colonialism which affected broad sectors of the local African population. These grievances had deep roots in the past, specifically working conditions which often verged on forced labour, or the Statute of Indigenous Peoples which signified that, despite the official Portuguese rhetoric of racial equality, the vast majority of the native African population of Angola and Mozambique did not have the same legal status as the European Portuguese. However, the main change at the beginning of 1961 was in the global and regional context after the Congo had become independent from Belgium the year before, providing a sanctuary on the other side of the northern and eastern borders of Angola for those aiming to organize an armed independence movement. Together with the Congo, other African colonies also became independent in the year 1960, which became known as the "Year of Africa". The movement to end colonialism in Africa was gaining decisive momentum and broad international support.

The international press was also expected in larger numbers than usual in the Angolan capital of Luanda, following rumours that the Santa Maria liner, seized by an anti-Salazarist and anti-Francoist commando led by the exiled Portuguese officer Henrique Galvão, would be heading for Angola. A UN debate on Portuguese colonialism was also imminent in New York. Moreover, the Union of Angolan Peoples headed by Holden Roberto, largely responsible for the initial armed uprising in Angola, was receiving international support, not only from the newly-independent Congo where it was based, but also from some of the UN peacekeepers stationed there, namely those from Tunisia (which had been independent from France since 1956). The UPA leader believed that the Portuguese, facing growing international pressure to decolonize, would not be able to resist armed struggle for long, as had been the case with the Belgians in the Congo, where he was living in exile together with an important Angolan diaspora.

The international connections enjoyed by Salazar and his regime are indispensable in understanding why this was not the case, and why the Portuguese state was able to fight on for more than a decade against the independence of the territories it controlled in Africa. After all, despite the official propaganda of Portugal standing alone, most of the weapons used by the Portuguese military in these late colonial wars were imported.

One prime example of Salazar's rhetoric of heroic isolationism was the speech delivered in February 1965 in which he affirmed that, since 1961, "we have been fighting, without spectacle or allies, proudly alone" in the "battle" for Africa. Paradoxically, this speech is filled with references to the global Cold War. Nevertheless, the "proudly alone" propaganda slogan has made its mark on the Portuguese collective memory. It has proved so resilient because during the final years of the Salazar regime Portugal was, in actual fact, increasingly criticized abroad for remaining on the fringes of the new international norms which stipulated swift independence for colonial territories. In 1973, the new state of Guinea-Bissau, unilaterally proclaimed by the African Party for the Independence of Guinea and Cape Verde (PAIGC), was recognized by over 80 UN member states, more than those who still had diplomatic relations with Portugal. In New York, informal consultations were being held on the possibility of the UN General Assembly accepting Guinea-Bissau and suspending Portugal, as in the case of South Africa. However, global politics cannot be reduced to the UN General Assembly.

Salazar and his associates knew that the rhetoric of standing proudly alone was useful internally, but also that Portugal was too weak to dispense with powerful foreign allies. It needed investment and the international markets to enable the economy to continue to grow and provide employment for a rapidly increasing population. If Portugal had not been a member of the European Free Trade Association since 1960, it would not have been possible for the Portuguese GDP to oscillate between a minimum of 2.4% and a maximum of 10.6% during the 1960s. It would also have been impossible for Portugal to continue fighting the armed Independence movements in Angola, Guinea-Bissau and Mozambique for more than a decade without importing sophisticated weaponry.

The country did not produce the military equipment required to plan and sustain a vast overseas expeditionary force engaged in contemporary counter-insurgency. In 1961 the Armed Forces did not have the necessary transport aircraft, helicopters, light automatic weapons and trucks needed for this purpose, and the Portuguese government therefore had no alternative other than to negotiate agreements abroad to buy them. Alouette helicopters and Berliet trucks from France, for example, were essential for Portuguese counter-insurgency in Africa. It also had to negotiate the transfer of know-how and rights to enable some of the equipment to be manufactured in Portuguese territory, in partnership with countries such as Germany. This was the case with the production of the *G-3* rifle at the Braço de Prata plant, the service weapon most widely used in the 1961–1974 campaigns and by the Portuguese military in the years that followed, which was only fully replaced in 2019.

The idea of a unique Portuguese military doctrine in the field of counter-insurgency still exists and is accepted by important authors such as John Cann. However, this is, in my view, largely a myth. Even the idea of great economy of force in this type of campaign, which contains a great deal of truth and contrasts in particular with the American way of war in Vietnam, was also present in the French and British wars of decolonization. Sending expeditionary forces to fight thousands of kilometres away was always a major logistical challenge that had to be managed with great economy of costs for it to remain sustainable for most powers that were not as wealthy as the US.

Moreover, in addition to obvious parallels between the Portuguese and, in particular, the French military doctrines, it is possible to actually document significant international links in the development of Portuguese doctrinal guidelines for counter-insurgency. Without taking these international connections of the Portuguese military into account, above all those linking it with the French Armed Forces, it is impossible to explain the rapid development of Portugal's counter-insurgency doctrine in 1959–1961, at a time when its Armed Forces had no direct previous experience of this kind of warfare. This is very important in explaining how Portuguese troops managed to respond effectively to these new challenges, despite initial difficulties and contrary to the expectations of many, including many foreign powers.

The 1959 Portuguese military mission to French Algeria, where French troops were fighting the guerrilla independence movement, was especially significant in this process of doctrinal diffusion and development. Portuguese soldiers attended the Arzew Training Centre for Pacification and Preparation in Counter-Guerrilla Warfare run by the French military. This resulted in a key report stressing the importance of psychological warfare tactics based on deploying reserves of combat forces comprising mobile troops, and a network of territorial units with mainly peacekeeping functions that involved contact with and control of the local population. This French connection was instrumental in shaping the creation of the Special Operations Training Centre in Lamego, where the first Portuguese army units were trained for the guerrilla war. When war broke out in Angola in March 1961, officers from this Special Ops Centre were dispatched as travelling instructors. Several of them with French counter-insurgency connections – including the future general Franco Pinheiro who had been involved in writing the 1959 report after his Algerian experience – were part of a working party that had been set up at the Institute of Advanced Military Studies to prepare texts for a special course in counter-insurgency, for the academic year 1961–1962. From 1963 onwards this was developed into the official military manual known as the EGS, *O Exército na Guerra Subversiva* (*The Army in Subversive Warfare*), a relatively successful attempt to combine actual experience with lessons from abroad that explicitly recognizes the influence of British, North American and French military doctrines.

These foreign connections also helped legitimize the radical change in the type of training and priority mission of the Portuguese Armed Forces, from conventional warfare in Europe to the guerrilla warfare in Africa, despite the usual corporate resistance. The war in Angola, in addition to other conflicts during the Cold War, contributed to the growing number of asymmetrical armed conflicts which have become the main form of armed violence on a global scale since the end of the Second World War. In fact, conventional wars between professional state armies represent less than 20 percen of armed conflicts since 1945. Hence, in recent decades these counter-insurgency campaigns have obliged the professional armed forces of European states to adapt to major changes in terms of force profile, equipment and doctrine in order to adjust effectively to this new type of combat. Portugal was therefore one of the pioneers in developing this new type of post-1945 warfare, in which there is no official declaration of war and the enemy is a clandestine organization intent on conquering power by resorting to surprise attacks and political subversion. It is a type of conflict in which there are no clearly defined front lines, insurgents fight amongst the civilian population and there are no decisive battles, only multiple surprise attacks designed to undermine the enemy's will to fight. This strategy of wearing down colonial powers forced into, or threatened with, protracted armed struggle in order to maintain control of overseas territories thousands of kilometres away helps to explain the emergence of a post-colonial and post-imperial global political order.

Portugal played a key role in the creation of this new global order, since it not only resisted it for decades but did so as a colonial empire in denial, forcing a clarification of these new norms. From 1951 onwards, the Portuguese state stipulated in its Constitution that it no longer possessed colonies, despite the fact that it was only when armed struggle began in 1961 that it abolished the Statute of Indigenous Peoples which, until then, had deprived a large number of native Africans of equal rights. Therefore, it never admitted the possibility of a negotiated independence. The Portuguese position forced an explicit clarification of the new global political order in a post-colonial and post-imperial sense. Obviously, a post-imperial global order does not mean that major powers have disappeared, but it has significantly changed what they can do with their great power in a way that is recognized as legitimate by other states. More precisely, what has disappeared is the possibility that formal empires can be established and gain legal recognition: the US can still invade Iraq with ease, for example, but it cannot formally annex Iraqi territory. This current post-imperial order was formally enshrined in a series of resolutions issued by the UN General Assembly in December 1960. They emerged in response to the Portuguese regime's resistance to rapid, unconditional decolonization. When it became clear, at the beginning of 1961, that Salazar would fight to prevent the decolonization of Angola and various other colonial territories and, above all, when it became obvious that the *Estado Novo* would continue to deny that it possessed colonies, the majority of UN members felt obliged to issue a clear definition of what a colony was and make explicit which new criteria should govern the principle of self-determination. The key role played by Portugal in this process is evident in UN General Assembly Resolution 1542, which stipulated that, in accordance with the criteria laid down in Resolutions 1514 and 1541, Portugal possessed a number of colonies and was obliged, in the light of these new international standards, to proceed rapidly towards accepting their independence.

After this, Portugal became a pariah state, not in the sense, as we have seen, of being completely isolated, but in terms of existing on the margins of universally accepted global standards and therefore subject to strong international pressure. Portugal was a successful pariah state, offering lessons still relevant today on how peripheral actors can resist international pressures for a considerable period of time. Salazar managed to hold out against this pressure for more than a decade, opting for a series of bilateral relations with major global or regional powers such as the US, Great Britain, France and Germany, which all had the power to veto the UN resolutions that were most threatening to the interests of the regime, and to provide it with vital military equipment. It was, paradoxically, through this intransigent defence of the Portuguese overseas territories that the Portuguese ruling elite moved diplomatically closer to the Paris-Bonn axis that presided over the building of a more integrated Europe which Portugal, minus its colonial empire, would soon join, strengthening its network of alliances in a very different political context.

Bruno Cardoso Reis
Centre for International Studies of ISCTE, University Institute of Lisbon

Bibliography

CANN, John P., *Counterinsurgency in Africa: The Portuguese Way of War 1961–74*, Warwick, Helion, 2012.

GOMES, Costa, *O Último Marechal* [interview], Maria Manuela Cruzeiro, Lisbon, Notícias, 1998.

OLIVEIRA, Pedro Aires, TOMÁS, António, *1961: Portugal Uma Retrospectiva*, Lisbon, Público/Tinta da China, 2019.

REIS, Bruno Cardoso, "As primeiras décadas de Portugal nas Nações Unidas: Um Estado pária contra a norma da descolonização (1956–1974)", in JERÓNIMO, Miguel Bandeira,

PINTO, António Costa (org.), *Portugal e o Fim do Colonialismo: Dimensões Internacionais*, Lisbon, Edições 70, 2014, pp. 179–215.

Idem, "The myth of British minimum force in counterinsurgency campaigns during decolonisation (1945–1970)", *Journal of Strategic Studies*, vol. 34, no. 2, 2011, pp. 245–279.

1966
Eusébio, Lusotropicalism and the Globalization of Sports Idols

Like other idols of his time, such as the Brazilian Pelé, Eusébio was soon feted by the crowds. Fans followed him in the stadiums, but also in the press, on the radio, and later on television. The increasing media coverage of sports retrospectively reinforced the centrality of football and its idols in everyday Portuguese life, and also internationally.

Born in 1941 in the poor suburbs of the city of Lourenço Marques, the capital of the Portuguese colony Mozambique, Eusébio da Silva Ferreira achieved the status of an icon in global popular culture in the 1960s. The dazzling career of this black football player coincided with the Portuguese military campaign to defend part of its colonial empire. Oliveira Salazar's *Estado Novo* had been fighting in Angola since 1961, extending its military action to the colonies of Guinea and Mozambique in 1963 and 1964. Eusébio left the neighbourhood of Mafalala on the outskirts of Lourenço Marques and travelled to Lisbon at the end of 1960, to play for SL Benfica. The following year, the club became a UEFA European Cup winner, beating Real Madrid in the final held in Amsterdam. In 1966, he joined the Portuguese national team, which reached third place in the first widely televised FIFA World Cup. At the end of the competition, which was held in England, he was declared the top scorer. His talents were reported in thousands of newspaper pages throughout the world and his greatest moves were replayed on television channels and in cinemas. To this day, Eusébio is considered the best African player of all time. The triumphs of Benfica and the national team created a multifaceted nationalism, in which Eusébio played an important role. The state fast-tracked his military service in 1963, although he enjoyed the privilege of never having to fight and only remained in the army for a short time. The sportsman also took part in campaigns organized by the National Women's Movement in support of Portuguese soldiers. As a member of the national team, he was awarded the Silver Medal of the Order of Prince Henry in 1966, presented by Salazar, who praised the achievements of the athletes in England that had created a positive image for Portugal in the eyes of the international press, a rare asset during the era of colonial wars. According to Eusébio, it was Salazar himself who declared him a national asset, which meant he could not transfer to other European clubs and improve his financial situation, as the player had wished.

Nationalism based on sport was expressed through other mechanisms. In press articles, the multiracial Portuguese team that captivated England was presented as the product of a unique and singular empire where racial harmony prevailed. The same representation of a harmonious, exotic and integrated colonial land predominated in

Eusébio's autobiography, *My name is Eusébio* (1966), a best-seller based on a series of interviews with the *Emissora Nacional* journalist Fernando Garcia, which was translated and published in many countries.

This creation of the "Portuguese world" through the biography and career of an exceptional athlete conformed with the rhetoric used by the government at the time to justify the continuing existence of its empire in the contentious arenas of public opinion and international diplomacy. The propaganda discourse, highlighting the unique nature of Portuguese colonialism, was broadly described as "Luso-tropicalism", a term used by the Brazilian sociologist Gilberto Freyre, initially to refer to Brazilian cultural identity. Examining the historical origins of Brazilian national frameworks, Freyre's project was influenced by the culturalist perspective predominant in North American anthropology, due to the fact the author had studied anthropology at the University of Columbia in New York, where he discovered Franz Boas and his work. In certain books, some sponsored by the Portuguese state, the sociologist provided a more specific definition of the concept and extended it to other Portuguese colonial contexts. The *Estado Novo* propaganda machinery, in particular the National Secretariat for Information and the General Overseas Agency, resorted to other means to disseminate the concept of the uniqueness of Portuguese colonialism.

National popular culture, transmitted by radio, newsreels, the press and television, played an important part in publicizing Lusotropicalism. As a symbol of social and racial integration in Portuguese territory, Eusébio was converted into an agent of Lusotropicalism for the masses. It should also be noted that his international fame was subject to other forms of appropriation. His "Black Panther" nickname, created by the *Daily Express* journalist Desmond Hackett following a match between Portugal and England at Wembley in 1961, had other associations: the North American political movement known as the Black Panthers was founded in 1966, only a few months after the World Cup in England.

In specific historical circumstances, the longstanding colonial project of a nation boasting eight centuries of history was also used to justify the performance of one football player. It was argued that Eusébio was the product of a unique national history and imperial culture. His story exemplified the opportunities that Portuguese colonial society offered to Africans, including the possibility of representing the nation on equal terms with Portuguese individuals of other origins. This was a rare occurrence in European national teams: it was not until 1978 that a black player featured in the English national team. As in Portuguese colonial society, the players in the national football team all worked towards a common goal, thus displaying this equality.

The link between Eusébio 's life story and the history of Portuguese colonialism is undeniable, although it cannot be explained by the nationalist narrative of the state. From the outset, it is important to interpret this relationship within the context of daily life in the colonial societies created by Portuguese expansion, which was very different to the representations produced by propaganda. In the case of the Benfica player, this would demand examining the foundations of the highly discriminatory and segregated world of Lourenço Marques, where Eusébio grew up. Yet, this alone would not be sufficient to explain the footballer's extraordinary path which led to the historic encounter between Eusébio's fame and the Lusotropicalist propaganda of the state.

In order to understand this trajectory, it is essential to abandon explanations limited to the confines of national or imperial history. This new Portuguese hero, famed for his performance in a profession that was so different from those in which other heroes of the nation had made their names, can only be explained by the fact that Portugal and its colonies were spaces in which the social practices and institutional processes that would define a global time were being developed. The age of modern sports belongs to this global era. Norbert Elias and Eric Dunning have called the dynamic involved in the expansion of the practice and consumption of such activities the sportization process The networks of relationships underpinning this process in Portugal and its colonies were responsible for the path that enabled a poor Mozambican with *indígena* status to reach the rank of a national and imperial hero who was recognized worldwide.

The importance of this transnational process highlights the autonomy of a particular activity in global expansion, one that produces specific outcomes that cannot be reduced to a reflection of other historical dynamics. Explanations focussing exclusively on national political history, such as those that might suggest that it was the regime which invented Eusébio and his sporting career, mask the importance of these global processes. Eusébio did not achieve his status by acting as a servant educated by the state (a politician, soldier or scientist), but as an outstanding interpreter of a modern sport that was part of popular culture in the process of massification, broadcast by media operating on an international scale, planting Eusébio in the imagination of millions of people.

An orthodox version of football was codified in the third quarter of the nineteenth century by the English public schools, then spread rapidly throughout the world. The founding of structures to oversee the application of the rules of the game and federate all the regulatory bodies involved in this process in a national context created the basis for the global expansion of the football association. In Portugal, as in other parts of the world, the pioneering work of the English communities in publicizing the sport contributed towards the organization of the first games, clubs and competitions at the end of the nineteenth century. The country quickly adopted the game, and clubs and associations were formed in the main cities, becoming more firmly established following the creation of a national federation in 1914, and district associations (the Lisbon Football Association was created in 1910, and its counterpart in Porto in 1912).

This movement was spurred on by the involvement of a growing public who saw the relationship with their club as an important part of their everyday identity. The effect of representation triggered an inevitable process of professionalization which helped the game expand beyond the amateur strongholds where it was initially played, leading to the emergence of what were essentially professional clubs. In Portugal, the three clubs which remain the most popular to this day were founded between the end of the nineteenth century and the beginning of the twentieth century: FC Porto in 1893, SL Benfica in 1904, and Sporting CP in 1906. Some researchers have contested the dates for Porto and Benfica, suggesting 1906 and 1908 respectively as alternatives.

The unstoppable sportization process soon reached the Portuguese colonies, which had been organizing games and competitions since the beginning of the twentieth century. The first clubs and associations were also created there. In Lourenço Marques, where Eusébio grew up, the sportization process was influenced by a radically segregated social structure. Social and racial discrimination resulted in the existence of two football associations, one for the white settlers and another for Africans from the suburbs. Very few players moved from one to the other: those who managed to do so were almost all of mixed race and had assimilated status. Despite the discrimination, interest in this game, which was easy to play and affordable, grew amongst Africans. They appropriated it, together with its rules, organized clubs, competitions and associations, and a few individuals became excellent players. This was the case with Eusébio, whose talent did not go unnoticed by managers and officials of clubs searching for the best athletes to represent them. Due to his outstanding qualities, Eusébio joined Sporting of Lourenço Marques in 1957, aged only fifteen. To the fans, these players possessed exceptional power: they offered daily joys, shared in their social relationships. It was the same in Portugal and almost the entire world.

It is the specific terms of this sportization process which explain the emergence of Eusébio's talent, revealing how he learned the game within the context of the institutional structures created to promote the development of football. It was his undisputed merits that led him to Lisbon and Benfica. At the Estádio da Luz, he trained under the Hungarian Béla Guttmann, a believer in professionalism, master of tactics, and one of the Magyars, almost all representatives of the European Jewish diaspora, who helped transform Portuguese football, making it more professional and effective.

Like other idols of his time, such as the Brazilian Pelé, Eusébio was soon feted by the crowds. Fans followed him in the stadiums, but also in the press, on the radio, and later on television. The increasing media coverage of sports retrospectively reinforced the centrality of football and its idols in everyday Portuguese life, and also internationally. Football not only developed a nucleus on a national level, but also created shared international networks, enabling Eusébio to become a global idol. Mistrusting football, a collective game prone to encouraging disorderly behaviour, and a mobilizer of the masses, susceptible to political infiltration, the *Estado Novo* nevertheless realized it could take advantage of this fever to convey a nationalist narrative, reproduced by its own press, and thus defend its Lusotropicalist representation of the empire. The difficulty involved in producing a history which re-establishes the connection between, on the one hand, the story of Eusébio and the sportization process in Portugal and its colonies, and, on the other hand, his career and the reality of Portuguese colonialism in Lourenço Marques, is one reason why stories of Eusébio's life continue to present an idealized narrative of Portuguese colonialism.

Nuno Domingos
Instituto de Ciências Sociais, Universidade de Lisboa

Bibliography

CARDÃO, Marcos, *Fado Tropical: O Luso-Tropicalismo na Cultura de Massas (1960–1974)*, Lisbon, Unipop, 2015.

CASTELO, Cláudia, *O Modo Português de Estar no Mundo: O Luso-Tropicalismo e a Ideologia Colonial Portuguesa (1933–1961)*, Porto, Afrontamento, 2001.

DOMINGOS, Nuno, *Football and Colonialism: Body and Popular Culture in Urban Mozambique*, Athens, Ohio University Press, 2017.

ELIAS, Norbert, DUNNING, Eric, *The Quest for Excitement: Sport and Leisure in the Civilizing Process*, Oxford, Basil Blackwell, 1986.

PENVENNE, Jeanne Marie, *African Workers and Colonial Racism: Mozambican Strategies and Struggles in Lourenço Marques, 1877–1962*, London, James Currey, 1995.

1974
The 25th of April: Transition to Democracy

Affiliating the April Revolution to the series of transformations inaugurated with the military defeat of conversative authoritarian regimes in the course of the Second World War, José Medeiros Ferreira presents it as the last European revolution.

On 25th April 1974, the Armed Forces Movement carried out a coup d'état that lasted less than twenty-four hours, putting an end to one of the longest dictatorships in Europe (1926–1974). It is generally agreed that the event was triggered by the Colonial War, which started in Angola in 1961 and rapidly spread to new fronts in Guinea (1963) and Mozambique (1964), and which had no military solution in sight. Contributing decisively to the radicalization of the opposition to the *Estado Novo* and increase in social unrest, the war had a mortal effect upon the Armed Forces, one of the central pillars of the regime. It was in response to new legislation which aimed to supply more officers to the battlefronts in Africa that, in September 1973, the Captains' Movement, or Armed Forces Movement, was born.

The conspiracy phase of the Movement was relatively short. At the beginning of 1974, it entered a rapid process of politicization. Signs were beginning to accumulate that the end of the regime was imminent, given its intransigence in maintaining the war effort: the publication on 22nd February of *Portugal and the Future* by António de Spínola, the ceremony on 14th March known as the "rheumatic brigade", the removal of the generals Costa Gomes and António de Spínola from the Chief of Defence Staff of the Armed Forces (15th March) and the false start by the 5th Infantary Regiment from Caldas da Rainha (16th March).

The international backdrop to all this was the oil crisis of 1973, an event which, according to Odd Arne Westad, "put an end to the regime" since "Portugal had no way of keeping the population supplied with subsidized fuel, while at the same time providing soldiers to fight in Africa".

The impact of the captains' intervention rapidly transcended national boundaries in a world divided by the Cold War and shaken by the recent oil crisis. However, those that hastened to draw parallels between these events and those which, a year before, had occurred in Chile (Pinochet's coup), were quickly enlightened, first and foremost because in the Portuguese coup had been carried out by middle- and low-ranking officers of little significance in the hierarchy of the Armed Forces, and without any interference from political movements or parties. What is more, contrary to predictions and quite unlike the most common models of military intervention in processes of political change, the captains of the April Revolution presented a programme of democratization which envisage not only the restoration of fundamental freedoms but also the constitution of a civil government and holding of free elections. Similarly unpredictably, after more than a decade of fighting on the African fronts, the military initiated a process of decolonization which soon resulted in independence for the former colonial peoples. The prospects that this might lead to a new transitional model became increasingly likely when it became clear that the fall of the dictatorship in Portugal had given rise to a turbulent revolutionary process (1974–1975). This unique situation surprised not only the academic community, but also top world leaders, who struggled to integrate the Portuguese case into the established interpretative grid.

According to Kenneth Maxwell, one of the most important characteristics of the 25th of April was its international impact, since it played "a significant and precocious part in the great ideological conflict of the twentieth century". However, even without subscribing to the thesis that foreign forces had played a fundamental role in bringing about the events of 25th April 1974, it is impossible to ignore the importance of the international context or the impact of the Portuguese revolution on the world stage.

The collapse of the Portuguese dictatorship occurred at a particular moment in the Cold War, a turning-point following a period marked by a loss of capacity on the part of the two superpowers to exert world hegemony, the debilitation of the United States in the face of the Vietnam War crisis and Watergate affair, the strengthening of the European Economic Community and rapid implementation of the USSR's strategy in Europe through détente. In such a context, the Portuguese situation (and particularly its African colonial aspect) threatened to destabilize the international balance of forces.

Despite giving it considerable importance, given its geostrategic position and NATO membership, the United States did not immediately realise what was going on in Portugal. However, they ultimately became a support for the forces in the country that were fighting for the establishment of a pluralist democracy, along with countries like the German Federal Republic and organizations like the Socialist International. Led by the Soviet Union, the eastern bloc also meddled in the political struggle, helping the Portuguese Communist Party. Portugal thus became a battleground in the East-West conflict, a kind of laboratory in which international actors could explore new formulas, but also a negative example for all subsequent democratic revolutions.

The extensive coverage given to the April Revolution by the international media, and the formal and informal networks set up between parties, organizations and diverse international actors, are clear signs of its foreign impact. The matter becomes more complex if we take into account that the fall of the dictatorship and prevalence of the Programme of the Armed Forces Movement over the federalist theses of António de Spínola (July -September 1974) paved the way for rapid decolonization. For Portugal, this meant the end of the imperial cycle and creation of conditions for the democratization and modernization of the country which, a decade later, became a member of the European Union (1986). On the international level, the prospect of the emergence of five new independent countries on the continent of Africa altered zones of influence and the balance of forces. The two blocs entered into open dispute for the enlargement of their areas of influence, nourishing civil wars and foreign armed interventions.

As Kenneth Maxwell observed, 25th April had "widespread and long-lasting international ramifications". In the end, the "triumph for anticommunist democrats" in the political struggle of revolutionary Portugal, together with "the initial victory of the communist-backed forces in Angola in the same period" mobilized "many of the forces which would help bring about the end of the Cold War in Europe", revigorating democracy and "escalating the costs of proxy conflicts in the third world". It is important to point out that studies of 25th April 1974 have tended to oscillate between two opposing interpretations. On the one side are those who, like António Costa Pinto, emphasise its pioneering role, presenting it as a precursor of the third wave of transitions to democracy, while on the other are those (like Medeiros Ferreira or Hermínio Martins) who highlight its belated nature, associating it with revolutionary movements of the past. Adopting the expression coined by Samuel Huntington, the first group presents the April Revolution as inaugurating a third wave of democratizations in the last part of the twentieth century. Preceding the end of the Greek Military Dictatorship by three months, the democratic transition of Adolfo Suárez in Spain by two years, and the South American and Eastern European transitions by one and two decades, respectively, the Portuguese experiment opened up new angles of analysis about political change and (particularly) democratization processes. Since then, the Portuguese and Spanish examples have protagonized the most common types of democratic transitions, presenting themselves as models of rupture and negotiation. In Portugal, the sudden collapse of the dictatorship triggered a revolution, while in Spain, which was affected (especially negatively) by the diffusion or contagion of the Portuguese experiment, there was a gradual negotiation between authoritarian and democratic elites.

The Greek experiment was closest to the Portuguese model of rupture, although without the crisis that followed, or rather, without a revolutionary process. The "pact" model, inspired by the way the Spanish elites made a complete break with Francoism from within its own institutions, is the one that predominates in subsequent transition processes in Latin America and Eastern Europe. In several cases (such as Chile, Argentina, Brazil, etc), the authoritarian elite significantly conditioned the institutionalization of democracy.

An important aspect of the thesis that presents the Portuguese case as a precursor of the third wave of transitions is the idea that that the collapse of the dictatorship followed a systemic rupture and triggered a revolutionary process characterized by a crisis of State, the politicization of the Armed Forces and the radicalization of social movements.

During the months of the Portuguese revolution up to 25th November, various processes and solutions were envisaged, polarizing positions in military circles and amongst social movements and parties. On the one hand, the defenders of a model inspired in the state socialism of the Soviet type considered the existence of a military vanguard as a unique opportunity to fulfil its objectives. This project was promoted by sectors connected to prime minister Vasco Gonçalves and counted on the support of the Portuguese Communist Party. A more ideologically diffuse group, involving revolutionary military units with considerable fighting power, advocated a self-managed socialist revolution. This cohered around the figure of Otelo Saraiva de Carvalho, commander of the Continental Operational Command and parties of the far left, such as the Revolutionary Party of the Proletariat/Revolutionary Brigades, the Socialist Left Movement, the Popular Democratic Union and Popular Socialist Front. Finally, among the myriad of projects that emerged in that context, there were the supporters of a pluralistic social democratic regime, to be implemented by free elections. Represented in the military by the Group of Nine (whose members were also known as Melo-Antunists or moderates), they had the strategic support of parties like the Socialist Party. These other realities have led some authors to question the idea that Portugal was a precursor of the third wave of transitions to democracy, highlighting instead its belatedness.

Affiliating the April Revolution to the series of transformations inaugurated with the military defeat of conversative authoritarian regimes in the course of the Second World War, José Medeiros Ferreira presents it as the last European revolution. For him, the 25th of April was an "imperfect revolution" which triggered profound alterations not only in politics but also in values and in society.

Likewise, Hermínio Martins interprets 25th April as a 1945 (downfall of dictator-ships) "renewed with ingredients of 1968", dates that were lost in Portugal in their original editions and which would be compressed into a period of eighteen months "experienced by many with extraordinary intensity". The emancipation of all the structures of authority and festivalization of politics – with politics on the street in the form of permanent "general assemblies" – the revolt against hierarchies, emergence of feminism and occupation of schools, universities, organs of state and companies, all attest to this.

Thus, rather than a pioneer, the 25th of April should be presented as the last example of a series of decolonizations of empires and of a failed transition to socialism (the "last Leninist theatre" or a "Cuba in Southern Europe", in the words of French journalist Dominique Pouchin).

Maria Inácia Rezola

Institute of Contemporary History, Nova University Lisbon and
School of Communication and Media Studies

Bibliography

FERREIRA, José Medeiros, "Portugal em transe", in MATTOSO, José (ed.), *História de Portugal*, vol. 8, Lisbon, Círculo de Leitores, 1993, pp. 1–285.

MAXWELL, Kenneth, *The Making of Portuguese Democracy*, Cambridge, Cambridge University Press, 1995.

PINTO, António Costa, MORLINO, Leonardo (ed.), *Dealing with the Legacy of Authoritarianism: The 'Politics of the Past' in Southern European Democracies*, London, Routledge, 2013.

REIS, António (ed.), *Portugal: 20 Anos de Democracia*, Lisbon, Círculo de Leitores, 1994.

WESTAD, Odd Arne, *A Guerra Fria: Uma História do Mundo*, Lisbon, Temas e Debates, 2018.

1986
Portugal's Membership to the European Economic Community

The slogan "Europe with us", launched by Mário Soares in 1976, set the tone for a longlasting commitment which counted particularly upon the political guarantee and endorsement that Europe would provide in order to prevent the spectre of totalitarianism.

Once the turbulent phase that had naturally followed the April Revolution of 1974 was over, Portugal moved firmly towards achieving one of the main purposes inher-ent in the construction of a democratic regime: full membership of the European Economic Community (EEC). The mediatic ceremony for the signing of the acces-sion treaty, which took place in the cloister of the Jeronimos Monastery on the 12th of June 1985, was the culmination of a negotiation process that would reveal itself to be the most significant consequence of the democratic opening-up of the country, enabling it to modernize and develop.

The desire to participate in European projects was first manifested during the authoritarian regime of the *Estado Novo*, with Portugal's presence at the creation of the European Free Trade Association in 1959. For the mentors and executors of the commitments arising from this participation (namely José Gonçalo Correia de Oliveira and Valentim Xavier Pintado), this was the affirmation of the conviction that Portugal could benefit from belonging to a free trade area, which would stimulate a dynamic of growth in the various sectors of the Portuguese economy. The effects were soon felt, as the growth that was noted in the golden years of the sixties was not a fortuitous outcome. It has now been amply demonstrated that it was this opening-up to the exterior, this gradual integration of the Portuguese economy into the European space created by the European Free Trade Association, that attenuated the disparities in the levels of per capita income and productivity indexes between Portugal and its main international partners. The growth model then followed, duly framed in development plans that prescribed goals and tools of economic policy, was based on a strong component of public and private investment in sectors with a significant preponderance of physical capital (transport, energy and communication infrastructures, machinery, equipment). Thus, the aim was to recover the pace of economic recovery that had been experienced in most European countries in the immediate post-war period. The process of European construction and integration underwent decisive moments during this period, and Portugal participated attentively, if somewhat timidly. With its entry into the European Free Trade Association, however, a decisive signal was given in the recognition of the strategic importance of its membership of a broader economic space.

After the April Revolution of 1974, there were two major alterations to the assumptions underpinning the successful growth model of the previous decade. Firstly, there was the loss of the African colonial market, which till then had helped structure the formation of broader national and international markets in which private economic groups and interests that supported the regime were acting. Secondly, there was the dissipation of the authoritarian political framework, which had imposed limits on the freedom of action of economic, social, political and cultural agents, and which impeded the modernization of the Portuguese economy and society. This meant that the challenges that Portugal faced in the period immediately after the April Revolution of 1974 involved the perception that the choices to be made implied simultaneously the break-up of the Atlantic colonial alliance and the reinforcement of the institutions that guaranteed the full functioning of a political regime based on principles of freedom and democracy.

The main signs that the options would have to be framed in the European economic and political space were given by Mário Soares, minister of Foreign Affairs in the First Provisional Government, who travelled to Brussels at the beginning of May 1974 for the first contacts with those responsible for the European Community. There he expressed Portugal's desire to forge closer bonds with the countries belonging to the EEC and benefit from their help, with a view to legitimizing the changes that were under way. A new meeting took place in Brussels on the 26th of June 1974 between the Portuguese delegation, represented by prime minister Adelino da Palma Carlos and the minister for Foreign Affairs Mário Soares, and, on the side of the European Commission, its president François-Xavier Ortoli and vice-president Christopher Soames. This meeting resulted in a good understanding between the two sides about Portugal's desire to draw closer to the European institutions and the availability of the European Economic Community to provide assistance in this respect, including, naturally, through financial support.

The turbulence of the first few months of the revolution and the replacement of Palma Carlos by Vasco Gonçalves as the head of the provisional governments created a stand-by situation that forced European spirits to cool down a little. It would only be after the Hot Summer of 1975 and the removal, on 19th September, of Vasco Gonçalves (supported by the Portuguese Communist Party) and his replacement by the more moderate Pinheiro de Azevedo, that European support for the young Portuguese democracy became effective. The declaration that made this explicit, in October 1975, is especially significant, as expressed in the Bulletin of the European Commission: "The Community's attitude towards Portugal is based on the hope and fervent desire of the Nine that economic progress in this country can effectively prosper in a context of democratic prosperity. For this reason, the European Council of 17th July declared its availability to grant the help requested to the Portuguese Government, and since then has reaffimed the fundamental political attitude of the Community [...] based on the criteron that support is only given to countries governed by a pluralist democratic system. For this reason, and in the light of the developments in the Portuguese situation, the Community, in the ministerial meeting of 6th and 7th October in Luxembourg, has informed the Minister of Foreign Affairs Melo Antunes that it would make available to the Portuguese government a total of 180 million European currency units [ECU] including subsidized loans and interest."

Once the doubts and uncertainties had dissipated about the viability of alternative international strategic alignments, Europe thus provided its first support for the construction of the Portuguese democracy. On the Portuguese side, Mário Soares and the Socialist Party continued the diplomatic and political efforts at an approximation which was judged vital for the survival of a project of building a pluralist democracy in accordance with the ideals of European social democracy. The slogan "Europe with us", launched by Mário Soares in 1976, set the tone for a longlasting commitment which counted particularly upon the political guarantee and endorsement that Europe would provide in order to prevent the spectre of totalitarianism – something that was more important than the financial support that could result from Portugal's integration into Europe.

In September 1976, Portugal and the European Economic Community signed a new economic and financial cooperation protocol, in anticipation of the formal application for accession of Portugal as member of the European Community, presented by the prime minister Mário Soares on 28 March 1977.

The process of negotiating Portugal's accession became definitive in nature after 1980, in na context marked by the exchange mechanism crisis and financial rupture of some severity, which Portugal managed to overcome thanks to the stabilization agreements celebrated with the International Monetary Fund in 1977 and 1983.

In this context, the financial assistance provided by the European Economic Community between 1980 and 1984, for the modernization of economic structures in the agricultural and industrial sectors and the training of human resources, was a foretaste of the benefits that would come with full membership, sealed on the 1st of January 1986.

The long pre-accession period was, in a way, justified by the increased difficulties resulting from the enlargement of the EEC to the countries of the south, which brought different problems for negotiations. Thus, Portugal had to wait for the outcome of conversations that were particularly complex in the case of Spain. This experience of enlargement resulted in important lessons for the whole internal process of adaptation of the EEC structure and institutions, aiming at a gradually intensifying process of economic and political integration, which would culminate in the preparation of a single market and single European currency. Portugal's participation in this process can undoubtedly be credited with many positive effects.

In addition to longlasting political significance, Portugal's entry into the EEC also brought immediate benefits on the economic and financial fronts, coinciding with a particularly favourable outside context due to the reduction in international oil prices. Since 1986, there had been a strong increase in exports (particularly to Spain), a clear recovery from the imbalance in the balance of payments, and a marked flow of foreign investment. The attribution of European structural funds also enabled a series of public investments in areas decisive for the development of the Portuguese economy. All of these factors together dictated the launch of a new process of convergence in relation to European growth rates, with significant gains on the level of income and patterns of consumption of large sectors of the Portuguese population.

The protagonism assumed by Mário Soares in the defence of a European project for Portugal was substantiated in the public signing of the accession agreement on 12th June 1985. From the end of that year, it fell to the new prime minister Aníbal Cavaco Silva, leader of the Social Democratic Party, to assume leadership of the process of effective integration, seeking to take as many benefit and advantage as possible.

Portugal's relative backwardness made it particularly eligible for the obtention of financial compensations and structural funds for the modernization of the economic and social fabric. The new rules and European institutional framework led to processes of constitutional and structural reform which contributed to Portugal's integration into an increasingly globalized world. The good news from Europe was assimilated with growing optimism and a broad consensus, ensuring high levels of satisfaction within the country as regards the consequences of the integration process.

The inauguration of the Belém Cultural Centre in 1992, which in that year served as the stage for the Portuguese presidency of the European Community (as it was designated after the Treaty of Maastricht of February 1992), is another symbolic milestone that marks the full maturity of Portugal's European citizenship, achieved after a narrow period of very rapid change. The distance from the Monastery of Jeronimos to the Belém Cultural Centre is very short, but the route to modernization traversed between 1985 and 1992 was very intense.

The decisive years following 1986 may be critically reassessed, particularly if we consider how much more might have been achieved if the structural funds and those destined for the modernization of infrastructures had been applied differently (particularly as regards the road network). However, speculating about alternative scenarios will not alter the unequivocally positive nature of the European legacy in the formation of the democratic regime in Portugal.

JOSÉ LUÍS CARDOSO
Instituto de Ciências Sociais, Universidade de Lisboa

Bibliography
BARRETO, António, "Portugal, a Europa e a democracia", *Análise Social*, vol. 29, no. 129, 1994, pp. 1051–1069.
LOPES, José da Silva (ed.), *Portugal and the EC Membership Evaluated*, London, Pinter Publishers, 1993.
MAGONE, José, "A integração europeia e a construção da democracia portuguesa", *Penélope*, no. 18, 1997, pp. 123–163.
PRIDHAM, Geoffrey, *Encouraging Democracy: The International Context of Regime Transition in Southern Europe*, London, St. Martin's Press, 1991.
TEIXEIRA, Nuno Severiano, "Portugal no mundo", in PINTO, António Costa, MONTEIRO, Nuno Gonçalo (dir.), *História Contemporânea de Portugal*, vol. 5, Lisbon, Penguin Random House, 2015, pp. 57–78.

1988
On the Internationalization of Portuguese Literature: Pessoa, Saramago and Lobo Antunes

Pessoa emerges increasingly as someone that incarnates the great drama of modern man, fragmented and in search of meaning for his existence. Lobo Antunes has something to do with the absence of meaning, but his universe is more circumscribed to the Portuguese space. Saramago does not share this problem because his Marxist beliefs supply him with an ideology that can offer a response to this type of human restlessness.

Aquilino Ribeiro is supposed to have said that the Portuguese language was the mausoleum of a great literature. And it is only in recent decades that this scenario has started to change. In fact, the works of two of the greatest literary figures of Portuguese history, Camões and Eça de Queiroz, though known to international specialists, are not listed amongst the most acclaimed authors of the Renaissance or nineteenth century (the *Lusiads*, for example, is rarely mentioned amongst the world classics of the genre). Today, however, both Camões and Eça figure in the series Penguin Classics – another sign of change.

It was only in the last quarter of the twentieth century that this situation began to alter, culminating in the award of the Nobel Prize to José Saramago in 1998. This internationalization had first made itself felt in France, which, unexpectedly awoke to Portuguese literature at the end of the eighties. A series of literary events triggered this interest, nourished by the publication of various translations of (mostly contemporary) Portuguese authors. António Lobo Antunes, for example, has enjoyed a prestige never before obtained by any novelist translated into French.

The publication of Harold Bloom's *Western Canon* (1994) symbolized this turning-point, not only for the Anglophone world but also beyond, since it had global impact. Various Portuguese authors figure in Bloom's canon: Camões, Eça, Pessoa and Saramago occupy prominent positions, as do Jorge de Sena, Sophia de Mello Breyner and Eugénio de Andrade, though Lobo Antunes is strangely absent. The translations of Lobo Antunes by Gregory Rabassa (the celebrated translator of Gabriel García Márquez) came too late for Bloom. Nominated various times for the Nobel Prize, Lobo Antunes only saw his name mentioned by the Swedish Academy in the justification presented when they awarded the prize to Günther Grass. According to the Academy's press release, Grass was "a much-admired predecessor of great literary figures of the world such as García Márquez, Rushdie, Gordimer, Lobo Antunes and Kenzaburo Oe". The fact that the editors of the *New York Times* made a telephone call to Lobo Antunes when the Nobel prize was awarded to Saramago and not to him (as revealed, in an unsigned commentary) attests to his international status. It is also indicative of the attention given to Portuguese literature, which is, out of all the Lusophone literatures, the one that has received the most international recognition. There has as yet been no Brazilian Nobel laureate – a great injustice. Equally strange, and even serious, is the almost total absence of Brazilian writers – not even Machado de Assis is there – from Bloom's canon. Carlos Drummond de Andrade is the only representative of that country. But this reveals more about Bloom's lack of attention, or about the inaccessibility of good English translations of Brazilian authors.

As for Lobo Antunes, though he enjoys an undeniably international reputation, particularly in the Francophone world, his recognition in the Anglophone world has not been on the same level. The critical reception of his work has not been particularly warm, and in the *New York Times*, the reaction, when some translations were launched, was not very positive at all (see for example, the review by Will Blythe of *What can I Do when Everything's on Fire?* or the one by Floyd Skloot about a collection of chronicles and other writing. The Irishman Oliver Farry even raised the question in the literary magazine *The Millions*.)

There are, however, two twentieth-century Portuguese authors that have achieved general international acclaim. One of them, José Saramago, was catapulted to world stardom when he received the Nobel prize. This recognition always brings with it a kind of consecration, though not necessarily longlasting. Thanks to it, translations into English, which were relatively few and far between in the years preceding the award, became generally available in book shops everywhere (including in airports), transforming Saramago into a well-known and much mentioned author.

The international recognition of Fernando Pessoa has been much slower and less mediatic, and naturally, without the impact of awards, since in life he published only *Mensagem* (*Message*), in the year preceding his death, and for this reason, never received any prize outside Portugal. In any case, *Mensagem* is the part of Pessoa's oeuvre with the least international appeal on account of its subject-matter, the context in which it was honoured, and the critical misreadings that it suffered. The translations of Pessoa's oeuvre began to appear belatedly and were, for decades, the result of laborious efforts by Lusophile enthusiasts, released by small foreign publishing houses. Little by little, however, he was projected across borders and it would be no exaggeration to say today that he is the Portuguese author with most international resonance, the most universally acclaimed, outside the Lusophone space. This is a bold claim, which does not rest on any solid empirical base, since the process of surveying the bibliographic data about Pessoa is still ungoing – unlike the case of Saramago, where there is concrete data. In fact, according to the Saramago Foundation, which has been collecting bibliographic data about the translations of his work, around fifty books (practically his whole oeuvre) have been translated with editions in around sixty countries. In the case of Pessoa, the journal *Pessoa Plural* (dedicated exclusively to the publication of Pessoan studies and previously unpublished works by the poet) invited Antonio Saez Delgado of the University of Évora to guest-edit a special issue about the reception of Pessoa outside the Lusophone space.

When contacted to provide the state-of-the-art on the matter, Saez Delgado wrote: "Fernando Pessoa's literary work has achieved a truly extraordinary level of international recogition in the context of Portuguese literature. There are numerous translations of his works in the most various linguistic and cultural contexts, as well as essays about the author. The presence of his titles clearly appears as one of the most important international references of the twentieth-century, in open dialogue throughout the world with the works of a notable collection of Pessoa reader-writers. In this context, it becomes extremely necessary to begin to systematize these phenomena of reception".

In the last two decades, two international conferences, one about Saramago and the other about Pessoa, may be revealing. The first was held in the University of Massachusetts in Amherst in 1996, with a programme of fifteen papers, mostly by foreign academics, though there were also various Brazilians and Luso-Americans. The second, about Pessoa, held in 2005 in Leipzig, Germany, involved some thirty academics. In each case, it was the first time that I had seen more foreigners than Portuguese scholars discussing Portuguese literature. The Leipzig colloquium was actually organized by two foreigners: the Colombian Jerónimo Pizarro and the German Steffen Dix. What is more, it is the group of foreigners that works in collaboration with Pizarro, or under his influence, that has contributed the most to date to the divulgation of the work of Pessoa. The only international journal exclusively dedicated to him, *Pessoa Plural*, published in Brown University (USA), is edited by Pizarro, in cooperation with two other Lusophone academics. That journal has made accessible online the largest collection of previously unpublished texts by Pessoa available on the Internet. Most of the critical editions of Pessoa are also the work of Pizarro (including five volumes to be brought out by the prestigious New York publisher *New Directions*), though we should also mention the role played by Richard Zenith in the Anglophone world. Particularly worthy of mention are the translations today available in Penguin of the *Livro do Desassossego* (*Book of Disquiet*), amongst others. In the Hispanic world, where much of the pioneering work was undertaken by Ángel Crespo, the Pizarro group has promoted a considerable number of translations.

The first non-Portuguese biographer of Pessoa was the South African Hubert Jennings. The publication of the book was hampered by the death of the editor immediately after the April Revolution of 1974, but it finally came out with Gávea-Brown of the Department of Portuguese and Brazilian Studies at Brown University, under the coordination of Carlos Pitella Leite. The first international conference on Pessoa's English writing was organised by Patricio Ferrari (an Argentinian who today lectures at Rutgers University in the USA) together with Pizarro at Brown University, during the period when he was a grantholder and then postgraduate student in that university. The texts presented at this event are published in *Fernando Pessoa as English Reader and Writer* (Gávea-Brown, 2018). The Tagus Press, of the University of Massachusetts Dartmouth, has also published translations of Pessoa's work and studies about him, while in the United Kingdom, the anthology of texts coordinated by Eugénio Lisboa in collaboration with L. C. Taylor, *A Centenary Pessoa*, at Carcanet Press, should not be overlooked.

It would be unfair not to mention too the pioneering work of Luso-American George Monteiro in introducing Pessoa to the Anglophone world through his two precious collections, *The Presence of Pessoa: English, American and South African Literary Responses* and *Fernando Pessoa and Nineteenth-Century Anglo-American*

Literature, both published by the University Press of Kentucky in 1998 and 2000 respectively. With Sussex Academic Press, George Monteiro also published *From Lisbon to the World: Fernando Pessoa's Enduring Literary Presence* (2018). As well as translating Pessoa to English, Monteiro also organized the first international symposium about the poet (Brown University, 1977), and edited the proceedings from it (*Fernando Pessoa: The Man Who Never Was*, 1982). Mention should also be made here of Edwin Honig (USA) and Jonathan Griffith (United Kingdom), as well as Robert Brechón (France) and Octávio Paz, in the hispanic world, all of whom have been important in the internationalization of Pessoa.

A significant symbolic incident that testifies to the universality of Pessoa, and which paradoxically reverts into an example of importance for the Portuguese language, was the revelation that was made to me during the Leipzig colloquium by the Chinese Christina Zhou, who presently teaches Chinese at the University of Coimbra: "I read 'Ode Marítima' in Mandarin," she said, "and promised myself that I would study Portuguese because I decided that I had to read that great poem in its original language".

Saramago today has a great many readers around the world and a particularly strong presence in Spain and Central and Southern America. He has perhaps not made such a mark in France as Lobo Antunes, but, in the Anglophone world, works like *Memorial do Convento* (*Baltazar and Blimunda*), *O Ano da Morte de Ricardo Reis* (*The Year of the Death of Ricardo Reis*) and *Ensaio sobre a Cegueira* (*Blindness*) have been publishing successes, due mostly to the two excellent translators, Giovanni Pontieri and Margaret Jull Costa. This is something of a novelty, because, till recently, the great foreign authors benefitted from being translated by great Portuguese writers, while the inverse did not occur. An important sign of the universalization of Saramago and Pessoa came when the essayist George Steiner wrote about Pessoa in the magazine *The New Yorker* of 8 January 1996, beginning in the following terms: "It is rare for a country and a language to acquire four major poets on one day". Steiner ends his text alluding to Saramago (note: this was two years before he won the Nobel Prize): "José Saramago's *The Year of the Death of Ricardo Reis*, which was translated into English in 1991 by Giovanni Pontiero, is among the great novels in recent European letters. It tells of Ricardo Reis's homecoming from Brazil, of eros and Fascism in Lisbon, and of the encounter between Reis and his dead begetter. Nothing more perceptive has been written about Pessoa and is country shades. In Fernando Pessoa's words: *If things are splinters of | The knowing universe, | Let bits of me be me, | Unfocused and diverse.*

The increased attention given to Portuguese literature and its translations is far from being limited to these writers. It would be time to consider the reasons for the international interest in these two authors, but this would require a much longer text and the analysis of critical reception, particularly in the languages most spoken around the globe (something that could constitute the work of many dissertations). Pessoa emerges increasingly as someone that incarnates the great drama of modern man, fragmented and in search of meaning for his existence. Lobo Antunes has something to do with the absence of meaning, but his universe is more circumscribed to the Portuguese space. Saramago does not share this problem because his Marxist beliefs supply him with an ideology that can offer a response to this type of human restlessness. Because he transmits it in a brilliantly appealing fiction, it finds an echo in various publics, particularly in those that are especially touched by this agenda. This is perhaps why Saramago is more appreciated in Latin America and

Lobo Antunes in France, for example. Of the three, Pessoa seems to exert a more universal, and perhaps more longlasting, appeal. In addition to the fascination exerted by his heteronymy, which takes further than anyone the psychological problem of fragmentation of the ego, his *Book of Disquiet* echoes much of the fundamental problem of the postmodern human being.

Onésimo Teotónio Almeida
Brown University

Bibliography

BLOOM, Harold, *The Western Canon*, New York, Harcourt Brace & Company, 1994.
BLYTHE, Will, "My father, the diva", Sunday Book Review. *The New York Times*, 21 Nov. 2008.
FARRY, Oliver, "Lost in translation. The curious obscurity of António Lobo Antunes", *The Millions*, 4 May 2012.
"Literature. Better luck next Nobel", Sunday Magazine. *The New York Times*, 6 Dec. 1998.
SKLOOT, Floyd, "Chronicles", Sunday Book Review. *The New York Times*, 25 Feb. 2009.
STEINER, George, "Foursome: The art of Fernando Pessoa", *The New Yorker*, 8 Jan. 1996, pp. 76–80.

2011
Portuguese Emigration: Global Interconnections

With free circulation in the European space, Europe once again became the destination of choice in this new phase of Portuguese emigration. The flows declined briefly with the global crisis at the end of 2008 (which generally affected the whole North Atlantic framework of the United States and Europe) but recovered after 2011, soon returning to former rates.

Emigration is the act of leaving one's place of origin with the intention of settling, temporarilty or permanently, in another country. The term is applied, historically and conventionally, to human movements that took place after the advent of the nation states and the consequent appearance of borders, something which, in an increasingly globalized world, now runs the risk of assuming unexpected contours. On the one hand, the general opening-up of borders and free circulation of people and goods in Europe has tended to attenuate boundary delimitations. On the other, the economic and security needs of the individual states have led to the creation of increasingly sophisticated systems for controlling these movements. In addition to this, the increase in the capacity of communication and circulation of people, the continual relocation of work and leisure places, increase in life expectancy and growing fragmentation and dispersion of the family, all combine to form a future society that is difficult to envisage today.

Portugal, with its base in successive migrations of European peoples (first the so-called 'barbarians' and then from north Africa and the Middle East) has always had a great capacity for resilience, and for adaptation to new situations, with land borders that were defined long before the appearance of the eighteenth and nineteenth century nationalisms. The border that was constituted during the Middle Ages and sealed by the Treaty of Alcanices in 1297 has survived, with only small adjustments, to the present day, making it one of the oldest in Europe. Having assured the land border, King Denis then set his sights on the maritime defence, calling to Portugal an Italian admiral and ordering the plantation of the Leiria pine forest.

The long Portuguese coastline and the good ports strategically placed near the mouths of the great rivers (which, for security reasons, were almost always placed in areas a little withdrawn from the seafront) allowed privileged contact with the Mediterranean and Atlantic worlds from very early on.

At the end of the Hundred Years War, which was marked in Portugal by the crisis of 1383, the '*arraia miúda*' (lower classes) led by a group of traders and scholars, elected a new king, King John, Master of Avis, who represented a novelty in the European context. An international alliance was forged with England in order to oppose the other claimant to the throne, the king of Castile, and once that war was won, King John I married an English princess. Portugal thus ceased to be a medieval-style land kingdom to become an increasingly maritime country.

It was these conditions that enabled Portugal to become the pioneer of the European expansion in the fifteenth and sixteenth centuries. Italian sailors, Jewish and Islamic geographers and cartographers, and financiers from central and northern Europe all participated in this expansion, under the close supervision of the Crown, constituting a very mixed and active society. It was not by chance that the daughter of King John I and Phillippa of Lancaster married Phillip III, Duke of Burgundy, in 1430, consolidating Portugal's maritime vocation. In Bruges, and later in Antwerp, the Portuguese established an entrepôt to oversee the distribution throughout northern Europe of products from the new Portuguese dominions. The bases of the Portuguese emigration phenomenon are thus very ancient and rooted in the settlement of new territories, progressively established as captaincies, fortified trading posts, vice-royalties, kingdoms and states.

The Portuguese expansionist movement began with the conquest of Ceuta in 1415 and the settlement of the archipelago of Madeira from 1420 or 1425. Thereafter, the archipelagos of the Azores, Cape Verde and São Tomé and Príncipe were also settled, providing essential support to the strongholds of northern Africa and the fortified trading posts along the African coast, which, in the space of a few decades, extended all the way to the Indian Ocean. The peace treaty of Alcáçovas–Toledo (1479) that followed the Spanish War of Succession defined the areas of expansion of the Iberian kingdoms, just as Portuguese caravels initiated their voyages of exploration on both sides of the Atlantic (from the 1470s and 80s). With the arrival of the Spanish ships in the Antilles in 1492, a new treaty was negotiated, defining the so-called meridian of Tordesilhas, broadened by Portugal to include the lands of Brazil, where there was already Portuguese settlement.

Throughout the sixteenth century, Portuguese interests extended to the settlement of Brazil, in the face of competition from the French, who disputed that territory. As had been done in previous decades for the State of India, it was now necessary to send royal agents, military and religious personnel, traders and others, from mainland Portugal and the Atlantic islands to Latin America, which created a strong demographic imbalance in the country, denounced by poets and chroniclers of the period. This can be verified by analysing the available data about these departures: Vitorino Magalhães Godinho calculates that, between 1500 and 1580, when Iberian union occurred, of the more than million inhabitants in the country, around 300,000 had left for the new dominions.

The Portuguese emigration figures remained high in the following periods, with variants that are difficult to calculate, since the opening-up of Castile's overseas territories to the Portuguese prompted a mass invasion of them. This resulted in a continuing increase of territorial space in Brazil, which continued up to the end of the eighteenth century. Thus the routes of population circulation were now different, with a transfer almost en masse of Portuguese interests from the Indian Ocean to the Atlantic. In fact, there was a great increase in population mobility between the two sides of the Atlantic, since the manpower needs of that enormous Brazilian space required the importation of large numbers of African slaves.

Throughout the eighteenth century, successive laws were passed to contain the migratory flows between Portugal and Brazil, though with the discovery of important deposits of gold and precious stones in the interior of that territory, the Portuguese mainland ran the risk of becoming seriously depopulated. In question was the royal cabinet's progressive drive towards centralization, which the Pomblaine consulate tried to finalise with various police laws and the extinction of the Society of Jesus, aiming to staunch the flow of Portuguese sailors, recruited illegally in all the ports of the mainland and islands by the powerful Royal Navy.

The various prohibitions on populations leaving the kingdom produced few results and, at the beginning of the nineteenth century, even the Portuguese court emigrated to Brazil. The consequences of that attitude were enormous. When the court had to return to Lisbon with the liberal revolt and summoning of the Constituent Courts, Brazil became independent, if it had not already been, since, when this transfer occurred, the traditional roles had already inverted.

Portuguese emigration, especially to Brazil, declined with Independence, but recovered from the middle of the nineteenth century and increased substantially in the final years of that century. With economic expansion based on the cultivation of coffee and cotton, manpower needs increased, but were confronted with the restrictions imposed by some European countries on emigration to South America, where immigrants were treated like slaves. Brazil, however, having abolished slavery in 1888, needed manpower, and once again resorted to Portuguese labour. In this period, despite the legendary figure of the emigrant to Brazil who sent large sums back to the homeland for the acquisition of property, many thousands of emigrants were also repatriated for having failed to make their fortune in that country.

At the turn of the nineteenth and twentieth century, the transoceanic movement of Portuguese emigration acquired new destinations, such as the US, Venezuela, Canada and South Africa, giving way, in the twentieth century, to an intra-European surge. Brazil continued to dominate the trend until 1912, losing favour as a destination with the First World War (1914–1918). Though Portuguese emigration generally picked up with the unemployment crisis of the 1930s, it declined again with the outbreak of the Second World War in 1939 and the paralysation of sea transport, picking up once more from 1949. Though there were oscillations in destinations, Europe remained the main one, particularly France. There were also government incentives that tried to present the overseas provinces as a new destination of choice, which it had not done in previous decades and centuries.

The government stimuli to divert the flow of migration to the overseas provinces had started in Angola as a response to the danger of infiltration in the south by South

African Boers, fleeing harassment by English military forces. Planned in 1881, it advanced with the preparation for the Berlin Conference (1884), transporting numerous settlers from the Island of Madeira to the area of Moçâmedes, from where they climbed the plateau of Huíla to found the city of Sá da Bandeira (today Lubango). Similar efforts were made in following years for other places in Angola and Mozambique.

The traditional Portuguese emigration was interrupted with the April Revolution of 1974, but began to grow steadily after Portugal's accession to the European Economic Community. With free circulation in the European space, Europe once again became the destination of choice in this new phase of Portuguese emigration. The flows declined briefly with the global crisis at the end of 2008 (which generally affected the whole North Atlantic framework of the United States and Europe) but recovered after 2011, the year the country was 'rescued' by the Troika, soon returning to former rates.

With so many study groups and observatories charting emigration patterns, it remains to be seen if we today are actually referring to the same entity as we were before. In fact, it seems clear that we are not. The basic idea of emigration described in the first paragraphs of this text took place in a completely different circumstances to that which is experienced today, which focuses much more on work mobility and transnationality. Exploratory studies into the recent wave of young skilled emigration to Europe, for example, triangulating data acquired through ethnographic observation, survey by questionnaire and interviews of a biographical nature, have sought to characterize the protagonists with regards social and demographic origins, educational trajectory, insertion or otherwise into the labour market, reasons for emigrating, process involved and integration status, and has already produced an abundance of literature on the subject. A distinction is made between pull factors (factors that attract this type of worker) and push factors (those that repel them from their country of origin), facts which are associated with (amongst other things) differentials of material and symbolic resources between countries. Here, the constraints operating on the earlier form of emigration continue to play a role, though in a less decisive fashion.

The physical circumstances and mental outlook of these new emigrants would seem to be very different from those of former generations. However, unconsciously, they continue to receive strong influences that they cannot or do not want to bar. If that did not happen, in the literature produced, particularly by the media, it would not cease to be mentioned, and perhaps, with a greater weight than we might expect. In any case, in the international quest for new work opportunities, new projects, etc., the weight of common history continues, consciously or unconsciously, to be present.

Rui Carita
University of Madeira and Centre for Lusophone and European Literatures
and Cultures, Faculty of Letters, University of Lisbon

Bibliography

GODINHO, Vitorino Magalhães, *Estrutura da Antiga Sociedade Portuguesa*, 3rd ed., Lisbon, Arcádia, 1977.

Idem, "L'émigration portugaise (xv–xx siècles). Une constante structurelle et les réponses aux changements du monde", *Revista de História Económica e Social*, no. 1, 1978, pp. 5–32.

SERRÃO, Joel, *Emigração Portuguesa*, 3rd ed., Lisbon, Livros Horizonte, 1977.

Idem, *Testemunhos sobre a Emigração Portuguesa: Antologia*, Lisbon, Livros Horizonte, 1976.

The Editors, Scientific Coordinators and Contributors

The Editors

Carlos Fiolhais, PhD at Goethe University, Frankfurt/ Main (1982), is Full Professor of Physics at the University of Coimbra. He was Director of the General Library of this University and he is Director of "Rómulo – Centro Ciência Viva" of the same University and of the collection "Ciência Aberta" (Gradiva Publishers). He is the author of several pedagogical and scientific books, some of them on the History of Science. He won the awards José Mariano Gago for Science Dissemination (2018), Ciência Viva-Montepio (2017), the Golden Globe of SIC (2005) and the Order of Henry the Navigator (2005).

José Eduardo Franco is Full Professor of the Aberta University and Director of the CIPSH Chair for Global Studies in this institution. Currently he coordinates the Doctoral Program in Global Studies in the Aberta University. He is member of the Portuguese Academy of History. He has coordinated large-scale research projects such as the *Historical Dictionary of Religious Orders in Portugal, The Complete Works of Father António Vieira* in 30 volumes, and the *Vatican Secret Archives* in three volumes. He was awarded the Medal of Cultural Merit of the Portuguese State, and in 2018 the José Mariano Gago Prize of Science Dissemination.

José Pedro Paiva is Full Professor at the University of Coimbra and Scientific Head of the Centre for History of Society and Culture. He was visiting professor at the University of São Paulo, fellow of the John Carter Brown Library and of the Nederlanse Organisatie voor Wetenschappelijk Onderzoek, and Dean of the Faculty of Arts and Humanities of the University of Coimbra. His research focuses on Religious History, Inquisition, Portuguese Seaborne Empire, Iberian Union (1580–1640) and Early Modern Witchcraft. He is the PI of the project *ReligionAJE: Religion, Ecclesiastical Administration and Justice in the Portuguese Seaborne Empire (1514–1750)*, PTDC/HAR-HIS/28719/2017 sponsored by FCT and FEDER.

The Scientific Coordinators

João Luís Cardoso is Full Professor and Vice-Rector of Universidade Aberta (Lisbon). He coordinates the Master in Heritage Studies and the Doctorate in History. His scientific activity as an archaeologist is embodied by more than 700 scientific articles published in Portugal and in some of the most important international journals, and around twenty books focusing on various themes from Prehistory to History of Archeology and Zooarcheology. He is fellow of the Royal Academy of History (Madrid), the German Archaeological Institute (Berlin), the Lisbon Academy of Sciences, and the Portuguese Academy of History.

Carlos Fabião is Professor at the History Departament of Lisbon University. Director of the Graduation degree on Arcaheology and Director of Lisbon University Archaeological Centre (UNIARQ). He has been invited lecturer by the American Institute of Archaeology (AIA) and invited professor at Universidade de São Paulo, Universidade de Campinas, Universidad de Sevilla and Universidad de La Laguna. He was the responsible for some Archaeological Exhibitions both in Portugal and Spain. His main research interests are Roman and Late Antique History and Archaeology and also the History of Portuguese Archaeology.

Bernardo Vasconcelos e Sousa is Associate Professor at the School of Social Sciences and Humanities of Nova University, Lisbon, and Head of the Master's Program on Medieval History. He was the Director of *Torre do Tombo*, the Portuguese National Archives, President of the Institute of Medieval Studies and the editor of *Medievalista* (published since 2005). His research focuses on social history, particularly the Portuguese nobility of the 14th and 15th centuries, monastic institutions, and the building process of the Kingdom of Portugal. He is member of the Portuguese Academy of History and of the International Academy for Genealogy.

Cátia Antunes is Full Professor of Global Economic Networks: Merchants, Entrepreneurs and Empires at the Institute for History, at Leiden University. She is particularly interested in the comparative history of empires from a global perspective. Her work has been generously supported by the European Research Council and the Dutch Research Council. She is currently the principal investigator of the project *Exploiting the Empire of Others* that raises the question of transmissibility of gains and social systems across different European empires between 1415 and 1800 in an attempt to demystify the transition from colonialism to imperialism.

António Costa Pinto is Research Professor at the Institute of Social Sciences, University of Lisbon. He has been a visiting professor at Stanford University, Georgetown University, a senior associate member at St Antony's College, Oxford, and a senior visiting fellow at Princeton University, the University of California, Berkeley and New York University. His research interests include fascism and authoritarianism, political elites and democratization. He authored *The Blue Shirts: Portuguese Fascism in Inter-war Europe* (2000), *The Nature of Fascism Revisited* (2012), *Latin American Dictatorships in the Era of Fascism* (2020) and he co-edited with Federico Finchelstein *Authoritarian and Corporatism in Europe and Latin America: Crossing Borders* (2019).

The Contributors

Almeida, Onésimo Teotónio is professor at Brown University.

Amaral, Luís Carlos is professor at University of Porto, and researcher at CITCEM – Transdisciplinary Research Centre "Culture, Space and Memory", University of Porto, and at CEHR – Centre of Religious History Studies, Catholic University of Portugal.

Andrade, Amélia Aguiar is professor at Faculty of Social Sciences and Humanities, Nova University Lisbon, and researcher at Institute of Medieval Studies.

Arruda, Ana Margarida is professor at University of Lisbon.

Barros, Amândio J. M. is professor at School of Education, Polytechnic Institute of Porto, and researcher at CITCEM – Transdisciplinary Research Centre "Culture, Space and Memory", University of Porto.

Bethencourt, Francisco is professor at King's College London.

Bicho, Nuno is professor at Faculty of Humanities and Social Sciences, University of Algarve, and researcher at Interdisciplinary Centre for Archaeology and Evolution of Human Behaviour.

Braga, Isabel Drumond is professor at University of Lisbon, and researcher at Centre for History, University of Lisbon, and at Interdisciplinary Centre for History, Culture and Society, University of Évora.

Branco, Maria João is professor at Faculty of Social Sciences and Humanities, Nova University Lisbon, and researcher at Institute of Medieval Studies.

Brites, Joana is professor at Faculty of Arts and Humanities, University of Coimbra, and researcher at Centre for Twentieth-Century Interdisciplinary Studies.

Candido, Mariana P. is professor at Emory University.

Cardim, Pedro is professor at Nova University Lisbon.

Cardoso, José Luís is professor at Instituto de Ciências Sociais, Universidade de Lisboa.

Carita, Rui is researcher at University of Madeira and at Centre for Lusophone and European Literatures and Cultures, University of Lisbon.

Carvalho, António Faustino is professor at University of Algarve.

Carvalho, José Madruga is an independent researcher.

Carvalho, Pedro C. is professor at Faculty of Arts and Humanities, University of Coimbra.

Carvalho, Rita Almeida de is researcher at Instituto de Ciências Sociais, Universidade de Lisboa.

Cascalheira, João is professor at Faculty of Humanities and Social Sciences, University of Algarve, and researcher at Interdisciplinary Centre for Archaeology and Evolution of Human Behaviour.

Catroga, Fernando is professor at University of Coimbra, and researcher at Centre for the History of Society and Culture.

Cavaco, Timóteo is researcher at Institute of Contemporary History, Nova University Lisbon.

Clementino, Kleber is professor at Federal Rural University of Pernambuco.

Coelho, Maria Helena da Cruz is professor at University of Coimbra, and researcher at Centre for the History of Society and Culture.

Costa, Palmira Fontes da is professor at Nova University Lisbon.

Curto, Diogo Ramada is professor at Faculty of Social Sciences and Humanities, Nova University Lisbon, and researcher at Portuguese Institute for International Relations.

Domingos, Nuno is researcher at Instituto de Ciências Sociais, Universidade de Lisboa.

† Domingues, Francisco Contente was professor at Faculty of Arts and Humanities, University of Lisbon.

Dores, Hugo Gonçalves is researcher at Center for Social Studies, University of Coimbra.

Duarte, Luís Miguel is professor at University of Porto.

Duarte, Marco Daniel is researcher at Department of Studies of the Shrine of Fatima and at Centre for Lusophone and European Literatures and Cultures, Faculty of Arts and Humanities, University of Lisbon.

Fernandes, Hermenegildo is professor at Faculty of Arts and Humanities, University of Lisbon, and researcher at Centre for History.

Fernandes, Paulo Jorge is professor at Nova University Lisbon, and researcher at Institute of Contemporary History.

Fontes, João Luís Inglês is professor at Faculty of Social Sciences and Humanities, Nova University Lisbon, and researcher at Institute of Medieval Studies, Nova University Lisbon, and at Centre for the Study of Religious History, Catholic University of Portugal.

Françozo, Mariana is professor at University of Leiden.

Garrido, Álvaro is professor at Faculty of Economics, University of Coimbra.

Gaspar, Joaquim Alves is researcher at Interuniversity Center for the History of Science and Technology, University of Lisbon, and PI of the ERC project *Medea-Chart*.

Gomes, Saul António is professor at Faculty of Arts and Humanities, University of Coimbra, and researcher at Centre for the History of Society and Culture.

Gori, Annarita is researcher at Instituto de Ciências Sociais, Universidade de Lisboa.

Guerra, Amílcar is professor at Faculty of Arts and Humanities, University of Lisbon, and researcher at Centre for Archaeology.

Herzog, Tamar is professor at Harvard University.

Jerónimo, Miguel Bandeira is professor at Department of History, European Studies, Archaeology and Arts, Faculty of Arts and Humanities, University of Coimbra.

Leitão, Henrique is professor at Faculty of Sciences, University of Lisbon, and researcher at Interuniversity Center for the History of Science and Technology.

Lombardo, Eleonora is researcher at Institute of Philosophy, University of Porto.

Loureiro, Rui Manuel is professor at Manuel Teixeira Gomes Higher Education Institute and researcher at CHAM – Centre for the Humanities, Nova University Lisbon.

Lousada, Maria Alexandre is professor at University of Lisbon.

Marcos, Rui de Figueiredo is professor at Faculty of Law, University of Coimbra.

Martins, Fernando is professor at University of Évora, and researcher at Interdisciplinary Centre for History, Culture, and Societies.

Meirinhos, José Francisco is professor at University of Porto, and researcher at Institute of Philosophy.

Miranda, Bruno is professor at Federal Rural University of Pernambuco.

Miranda, Susana Münch is researcher at CSG/GHES – Research Center of Economic and Social History, Lisbon School of Economics and Management, University of Lisbon.

Monteiro, João Gouveia is professor at University of Coimbra, and researcher at Centre for the History of Society and Culture.

Norte, Armando is researcher at Centre for the History of Society and Culture, University of Coimbra, and at Centre for History, Faculty of Arts and Humanities, University of Lisbon.

Oliveira, António Resende de is professor at University of Coimbra, and researcher at Centre for the History of Society and Culture.
Oliveira, Luís Filipe is professor at University of Algarve, and researcher at Institute of Medieval Studies, Faculty of Social Sciences and Humanities, Nova University Lisbon.

Pereira, Edgar Cravo Bertrand is researcher at Centre for the History of Society and Culture.

Pereira, Gaspar Martins is professor at Faculty of Arts and Humanities, University of Porto, and researcher at CITCEM – Transdisciplinary Research Centre "Culture, Space and Memory".

Pires, Hélio is researcher at Institute of Medieval Studies, Faculty of Social Sciences and Humanities, Nova University Lisbon.

Polónia, Amélia is professor at Faculty of Arts and Humanities, University of Porto, and researcher at CITCEM – Transdisciplinary Research Centre "Culture, Space and Memory".

Rebelo, António Manuel Ribeiro is professor at Faculty of Arts and Humanities, University of Coimbra, and researcher at the Centre for Classical and Humanistic Studies.

Reis, Bruno Cardoso is professor at ISCTE – University Institute of Lisbon and researcher at Centre for International Studies.

Rezola, Maria Inácia is professor at School of Communication and Media Studies, and researcher at Institute of Contemporary History, Nova University Lisbon.

Richardson, Noelle is professor at Utrecht University.

Rossa, Walter is professor at University of Coimbra.

Sá, Isabel dos Guimarães is professor at Department of History, University of Minho, and researcher at Communication and Society Research Centre.

Salvado, João Paulo is professor at University of Évora and researcher at Interdisciplinary Centre of History, Cultures and Societies.

Santos, Maria José Azevedo is professor at University of Coimbra, and researcher at Centre for the History of Society and Culture.

Sardica, José Miguel is professor at Faculty of Human Sciences, Catholic University of Portugal.

Serrão, José Vicente is professor at ISCTE – University Institute of Lisbon.

Silva, Filipa Ribeiro da is researcher at International Institute of Social History, Royal Netherlands Academy of Arts and Sciences, The Netherlands.
Silva, José Custódio Vieira da is professor at Nova University Lisbon.

Silva, Manuela Santos is professor at Faculty of Arts and Humanities, University of Lisbon.

Sobral, Luís de Moura is professor at University of Montreal.

Sottomayor-Pizarro, J. A. de is professor at Faculty of Arts and Humanities, University of Porto, and member of Academy of Sciences of Lisbon and of Royal Academy of History of Madrid.

Souza, Laura de Mello e is professor at Sorbonne University.

Tavim, José Alberto Rodrigues da Silva is professor at University of Lisbon, and researcher at Centre for History.

Teixeira, Nuno Severiano is professor at Nova University Lisbon, and researcher at Portuguese Institute of International Relations.

Valladares, Rafael is researcher at EEHAR – Spanish Institute of Roman Archeology, and Spanish National Research Council.

Ventura, António is professor at Faculty of Arts and Humanities, University of Lisbon, and researcher at Centre for History.

Viegas, Catarina is professor at Faculty of Arts and Humanities, University of Lisbon, and researcher at Centre for Archaeology.

† Vieira, Alberto was researcher at Centre for Studies of Atlantic History.

Vilaça, Raquel is professor at University of Coimbra.

Index

1755 Lisbon Earthquake, 166, 252, 263–266
1911 Law on the Separation of Church and State, 202, 308

A Corunha (A Coruña), 71, 92, 93
Abreu, António de, 206–207
Abrilada/April Revolt, 287
Aemilius Paullus, 38, 46
Afonso Henriques (Afonso I of Portugal) (king), 87, 99–100, 106–107, 112–115, 119–120, 123–124, 130–131, 149, 333–334, 337
Afonso II (king of Portugal), 87, 89, 96–97, 99, 129, 148
Afonso III (king of Portugal), 87, 89, 121, 129, 131, 133, 139, 149–150
Afonso IV (king of Portugal), 117, 154, 156
Afonso V (king of Portugal), 99, 102, 143, 174–176, 178, 198, 243
Afonso VI (king of Portugal), 243
Afonso of Portalegre (King Denis brother), 150
Africa, 10, 35, 39, 41–44, 55–57, 66, 68, 74–8, 81–82, 88–89, 90, 98, 101, 111, 112, 129, 148, 151–152, 160–228 *passim*, 238–247, 259, 260, 261, 265, 280, 299–302, 309, 317, 319, 320, 331, 347–349, 355–356, 366– 367
Agadir (Cabo de Aguer), 169, 216–217, 317
Agriculture, 14–15, 18–19
Al-Andalus, 89, 90–92, 113, 119, 148–149
....Abbasid, Abbasids, 90–91
....Andalusia, 27, 32, 35, 42, 59, 76, 121, 149, 167
....   Córdoba, 22, 90–91, 93, 148–149
....   *Gharb*, 86, 92
    Berber empires, 91
....   Almoravid, 91, 161
....   Almohad, 91, 161
Prophetic Chronicle, 89, 93–94
....*Taifa, taifas*, 148–149

Alans, 76
Alcácer do Sal, 25–26, 47, 52, 60, 94, 109–110, 196
    Necropolis, 25–26
    Salacia, 47, 52
Alcalá del Río, 38
....*Ilipa*, 38, 40
Alcobaça, 101, 123, 141, 153
Alentejo, 16, 18, 22, 27, 32, 42–43, 59, 61, 93, 126–127, 149–150
Alexander III (pope), 115
Alexander VI (pope), 179, 200
Alfonso VI (king of León and Castile), 103–105, 115, 132
Alfonso VII (king of León and Castile, emperor), 107, 114–115, 149
Alfonso X, el Sabio, the Wise (king of Castile), 116–17, 139, 149
Alfonso XIII (king of Spain), 307, 309, 317
Algarve, 12, 16, 18, 27, 39, 43, 52, 59, 61, 64, 91–92, 109–110, 127, 149, 161, 167, 169, 195, 311–312, 333
Aljubarrota, 88, 155–156, 159
Aljustrel, 32, 64, 109
Almada, 23, 25, 109
Almeida, 150, 157
Almeida, António José de, 257
Almeida, D. Francisco de, 179, 206
Almeida, João Ferreira de, 292
Almohad, Almohads, 91, 109, 119, 149, 161
Almoravids, 102
Alps, 21, 62–64, 311
Alto da Vigia, 49–50, 72
Álvares, Manuel, 213
Amarante, 314
....Manhufe, 314–316
America, American continent, 4, 31, 165–228 *passim*, 241, 245–247, 253, 262, 265, 271, 276, 284–286, 331, 365, 368
....American Revolution, 282
....Discovery of America, 206, 228–229, 238

....New World, 165, 192, 195, 199, 206–207

Amsterdam, 183, 210, 229, 250, 351

anarchism / anarchists 303, 305, 308

Anatolia, 15, 27, 90

Anchieta, José, 215

Andrade, António de, 214, 236

Andrade, Gomes Freire de (general), 285

Anglicanism, 293

Anglo-Portuguese Alliance, 317, 319

Angola, 164, 177, 186, 201, 204, 214, 242, 254, 257, 265, 282, 301, 310, 322, 347–351, 355–356, 368–369

Animal husbandry, 14

....animal "secondary products", 16

....domestic species, 14, 15, 64, 68

Anthony of Lisbon and Padua (Saint), 88, 133–136

anticlericalism, 280

Antilles, 179, 185, 192, 206, 331, 367

António, D. (Prior do Crato), 227, 276

Antunes, António Lobo, 362–363, 365–366

Antwerp, 210, 222, 250, 367

April Revolution, 355–359, 364, 369

....25th April 1974, 281, 355–358

Arabia, 152, 224

....Arab-Islamic civilization, 112, 115

....Arabian Peninsula, 10

....Arabic language, 86, 89–90, 93, 113, 128, 216

....Arabic literary culture, 91

....Arabs, 83, 90, 139, 195

Aragon, 87, 91, 112, 118, 148–150, 161, 178–180, 238

archaeology, 31, 41, 53, 56, 61, 76, 78

architecture, 24–28, 53–54, 128

....aesthetic forms, 89–99, 102

....cathedrals, 100–102, 132

....chapels, 100–101

....cloister, cloisters, 101, 142

....funerary, 27–28

....mendicant, 102

....Portuguese Gothic art and cathedrals, 101–102

....Romanesque, 99–101

....Monastery of Lorvão, 98, 101, 153

....Monastery of Santa Cruz (Coimbra), 97–99, 101, 115, 124, 130, 132, 134–135, 141, 152–153, 196

architecture and visual arts under King John V's patronage

....Alvor Palace (Lisbon), 252

....*Azulejos*, 253–254

....Baroque, Monumental Baroque decoration, 165, 183, 251–254

........"Joanine" style

........*quadratura* paintings, 252

........Solomonic Baroque, 254

....Mafra's Convent and Palace, 251–255

....Nasoni, Niccolò, 252

Argentina, 283, 322–323, 357

Arguin, 169, 175, 198, 203

Arianism, 79–80, 82

Aristotle, 66–67, 213, 235

Armed Forces Movement, 355–356

Arriaga, Manuel de, 309

Arruda, Miguel de, 218–219

Asia, 10, 21, 31, 55, 87, 98, 129, 151–247 *passim*, 259–261, 265

....Asian languages, 220

........Chinese, language, 235

........First Portuguese–Chinese dictionary (1583–1588), 143, 235

........Mandarin, 235

........Vietnamese–Portuguese–Latin dictionary and catechism, 215

Asilah, 39, 160, 182, 188, 217

Assisi, 125, 134, 139

Astorga, 76, 112, 149

Asturias, 36, 49, 58, 89, 148

....*Asturica Augusta*, 73

Atlantic, 18, 21, 23, 31, 33, 41, 51, 59, 65–67, 69–71, 78, 93, 119, 121–122, 148, 151, 160–186 *passim*, 200, 203–206, 216, 238, 245, 251, 263, 275, 284, 286–287, 311, 317, 328–330, 335, 340–344, 359, 367–369

Atlantic Islands, 165, 167, 169, 203, 213, 254, 259–260

....Ano Bom, 175

....Azores, 164, 167, 170, 179, 198, 201, 213, 227, 250, 254, 256

....Canary Islands, 162, 169, 178–179, 195

....Cape Verde, 129, 164–165, 169, 175, 177, 179, 194, 197, 201, 203, 213, 257, 260

....Madeira, 164–165, 167–170, 195, 198, 201, 204, 213, 232, 255

........Madeira's settlement, 167–170

....Príncipe (Island), 175

....São Tomé (Island), 164–168, 175, 177, 195, 201–204, 242, 260

....São Tomé and Príncipe (Archipelago), 260, 282, 335, 367

Augustus, 36–38, 46, 49, 51–52, 59, 71

....Augustan period / Augsutan era, 46–47, 52–53, 73

Austria, 238, 240, 284, 288, 290, 296, 307, 309, 344–345

....Austria-Hungary, 299, 306

Aveiro, 63, 190, 253, 336

Avignon, 101, 125, 132

Axis (Germany, Italy, and Japan), 343–344

Azemmour, 169, 207, 216–217

Azevedo, Pinheiro de, 360

Azores, 317, 341, 367

Badajoz, 40, 91–92, 114, 149–150, 208
Baetica, 39, 42–43, 59, 60, 64, 73, 75–76
Bahia, 167, 170, 214, 243, 252, 254–255
Baiões, 22–23
Balearics, 91, 93, 149
Balkans, 15, 79, 90, 306
Baltic, Baltic States, 9, 23, 250, 268, 281
Bangladesh, 200, 227
Barbarians, 32, 75–76, 80
Barcelona, 82, 303, 307
Barros, João de, 175
Battles, 35, 38, 57–58, 242
Beatrice of Castile (daughter of Alfonso X),
      149, 156, 158
Beccaria (marquis), 295–296, 298
Beijing, 201, 235–236
Beja, 21–22, 27, 52, 61, 64–65, 149, 214
....*Pax Iulia*, 52, 61, 65
Belém Cultural Centre, 335, 361
Belém Tower, 217, 334–335
Belfastada, 289
Belgium, 231, 270, 299, 322, 347
Bell Beaker, 17–19
Benevides, Salvador Correia de Sá e, 242, 244
Benoliel, Joshua, 304
Berbers, 74, 83, 89, 90, 161
Beresford (marshal), 285
Berlin, 280, 300–302, 305, 307, 315, 323
....Berlin Conference (Conference of Berlin),
      280, 299, 301–302, 369
Bible Society (*Sociedade Bíblica*), 292–293
Bismarck, Otto von, 299–301
Black Sea, 66, 79, 152, 191–192
Bocage, Barbosa du, 300–301
Bocchus, Cornelius, 32, 47
Bologna, 132, 140–141
Bombarral, 10, 13
Bordeaux, 183, 303, 337
borders, 92, 107–110, 113, 118, 121, 123,
      148–150, 155, 166, 178, 184, 193,
      218–219, 229, 236, 238, 247, 255, 259,
      269, 277, 284, 305, 309, 319, 326, 347,
      363, 366–367
Bourbon-Naples (House of), 277
Bourdin, Maurice (Bishop of Coimbra), 97,
      104
Braga, 20, 33, 54, 73–74, 76–80, 100, 104,
      138, 149, 214, 253
....*Bracara Augusta*, 33, 73, 78
Braganza (Dynasty, House of), 216–217, 229,
      241–244, 277
Brazil, 164–294 *passim*, 305, 309, 322, 334,
      357, 365, 367–368
Britannia, 38, 41, 59, 71
British Isles, 20, 66, 95
British Ultimatum, 301–302, 308
Brittany, 18, 329

Bronze Age, 9, 20–27, 69
Brussels, 315
....Brussels Anti-Slavery Conference, 302
....Brussels Geographic Conference, 299
Buenos Aires, 229, 245–246, 322
Buíça, Manuel, 303–304
bull, 115–116, 118, 134, 136, 159, 172, 176,
      179, 198–199, 209, 230–232, 292
Burgos, 207, 222
Burgundy (Ducal house of), 100, 103, 129,
      132
Byzantine, 79, 80–82

Cabral, Pedro Álvares de, 184, 187, 193,
      206
Cáceres, 52, 60, 109, 149
....*Norba Caesarina*, 52
Cádiz, 9, 24, 35, 70–71, 168, 248
Caetano, Marcelo, 338
Cairo, 160–161
Calouste Gulbenkian Foundation, 313
Calvinism, 243
Cambridge, 141, 156
Camões, Luís de, 48, 70, 117, 158, 221,
      223–225, 362
Canada, 322–323, 341, 368
Canning, George (prime minister), 283, 288
Cantabria, 36, 58–59, 63
Cantino, Alberto, 191, 193
Cape, 49, 67, 71–72, 77, 171, 175, 241
....Bojador, 164, 171–174, 176, 198–199
....Good Hope (Cape of Storms), 171–172,
      179, 185, 205, 208
Cape Verde, 282, 367
Carbonari/Carbonária, 303
Cardoso, Amadeo de Souza, 313–316
Caribbean (sea, islands), 165, 167, 170, 184,
      191–192, 202–204, 262
Carletti, Francesco, 226, 228
Carlists, 289–290
Carlos, Adelino da Palma, 359–360
Carlota Joaquina (queen), 287–288
Carolingian (Empire), 90, 93, 97
Cartagena, 32, 35, 59, 63, 81, 229
....*Carthago Nova*, 35
Carthage, 27, 34–35, 38, 43
Carthaginensis, 73, 75–76
Cartography, 164, 180, 194, 236
....Cantino Planisphere, 190–194
....Ptolemy, 49, 172, 191–192
Carvalho, Otelo Saraiva de, 357
Cassels, James, 293
Cassiterides, 31, 36, 70
Castile (kingdom), 87–88, 91–92, 103,
      108–109, 111, 117–118, 122, 125, 128,
      133, 146–201 *passim*, 211, 226–228, 238,
      242

Castile-León, León and Castile (kingdom), 88, 92, 103, 105, 107, 114, 118, 132, 139, 148

Castilho, João de, 217–218

Castilians, 156–159, 161, 195

Castro, D. João de, 173

Castro, Inês de, 102, 156–157

Catalan (county, principality), 91, 148

Catalonia, 34–35

Cathedral, 97–101, 105–108, 115, 120, 129, 134, 137–139, 143, 153, 158, 252, 254

Catherine of Braganza, 217

Catholic Monarchs, 177–179, 200

Catholicism, Catholic faith, 79, 88, 90, 126, 134, 181, 189, 191, 199, 202, 228, 238, 271, 281, 291–292, 323

Catholics, 79–80, 239, 255, 286, 293, 321–323, 325–327, 329

Catholics and Protestants, 231, 239, 250

Caverio, Nicolay de, 194

Celtiberia / Celtiberians, 35, 39, 45, 58

Celtic, 39, 45, 101

Celtici Neri, 49

Ceramics, 17, 42–44, 52, 54, 61, 64–66, 78

....Palmela bowls, 19

....Phoenician ceramic graffito, 27

....Phoenician model, 26

....pottery, 30, 42–43

........amphoras, 31, 42–44, 56, 61, 64, 68, 71, 78

....*sigillata*, 43, 78

Cerejeira (cardinal), 327

Cervantes, Miguel de, 214, 225, 336

Cesar, Julius, 230

Ceuta, 88, 111, 159–162, 164, 188, 198, 200, 216–217, 219, 367

Charles (king), 302–308

Charles I (king of Spain), 207

Charles V, 180, 218, 265, 290

Chaves, 32, 63, 75, 77, 79

....*Aquae Flaviae*, 32

Chicago, 313, 315

Chile, 283, 355, 357

China, 151–152, 164, 179, 186–187, 192, 195, 198–201, 206, 214, 226, 228, 233–237, 240, 305, 307

....Chinese Empire, 186, 240

....Chinese Rites controversy, 236

Christ, 110, 124–125, 224

Christendom, 111, 115, 119, 123, 142

Christian Kingdoms, 91, 124, 148

Christianity, 33, 80–81, 83, 88, 123, 128, 131–132, 137, 139, 150, 159, 181–182, 198–199, 213–215, 223–225, 228, 235

Christians, Christian communities, occupation, 33, 76–78, 80–81, 87, 89–91, 111, 114, 120–121, 125, 128, 137–138, 161–162, 181–182, 198–201, 211, 224, 291, 293, 295

Churches, 286, 292–293, 308, 323, 333

....Catholic Church, 78–79, 88, 110, 123, 125–126, 131–132, 137–143, 153, 198–200, 202, 209, 214, 230–231, 234, 271, 273, 280, 291, 326–328

....Church of England/Episcopalian, 292

....Danish Lutheran, 292

....Dutch Reformed Church/Calvinist, 292

....French Huguenot, 292

....Protestant churches, 291–292

....Reformed churches, 292

Churchill, Winston, 309

Civil Code, 294

Clairvaux, Saint Bernard of, 101, 120, 123

Claudius, 41, 59, 71

Clement XIV (pope), 270

climate, 8, 311–312, 344

Clinton (general), 288–289

Cluny (Abbey of), 97, 100, 104, 124

Coa (river), 12, 149–150

Cochinchina, 201, 215, 234

Coffyn, André, 22, 23

Coimbra, 77, 88, 94, 97–101, 103–104, 106, 109, 113–115, 124, 130, 132, 134–136, 141–143, 153, 157, 195, 209, 211, 213–214, 231, 234–235, 252, 258, 296–297, 337

....*Aeminium*, 77

Collegiate Church of Saint Mary of Guimarães, 138–139

Colonia de Sacramento (Colony of Sacramento), 165, 244–246

colonialism, 282, 300, 345, 347, 349, 352, 354

colonies, 280, 282, 285–286, 317–320, 327, 330, 342, 349–351, 353–354

....anti-colonial, 340, 347

Colonization, Colonial expansion, 66, 88, 95, 229

Columbus, Christopher, 86, 168, 178–179, 185, 192, 205–208

communications, 1, 2, 304, 311, 313, 359, 366

communism, 282, 324, 326–327

Concert of Nations, 290, 320

Concordat, 327, 333

Congo, 188, 204, 271, 299–302, 347

Congress of Vienna, 284, 300

Conímbriga, 26, 53–54, 76–78

Constantinople, 82, 90–91, 152, 161

constitution, 285–287, 297, 305, 308–309, 326, 349

....Constitutional Charter, 286–289, 293, 297, 305

Convention of Evoramonte, 290

Convents, 107, 109–110, 196

Conventus, 60–61, 65, 73, 76

Copper Age, 8
Cordeiro, Luciano, 300–301
Córdoba, 22, 59, 73–74
corporativism, corporatism 280, 281, 326, 328, 331
Coruche, 110, 181–182, 197
Costa, Afonso, 331
Costa, Alfredo, 303–304
Council, 80–82, 108, 124–125, 128, 139, 189, 197, 199, 226, 230–231
Count of Ericeira [D. Luís de Meneses], 243, 249
Count of Lippe, 256
Count of Óbidos [D. Vasco Mascarenhas], 243–244
Count of Palmela, 284
counter-insurgency, 348–349
coup/coup d'etat, 280–281, 287–289, 303, 305, 307, 355
court, 80–82, 87, 91, 111, 121, 131–133, 156, 162, 229, 235–236, 247, 251, 253, 264–265, 268, 274–277, 283–289, 368
Courts (*Cortes*), 139, 154, 157, 168, 176, 226, 228, 256, 286, 289, 368
Coutinho, Domingos de Sousa (marquis of Funchal), 276, 283
Coutinho, Rodrigo de Sousa (count of Linhares), 276, 283
Couto, Diogo do, 225
Crusades, 114, 116, 119–120, 123, 139, 141, 159, 167
Cunha, Luís da, 283
Cunha, Martim Vasques da, 157
Cunliffe, Barry, 70
Curia (Roman Curia), 115, 120, 137, 139, 179, 271, 273
cursus honorum, 73, 75
Cusa, Nicholas of, 230
Cyprus, 21, 119

D'Ailly, Pierre (Cardinal), 230
D'Este, Ercole (duke of Ferrara), 191, 193–194
Damásio, António, 339
Danube, 31, 76
death penalty, 294–298
Decimus Junius Brutus, 36, 40
decolonization, 280–282, 284, 286, 340, 343, 346–348, 350, 355, 358
decrees, 284, 290, 295, 297, 326
Delaunay, Robert, 314–316
Delaunay, Sonia, 314–316
Delgado, Humberto, 343
democracies, 280–282, 308, 325, 342–343, 347, 356–357, 359–360
....democratizations, 281, 306, 340, 355–357
....third wave of democratizations, 280–281

Denis (king of Portugal), 98, 121, 129, 131, 141–142, 144–145, 150, 367
Denmark, 71, 87, 283, 299
Descartes, René, 213
Dias, Bartolomeu, 205
Dias, Manuel, 233–236
dictators / dictatorships, 55, 280, 323–328, 335, 342, 355–358
Diet of Worms, 292
diocese / diocesis, 73–75, 77
Dioclician, 72–74
diplomacy, 292, 302, 317, 329, 345, 352
DNA, 8, 10, 18
Domingues, Afonso, 102
Dominican Republic, 195, 200
Dominus ac Redemptor (Brief), 270
domus, 54, 61
Douro (river), 32, 59, 71, 76–77, 89, 92–94, 104, 106, 108, 149, 267, 287....
Dudley (lord), 288
Duke of Alba, 227
Duke of Braganza, 216, 241–242
Duke of Cadaval, 249
Dutch, 181, 238, 241–244, 250, 255
....Dutch Empire, 183, 203
........Dutch Brazil, 183–184, 241–243
........Dutch West India Company, 241–243
Dynasty of Avis, House of, 118, 122, 125, 132, 158–159, 226–227, 243
Dynasty of Braganza, 118

Eanes, Gil, 173
Earl of Cambridge, 156
East, 8, 10, 14–15, 22, 24, 33, 90, 110, 119, 164, 185–236 *passim*, 292, 306, 345
eastern bloc, 281, 356
Eastern Question, 289
Ebro (river), 12, 34–35, 39, 45, 92
Ebro Frontier Model, 12
Economy, 8, 16, 86, 119, 145, 154, 173, 185, 187, 203, 241, 259–260, 268, 284, 306, 311, 318, 325–326, 328, 331, 333, 348, 359, 361
....agropastoral economy, 16
....economic expansion, 299, 368
....economic growth, 281
....geo-economy, 330
....investment, 281, 348, 359, 361
....market economy, 282
....plantation economy, 187, 203
Ecuador, 247, 282
Edward III (king of England), 154
Edward VII (king), 309
Egitania, 77
Egypt, 21, 57, 90, 152, 160
Eisenhower, 345
Elbe (river), 71

Elcano, Juan Sebastian, 194, 205, 208, 228
Elevator Coup, 304
Elizabeth (empress), 307
Elvas, 157, 208, 214
Emden, Johannes de, 220
emigration, 281, 289, 366–369
empires, 282–287, 298, 306–307, 309, 317,
    319–320, 323, 331, 333, 335, 349–352,
    354, 358
England, 20, 23, 87–88, 119, 141–142, 146,
    152–154, 156–158, 180, 217, 248–249,
    256, 276
....English Empire, 183, 203
Enlightenment, 263, 271, 273, 295
....Kant, Immanuel, 263
....Rousseau, Jean-Jacques, 263
....Voltaire, 214, 263, 295
Entente Cordiale, 308, 317
Ephorus, 49
Epidemics, 87, 151–154, 186
....Black Death, 87, 151–153, 155
epigraphy / epigraphs / epigraphic, 30–31, 33,
    46–47, 50–53, 59, 73–74, 82
Equator, 178–179, 192, 194, 322
Espinha, José da, 236
Espinho, 311, 315
Estado Novo (Salazarian regime), 37, 202, 258,
    260, 274, 280, 323–327, 329, 331,
    333–335, 339, 343–344, 346, 350–352,
    354–355, 359
Estaus Palace, 182
Estremadura, 12, 16, 110
Estremoz, 54, 61
Ethiopia, 195, 215, 224, 271
Eurasia, 152, 185, 187
Europe, 4–23 *passim*, 31, 41–42, 44, 48–49,
    63, 68, 71, 72, 86–156 *passim*, 161–296
    passim, 303–369 *passim*
....European integration, 340–341, 359–361
....European powers, 280, 296, 299–300, 340
European Free Trade Association (EFTA),
    281, 346, 348, 359
European Recovery Program, 344
European Union, 282, 331, 356
....Bulletin of the European Commission, 360
....European Commission, 359
....European Community, 359–361
....European Community Presidency, 335
....European Council, 360
....European Economic Community (EEC),
    313, 335, 356, 358–361, 369
....United States of Europe, 369
Eusébio (Eusébio da Silva Ferreira), 281, 351–
    354
Évora, 11, 52, 101, 110, 114, 143, 149, 168,
    209, 213, 252, 254
....*Ebora Liberalitas Iulia*, 52

Expositions Mouvantes, 315–316

fado, 281, 323
Faleiro, Rui, 207
Fano (Pesaro), 217
Farinha, Afonso Peres, 109–110
Farming, 14, 115
Faro, 43, 60, 73, 92, 214
....*Ossonoba*, 43, 73
fascism, 280–281, 325–327, 335, 365
Fátima, 11, 280–281, 321–324
Ferdinand I (king of Portugal), 117, 146, 156
Ferdinand II (king of León), 112, 114, 149
Ferdinand III (king of León and Castille), 92
Ferdinand IV (king of Castile and León), 150
Ferdinand VII (king), 284, 287, 290, 292
Ferdinand of Aragon (Catholic king),
    178–179, 227–228
Fernandes, Crisóstomo, 220
Fernandes, Valentim, 50
Fernandes, Vasco, 110
Fernando Pó (Island), 175
Ferrão, António Fernandes da Silva, 297
Ferrara (Duchy of), 191, 193–194, 210
Ferreira, António, 224–225
Ferreira, Cristóvão, 237
Ferro, António, 325, 327, 332
Ferry, Jules, 300, 308
Fez, 161–162
Figanière, Frederico Francisco de la, 118
Figueira da Foz, 71, 196, 311
Figueiredo, António Pereira de, 272
Filangieri, 295
finis terrae, 31, 48, 60, 69, 72
Finland, 152, 344
First Republic, 309–310, 321, 323, 326, 331,
    333, 337
fish (industry, products), 33, 42–44, 52,
    60–61, 64, 78, 328–332
Flaking industries, 11–12
Flanders, 250, 309
Flavian dynasty, 52–53
Flemish, 119–120, 123, 168, 249–250
Fonseca, Ângelo da, 337
Fonseca, Christophe, 313
Fonseca, Isaac Aboab da, 183
Fontana, Roberto, 232
food habits / eating habits, 25, 42
food production / food products / food
    resources, 14, 33, 41–43, 52, 56, 61, 64
Foreign Office, 284, 308, 318
foreign policy, 283, 308–310, 317–320,
    340–343, 345
Forlì, 133–134
forum, 53–56, 74, 77
France, 4, 12, 19, 20, 38, 45, 80–157 *passim*,
    180, 183, 201, 218, 231, 237, 239, 248,

France (continued)
  256, 262– 309 *passim*, 317, 321, 326,
  330, 333, 337, 344, 347–348, 350, 362,
  365, 368
....French invasions, 256, 275–276, 283
........Treaty of Fontainebleau, 276
....French overseas empire, 183, 203, 271
....French Revolution, 256, 265, 282
Francisco de Holanda, 50, 217
Franco, João, 303–304
Franks, Frankish, 76, 79–80, 90, 94, 103–105,
  124
Frederick II Hohenstaufen (emperor), 134
free elections, 355, 357
Freemasonry, Freemasons/Masonic, 255–259,
  303–304, 307–308
Freire, Mello, 296
Freitas, Augusto César Barjona de, 294, 298
Freitas, Serafim de, 180
Fribourg, 296
Froilaz, Pedro (count of Trava), 105–106
Fróis, Luís, 215
Frutuoso, Gaspar, 208
Fuero Juzgo (códice), 117
Funai (Japan), 201, 214, 237
Funchal (diocese), 200–201
Funchal, 168–169, 200–201, 214, 232, 276,
  291, 293, 312
Fundação Nacional para a Alegria no Trabalho
  [National Foundation for Joy in Work]
  (INATEL), 312

G. Marius, 55
G. Sulpicius Rufus, 74
Galba, 39–40
Galicia, 92–93, 95, 103–107, 112–114, 133,
  150
....Galician language, 128, 132
....Galician-Portuguese, 87, 96, 99, 127–128,
  130–132
Gallaecia, 33, 73, 75–76, 78, 80
....*Callaecia*, 73–74, 76
Galvão, Henrique, 347
Gama, Vasco da, 179, 184, 186, 191,
  205–206, 224
Gamarra, Fernando, 178
Garrett, Almeida, 310
Gaudí, Antoni, 315
Gauguin, Paul, 314
Gaul, 38, 43, 57, 71, 76, 79–80
....Gauls, 34, 57, 70
Gaunt, John of (duke of Lancaster), 118,
  158
Genetics, 8, 12, 15
Genova, 290
George III (king), 283
George V (king), 309

Geraldo Geraldes (Geral de Fearless), 114,
  149
Germania, 38, 71
Germany, 10, 37–38, 99, 280, 290, 299,
  301–302, 307, 309, 312, 318, 320, 323–
  324, 326–327, 344, 348, 350, 364
....Federal Republic of Germany, 281, 356
....Germany (Catholic states), 231
Ghobrial, John-Paul, 3
Gibraltar, 12, 26–27, 33, 55, 67, 74, 93, 121,
  161, 292
....Pillars of Hercules, 33, 67
Giglio, Luigi (Lilio), 231
Global History, 2–4, 164–166, 174, 233–234,
  266, 280, 314, 346
global order, 281, 349–350
Globalization, 1–2, 86, 164–166, 171,
  173–174, 187, 190–191, 205, 208, 220,
  228–229, 234–235, 282, 312, 314, 322,
  346
....Proto-globalizations, 24
....Worldwide monarchy, Hispanic *Universi*
  Globus, 226–229
Globalization of food products, transplantation of cultures and dietary habits,
  165, 195
....brazilwood, 177, 250
....cloves, 179, 206
....coffee, 167, 195, 203
...."Columbian exchange", 186
....Luxury goods, imports, 186
....Melegueta pepper, 176–177
....monoculture system, 167, 203
....nutmeg, 206
....rice, 165, 195–197
....sugar, sugar cane, production, 122, 165,
  167–170, 185, 188, 195, 203–204,
  241–244, 250
....tobacco, 167, 203
Globalization of Knowledge, 220–222
....*Colóquios dos Simples/Colloquies on the*
  Simples, Drugs and Materia Medica of
  India, 220–222
....Medical and botanical knowledge, 220
....Printing press, 165, 220
....Saint Paul's College press, 220
Globalization of science, 233–237
....Astronomical Observatory of Beijing,
  235–236
....Classes on the Sphere, *Aula da Esfera*, 214,
  234
....Clavius, Christopher, 231, 234–235
....Copernicus' heliocentric theory, 234, 236
....Euclid, 235
....(European) Scientific Revolution, 233–235
....first European hospital in Japan, 237
....Galileo, 233–236

....Jesuit astronomers, 235–236
....Mathematical board, 235–236
....Ptolemy's geocentric model, 234, 236
....Sacrobosco, 172, 235
....Translation of scientific works, 235
Globalization of time measurement, 230–233
....Gregorian Calendar, reform, 165, 230–233, 235
....Gregory XIII (pope), 230–232
....Julian calendar, 230, 232–233
....*Kalendarium gregorium perpetuum*, 231–232
....*Lei do Rei de Portugal Filipe I sobre os 10 Dias do Calendário (The Law of King Philip I of Portugal on the 10 Days of the Calendar)*, 232
Goa Military Hospital, 221–222
Godinho, Vitorino Magalhães, 2, 367
Godoy, 283
Goethe, 296–297
Góis, Bento de, 214
Gold Coast, 175, 204
Gomes, Costa, 355
Gomes, Fernão, 174–177
Gomes, Laurentino, 275
Gonçalves, João, 220
Gonçalves, Nuno, 99, 102
Gonçalves, Vasco, 357, 360
Gothic style, 97, 99, 101–102
Goths, 33, 79–83, 103
Gouveia, Aires de, 297
Graeco-Latin, 30, 48
Granada, 91, 111, 148, 159–161, 169, 199, 292
Grão-Pará Company, 272
Greece, 21–23, 55, 82, 223–224, 281, 287
Greenland, 62–64, 191, 193
Gregorian reforms, 100, 131–132
Gregory X (pope), 138–139
Grienberger, Christoph, 234
Grotius, Hugo, 180
Guadalquivir (river), 38, 42–43, 58, 60, 64, 71, 77, 93, 110
....*Baetis*, 58
Guadiana (river), 26, 80, 109–110
Guaraní (people), 271
Guimarães, 95, 104, 106, 113, 138–139, 153, 333
Guinea, 168–169, 174–177, 179–180, 197
Guinea-Bissau, Guiné, 204, 260, 282, 348, 351, 355
Gusmão, D. Louisa de, 243
Guzmán, Dominic of, 125

Habsburg (House of), 226–229, 237–239, 241, 250
Hadrian V, 139
Haiti, 195, 200

....Haitian Slave Revolt, 282
Hamburg, 183, 210, 229, 315
Handwritten Text, Handwriting, 96–99
....Apocalypse (manuscript of Lorvão), 101
....*Book of Birds (Livro das Aves)*, 101
....French illumination, 101
....Scribe, scribes, 96–97, 99, 142
Hannibal, 34–35
Hansa, Hanseatic League, 145, 152
Haro, Cristóbal de, 207
Harrison, Richard J., 17–18
Hašek, Jaroslav, 305
Hastings, Gilbert of (bishop of Lisbon), 100
Hebrew (language), 128, 183
Heidelberg, 10
Heidelberg Man, 8
Henriques, Urraca (princess), 106
Henriquez, D. Henrique, 178
Henry IV (king of Castile), 178
Henry (cardenal, king), 209, 226, 232
Henry (count of Trastámara), 156
Henry of Burgundy (count Henry), 87, 100, 103–106, 112–113
Heracleium at Gades, 67
Heresy, 111, 134, 141, 210, 243
Hermenegild, 81
Hispania, 35–91 *passim*, 103, 105, 107, 118
....Arab-Berber conquest, 90
....Diocletian provincial reorganization, 89
Hispaniola, 195, 200
Hitler, 324–325, 327
holidays, 304, 311–312, 315
Holland, 17, 201, 242
Holocene, 13
Holy Alliance, 284
Holy Empire, 292
Holy Land, 72, 94, 107–111, 114, 120, 123, 139
Holy Roman Emperor, 91, 139, 239
Holy Roman-Germanic Empire, 87, 240, 248, 250
Holy See / Vatican, 110, 114–115, 123, 125, 198, 200, 231, 289, 309, 327, 333
Homo sapiens, 8
Hormuz, 190, 201, 206, 219
House of Braganza / Braganzas, 285, 290, 308–309, 333
Huelva, 9, 24, 27, 63, 322
Huesca, 56
....Huesca "school", 46
....*Osca*, 56
Hugh (Saint, Abbot of Cluny), 100, 105
Hugh of Fouilloy, 101
Huguet, 102
Hungary, 231, 269, 344
Hydatius, 32, 75, 77–79

Iberian Pact, 333, 342
Iberian Peninsula, 8–119 *passim*, 127–129,
    131–133, 138, 141, 148–149, 153, 156,
    159, 167, 183, 195, 229, 243, 284, 287,
    290, 308–309, 317, 319, 336, 342
....Iberian kingdoms, 107, 110, 115, 178, 213,
    219, 275, 290, 367
Iberian Union, dual monarchy, "Union of
    Crowns", 113, 165, 201, 219, 226–229,
    246, 250
....Portuguese autonomy, 162, 219, 229, 242,
    275
Iceland, 31, 70, 152, 329
Idanha-a-Nova, 21, 23
Idanha-a-Velha, 77–78
imperialism, 284, 286, 324, 342
India, 164–206 *passim*, 220–222, 224–225,
    227–228, 233, 235–236, 238, 247, 271,
    322, 367
Indian Ocean, 1, 66, 148, 151–152, 164, 171,
    173, 181, 185, 187, 191, 200, 367–368
Indigenism, Indigenous culture, settlements,
    15, 25, 27
Indo-European language, 45
Indonesia, 200, 205–206
Industrial Revolution, 64, 283
industrialization, 305–306
....industries, 33, 42, 52, 63–64, 284, 331, 334
Innocent V (pope), 139
Inquisition, 165, 182, 209–212, 222, 255, 264,
    292
International Association of the Congo (IAC),
    299–301
International Monetary Fund, 360
Ipiranga, 286
Ireland (Republic of), 344
Iron Age, 25
Isabel II, 290
Isabella (Catholic queen), 178–179
Isabella (half-sister of Henry IV of Castile),
    178
Isidore of Seville, 79, 82–83
Isidro, Charles Maria (prince), 290
Islam, Islamism, 86–87, 89–90, 111, 121, 139,
    161, 174, 176, 210, 224–225
....Islamic culture, Islamic world, Islamic rule,
    87, 89–91, 137, 140, 161
Italy, 4, 21, 23, 35, 57, 88, 90, 93, 97, 102,
    129, 133–136, 141–142, 153, 161, 191,
    217–218, 231, 233–234, 236, 281–282,
    290, 295, 299, 303, 306–307, 309, 312,
    322, 325–327, 330, 333, 344
....Italian Peninsula, 34–35, 42–43, 55, 139,
    152, 217
Iulius Saturninus, 74
Ivory Coast, 204

Jaboatão dos Guararapes, 242
Jacobinism, 307
Jaen, 91
Jaime, D. (duke of Braganza), 216
James II of Aragon, 150
Japan, 164, 179, 186, 188–190, 192, 199–201,
    213–215, 226, 228, 233–234, 236–237,
    271, 314, 322, 344–345
Jardo, Domingos, 143
Járnsíða, Björn, 93
Jerez de la Frontera (Mesas de Asta/Hasta),
    39–40, 46
Jerusalem, 107, 110–111, 119–120, 159
Jewish culture, Judaic culture, influence, 87,
    133, 140, 291, 315, 330, 367
Jews, 139, 152, 181–184, 211
....Jews expulsion, 181–184
........Conversion to Christianity, New
    Christians, Converts, 181–184, 209–211,
    221, 229
....Judaism, 183, 209–211, 222
John (prince regent), 266, 274–275
John I (João I) (Master of Avis, king of
    Portugal), 102, 111–112, 116, 118, 146,
    155–159, 162, 172, 200, 367
John I (Juan I) of Castile, 118, 155–158
John II (king of Portugal), 178–180, 205, 217,
    243
John III (king of Portugal), 180, 182, 213,
    217, 243
John IV (king, duke of Braganza), 241, 243,
    333
John V (king of Portugal), 201, 251–254
John VI (king of Portugal), 256, 265, 285,
    287–288
....Prince regent John, 283–285, 287, 297
John XXI (pope), 88, 137–140
....Pedro Hispano, 137–138, 140
John of Biclaro (João de Santarém), 82
John of the Rules (João das Regras), 157
Jordão, Levy Maria, 297
Jórsalafari, Sigurðr (king), 94
Joseph I (king of Portugal), 256, 267,
    270–271, 295
Joseph II, 296
Julian Calendar, 57
Julio–Claudian dynasty, 53
Julius Caesar, 34, 36, 52, 57, 70
July Revolution, 289
Justinian I, 33, 80, 152

Kalley, Robert, 293
Kenya, 172, 201
Kepler, 231
Khrushchev, 345
Kpengla (king), 266
Kraft durch Freude [Strength through Joy], 312

Kristiansen, Kristian, 23
Ksar es-Seghir, 188, 217
Kunstman IV, 207
Kurzman, Charles, 280

L. Cornelius Sulla, 55, 57
L'Écluse, Charles de (Carolus Clusius), 220, 222
La Gravette (site), 12
La Micoque (site), 11
La Plata (river), 285
Labrador, 329–330
Ladeia (region), 113
Lagos (Bay of), 27
Lagos (Portugal), 173, 175
Laguna, Andrés, 221
Lajes Agreement, 340–341
Lamego, 78, 153, 349
Lancaster, Philippa of, 102, 116, 118, 158, 367
Lapa do Picareiro (site), 11–13
Lapedo child, 12
Las Casas, Bartolomé de, 225
Las Palmas, 168
Last Glacial Maximum, 13
Latin America, 281, 314, 325, 357, 365, 367
Latin authors, 127
Latin Church, 88, 139
Latin language, 32, 44–47, 76, 78, 87, 90, 93, 97, 127–130, 132
Latin literature, 36, 130
Le Goff, Jacques, 88
Le Moustier (site), 11
Le Solutré (site), 13
League of Nations, 302, 320, 340, 343, 345
Leceia, 18–19
Legitimism / legitimists, 287, 289, 290
Leiria, 12, 102, 113, 141, 157, 321–322, 367
leisure, 311–312, 334, 366
Leite, Duarte, 193
Lembo, Giovanni, 234
Leme, Rui, 178
Leo X (pope), 230–231
León (kingdom), 87, 91, 109, 112, 114, 149–150, 158
León, Pero de, 178
Leopardi, Giacomo, 275
Leopold II (king), 296, 299–301
Leovigild, 79, 81–82
liberalism, 280, 306, 314
....anti-Liberal, 284, 287, 290
....demo-liberalism, 328
....economic liberalism, 326
....Liberal, 289–290, 292, 296
....liberal democracy, 324–325
....Liberal governments, 287–288
....liberal revolutions, 256, 280

Lima (Peru), 228
Lima (river), 113
Lima, Manoel de Oliveira, 274–275
Lima, Sebastião de Magalhães, 303–304, 308
Limoeiro (jail), 297
Limoges, 100–101
Limousin (region), 136
Lisbon, 25, 43, 60–61, 71–149 *passim*, 157, 160, 162, 167–169, 170, 175, 178, 182, 188–190, 196, 205–318 *passim*, 321, 327, 330–331, 334–339, 341–342, 351, 354, 365, 368
....*Olisipo*, 42, 61, 71, 74
....*Olisiponensis*, 71–72
....*Olysipona*, 78
Lisbon Academy of Sciences, 215
Lisbon castle, 264
Lisbon Geographic Society, 301–302
literature, 297, 305, 324, 336, 339, 362–365, 369
Liturgy, 97, 100, 124, 130, 132, 136, 230, 253
Livorno, 183, 210
Livy, 38
Llanete de los Moros, 22
Lo Schiavo, Fulvia, 22
Lóðbrók, Ragnar, 93
Loescher, Robert, 313
Lombada de Ponta do Sol, 168
London, 145, 183, 229, 255, 268, 271, 283, 289, 290, 292–293, 299–300, 305, 307–309, 315, 317, 331, 338
Longobardi, Niccolò, 236
Longroiva, 108
Lordemão, 94–95
Louis I (king), 294, 297–298
Louis VII (king of France), 116
Louis XIV of France, 201, 251, 253
Louis XVIII, 287
Loulé, 181–182
Loureiro, João de, 215
Loures, 12
Loyola, Ignatius of, 212, 270
Luanda, 170, 214, 242, 254, 260, 347
Lucius Sestius Quirinalis, 49
Lucullus, 39
Lugo, 76, 149
Luís Filipe, 302
Lusignan, Guy of (king of Jerusalem), 159
Lusitania, 32–33, 38–39, 43, 46–48, 50, 52, 54, 59–60, 65, 73–76, 78
....Late Lusitanian, 64
....Lusitanian cities, 39, 53, 61
....Lusitanian Wars, 35–37, 40
....Lusitanians, 31, 38–40, 43, 47, 55, 223, 225
Lusotropicalism, 352, 354
Luther, Martin, 291–292
Lyco, 38

Macao, 190, 198, 201, 214, 229, 234–236, 265, 335
Maçãs (beach), 49
MacDonnell, Jacobite, 289
Macedonia, 57
Machado, Bernardino, 257
Machico, 168
Mactan (Island), 208
Madeira, 122, 310–312, 367, 369
Madrid, 229, 235, 238, 245, 271, 275, 305, 307–309, 337, 351
Mafra, 110, 165, 251–253
Magalhães, Gabriel de, 236
Magellan, Ferdinand, 192, 194, 205–208, 228, 236
Maggiolo, Vesconti, 194
Maghreb, 119, 122, 185
Maia, Soeiro Mendes da, 104
Malacca, 129, 164, 179, 190, 199, 201, 206–207, 233, 292
Malaga, 27, 91, 292
Malagrida, Gabriele, 272
Malagueta Coast, 177
Malay Archipelago, 206–207
Maldives, 186
Maldonado, Rodrigo, 178
Malhoa, José, 311
Mallorca, 140, 152
Mameluke Empire, 152
Manchu conquest, 240
Mandinka, 193
Manila, 186, 190, 228–229
Manilius, 39
Mansilha, Friar João de, 268
Manuel I, Emanuel I (king of Portugal), 112, 179, 181–182, 193, 199–200, 206–207, 217, 227, 231, 243, 291
Manuel II (king), 307–309
Manueline, 295
Mar del Sur, 206
Maranhão, 242
March of Treviso, 134
Marcus Atilius, 39
Marcus Crassus, 57
Mardel, Carlos, 255
Mare clausum, 174, 176, 199
Mare liberum, 201
Maria I (queen), 296–297
Maria II (princess/queen), 288–289, 297
Maria da Fonte (uprising), 290
Maria Teresa, 290
Marialva (castle), 149
Marian cult, 280
Mariette, Jean, 252
Marine Isotope, 11
Marinetti's futurist manifesto, 314
Mark Antony, 57

Marks, Anthony, 11
Marquis of Alegrete, 249
Marquis of Pombal (Sebastião José de Carvalho e Melo), 144, 211, 213, 215, 255, 263, 267–272, 283, 295, 331
Marriage (Royal), marriages, 87, 103, 115–118, 156
Marseille, 31, 66, 70, 330
....*Massalia*, 66
Marshall Plan, 340–341, 344
Martins, Lourenço, 111, 110
Martins, Oliveira, 274
Martone, Hugo de, 108
Mary I (queen of Portugal), 274
Mary of Portugal (queen of Castile), 117
Massaliote *Periplus*, 70
Matisse, Henri, 314
Matos, Gregório de, 214
Mattioli, Pietro Andrea, 221
Mattoso, José, 104, 106
Maurras, Charles, 325
Mauretania Tingitana, 74
Mauri, 74
Maurienne, Matilda of (queen), 115–116, 123, 132
Mauritania, 76, 169, 175, 198
Mazagan (fortress, port), 165, 169, 216–219
Mazagan process, project, 217–218
McKinley, William, 307
McLuhan, Marshall, 1
Medellin, 52
....*Metellinum*, 52
Medical authorities (classical Greek, Latin, Arab and Christian), 138
Medici, Cosimo III de' (grand duke), 269
Medieval universities, 88, 137–143, 180, 221
Mediterranean, 9, 15, 18–48 *passim*, 57, 63, 65–66, 68–72, 79–82, 89–91, 93–94, 111, 119, 121–122, 167, 173, 183, 185, 191–192, 203, 210, 238, 249–250, 275, 309, 311, 317, 325, 330, 367
....*mare nostrum*, 70
....Mediterranean civilization, heritage, 90, 102, 121, 130, 151–152, 160–162
Melo, Fontes Pereira de, 302
Mendes, Paio, 106
Menezes, Francisco Barreto de, 243
Mérida, 43, 52, 54, 59–61, 73–74, 77–80, 82
....*Augusta Emerita*, 43, 52, 60–61, 73–75, 78
Merovingian, 82
Mértola, 27, 52, 60, 64, 82, 109
....*Myrtilis*, 52
Mesolithic, 13, 16
Messina, 134, 152
metals, 20, 30, 42, 62–63
....antimony, 62–64
....bronze, 20–21, 31–32, 36, 64

....copper, 31–32, 36, 64, 69
....gold, 20–21, 24, 32, 36–37, 62–63
....lead, 20–21, 32, 36, 56, 62–63, 64
....silver, 32, 35–36, 62–63, 69
....tin, 20–21
Methuen, John, 248–249
Métissage, mestiço, miscegenation, 2, 165, 261
metropole, 284–285, 292, 294, 306
Metternich, 288
Mexico, 190, 228, 280, 283, 307
Micer Pessagna, 121
Michael (king of Portugal), 256
Michel, Saint, 153
Migrationism, 15
....emigrants, 332, 368–369
....immigrants, 368
....interpretative models, 15
....migration process, 16
Miguel (prince/king), 287–290
Milanese, 122
Milharós, 11
militar / military, 36–38, 40, 42, 55, 57, 71, 80,
    281, 284–285, 287, 289, 301, 307,
    309–310, 318–319, 325, 341–343, 345,
    347–351, 355, 357, 367
Military Orders, 88, 107, 109, 110–112, 115,
    125, 131
....Alcántara, 158
....Avis, 107, 109, 110–111, 198
....Calatrava, 107, 110
....Christ (Order of; soldiers of), 111, 161,
    198–200
....Donation, Donations, 107–110, 123–124,
    189, 271, 273
....Évora-Avis Militia, 107, 109–110
....Hospital, Hospitallers, brothers of the
    Hospital, 108–111, 131
....Rodhes and Malta, 111
....Santiago, brothers of, 107, 109, 111, 131,
    198
....Temple, Templars, 107–111, 113, 120
Millenium Museum of Beijing, 235
Mina Coast, 204
Minas Gerais, 253, 259
mines, 32–33, 42, 63–64
minerals, 23–33, 35–36, 42, 54, 60–61, 63,
    71
Ming dynasty, 240
Minho (region), 105, 260, 311
Minho (river), 36, 41, 63, 77, 93, 103–107,
    114, 149
Miranda do Corvo, 113
Miranda, Francisco de Sá de, 224–225
Miróbriga, 54
Misericórdia Brotherhoods, 188–191
Mithridates, 55–56
Mittermaier, 298

Mixed perspectives, 16
Modena, 191, 194
Modern expansion of Christianity, 198,
    214–215
....Catholic missions, missionaries, 198, 200,
    202, 212–215, 222, 234–236, 246
....Congregation for the Propagation of the
    Faith, 201
....Evangelization, 199, 212–213, 215, 220
modernism, 313–314, 316
Mogadouro, 108
Mohammed (Prophet), 91, 161
Moissac, 100–101
Molecular biology, 8, 10
Molesme, Robert of, 124
Molina, Maria de, 150
Moluccas, 164, 179, 180, 190, 201, 205–208,
    228
Mommsen, Theodor, 30
monarchies, 284–286, 290, 303, 306–307,
    309, 317–318
....anti-monarchism, 307–308
....monarchists, 286, 307, 318
Monastery, 97, 100–102, 108, 120, 134, 141,
    149, 264, 334, 358, 361
Mondego (river), 9, 16, 25–26, 71, 93–94,
    104, 108, 113–114, 195
Moniz, Egas, 214, 336–339
Montaigne, Michel de, 225
Montánchez, 149
Monteiro, George, 364–365
Monteiro, J. P. Franco, 118
Montepaolo (Hermitage of), 133–134
Montesquieu, 295
Moquat, Jean, 169
Mora, Ângel Herreros de, 293
Moreton, Robert Hawkey, 293
Morin, Edgar, 4
Morocco, 111, 134, 160–161, 167, 169, 175,
    183, 201, 216–217, 219
Moura, 27, 149–150
Mozambique, 201, 219, 224, 257, 260, 265,
    282, 297, 301, 310, 322, 347–348, 351,
    355, 369
Mozarab, Mozarabs, 87, 93, 124
Mozarabic style, 100–101
Mughal Empire, 186, 240, 247, 271
Münster, 238–239
Murcia, 91, 148, 150
Museu Nacional de Arte Antiga (Lisbon), 99,
    102, 252
Muslims, Muslim populations, 79, 95, 100,
    104, 108, 113–114, 119–120, 124, 128,
    132, 134, 148, 159–160, 162, 167, 169,
    198–199
....Muslim invasions, 105, 108, 148
....Muslim piracy, 161–162

Muslims, Muslim populations *(continued)*
....Muslim presence, erudite circles, traders,
       101, 111–113, 115, 128, 130, 132, 162
Mussolini, 325, 327

Nanjing (diocese), 201
Naples (kingdom), 42, 270, 273, 275,
       287–288, 330
Napoleon, 256, 276, 283–284
Napoleon III, 307
Nassau-Siegen, John Maurice, 241–242
National archives, 1, 91, 96, 98, 150, 194,
       252, 264–266
nationalisms, 293, 308, 351, 367
NATO (North Atlantic Treaty Organization),
       Atlantic Alliance, 281, 340–346, 356
navigation, 284, 299–301, 305
Nazaré, 11, 311
Nazi (party, regime), 326–327, 333
Neanderthals, 8
Needham, John, 235
Negreiros, Almada, 313, 316
Negreiros, André Vidal de, 242–243
Neolithic, 14–17, 20
Nero, 289
Netherlands, 4, 18, 71, 180, 231, 241–242,
       299, 321
Neuville, Hyde de, 287
New France (Canada), 201
New Holland, 242, 250, 270
New York, 308, 315–316, 347–348, 352, 364
Newfoundland, 191–193, 328–330
news agencies, 305
newspapers, 303–305, 308, 313–314,
       321–322, 332, 336–337, 351–352,
       363–365
Newton, Isaac, 68
Nicholas II (pope), 199
Nicholas IV (pope), 141–142
Nicholas V, 198
Niebla, 149
Nobel Prize, 30, 336–339, 362–363, 365
Nobili, Roberto, 214
Nóbrega, Manuel da, 214
Normandy, 95
Norway, 31, 152, 299, 329
Notitia Dignitatum, 73
Novais, Fernando, 275
Nunes, Pedro, 1, 143, 173, 232, 234
Nuoro, 22

Oceania, 10, 213
Octavian, 57, 59
Odrinhas Museum, 50
Oeiras, 18–19
Oita (Japan), 237
Olaf, Saint, 94

Olinda, 243, 255
Oliveira Cave, 10, 12
Oliveira, Manuel de, 197
Olivença, 188, 284
Oran, 162
Ordenações Filipinas, 176
Ordinations, 181, 295
Ordonho I, 93
Organization for Economic Co-operation and
       Development, 344, 346
Oriental influence, 26–27
Orta, Garcia de, 183, 220, 222
Orta, Tomás da, 232
Ortigão, Ramalho, 310–311, 331
Osnabrück, 238–239
Osuna, 40, 65
....*Urso*, 40, 65
Ottoman Empire, Turkish Empire, 181, 183,
       195, 240, 299
Ottomans, 162
Ouguela, 150
Ourique, 27, 113
Ouro Preto, 253
Overseas Council (*Conselho Ultramarino*),
       259–260, 262
Oviedo, 89

Pach, Walter, 315
Pacific Ocean, 164, 171, 192, 203, 208
Paço de Sousa (Benedictine Church), 100
Pact of Succession, 105
Padua, 133–136
Pais, Álvaro, 143
Pais, Gualdim, 108, 110
Pais, Sidónio, 257, 280, 319, 337
Paiva, João Soares de, 128, 131, 133
Palace and Convent of Mafra, 165, 251–253
Palaeolithic, 8, 10, 13
Palencia, 141
Palermo, 275
Palestine, 152
Palmela (castle), 109
Pancorbo, Bartolomeu, 268
Panoias, Constantim de, 104
Papacy, 115, 123–126, 134, 139–140, 159
Papal States, 272
Paraguay, 245, 282, 322
Paraíba, 242, 274, 277, 322
Paris, 137, 140–141, 201, 255, 283, 288, 303,
       305, 307–308, 313–315, 337–338, 350
parliament, 297–298, 321, 326
....Chamber of Deputies, 289, 297
....Constituent Assembly, 285, 309, 337
....Corporative Chamber, 326
Parma (Duchy), 270, 273
parties, 280, 282, 300, 303–304, 320, 325,
       328, 349, 355–357

....African Party for the Independence of
      Guinea and Cape Verde (PAIGC), 348
....Centrist Party, 337
....Evolutionist Party, 337
....Popular Democratic Union, 357
....Popular Socialist Front, 357
....Portuguese Communist Party, 342,
      356–357, 360
....Portuguese Republican Party, 308–309
....Progressive Party, 301, 304
....Regenerator Party, 300
....Revolutionary Party of the
      Proletariat/Revolutionary Brigades,
      357
....Social Democratic Party, 361
....Socialist Left Movement, 357
....Socialist Party, 357, 360
Paul, Saint, 143
Paul III (pope), 212
Paul V (pope), 209
Paul VI (pope), 323
Payns, Hugues de, 107
Peace of Westphalia, Westphalia Treaties,
      166, 237–240
Pecetto, Lucie, 315
Peculiar, João, 114–115
Pedro (prince, duke of Coimbra), 143
Pedro and Inês, 102, 157
Penafiel, 107, 300–301
Penal Code, 293, 296–297
Peniche, 43, 61, 64, 254
Pereira, Duarte Pacheco, 278
Pereira, Gonçalo, 110
Pereira, Nuno Álvares (Constable), 157–158
Pereira, Tomás, 214, 236
Peres de Trava, Fernando, 106
Peres, Bermudo, 106
Pernambucan Revolt of 1817, 256, 285
Pernambuco, 241–244, 255
Persia, 90, 224
Persian empire, civilization, 89–90
Persian Gulf, 192
Persian Revolution, 307
Peru, 213, 228, 247, 283, 322
Perugia, 139
Pesaro, 217
Pessoa, Fernando, 48, 258, 339, 362–366
Peter (count of Barcelos), 131
Peter (prince regent's heir, Royal court
      transfer context), 274, 276
Peter I (emperor) / Peter IV (king), 285–286,
      289–290
Peter I (king of Portugal), 102, 118, 156–157
Peter II (king of Portugal), 201, 243, 248–249
Peter V (king), 297
Peter I of Aragon (king), 199
Peter of Castile (king), 156

Philip I (of Portugal; II of Spain), 226–228,
      232, 265
Philip III (king of France), 139
Philip III (of Portugal; IV of Spain), 227, 235,
      238
Philippine Dynasty, 228, 241, 244
Philippines, 208, 226, 228–229
Phoenicians, 9, 22, 24–27, 49, 63, 65
Picasso, Pablo, 314
PIDE (International and State Defence
      Policy), 258
Pimentel, António de Serpa, 300
Pina, Francisco de, 215
Pinto, Fernão Mendes, 225
Pires, Tomé, 207
Pius XII (pope), 136
Plate (river), 245–246
Pliny the Elder, 32, 36, 47, 49, 52, 66, 71–72
Pluricontinentalism, pluricontinental diaspora,
      23, 184, 186, 261
....*estrangeirados*, 260
....Portuguese global diaspora, emigration,
      259–262
....Portuguese identity, 254, 260–262
....Portuguese presence, 165, 220–221,
      227–228, 246, 262
....retornados, 262
Polo, Marco, 191, 235
Polybius, 8, 30, 56
Pompey, 56–58
Ponta Delgada, 214, 254
Ponte de Reguengo, 197
Port wine, Port wine demarcated region, 260,
      267–270, 272
Portalegre, 214, 293
Portel, Pero Anes de, 133
Portimão, 11, 214
Porto, 76–77, 101, 104, 115, 129, 144,
      146–147, 158, 190, 214, 248–249, 252–
      253, 256–257, 267–268, 272, 284–285,
      291, 293, 330, 331, 337, 353
Portus Cale, 77
Porto de Mós, 13, 22, 155, 157
Porto Seguro, 184
Portugal, Afonso de, 110
Portuguese America, 170, 190, 204, 238, 259,
      276–277
Portuguese and Spanish navigators and
      exploratory voyages, 191, 193, 205, 208
Portuguese border, 107, 109–110, 148–150
....Aiamonte, 150
....Castilian border, 150
........Olivença, 150
....*Condado/Terra Portucalense*, Portucale, 87,
      91, 103–106, 112, 149
....Battle of São Mamede, 107, 112
....Galician border, 113

Portuguese border *(continued)*
....Gallaecia, 149
....León (kingdom), 87, 91–92, 109, 112, 114, 149–150, 158
....Lusitania, 149
....Treaty of Alcáçovas, 151, 367
....Treaty of Alcañices, 48, 88, 150, 367
....Treaty of Badajoz, 149
....Treaty of Tordesilhas, 151
Portuguese-Castilian wars, 111, 147, 156
....Battle of Alcântara, 227
....Battle of Aljubarrota, 88, 108, 155–158, 159
........Master of Avis, (John I of Portugal), 111, 156–157
........Medieval chroniclers, 155
...........Ayala, Pero López de, 155
...........Froissart, Jean, 155
....Battle of Atoleiros, 157
Portuguese Crown, 88, 96, 111–112, 115, 122, 129, 144–145, 162, 167–168, 170, 174–175, 177–178, 185, 188–190, 194, 200–201, 205, 220, 242–243, 250, 260, 264, 273
Portuguese dynastic crisis, 122, 146, 226, 241
Portuguese economic development, 248
....British markets, 268–269
....English cloth and textile traders, 248–249
....French wine, 248–249
....German banking houses, 249
....Methuen Treaty, 248–251
....Portuguese market, markets, 249, 270
....Portuguese wines, wine, 248–250
Portuguese Empire, 184, 186, 200–201, 221–222, 227, 243, 248, 259–261, 276
Portuguese Evangelical Alliance, 293
Portuguese Expeditionary Force, 309, 321
Portuguese exploration, 165, 193
Portuguese (imperial) colonies/territories, 165, 202–204, 250, 254, 257, 259–261, 264–265
....African colonies, 260, 280–281, 283, 318–319, 347, 353
....American colonies, territories, 187, 200, 241–247, 259
....Asian colonies, 247
....Atlantic colonies, 203, 209
....Atlantic expansion, 175
Portuguese influence, 166, 172, 191, 204, 219
Portuguese language, 97, 126, 128–129, 132, 183, 186, 222, 235, 275
Portuguese Literature, 129–130, 133
....Castilian court, 131
....Castilian historiography, 133
....ecclesiastical writing, 131
....Erudite Jewish and Muslim circles, 130, 132
....French court, 133
....Galician-Portuguese cultures, 130

....Interest in Arab culture, 133
....Latin culture, 130, 132
....libraries, 130, 132–133, 141
....Literary genres, 130
........annals and narratives, 130
........chivalric romances, 131
........chronicle tradition, writing, 131
...........*Chronicle of the Conquest of the Algarve,* 131
...........*Crónica Geral de Espanha,* 131, 133
...........didactic and moral works, 132
..........."First Portuguese Chronicle", 131
...........hagiographies, hagiographic narratives, 130–132, 135–136
...........legal literature, 131
...........Lopes, Fernão, 155
...........poetry, 132
...............popular oral culture, minstrels, song-books, 130
...............troubadours, 131, 133
...........technical treatises, 132
...........works of philosophy, apologetics and medicine, 131
........Portuguese nobility, 131, 156
........Portuguese University (General Studies), 88, 98, 130, 132, 142–143
........Urban preaching, 132
....Portuguese literary circles, 130–133
Portuguese maritime/overseas expansion, 88, 122, 145–146, 167, 170–171, 174, 188, 220, 222, 249, 251, 259–260, 262, 264–266
....African expeditions, 159, 162
........Zurara, Gomes Eanes de, 162
....Atlantic trade, 146, 167–169, 174–177, 186, 203
........Cape route, 176–177, 185, 189, 205–206
........*Carreira da India,* 177
....Conquest of Ceuta, 86, 111, 122, 158–159, 198, 216
....Discoveries, Age of Discoveries, Maritime discoveries, 102, 143, 192, 199, 220, 243, 333–335
....naval construction, 95, 121, 144–147, 161–162
....Overseas conquests, expansion, policies, 88, 112, 146
....South Atlantic navigation, 175, 177, 185, 203, 250, 276
Portuguese Protestant Association, 293
Portuguese Royal Court transfer to Brazil, 264, 274–277
Portuguese Travel Literature, 225
Portuguese University, 98, 130, 132, 140–143
....Coimbra, 88, 140–143, 234, 252
....Évora, 143
....Lisbon, 98, 221

Portuguese voyages, 173, 220
....António de Abreu expedition to the
    Moluccas, 206
....António de Andrade's arrival in Tibet, 214,
    236
....Bartolomeu Dias' voyage beyond the Cape
    of Good Hope, 205, 207
....Magellan circumnavigation, 205–208
....Pedro Álvares de Cabral's first voyage to
    Brazil, 184, 187
....Vasco da Gama's voyage, 185, 187, 224
Portuguese World (exhibition), 327, 334–335
Posidonius, 40, 50, 67
post-war, 307, 321, 340–341, 359
Potsdam Conference, 345
Prado Jr., Caio, 275
Praia Rei Cortiço (site), 11
pre-Roman times / pre-Roman world / pre-
    Roman era, 47–48, 52, 60
press, 287, 304–305, 321, 347, 351–352, 354,
    363
Princes of Avis, 129, 161
....Edward (king), 132, 158–159, 161–162
....Ferdinand (infant), 159
....Henry, the Navigator, 112, 143, 159–161,
    172–173, 175–176, 198, 333
....John, prince, 159
....Peter, prince (regent), 132, 159, 161–162,
    176
Proença, Raul, 310, 338
Promontory, 31, 48–49, 72
Protestantism / Protestants, 231, 238–239,
    255, 291–294
Prussia, 276, 284
Punicus, 39
PVDE (*Polícia de Vigilância e Defesa do Estado
    /* Surveillance and State Defence Police),
    326–327
Pyrenees, 76, 87, 112, 115, 132
Pytheas, 31, 66–67, 70

Quadruple Alliance, 284, 290
Queirós, Eça de, 331, 362
Quintus Sertorius, 46, 55–56
....Sertorian rebellion, 56

radiclism / radicals, 281–282, 285, 303, 307,
    309, 325–327, 341, 349, 355, 357
Ramusio, Giovanni Battista, 220
Ravena, Benedetto da, 218
Raymond of Burgundy, 103, 105
Reccared, 79, 81, 90
Reccopolis, 81
Recife, 241, 243, 253–254
Reconquest, 95, 100, 132, 148–149, 162
....Almohad Empire, 149
........Almohad fortress of Badajoz, 149

........"Badajoz disaster", 114
....Battle of Alarcos, 110
....Battle of Navas de Tolosa, 149
....Battle of Salado, 109, 117, 131
....Conquest of Alcácer do Sal, 109, 120
....Conquest of the Algarve, 121, 149
....Conquest of Coimbra, 113
....Conquest of Lisbon, 119–120, 123
....Conquest of Santarém, 108
....Conquest of Seville, 110
....Conquest of Toledo, 103
....Leonese *Reconquista*, 114
....Palmela recovery, 109
Red Sea, 10, 192, 206, 219
Redondo, 126
Regenerator government, 302
regicide, 303–305, 307
regime, 281, 288–289, 303–305, 307–310,
    317, 319–320, 324–327, 341–344,
    346–347, 350, 353, 355, 359
....Ancien Régimes, 280, 283, 289
....authoritarian, 281, 320, 326, 346, 357, 359
....authoritarian regime, 340–341, 344, 347,
    357, 359
....authoritarianism, 285, 341
....colonial regime, 281
....constitutional regime, 287
....democratic regime, 358, 361
....dictatorial regime, 281, 326
....nationalist regime, 326
....Nazi regime, 327
....political regime, 307, 325, 346, 359
....protectionist trade regime, 299
....Republican regime, 308, 319
....Salazar regime, 331, 348
....social democratic regime, 357
Reid family, 311
Reinel, Pedro, 207
Religious orders, 88, 112, 115, 123, 198,
    200–201, 209, 211–213, 215, 246, 271
....Benedictine rule, 109, 124
........Benedictine churches, life, monks, 100,
    109, 125
........Cister, Cistercian, Cistercians, 101, 120,
    123–125, 129, 143, 149
........Cluny, Cluniac Order, 100, 104–105,
    124, 129
....Loios, Congregation of the Secular Canons
    of Saint John Evangelist, 126
....Mendicant orders, 101-102, 125, 131–132,
    142
........Carmelites, 125
........Dominican (order), Dominicans, 101,
    126, 131, 142–143, 212
........Franciscan (Order), Franciscans, 101,
    126, 131, 134–136, 142, 213....
........Trinitarians, 125

Religious orders *(continued)*
....Saint Augustine rule, 124–125
........Augustinian Order of Regular Canons, 134
........Hermits of Saint Augustine, 125
........Saint Jerome (Order of), 126
....Theatines, 212
Relvas, José, 308
Remismund, 77
Renaissance, 86, 97, 102, 129, 137, 140, 217, 235, 315, 362
republicans, 280, 285–286, 303–304, 306–310
Resende (viscount), 288
Resende, André de, 53
Restoration of 1640, Restoration period, 219, 229, 242, 275
Rhine, 18, 31, 71, 76
Rhodes, Alexandre de, 215
Rhône, 93
Ribeira (Royal Palace of the), 122, 252, 263
Ribeiro, Aquilino, 97
Ribeiro, Diogo, 194
Ribeiro, José Cardim, 50
Ribeiro, Orlando, 69
Ricci, Matteo, 143, 214, 235
Rio de Janeiro, 190, 195, 214, 242, 244, 252–255, 264–265, 274–277, 283–286, 305, 308
Rio Maior, 12–13
roads / routes, 31, 36, 41–42, 52, 60–61, 66, 70, 75
Robert (Lisbon cathedral chief architect), 100
Roberto, Elias, 142
Robinson, George, 293
Roch, Saint, 151
Rocha, Félix da, 236
Rodrigues, André, 236
Romance language, 44–45, 127–129
Rome, 30, 34–36, 38–43, 45–47, 51, 54–57, 60, 62, 64, 66–67, 71, 73, 223–224, 290, 308
....*civitates*, 47, 61, 77, 78
....*ius Latii*, 52–53
....Roman army, 35, 59
....Roman cities, 53, 62, 77
....Roman conquest, 32, 34–36, 42, 45, 49
....Roman culture, 32, 46, 60, 76
....Roman Empire, 33, 35, 41, 49, 51, 53, 57, 59, 63–64, 72, 76, 80–82
........construction of the Roman Empire, 71
........downfall of the Roman Empire, 62–63
........early empire, 42–43, 62, 64
........Eastern Roman Empire, 80, 82–83
........*Pax Romana*, 63
........territories of the Roman Empire, 30
....Roman periods
........Late Roman period, 42
........post-Roman period, 81
........Republican period, 39, 42, 46, 59–62
........Roman Imperial period, 42, 51, 53, 60
........Roman period, 38, 42, 46, 62–63, 65
....Roman provinces, 32, 76, 80
....Roman times / Roman world / Roman era, 32, 42, 44, 46, 53, 58–59, 62, 311
....Senate, 34–35, 56
....*termini Augustales*, 52, 61
Rome (Church), 107, 109, 111, 120, 123, 132, 159, 182, 199–202, 207, 209–211, 231–232, 235–236, 251, 253
Rome College, 234–235
Rosa, Sousa, 303
Rose-Coloured Map, 301
Rotterdam, Erasmus of, 225
Roughton, Ellen, 293
Rousseau, Henri, 314
Rowland, Robert, 209
Royal Academy of History, 252
Royal exile, 164
royal family, 283, 287, 303–304, 307
Royal Mint, 274
Royal Patronage, Portuguese royal patronage, 165, 198–202, 252–253
royalism / royalists, 287, 289–290, 318
Rubino, Giovanni, 236
Rudolph I of Habsburg, 139
Rufus Festus Avienus, 70
Ruggieri, Michele, 235
Russell, Richard, 311
Russia, 10, 152, 236, 262, 276, 280, 284, 296, 299, 303, 307, 314, 336
Russian Empire, 240

Sado (river), 25, 43, 61, 64, 71, 109, 195–196
Safi, 169, 201, 217
Sagres, 178
Saint Louis (king of France), 87
Saint Vincent Panels, 99, 102
Saladin, 159
Salamanca, 108, 114, 141–143, 221
Salanova, Laure, 17–19
Salazar, António de Oliveira, 280, 323–325, 327, 331–334, 340–343, 346–348, 350–351
....Salazarism, 281, 325–326
Salerno, 141
Salon des Indépendants, 314–315
Sampaio, Souza e, 296
Sancho I, 109–110
Sancho IV (king of Castile), 150, 156
Sangmeister, Edward, 18–19
Santa Cruz de Cabo de Aguer, 216
Santa Cruz de Tenerife, 168
Santa Teresa, Friar João José de, 243

Santarém, 25, 52, 61, 67–68, 102–104, 110, 114, 149, 157, 195–197, 214, 321

....*Scallabis*, 52, 61

Santiago de Compostela (Church), 100, 104, 106, 129, 153

Santos, António Ribeiro dos, 296–297

Santos, João Cid dos, 339

Santos, Machado, 307

Santos, Reynaldo dos, 339

São Fins dos Galegos, 150

São Francisco (river), 241, 243

São João del Rei (Brazil), 252

São Jorge da Mina, 169–170, 177, 219, 241

São Julião da Barra (Fort), 219

São Mamede (Guimarães), 106

São Miguel (Island), 254

São Paulo, 214, 229

São Salvador da Bahia, 188, 190, 201, 219, 243, 255, 274, 277

Saraiva, António José, 210

Saraiva, António Ribeiro, 289

Saramago, José, 310, 336, 362–365

Sardinia, 21–22, 34, 275, 277

Savoy, 87, 115–116, 132, 277

Schall, Adam, 214

Schall, Johann Adam, 236

Schmidt, Hubert, 18

Schreck, Johannes, 236

Seabra (viscount), 294

Sebastian (king of Portugal), 227

Secret Convention, 283–284

Secretariat of National Propaganda/National Secretariat for Information, 325, 327, 332, 351

Sérgio, António, 274

Serpa, 21, 149–150

Serra de Ossa, 125

Sestian altars, 49

Setúbal, 26, 109, 169, 196, 214, 254

Seville, 40, 65, 79, 81–83, 91–93, 109–110, 142, 149, 194, 207–208, 225, 229

Sextus Pompeius, 58

Shaoguan, 235

Siam, 201, 261

Sicily, 23, 34, 132, 152, 275, 277, 287

Siena, 138, 141

Sierra Leone, 175, 193, 203–204

Silhouette (French traveller), 275

Silva, Aníbal Cavaco, 361

Silva, José de Seabra da, 272

Silveira family, 287

Silves, 92, 109–110

Sintra, 50, 94, 119

Siqueira, João Soares de, 178

Sissi (empress), 305

Slavery, 164, 169–170, 198, 204, 286, 300, 368

....African coastal markets, 204

....African enslaved, captives, enslaved populations, 165, 167–170, 177, 187, 203–204, 228, 238

....Enslaved *mouriscos*, Muslim captives, 169

....Fugitive enslaved communities, 204

....Pernambuco "insurrectionists", revolt, 166, 241–244

....São Tomé enslaved revolt of 1517, 165–166, 202–204

....slave trade, 88, 93, 185–186, 202–203, 271, 299, 300, 331

Soares, Mário, 335, 359–361

socialism, 307, 325–326, 357–358

Society of Jesus (Jesuits), 189, 201, 212–215, 220, 226, 232–236, 245–246, 270–273, 368

....Supression, 201, 214–215, 270–273

Soure (town, castle), 107–108, 113

Sousa, João de, 178

Sousa, Martim Afonso de, 221

Sousa, Rui de, 178

Sousa, Tomé de, 276

Sousa-Portel, Branca (count of Barcelos's wife), 131

South Africa, 162, 262, 282, 348, 368

Souza, João de, 243

Soviet Union (URSS), 281–282, 340, 342, 344–345, 356

Spain, 4, 22, 45, 57, 59–60, 63, 77, 94, 102, 118, 148, 150, 153, 183, 206–207, 211, 228, 231–232, 240, 244–246, 248–249, 265–336 *passim*, 342, 344, 357, 361, 365

....Spanish America, 185, 195, 200, 204, 211, 227, 239

........Spanish Indies, 186, 228

........Spanish West Indies, 202–204

....Spanish Empire, 200, 241

....Spanish Inquisition, 209, 211

....Spanish monarchy, 237–239, 241

Spínola, António de, 355–356

sport, 281, 312, 323, 351, 353–354

....football, 281, 323, 351–354

Stalin, 324, 345

State of India, 185, 188–190, 206, 209, 214, 220, 229, 232, 238, 260

....Calicut, 184, 193

....Cochin, 189, 201–202

....Daman, 219

....Diu, 219

....Goa, 189–190, 201, 206, 209, 214, 220–221, 232–233, 235, 265

....Sri Lanka, 265

....West Coast of India, 206

Statute of Indigenous Peoples, 347, 349–350

Stein, Gertrude, 315

Stein, Leo, 315

Steiner, George, 365
Strabo, 30, 36, 48–50, 58, 60, 66–68, 70
Suebi, 33, 75–79, 80–81
Sweden, 239, 299, 344
Switzerland, 316, 336, 344
Syria, 23, 27, 31, 57, 90, 98, 108, 116, 152

Tagus (river), 9, 16, 18–20, 25, 36, 39, 43, 49,
    59–61, 63–64, 67–68, 78, 80, 93, 103,
    108–110, 114, 119–120, 122, 149, 195,
    263, 283, 288, 334
Tangier, 160, 188, 200, 216–217, 219, 292
Tangiers, 111
Tariq bin Ziyad, 89
Tarraconensis, 43, 59, 73, 75
....Tarraco, 73–74
Tavira, 26, 43, 161
Távora family, 295
Teles, Baltazar, 215
Teles, Leonor (queen), 156
Telmo, José Ângelo Cottinelli, 333–334
Terceira Island (Azores), 254
Terreiro do Paço, 303–305
Thailand, 200–201, 261, 344
Theodoric II, 79
Theresa of León (countess), 103–108,
    112–113
Tiberius, 71
Tibet, 214, 236
Tierra Firme (Province of), 202–203, 206
Timor, 164, 184, 265
Todos-os-Santos (Bay of), 232
Tojar, Vicente Gomez y, 292–293
Toledo, 79–82, 91–92, 103
Toledo, Fernando Alvarez de, 178
Tomar, 11, 78, 100, 108, 113, 157, 199, 226,
    228
Torga, Miguel, 298
Torralva, Diogo de, 218
Torres Novas, 10–11, 13, 19
Torres Vedras, 13, 153
Torres, Fernando de, 178
Toulouse, 79, 100, 132, 141
....Tolosa, 79
tourism, 310–312, 335
Trade, traders, 8–9, 20, 23, 41–44, 46, 52, 60,
    70, 78, 82, 88, 121, 144–145, 152,
    160–190 *passim*, 196, 203–204, 206–208,
    213, 221–222, 228, 233, 239, 241–250,
    255, 263, 267–269, 284, 299–301, 308,
    328–332
....Asian luxury goods, 187, 228
....Asian spices, spices, 167, 173, 179, 185,
    195, 206, 208, 221
....Atlantic commerce, 95, 119, 128, 145
........gold, 122, 160
........silk and spices, 160

........wheat, 160, 162
....Brazilian gold, 249–251
....*feitorias*, 200
....Maritime trade, 144–147, 188
....Merchants Exchange, 88, 144–147
........merchants, 120–121, 144–147, 152,
    160–162
....network of fortress and trading posts, 221
....networks, 121, 145, 167
....(new) Atlantic economy, 203
........European markets, 168–170, 204, 250
........Manufacturing production, 187, 203–204
....ports, 121, 144–147, 152, 162, 165, 177,
    250
....Portuguese trade, traders, 144, 168–169,
    228
....routes, 151, 168–169, 173, 175, 213,
    247–248
....Spanish silver, 228–229
....sugar trade, 167–170, 188, 204, 242, 250
...."trade of the Kingdom", 147
Trancoso (site, castle), 149, 157
Trastâmara, Joana de, 178
Trava brothers, 112–113
Travas (family), 106
Treaty, 34, 148, 156, 178–180, 208, 236, 245,
    271, 283–284, 299–301, 340–341, 359,
    361
Tordesillas, 176, 178, 180, 192, 194,
    206–207, 244–246
Tripoli, 108
Tripolitania, 42
Troika, 369
Tui, 77, 113–114
Tunisia, 43, 161, 167, 347
Turdetani, 38–39, 58
Turdetania, 67
Turkey, 23, 55, 307, 344
Tuscany, 132, 269, 296

Umberto I (king), 303, 307
UN (United Nations), 340–348, 350
Unesco World Heritage (Mafra), 252
UNESCO's World Heritage status (Coimbra),
    144
United Kingdom, 262, 281, 311–312, 344,
    364–365
....Britain, 288, 300, 302, 317–319, 326
....England, 20, 23, 38, 281–284, 288–290,
    292, 296, 308–309, 311, 330, 340, 342,
    351–352, 367
....Great Britain, 31, 34, 57, 70–71, 269, 275,
    284, 287, 293, 299, 301, 308, 350
United Kingdom of Portugal, Brazil and the
    Algarves, 284–286
United Provinces (Republic of the), 241, 243,
    248

United States of America / USA, 4, 281–283, 286, 289, 299, 301, 303, 308–309, 314, 322, 336, 339–342, 344–345, 348, 350, 356, 364–365, 368–369
Universal Declaration of Human Rights, 312
Urraca of León (queen), 103, 105, 112
Uruguay, 244–245, 271, 282, 285
Utrecht, 275

Valencia, 56, 91, 148–150
Valignano, Alessandro, 214, 233
Valladolid, 141, 150, 207
Vandals, 76
....Silingi, 76
Varthema, Ludovico, 207
Vasconcelos, Jorge Ferreira de, 225
Vega, Lope de, 227
Veiga, Alves da, 308
Velázquez, Isidro, 227
Venezuela, 282, 368
Verbiest, Ferdinand, 236
Verona List, 73
Versailles Peace Conference, 307
....Treaty of Versailles, 320, 337
vicarius Hispaniarum, 74
Vicente, Gil, 225
Vico, Guido de (Cardinal), 114
Vieira, António, 1, 214, 276
Vieira, João Fernandes, 242–243
Vienna, 271, 284, 288–289, 307
Vietnam, 200–201, 215, 234, 348
Viking Age, 92–95
Vikings, 72, 87, 92–95
Vila Franca de Xira, 19, 25, 197
Vila Pouca de Aguiar, 63
....Jales, 32, 63
....Tresminas, 32, 63
Vila Real (count), 288
Vila Seca (baron), 288
Vilafrancada, 256, 288
Vincent (Saint martyr, patron of Lisbon), 99, 102, 142
vintism / vintist, 285–287
Viriathus, 37–38, 40, 45
....Viritathan Wars, 40
Viseu, 78, 153
Visigothic Kingdom, rule, 89–90
Visigoths, 33, 76–77, 79–80, 82–83, 119, 128
Viterbo, 139
Vizinho, Diogo Mendes, 231–232

wars, 280–281, 283–284, 289, 315, 318–321, 333–334, 340–341, 344, 348–349, 355, 367
....Balkan War, 307
....Cisplatine War, 285
....civil wars, 32, 36–37, 55, 57–58, 280, 289–291, 333, 356
....Cold War, 281–282, 341, 346–347, 349, 355–356
....Colonial War, 281, 323, 347, 351, 355
....First World War / Great War, 280, 306–307, 309, 315, 318, 320, 325, 331, 333, 337, 368
....Hundred Years War, 87, 121, 155–157, 367
....interwar (time), 324–326, 328, 335
....Korean War, 345
....Napoleonic wars, 280, 287
....Numantine Wars, 35
....Peninsular War, 284
....Punic Wars, 34–35, 38, 63
....Second World War (World War II), 260, 281–282, 312, 327, 333, 340–341, 343–344, 346, 349, 356, 368
....Spanish Civil War, 290, 327
....Spanish War of Succession, 367
....Thirty Years' War, 238
....Vietnam War, 356
....War of Mascates, 244
....War of Spanish Succession (1701–1714), 248
Wellesley, Henry, 288
Wellington, 289
Wesleyan Methodist Missionary Society, 293
West, 22, 33, 48, 80, 88, 107, 115, 119–120, 342, 345, 356
Western Schism, 125, 159
Wicki, Joseph, 233
Wild [domestic animals] ancestors, 15
Wittenberg, 291

Xavier, Saint Francis, 189, 214, 236

Young Men's Christian Associations, 293

Zamora, 106–107, 112, 114
Zilhão, João, 11–12, 16
Zurara, Gomes Eanes de, 172–173